Using Corel WordPerfect® 7

Using
Corel
WordPerfect 7

Joshua C. Nossiter

Using Corel WordPerfect 7

Copyright© 1996 by Que® Corporation.

All rights reserved. Printed in the United States of America. No part of this book may be used or reproduced in any form or by any means, or stored in a database or retrieval system, without prior written permission of the publisher except in the case of brief quotations embodied in critical articles and reviews. Making copies of any part of this book for any purpose other than your own personal use is a violation of United States copyright laws. For information, address Que Corporation, 201 W. 103rd Street, Indianapolis, IN 46290. You may reach Que's direct sales line by calling 1-800-428-5331.

Library of Congress Catalog No.: 95-72574

ISBN: 0-7897-0141-3

This book is sold *as is*, without warranty of any kind, either express or implied, respecting the contents of this book, including but not limited to implied warranties for the book's quality, performance, merchantability, or fitness for any particular purpose. Neither Que Corporation nor its dealers or distributors shall be liable to the purchaser or any other person or entity with respect to any liability, loss, or damage caused or alleged to have been caused directly or indirectly by this book.

98 97 96   6 5 4 3 2 1

Interpretation of the printing code: the rightmost double-digit number is the year of the book's printing; the rightmost single-digit number, the number of the book's printing. For example, a printing code of 96-1 shows that the first printing of the book occurred in 1996.

All terms mentioned in this book that are known to be trademarks or service marks have been appropriately capitalized. Que cannot attest to the accuracy of this information. Use of a term in this book should not be regarded as affecting the validity of any trademark or service mark.

Screen reproductions in this book were created using Collage Plus from Inner Media, Inc., Hollis, NH.

Composed in *ITC Century*, *ITC Highlander*, and *MCPdigital* by Que Corporation.

Credits

President
Roland Elgey

Vice President and Publisher
Marie Butler-Knight

Publishing Director
Lynn E. Zingraf

Editorial Services Director
Elizabeth Keaffaber

Managing Editor
Michael Cunningham

Director of Marketing
Lynn E. Zingraf

Acquisitions Editors
Stephanie Gould
Martha O'Sullivan

Senior Product Development Specialist
Lorna Gentry

Production Editor
Mark Enochs

Copy Editor
San Dee Phillips

Assistant Product Marketing Manager
Kim Margolius

Technical Editor
Robert Hartley

Technical Specialist
Nadeem Muhammed

Operations Coordinator
Patty Brooks

Editorial Assistant
Michelle Newcomb

Book Designer
Ruth Harvey

Cover Designer
Dan Armstrong
Jay Corpus

Production Team
Marcia Brizendine
Jessica Ford
Daryl Kessler
Michelle Lee
Christine Pesetski
Paul Wilson

Indexer
Chris Barrick

For Madeline: in a word, perfect.

About the Author

Joshua C. Nossiter received a B.A. in English from Dartmouth University and an M.B.A. in finance from Columbia University. He has worked in broadcasting in California and in public finance on Wall Street. His interest in computers dates back to the 1970s, when he first began using the Dartmouth mainframe system. Josh now lives in San Francisco with his two children, where he writes about software, among other things.

Acknowledgments

Any writer would be thrilled to find an editor who tolerates authorial foibles, provides essential encouragement, and spots blunders before it's too late. Que books somehow assemble a whole team of such editors. Their writers are lucky. Also grateful.

I was lucky enough to draw Lorna Gentry, Senior Product Development Specialist. Lorna takes a pile of manuscript and figures and turns it into a book, and does it with infectious enthusiasm. Her praise for the good is unstinting. Her criticism of the not-so-good is invaluable.

Robert Hartley of Corel Corporation, Technical Editor, saved me from error whenever I went astray. He also made many valuable contributions to the text. His mastery of WordPerfect's newest version, and his willingness to share it, made for a stronger book in every way.

San Dee Phillips, Copy Editor, combines the twin graces of the best copy editors: she wields her editorial blue pencil with both restraint and thoroughness. Her encouragement was a real spur in the last lap.

Acquisitions Editor Stephanie Gould got the project off the ground, and kept it there in the early going. Her successor on the book, Martha O'Sullivan, might be the only acquisitions editor in the world who doesn't feel obliged to share her enthusiasm for meeting deadlines. Her occasional cheery phone calls were enough to keep the authorial nose to the word processing grindstone.

Production Editor Mark Enochs juggled the many last minute changes with the skill I've come to take for granted from the Que team.

Not for the first time, Andy Zack, Literary Agent, shouldered the burden of the business end with perfect aplomb.

We'd like to hear from you!

As part of our continuing effort to produce books of the highest possible quality, Que would like to hear your comments. To stay competitive, we *really* want you, as a computer book reader and user, to let us know what you like or dislike most about this book or other Que products.

You can mail comments, ideas, or suggestions for improving future editions to the address below, or send us a fax at (317) 581-4663. For the online inclined, Macmillan Computer Publishing has a forum on CompuServe (type **GO QUEBOOKS** at any prompt) through which our staff and authors are available for questions and comments. The address of our Internet site is **http://www.mcp.com** (World Wide Web).

In addition to exploring our forum, please feel free to contact me personally to discuss your opinions of this book: I'm **lgentry.que.mcp.com** on the Internet, and **74671,3710** on CompuServe.

Thanks in advance—your comments will help us to continue publishing the best books available on computer topics in today's market.

Lorna Gentry

Product Development Editor
Que Corporation
201 W. 103rd Street
Indianapolis, Indiana 46290
USA

Contents at a Glance

Introduction 1

I Everything You Need to Get Started 9
  1 This Is No Ordinary Blank Page! 11
  2 Creating a New Document 31
  3 WordPerfect Help Is All Around You 49

II Editing and Formatting for Perfect Documents 65
  4 Good Writing Means Rewriting: Editing Text 67
  5 Formatting for Characters with Character 87
  6 What's My Line? Formatting Paragraphs for Precision and Punch 103
  7 Setting Up the Page 123

III Getting the Words Right on Screen and Page 143
  8 Choose Your Words...Easily! 145
  9 The Printer's Craft 165

IV Let WordPerfect Do Some of the Work for You 183
  10 Templates: The Express Route to Fancy Documents 185
  11 Documents with Style(s) 199
  12 WordPerfect's Labor-Saving Devices 213
  13 Merges, for Letters by the Bushel 231

V How to Be a Desktop Publisher 245
  14 When Only Columns Will Do 247
  15 Dress Up That Text! 263
  16 Jazz Up a Document with Graphics 285
  17 In a Table, Anything Goes—with Ease 305

VI Getting the Most Out of WordPerfect 331

      18 Documents, Big and Small, Few and Many 333

      19 Presentations 7 for Instant Artists 359

VII Expert WordPerfect Features for Non-Experts 379

      20 Customizing WordPerfect 381

      21 Import, Export, Convert: Sharing Files Between Programs 401

      22 Share Documents with the Office and the Rest of the World 415

Action Index 439

Index 445

Table of Contents

Introduction

What makes this book different? 3

How do I use this book? 4

How this book is put together 4

Special book elements 7

Part I: Everything You Need to Get Started

1 This Is No Ordinary Blank Page! 11

What can WordPerfect do for me? 12

    Where do I start? Running WordPerfect 12

    Put dear old DAD in its place 13

    I want a WordPerfect icon on my desktop 15

    How do I get out of here? 16

What's in the WordPerfect window? 16

    Why don't I see all those buttons in my copy of WordPerfect?! 17

    The WordPerfect window 18

    Why does my mouse pointer keep changing shape? 20

    What do the buttons do? 21

    Gray QuickSpots, Red under-hatchings, and the Shadow Pointer 21

        Other handy tools in shades of gray 23

Menus and QuickMenus, for all WordPerfect's features 23

    My right mouse button actually *does* something? 24

Dialog boxes do many commands at once 25

I want to see more (or less) of this document 26

    Telescope the screen with Zoom 27

    Scrolling turns the on-screen page 28

        Moving the insertion point as you scroll 29

2 Creating a New Document   31

How do I enter text in a WordPerfect document?   32
   Do-it-yourself documents   33
   Use WordPerfect Expert templates for documents by the numbers   35
      Bonus timesaver! Save typing with copy and paste   39

Document finished? Save it   41
   What do I name my file?   42
   How do I get out of this document?   43

WordPerfect has a built-in file manager   44
   How do I get my latest documents back?   44
   I need a document from weeks ago   44
   I can't remember what I called my file!   45
      QuickFinder's search came up empty-handed! Now what do I do?   46

I'm ready to print my document   47

3 WordPerfect Help Is All Around You   49

On-screen help for what you see on the screen   50

The PerfectExpert, a know-it-all in a can   52
   Okay Mr. Expert, show me how to do labels   52
   Let Guides and QuickTasks do the work for you   53

Press F1 for all the help   55
   How do I...   55
   Help by example   57

Searching for Help   58
   Help! I'm lost in Help!   59
   If you're used to doing things in a different program, try Upgrade Help   60
   Dialog boxes have you stymied? Try help in a box   61

WordPerfect is wired for Help   62
   How do I connect to WordPerfect's online help?   63

Part II: Editing and Formatting for Perfect Documents

4 Good Writing Means Rewriting: Editing Text 67

Inserting, for everyday writing 68
    How do I move the insertion point where I want it? 68
        Typeover, an occasional option 70

Deleting text: no white-out needed 71
    Changed your mind? Undo or Undelete 71

Selecting text for alterations—minor and major 73
    Select with the keyboard 73
    Select with the mouse 74
    QuickSelect is for slower fingers 74
    Select from the QuickMenu 74
    Selecting text is a drag 74
    Go To, the insertion point express 75

What can I do with selected text? 76
    Cut and Paste it 77
    Make a smudge-free copy 77

Undo and Redo forgive mistakes, repeat successes 77
    I want those edits back! 78
    How many times can I change my mind? 79

Reveal codes take you behind the scenes 79
    Opening the reveal codes window 79
    Now that I can see the codes, what do I do with them? 81
        True confessions: how I used reveal codes to delete the tab bar icon 81

Find and Replace: better than any lost and found 82
    First Find it... 83
        Getting specific with Find 84
        Finding, finding, found! 85
    ...then Replace it 86
        Using Replace to delete words 86

5 Formatting for Characters with Character   87

Formatting at the push of a button   88
   Put a boldface on it   89
   When (and how) do I add italics?   89
   Underline for emphasis   90

What are fonts?   91

How do I change font faces and sizes?   92
   How can I tell what those font faces look like?   94
   Other font options   95
   I cooked up a great font! How do I get it back again?   96

WordPerfect has a font for every occasion   97

Drop-caps are characters with real character   98
   How do I get a drop-cap?   99

6 What's My Line? Formatting Paragraphs for Precision and Punch   103

How do I set the margins?   104
   Margins line up fast with Guidelines   104
   Mousephobic? Margin setting for those who hate dragging   106
   Tab stop changes to make? Call up the ruler bar   107

Everything you always wanted to know about indents   109
   Pick your indent option from the QuickSpot menu   110
      I want to indent a new paragraph   112

Centering and flush right: where does your text stand?   112
   Take me to your (dot) leader   112
   Center a line: the middle of the road   113
   How do I justify my work?   114
   Justified lines are ragged no more   115

Bullets and numbers add punch to paragraphs   116
   Speeding (or at least Quick) bullets   117
   You've got it on a (numbered) list   119

How to add paragraph borders without incident   120

7 Setting Up the Page   123

The Page Toolbar, for page setup at your fingertips   124

Pick a number, any page number   124
- Close-Up: the Page Toolbar   125
- Dress up that page number   126
- Where on the page should the page number go?   127
- Create your own page numbering format   128
  - These page numbers need a face-lift   129
  - What if I want the page numbers to start at something other than 1?   130

What's a header (or a footer)?   130
- Where do the header and footer go?   131
  - How do I add a second header?   132
  - Put your footer down on that page   134
- How do I edit headers?   135

I don't want all these gadgets on every page   136

How do I double-space this page?   136
- My page looks unbalanced   137

I want to keep my text together   138
- How to prevent widows and orphans   138
- Block Protection: lock up text, not doors   139
  - What is conditional end of page?   139

Decorate the page with a border   140

Part III: Getting the Words Right on Screen and Page

8 Choose Your Words...Easily!   145

Spell-As-You-Go, the red pencil maven   146

Spell Checker is handy, but not infallible   147
- Spell Checker corrects typos and misspellings   148
- Spell Checker flags some correctly spelled words, too!   150
- Spell Checker finds all kinds of errors— even nonerrors   151
- Proofread, to catch what Spell Checker misses   152

QuickCorrect corrects as you type   153
    Add your own mistakes to the QuickCorrect list   153
        What else does QuickCorrect correct?   154

I can't think of the right word!   155
    Use the Thesaurus to say it another way   155
    Put the Thesaurus to work on your document   157

It's English, but is it Grammatikal?   158
    How do I use Grammatik?   158
    My letter is informal. Can I tell Grammatik to lighten up?   161
        Grammatik offers a lot of interesting information   161

All I really want is a word count for this document   162

9 The Printer's Craft   165

Pick your printer   166

How do I print this document?   167
    My printer's not printing! What do I do?   168
    Look before you leap: previewing your document layout   169

I don't want to print the whole document   171
    Refine print selections with Advanced Multiple Pages   171
        All I want to print is one section of a page   173
    How do I print more than one copy?   173
    Other nifty print options   173
        Here's a paper saver: print on both sides of the page   174

How do I print labels and envelopes?   175
    Perfect envelopes, fast   175
    Printing labels is easy   176

Can I print several documents at once?   180
    The last lines of my print job look lonely on their own page   180

Part IV: Let WordPerfect Do Some of the Work for You

10 Templates: The Express Route to Fancy Documents   185

What exactly is a template?   186
    When do I use templates?   186
    Can I edit template information?   190
Newsletter to write? Call in the expert   190
Can I create my own template?   195

11 Documents with Style(s)   199

WordPerfect's canned headings, for instant style   200
QuickFormat provides quick style   201
    QuickFormat starts with formatting   201
    QuickFormat's magic trick: automatic updating   203
    Can I copy formatting from character to character?   204
    What is fill, and how do I use it?   205
Just what is a style?   206
    What can I do with styles?   207
QuickStyles, for styles the quick way   207
    How do I apply my new style?   208
    I hate this style. How do I get rid of it?   210
This style needs restyling   211
    Concoct your style from scratch   211
    I want this style in another document   212

12 WordPerfect's Labor-Saving Devices   213

Save typing with abbreviations   214
    Abbreviate your typing chores: use abbreviations   216
    How about expanding all my abbreviations at once?   217
    I need to change these abbreviations   218
    I want this abbreviation in another template   218
What's a macro?   219

How can I create my own macro?   220
    How do I play it back?   223

This macro could use a few alterations   224
    Can I edit my macros?   225
        WordPerfect has an online macro guide   226

Your little black book is a click away   227
    Add address entries to build your book   227

13 Merges, for Letters by the Bushel   231

What happens in a merge?   232
    When do I use a merge?   232

Merges start with a data file...   233
    ...And the data file is your Address Book   233

Form files are document shells   234
    How do I make a form file?   235
    While we're at it, how about envelopes by the bushel, too?   239

Select your records; then bring it all together with a merge   241
    What do I do with this merge?   242
    Merge bells and whistles   243

Part V: How to Be a Desktop Publisher

14 When Only Columns Will Do   247

Why newspapers love newspaper columns   248

Fast columns with no fussing   250
    Where's the Power Bar Columns button?   252
    How can I tell where column formatting begins and ends?   252
    How do I end one column and start another one?   254
    Default columns settings are usually fine...   254
    These columns need adjustment   255

How do I fine-tune my columns?   257
  The Columns dialog box is the column control panel   257
  How do I move around in these columns?   258
  These columns need borders   259
  How do I get these parallel columns to work?   261

15 Dress Up That Text!   263

Call in the typographer? No need. It's you!   264
  I want to see what this font looks like before I use it   264
  How about a different color for this font?   265
  What are those symbols by the font names?   267
    How do I add more fonts?   268

TextArt, for text with an artistic bent   269
  Bending TextArt to your will   269
  Editing TextArt   271

Create fancy stationery with watermarks   273
  WordPerfect images make great watermarks   273
  How do I create my own watermark?   277

WordPerfect puts a typesetter on your desk   278
  That's *kerning*, not kernel, Colonel   278
    Line Spacing? Leading? What's that all about?   280
    How about letterspacing?   280

Pardon my French: inserting special characters   281
  How can I use the Characters dialog box more efficiently?   282

16 Jazz Up a Document with Graphics   285

Here's your line: graphics lines   286
  How do I get a line on more lines?   287
  This line needs some work: move, resize, or delete it   288
  I want a fancier line   289
    I need to create my own line style   290

When text needs a pickup… add a picture   291

How do I fit this graphic on the page?   292
    This graphic pushed my text aside!   292
    How do I resize this graphic?   294
    This graphic looks like a reflection in a fun house mirror   296
        I can't get this image quite right   296
    I just can't get this graphic right!   297
    How do I move a graphic around?   298
    What about a caption?   299

Just what is a graphics box?   300
    I need to make this text stand out   300
    How do I get rid of graphics boxes?   302
        I can't find an image I like. Where can I find more graphics?   302

17 In a Table, Anything Goes—with Ease   305

What exactly is a table?   306
    Create a quick table   306

How do I edit this table?   310
    How do I add rows and columns to this table?   311
    Anatomy of a WordPerfect table   312
    This cell doesn't look big enough for my data...   314
    I want wider cells   315
        Adjusting column widths is a drag   316

Tables are spreadsheets, too   317
    The formula bar turns tables into calculating machines   317
    How do I add up a column of numbers?   318
    How do I write my own formula?   320
    Can I copy this formula?   321
    SUM is just the beginning   323

Can I put this table in another document?   323

This table could use a facelift   325

What else can I do with tables?   327
    Can I turn these parallel columns into a table?   328
    Tables don't have to look like tables   328
    My data is out of sorts   329

Part VI: Getting the Most Out of WordPerfect

18 Documents, Big and Small, Few and Many   333

Outlining organizes documents   334
    How do I create an outline?   334
    Finished the outline? Add body text   338
    How do I get rid of these outline numbers and letters?   340
        I need to move this outline item   341

This big document is cumbersome   342
    How do I create a master document?   342
    I want my document in one piece!   345
    What can I do with this expanded document?   347
    Put the expanded document away again   347
        Viewing a condensed master document   348

I need a table of contents   349

I want to see lots of files at the same time   352

How do I manage all these files?   353
    Create a new subfolder for files of one type   354
    Let QuickFinder gather your files together   355

19 Presentations 7 for Instant Artists   359

What can I do with a drawing program?   360
    Can't find the image you want? Make your own!   360

What else can I do with Presentations?   368
    How can I reshape this object?   368

Can I make charts in WordPerfect?   370
    Use WordPerfect's built-in chart for fast results   370

What else should I know about charts?   376

Part VII: Expert WordPerfect Features for Non-Experts

20 Customizing WordPerfect 381

    I want to see more words and fewer gadgets 382

        Can I save my document window's custom look? 383

    Speed up your work: keep your most used features in reach 385

        How to create a custom Toolbar 385

        How about changing an existing toolbar? 389

    Tired of the same old buttons? Change 'em! 389

        Power Bar remodeling is possible, too 391

        Change the status of the Status Bar 392

    Short of buttons? Create your own 393

        Can I change the way this button looks? 394

    Custom math quizzes? Use the Equation Editor 397

        Create a simple equation with the Equation Editor 398

21 Import, Export, Convert: Sharing Files Between Programs 401

    How can I turn this file into a WordPerfect 7 document? 402

        My file isn't being converted into WordPerfect 7 automatically 404

        I need to save this WordPerfect document in another format 404

        WordPerfect saves you from Save errors 405

    Can I copy from one program to another? 406

        How do I put my Quattro Pro object in a WordPerfect document? 407

        Edit embedded objects with the application that created them 408

    What's a link? 410

        Link one application to another for fast updates 410

        Keep up your links, or break them 412

    Can I stick my Presentations graphic in a WordPerfect document? 413

22 Share Documents with the Office and the Rest of the World   415

Save shoe leather, postage stamps with e-mail   416
    How do I send an e-mail note from WordPerfect?   417
    I'm e-mailing this document to another WordPerfect user   420
    Envoy, for e-mail recipients who don't use WordPerfect   421

I want the whole world to read this document!   424
    WordPerfect is your Web connection   424
    How do I publish my document on the Web?   426

Hypertext links send readers on side trips   430
    Bookmark links turn ordinary text into Hypertext   431
    I happen to know this great Web site…   435

Building a home page? Call in the Web Page Expert   437

Action Index   439

Edit documents   439

Format characters   439

Format documents   440

Cut down on typing chores   440

Insert graphics   441

Print   441

Manage documents   442

Change the way you work with WordPerfect   442

Share Documents with the Office and the World   443

Index   445

Introduction

Most of us have jobs to do, and a computer to do it with. We'd also rather be somewhere other than in front of the computer screen as fast as we can get there. The computer enthusiast doesn't understand this. Enthusiasts aren't happy unless they're wrestling with some involved software feature in an obscure corner of a giant program. Enthusiasts love the challenge. Everybody else would rather be whacking a golf ball. Or shopping.

Since computer enthusiasts write all our software, it's not too surprising that their efforts, however brilliant, aren't always easy to figure out. Which leaves the rest of us, trying to get a job done as fast as possible, with an urgent question: how do I do it!?

Using Corel WordPerfect 7 for Windows 95 was written to answer that question. Not that WordPerfect is at all hard; this latest version is one of the most intuitive word processors ever. Once you know what button to press and where to find it, you'll get dazzling results in no time at all.

But there's a lot here. WordPerfect does almost anything imaginable with text and graphics, and you usually get several different ways to do it. There are loads of features you'll use all the time, and some that you'll use rarely—or never. WordPerfect does so many different things that figuring out how to do any one of them is not always obvious. This book cuts through the clutter to give you just the information you need.

It's an approach that makes WordPerfect's myriad features accessible, not intimidating. Some WordPerfecters never go much beyond the basics, because the program's advanced features seem too daunting. *Using Corel WordPerfect 7 for Windows 95* shows you exactly how to apply those advanced features to your work, with clear, step-by-step instructions. That'll help you get the most out of the program.

WordPerfect is a window on the world

PCs used to be like country cottages: solitary, and a little bit removed from the world. With the Corel WordPerfect Suite, PCs move to the big city. The whole world is just on the other side of your modem. Solitary no longer, your

PC is linked to millions of other computers around the globe. The Internet, that vast global network of computers, makes every PC another potential link in the chain. With the right software and a modem, you become part of the most exciting thing to hit computing since the silicon chip.

The Corel WordPerfect Suite is the right software. The suite has a built-in Web browser, a program that puts the World Wide Web on your computer screen. You can send e-mail, and even publish your work on the Web. Best of all, everything—e-mail, the WordPerfect Internet publisher, and the Web itself—is easy to use. It's a simple matter of point-and-click.

So sorry, no rooms available—take this suite instead!

It's every traveler's dream: you check into a hotel and discover that you've been upgraded from a single room to a roomy suite. That's exactly what happened when you bought the Corel WordPerfect 7 Suite. Along with the WordPerfect word processor, you have a slew of other useful programs to help you get your work done. The rest of the Corel WordPerfect Suite includes:

- **Quattro Pro** is one of the best spreadsheet programs around. A spreadsheet, if you haven't used one before, is like a word processor for numbers. It lets you edit and calculate numeric data with the same ease a word processor brings to typing and editing text.

- **Presentations** is a powerful graphics program. It has all the tools you need to create your own works of art, and it comes with a library of ready-made images that you can customize to suit. You can pop Presentations graphics into WordPerfect documents, or design entire slide shows and multimedia presentations.

- **AT&T WorldNet Services** is software that lets you navigate the millions of pages of information and entertainment on the World Wide Web. It's also an Internet service provider: a gateway to those millions of Web pages. Everything you need to set up an account with AT&T WorldNet services is included. Like a cable TV account, you pay a monthly fee to "tune in" to the World Wide Web. Your account also gives you an e-mail address, so that you can send and receive mail over the Internet.

- **Envoy** is a remarkable program that packages your WordPerfect documents in a special viewer. Saved as an Envoy file, a WordPerfect document will be viewed exactly as you created it by anyone, including those who have neither WordPerfect nor Envoy installed on their computers.
- **Dashboard** puts all your programs in one handy little window. It lets you run any software application on your computer with a single click.

And that's not all. Sidekick 95 Internet is an electronic calendar and organizer that meshes seamlessly with the Internet. You'll also find hundreds of fonts, decorative graphics, and clip-art images. There is indeed a lot here, and it's all worth exploring.

What makes this book different?

If you phone a computer buff pal with questions about WordPerfect, you want straight answers, not a lot of jargon. Otherwise, you'd probably hang up. I wrote *Using Corel WordPerfect 7 for Windows 95* just as I'd answer telephone queries from my WordPerfect-using friends: with plain English that gets right to the point.

You don't have to spend a lot of time with this book. It's designed so that a quick look shows you the fastest and easiest ways to create and edit documents, and send them around the office and the world.

What's more, you'll find plenty of tips to speed up your work, cautions to help you avoid trouble, and Q&As to solve mysteries. When you want some background, sidebars have tidbits of information I couldn't fit in anywhere else.

If you're new to WordPerfect, you'll discover that learning the program is fun. Experienced WordPerfect users will find that WordPerfect 7 is packed with new features. From integrated e-mail and the Internet Publisher, to QuickSpots (handy little buttons that put a menu of formatting tools wherever you happen to be working), this latest version of the software is the most powerful yet. *Using Corel WordPerfect 7 for Windows 95* helps you harness that power.

How do I use this book?

Most of the time you'll want fast help with a specific chore. The Action Index at the back of the book is a good place to start. It lists common word processing tasks, and directs you right to the page where you'll find the task explained. If you can't find what you want in the Action Index, check the Table of Contents next. It's very detailed, and chances are your job will be listed there.

When you have some spare time, try browsing. Each chapter of the book is divided into sections. Look through the section headings, and you'll find WordPerfect features you might not have known about. You might also discover ideas about using WordPerfect to tackle your work in new ways.

Of course, there's nothing to stop you from sitting down and reading a chapter through from beginning to end. To really master WordPerfect, that's the way to go. I can't promise you a thriller, but I've tried to keep things lively.

How this book is put together

When you have a big project to do, you probably break it up into smaller parts and tackle them one at a time. WordPerfect is a big program, and that's how this book is set up. There are ten parts:

Part I: Everything You Need to Get Started

Whether you plan on occasional visits or extended daily sessions, here's the place to find out what you're getting into. You'll learn how WordPerfect works, the basics of creating a document, and how to get help fast, whenever you need it.

Part II: Editing and Formatting for Perfect Documents

These are the things you'll do when you fire up WordPerfect every day. From short memos to epics, WordPerfect can handle whatever you throw at it. If you make a mistake, or need to make changes of any kind, you'll see that editing is easy and quick. And with a few basic formatting tools, you can turn out handsome pages in no time.

Part III: Getting the Words Right on Screen and Page

Writing is all about words. Finding and spelling the right words is painless with WordPerfect's spell checker and thesaurus. Grammatik, WordPerfect's grammar checker, even helps you arrange your words correctly in sentences. A wealth of formatting features is a click or two away, to help you create documents that are as attractive to look at as they are easy to read. And when it's time to print, the chapter on printing will help you produce good-looking pages, labels, and envelopes.

Part IV: Let WordPerfect Do Some of the Work for You

When you want a professional-looking document without spending a lot of time tinkering with formatting, WordPerfect's templates are the answer. A template gives you perfect, ready-made formatting—just type the text and you're done! Features like macros and Abbreviations even do some of your typing for you. If you want to design your own document formatting, WordPerfect's Styles save and apply your formatting creations.

Part V: How to Be a Desktop Publisher

Columns organize pages neatly and readably, and WordPerfect makes working with columns a straightforward chore. Tables go columns one better; a table is not only a great organizing tool, but WordPerfect tables can turn your documents into spreadsheets. Pop up a table, enter your data, and use WordPerfect's built-in calculator for everything from addition and subtraction to financial calculations.

How do you produce 50 letters, each one personalized with the recipient's name and address? You can spend a few days on the project and type 50 different letters. Or you can use WordPerfect's Merge feature and do the job in minutes. When you want to mass-produce documents that look custom-made, Merge takes care of the job effortlessly.

Part VI: Getting the Most Out of WordPerfect

Build a kid's playhouse, and you can get by with a hammer and saw. Build an office building, and you need more powerful equipment. Big documents need special tools, and WordPerfect has them. There are automated outlines, instant tables of contents, and other useful features to help you cope with big writing jobs. And as your writing jobs pile up, WordPerfect has a handy file manager to keep you on top of your work.

Even the best writing benefits from attractive fonts and eye-grabbing graphic effects. From fancy borders to colorful pictures, WordPerfect puts a collection of decorative graphics at your fingertips. Adding graphics to text is as easy as clicking and dragging. You'll also find everything you need to dress up the text. And with WordPerfect's amazing TextArt, you can even turn text *into* graphics.

Graphics can be as informative as they are decorative. That's exactly what a chart is: a picture that tells a story. There's no great trick to creating a spectacular chart in WordPerfect; just type your data, point, and click. With Presentations, WordPerfect's drawing program, even nonartists can whip up attention-getting artwork in minutes. And because everything in WordPerfect works together, you can easily pop charts and drawings into your documents.

Setting up perfect pages used to be the province of skilled layout artists. With WordPerfect, you get a battery of tools that help you produce pages of near-typeset quality. That's what desktop publishing is all about, and WordPerfect takes all the mystery out of it.

Think of WordPerfect as an electronic desk, with all your writing and drawing tools ready for use. Just like your desktop, you can customize WordPerfect to set up your tools the way you want them.

Part VII: Expert WordPerfect Features for Non-Experts

When you need material from another Corel WordPerfect Suite application, copy it right into WordPerfect and work on it there. Exchanging files between WordPerfect and the other programs is as easy as working on someone else's file at your own desk.

And when you're ready to send your document down the hall, or to the other side of the world, you can do it without leaving WordPerfect. Even the greatest writers struggled to find readers. WordPerfect puts a reading audience of millions a few clicks away. There's built-in e-mail for your electronic correspondence, and the WordPerfect Internet Publisher to publish your work for the perusal of the teaming legions on the World Wide Web.

Indexes

Besides the usual index of key words and topics, which you'll find in the usual spot at the back of the book, there's also a handy Action Index. It's a listing of specific WordPerfect chores you'll want to do, together with the page in the book that tells you exactly how to do them.

Special book elements

Using Corel WordPerfect 7 for Windows 95 has a number of special elements and conventions to help you master the program with ease.

TIP **Tips point out information often overlooked in the documentation.** Some tips are shortcuts that help you use WordPerfect more efficiently; others help you solve or avoid problems.

CAUTION **Cautions alert you to the possible dangers of a command or a procedure,** especially when the result might be the loss of your hard work! Cautions also warn you to avoid options or features that cause unnecessary complications.

Q&A **What are Q&A notes?**
Cast in the form of questions and answers, Q&As suggest ways to avoid common problems. They also provide quick fixes for problems you might have already run into.

❝ **Plain English, please!**
When technical terms and jargon are unavoidable, these notes explain what it all means in plain English. ❞

Throughout the book, we'll use a comma to separate the parts of a pull-down menu command. For example, to send your document via e-mail, you'd click File, Send. That means "Pull down the File menu, and choose Send."

And if you see two keys separated by a plus sign, such as Ctrl+X, that means to press and hold the first key, press the second key, then release both keys.

Right-click means clicking the right mouse button.

And when we talk about dragging, we mean holding down the left mouse button and moving the mouse pointer.

Sidebars are interesting nuggets of information

Sidebars are nonessential but relevant reading, side trips you can take when you're not at the computer or when you just want some light relief. You'll often find technical details or interesting background information.

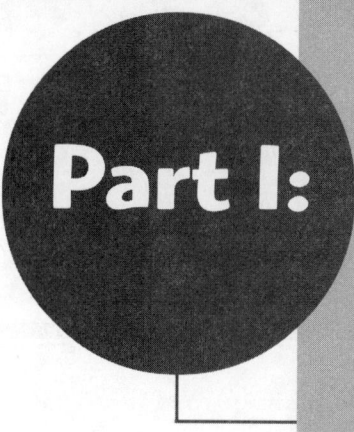

Part I: Everything You Need to Get Started

Chapter 1: **This Is No Ordinary Blank Page!**

Chapter 2: **Creating a New Document**

Chapter 3: **WordPerfect Help Is All Around You**

1

This Is No Ordinary Blank Page!

● **In this chapter:**

- How do I start WordPerfect?

- What am I looking at in the WordPerfect window?

- Menus? Toolbar? Power Bar? Explain, please!

- Why do my typed words sprout little red lines?

- I need to see more of my document

Driving a car is easy once you learn what all the buttons and levers do. Get acquainted with WordPerfect's controls, and you'll be as comfortable at the keyboard as you are behind the wheel . . . . ▶

Before the car, people walked. T.H. White wrote about a pre-automobile Englishman named Allerdyce, who went hunting and walked 30 miles. After a bite to eat, he walked another 60 miles to get home. He did the chores, walked 16 miles to a ball, danced, walked home in the morning, and then spent the day partridge shooting. All told, he covered 130 miles in three days and two nights.

Great exercise, but if he'd had a car, he would have used it.

Writing with pen and paper is like walking. You get where you're going, but slowly. If you take a wrong turn, retracing your steps means a lot of crossing out. Writing with WordPerfect is more like driving a car. Spend a few minutes learning which buttons to push, and you get to where you're going quickly and effortlessly. Make a mistake, and a click or two of the mouse sets you back on the right road again. And this new model of WordPerfect comes fully equipped; every imaginable option and accessory is at your fingertips.

What can WordPerfect do for me?

From a quick memo, to a lengthy report, to a newsletter complete with headlines and graphics, WordPerfect gives you everything you need to get the job done quickly. WordPerfect checks your spelling, finds you the right word, and even examines your grammar. It's easy to add color and graphics to give your writing jobs extra pizzazz. And when you're ready to share your document with others, WordPerfect has all the tools you need to send a document around the office—or around the world.

WordPerfect helps make your good work even better.

Where do I start? Running WordPerfect

Windows 95 was designed to make PCs easier to use. By and large it succeeds, but the road to simplicity has a few twists and turns. Take the simple chore of running a program. It's easy to launch programs in Windows 95, but there are many (many!) ways to do it. It's like picking alternate routes on a map. They all lead to the same destination, but you have different ways of getting there.

A single program can wind up on the Start, Programs menu, on the Start menu itself, and also appear as an icon on the Windows 95 desktop. The

Corel WordPerfect Suite adds yet another wrinkle (assuming you chose a typical installation of the suite); if you chose a custom installation, or only installed WordPerfect, you may see something different. The installation program puts the DAD, or Desktop Application Director, right on your Windows 95 Taskbar.

The DAD is crowded with icons that you click to launch WordPerfect, Quattro Pro, Envoy, and the other applications in the Corel WordPerfect Suite—maybe too crowded; those little icons are hard to see. If you can't tell what an icon on the DAD is for, point at it for a label.

If you don't want to launch WordPerfect from the DAD, the installation program also added the Corel WordPerfect Suite 7 folder to your Windows 95 Start menu. To run WordPerfect, click the Start button, select the Corel WordPerfect Suite 7 folder, and click the WordPerfect 7 icon, as shown in figure 1.1.

Fig. 1.1
It's hard to miss the Corel WordPerfect Suite 7 folder; the installation program puts it right on the Start menu!

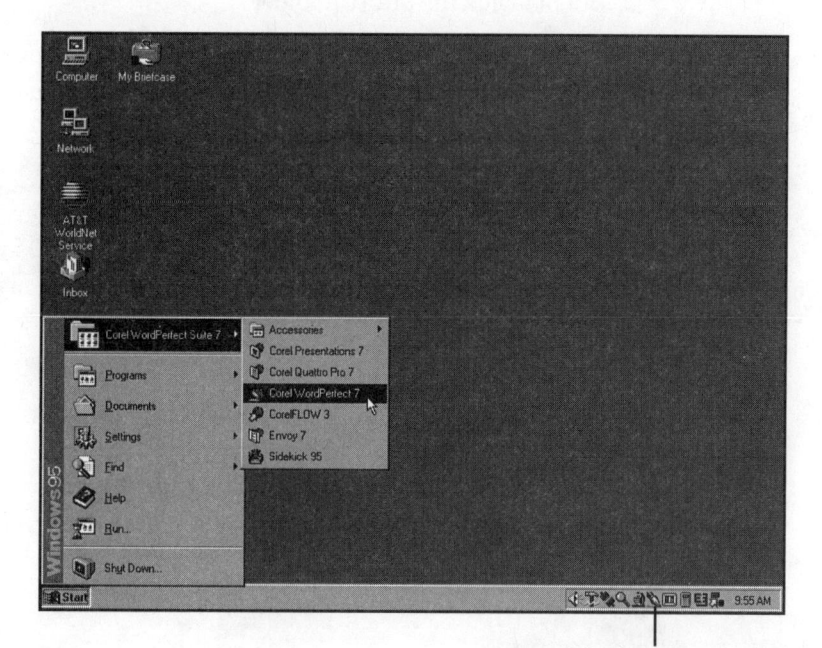

Here's the WordPerfect icon on the DAD; click it to start the program.

Put dear old DAD in its place

You'll notice something about the Desktop Application Director right away. Like many of its namesakes, this DAD hangs around whether you want it or not. Turn your computer on, and there's the DAD, sitting on your Taskbar. Chances are, you'll find the DAD useful, especially if you're a frequent user of WordPerfect, Quattro Pro, and the other programs in the Suite.

On the other hand, the DAD hogs a lot of Taskbar space, as well as a small chunk of precious system memory. To clear it off the Taskbar, right-click the DAD and choose E_xit DAD. That gets rid of the DAD only temporarily; the next time you turn your machine on, it'll be back in its usual spot.

There's a longer-term fix. To prevent the DAD from appearing whenever you turn you computer on:

1 Right-click the Start button on the Taskbar and choose O_pen.

2 In the Start Menu window that pops up, double-click the Programs folder. The Start Menu/Programs window appears.

3 Double-click the StartUp folder.

4 In the Start Menu/Programs/StartUp window that opens, right-click the Corel Desktop Application Director icon and choose D_elete, as seen in figure 1.2.

Fig. 1.2
Any programs placed in the StartUp folder run automatically whenever Windows loads.

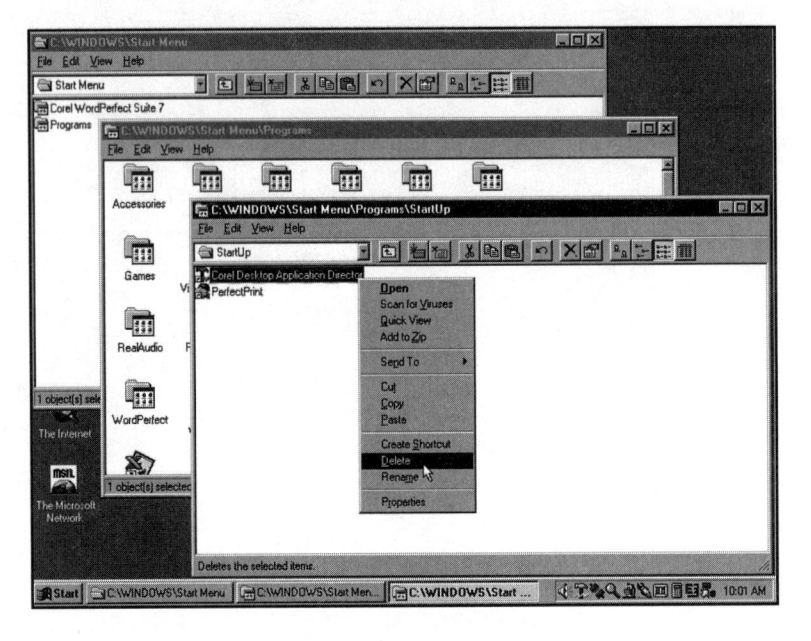

5 Click the Close button in each of the windows you've opened, and you're done.

The DAD will no longer appear automatically when you turn on your computer. You can get it back at any time: click Start, Corel WordPerfect Suite 7, Accessories, Corel Desktop Applications Director to plop it right back on to the Taskbar.

> **TIP** **If you leave the DAD in the StartUp folder, you can still prevent it** from running automatically on those occasions when you don't want it. To stop the DAD from appearing, wait for the desktop background to appear while Windows loads. Before the desktop icons pop up, press and hold the Ctrl key on the keyboard. Release the Ctrl key when the hourglass disappears. That trick stops anything in the StartUp folder from loading automatically.

You can also cut the DAD down to size. Right-click the DAD and choose Properties. In the DAD Properties dialog box that pops up, clear the check boxes for the programs you don't plan to use much (just click the check boxes to get rid of those little xs). Click the Close button in the DAD Properties dialog box when you finish. The icons for the programs you've deselected won't appear on the DAD until you put them back again.

> **TIP** **If you find your Start menu getting a little crowded, just move the** Corel WordPerfect Suite 7 folder (or any program icon or folder) to the Start, Programs menu, where most of your applications live. Right-click the Start button and choose Open. In the Start menu window that opens, drag the Corel WordPerfect Suite7 folder onto the Programs folder. Release the mouse button, and then close the Start menu window. The next time you want to run WordPerfect, click Start, Programs, aim your pointer at the Corel WordPerfect Suite 7 folder, and click the WordPerfect 7 icon.

I want a WordPerfect icon on my desktop

As if you really wanted yet another way to launch WordPerfect! But, many of us like to have program icons right on the desktop, where we can double-click them to run programs without searching through the Start menus and submenus.

If you're not planning to use the DAD and you'd like a WordPerfect icon on your desktop:

1 Right-click the clock on the Taskbar, and select Minimize All Windows to go to the desktop if you're not already there.

2 Right-click the Start button and choose <u>O</u>pen.

3 In the Start menu window that opens, double-click the Corel WordPerfect Suite 7 folder.

4 Click the WordPerfect 7 icon to select it. Now, press and hold the Ctrl key and drag the WordPerfect 7 icon out of the window and onto the desktop, as shown in figure 1.3.

Fig. 1.3
Ctrl+dragging an icon onto the desktop copies the icon instead of moving it.

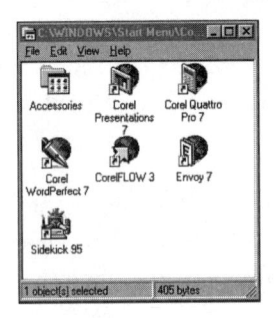

5 Release the Ctrl key and the mouse button, and a copy of the WordPerfect icon appears on the desktop. The original stays in the Corel Office 7 folder on the Start menu. To finish the job, click the Close buttons to close any open windows.

Now, you can run WordPerfect from the DAD, the desktop, or the Start menu. With all those choices, you'll have no excuses to avoid your work.

How do I get out of here?

Once you get WordPerfect running, you'll want to know your way out. To exit WordPerfect, select <u>F</u>ile, E<u>x</u>it, or click the Close button, that little X in the right corner of the WordPerfect title bar. Keyboard fans can press Alt+F4 to exit WordPerfect (or any other program, including Windows).

What's in the WordPerfect window?

Writers liked older versions of WordPerfect because the program displayed a (nearly) blank screen. Like the blank sheets of paper we used to roll into typewriters, the view was uncluttered, hence not distracting. On the other hand, you had to refer to a little slip of cardboard to remember the commands.

The not-distracting-look has gone the way of the typewriter. When you run WordPerfect now, that blank page is framed by a host of useful gadgets (see the following figure).

Why don't I see all those buttons in my copy of WordPerfect?!

The screen you see in the WordPerfect window on the next page might not look exactly like the WordPerfect screen you see on your own monitor. That's because your monitor might be set to a lower **screen resolution**. The higher the screen resolution setting, the more information the monitor displays. WordPerfect is designed to display all its Toolbar and Power Bar buttons at a screen resolution of 800 × 600 or higher; if your screen resolution is less than 800 × 600, you won't see as many Tool or Power Bar buttons. You don't lose out on any features, because they're all accessible from the menus. You're just missing a few buttons.

If you're not seeing all the WordPerfect buttons on your screen, you can adjust your screen resolution to a higher setting. Make sure your graphics card and monitor support resolutions are greater than 640 × 480. A quick look through your computer's manual should tell you what you need to know.

> ### 66 Plain English, please!
> The image you see on your monitor looks solid, but it's actually composed of thousands of tinier images, called **pixels**. Pixels are like the little dots that form an image in a newspaper. Look closely at any photo in today's paper, and you'll see the dots. Hold the photo farther away, and it looks like a solid image. Computer monitors work more or less the same way. **Screen resolution** is simply the number of pixels that the monitor displays, measured in terms of the number of horizontal pixels by the number of vertical pixels. A resolution of 800 × 600 means the monitor displays 800 pixels across the screen by 600 pixels down the screen. 99

To increase your screen resolution in order to see all the WordPerfect buttons:

1. If you're not already at the Windows desktop, right-click the clock on the Taskbar and choose Minimize All Windows.

2. Right-click the Windows desktop and choose Properties on the shortcut menu.

The WordPerfect window

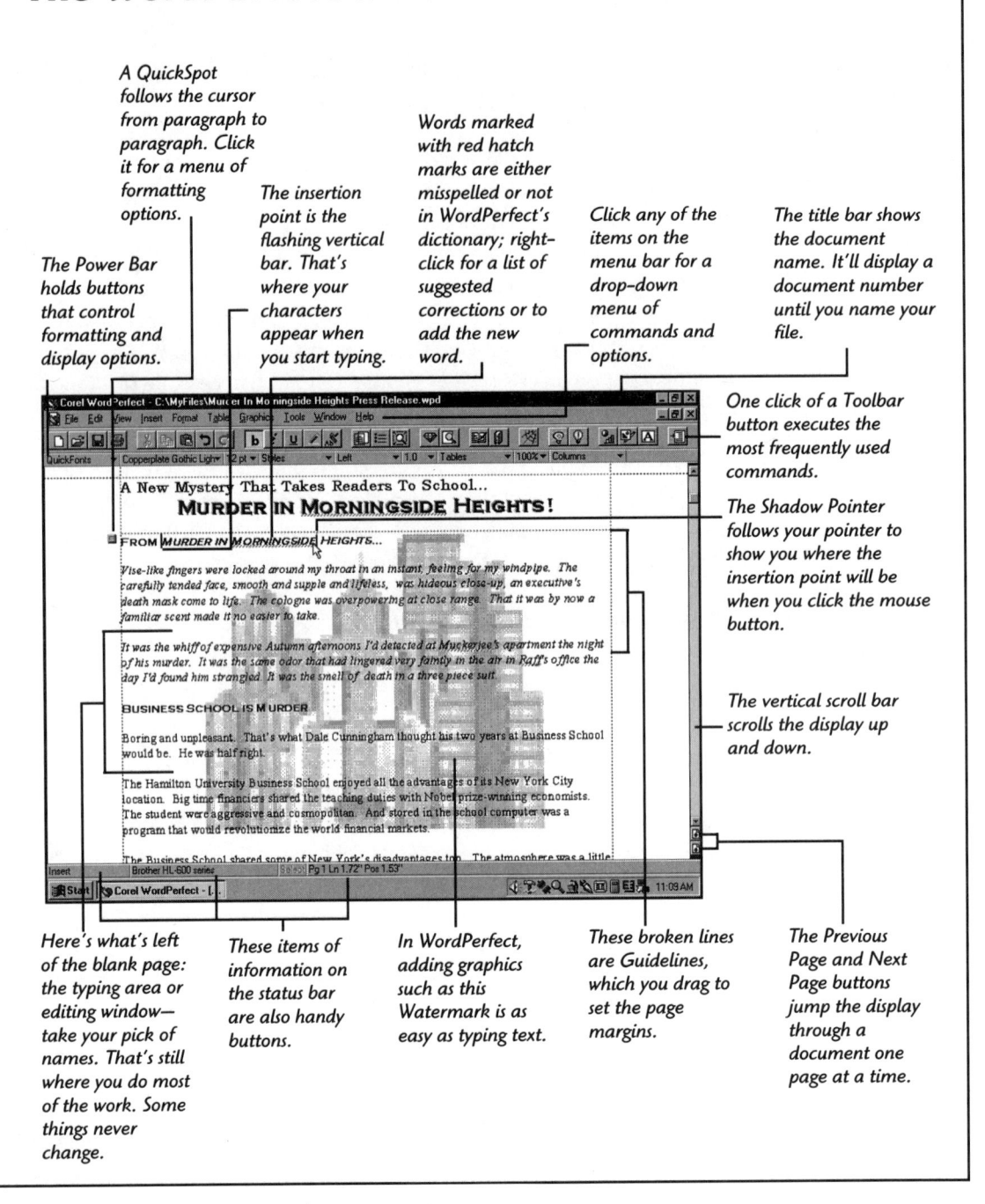

A QuickSpot follows the cursor from paragraph to paragraph. Click it for a menu of formatting options.

The insertion point is the flashing vertical bar. That's where your characters appear when you start typing.

Words marked with red hatch marks are either misspelled or not in WordPerfect's dictionary; right-click for a list of suggested corrections or to add the new word.

Click any of the items on the menu bar for a drop-down menu of commands and options.

The title bar shows the document name. It'll display a document number until you name your file.

The Power Bar holds buttons that control formatting and display options.

One click of a Toolbar button executes the most frequently used commands.

The Shadow Pointer follows your pointer to show you where the insertion point will be when you click the mouse button.

The vertical scroll bar scrolls the display up and down.

Here's what's left of the blank page: the typing area or editing window—take your pick of names. That's still where you do most of the work. Some things never change.

These items of information on the status bar are also handy buttons.

In WordPerfect, adding graphics such as this Watermark is as easy as typing text.

These broken lines are Guidelines, which you drag to set the page margins.

The Previous Page and Next Page buttons jump the display through a document one page at a time.

3 In the Display Properties dialog box that pops up, click the Settings tab.

4 Drag the Desktop area marker to the right until the display reads 800 × 600, as shown in figure 1.4.

Fig. 1.4
If your graphics card and monitor support a higher resolution, this is the place to make the adjustment.

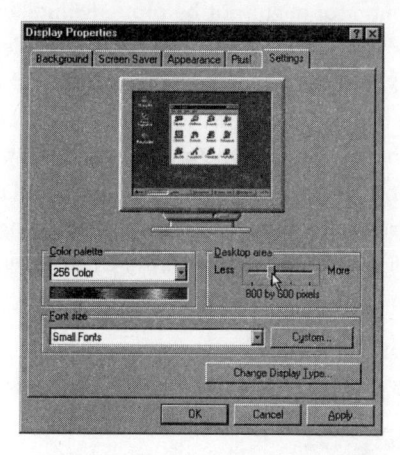

5 Click OK on the Settings tab, and a Display Properties message box pops up to tell you that Windows is about to resize your desktop. Click OK in the message box.

6 Click Yes in the Monitor Settings message box that appears next, and your new screen resolution is set.

You can always reverse the steps we just took if you don't like the new setting. And if your system can't handle a higher resolution, it's no great loss. All the WordPerfect features are still only a click or two away on the menu bar.

There are also many customization options that display as many, or as few, Toolbar and Power Bar buttons as you like (see Chapter 20 for more information).

> **TIP**
> **If your system doesn't suport higher screen resolutions, you can** add a scroll bar to the WordPerfect 7 Toolbar. The scroll bar lets you access all the Toolbar buttons, even if you can't see them all at the same time. To add the Toolbar scroll bar (it's easier done than said!), right-click the Toolbar and choose Preferences on the Quickmenu. In the Toolbar Preferences dialog box that appears, click Options. Click the Show scroll bar check box in the Toolbar Options dialog box. Click OK, and close the Toolbar Preferences dialog box. Two scroll arrows appear at the right of the Tollbar; click them to scroll the Toolbar buttons.

Q&A *I adjusted the screen resolution, and now I can't see everything on the screen!*

If your monitor hasn't adjusted automatically to a higher screen resolution, your particular monitor might not be properly installed in Windows. That's easy to fix: click Start, Settings, Control Panel. Double-click the Display icon in the Control Panel; then click the Settings tab in the Display Properties dialog box (see figure 1.4—we just took a different route to the same place). Click Change Display Type and take a look at the Monitor Type listing. If that isn't your monitor, click Change. Scroll down the lists of Manufacturers and Models in the Select Device dialog box, select your monitor, and click OK. Click Close in the Change Display Type dialog box, and click OK in the Display Properties dialog box.

Why does my mouse pointer keep changing shape?

If you move the mouse pointer around the window, you'll notice that it mutates from a white arrow to a two-headed black arrow as it travels from the Tool, Power, scroll, and status bars to the Guidelines in the typing area. As the white arrow, the pointer selects menu options or executes commands when clicked. When it's a two-headed arrow, drag it to change your margins.

Position the pointer over a blank space on the Toolbar, and it undergoes another transformation. When the pointer turns into that grabby-looking hand, you can drag the Toolbar to a different location. If, for example, you find all those buttons at the top of the window distracting, try dragging the Toolbar to the bottom of the window. You can also drag the Toolbar to the right or left side of the screen (see figure 1.4), or leave it "floating" in the middle of the screen.

Q&A *I dragged my Toolbar away from the top of the screen—now, how do I put it back again?*

If you have the Toolbar positioned at the left, right, or bottom of the screen, just use that grabby-looking hand to drag it back to the top. Once the gray outline of the Toolbar (which appears as you drag it) stretches out to the width of the screen, the Toolbar will snap back into its original position when you release the mouse button. If you've left the Toolbar floating in the middle of the screen, point at the Toolbar's title bar and drag that to the location of your choosing.

What do the buttons do?

You've probably noticed something else as you move the mouse pointer around the window. When you point at a button, a little label appears with the button's name and description. That's called a **QuickTip,** as shown in figure 1.5.

Fig. 1.5
Here's the Toolbar at the left of the screen; point at any button to get a QuickTip, a handy description of the button's function.

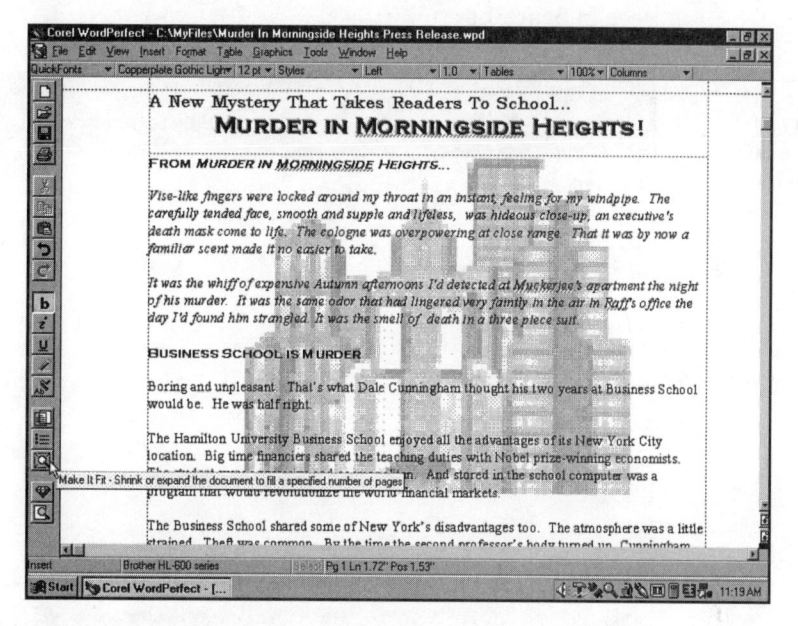

> 66 ***Plain English, please!***
>
> Those items on the Toolbar that we've been calling **buttons** are also called **tools**, hence "Toolbar." You might also see them referred to as **icons**, because they're little pictures. By whatever name, they put most WordPerfect features at your finger tips. The items on the Power Bar are also buttons, but they work a little differently. Click a Power Bar button, and you get a drop-down list of options to choose from. Between the Menu, Tool, Power, and Status bars, you'll never go thirsty for features in WordPerfect. 99

Gray QuickSpots, Red under-hatchings, and the Shadow Pointer

Some WordPerfect features are activated without your having to click a button or choose from a menu. Start typing, and you'll notice a few interesting things going on. You might find that some words have sprouted red cross-hatchings underneath them. That's WordPerfect's new Spell-As-You-Go feature, and it means that the word is either misspelled or contains a capitalization error. Try it: type **Ameria the beautiful.**

"Ameria" appears with the red cross-hatching, indicating that it's misspelled. Right-click the word, and you get a list of correctly spelled alternatives, as seen in figure 1.6.

Fig. 1.6
Fixing typos and misspellings is quick and easy with Spell-As-You-Go.

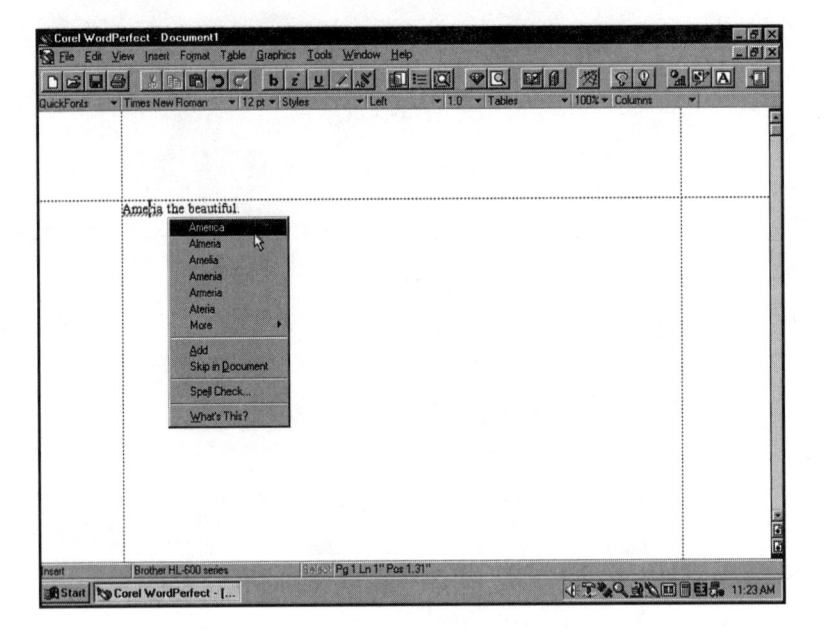

Click the word "America" on the QuickMenu list, and your misspelling is instantly corrected. Of course, not everyone wants to correct typos on the fly in this way. WordPerfect has a powerful spell checker that can correct all your errors after you finish typing the document (see Chapter 8). If you prefer to write first and check your spelling afterward, click Tools, Spell-As-You-Go to turn the feature off.

Once it's off, the check mark next to the menu item is cleared. To turn it back on, just click Tools, Spell-As-You-Go again. The check mark reappears, letting you know the feature is active once more.

7 Other handy tools in shades of gray

Type some text in the WordPerfect editing window, put the pointer over the text, and you'll notice a small gray button that appears to the left of the Guideline (see the graphics page). That's a **QuickSpot**; click it and you'll get a menu of the paragraph formatting features that we'll take a look at in Chapter 6.

Now move the pointer over the text you've typed. That faint gray bar you'll see next to the pointer is the **Shadow Pointer.** It's there to show you where the insertion point will be if you click the left mouse button (take a look at the figure on page 18 to see a QuickSpot and the Shadow Pointer).

Menus and QuickMenus, for all WordPerfect's features

Restaurant menus group choices by type: appetizers, main courses, and so on. WordPerfect menus do the same thing, which makes it a lot easier to find what you're looking for among the program's many features.

Click any item on the menu bar to get a menu of related features. You'll find commands to open, close, and save files under the File menu, for example. If you're not sure what a command on a drop-down menu does, point at it: a description of the command pops up right alongside the menu.

Some menu items display the keyboard shortcut associated with them, like the File, Close command's Ctrl+F4 shortcut. That means that you can hold down the Control key and press F4 to close a file, instead of using the mouse to click File, Close. The key strokes have exactly the same effect as the mouse clicks, so just choose the method you're most comfortable with. Figure 1.7 shows a menu item, along with its pop-up description and keyboard shortcut.

Q&A Why are some menu items dimmed? And why doesn't anything happen when I select them?

Dimmed menu items are features that temporarily can't be used. For example, before you type any text, the Cut and Copy commands are dimmed in the Edit menu, since you don't have any text to cut or copy.

Fig. 1.7
Just point to get a description of the highlighted command in any menu.

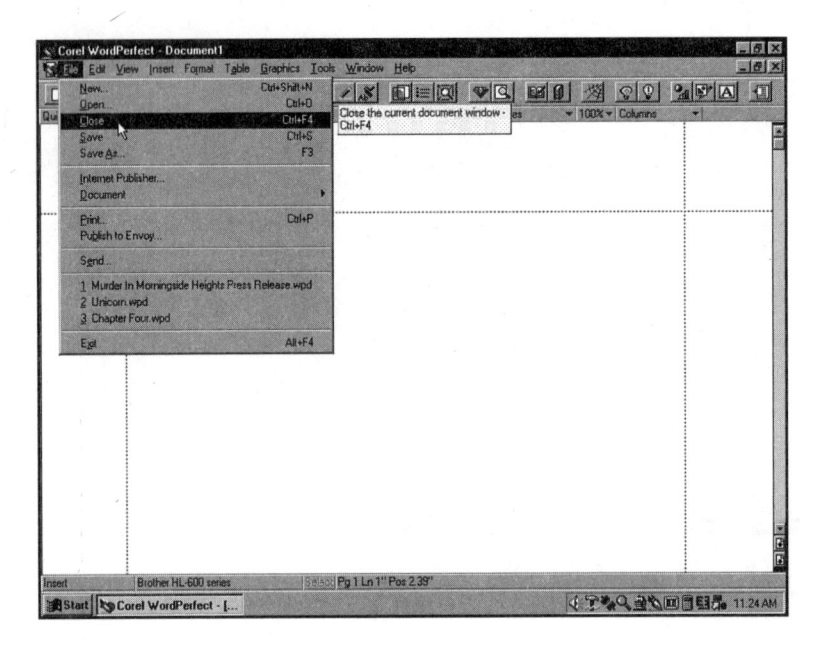

> ❝ **Plain English, please!**
>
> We promised to avoid computer jargon, but some terms are, well, unavoidable. Here's a recap of the computer-ese used so far: a **keyboard shortcut** is a combination of keyboard key strokes that you use instead of clicking menu commands or Toolbar buttons. A **pull-down menu** is a menu you see when you click an item on the menu bar. Also, you don't really have to pull it down—it drops down by itself. When you do click a menu item, you **execute**, or activate, a feature. We've been talking about **clicking**, which you probably know by now means to click the left mouse button. To **drag**, hold down the mouse button and move the pointer. You can drag through text to select it. You also drag to move things around on the screen. ❞

My right mouse button actually does something?

Here's another of WordPerfect's nice surprises: the right mouse button is a handy tool. Try pointing at the Toolbar, then click the right mouse button. A QuickMenu pops up with a list of all the WordPerfect Toolbars. Each Toolbar has buttons for different tasks, such as working with tables, preparing legal documents, or designing publication-quality documents.

If there's text in the editing window, point at the left margin (directly to the left of your text) and right-click for a QuickMenu with a choice of selection options and the Margins command. Point anywhere else in the editing window, right-click, and you get the QuickMenu shown in figure 1.8.

Fig. 1.8
QuickMenus pop up with a right click of the mouse.

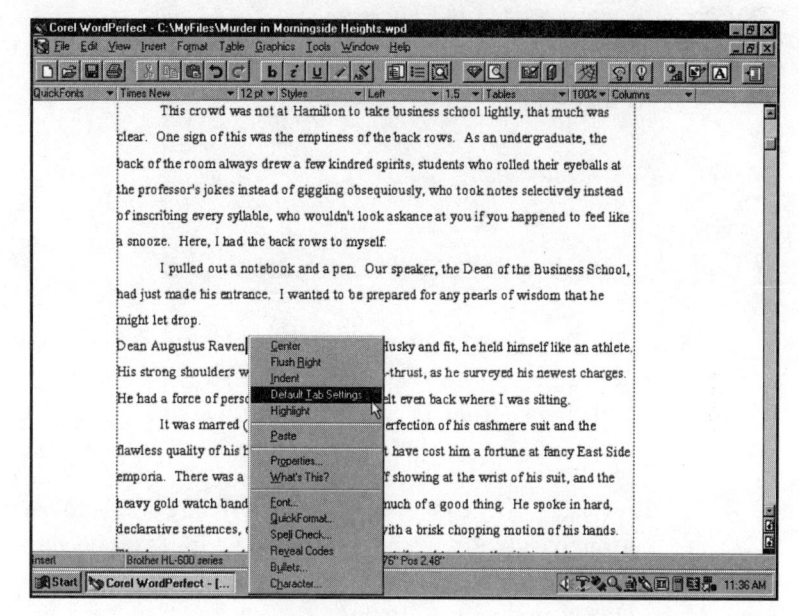

There are QuickMenus for the Power and status bars as well. Point at either one, and right-click for QuickMenus that let you add or remove items on the bars, or hide the bars entirely in case you need a bigger space to type in.

Dialog boxes do many commands at once

A lot of WordPerfect commands require more information from you before the program can execute them. Whenever that happens, a dialog box pops up. Click Format, Font, for example, and you'll get the Font dialog box shown in figure 1.9.

Dialog boxes often have **check boxes**, like the ones under Appearance in figure 1.9. Click a box to select or deselect an item. The ✔ in the check box next to Bold shows that Bold is selected.

Click an item under Font Face to select it, and your selection is highlighted. The preview box, at the lower-left corner, shows what you selected.

Fig. 1.9
The Font dialog box holds a host of options to control the size and appearance of the characters in your document.

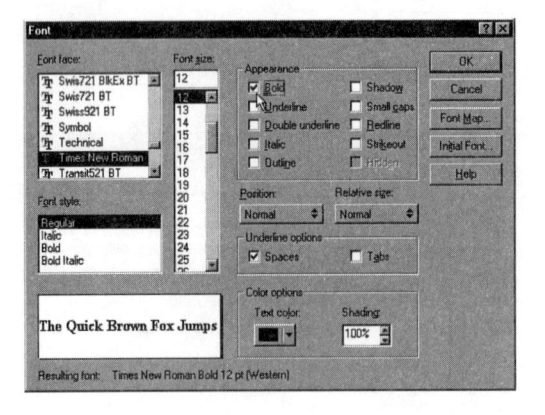

Some dialog boxes have edit boxes, like the Font size edit box in figure 1.9, where you can type text. That particular edit box also gives you a scrolling list to choose from, in case you don't feel like typing numbers. Most dialog boxes also have special push buttons, such as OK, Cancel, or Help.

The easiest way to move around in a dialog box is to use the mouse. Click a button, check box, or list item to select it. If you need to type in text, click the edit box where the text goes. That puts the insertion point in the edit box, and you can just start typing.

When you finish with a dialog box, click the OK button. To back out without making any changes to the document, click the Cancel button, or simply press the Escape (Esc) key. And if you have any questions about the dialog box, click the Help button.

I want to see more (or less) of this document

Change your point of view, and you see things differently. WordPerfect gives you several ways to look at your documents. Click View on the menu bar and take your choice of three display options:

- Draft shows you your text, but it doesn't display the margins, which means you won't be able to see headers, footers, or footnotes.

- Page displays all your text, including everything in the margins. When you start up WordPerfect, the display is in Page mode until you change it.

- T<u>w</u>o Page displays two pages of a document at once, as shown in figure 1.10. You can make editing changes in Two Page mode, but it's next to impossible to see body text.

Fig. 1.10
Two Page mode gives you the big picture of your document.

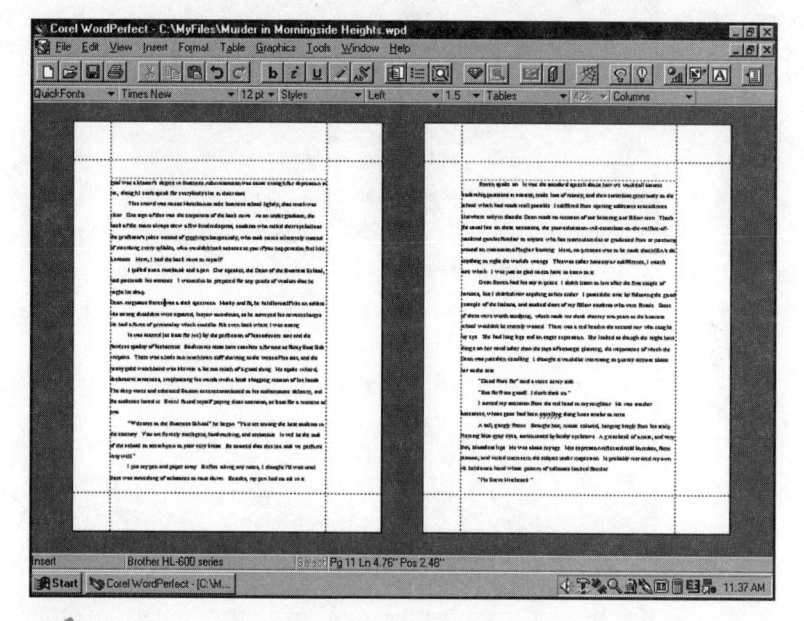

TIP To flip quickly between <u>P</u>age and <u>D</u>raft modes, press Ctrl+F5 for Draft mode or Alt+F5 for Page mode.

Telescope the screen with Zoom

Ever try looking at the same thing from either end of a telescope? WordPerfect's Zoom control has the same effect on your document.

The Page/Zoom Full button on the Toolbar switches you to a full page view of your document, just as it would look in print. That's handy for previewing a print job before you start using up paper. Click the Page/Zoom Full button again to return to your previous document view.

You can also change the normal view with the Zoom button at the right end of the Power Bar. Click the button, and take your choice of zoom levels from the pull-down menu shown in figure 1.11.

The **zoom percentage** is the ratio of the screen display to the printed page. Lower the ratio to see more of the page; increase the ratio to see a smaller area in magnified detail. Figure 1.11 shows you what Zoom control is all about.

Fig. 1.11
A document zoomed to 150%. Use the Power Bar Zoom button to see document detail, or the big picture.

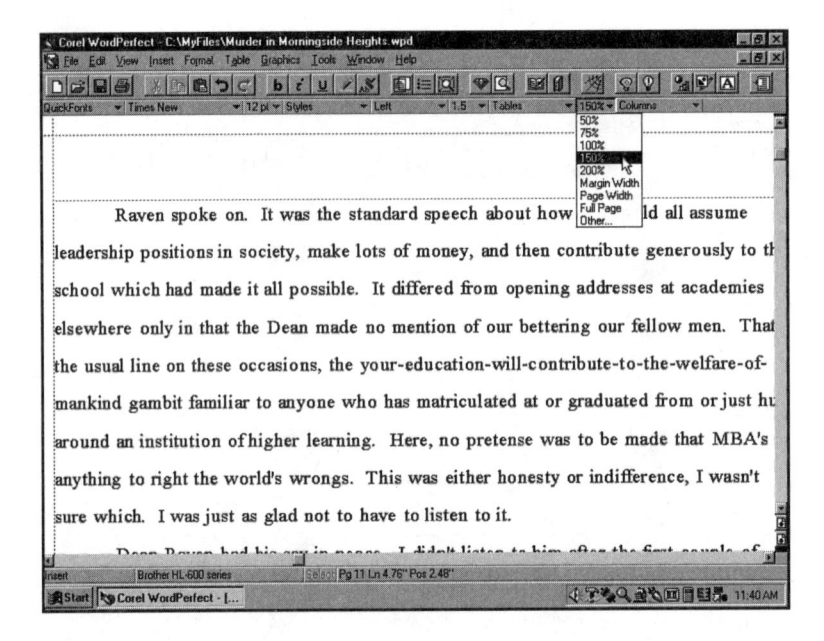

If you want to adjust the zoom ratio to some value other than the choices on the Power Bar button, click View, Zoom. That pops up the Zoom dialog box, in which you can set the magnification level to anything you want.

Scrolling turns the on-screen page

Getting from page one to page two in a book is pretty straightforward; you just turn the page. Turning pages in a WordPerfect document is just as straightforward. Click the Previous Page or Next Page buttons on the scroll bar to get from page to page in a document.

The problem is, in normal view you won't see an entire page of a document on the screen. The Previous Page and Next Page buttons take you from the top of one page to the top of the next page, but you see only one window's worth of the page, about a third of it, at a time.

That's okay though, because WordPerfect gives you plenty of ways to scroll through a document:

- Click the scroll bar up and down arrows to scroll through the document one line at a time.

- Click the scroll bar between the up and down arrows to advance or retreat one window at a time. Click above the scroll button to move back through the document; click below the scroll button to advance forward.

- Drag the scroll button up or down to advance or retreat through the document by variable amounts.

Q&A ***How come WordPerfect seems to jump around when I scroll from page to page?***

You're in Page mode. Click View, Draft to switch to draft mode. With no margins to display, scrolling through WordPerfect might seem smoother.

These scrolling options don't move the insertion point through the document. You may be seeing a different part of the document, but if you type something, WordPerfect jumps back to the last place you left the insertion point.

Moving the insertion point as you scroll

As you press the keyboard arrow or the Page Up and Page Down keys, the insertion point *will* move through the document. If you move the insertion point past the window-full of document you happen to be looking at, the document scrolls to the new position automatically.

There are some other ways to move the insertion point through a document, which we'll look at in Chapter 2.

2

Creating a New Document

● **In this chapter:**

- How do I enter text?

- I need to create a new document

- I want to save the document with a name I'll remember

- How do I get my document back when I can't remember its name?

- Okay, I'm ready to print

- How can I tell one dialog box from another?

WordPerfect can't come up with the ideas for your new document, but it does make translating those ideas into words a lot easier. . . . . ▸

From cave paintings on, we've always tried to set our thoughts down on something permanent. Recording an idea, in pictures or writing, makes it clearer. Dr. Samuel Johnson, who wrote the first modern dictionary of the English language, once said, "No man but a blockhead ever wrote except for money."

Great man though he was, even Dr. Johnson could be wrong. We write for a lot of reasons, not the least of which is that writing, by capturing our thoughts, helps us think.

As you'll see in this chapter, WordPerfect can make writing easier. WordPerfect's polished documents make captured thoughts clearer, for ourselves and for our readers.

How do I enter text in a WordPerfect document?

The best way to start writing is to start writing. If you don't like what you've written, you can always go back and change it. Two hundred years ago, editing with a quill pen must have been a bit of a chore. (That might explain Dr. Johnson's attitude.) Changing things around in WordPerfect is a breeze. Setting your words down in a clear and attractive way is just as easy.

There are two ways to tackle a new document in WordPerfect. One way is to wing it and just type. The words appear in the editing window. When you finish typing, you can edit your work, save it, and print it, all with a few clicks of the mouse.

But if you want a polished document, WordPerfect's templates provide professional-looking results with a minimum of fuss. Templates are preformatted document shells, in which all the margins, tabs, spacing, and other settings are already taken care of. Just add text, and you're done.

Whichever method you use to create a new document, there are two things to keep in mind when you type in WordPerfect:

- WordPerfect is smarter than a typewriter. Just keep typing, even when you get to the end of a line. The typed text "wraps" automatically to the next line. When you get to the end of a paragraph, press Enter. That forces the insertion point to move to a new line so that you can start the next paragraph.

- To indent paragraphs, or to align text vertically, press the Tab key, not the Spacebar. *Do* use the Spacebar to add a space after commas or two spaces after periods as you'd do normally. Just don't use the Spacebar to set off the first line of a paragraph or to align other text. It may look correct on your screen, but the alignment may be off if you change fonts or when you print.

Do-it-yourself documents

If we wrote a letter by the wing-it method, here's a little exercise to show what we'd do. Feel free to follow these steps and type what's in boldface for the exercise. If you make a typing mistake, press Backspace or Delete to correct it:

1. Click Insert, Date, Date Text to stick the date in the document at the insertion point. Then press Enter twice to move down two lines.

> **TIP** For a date that "updates" automatically, click Insert, Date, Date Code. That inserts today's date, but if you open the file on subsequent dates, those days' dates will be inserted in its place.

Hard or soft, every line has a return

When you type past the right margin, WordPerfect inserts what's called a **soft return** to move the insertion point to the next line. If you add text or make changes in the paragraph, those soft returns move automatically to accommodate the changes, jumping words up or down to the next line as needed.

Pressing Enter at the end of a paragraph inserts a **hard return**. Hard returns stay where you put them until they're deleted. Because hard returns don't move, you can make changes in a paragraph but still keep the paragraph together.

Think of the sentences in a paragraph as a continuous line, like a long strand of cooked spaghetti. Soft returns bend the strand at the end of each line without breaking it. Hard returns snap the strand wherever you press Enter.

2 Type the salutation: **Dear Dr. Johnson,** and then press Enter twice to move down two lines.

3 Press Tab and type the first paragraph. Don't press Enter at the end of the lines; just keep typing to the end of the paragraph. Type: **We have nothing but admiration for the poems, essays, stories, and epigrams you have left us. Your pioneering dictionary was truly heroic. The changes it made to the English language are still with us, two hundred and forty years later.**

4 Press Enter to end the first paragraph, and press Enter again to move down one more line.

5 Press Tab and type the second paragraph: **We cannot agree with you, however, when you say that any writer who doesn't write for money is a blockhead. Simply by clarifying thought, writing is priceless—even if you don't get paid for it.**

6 Press Enter twice to move down two lines and type **Sincerely,**. Our letter looks like figure 2.1.

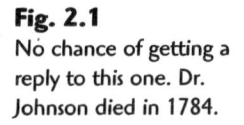

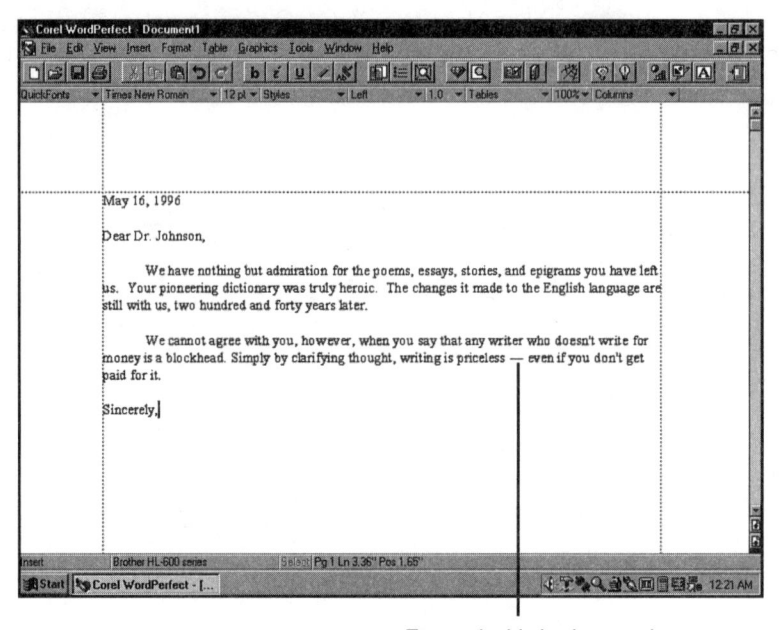

Fig. 2.1
No chance of getting a reply to this one. Dr. Johnson died in 1784.

Type a double hyphen, and WordPerfect converts it to an em dash automatically.

Of course, a letter written this way leaves us with a few questions. How about the recipient's address? And we'll want the return address in there somewhere. WordPerfect gives us one-inch margins without being asked. But do we really want the letter scrunched up at the top of the page, which is what we'd get with our letter?

Click the Page/Zoom Full button to view the document as shown in figure 2.2, and you can see that our letter's layout could use some work. Let's call in the Expert!

Fig. 2.2
This is how the letter would look on the printed page.

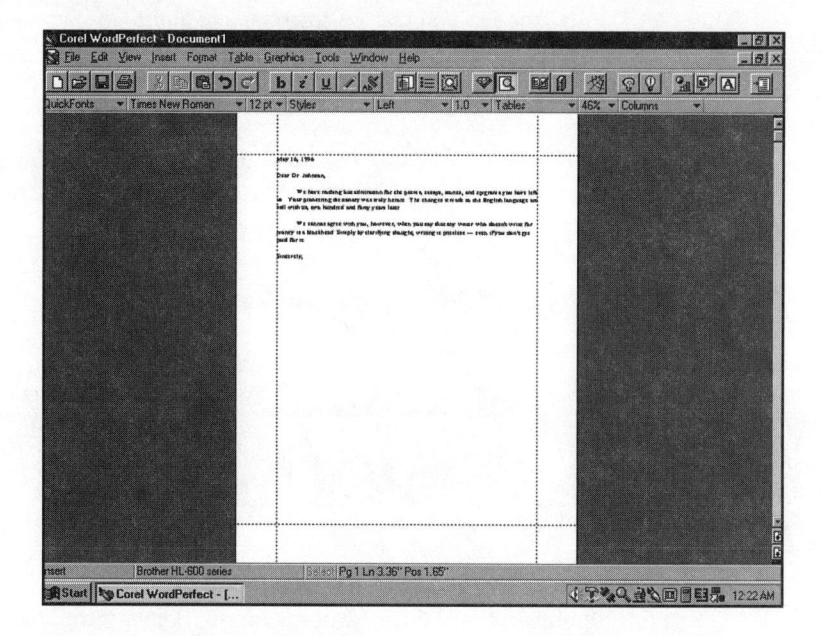

Click the Page/Zoom Full button again to return to the normal view.

Use WordPerfect Expert templates for documents by the numbers

WordPerfect has a second way to tackle new documents that settles all such questions without our having to bother about them. We can use a letter **template** to handle all the layout issues for us. With a template, all we have to do is compose the body of the letter; WordPerfect does the rest of the job.

Let's try that same letter the WordPerfect way. The result will be a professional-looking document, created with no more effort than the wing-it version we've already churned out. We'll also add some personal information that will speed things up the next time you use the Letter Expert template.

66 Plain English, please!

A **template** is any tool used to fit a piece of work to a desired shape. A template is usually an outline or model of the finished product; when the outline is filled in, the result resembles the model. 99

TIP **Incidentally, the first button on the Toolbar is the** New *Blank* Document button, not to be confused with the New Document button we've just clicked. Clicking the New Document button lets you choose any template and then start your document. Clicking the New Blank Document button opens a new document with the default template.

1 Click the New Document button on the Toolbar. That pops up the Select New Document dialog box, with a variety of template choices arranged in related groups (see fig. 2.3).

Fig. 2.3
The Select New Document dialog box gives you a choice of templates and experts.

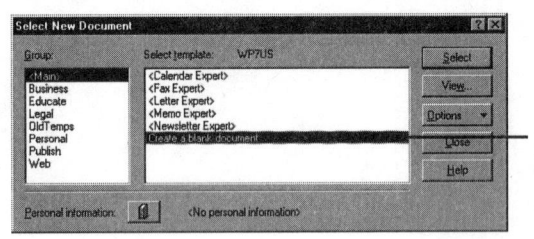

You can take your pick of templates, including Create a blank document (which gives you the default template you see whenever you first run the program).

2 Under Group in the New Document dialog box, choose "Main," and then double-click <Letter Expert> on the Select template list.

3 It's no fun typing your own name and title at the bottom of every memo and letter you send, and WordPerfect spares you the trouble. All you do is type the information once, and it'll be stored in the WordPerfect Address Book. Click OK in the Personalize Your Templates message box that pops up, and select Person in the New Entry dialog box that appears next, as seen in figure 2.4.

4 Click OK in the New Entry dialog box and the Properties for New Entry dialog box appears. Here's where you enter your name, title, company, address, phone; whatever information you want on letterheads and return addresses, as seen in figure 2.5. Use the Tab key to move from one edit box to another on the form, or just click in the box you want to type in.

Chapter 2 *Creating a New Document* **37**

Fig. 2.4
The WordPerfect Address Book stores all your important names and addresses, including your own, and every new entry starts with this dialog box.

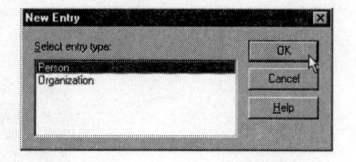

Fig. 2.5
Enter as many details of your own life as you like: typing it in now saves you from having to do it again for your next letter.

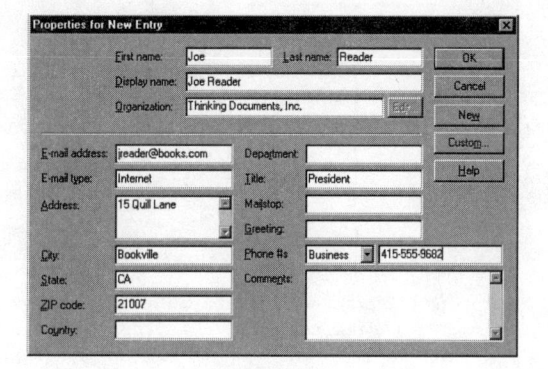

5 Click OK in the Properties for New Entry dialog box to save your personal information, and click OK in the Corel Address Book. Unless it changes, you'll never have to type your name and return address again—WordPerfect stores it for use with this and other templates.

6 With the Address Book closed, WordPerfect's gears whirl for a moment, and then the Letter Expert dialog box pops up. In the To edit box, type your recipient's name and address. Add the salutation in the Greeting edit box, as shown in figure 2.6.

7 Once you've typed your recipient's address and greeting, click Finished in the Letter Expert dialog box. In moments, all the elements of the letter—greeting, closing, and so on—are properly formatted and displayed. All we need now is the body text, as shown in figure 2.7.

Fig. 2.6
When you have data in the WordPerfect Address Book, you'll just click the Address Book button to insert recipients' names and addresses.

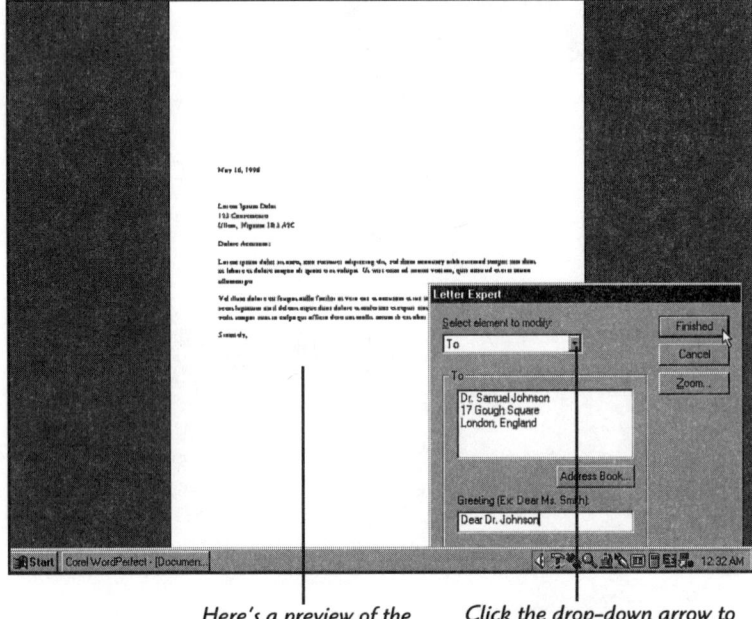

Here's a preview of the letter's layout, with WordPerfect's own ersatz body text.

Click the drop-down arrow to add courtesy copy notations, or to change items such as the letter closing.

Fig. 2.7
The Letter Expert adds the date and throws in the closing automatically.

The default closing is "Sincerely" but you can change that (see fig. 2.6).

The Letter Expert adds the sender's name and title, which it takes from the personal information we filled out in the Address Book.

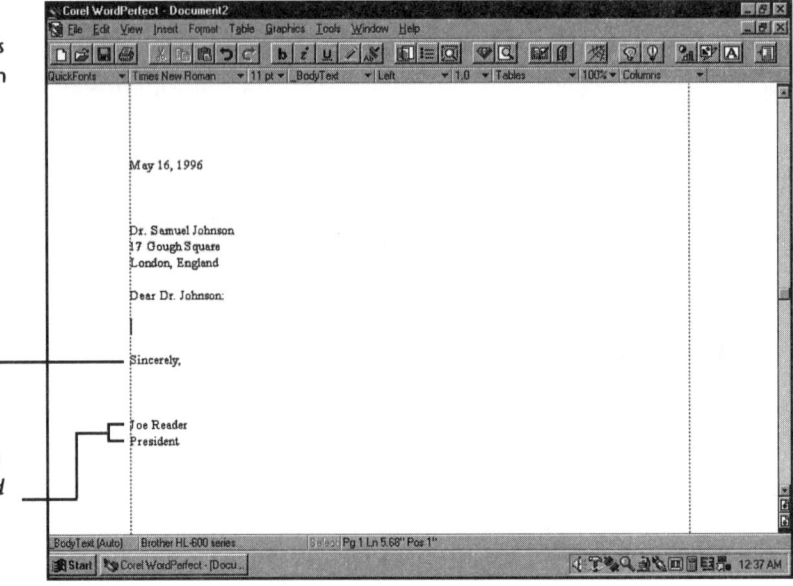

Bonus timesaver! Save typing with copy and paste

We have a perfect letter layout. Now we just add the body text for a perfect letter. We want those two paragraphs we've already typed to appear between the salutation and the closing of the letter. We could retype them, but why bother? Instead, we'll save time and effort by copying the paragraphs from Document 1 and pasting them into our template letter in Document 2.

> **TIP** To switch quickly from one document window to another, press Ctrl+F6. You can keep as many as nine documents open at a time in WordPerfect. When you start WordPerfect, you're automatically in Document 1, and each new document you open is numbered 2, 3, and so on.

To copy text from Document 1 to Document 2, first go to Document 1.

1. Click Window, 1 Document 1 to display our first letter.

2. Move the mouse pointer to the left margin of the first paragraph of text and click to put the insertion point there. The flashing cursor should be immediately to the left of the tab preceding We.

3. Hold down the Shift key and press the down-arrow key to highlight both paragraphs of text (see fig. 2.8).

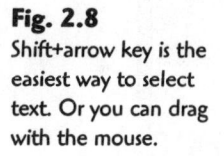

Fig. 2.8
Shift+arrow key is the easiest way to select text. Or you can drag with the mouse.

4. Now click the Copy button on the Toolbar.

5. Click <u>W</u>indow, <u>2</u> Document 2 (or press Ctrl+F6) to switch to our template letter.

6. The insertion point should be between the salutation and the closing—that's where the Letter Expert leaves it. If it's not, just click between the salutation and the closing to put the insertion point in the right place.

7. Click the Paste button on the Toolbar. The copied text is pasted into the letter, as shown in figure 2.9.

Fig. 2.9
Copying and pasting text is easy to do, and it saves a lot of time and typing.

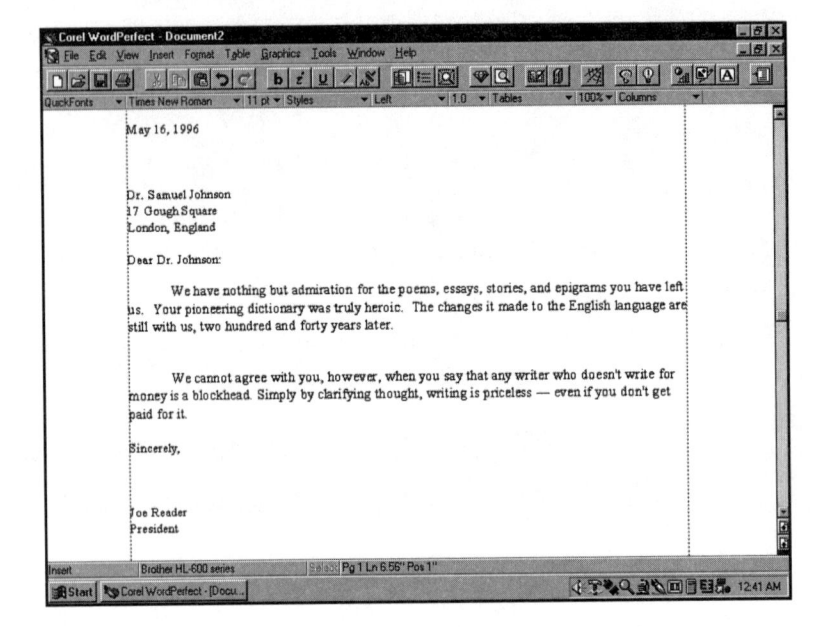

> **TIP** **Even if you love mice and hate keyboard shortcuts, try these** keyboard copy, cut, and paste methods anyway—with frequent use; they'll grow on you. Highlight your text, and then press Ctrl+C to copy it or Ctrl+X to cut it. To paste it in elsewhere, press Ctrl+V.

Check out the difference between our Letter Expert template letter and our wing-it effort as shown in figure 2.10.

Fig. 2.10
Same letter, but different layouts. The template version looks much more professional.

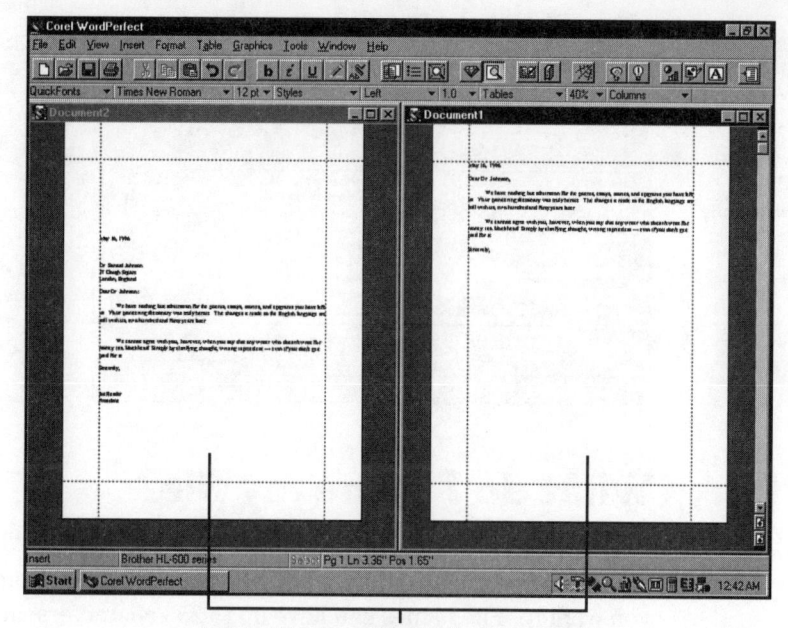

I clicked Window, Tile Side by Side, and put both documents in Page/Zoom Full view so you could see them side by side.

Document finished? Save it

It's very convenient to have WordPerfect number successive documents 1, 2, 3, and so on. That makes it easy to switch back and forth between them. On the other hand, the name Document 1 doesn't tell us much. We need to save our letter with a new name.

Click the Save button on the Toolbar for the Corel Office Save As dialog box shown in figure 2.11.

Here's where we name our new document. In the Name edit box down at the bottom of the screen, the characters ***.wpd** are highlighted (see fig. 2.11). That inscrutable notation is a relic from the days of DOS, Windows's predecessor, and it simply means "all files of any name of the WordPerfect Document (.wpd) type." It'll disappear as soon as you start typing your file name.

Fig. 2.11
The Corel Office Save As dialog box lets you name a new document; it also displays existing saved documents if you have any.

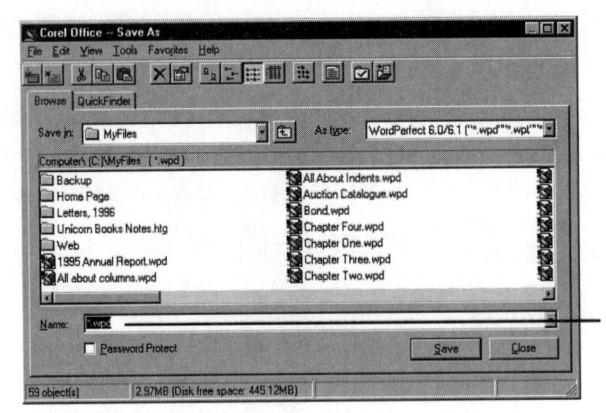

Type your file name in the Name edit box. You'll type over any highlighted characters that are already in the edit box.

What do I name my file?

Readers who have suffered through earlier versions of Windows and DOS are in for a nice surprise: you can call your new document pretty much anything you want to. File names can have up to 255 characters, including spaces. Just don't include any of the following characters: / : * ? " < > |. Those characters are illegal, but otherwise, anything goes. You can be as prolix—"Letter to Dr. Johnson on the subject of writing for money"—or as terse—"Dr. Johnson letter"—as you like.

Just type your file name in the Name edit box and click the Save button. WordPerfect automatically saves your document in a folder called **MyFiles**, and there it'll stay until you move or delete it.

Windows stores all your files in folders, many of which contain subfolders, which in turn can hold sub-subfolders, and so on. It's a system like your own filing cabinet, although you probably don't stick one file folder inside another the way Windows does. When you start to accumulate lots of different documents of different types, you'll probably want to create new folders for them. That makes it easier to keep everything organized. For now, the **MyFiles** folder is a fine place to store your documents.

Once you type a file name and click Save in the Corel Office—Save As dialog box, you'll notice that the title bar no longer displays Document 1, but shows our new name instead, as seen in figure 2.12.

Fig. 2.12
The title bar reflects your file's new name as soon as you save it.

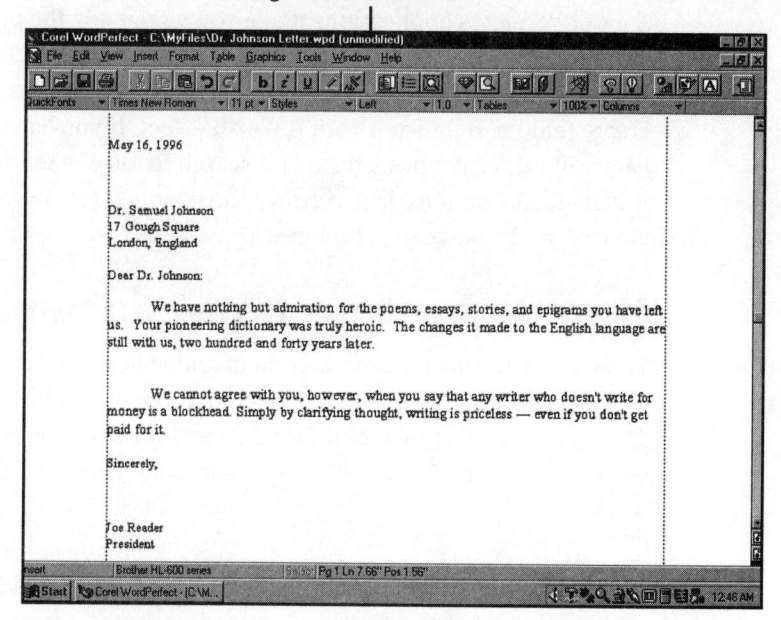

The "unmodified" in the title bar disappears when you make changes in the document.

How do I get out of this document?

The document is finished and saved, and you're ready to go home for the day. All you need to do is exit. WordPerfect gives you several ways out:

- To exit the program, click the Close button, that top X at the upper right-hand corner of the title bar.

- Or click File, Exit, or press Alt+F4 to leave the program.

- Maybe you're through with the document but you have more work to do. To exit the active document but stay in WordPerfect, click File, Close, or press Ctrl+F4. You can also click the lower of the two Close buttons at the upper-right of the screen.

You can always refer back to these directions to the exits, but if you're still working your way through this chapter, don't leave WordPerfect quite yet.

WordPerfect has a built-in file manager

A lot of Windows applications make you go outside the program to the Windows Explorer or My Computer to take care of file chores. Not WordPerfect. You can delete, move, rename, or print files, even rename and create folders, right from within WordPerfect. If you can't remember a file name, WordPerfect has a powerful search feature that'll find your file for you. And if all you want to do is retrieve the documents you've been working on most recently, you can get them with two clicks of the mouse.

How do I get my latest documents back?

You named and saved your document and shut down WordPerfect. Now you're back from lunch and you need that document opened again. Click File. The bottom of the File menu lists the last four documents you've worked on, even if you closed WordPerfect. Click the one you want and get back to work.

I need a document from weeks ago

Now let's speed up the clock. Weeks have passed, we've created a slew of new files, our letter to Dr. Johnson is buried under a pile of new documents, and we want it back. When you want a file that doesn't happen to be among the last four you've worked on, click the Open button on the Toolbar. That pops up the Corel Office—Open dialog box shown in figure 2.13.

No, you're not having a spell of déjà vu. The Open dialog box looks just like the Save As dialog box and their triplet sibling, the Insert File dialog box. In each case, you're getting what WordPerfect calls the file management dialog boxes, which act collectively as the program's file manager.

We'll take a look at file management in detail in Chapter 18. For now, we're trying to find a file that's not on the File menu list. If you recognize the file in the Open dialog box, just double-click it. If you think, but aren't completely sure, that the selected file is the one you want, click the Preview button on the Open dialog box toolbar. A preview window pops up, and you can glance at the file's contents.

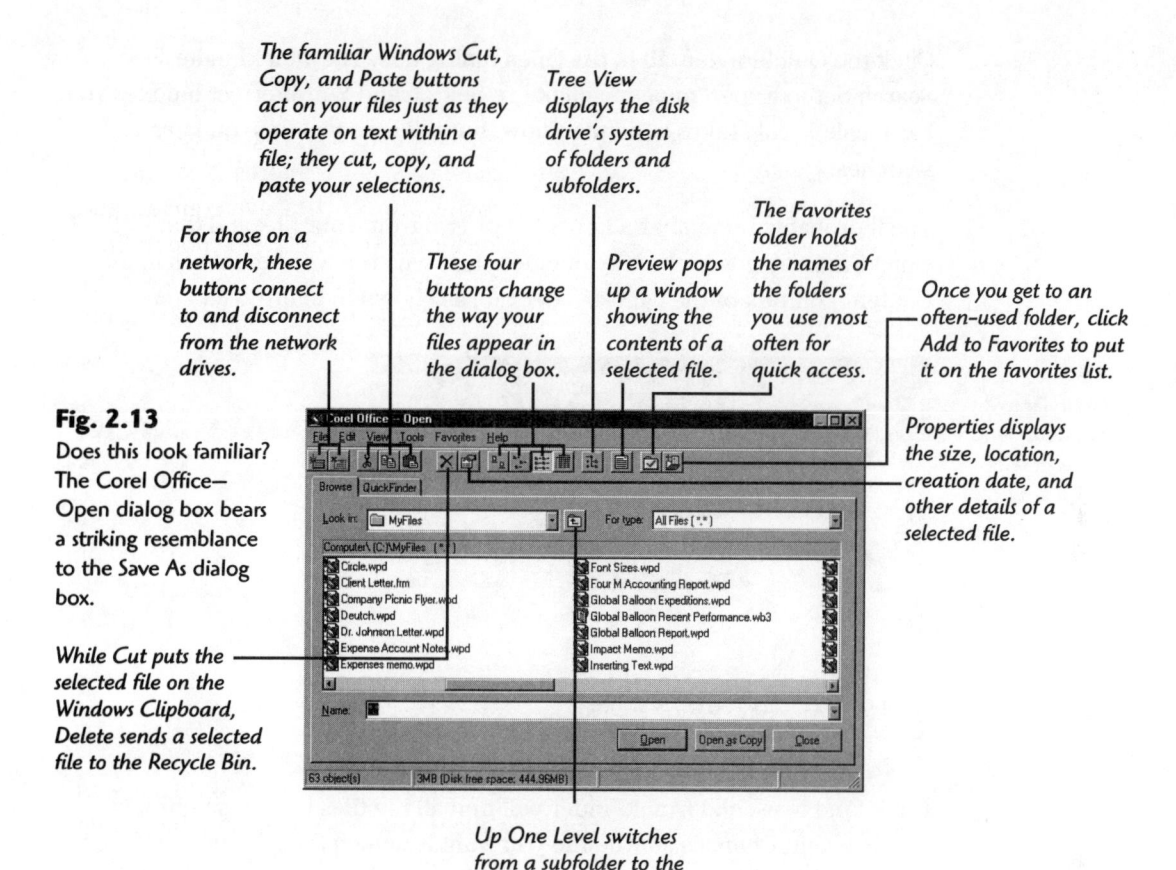

Fig. 2.13
Does this look familiar? The Corel Office—Open dialog box bears a striking resemblance to the Save As dialog box.

The familiar Windows Cut, Copy, and Paste buttons act on your files just as they operate on text within a file; they cut, copy, and paste your selections.

Tree View displays the disk drive's system of folders and subfolders.

For those on a network, these buttons connect to and disconnect from the network drives.

These four buttons change the way your files appear in the dialog box.

Preview pops up a window showing the contents of a selected file.

The Favorites folder holds the names of the folders you use most often for quick access.

Once you get to an often-used folder, click Add to Favorites to put it on the favorites list.

Properties displays the size, location, creation date, and other details of a selected file.

While Cut puts the selected file on the Windows Clipboard, Delete sends a selected file to the Recycle Bin.

Up One Level switches from a subfolder to the folder that contains it.

> **TIP**
>
> **Backing up files to a tape or floppy disk takes a minute or two.** Re-creating lost files is just too painful to contemplate. There are all kinds of backup programs available, including Windows' own. But if you just want a quick copy of a file or two on floppy disk, you can do it right from the WordPerfect Open dialog box. Insert a floppy disk into your disk drive, right-click your file in the Open dialog box, and choose Send To. Click 3 1/2 Floppy on the Send To menu to copy the file to your diskette.

I can't remember what I called my file!

If you can't remember your file name at all, WordPerfect has a detective service that can track it down for you. It's called QuickFinder; supply it with a clue or two, and you'll recover that lost file in moments.

Click the QuickFinder tab in the Open dialog box. The QuickFinder Fast Search Setup Expert appears; click Pre-Search and WordPerfect indexes your hard disk. It only takes a moment now, but it'll save you time on later searches.

You'll probably remember a key word or two from your file, and that's all QuickFinder needs in the way of clues. Just type the word or words in the Content edit box of the QuickFinder tab, as shown in figure 2.14.

Fig. 2.14
Use QuickFinder to track down documents whose names or locations you can't remember.

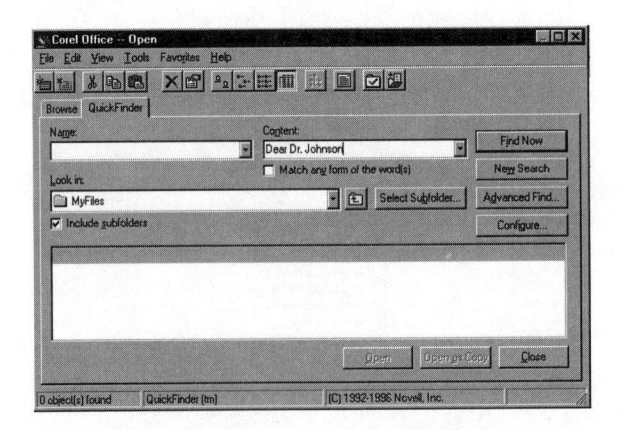

Click Find Now, and QuickFinder will find all the files in which your key words occur. Chances are the file you want is among them; double-click it to open the file.

QuickFinder's search came up empty-handed! Now what do I do?

By default, QuickFinder looks for files in the MyFiles folder. But maybe you saved your lost file in a different folder, or you're looking for files in a different location altogether (if you have old WordPerfect 6.1 files, for example, they're probably in a folder called OFFICE/WPWIN/WPDOCS).

That's no problem. Just tell QuickFinder to look elsewhere for the file. Click the drop-down arrow by the Look in edit box in the QuickFinder tab and select a different folder. Now click the Include subfolders check box; then click Find Now. QuickFinder will search the selected folder and all its subfolders for that errant file.

I'm ready to print my document

Want to print the whole document, one page, or a range of pages? Click the Print button on the Toolbar. That gets you the Print dialog box (see fig. 2.15).

WordPerfect uses your Windows default printer automatically, so the printer you've installed in Windows is the printer WordPerfect will use.

To print the whole document, click the Print button in the Print dialog box (it's actually the Print button in the Print *tab* of the Print dialog box, but there are too many Prints in that sentence already).

Full Document is the default choice in the Print dialog box, but if that's not what you want, there are plenty of options. Click the drop-down arrow under Print for the choices shown in figure 2.15.

Fig. 2.15
Print the current page, the whole document, or anything in between from the Print dialog box.

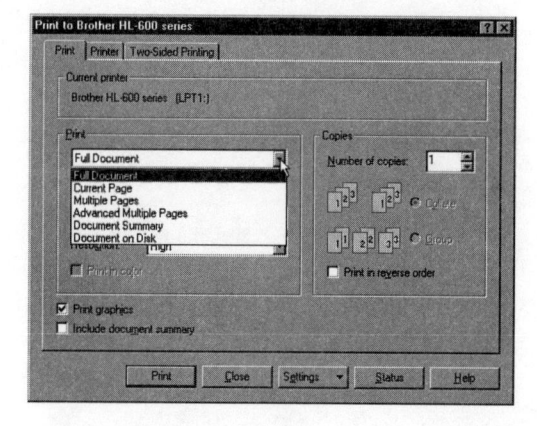

- Select Current Page, and click the Print button to print only the page where you last left the insertion point.

- Select Multiple Pages if you want to print more than one page, but not all the pages, in a document. You can specify exactly which pages to print in the Page range edit boxes.

> **Q&A** *I only want to print a few pages, but the Page range option seems to be grayed-out!*
>
> Just click in the Page range edit boxes and type the page numbers you want to print. WordPerfect will automatically select the Multiple Pages option in the Print drop-down list, and the Page range option will spring to life.

3

WordPerfect Help Is All Around You

● In this chapter:

- Have a question? Ask the PerfectExpert!

- Quick! Remind me what this button does

- How do I get help fast?

- This dialog box has me boxed in

- Help is online, anytime

Features are thick on the ground in WordPerfect, and you'll need help to find your way. Like an ideal scout, WordPerfect Help knows all the best routes, and it never leaves your side . . . . ▶

A strolling newspaperman stopped to watch a kids' baseball team take batting practice one afternoon. The sound of whiffing bats was deafening.

A silver-haired onlooker picked up a bat, and with a few sweet swings showed the kids what they were doing wrong. Every journalistic instinct aroused, the reporter moved closer. The silver-haired gent put his finger to his lips and shook his head. Some things are more important than a good story. The reporter nodded and walked away.

It was all in a day's work for Joe DiMaggio, the quiet batting expert. But the reporter, my father, never forgot that moment. Unlike those kids, we're not likely to get Hall-of-Fame-caliber help just when we most need it. We'll have to settle for WordPerfect Help instead, which just might be the next best thing.

On-screen help for what you see on the screen

When you begin using WordPerfect, your most frequent question is likely to be "What does *that* do, and how do I use it?"

Point at a button on the Toolbar; you see a little label (or **QuickTip**) with the button's name and a description of what it does. If that just raises more questions, WordPerfect supplies a nifty tool you can use to get the answers.

Press Shift+F1, and the mouse pointer grows a little question mark, as shown in figure 3.1.

Now, click anything—a Toolbar, Power Bar, or status bar button, the editing window, a Guideline—anywhere at all on the screen. You'll get either a QuickTip or a Help window with a description or with complete details on how to use that WordPerfect feature. Clicking the Make It Fit button with the pointer question mark brings up the help explanation shown in figure 3.2.

Fig. 3.1
Press Shift+F1 and click an on-screen button when the QuickTip doesn't provide enough information.

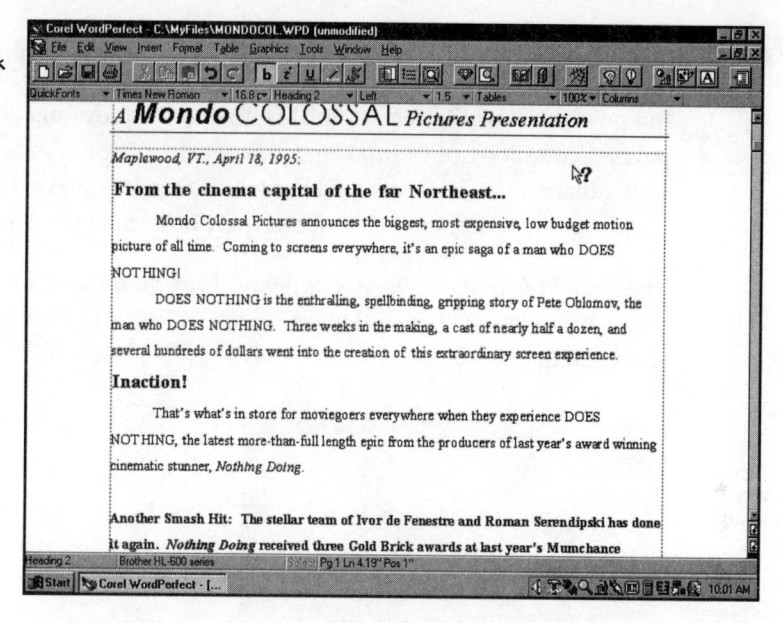

Fig. 3.2
These handy help windows describe WordPerfect features and provide complete instructions.

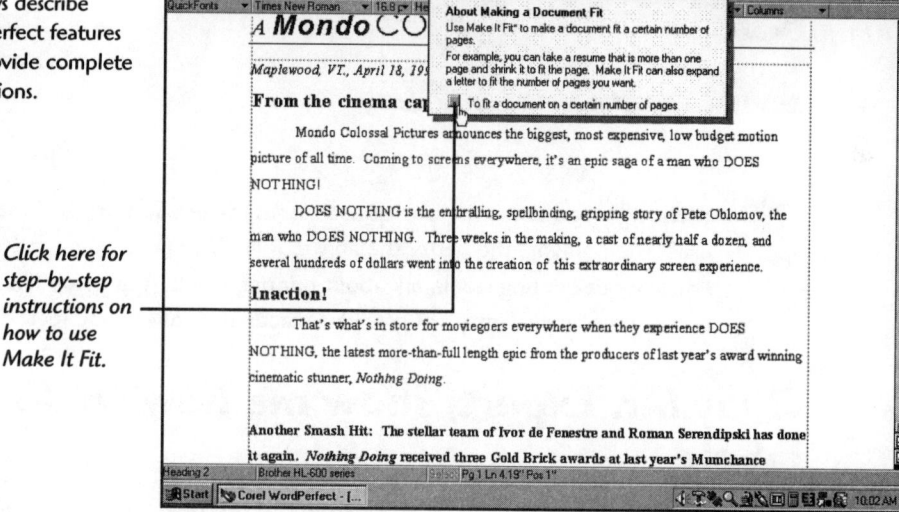

Click here for step-by-step instructions on how to use Make It Fit.

The PerfectExpert, a know-it-all in a can

Suppose the WordPerfect manual is nowhere handy, and good old Uncle Fred palmed your copy of *Using Corel WordPerfect 7 for Windows 95* on his last visit. Meanwhile, you have a pile of labels to print and no idea how to do it. No problem. Just click the PerfectExpert button on the Toolbar.

The PerfectExpert dialog box appears. Type your question in the What do you want to know? box and click Search. A list of likely topics appears, as shown in figure 3.3.

Fig. 3.3
The PerfectExpert takes questions any way you phrase them. It'll tell you no lies, though you may not get exactly the answer you want.

If the PerfectExpert displays an icon like this one, double-click it for a demonstration.

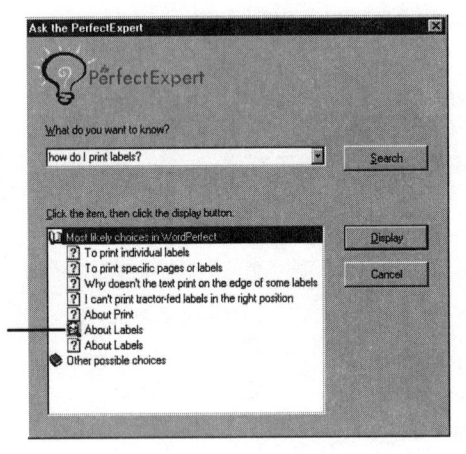

TIP Although you can ask your question any way you like, the more exact the phrasing, the better the answer is likely to be. If you want to know about printing labels, ask about printing labels. A question like "How about some labels?" may not give you exactly the answers you seek.

Okay Mr. Expert, show me how to do labels

The PerfectExpert retrieves what it considers to be the most likely topics that address your question. It's not perfect; if your question isn't specific enough, you'll get a list of topics that may be irrelevant. If that's the case, click the Other possible choices book icon in the Ask the PerfectExpert dialog box. You'll get another list of topics, some of which may be more pertinent to your search.

If one of the PerfectExpert's topics is marked by a little illuminated magnifying glass, such as the first About Labels topic in figure 3.3, double-click it. You'll get a PerfectExpert Guide like the one in figure 3.4.

Fig. 3.4
The PerfectExpert not only finds information, it'll even do the chore for you.

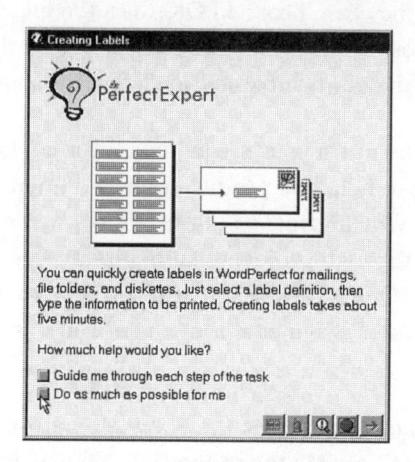

Click Do as much as possible for me; that option saves you a few clicks, and it's also more fun. The PerfectExpert Guide offers a polite "Allow Me," and then takes control of your pointer and sends it skittering across the screen. You'll think your mouse is possessed. The Guide points and clicks its way through the label chore, pausing only when you need to make a decision about label type and formatting. Once the Guide finishes setting up the label, type the text that you want to appear on the label, click the Print button on the Toolbar, and go home.

Unlike some tours, you can quit this one the moment it becomes tedious; just click the red stop sign icon.

Let Guides and QuickTasks do the work for you

There are Guides for many other WordPerfect chores, from inserting bullets to creating watermarks. To browse all the Guide topics, click the Show Me button on the Toolbar, or press F1 for the Help Topics dialog box, and click the Show Me tab. Select the Guide Me through each step of the task option, and scroll down the list to view the Guides.

> **TIP** **If you don't see the Show Me button on your Toolbar, right-click** the Toolbar and choose Preferences on the QuickMenu. Select Options in the Toolbar Preferences dialog box. In the Toolbar Options dialog box that appears, click Show scroll bar and OK. Click Close in the Toolbar Preferences dialog box, and you'll see two scroll arrows on the right side of your Toolbar. Click the down arrow and you'll find the Show Me button.

Like a secretary who can turn your scrawl into a formal letter, Guides apply WordPerfect features to help you produce polished documents. For more complicated jobs, try WordPerfect's built-in project manager: QuickTasks. QuickTasks lead you through projects that might involve several different WordPerfect features. QuickTasks even draw on the other programs in the Corel WordPerfect Suite 7, whenever they're needed to help accomplish a task.

To view the list of QuickTasks, click the Show Me button on the Toolbar, or press F1 and click the Show Me tab of the Help Topics dialog box. Select the Do it for me option, as seen in figure 3.5.

Fig. 3.5
Let QuickTasks help you complete projects that involve several features of the WordPerfect Suite.

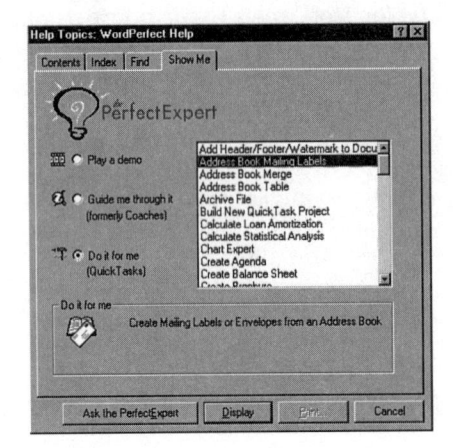

> **TIP** **If you're using the DAD, click the Corel QuickTasks button (it's** that little hammer). That pops up the QuickTasks dialog box. They're the same QuickTasks you get on the Show Me tab of the Help Topics dialog box in WordPerfect, though the QuickTasks dialog box organizes the tasks on tabs, by function.

Double-click any of the QuickTasks on the list, and WordPerfect accesses all the features and runs all the Corel WordPerfect Suite 7 programs needed to do the job. The Address Book Mailing Labels QuickTask highlighted in figure 3.5 is particularly slick. It uses WordPerfect's merge feature to turn your Address Book entries into mailing labels, automatically (see Chapters 12 and 13 for more information about merges and the Address Book). You're prompted to make a couple of decisions along the way, but all the work of producing finished mailing labels is pretty much done for you.

QuickTasks live up to their name. They take involved, multistep jobs and reduce them to a few clicks.

Press F1 for all the help

Helpful as they are, Guides and QuickTasks cover a relative handful of WordPerfect features. For comprehensive help, press F1 for the Help Topics dialog box and click the Contents tab. You'll find the library of online references shown in figure 3.6.

Fig. 3.6
The Help system covers just about anything you can do in WordPerfect.

How do I...

Double-click How Do I on the Help Topics dialog box's Contents tab. Like a shelf of instruction manuals, How Do I is a complete set of step-by-step instructions on WordPerfect tasks.

Double-click any topic, and the corresponding book icon springs open to show all the subtopics, like chapters in a book. Double-click any of those chapters and a list of all the subjects covered in the chapter appears, as shown in figure 3.7.

Fig. 3.7
Working your way through Help can be like peeling away an onion layer by layer. No tears though.

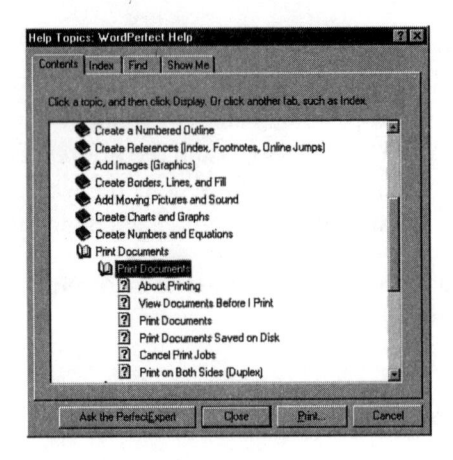

Now, double-click any of those subjects and you'll see a Help window with instructions, general information, and an icon to take you to a list of related topics.

You'll also see **glossary terms**, shown with a broken underline. Click a glossary term and a definition pops up, as shown in figure 3.8.

Fig. 3.8
If Help uses an unfamiliar term, chances are, it'll have a broken underline. Click the term for a definition.

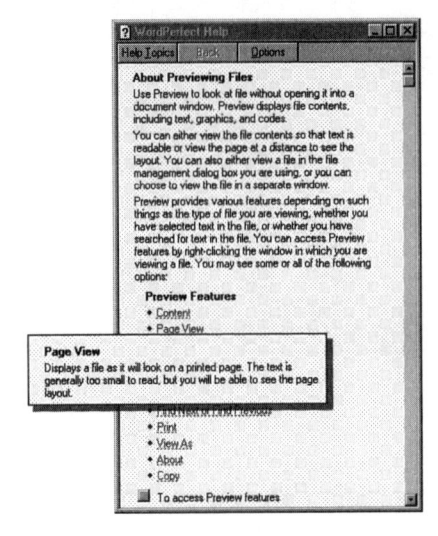

When you're through with Help, press Esc to close the Help window and return to your document.

Help by example

Ever find that you know you want something, but since you can't name it, you can't ask for it? Help is helpful even in situations like that. Say you want to create a paragraph with a large first letter, but you can't remember what the confounded things are called. You could try the PerfectExpert with a question like, "How do I create large letters at the beginning of a paragraph?" and then browse the topics that the PerfectExpert comes up with.

But we're in a hurry. Press F1 for the Help Topics dialog box, click the Contents tab, and double-click Examples. You'll see seven examples of common types of documents, shown as pictures in the Examples window. Click any of the pictures, and a blow-up appears to the right of the original pictures, with arrows pointing to each of the specialized elements in the document.

One of the sample documents has just the kind of large-first-letter-of-a-paragraph you're looking for. Click the sample; then click the arrow by the large first letter for instructions on how to create that element, as shown in figure 3.9.

Fig. 3.9
Drop-caps can do a lot to pep up a page, even if you can't remember what they're called.

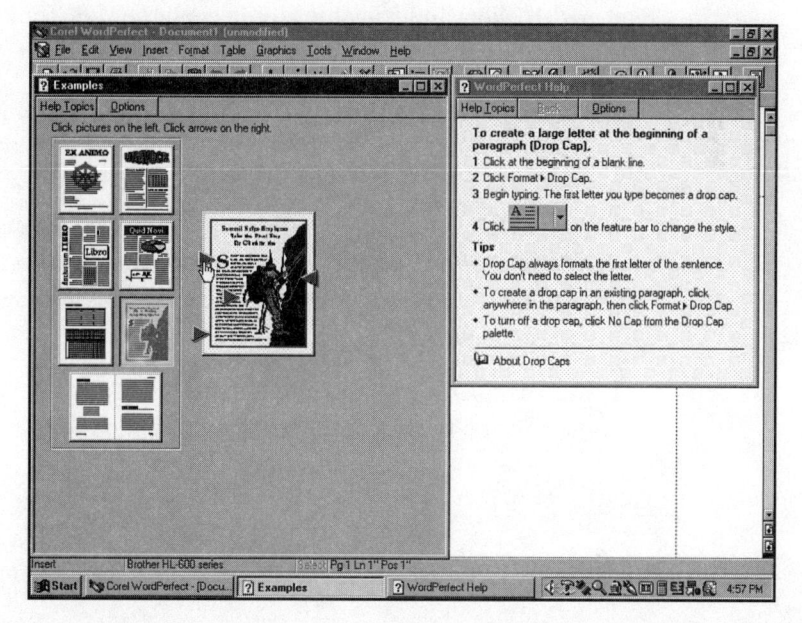

Searching for Help

If you know what you're looking for, press F1 for the Help Topics dialog box and click the Find tab. If it's the first time you've used Find, the Find Setup Wizard dialog box appears. Just accept the recommended Minimize database size option and click Next and then Finish (see fig. 3.10).

Fig. 3.10
Before Find can find anything for you, WordPerfect has to index the words in the online Help system.

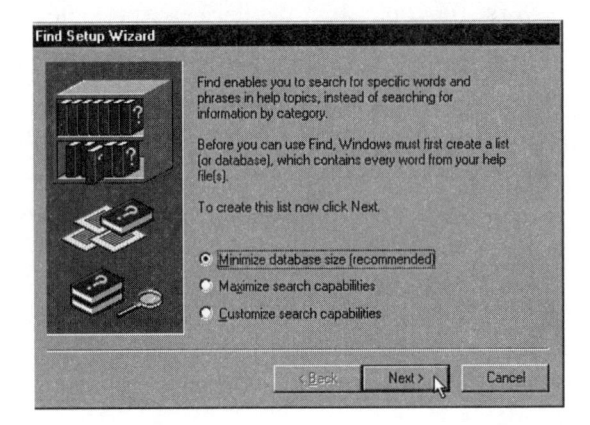

Find goes to work indexing the words in all the Help topics. It might take a little while, but eventually the Find dialog box appears.

Here's the express route to useful help. Using Find is a three-step job:

1 Type the first few letters of your topic in the Type the word(s) edit box.

2 Words that match those letters appear on the Select some matching words list. Click the word you want. If there are several words that match what you're looking for, click the first one and Ctrl+click each additional word.

3 Browse the topics that appear in the Click a topic list. When you spot the one you're after, double-click it to open the relevant Help window.

Figure 3.11 shows you how to use Find.

Fig. 3.11
Find is one of those features that's easier to use than it looks.

Type the beginning of your word here.

Select one or more of the words that appear here.

Double-click the topic you want when it appears here.

Help! I'm lost in Help!

There's a lot of help in WordPerfect Help, and once you start flipping from topic to subtopic, it's easy to lose sight of the subject you were after in the first place.

Click the Back button in any WordPerfect Help window to work your way back through all the help topics you've looked at, one by one.

If you're in a topic you think you might want to revisit, click Options, Define a Bookmark, OK. Forage through the Help system to your heart's content; when you want to return to the marked topic, click Options, Display a Bookmark, and double-click the topic name. You can also click Options, Print Topic, OK to print any help topic.

Q&A *I had a Help window pop up, but when I switched away from WordPerfect, it disappeared when I came back. What gives?*

WordPerfect Help is actually a program in its own right. Switching away from Help is just like switching away from any other Windows application. Simply click the WordPerfect Help icon that'll appear on the Taskbar to get the Help window back.

TIP If you want to display your help topic alongside your work as you go through the steps of a task, click Options, Keep Help on Top, On Top in any Help window. That puts the Help window over your WordPerfect document. If the window gets in the way, drag an edge to change the window's size, or drag the title bar to move the window out of your way.

If you're used to doing things in a different program, try Upgrade Help

If you've been using another word processing program, or if you've just upgraded from an earlier version of WordPerfect, click Help, Upgrade Help for the PerfectExpert's Upgrade Help dialog box (see fig. 3.12).

Fig. 3.12
Here's specific help on how to do chores in WordPerfect 7 that you've been doing in other programs.

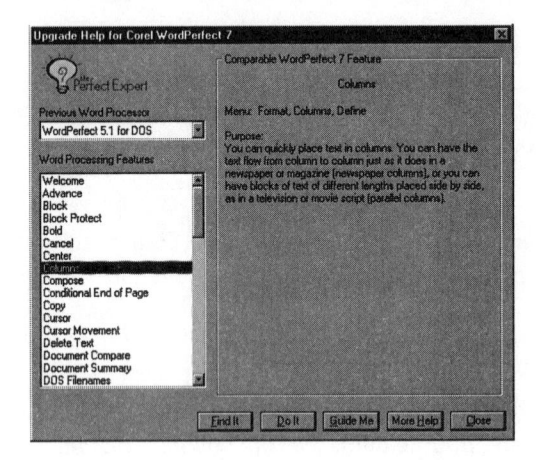

Click the Previous Word Processor drop-down arrow and select your old program. Then, click the feature you want to know about on the Word Processing Features list.

Now you get a choice: there are Find It, Do It, Guide Me, and More Help buttons at the bottom of the dialog box. They'll either take you to instructions and explanations, or, in the case of Do it, actually do the chore for you.

Help in WordPerfect is not only helpful, it's also fun to play around with. Try it.

Dialog boxes have you stymied? Try help in a box

It's amazing how many features WordPerfect packs into one program. Of course, to access some of those features, you have to navigate menus and submenus, dialog boxes that lead to other dialog boxes, and perhaps an icon or two as well. There'll be times on your travels across the WordPerfect landscape when your next step isn't entirely clear.

Suppose you've successfully negotiated layers of menus and submenus and icons, finally arrived at the last crucial dialog box that holds the key to what you're trying to accomplish—and you get stuck. How can you tell what you're supposed to do in a dialog box? Click the dialog box's Help button. That takes you straight to instructions and explanations for that particular dialog box.

If there's an option in the dialog box that requires further explication, click the little question mark in the dialog box's title bar. The question mark follows your pointer around; click any obscure option for a brief description, as shown in figure 3.13.

Fig. 3.13
With help in a box, dialog boxes will never box you in.

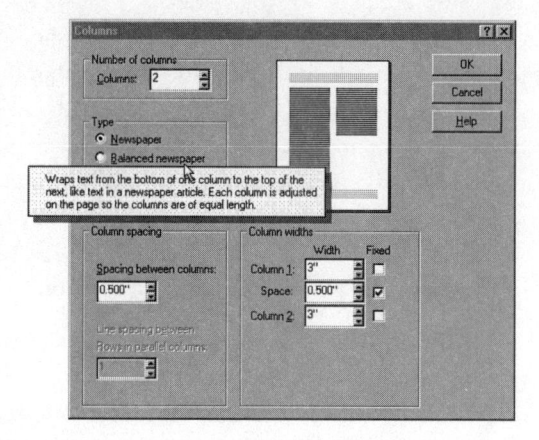

WordPerfect is wired for Help

Unless you've been on vacation with Rip Van Winkle for the past few years, you've heard a good deal about the Internet. What began life as a research tool and mail system for academics and scientists is now a TV substitute, a potent force for good or evil, a great time waster, a bottomless well of information, or a wonderful toy, depending on your point of view.

What's overlooked amidst the hype is the fact that the Internet, and especially its user-friendly aspect, the World Wide Web, is a very handy source of practical information. The Web has stock quotes, restaurant reviews, Finnish census data—and help for WordPerfect users.

WordPerfect 7 has a built-in connection to the World Wide Web that takes you directly to the Corel WordPerfect Documentation Web page. There, you'll find libraries of tips, news, and technical papers on every aspect of WordPerfect. No matter how rarefied your problem, chances are there's a discussion of it on the WordPerfect Web page.

66 Plain English, please!

The **Internet**, about which you've heard so much, is a vast international network of computers, strung together over the phone lines and accessible to anyone with a modem. The **World Wide Web** is the Internet's graphical face, a bit like using a color TV to access the cable network instead of an old black and white model. A **Web page** is a site on the great Internet network, like a radio station on the FM dial. Instead of tuning to 88.5 as you would to find a radio station, you go from Web page to Web page simply by clicking pictures or words. You can do that because Web pages, unlike radio stations, are all connected together on the network.

A **Web browser** is a software program that enables you to view the information on the World Wide Web's pages. **CompuServe** is another online information service; subscribers pay fees to read news, sports, periodicals, and messages from other subscribers on their computers. WordPerfect has its own **forum** on CompuServe, an electronic bulletin board for messages and articles by WordPerfect users and employees. 99

How do I connect to WordPerfect's online help?

The World Wide Web is not only full of useful information, it also makes it pretty easy to find what you need. WordPerfect makes the task of getting online a complete no-brainer. For the online help connection to work, you'll need a modem and a CompuServe account, or an AT&T WorldNet Service account, or both (if you have another Web browser and service provider, that'll work, too). Software for the AT&T WorldNet service comes with the Corel WordPerfect Suite—see Chapter 22 for details.

Once you've installed CompuServe or the Web browser or both, click Help, Help Online. The Help Online dialog box pops up (see fig. 3.14). If you haven't used online help before, click Configure in the Help Online dialog box. WordPerfect hunts down your Web browser and CompuServe software and automatically installs its own hookup to them.

Q&A ***I don't have CompuServe or a Web browser. How do I get them?***

The Corel WordPerfect 7 Suite includes the AT&T WorldNet Service browser. See Chapter 22 for information on installing it and signing up for an Internet account. CompuServe will send you its free software, and sign you up for the service via modem once you receive it. Call the 800 directory (800-555-1212) and ask for CompuServe's 800 number. Then call CompuServe and request the software. Although the software is free, you'll have to pay a monthly fee for CompuServe and the Internet, and there may be hourly charges as well. Make sure you get all your questions about fees answered before surrendering a credit card number.

Choose either Internet or CompuServe on the Select a service drop-down list, as shown in figure 3.13.

Click Connect in the Help Online dialog box, and you're on your way to the WordPerfect Forum on CompuServe, or the WordPerfect page on the World Wide Web.

Fig. 3.14
Click Configure, and if you have them installed, either one or both of these choices appear in the dialog box automatically.

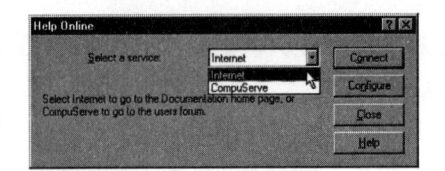

Part II: Editing and Formatting for Perfect Documents

Chapter 4: **Good Writing Means Rewriting: Editing Text**

Chapter 5: **Formatting for Characters with Character**

Chapter 6: **What's My Line? Formatting Paragraphs for Precision and Punch**

Chapter 7: **Setting Up the Page**

4

Good Writing Means Rewriting: Editing Text

● **In this chapter:**

- How do I select text?

- I have a lot of deletions to take care of

- I need those deletions back!

- How do I cut and paste?

- My document looks strange, and I can't figure out why!

- I want to change a word throughout a document

What the food processor does for preparing food, the word processor does for editing text: it makes the job fast, fun, and accurate . . . . ➤

There's one thing every writer has in common. Whether it's a three-line memo or a three-volume novel, **writing it means rewriting it.**

P.G. Wodehouse wrote over 80 novels at his typewriter (including those Jeeves and Wooster stories beloved by Masterpiece Theater). His style is famous for its witty ease; he called his stories musical comedies without the music. To get that effect, he wrote—and wrote again. Wodehouse sometimes rewrote a page eight times before he was satisfied. When he finished a page, he'd tape it to the wall at an angle. Each rewrite would be taped alongside at less of an angle. When the page was right, it went on the wall perfectly straight.

WordPerfect spares us from having to use dodges like that. Rewriting, editing, and shifting text around is fast and easy. Our results won't read as effortlessly as Wodehouse's, but it'll take much less effort to get them.

Inserting, for everyday writing

Typing new text into a WordPerfect document is like shoving aside books on a shelf to make room for a new one. As you type, characters are entered at the insertion point, and any text that's already in the document gets pushed to the right.

That also goes for spaces, tabs, or blank lines—insert any of them into a document, and existing text is shoved to the right (or down, in the case of blank lines). Figure 4.1 shows where existing text moves when you insert more text and a blank line.

How do I move the insertion point where I want it?

WordPerfect 7 makes it very easy to place the insertion point with precision. Slide your pointer over a line of text, and the **shadow pointer** (see fig. 4.1), that gray echo of the flashing black cursor, faithfully follows the pointer.

Chapter 4 *Good Writing Means Rewriting: Editing Text*

Fig. 4.1
Add new text, spaces, blank lines, or tabs; existing text moves aside to make room for it.

If I type **(this text is in bold)**, *the words* and *any text...* *are shoved to the right to make room.*

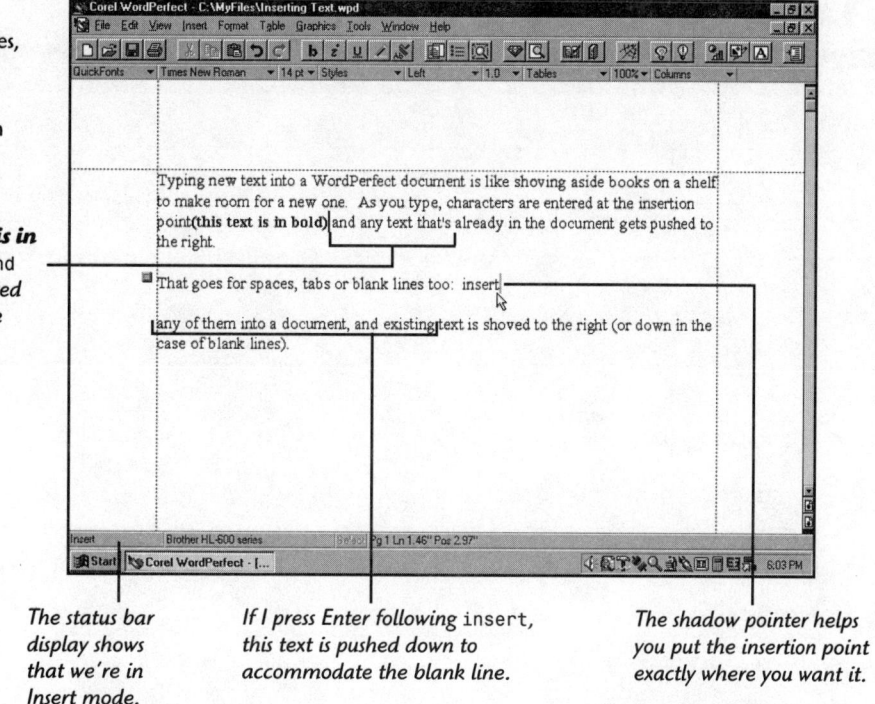

The status bar display shows that we're in Insert mode.

If I press Enter following insert, *this text is pushed down to accommodate the blank line.*

The shadow pointer helps you put the insertion point exactly where you want it.

The feature is especially helpful when you're trying to spot the insertion point in the middle of a long word in a thick block of text. Typed "remunration," leaving out an "e?" Move the mouse pointer until the shadow pointer is between the "n" and the "r," click the mouse key, and type the "e." That's a fast way to get the insertion point from one place to another, and a big improvement over the I-beam that other word processors use. Where the old I-beam tended to obscure what you were trying to read, the shadow pointer lets you place the insertion point without hiding a thing.

If you need to move the insertion point past the current window of text, or if you don't want to lift your fingers from the keyboard, check out the other options listed in table 4.1.

Table 4.1 Moving the insertion point around a document

To move the insertion point...	Press
One word to the right	Ctrl+right arrow
One word to the left	Ctrl+left arrow
To beginning of next paragraph	Ctrl+down arrow
To beginning of previous paragraph	Ctrl+up arrow
To end of line	End
To beginning of line	Home
To beginning of document	Ctrl+Home
To end of document	Ctrl+End
To top of next page	Alt+PageDown
To top of previous page	Alt+PageUp
To top of editing window	PageUp
To bottom of editing window	PageDown

You'll notice that when you move the insertion point past the current window, the display scrolls along with the insertion point. To scroll the display without moving the insertion point, use the scroll bars.

Typeover, an occasional option

When you start up WordPerfect, the program is in Insert mode—inserted text or spacing moves existing text down or to the right.

Double-click the status bar Insert button (refer to fig. 4.1), and WordPerfect switches to **Typeover** mode. The status bar displays Typeover, and any new text you type or spacing you add overwrites existing text instead of pushing it aside. Like a painter painting over an old canvas, existing text is blotted out as you type in the new.

Typeover might be handy for a quick, one-word editing job. Trouble is, if the new word is longer than the old one, the extra characters wipe out part of the next word on the line. It's safer to use Insert mode to add new text, and then delete any existing text you don't want.

TIP If you accidentally type over text in Typeover mode, click the Undo button on the Toolbar.

TIP To toggle between Typeover and Insert modes, press the Insert key on your keyboard.

Deleting text: no white-out needed

Remember all the gear we used to use to delete typescript? There was the bottle of white-out that always dried up, the strips of white correction tape that stuck to the fingers, and good old corrasable bond paper, guaranteed to smudge every time.

With WordPerfect, we can heave all that stuff out with the rest of the trash. Deleting in WordPerfect is cleaner and easier. Best of all, when you delete something and change your mind, you can get it back again.

Press the Delete key to delete one character to the right of the insertion point; press Backspace to delete one character to the left of the insertion point. The other deletion options are shown in table 4.2.

Table 4.2 Deleting text in WordPerfect

To delete...	Press
The word adjacent to or enclosing the insertion point	Ctrl+Backspace
From the insertion point to the end of the line	Ctrl+Delete
Any highlighted text	Delete

Changed your mind? Undo or Undelete

The glory of the word processor is also its curse. It's so easy to delete things, we sometimes wipe out text without meaning to. If you've just zapped something by accident, you can get it back fast. Click the Undo button on the Toolbar, and your last action is instantly undone.

The Undo button on the Toolbar only works for the very last action. Tough critics of their own writing are likely to want something back that they've deleted several edits ago.

That's no problem. Just click Edit, Undelete. The deleted text reappears highlighted at the insertion point. You also get the Undelete dialog box shown in figure 4.2.

Fig. 4.2
The highlighted line was deleted; it's about to be undeleted.

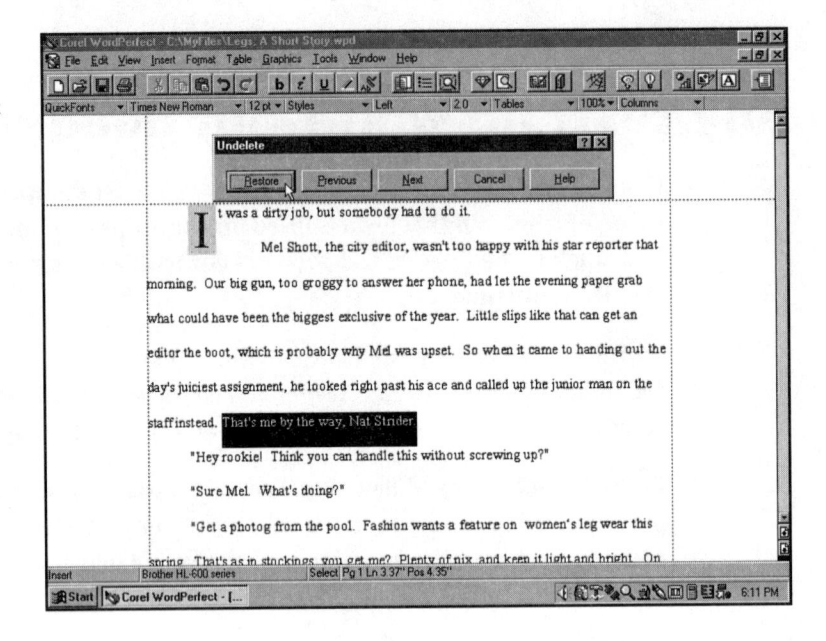

Click Restore to reinsert the deleted text at the insertion point.

Undelete can restore your last three deletions. Click Next or Previous to cycle through them until you find what you want to restore.

TIP If the Undelete dialog box is blocking text you want to see, point at the dialog box title bar and drag the dialog box out of the way.

Selecting text for alterations—minor and major

Editing in WordPerfect is speedy because the program lets you operate on as much, or as little, of a document as you want. Whether you're moving, deleting, copying, or formatting, the basic idea is the same: select the text and then apply the command to the selection.

Select with the keyboard

Selected text is highlighted so you can see what you're doing. Shift+Arrow key selects text in whatever direction the arrow is pointing. Pressing Shift in combination with any of the insertion point movement commands in table 4.1 highlights everything from where the insertion point started to where the command moved it.

Shift+End, for example, selects the text from the insertion point to the end of the line. Ctrl+Shift+End selects everything from the insertion point to the end of the document. Figure 4.3 shows a selected paragraph in a document.

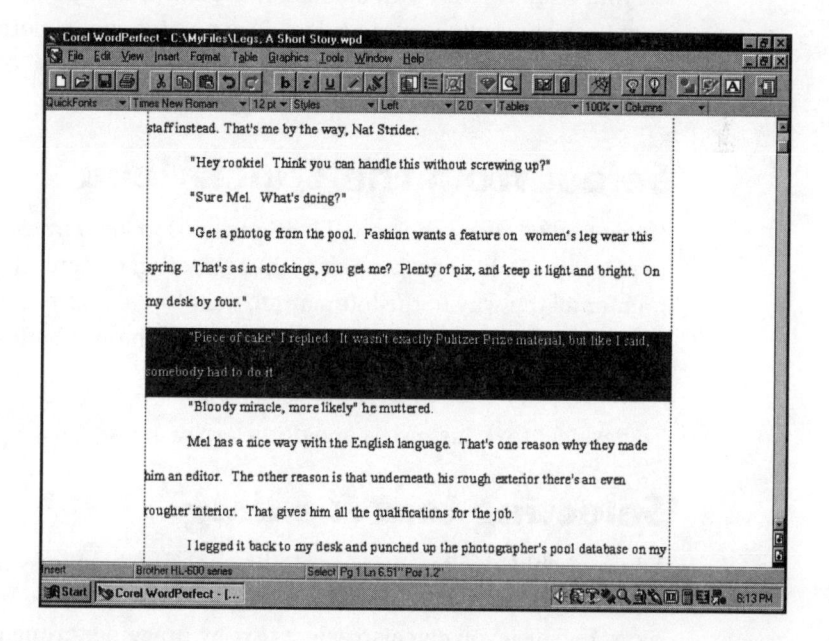

Fig. 4.3
Selected text is highlighted so you can see exactly what you're doing.

Select with the mouse

You can also use the mouse to select text:

- Double-click a word to select the entire word to the beginning of the next word.
- Triple-click a sentence to select the whole sentence to the beginning of the next sentence.
- Quadruple-click a paragraph to select the entire paragraph to the beginning of the next paragraph.

That triple-click to select a sentence is particularly handy. With some word processors, selecting a single sentence in a paragraph without unintentionally grabbing parts of the adjacent text can be tricky. The WordPerfect triple-click makes sentence selection foolproof.

QuickSelect is for slower fingers

Finding those multiple clicks something less than a snap? You can cut down on your clicking with QuickSelect: move the mouse pointer to the left margin, next to the text you want to select. The pointer, which normally points left, changes direction and points right. Now, click once to select a whole sentence or twice to select an entire paragraph.

Select from the QuickMenu

If you find all these click combinations hard to keep track of, or if you want to select a whole page, here's another selection option: shove the mouse pointer all the way to the left margin, next to the text you want to select. When the pointer points right, click the *right* mouse button. The QuickMenu shown in figure 4.4 appears.

To deselect text, just press one of the arrow keys.

Selecting text is a drag

You probably won't remember all the click combinations and insertion point movement commands, at least when you first start using WordPerfect. That's okay, because you can also select text by dragging through it. Click at the beginning of the selection, hold the mouse button down, and drag until you get to the end of the selection.

Fig. 4.4
Use this QuickMenu to select text as an alternative to the keyboard or multiple mouse clicks.

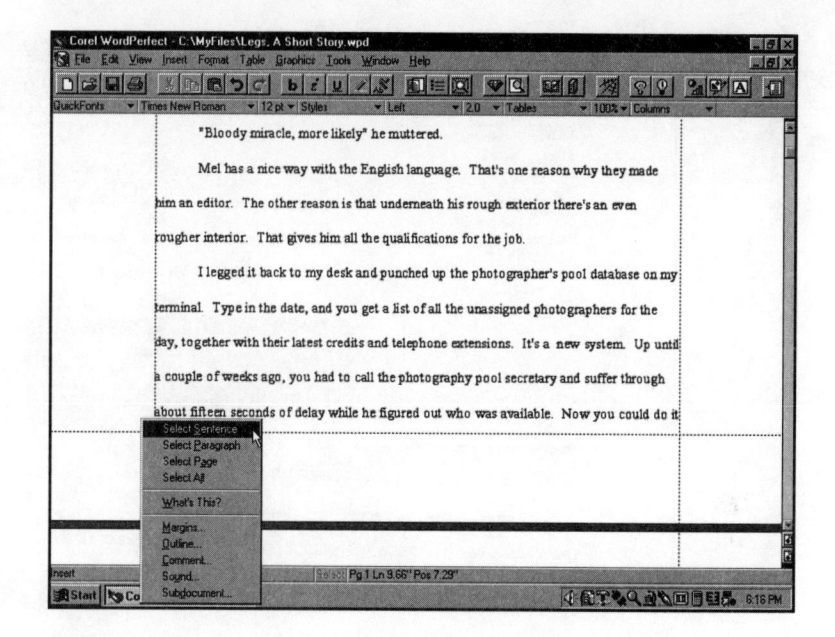

> **TIP** To add more to your selection without starting over after you release the mouse button, press Shift and drag again.

Go To, the insertion point express

Do you have a big, multipage document on your hands? When you know where you want the insertion point to go, and you want to get it there fast, double-click the page number display on the status bar at the bottom of the screen. Or press Ctrl+G. Either method pops up the Go To dialog box shown in figure 4.5.

Click Page number, enter the page you want to go to, and click OK to go straight to the beginning of that page. Click Position and choose one of the options on the list to move the insertion point to various spots in the document.

Fig. 4.5
Use the Go To dialog box for fast insertion point moves.

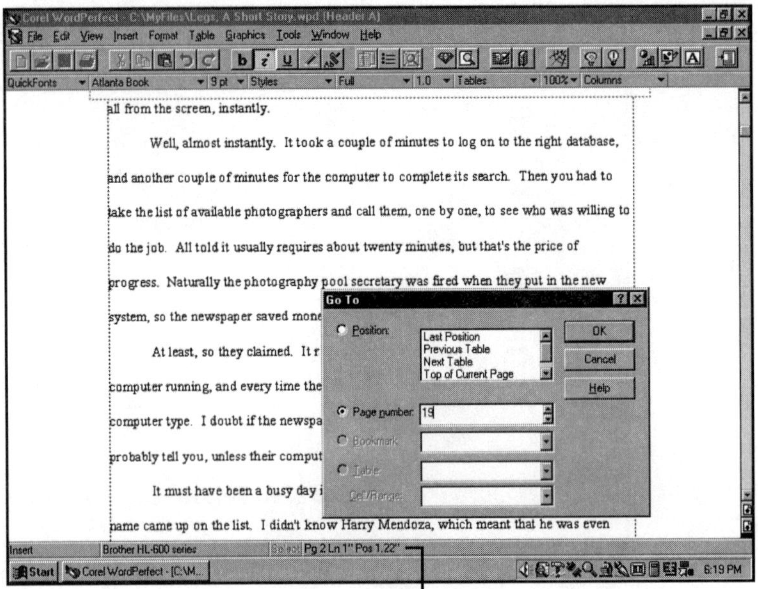

Double-click the page number display on the status bar for the Go To dialog box.

What can I do with selected text?

You have many options for selecting text in WordPerfect. Once selected, what do you do with it? The short answer is—just about anything you want to do. We know we can delete text by selecting it and pressing Delete. But that's just for starters.

One of the handiest, and oft-overlooked, uses for selected text? You can type over it. Select a sentence in a paragraph, type a new one, and the new sentence replaces the old one without disturbing any of the adjacent text. It works for a single word, or several—select the word or words, type new ones, and the new text replaces the old without affecting the rest of the sentence.

You'll see the old text disappear as soon as you start typing. The text you haven't selected is pushed aside to make room for the new text, no matter how much new typing you plan on doing.

Cut and Paste it

That glue stick and scissors can join the white-out in the trash can. Cutting and pasting in WordPerfect is a push-button affair. To cut text from one part of a document and paste it somewhere else:

1 Select the text by any of the various methods.

2 Click the Cut button on the Toolbar.

3 The cut text is moved to the Windows Clipboard and saved there until you need it.

4 Move the insertion point to where you want the text to reappear.

5 Click the Paste button on the Toolbar. The text reappears at the insertion point.

This works for anything from a single character to an entire document.

> **TIP** **Don't forget about those handy keyboard shortcuts: Ctrl+X to cut** selected text, Ctrl+C to copy it, and Ctrl+V to paste the cut or copied text at the insertion point.

Make a smudge-free copy

Copy and paste text the same way you cut and paste it. Just click the Copy button on the Toolbar after selecting your text. Move the insertion point to where you want the copy; then click the Paste button.

You get a perfect copy every time!

Undo and Redo forgive mistakes, repeat successes

Everybody does it. Something about what you've just written bugs you. So you start to slice and dice, deleting words and moving sentences and paragraphs around with cut and paste. Then, you look at it again and think "this was better the way it was before."

WordPerfect lets you change your mind about your last several editing changes. Select Edit, Undo/Redo History and the dialog box shown in figure 4.6 appears.

Fig. 4.6
Undo/Redo is a great tool for the editorially indecisive.

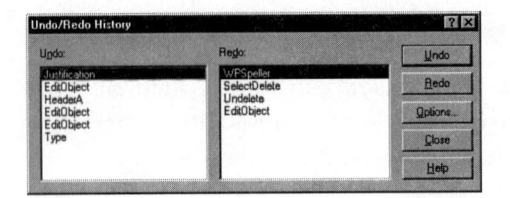

Your editing changes appear under Undo. Select an item, and all the preceding items are automatically selected as well. Click the Undo button in the dialog box, and all the editing changes you've selected are reversed. Deleted text will be restored, moved text will be moved back to where it was originally, and even format changes will be reversed.

Bear in mind that Undo is sequential. For example, you can't choose to undo only the fifth item in the list. If you do choose to undo the fifth item, items one through four will be undone as well.

I want those edits back!

Any editing you've undone will appear under Redo in the Undo/Redo History dialog box. If you change your mind again, select those edits under Redo and click the Redo button in the dialog box.

That restores the edits you've just undone. So what, you might be asking, is the difference between Undelete and Undo? Here's one big difference: Undelete restores deleted text at the insertion point. Undo restores deleted text to its original location.

TIP Don't forget that to undo or redo just your last action, click the Undo or Redo buttons on the Toolbar.

Undo and Redo let you edit fearlessly. Since anything you cut or move can be restored or moved back, you can tinker without worrying about doing permanent editorial damage to your document. If, however, you've made a complete hash of a saved document that was perfectly fine to begin with, press Ctrl+F4 and click No to exit the document without saving the changes. Now, you can reopen the previously saved version and start over.

How many times can I change my mind?

Undo is very forgiving. WordPerfect starts you off with 10 saved edits, but you can save up to 300 editing changes for later undoing or redoing. You can even save the changes right along with the document.

Click the Options button in the Undo/Redo History dialog box, and select the Number of Undo/Redo items you want to keep.

> **CAUTION** **The more Undo/Redo items you save, the bigger your document.** If you run into memory problems or find that WordPerfect is slowing down too much, try saving fewer Undo/Redo items.

Reveal codes take you behind the scenes

Actors on the stage look natural, but they're really just following stage directions. An actor walks off in a huff and it looks like part of the action. Actually, the director has told him, "Exit in a huff, stage right." What you see is controlled by someone behind the scenes.

WordPerfect documents are peppered with "stage directions" called **codes**. Codes are instructions to WordPerfect on what to do with text. WordPerfect inserts some codes automatically, like the soft-return codes at the end of lines of text. Some codes are inserted when you type a keyboard command. Press Enter, for example, and you're actually inserting a hard-return code.

Just as you don't see the stage directions when you go to a play, you don't see the codes in the editing window. Instead, you view and edit them in the **reveal codes** window. The reveal codes window puts you in charge of a document the way stage directions put a director in charge of a play. Like a director, you can alter the directions—by adding or deleting codes—to take control of your text. If your document looks or behaves oddly (maybe there's an indent where you don't want one, or a mysterious change of fonts), open the reveal codes window and get rid of the unwanted codes.

Opening the reveal codes window

Click View, Reveal Codes and the reveal codes window appears, as shown in figure 4.7.

Fig. 4.7
The reveal codes window lets you view and edit WordPerfect's "stage directions" for text.

The editing window insertion point

Drag here to resize the reveal codes window.

Hard-return code   *The reveal codes cursor*   *Soft-return code*   *Point at a code for a description of what it does.*

The text in the editing window is mirrored in the reveal codes window, but now you can see the codes that WordPerfect uses to control the text in documents.

Every code appears as a raised button. The reveal codes window cursor shown in figure 4.7 apes the editing window insertion point—as you move the insertion point in the editing window, the reveal codes window cursor moves through the text with it.

If you want to know what a code is for, point at it. A description appears alongside the code (refer to fig. 4.7).

And if you point at the border between the editing and reveal codes windows, the pointer changes to a double arrow. Drag the double arrow to resize the reveal codes window.

> **TIP** **There's more than one way to get at the reveal codes window.**
> Keyboardists can press Alt+F3 to open, and press again to close, the window. Devoted mousers can drag the thick black lines at the top and bottom of the vertical scroll bar (see fig. 4.8), or right-click in the editing window and choose Reveal Codes from the QuickMenu.

Fig. 4.8
These thick black lines on the vertical scroll bar are a bit hard to see; once you find them, they're a handy way to get the reveal codes window.

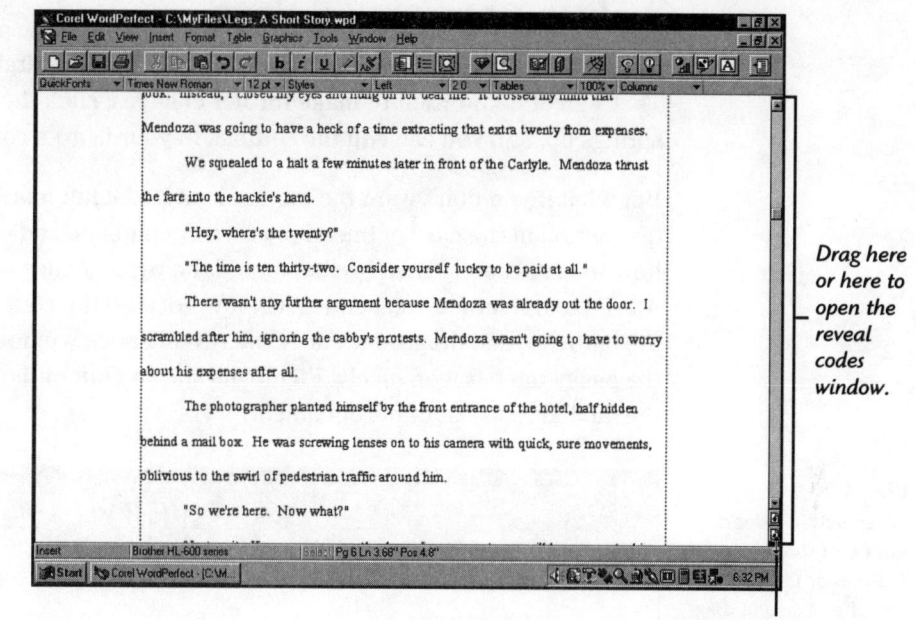

Drag here or here to open the reveal codes window.

The pointer turns into a double-headed arrow when you're in the right spot for dragging.

Now that I can see the codes, what do I do with them?

Wonderful as they are, word processors can sometimes drive you nuts. If you accidentally hit the Tab key, or lean on the Spacebar, or make a similar but not too obvious mistake, your document might look odd. Those unnecessary spaces or tabs (I tend to hit the Return key when I don't want it) can give documents a curiously gap-toothed appearance.

It's hard to see extra tabs and blank lines in the editing window, so pop up the reveal codes window, click the unwanted tab or hard-return code, and drag it out of the reveal codes window to get rid of it.

True confessions: how I used reveal codes to delete the tab bar icon

WordPerfect 7 is packed with features, which is good. And you can turn off most of the features if you don't want them, which is also good. Some features, however, are stubbornly resistant to elimination, and the tab bar icon is a case in point. When you change tab settings, the paragraph in which you made the change sports a tab bar icon in the left margin (see fig. 4.9). That's great if you want to make further changes: click the icon, the tab bar springs up, and you can edit tab settings to your heart's content.

But what if you don't want the tab bar icon in the left margin? I found it a distraction in the case of one of my own documents, and couldn't figure out how to get rid of it. Then I remembered the reveal codes window. I pressed Alt+F3 to open the reveal codes window, located the code responsible for the tab bar icon, and dragged it out of the reveal codes window. That got rid of the pesky tab bar icon nicely. Figure 4.9 shows your author poised to clear the tab bar icon out of his document.

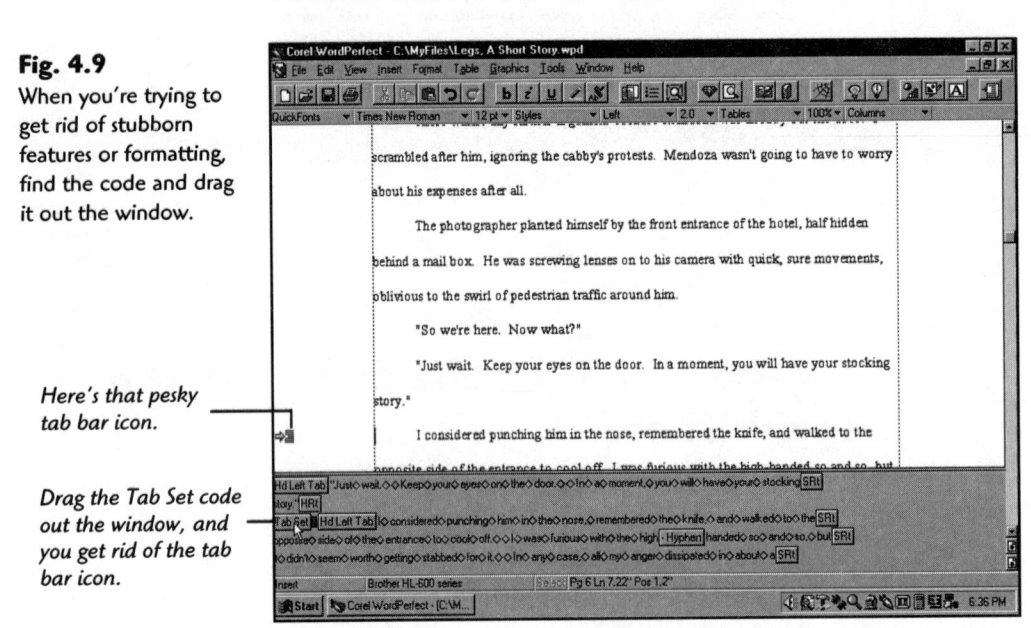

Fig. 4.9
When you're trying to get rid of stubborn features or formatting, find the code and drag it out the window.

Here's that pesky tab bar icon.

Drag the Tab Set code out the window, and you get rid of the tab bar icon.

Find and Replace: better than any lost and found

If I had to vote on the single handiest feature in WordPerfect, I'd pick the Edit, Find and Replace command. You use it to find every occurrence of a word or code in a document, automatically. You can then replace the word or code with whatever you substitute in its place. You can even get rid of every occurrence of the offending word or code by replacing it with nothing.

If you've just finished a 300 page novel and you decide that you hate your protagonist's name, use Find and Replace to change it to something better, wherever the name occurs. Or maybe you've written a long client letter, mentioned the client's name 50 times, and realized that you've misspelled it every time. It takes only a few seconds to Find and Replace the misspelled name with the correct spelling.

First Find it...

Suppose we have a short story on our hands, one of whose characters is an editor named Mel Shott. The name occurs many times throughout the story. After seeing the name "Mel" once too many times, we decide to replace it with "Oscar" throughout the document.

Select **E**dit, **F**ind and Replace and the Find and Replace Text dialog box appears. Type **Mel** in the F**i**nd edit box and **Oscar** in the Replace **w**ith edit box, as shown in figure 4.10.

Fig. 4.10
Notice how the Find and Replace Text dialog box has its own menu bar to accommodate all the options.

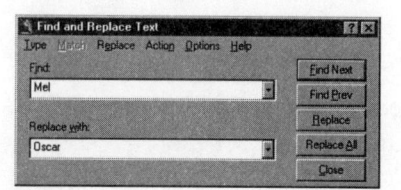

> **TIP** If you want to find text or a code without replacing it, click the **F**ind Next button.

Although the Replace **A**ll button looks tempting, we won't use it. Clicking Replace **A**ll does indeed replace all occurrences of whatever you've typed in the F**i**nd edit box with whatever's typed in the Replace **w**ith edit box.

But ***Find*** can be too thorough. It'll find ***every*** occurrence of (in this example) the letters "mel," no matter what the context. Figure 4.11 shows how Find's thoroughness can lead to problems.

Fig. 4.11
Find has found the "mel" in "smelled." Replace All would have given us "soscarled" here!

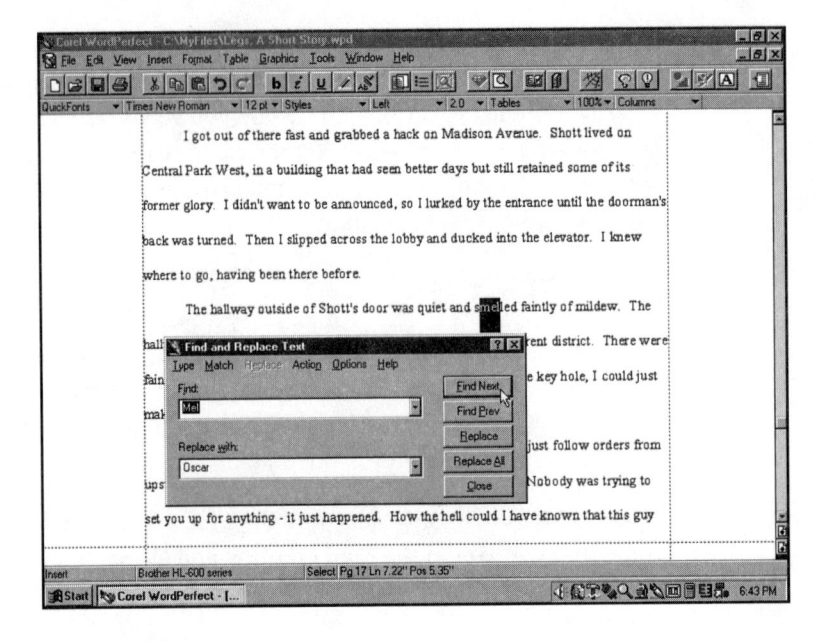

Getting specific with Find

Find's enthusiasm needs to be tempered with further instructions. Select Match for the following options:

- Whole Word is what we want here. Select it when you want to find a word like Mel, instead of the letters "mel" wherever they occur.

- Case matches either upper- or lowercase, not both. Since we're only interested in occurrences of the proper name Mel, capital M, we'll select Case to further refine our search.

- Font pops up the Font dialog box and lets you search for any font attribute you choose. For example, you can search for "Mel" in italics, or text in a specific typeface.

Remember those codes you saw in Reveal Codes? You can search for any of them with Find and Replace. Click Match, Codes in the Find and Replace Text dialog box to pop up the Codes dialog box shown in figure 4.12. Double-click any code on the list to enter it in either the Find or Replace with edit boxes. If you're hunting for specific codes in a document, this is a very handy tool.

Fig. 4.12
The Codes dialog box lists WordPerfect formatting and wild-card codes.

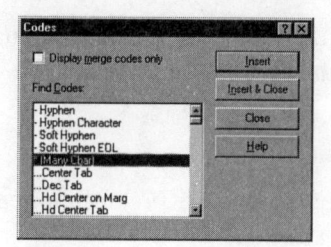

You can also use the Codes dialog box to search for words containing unknown characters. Suppose you're looking for a word in the document, but you're not sure of the spelling. Type the first letter or two; then, choose one of the **wild-card** codes from the Codes dialog box. Say you're looking for the word "bowdlerize," but you can't remember the exact spelling (I cheated and looked it up). Type **bow** in the F‍ind edit box and double-click the *(Many Char) code highlighted in figure 4.12. F‍ind will stop at each occurrence of the **text string** bow, followed by several other characters. That would turn up bowdlerize, but you'd also find bowsprit and bow-chaser.

> **Plain English, please!**
>
> A **text string** is a word or part of a word that you enter in a search. **Wild-cards** are substitute characters that represent unknown characters in a word or text string. The asterisk (*) represents a range of characters. For example, **mark*** finds market, marker, or marks. A question mark (?) represents just one unknown character. For example, **part?** finds parts or party, but not parties.

TIP Find starts its search at the insertion point and continues to the end of the document. If the insertion point doesn't happen to be at the top of the document, select Options, Begin Find at Top of Document.

Finding, finding, found!

Suppose you're describing a local election to an English chum. Where we say "so and so ran for Congress" the English say "so and so stood for Congress." WordPerfect lets you find every form of the verb "run" in a document so that you can replace it with equivalent forms of "stand" for your transatlantic pal.

Select T‍ype, W‍ord Forms in the Find and Replace Text dialog box. Type **run** in the F‍ind edit box and click F‍ind Next, and you'll come up with "run," "running," and "ran." Type **stand** in the Replace w‍ith edit box and you'll get "stood," "standing," and "stand" in the appropriate contexts. There are limits to this magic, however. Word Forms won't find the noun "runner" in this example, just the tenses of the verb.

...then Replace it

Once you specify exactly what it is you're finding and replacing, you have three choices for proceeding further:

- Click the Find Next button for the cautious approach. Find will stop at the first occurrence of the word and highlight it. Click the Replace button to replace it, or click the Find Next button to skip to the next occurrence of the word.

- Click the Replace button for the moderately cautious approach. Find will stop at the first occurrence of the word and highlight it. Click Replace again to replace the highlighted word.

- Click Replace All and throw caution to the winds. It's a good idea to save your document first, in case you want to return to the original version after Find and Replace finishes.

Using Replace to delete words

To delete a recurring word in a document, type the word in the Find box, leave the Replace with box blank, and click the Replace button at each occurrence of the word.

That replaces the word with nothing, which is the same thing as deleting it, at least as far as WordPerfect is concerned.

5
Formatting for Characters with Character

● **In this chapter:**

- I want to format text fast!
- When do I use italics? Underlining? Boldface?
- Just what is a font?
- I want to change fonts
- How do I know what font to use?
- Drop-caps create a nifty effect

Documents, like people, make an impression. Format your text for eye-appeal, and your readers' first impression will be a good one . . . . ▶

Formatting is everything to do with the appearance of a document. So does it really matter? At least one fine American writer thought so. E.E. Cummings' great World War I novel, *The Enormous Room*, used all kinds of formatting tricks to good effect. Cummings left out the spaces after commas to make his narrative livelier. He separated the lines in some of his dialogues with dashes to make the conversations more energetic, and capitalized certain words for emphasis. And Cummings did it all with a typewriter, which must have taxed his powers of invention.

WordPerfect makes formatting text easy and routine. There are also more formatting options in WordPerfect than you'll ever need. How might *The Enormous Room* have looked written with WordPerfect instead of a typewriter? We can't know for sure, but one thing is certain: Cummings would have had a field day.

Formatting at the push of a button

Suppose the local gym decided to experiment with the soap and shampoo supplied in the shower room. The new stuff is awful. A strong memo is called for, something along the lines of the one in figure 5.1.

Fig. 5.1
Don't laugh—it's a true story. Best to nip it in the bud with a memo that gets some attention before it's too late.

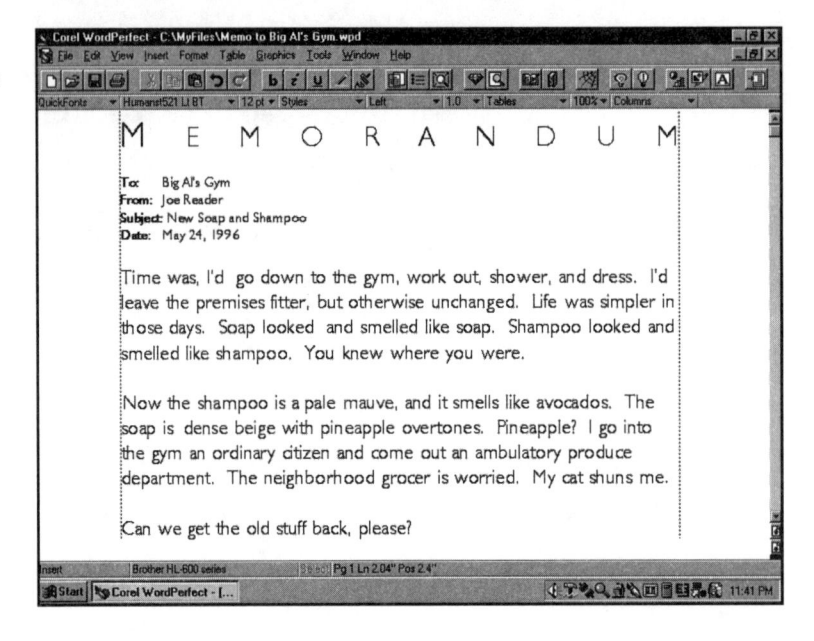

TIP To create a memo in the format shown in figure 5.1, click the New Document button on the Toolbar, double-click Memo Expert in the Select New Document dialog box, and follow the prompts.

Put a boldface on it

The memo in figure 5.1 expresses our feelings reasonably clearly, but we can pitch it a little stronger without rewriting.

Making text **bold** is an easy way to emphasize key words or phrases. Select the text you want to appear in boldface; then click the Bold button on the Toolbar. That's all there is to it.

Double-click the word "soap" in the memo to select it; then click the Bold button on the Toolbar for instant boldface.

To apply boldface to text you're about to type, you can click the Bold button on the Toolbar to turn on boldfacing, type the word, and then click the Bold button again to turn off boldfacing. You might find it easier to use Ctrl+B to turn boldfacing on and off while you're typing.

Q&A *I pressed Ctrl+B for bold, and now everything I type is bold! What do I do?*

You forgot to press Ctrl+B at the end of the text you wanted boldfaced. That turns off bold. To get rid of boldfacing on text, select the text and either click the Bold button on the Toolbar or press Ctrl+B. This works for italics and underlining too—select the text and then click the appropriate Toolbar buttons to apply or clear the formatting. The Bold, Italics, and Underline buttons toggle the formatting on and off.

When (and how) do I add italics?

Like boldface, *italics* add emphasis, but with a subtler effect. Use italics for book, newspaper, or magazine titles, and for foreign language words in English text. You can also use italics to express scorn, especially scorn for a particular choice of word or words. Book reviewers are fond of quoting awkwardly written or overwritten passages and italicizing them, as though to say, "Can you *believe* this trash?" Not nice, but effective.

Italicizing text works along the same lines as boldfacing text. Just select the text; then click the Italics button on the Toolbar.

Let's italicize the word "Pineapple" in the memo in figure 5.1 to emphasis our feelings about toiletries scented thusly. Double-click the word, and click the Italics button on the Toolbar.

You can click the Italics button on the Toolbar to turn italics on and off while you're typing, or press Ctrl+I.

> 66 **Plain English, please!**
>
> Boldface, italics, and underlining are the **attributes** or **appearance** of characters. 99

Underline for emphasis

Underlining for emphasis is pretty obvious. It's even a figure of speech, as in "let me underline this point." No surprises in applying underlining: select the text and click the Underline button on the Toolbar.

Double-click "please" in the last sentence of our memo to select it; then click the Underline button on the Toolbar to apply underlining.

Applying underlining as you type works just the same as applying boldfacing or italics; click the Toolbar button to turn on underlining, type, and then click again to turn it off. Or press Ctrl+U to turn underlining on and off.

The results of all this formatting work are shown in figure 5.2.

Fig. 5.2
It's not exactly E.E. Cummings, but this memo now packs a little more punch.

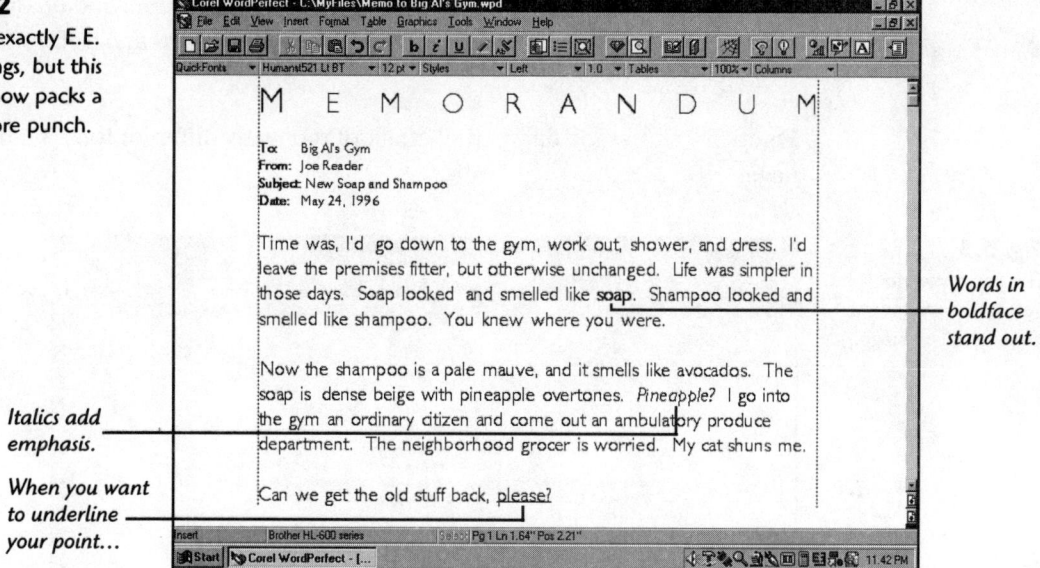

Italics add emphasis.

When you want to underline your point...

Words in boldface stand out.

What are fonts?

Build a house, and you might use stone, brick, and wood for the exterior. When you create a document, the exterior consists of **fonts**. It's a rare builder who uses just one material. In the same way, documents usually have a combination of different fonts and font sizes.

Just as you wouldn't put aluminum siding on a church, the choice of font depends on the tone of the document. Each font has its own personality, and you'll want to choose one that doesn't clash with your text. Shelley Volante might work for a wedding invitation, for example, but to announce a kids' weenie roast, Lucida Handwriting would be a better choice.

> 66 *Plain English, please!*
>
> Most typography mavens insist that a **font** is a typeface and all its attributes (size, boldface, italics, underlining, and so on). **Typefaces**, or **font faces**, are those character types whose names you see on the Power Bar and in the Font dialog box. Times New Roman is a typeface. Times New Roman in all its different sizes and appearances is a font. In practice, font, font face, and typeface are used interchangeably. 99

WordPerfect makes it so easy to change fonts that you can wind up overdoing it. Too many fonts in one document is distracting and makes for a cluttered page.

Figure 5.3 shows the distracting effect of too many different fonts on the page.

Fig. 5.3
The patchwork look gets in the way of the document's message.

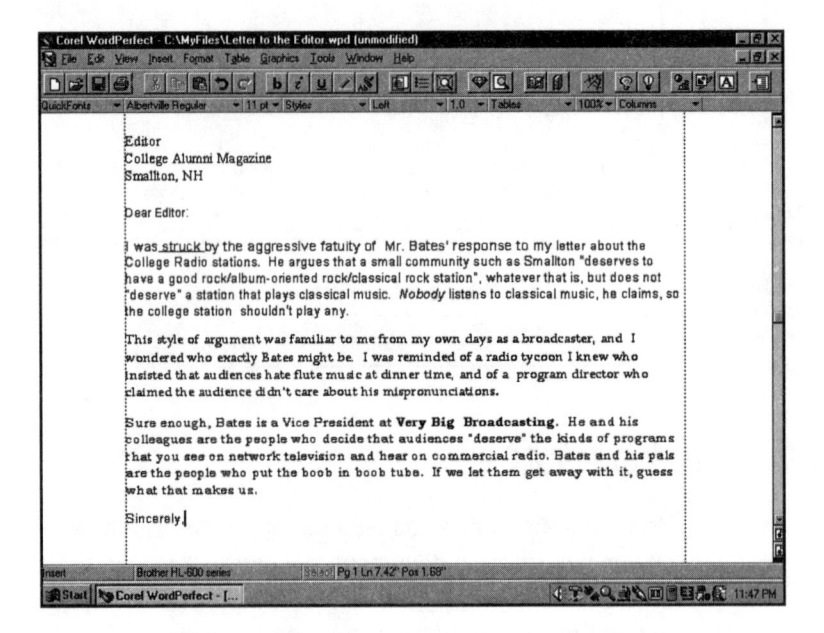

How do I change font faces and sizes?

WordPerfect comes with many different fonts. Windows has fonts of its own, and your printer has fonts too. When you install WordPerfect, the program sniffs out all your fonts so that you can use them all from WordPerfect.

When you start up WordPerfect, Times New Roman in 12-point size is the default. You'll see Times New Roman and 12 pt displayed on the second and third buttons at the left of the Power Bar. To switch to a different font face, click the Power Bar Font Face button for the drop-down list shown in figure 5.4.

Chapter 5 *Formatting for Characters with Character*

Fig. 5.4
The Power Bar Font Face button displays the current font face.

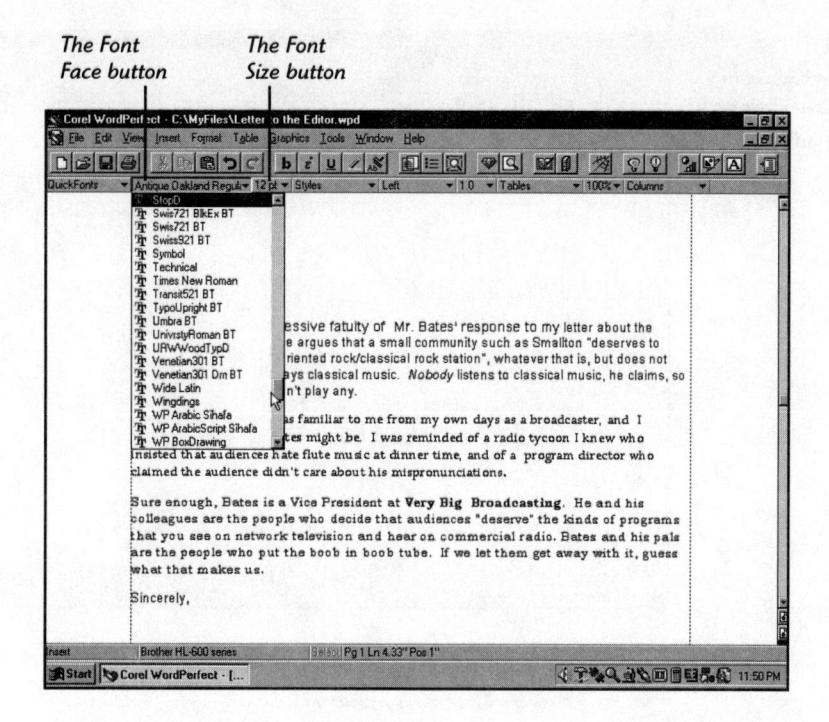

Click any of the font faces on the list for a new font. Font changes take effect in the following different ways:

- If the document is in only one font to begin with, the new font changes the text from the insertion point to the end of the document.

- If there are other fonts in the document, the new font changes all the text from the insertion point to the next different font.

- If you've selected text, the new font settings affect only the selection.

To change the font size, click the Font Size button on the Power Bar and select a point size from the list. Font size changes affect text in the same ways as font face changes. Either selected text or text from the insertion point to the end of the document, or to the next different font, will be resized.

Figure 5.5 shows the Power Bar Font Size button and Times New Roman in different point sizes.

Fig. 5.5
WordPerfect lets your documents whisper or shriek with different-sized type.

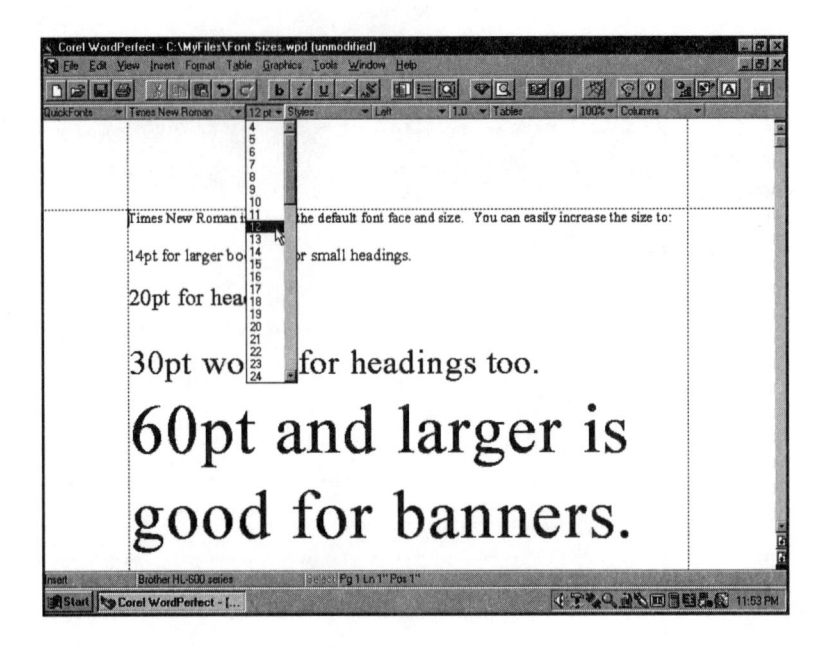

> 66 **Plain English, please!**
>
> **Point size** is typesetter's jargon for the size of the characters. There are 72 points in an inch; when a newspaper cranks up its headlines to a shriek, it uses 72-point, or one-inch, type. 99

How can I tell what those font faces look like?

The Power Bar makes changing font faces convenient and fast. But, unless you know what each of those many faces looks like, how do you know what you're getting when you select one?

Click Format, Font for the Font dialog box shown in figure 5.6.

Make your selection from the Font face list, and view the sample of the font face displayed at the bottom of the dialog box.

The sample changes to reflect your choice of Font size and Appearance as well. Experiment with Shadow and Outline for special effects. WordPerfect gives you a lot of flexibility, and if you don't like the results, you can either click Cancel before you leave the Font dialog box, or click the Undo button on the Toolbar to erase your alterations.

Fig. 5.6
Use the Font dialog box to preview and make font selections.

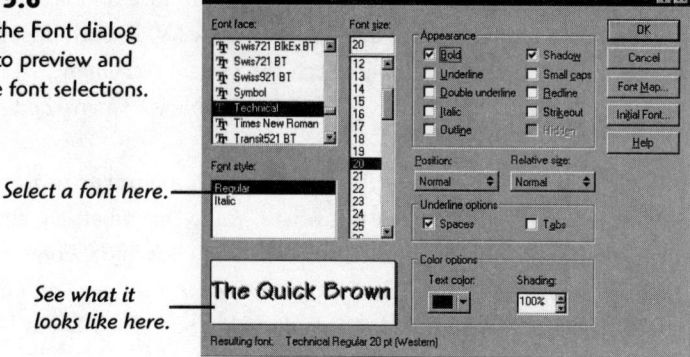

Select a font here.

See what it looks like here.

When you're happy with your efforts, click OK.

Other font options

From the Font dialog box, apply any of these effects to new or selected text:

- Click the Position button for Superscript or Subscript. Text is displayed and printed at 60% of the selected size, above or below the line, like the "2" in H_2O.

- Relative Size changes text to preset ratios of the selected size. For example, Relative Size, Extra Large makes text twice as large (200%) as the selected point size.

- Click the Text color button and select a color from the palette that pops up. The color appears on the button, and the colored text appears in the preview window and on the screen. Colored text won't print in color unless you have a color printer (see Chapter 15 for more on coloring fonts).

- Click the Shading arrows and set a value between 0 and 100% for fainter or darker text.

> **Q&A** *I changed the font for this whole document, but my page numbers, headers, and footnotes didn't change!*
>
> Font changes you make from the Power Bar or the Font dialog box don't affect text in headers or footers, including page numbers. To change the font for the entire document, headers and footers included, click Initial

Font in the Font dialog box and select a different font face and size in the Document Initial Font dialog box that appears. Click OK in both dialog boxes to save your choice. That only affects the current document. The next new document you open will have good old Times New Roman 12pt.

> **TIP** **You start out with Times New Roman, a good, all-purpose font,** whenever you fire up WordPerfect. But what if you want something else as the initial font for all your documents? Press F9 and click In<u>i</u>tial Font in the Font dialog box. Choose a different font; then click the S<u>e</u>t as printer initial font check box in the Document Initial Font dialog box. Click OK in both dialog boxes. The new font is now the default for the current, and all new documents. But only if the printer current at the time of the font change is selected. Change printers, and you go back to Times New Roman. Unless, of course, you set a new initial font for that printer as well.

I cooked up a great font! How do I get it back again?

You've concocted an elaborate mix of font face, size, and appearance in the Font dialog box, and then applied it to selected text. Further down in your document, you want the same font again for more selected text. You could go back to the Font dialog box and mix your font from scratch...

...but don't do it. Instead, click the QuickFonts button on the Power Bar. You'll see a list of the last 10 fonts you've used (see fig. 5.7).

The QuickFonts button works just like the Power Bar Font Face and Font Size button. Any font you select will change text from the insertion point to either the end of the document, or to the next different font. If you select text first, and then click a font on the QuickFonts button list, only the selected text changes. QuickFonts remembers your font face, size, and appearance, no matter how fancy your creation.

Fig. 5.7
Whenever you want to reuse a font, click the QuickFonts button and select it from the list.

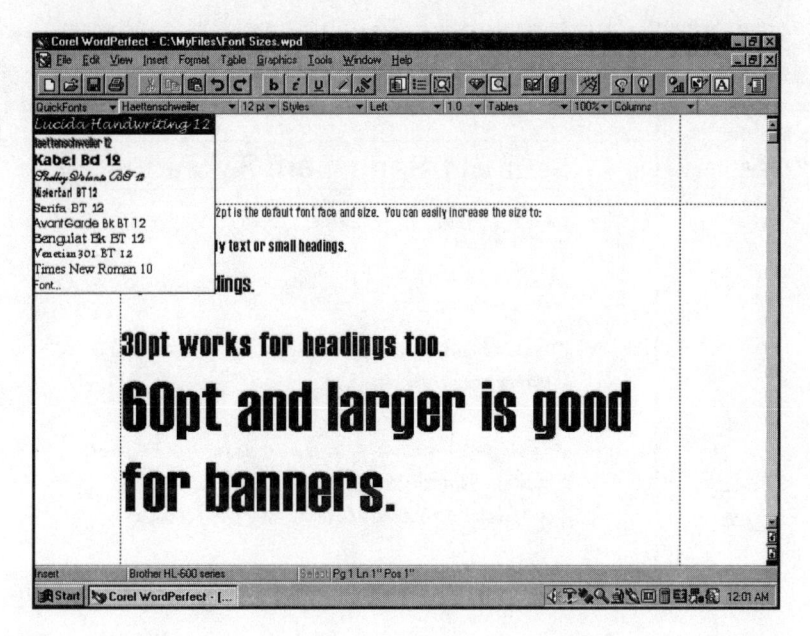

WordPerfect has a font for every occasion

Changing fonts is easy. Picking the best font for a particular job is a question of taste and judgment. Trial and error is a fine way of proceeding until you get to know the various fonts, especially since your choices are always reversible.

These general ideas might help narrow your choices:

- **Serif** fonts are usually used in body text. Serifs are those little "tails" at the beginning and ends of characters in typefaces such as Times New Roman. Because serifs guide the eye from one character to the next, serif fonts tend to be easier to read in the smaller, denser type of body text. You're reading a serif font right now.

- **Sans Serif** fonts don't have the little tails; Arial is a sans serif font. In bigger sizes, they can have an insistent look, which is why sans serif fonts are often used for headlines. They say "look at me." The heading for this section is printed in a sans serif font called Highlander Bold.

Fonts such as Algerian or Caslon are more decorative, for occasional use in titles or headings. Figure 5.8 illustrates some of the choices among serif, sans serif fonts, and decorative fonts.

Fig. 5.8
Experimenting with different fonts is the best way to find the right look for your text.

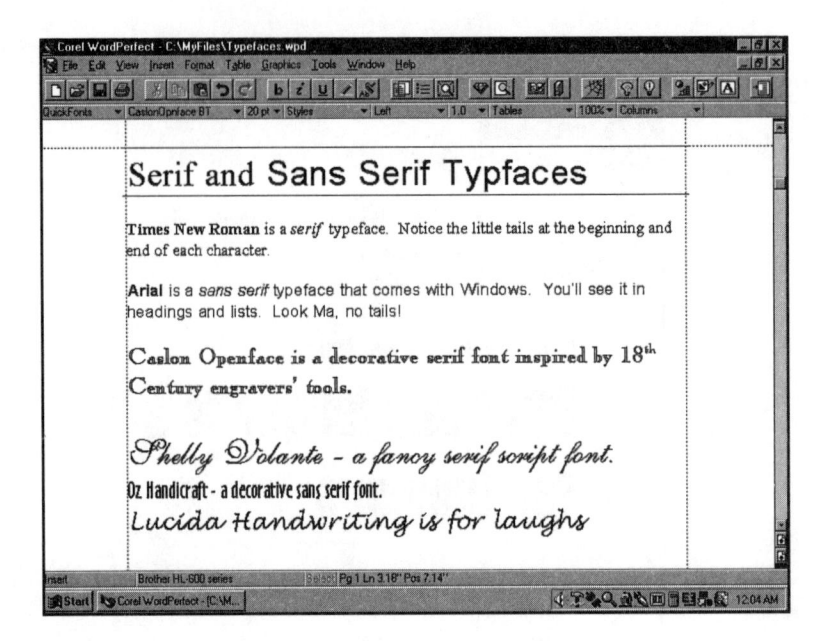

There are no hard and fast rules for any of this. **Typography**, the use and design of typefaces, is more art than science. Many newspapers use a famous serif typeface called Bodoni in headlines, for example, and you'll often see sans serif typefaces in body text.

WordPerfect makes it easy to experiment with font faces and their attributes, so go ahead and try different fonts. You can always change your mind later.

Drop-caps are characters with real character

Drop-caps, or dropped capital letters, are enlarged characters used at the beginning of a paragraph. Anyone who has read aloud to kids knows about drop-caps—publishers of fairy tale books love them. Drop-caps work well in any document because they break up dense body text in an attractive way.

In the Middle Ages, monks labored for months on magnificent decorated drop-caps. WordPerfect lets you do the job in seconds.

How do I get a drop-cap?

To create a drop-cap, type your paragraph. With the insertion point anywhere in the paragraph, click Format, Drop Cap.

That gives you an instant drop-cap and the Drop Cap feature bar, both of which are shown in figure 5.9.

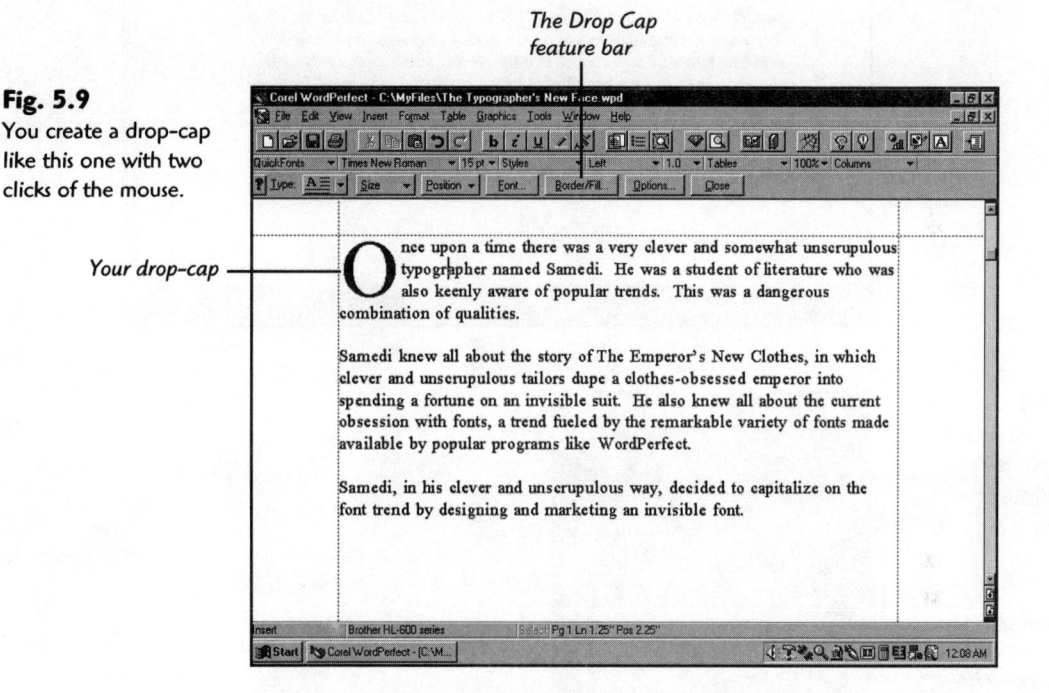

Fig. 5.9
You create a drop-cap like this one with two clicks of the mouse.

The Drop Cap feature bar

Your drop-cap

Click the Toolbar buttons to change the drop-cap's size and font, and the position of the drop-cap relative to the paragraph text. Click the Type button on the Drop Cap feature bar for the selection of drop-cap styles in figure 5.10.

> **TIP** If you want the first several letters of a paragraph formatted as drop-caps, click Options on the Drop Cap feature bar and enter a value for the Number of characters in drop-cap in the Drop Cap Options dialog box. Or click Make first whole word as drop cap to drop the first word.

Want some special effects? Click the Border/Fill button to pop up the Drop Cap Border/Fill dialog box. Click the Fill tab and browse the Available fill styles shown in figure 5.11.

Fig. 5.10
The Type button makes it easy to pick a size and position for your drop-caps.

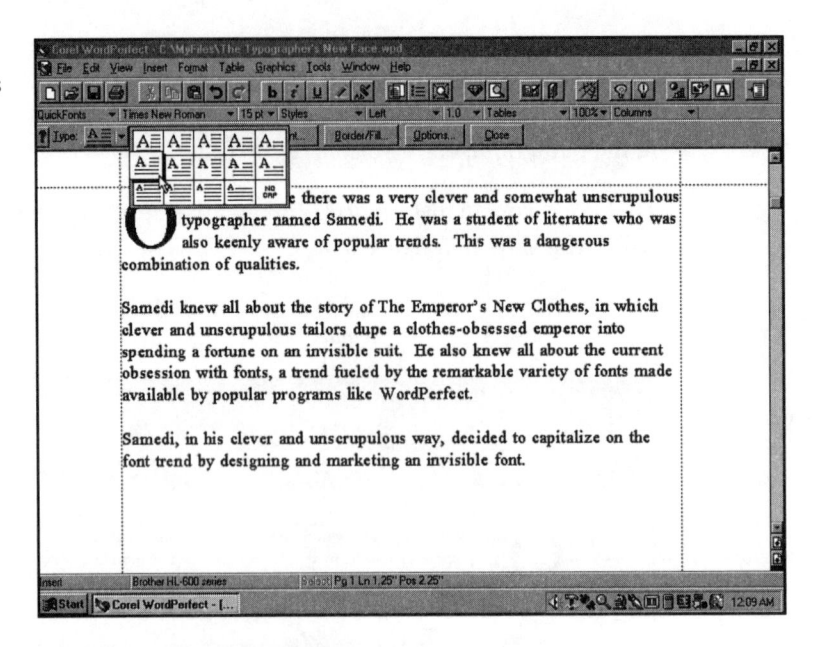

Fig. 5.11
Some of these drop-cap special effects are positively jaw-dropping.

The fill style name appears here when you make a selection.

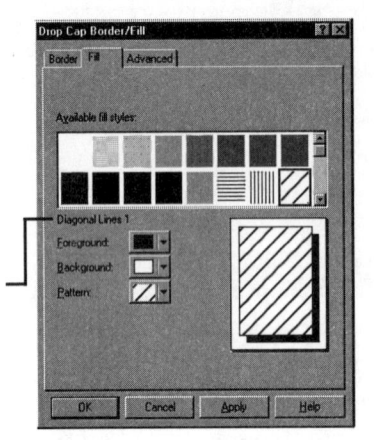

To create the effect in figure 5.12, I used Diagonal Lines 1 from the Fill tab of the Drop Cap Border/Fill dialog box and Shadow from the Border tab. I also changed the font to Oz Handicraft (click the Font button) and the font size to 4 Lines High (click the Size button).

The result isn't exactly an illuminated manuscript. On the other hand, you get your results quite a bit faster. When you've finished formatting your drop-cap, click Close on the Drop Cap feature bar to put it away.

Fig. 5.12
You can create nifty effects in no time with the Drop Cap feature bar.

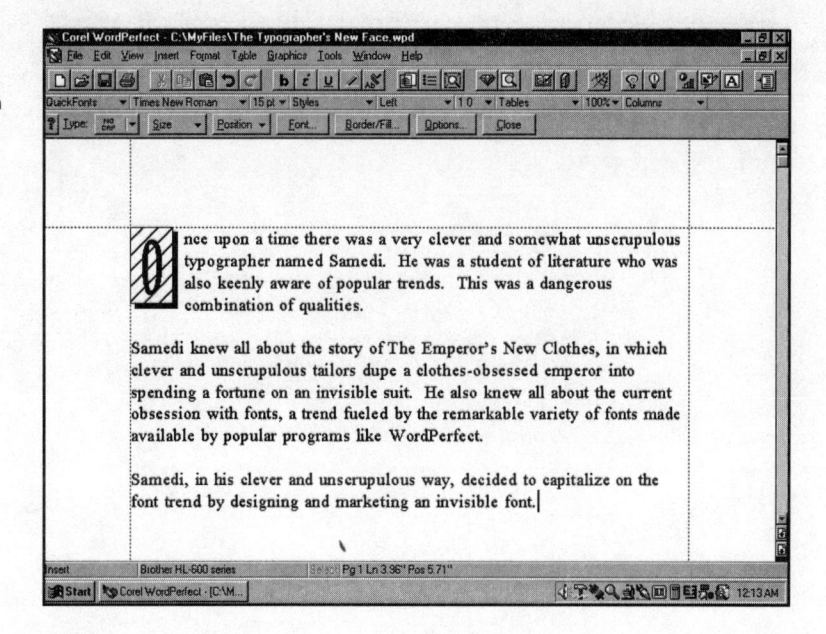

TIP **To change the formatting on a drop-cap after you close the Drop Cap feature bar,** simply double-click the drop-cap. That pops up the feature bar again.

6

What's My Line? Formatting Paragraphs for Precision and Punch

● **In this chapter:**

- I need new margins

- How can I indent this paragraph?

- What is justification?

- How do I center titles?

- I want a bulleted (or numbered) list!

- How can I tell one dialog box from another?

Staring at a blank wall isn't much fun, so we hang pictures. To give pages variety, we use paragraphs. With WordPerfect's formatting tools, you'll turn out picture perfect paragraphs every time . . . . ▶

A paragraph expresses a complete thought, or marks a break in a narrative or a discussion. Or does it? Henry James wrote paragraphs that go on for pages. He crammed more thoughts into a single paragraph than you sometimes find in other authors' novels. Colombian Nobel prize-winner Gabriel García Márquez wrote a novel called *Autumn of the Patriarch* with no paragraphs at all.

In fact, there are no strict rules about what makes a paragraph. It's really just a formatting convention. Paragraphs break up a page to make it easier to read. Since WordPerfect shines at formatting text, you'd expect it to be pretty helpful in formatting paragraphs.

And you'd be absolutely right.

How do I set the margins?

Paragraphs may vary in length and content, but all paragraphs are made up of lines. Formatting a paragraph begins with formatting lines. And since lines begin at the margin, that's where we'll start, too.

WordPerfect gives you one-inch left, right, top, and bottom margins. Those settings are fine for most uses, but there'll be times when you want to change the margins. If you're planning to put hole punches in your pages for a bound report, for example, you might want more than a one-inch left margin. Or you might be writing a document with densely packed text, like a contract. You might want less than one-inch margins in that case.

Margins line up fast with Guidelines

All the margin settings—left, right, top, and bottom—are easily changed, and as with many WordPerfect features, you get a choice of ways to change them. The fastest and easiest way to adjust your margins is with WordPerfect's new Guidelines feature. Guidelines are those dotted blue lines that frame the text in the editing window. They're like a vise for text: drag them left or right, up or down, and the lines of text they enclose compress or expand. With Guidelines, your on-screen page is completely adjustable.

If you don't see the Guidelines, just turn them on. Select View, Guidelines and click the Margins check box, as shown in figure 6.1.

Chapter 6 *What's My Line? Formatting Paragraphs for Precision and Punch* **105**

Fig. 6.1
They might be checked, but you won't see the table, column, or header/footer Guidelines unless your document includes those features.

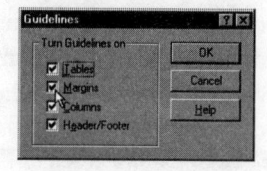

With the Guidelines visible, margin setting becomes a simple drag operation. Want a 1.5" left margin instead of the standard issue 1"? Move your mouse pointer so that it's directly over the left Guideline; when the pointer changes to a black two-headed arrow, click and drag the Guideline to the right. A helpful little QuickStatus box pops up to show exactly where you're moving the margin, as seen in figure 6.2.

Fig. 6.2
Drag a Guideline, and you can see precisely where on the page the margin will be.

The distance between text and the page edge appears whenever you drag a Guideline.

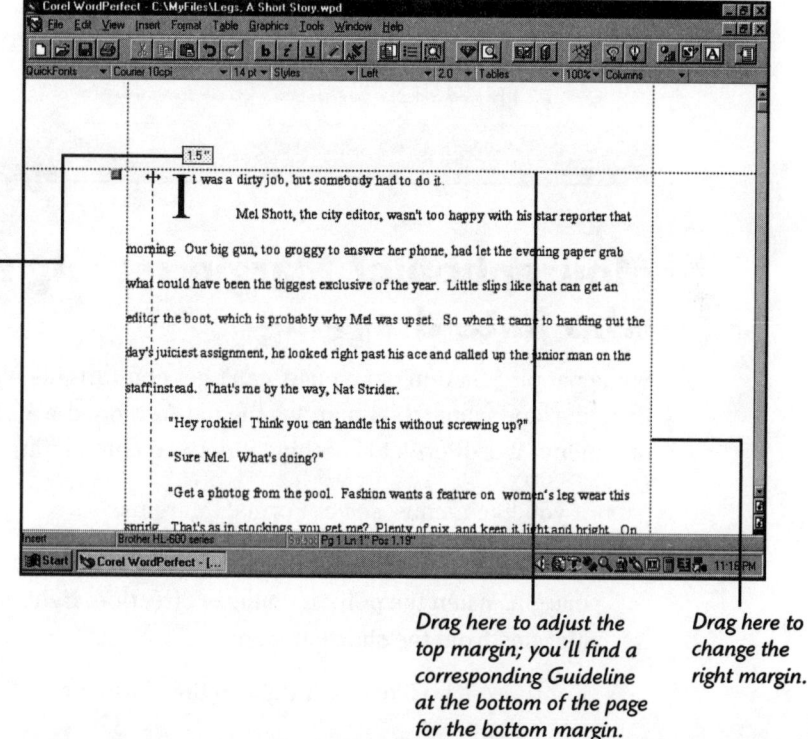

Drag here to adjust the top margin; you'll find a corresponding Guideline at the bottom of the page for the bottom margin.

Drag here to change the right margin.

Adjust your top, bottom, and right margins the same way—just drag the appropriate Guideline. Your margin adjustments take effect from the point where you drag the Guideline to the end of the document. To change the margin for the entire document, drag the Guideline at the very beginning of the document. If you drag the Guideline at a spot in the middle of the document, the margin above that spot won't change, as you can see in figure 6.3.

Fig. 6.3
Unless you want different margins at different points, drag Guidelines at the beginning of the document.

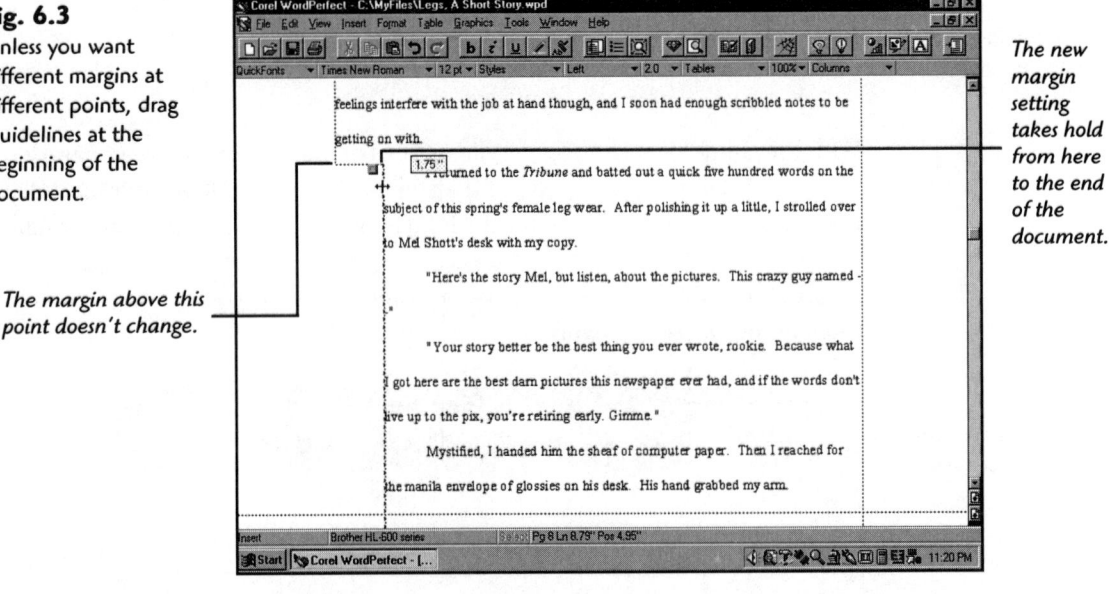

The margin above this point doesn't change.

The new margin setting takes hold from here to the end of the document.

Mousephobic? Margin setting for those who hate dragging

Some people just don't like mice, can't get comfortable with the idea of dragging, and want to set margins the old-fashioned way: from the keyboard or a menu. WordPerfect is nothing if not accommodating:

- If you like menus, select Format, Margins.
- Shortcut menu fans can slide the pointer all the way over to the left margin. When the pointer changes direction, right-click and choose Margins from the shortcut menu.
- For those who like to cut right to the chase, press Ctrl+F8.

Any of the above actions brings up the Margins dialog box seen in figure 6.4.

Either type new values in the Left, Right, Top, and Bottom edit boxes, or click the arrows to change the settings. The measurements are from the edge of the page to the text. As you change the margin settings, the sample page in the dialog box changes to reflect the new values.

Fig. 6.4
For some, the Margins dialog box might be the easiest margin adjustment option.

Any changes you make affect the current paragraph (the paragraph where the insertion happens to be) to the end of the document.

> **TIP** **WordPerfect displays measurements in decimals, but if you think** in fractions, type them. For example, if you type **1/4**, WordPerfect automatically converts that to .250".

To change margins for the whole document, move the insertion point to the very beginning of your text. If you select text before popping up the Margins dialog box, only the margins for the selected paragraphs are affected by new margin settings.

> **Q&A** *How do I get the original one-inch margins back after all these adjustments?!*
>
> If you just made the margin changes, use Undo to reverse them. If you've made other edits since changing the margins, open the Reveal Codes window (press Alt+F3) and delete any margin setting codes you see there.

Tab stop changes to make? Call up the ruler bar

WordPerfect gives you tab stops at half-inch intervals across the page. That's fine, until you need something different. You might, for example, want to tab from the left margin to the right margin with one press of the Tab key.

You can get rid of any or all the tab stops, or add more, with the ruler bar. To summon it up, select View, Toolbars/Ruler, click the Ruler Bar check box, and then click OK in the Toolbars dialog box.

Figure 6.5 shows the ruler bar on display.

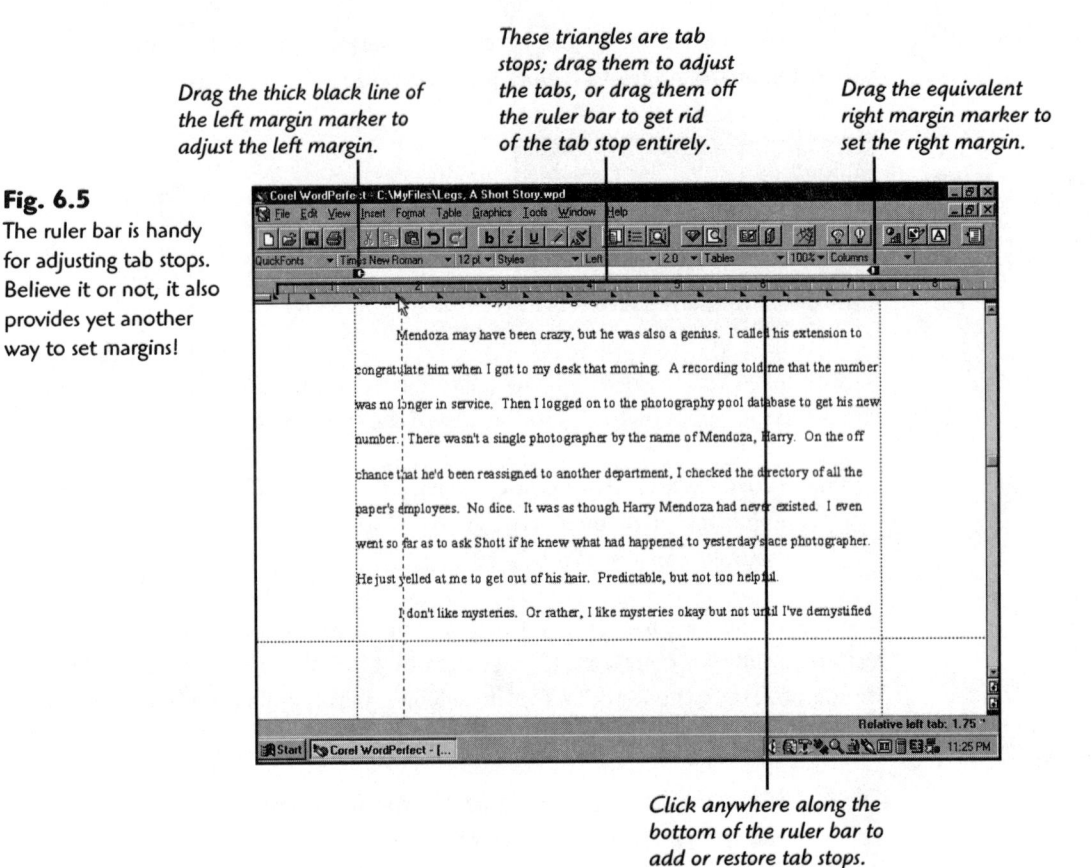

Part II Editing and Formatting for Perfect Documents

Fig. 6.5
The ruler bar is handy for adjusting tab stops. Believe it or not, it also provides yet another way to set margins!

Drag the thick black line of the left margin marker to adjust the left margin.

These triangles are tab stops; drag them to adjust the tabs, or drag them off the ruler bar to get rid of the tab stop entirely.

Drag the equivalent right margin marker to set the right margin.

Click anywhere along the bottom of the ruler bar to add or restore tab stops.

To clear individual tab stops, just drag the tab markers down off the ruler bar. If you want to add tabs, click anywhere on the bottom of the ruler bar. To get rid of all the tab stops, right-click the lower part of the ruler bar for the QuickMenu and select Clear All Tabs. And to put the ruler bar away again, right-click *anywhere* on the ruler bar and select Hide Ruler Bar.

7 You've changed tab stops on the ruler bar, put the ruler bar away, and now you have further tab stop changes to make. Skip the ruler bar and call up the tab bar instead. To the left of the paragraph where you changed tab stops, you'll see an arrow pointing at a little picture of an indented page.

Click the arrow, and the tab bar springs up, as seen in figure 6.6.

Click anywhere outside the tab bar to put it away.

Fig. 6.6
The tab bar icon only appears when you change tab stops with the ruler bar.

Click here for a menu of tab options.

Drag the markers back and forth to change tab stops; drag them off the tab bar to clear tab stops.

Click here to summon up the tab bar.

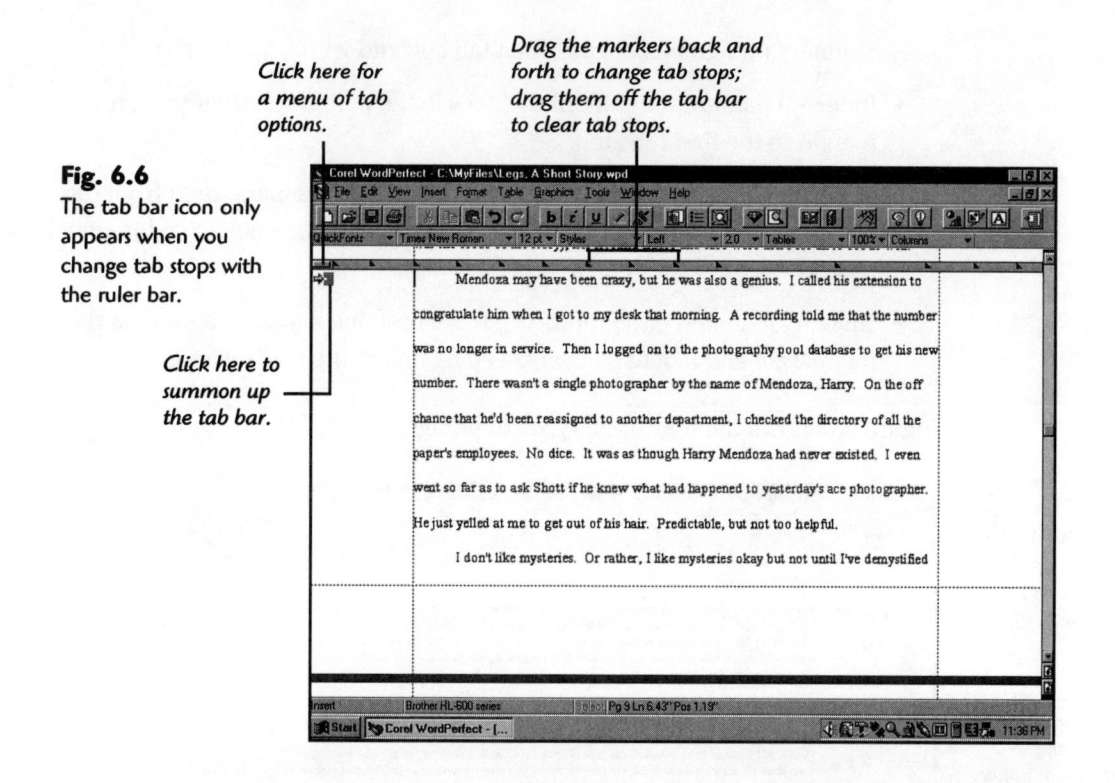

Everything you always wanted to know about indents

Paragraphs break up a page of text to make it easier on the eyes, but a long document with paragraph after paragraph of the same type can get a little wearisome, too. It's like sneaking away from your desk for ice cream. A welcome break, but a choice of just one flavor would get old fast.

Variety is good, for ice cream and for paragraphs. WordPerfect lets you create all kinds of different paragraphs with ease. You don't want to overdo it; too many different kinds of paragraphs in a document might lead to visual indigestion.

But the occasional indented, double-indented, or hanging-indented paragraph adds interest to the page and emphasis to key paragraphs. WordPerfect gives you a choice of indented paragraph formats:

- Ordinary paragraphs begin with a tab and end with a hard return.
- Indented paragraphs shift all the lines in the paragraph from the left margin to the first tab stop.
- Double-indented paragraphs shift all the lines in the paragraph from the left margin to the first tab stop and an equivalent distance from the right margin.
- Hanging-indented paragraphs begin the first line in the paragraph at the left margin and indent each succeeding line to the first tab stop.

Figure 6.7 shows the four basic types of paragraphs.

Fig. 6.7
Use the different indenting options to add emphasis and break up the page.

Here's a QuickSpot: click it for paragraph formatting tools, including indent options.

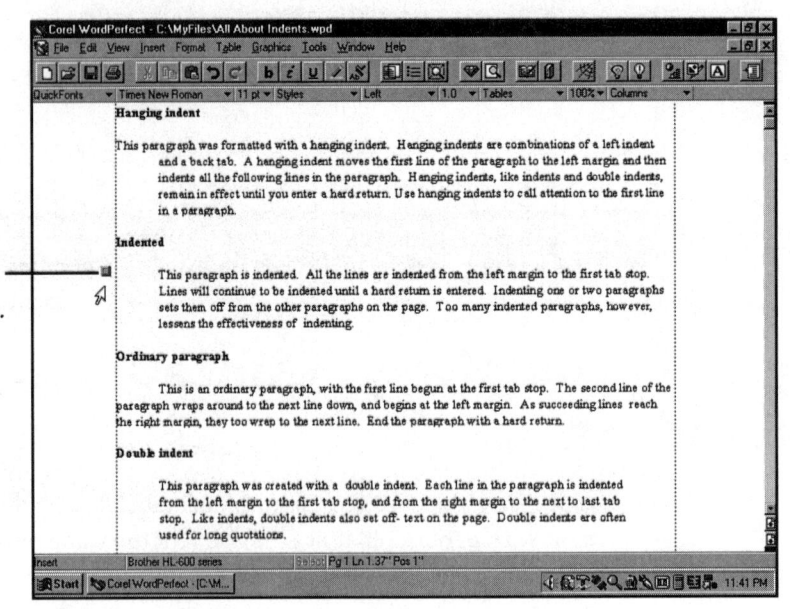

Pick your indent option from the QuickSpot menu

Glance over toward the left margin of the editing window, and if you've typed some text, you'll see a QuickSpot appear (take a look at figure 6.7). They're those little gray objects that seem to materialize and vanish mysteriously as your pointer moves around the screen. There's really no mystery about them.

QuickSpots appear when there's text on the screen, and move from paragraph to paragraph as you move your pointer. To use a QuickSpot to indent a paragraph:

1 Type your paragraph first, and don't bother with tabs or indents yet.

2 Click the QuickSpot adjacent to the paragraph you want to indent. That selects the paragraph and pops up the Paragraph dialog box.

3 Click the Indent button for the menu of indent options shown in figure 6.8.

Fig. 6.8
There's a complete set of paragraph formatting tools hiding behind every QuickSpot.

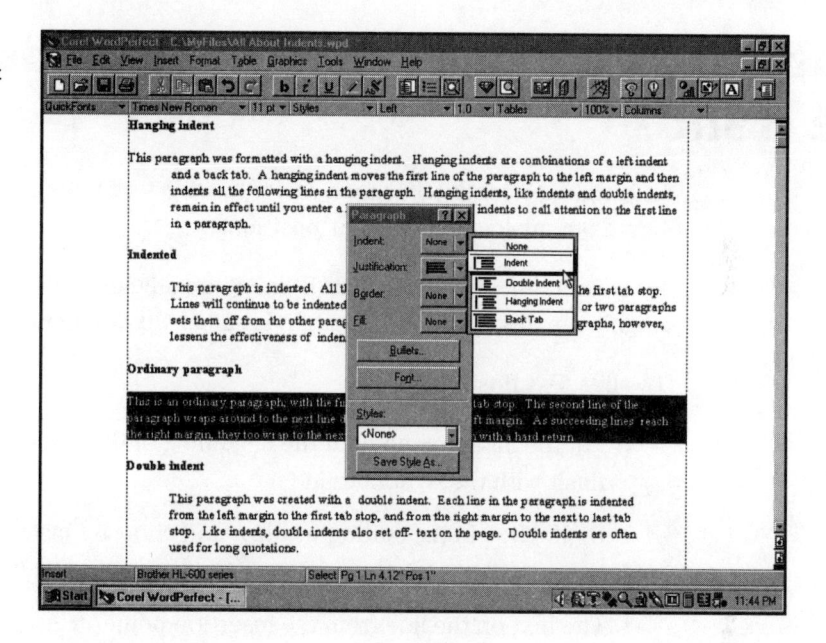

4 Choose an indent style from the drop-down list, and the selected paragraph is instantly transformed.

5 Click anywhere outside the Paragraph dialog box to put it away.

QuickSpots let you try different paragraph formats on for size. You can keep changing the indent style of the selected paragraph while the Paragraph dialog box is displayed, as many times as you like. Just remember to choose None on the Indent drop-down menu in between each change. Otherwise, the successive indents will squash your paragraph into a column!

> **TIP** **For an instant hanging indent, type a paragraph with no tabs or indents.** Press Tab at the beginning of any line in the paragraph *other than the first line*. All the lines in the paragraph except the first line will be indented one tab stop.

I want to indent a new paragraph

QuickSpots are convenient for altering existing paragraphs, but if you just want to indent a new paragraph, press F7 and start typing. All the other indent options for new paragraphs are available from the keyboard and the menu as well; click Fo_r_mat, P_a_ragraph to get them.

Centering and flush right: where does your text stand?

Left, right, or center, it's much easier to align text in WordPerfect than it is to figure out my local politicians' positions.

By default, lines of text in WordPerfect are aligned with the left margin. Aligning text with the right margin is called **flush right.**

To align text flush right:

1. Put the insertion point at the beginning of the text you want to align flush with the right margin.
2. Right-click in the editing window and choose Flush _R_ight on the shortcut menu.
3. The text on the line from the insertion point on is aligned with the right margin.

When you press Enter at the end of the line of text aligned flush right, you return to normal, left-aligned text.

> **TIP** **If you want flush right and left-aligned text on the same line, just** type the left-aligned text beginning at the left margin. Then right-click for the shortcut menu and choose Flush _R_ight. Start typing the rest of your text, and it'll be aligned with the right margin.

Take me to your (dot) leader

A **dot leader** is left- and right-aligned text on the same line, with a string of dots in between. You see dot leaders in tables of contents and directories, and it's a snap to put them into a WordPerfect document.

To create a dot leader:

1 Type your text at the left margin.

2 Click Format, Line, Flush Right with Dot Leaders. A line of dots will appear between the text at the left margin and the right margin.

3 Now, type the text you want at the right margin—the insertion point has moved there automatically. The right-most dots will be overwritten to make room for your text. Figure 6.9 shows you the dot leader effect.

Fig. 6.9
WordPerfect dot leaders always have the right number of dots per line, automatically.

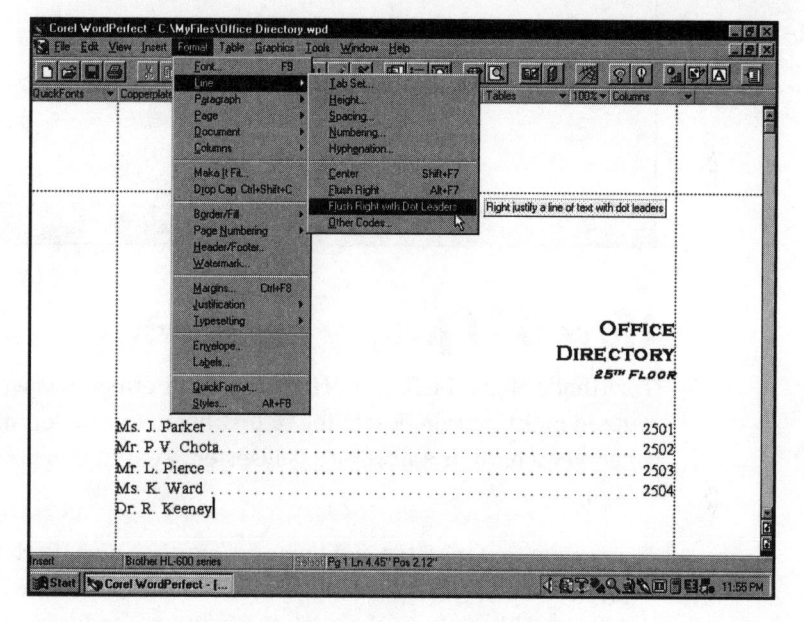

Center a line: the middle of the road

To quickly center a line of text:

1 Put the insertion point at the beginning of the text you want to center.

2 Right-click anywhere in the editing window and choose Center on the shortcut menu.

3 All the text on the line from the insertion point on is centered between the left and the right margins.

Pressing Enter at the end of a centered line returns the insertion point to the left margin for normal, left-aligned text. Figure 6.10 shows lines that are aligned left, centered, and flush right.

Fig. 6.10
Centered and flush right titles stand out on the page.

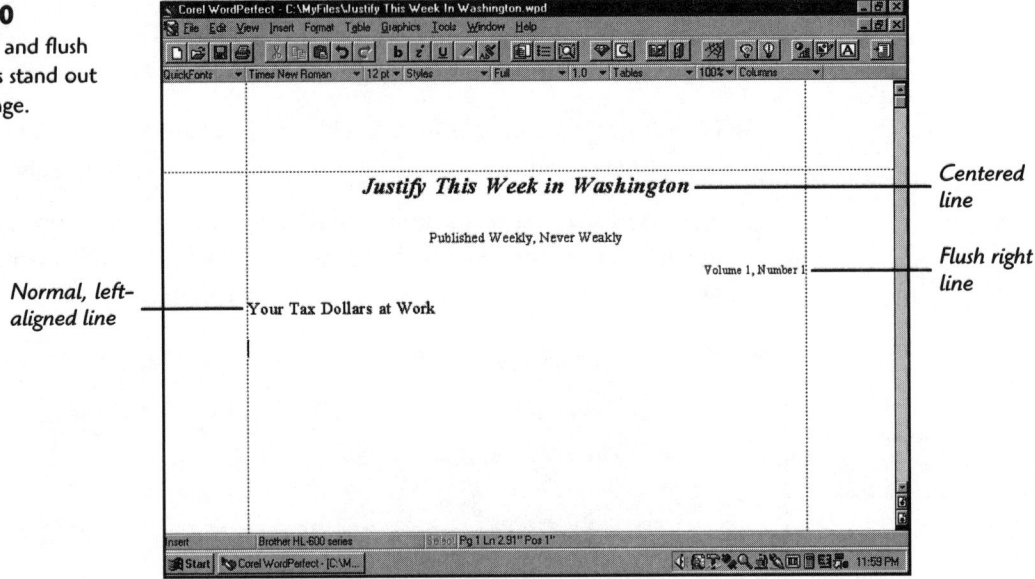

Screenshot of Corel WordPerfect showing "Justify This Week in Washington" document with callouts:
- Centered line → *Justify This Week in Washington*
- Flush right line → Volume 1, Number 1
- Normal, left-aligned line → Your Tax Dollars at Work

Also shown: *Published Weekly, Never Weakly*

How do I justify my work?

Text that's aligned left, the default in WordPerfect, has what's called a **ragged right** margin. Each line of text begins at the left margin, but ends wherever a hard or soft return is inserted. Text in this book has a ragged right margin.

If you align text with the right margin, another WordPerfect option, you get a **ragged left** margin. To do that, put the insertion point where you want your right-aligned lines to begin, click the Justification button (it's the button labeled Left, until you change it) on the Power Bar, and select Right from the drop-down menu. Figure 6.11 shows the Power Bar Justification button and the difference between ragged right and ragged left margins.

> **Plain English, please!**
>
> In printing and page-layout jargon, to **justify** means to adjust lines of text so that they line up evenly at the left or right margins, or with both margins.

Fig. 6.11
Alignment changes made with the Power Bar Justification button affect text from the insertion point to the end of the document.

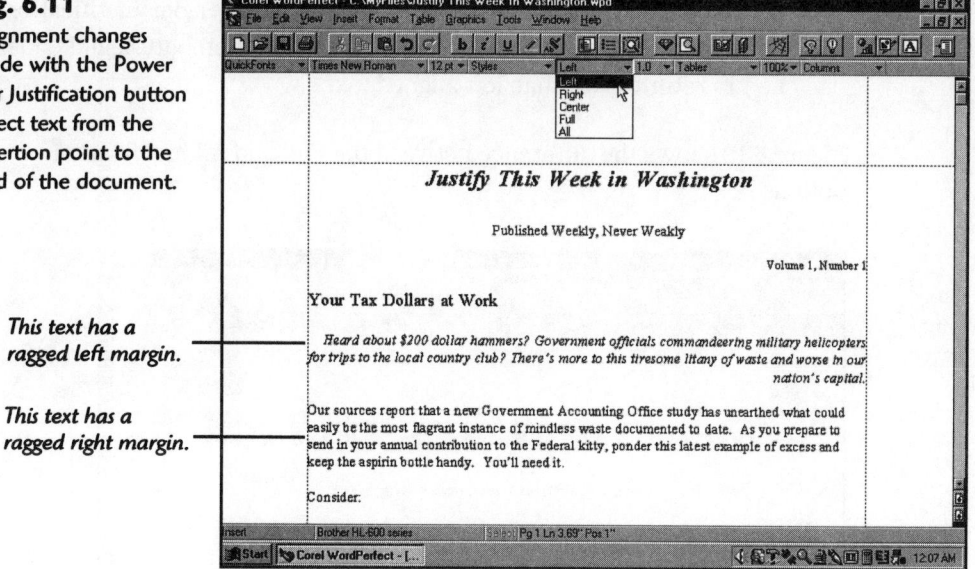

This text has a ragged left margin.

This text has a ragged right margin.

Justified lines are ragged no more

Fully justified lines are aligned with both the left and right margins, so that each line begins and ends at exactly the same horizontal position on the page. Fully justified lines are like lengths of string cut neatly with a scissors at both ends. They give the page a more formal look. There are two sorts of fully justified text formats in WordPerfect (see fig. 6.11), and, confusingly, one of them is called Full on the Power Bar Justification button:

- **Full** gives all lines that end in soft returns even left and right margins. But, the last line in a paragraph will end wherever you press Enter to insert a hard return. That last line won't, in other words, necessarily reach the right margin like the other lines in the paragraph.

- **All** forces even left and right margins on every line, including those that end in a hard return. **Justify All** stretches out the spacing between words and letters so that every line begins and ends at the left and right margins, even if the last line in a paragraph is a short one.

To justify text, either Full or All:

1 Put the insertion point at the beginning of the text you want justified.

2 Click the Justification button on the Power Bar for the drop-down list shown in figure 6.11.

3 Select either Full or All. For new text, click a Power Bar Justification option first; then start typing. Click the Justification button and choose Left to return to normal, left-aligned text.

Figure 6.12 shows the difference between the Full and All justification options.

Fig. 6.12
Justified lines look formal, but for most documents a ragged right margin is considered friendlier on the eyes.

The All option stretches text and spaces to fit between the margins, even on lines ending in hard returns like this one.

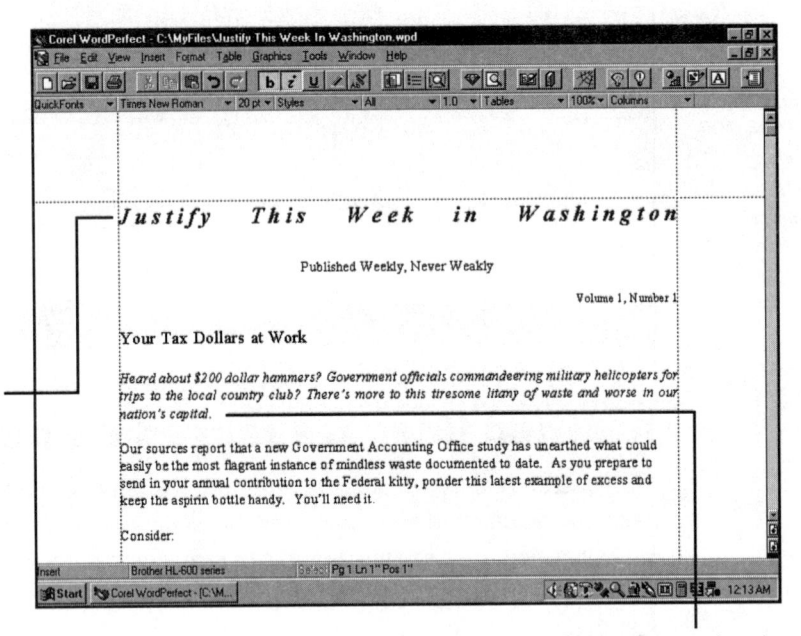

Full justification doesn't justify lines ending in hard returns.

Bullets and numbers add punch to paragraphs

The idea behind paragraph formatting, whether it's indenting or justifying, is to add variety to the page and emphasis to key points in a document. WordPerfect's Bullets and Numbers feature is a convenient way of painlessly doing both for certain types of paragraphs:

- Bullets, small graphics at the beginning of lines, hammer home successive points in an argument and draw attention to important sections of a document. You're reading bulleted text right now.

- Numbers at the beginning of lines outline successive steps in a series of directions or in a procedure. Numbers are also useful to list a series of distinct items.

For a speedy bulleted list, first type your list. Begin each line at the left margin, and press Enter at the end of every line. Now, select the whole list and click the Bullets button on the Toolbar. Each line gets a small square bullet. For anything fancier, read on.

Speeding (or at least Quick) bullets

WordPerfect will produce bullets of all kinds with minimal effort on your part. The **QuickBullets** feature converts asterisks to square bullet characters, automatically. Just type an asterisk; then press the Tab key. The asterisk transforms into a bullet, and you're ready to type your first bulleted line.

Press Enter after the first line, and the next line is automatically bulleted. You don't have to do a thing. Each succeeding press of the Enter key creates another bullet in the same way. To turn off the automatic bullets, press the Backspace key to delete the last, unwanted bullet.

Square bullets too square? That's not your only choice:

- For triangular bullets, press the > key, and then press Tab.
- For star bullets, press the + key and then Tab.
- For diamond bullets, press the ^ key and then Tab.
- For large round bullets, type an uppercase O and then press Tab.
- A lowercase o and then Tab gives you small, square bullets.
- Type a - [hypen] and then press Tab for an em dash-like bullet.

You can change bullets after you insert one; delete the bullet with Backspace, then type a different character and press Tab. As you add bullets to a document, they appear on the Power Bar Styles button drop-down list. And that's another way to change your bullet style: click the Styles button; then choose a different bullet style from the list.

Figure 6.13 shows the Styles button drop-down list and the different types of bullets QuickBullets can create for you.

Fig. 6.13
Like magic, QuickBullets converts standard keyboard characters to bullets.

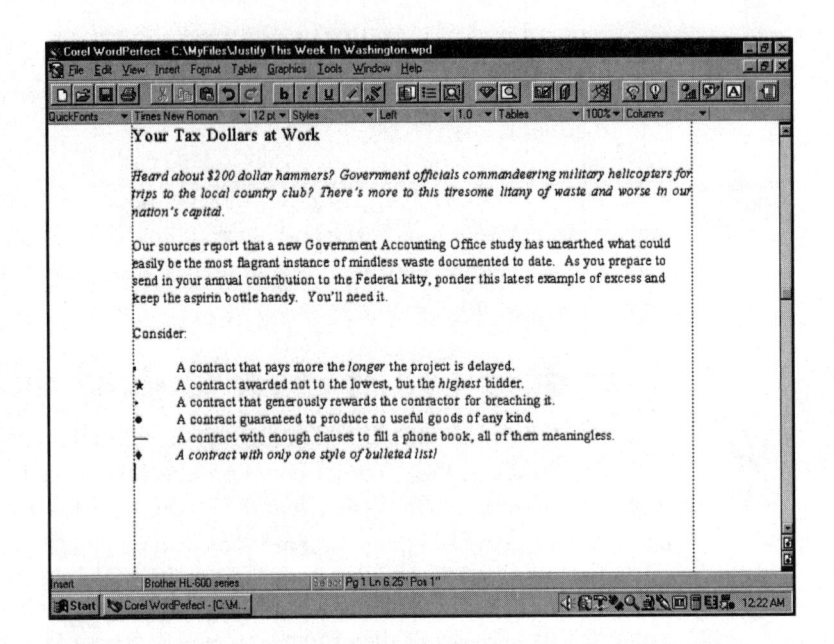

TIP If you find QuickBullets more of a nuisance than a help, you can turn them off. Click Tools, QuickCorrect. Click the Options button in the QuickCorrect dialog box, clear the QuickBullets check box, and click OK. Click Close in the QuickCorrect dialog box to finish off the job. You can always turn QuickBullets back on—or insert your own bullets. Click a QuickSpot and choose Bullets in the Paragraph dialog box to see your options.

CAUTION If you do turn off QuickBullets, you'll also turn off the automatic numbered lists described in the next section.

Q&A *I got my QuickBullet, but when I press Enter, I don't get a second bullet!*

For QuickBullets to work on consecutive lines, you need to type something on one line before moving to the next one. You can't, in other words, have a series of bullets with no bulleted items to go with them.

You've got it on a (numbered) list

Plenty of otherwise competent typists break down when it comes to touch-typing numbers. I'm among them. That's why I like WordPerfect's automatic numbered list. It not only keeps the numbering sequence straight, it also saves the trouble of typing the numbers.

Automatic numbering works just like automatic bullets. Type a number and a period, press Tab, and then type your first list item. Press the Return key, and the next line is automatically numbered for you.

You have a choice of numbering styles:

- Type **1.** and press Tab for a numbered list in the style 1,2,3,4....
- Type **i.** and press Tab for the sequence i, ii, iii, iv....
- Type **I.** and press Tab for I, II, III, IV and so on.
- Type **A.** or **a.** and press Tab; you'll get either A, B, C... or a, b, c....

Want a close parenthesis [)] or a hyphen [-] after your numbers instead of a period? Type either one after your first number or letter, and succeeding lines will use the same character. Figure 6.14 shows an automatic numbered list.

Fig. 6.14
You'll appreciate the way WordPerfect can do the typing for you—that 4 appeared when I pressed Enter at the end of line 3.

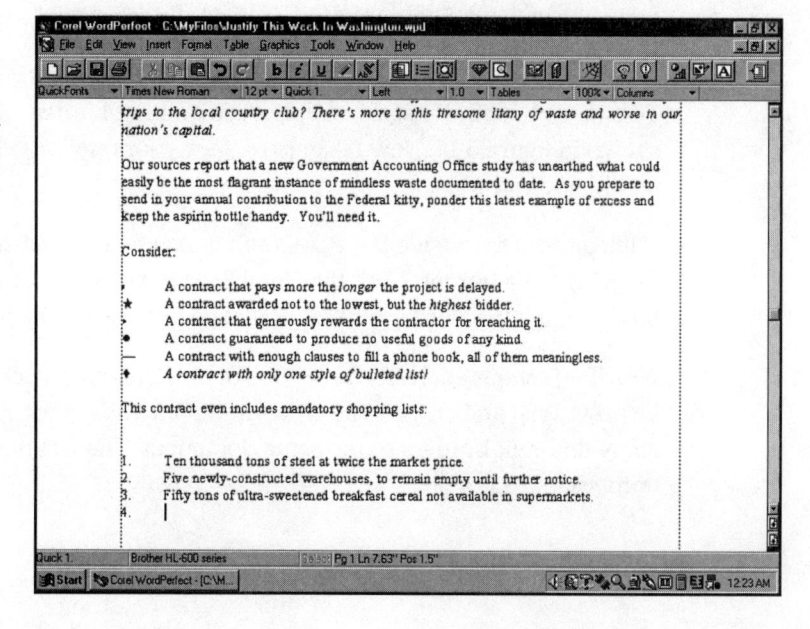

Like QuickBullet styles, the automatic numbering styles you use in your document will turn up on the Power Bar Styles button list. That's handy if you want to add items to an existing numbered list, even if you've already turned the automatic numbering off. Position the insertion point on the line after your last item, click Styles, select the numbering style, and the next number in the sequence will be inserted for you.

> **TIP** **Here's a speedy way to turn off QuickBullets and automatic numbering:** place the insertion point in the paragraph after the last list item, click the Power Bar Styles button, and choose <None>. This is especially useful if you forgot to turn off the bullets and you've already typed your next paragraph!

How to add paragraph borders without incident

Borders—lines around, under, or above a paragragh—set off a paragraph from the rest of the page. WordPerfect has border styles ranging from the gaudy to the austere, and they're all easy to access. To format a paragraph with a border, click the paragraph's QuickSpot; then, click the Border button on the Paragraph dialog box that pops up. Select a border from the palette that appears, and your paragraph is instantly formatted with the border of your choice.

To change the border style, simply click another border on the palette, as shown in figure 6.15. New borders replace your previous choice until you hit on the one you want.

Click anywhere outside the Paragraph dialog box to return to your document. To get rid of a border, click the QuickSpot next to the paragraph with the border, click the Border button, and choose None on the palette of borders.

WordPerfect has such an abundance of borders that making a choice may not be easy. Trial and error is the ticket here, but you'll want to avoid adding too many different borders to the same document. The last thing you want is a border incident.

Fig. 6.15
Borders are often used to give headers a decorative touch. Click the More button to see the wilder effects.

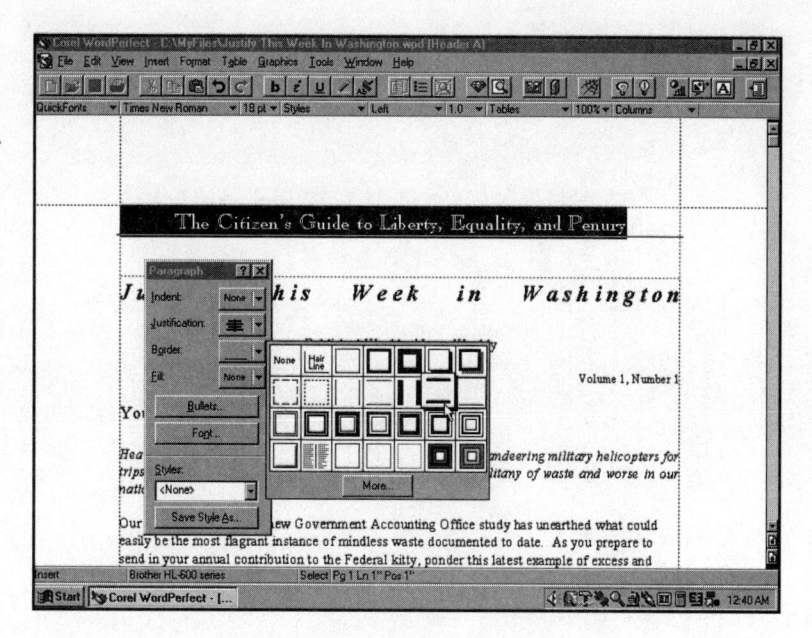

7

Setting Up the Page

● **In this chapter:**

- How do I number my pages?

- I want something fancier than plain numbers

- What's a header (or a footer)?

- How do I keep my text together?

- This page needs more white space!

- I want to throw a border around my page

Like a picture frame, a well-organized page focuses the reader's eye on your text . . . . ▸

Good writing is clear writing. And if a writer is hard to read, it's because his thinking is muddy. At least, that's what Lord Chesterfield argued, 250 or so years ago.

In Chesterfield's day, it was okay to make pronouncements like that and then drop the subject. Nowadays, we'd insist on some practical suggestions on clearer writing.

WordPerfect is one practical place to start. Easy-to-read writing begins with a well laid-out page. WordPerfect supplies plenty of page setup tools to sharpen a document's focus and to help make your meaning clear. Lord Chesterfield would have approved.

The Page Toolbar, for page setup at your fingertips

The Page Toolbar is the handiest way to use the page setup options. Point at the Toolbar, right-click for the Toolbar menu, and select Page. The Page Toolbar buttons appear on the Toolbar, as shown in figure 7.1.

Most of the page setup commands are available from the Format, Page menu, but you might find the Page Toolbar more convenient.

The Page Toolbar is especially useful when you're first setting up a document. To get the regular Toolbar back again when you finish setting up the pages, right-click the Toolbar for the Toolbar menu and select WordPerfect 7.

Pick a number, any page number

The easiest way to add focus to a page is to identify it with a page number. Numbering pages in WordPerfect is a snap. As with most WordPerfect features, you can choose from different page numbering options, and you also have different ways to get those options.

Close-Up: the Page Toolbar

For page setup jobs, pop up the Page Toolbar; the buttons appear at the right end of the standard Toolbar. When you finish setting up the page, right-click the Toolbar and choose WordPerfect 7 to get the standard Toolbar back.

Toolbar

Center Page
Centers from top to bottom

Page Numbering
Pops up the Page Numbering dialog box

Suppress
Turns off various page elements on selected pages

Subdivide Page
Breaks up the page into columns or rows

Force Page
Ensures that the current page always has an even or odd page number

Binding/Duplex
Provides for extra margin space to allow for binding and to print on both sides of a page

Keep Together
Keeps key paragraphs or selected text together on the same page

Paper Size
Adjusts page settings for different sizes of paper

Page Border
Puts a border around the page

Q&A *Why do I need to bother with page numbers when I can see what page I'm on right on the status bar?*

When you fill a page with text, WordPerfect automatically flows text to the next page. The page number is indeed displayed on the status bar, but those numbers won't print. For page numbers that print, you have to use Page Numbering.

Dress up that page number

Page numbers by themselves look a little bare, but WordPerfect gives you a wardrobe of formats to dress up those naked numbers. To see the available page numbering formats, click the Page Numbering button on the Page Toolbar, or click Format, Page Numbering, Select. Either way, you get the Select Page Numbering Format dialog box shown in figure 7.1.

Fig. 7.1
There's a closet full of page number formats here, in styles ranging from the austere to the rococo.

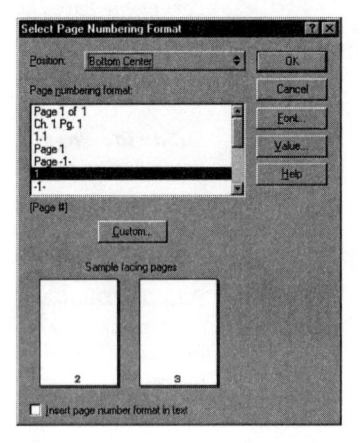

If all you want is plain page numbers at the bottom center of every page, press Ctrl+Home to go to the top of the document, pop up the Select Page Numbering Format dialog box, and click OK. If you want something fancier, read on.

How much information do you want your page numbers to convey? Take your pick from the Page numbering format list, and preview your selection in the Sample facing pages.

The Page 1 of 1 format is one option for more informative page numbers. It gives you page numbers with both the current page and the total number of pages in the document, as in `Page 4 of 10`.

CAUTION WordPerfect inserts page numbers beginning on the page where you start numbering in the Select Page Numbering Format dialog box. If the insertion point is on Page 3 when you start page numbering, Pages 1 and 2 won't get numbers. The program *is* smart enough to make the first page number 3 if you begin numbering on Page 3. But if you want your entire document to be numbered, position the insertion point at the very top of the document (press Ctrl+Home to get there) before diving into the Select Page Numbering Format dialog box.

Not only will your pages be numbered automatically, but WordPerfect also keeps track of the total number of pages in the document. If you have a 10-page paper and you delete Page 6, what was Page 7 of 10 automatically becomes Page 6 of 9.

The Page 1 of 1 style is especially useful in long documents with many sections and no obvious conclusion. Contracts spring to mind. The reader of such a document might not know she's missing a page or two unless the pages are numbered in the Page 1 of 1 format. It's also handy for long faxes, where pages sometimes have a way of vanishing mysteriously into the ether.

Where on the page should the page number go?

Once you decide on a numbering format, pick a spot on the page for your page numbers. Click the Position button in the Select Page Numbering Format dialog box to display a menu of page number position choices.

Click one of the position options, and the Sample Facing Pages window displays a preview of your choice. Figure 7.2 shows the Top Center option.

Fig. 7.2
There are a lot of choices here, but the sample pages let you experiment without committing yourself.

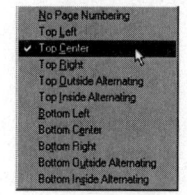

Putting your page numbers at the top center of every page is usually a safe choice. If you plan to bind or staple your document, consider one of the Outside Alternating options. They put the page number at the outside edge of every page, where the numbers are easy to read when the inside edges are bound together. Books often use alternating page numbers for that reason.

Once you make your choices of format and position, click OK. From the current page to the end of the document, each page will be numbered with automatically incremented numbers.

And if you don't like the way your choice of position and format turns out, just click the Page Numbering button on the Toolbar and try again.

Q&A Why can't I see my page numbers?

You're viewing the editing window in Draft mode. Page numbers and other nonessentials aren't displayed in Draft mode to reduce clutter and speed up the display. Select View, Page to flip to Page mode to display page numbering.

But, even though you can't see your page numbers in Draft mode, they'll print just fine.

Create your own page numbering format

You might have your own ideas about what text you want to accompany page numbers. You can, for example, have the document title repeat with every page number, as in Sales Report, Page 2.

First position the insertion point on the page where you want the numbering style to begin. Then, to add your own text to page numbers:

1. Click the Page Numbering button on the Toolbar or select Format, Page Numbering, Select.

2. Select a Position for your page numbers; then click the Custom button in the Select Page Numbering Format dialog box.

3. In the Custom Page Numbering dialog box, you'll see the [Page #] code in the Edit custom format and text edit box. Press the left or right arrow key to deselect the code; then type your text in the edit box on either side of the code, as shown in figure 7.3.

Fig. 7.3
I've added the text
- Sales Report,
Page -.

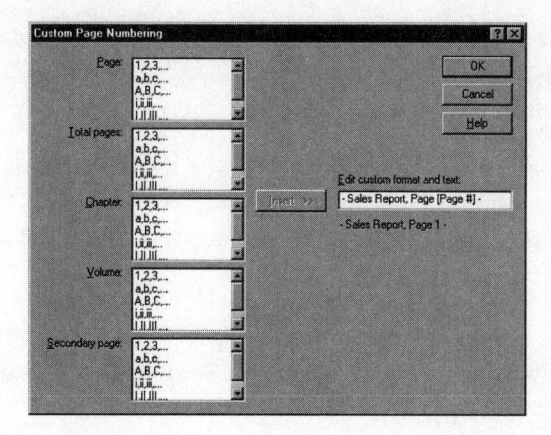

4   Your text, and the page number, appear below the edit box as you type it, so you get an inkling of how it'll look. Click OK when you're done; then click OK again in the Select Page Numbering Format dialog box. Your page number and text will appear on each document page in the position you've specified.

Q&A *I accidentally deleted the [Page #] code in the Custom Page Numbering dialog box! What do I do?*

Put the insertion point in the Edit custom format and text edit box at the spot where the code should be. Click the 1,2,3... format on the list of Page codes, and then click the Insert button. That reinserts the code for you.

Q&A *Why can't I see a preview of my page number text in the Sample Facing Pages windows?*

Before typing accompanying text in the Page Numbering Options dialog box, you have to select a Position in the Select Page Numbering Format dialog box. If the No Page Numbering option is selected, you won't see a preview.

These page numbers need a face-lift

You might want your page numbers in a font face that's different from the face you're using for body text. That adds variety to the page, and it makes the numbers more or less obvious, depending on what face you choose. Just click the Font button in the Select Page Numbering Format dialog box to pop up the Page Numbering Font dialog box. Take your pick of face, size, and appearance, and click OK when you're done.

What if I want the page numbers to start at something other than 1?

By default, WordPerfect numbers pages beginning with the number of the current page—that is, the document page the insertion point happens to be in when you start page numbering. That's perfectly logical, but on occasion, you may want to number your pages starting with a different number.

You might have several preface pages. Or you might have different sections of a report in different WordPerfect files, but you want to number all the pages in the report consecutively. To start each file with a different page number:

1. Click the Page Numbering button on the Toolbar.
2. Click the Value button in the Select Page Numbering Format dialog box.
3. Click the Page tab of the Values dialog box, and type your starting number in the Set page number edit box, as shown in figure 7.4.

Fig. 7.4
Once you know where to look, starting documents with a page number other than 1 is easy in WordPerfect.

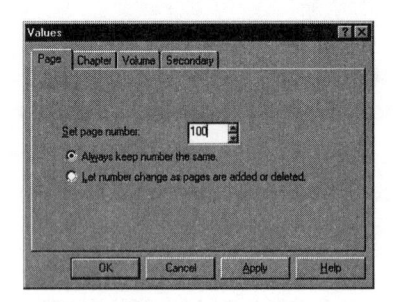

4. Click OK when you're done, and then click OK in the Select Page Numbering Format dialog box to insert the new page number.

What's a header (or a footer)?

We don't record answering machine greetings every time we receive messages. We record them once, and the greeting is repeated as often as needed. **Headers** and **footers** in documents work the same way—enter the information once, and it's repeated on every page. Like the greeting on your answering machine, headers and footers convey important, but repetitive, information.

Document titles, chapter titles, and author names are good choices for headers and footers. Page numbers also go in headers or footers. Headers and footers add a balanced look to the page.

Where do the header and footer go?

Create a header, and WordPerfect sticks it right below the top margin of the page. Footers go just above the bottom margin of the page.

You can have up to two different headers and two different footers per page. WordPerfect calls them Header A and Header B, and Footer A and Footer B.

To create a header:

1 Position the insertion point in the page where you want the header to begin. Click Format, Header/Footer and the dialog box shown in figure 7.5 appears.

Fig. 7.5
The Headers/Footers dialog box has more options than you'll probably need, but if you want four headers and footers to a page, you can have them.

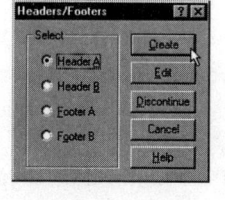

> **TIP** QuickMenu fans can right-click at the top of the editing window and select Header/Footer to get the Headers/Footers dialog box.

2 Select Header A and click the Create button. The Header/Footer feature bar appears automatically. You also get header Guidelines, in purple yet, as seen in figure 7.6. (If you don't see the Guidelines, click View, Guidelines, click the Header/Footer check box, and click OK.)

3 Type the text you want in the header. Use any of WordPerfect's formatting options, just as you would in body text. Once you finish typing your text at the header's left margin, press Alt+F7 to add text flush with the header's right margin for balance.

Part II Editing and Formatting for Perfect Documents

Fig. 7.6
The Header/Footer feature bar springs up when you create or edit a selected header or footer.

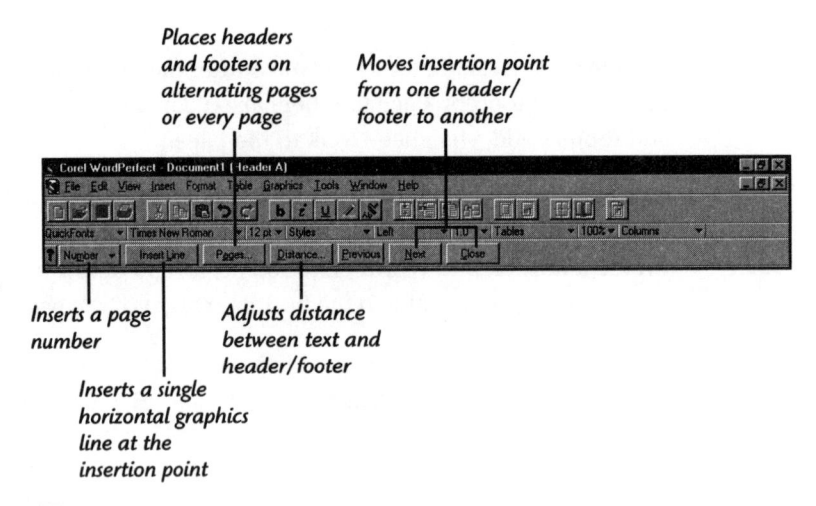

- Places headers and footers on alternating pages or every page
- Moves insertion point from one header/footer to another
- Inserts a page number
- Inserts a single horizontal graphics line at the insertion point
- Adjusts distance between text and header/footer

> **CAUTION**
> If you've already added page numbers with the Format, Page Numbering menu command and picked one of the top-of-the-page position options, the page number will print along with the header. This may result in a jumbled mess, so be careful not to use both page numbering and headers at the same location. The top-left page number position should especially be avoided if you plan on creating a header. Header text at the left margin will type right over the page number!

4 Click the Insert Line button to insert a horizontal graphics line to set your header off from the rest of the page if you like. And click the Pages button and select Odd Pages or Even Pages if you want the header to appear on alternating pages. By default, headers go on every page. If you plan on adding a second header on facing pages, select Odd pages to put Header A on page 1, 3, 5, and so on.

5 Click the Close button when you're done. Figure 7.7 shows a header with a previously added top-center page number, a line inserted from the Header/Footer feature bar, and text aligned flush right.

How do I add a second header?

The header in figure 7.7 shows the page number, document title, and author's name. Suppose you want to add, say, the company name in a header as well? If you placed Header A on odd pages, you can stick a Header B with additional information like that on even pages.

Fig. 7.7
Headers and footers add useful information, especially if a printed page gets separated from the rest of the document!

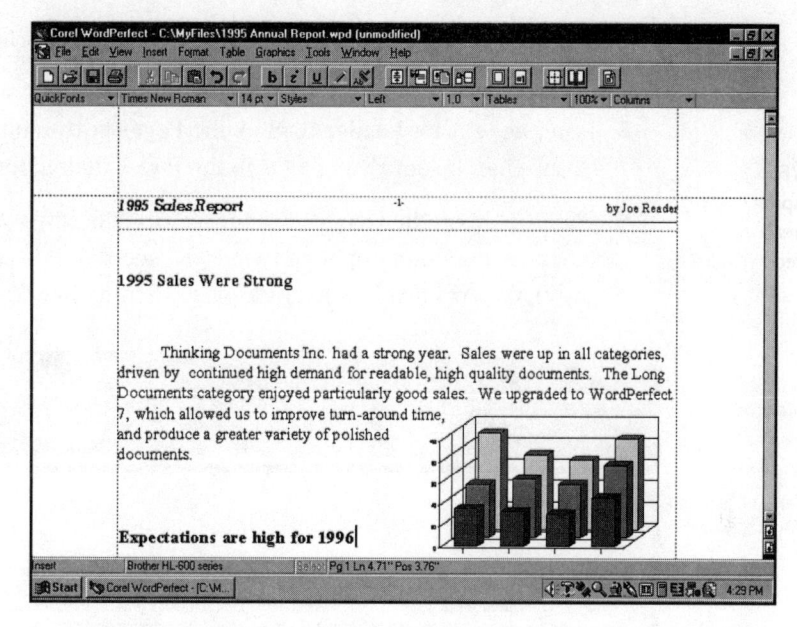

To add a header B:

1 Move the mouse pointer to the top of the editing window and right-click for the QuickMenu shown in figure 7.8.

Fig. 7.8
Right-click in the top margin for the QuickMenu.

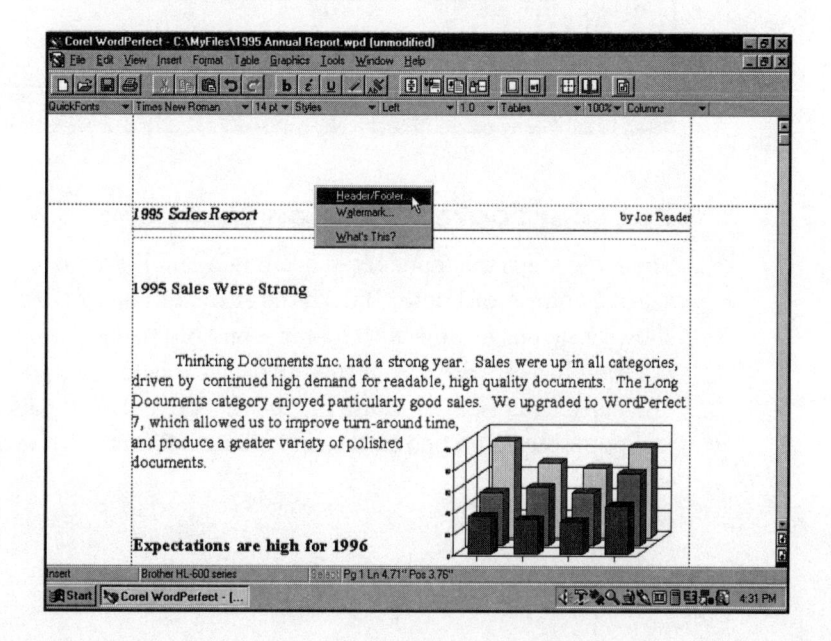

2 Select Header/Footer from the QuickMenu for the Headers/Footers dialog box. Click Header B and select Create.

3 Type the text for header B, click the Pages button on the Header/Footer feature bar, select Even pages in the Pages dialog box, and click OK.

4 Click Close on the Header/Footer feature bar when you're done. With the same document opened twice (the second time as a read-only copy), the two headers might look something like figure 7.9.

Fig. 7.9
Windowed view of two pages of the same document, showing that two headers are better than one.

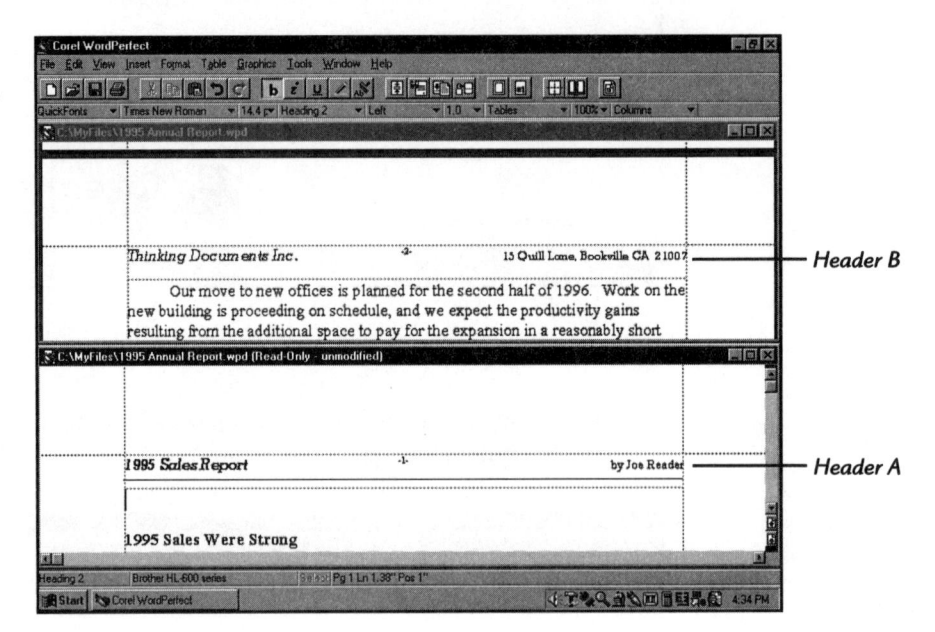

Put your footer down on that page

The same steps that concocted headers A and B create footers A and B. Just select Footer A or Footer B from the Headers/Footers dialog box. Figure 7.10 shows a two-page view with footer A on both pages. Even though the two different headers are on alternating pages, this footer appears on every page. You can also have alternating footers on odd and even pages if you want—just put footer A on odd pages, and create a footer B for even pages.

Fig. 7.10
Footers convey additional repetitive information and round off your pages.

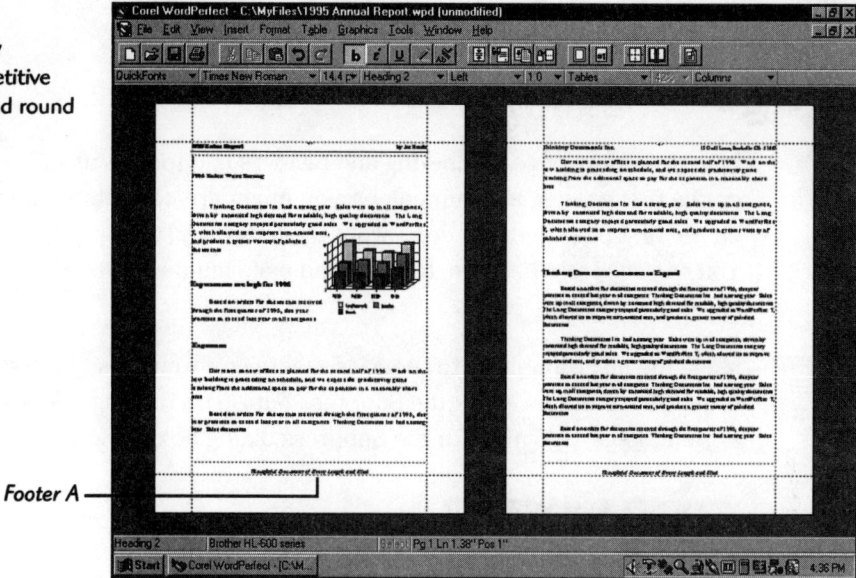

Footer A

How do I edit headers?

To edit header A, just click it (as long as you're in Page view). To get at header B, click anywhere outside of header A, right-click at the top of the editing window, and select Header/Footer from the QuickMenu. Select Header B in the Headers/Footers dialog box and click Edit. If you lose track of which header you're editing, check WordPerfect's title bar—that displays the current header. Click Close on the Header/Footer feature bar when you're done.

Q&A *I'm trying to edit header B, but I can't get the QuickMenu, and the menu bar command is grayed-out!*

You've just encountered a minor WordPerfect idiosyncrasy. If the insertion point is in header A (and if you've been editing header A, it very well might be), both the menu bar and QuickMenu Header/Footer commands are unavailable. Click anywhere outside header A to move the insertion point; then right-click at the top of the editing window for the QuickMenu (or choose Format, Header/Footer).

I don't want all these gadgets on every page

By convention, page numbering and headers and footers usually don't appear on the first page of a document. Or you might create a letterhead in a header on the first page, but you don't want the letterhead to appear on page two. You can suppress headers, footers, and page numbering on the first page, or any current page.

Move the insertion point to the page where you want to suppress page formatting features. Click the Suppress button on the Page Toolbar, or select Format, Page, Suppress for the Suppress dialog box shown in figure 7.11.

Fig. 7.11
Stop any of these page formatting elements from displaying or printing on the current page.

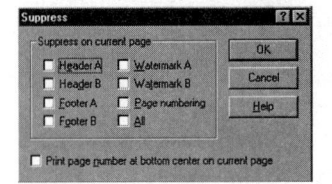

Select the features you want to suppress and click OK. Any headers, footers, or page numbering will be unaffected on the other pages in the document.

If you want to suppress these elements on other pages, you'll have to repeat the operation for each page. To discontinue a header or footer from the current page to the end of the document, click Format, Header/Footer, select the header or footer you no longer want, and choose Discontinue.

How do I double-space this page?

Pages that are densely packed with text can be hard to read. Want a quick way of adding white space to the page? Change the line spacing. By default, WordPerfect **single-spaces** the lines on a page. Lines display and print one line below the other.

That's easily changed. Click the Line Spacing button on the Power Bar (the button displays 1.0 until you change it) and choose 1.5 for one and a half spaces between lines, or 2.0 for double-spacing. Choose Other on the Power Bar Line Spacing button drop-down list, and you get the Line Spacing dialog box shown in figure 7.12.

Fig. 7.12
Automatically insert blank lines between lines of text in the Line Spacing dialog box.

Click the arrows or type a new value in the Spacing edit box. Line spacing is measured in numbers of lines, and you can enter any number, or fraction of a number—for example, **1.25 or 1 1/4**. For triple-spaced lines, enter **3** in the Spacing edit box. The preview window in the dialog box changes to reflect the new spacing value.

My page looks unbalanced

You've written a short letter, printed it, and all the text is scrunched up at the top of the page.

Centering the page is a quick fix. Click the Center Page button, or select Format, Page, Center for the Center Page(s) dialog box. Take your pick of centering options: you can center the Current Page, or the Current and Subsequent Pages.

Either option automatically centers the text on the page between the top and bottom margins, as shown in figure 7.13.

Fig. 7.13
Short letters are good candidates for page centering.

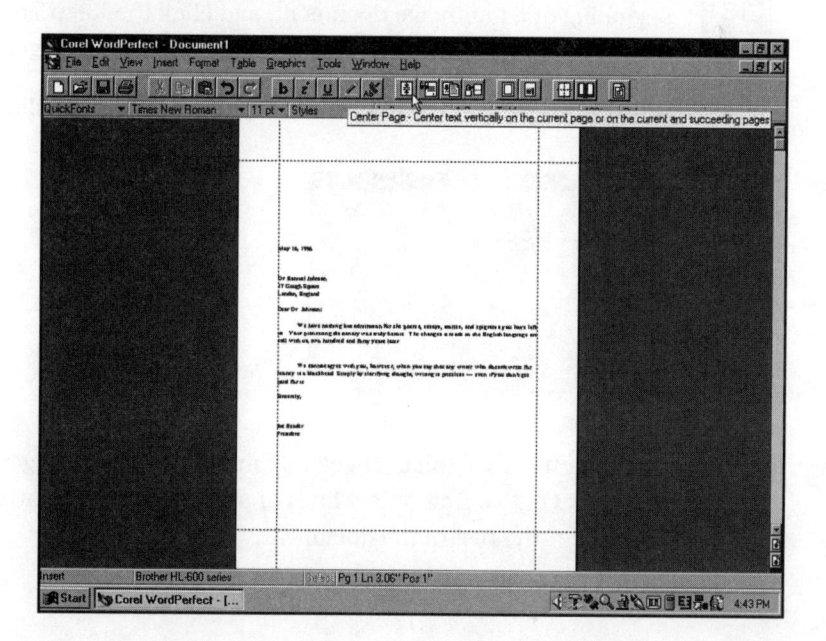

I want to keep my text together

Let's face it. Books on the subject of word processors, admirable though they may be, don't lend themselves to high drama. When you see references to block protection and widows and orphans, don't expect crime stories or gripping tragedy.

> **Plain English, please!**
>
> When you fill up a page of text, WordPerfect automatically starts the next line on a new page. A **widow** is the last line of a paragraph that appears by itself at the top of the next page.
>
> An **orphan** is the first line of a paragraph that winds up by itself at the bottom of a page. The rest of the paragraph has been moved to the top of the next page.

How to prevent widows and orphans

In WordPerfect, widows and orphans are produced not by wars or natural disasters, but by the way the program automatically flows text from one page to the next.

These minor tragedies are easily avoided. Put the insertion point at the beginning of a multipage document, and click the Keep Together button on the Page Toolbar. Or select Format, Page, Keep Text Together.

Either way, you get the Keep Text Together dialog box shown in figure 7.14.

Fig. 7.14
Keeping widows and orphans together in WordPerfect is no trouble at all—if only life were that simple.

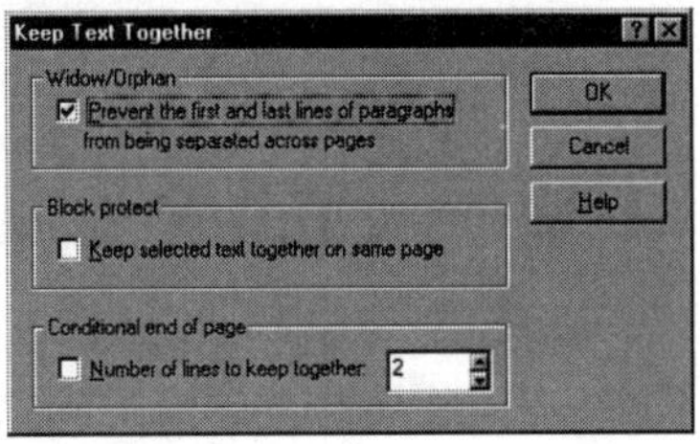

Click the Widow/Orphan check box in the Keep Text Together dialog box and click OK. No first or last lines of paragraphs will be widowed or orphaned for the rest of the document.

Block Protection: lock up text, not doors

Preventing widows and orphans is enough to keep text together in most situations, but there may be times when you'll want to keep entire paragraphs together. Tables, for example, or numbered lists, might look peculiar if they're separated on two pages.

Block protection keeps selected blocks of text together on the same page. To keep any block of text together on the same page:

1 Select the text you want to keep together.

> **TIP** **To select an entire paragraph, put the mouse pointer in the left** margin next to the paragraph you want to select, and double-click. If you're quick on the draw, quadruple-click the paragraph to select it.

2 Click the Keep Together button on the Page Toolbar, or select Fo_r_mat, _P_age, _K_eep Text Together.

3 Click the Block protect check box in the Keep Text Together dialog box (see fig. 7.15).

4 Click OK.

No matter what editing changes you make, on the page or throughout the document, the selected block of text will now stay together.

What is conditional end of page?

The third option in the Keep Text Together dialog box works like Block Protect, except that you keep only specified numbers of lines together on one side or another of the page break.

Say you have a title, then a blank line, and then a paragraph. You don't want the title to end up at the bottom of a page by itself. By keeping the first three lines of the paragraph together, the title and the paragraph won't ever get separated. Move the insertion point to the beginning of the first line. Pop up the Keep Text Together dialog box, and then click the _N_umber of lines to keep together selection box shown in figure 7.15. Enter the number of lines in the adjacent edit box and click OK.

Decorate the page with a border

Most governments take their borders pretty seriously, and decorate them with everything from passport controls to barbed wire. In WordPerfect, page borders are just for decoration. There are loads of borders available, from modest lines around the page to whimsical graphics that all but take over the page. WordPerfect's borders are wide open.

When you add a page border, it's applied to every page, from the current page to the end of the document. To add a border to the current and subsequent pages in a document, click the Page Border button on the Page Toolbar, or choose Format, Border/Fill, Page. Either way, the Page Border/Fill dialog box appears, as shown in figure 7.15.

Fig. 7.15
To see even more borders, click the Change button and browse the Border folder.

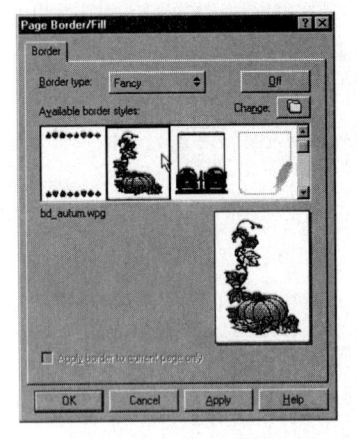

Click the Border type button to toggle between Fancy and Line borders. Scroll through the list of Available border styles, and click your choice to select it. Click OK, and the border appears in the current page, as seen in figure 7.16.

WordPerfect is a lot more straightforward than international diplomacy. To turn off a border in the current page to the end of the document: click the Page Border button on the Page Toolbar, or choose Format, Border/Fill, Page. Then, click Off in the Page Border/Fill dialog box. No government in the world gives its citizens that option, though if enough diplomats start using WordPerfect 7...

Chapter 7 *Setting Up the Page* **141**

Fig. 7.16
Some borders are discreet, others take over the page. WordPerfect has a border for everybody.

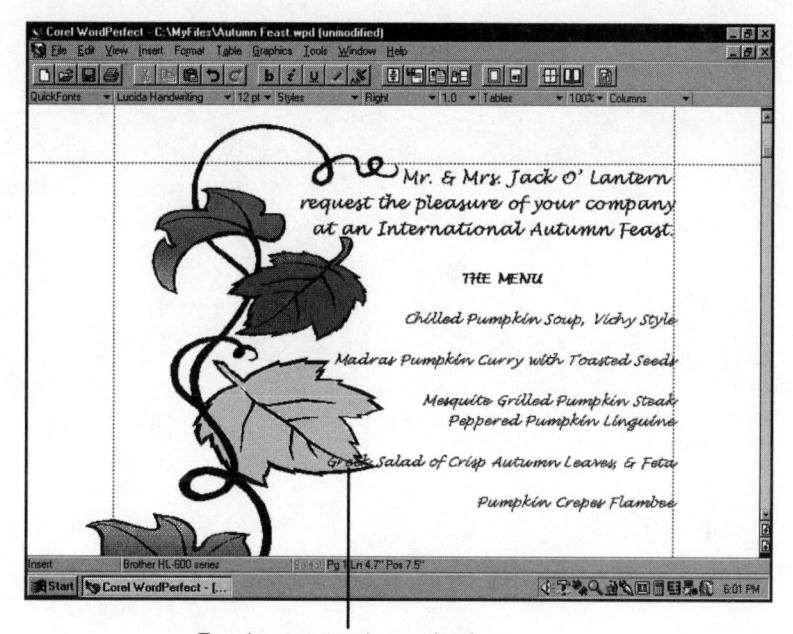

Typed text goes right over borders that hog a lot of page space.

Part III: Getting the Words Right on Screen and Page

Chapter 8: **Choose Your Words...Easily!**

Chapter 9: **The Printer's Craft**

8

Choose Your Words...Easily!

● In this chapter:

- WordPerfect checks spelling AND grammar?
- I wish I could do something about these typos
- I can't think of the right word!
- Have I written 500 words yet?
- How to "talk" to windows through dialog boxes
- How can I tell one dialog box from another?

Writers tear their hair out trying to find, spell, and use the right word. With a built-in thesaurus, and spelling and grammar checkers, WordPerfect saves many an authorial follicle . . . . ▶

The French are so fussy about French that they have laws against misusing the language. Americans are more freewheeling. E.B. White, that master of American English, compared correct American usage to crossing the street—getting to the other side is mostly luck.

H.W. Fowler wrote the book on English usage. His *A Dictionary of Modern English Usage* is the writer's bible. Here's what he says about grammar: "What are generally recognized for the time being as its conventions must be followed by those who would write clearly and agreeably."

WordPerfect has some nifty tools to help us follow the conventions of "clear and agreeable" English.

Spell-As-You-Go, the red pencil maven

When word processors with automatic spell checkers came along, students everywhere raised a cheer. No longer would their pristine essays and reports come back covered with little red (Sp.) marks. The eagle-eyed teacher with the poised red pencil had been foiled by an electronic gadget.

WordPerfect's Spell-As-You-Go feature is the teacher's revenge. Type a misspelled word, and WordPerfect whips out the red pencil. Even good typists and spellers will have noticed that certain words on their screens have little red cross-hatchings under them. That's Spell-As-You-Go's version of (Sp.), and it means the same thing: spelling error!

Spell-As-You-Go doesn't give grades, so you don't have to think up a good excuse for egregious misspellings. Instead, just right-click any word marked by Spell-As-You-Go and select the correct spelling from the word list that pops up, as shown in figure 8.1.

Spell-As-You-Go can be tailored to your documents:

- If it's a correctly spelled word that Spell-As-You-Go simply doesn't recognize, click Add on the Quickmenu to add it to the word list.

- For a word peculiar to that document, slang for example, or a nickname, click Skip in Document on the Spell-As-You-Go Quickmenu. Every occurrence of the word will thenceforth be ignored by WordPerfect's built-in red pencil.

Fig. 8.1
If you don't see the correction on the Spell-As-You-Go list, click More for additional possibilities.

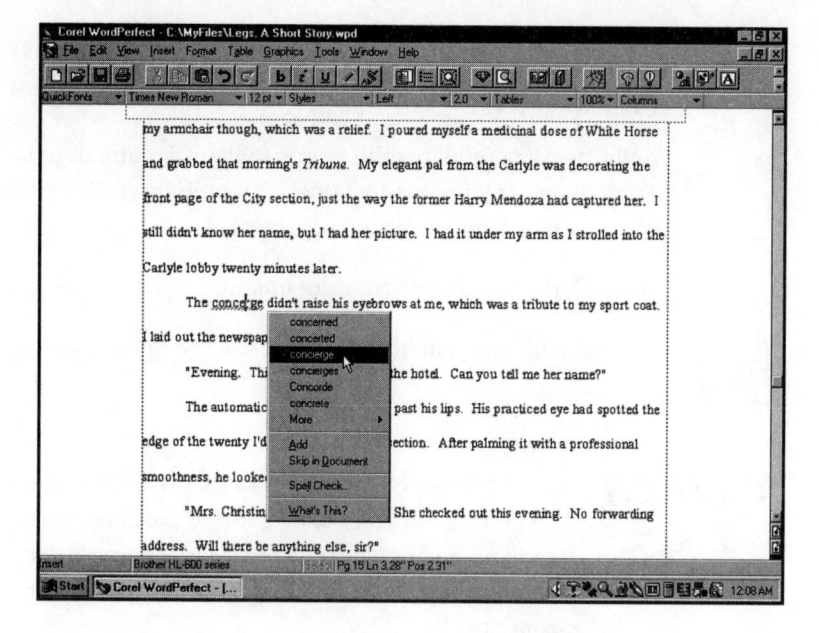

And of course, you can ignore those red markings yourself. You might find it more convenient to check for typos and misspellings when you're at the end of the document anyway, instead of interrupting your train of thought to make the corrections on the fly.

If you prefer to tackle misspellings at one fell swoop, use the spell checker (described here) when you finish writing.

> **TIP** **Unlike your former teachers, Spell-As-You-Go is easily shut off.** Click Tools, Spell-As-You-Go. That unchecks the Spell-As-You-Go menu item, putting it, and you, out of orthographic misery.

Spell Checker is handy, but not infallible

With over a hundred thousand words at its command, unfailing persistence, and, within limits, perfect accuracy, WordPerfect's Spell Checker makes a great adjunct to proofreading—not a replacement. You still have to read over your copy with care. You just won't have to worry about routine misspellings any more. Those who like to fix errors as they make them have Spell-As-You-Go. But for writers who like to bat out copy in a hurry, while it's still fresh in the mind, Spell Checker is a great comfort. It lets you write in a furious burst, saving the cleaning up for the end, when the ideas start to run out.

Spell Checker corrects typos and misspellings

Spell Checker compares the words in your document to the words in its built-in dictionary. If your spelling doesn't match its spelling, WordPerfect highlights the word and suggests a correction.

To check the spelling of your document:

1 Save the document before you run the Spell Checker.

CAUTION Spell Checker is a program in its own right. Even though Windows 95 is pretty good at it, running several programs at a time can sometimes lead to unpredictable results. To avoid losing valuable work, always save your documents before running Spell Checker, the Thesaurus, or Grammatik.

2 Click the Spell Check button on the Toolbar. The Spell Checker pops up, and Spell Checker immediately highlights the first misspelling in the document, as shown in figure 8.2.

They just don't spell like they used to

Not so long ago, spelling in English was largely a matter of taste. Writers winged it, and the spelling of the same word varied from writer to writer. The first modern dictionary of the English language, written in 1755 by Dr. Samuel Johnson, helped to change that. Johnson's great tool was the beginning of standardized spelling in English. Trouble is, knowing that a word *should* be spelled a particular way doesn't help us with knowing *how* to spell it. WordPerfect's Spell Checker goes a long way toward solving that little problem. You still need a good dictionary though. Spell Checker says nothing about pronunciation, for one thing. Dictionaries do. Johnson's dictionary, now somewhat dated, was famous for using quotations to show how words are used in context. That's often the best way to get at a word's meaning, and it's still a feature of the best dictionaries.

Fig. 8.2
Spell Checker doesn't waste time. Click the Spell Check button and it goes right to work.

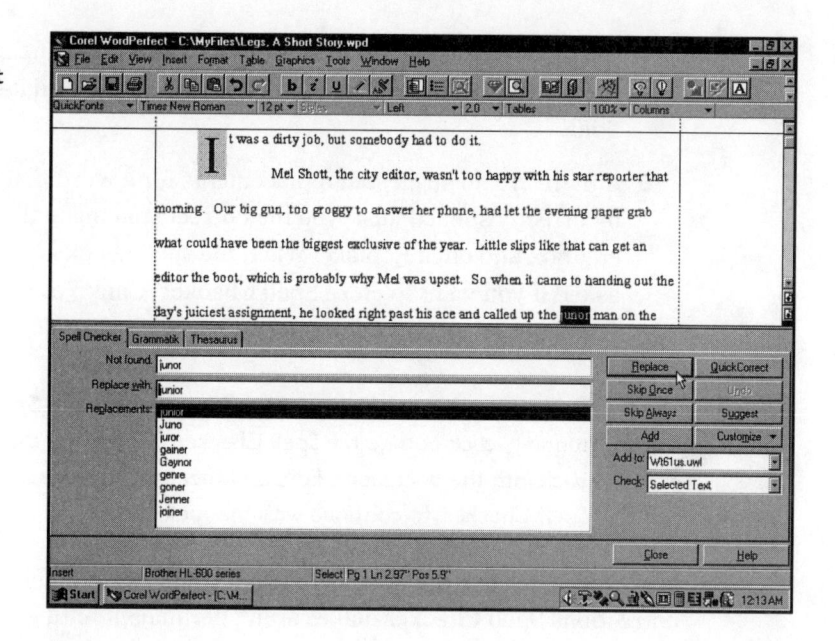

Q&A Why don't I see the Spell Check button on my Toolbar?

You have another of WordPerfect's many Toolbars on display instead of the standard, WordPerfect 7 Toolbar. To get the standard issue Toolbar back, right-click whatever toolbar you have on the screen and choose WordPerfect 7 from the QuickMenu.

TIP The Spell Checker appears at the bottom of the editing window. If

you want to move it, aim the pointer at the top of the Spell Checker; when the pointer turns into a hand, drag the Spell Checker elsewhere on the screen.

3. In figure 8.2, Spell Checker has seized on the typo "junor." It has guessed that we meant to type "junior," and displays the word in the Replace with edit box. Click the Replace button, and Spell Checker replaces "junor" with "junior."

4. Spell Checker then goes on to check the rest of the document. As each incorrect word is found, choose to replace it with the word in the Replace with edit box. If that's not the word you wanted, look at the list of Replacements. Select any of them; the word you click is placed in the Replace with edit box. Click the Replace button to substitute the

selected replacement for the word in your document. If you don't see the word on the list, click S__u__ggest for—you guessed it—more suggestions.

5 If there are no suggested replacements for a word that you know is incorrectly spelled, just type the correct spelling in the Replace __w__ith edit box and click __R__eplace. When the spell check is completed, you're asked if you want to close Spell Checker. Click __Y__es to shut down Spell Checker and return to your document.

> **TIP** To make editing changes in a document while Spell Checker is running, click outside the Spell Checker. That moves the insertion point back into the document. Edit, and then click the __R__esume button in the Spell Checker to continue with the spell check.

Don't forget to save the document again when Spell Checker finishes. The corrections Spell Checker makes aren't permanent until you save them.

Spell Checker flags some correctly spelled words, too!

Spell Checker will also seize on legitimate words that don't happen to be in its dictionary, as shown in figure 8.3.

Fig. 8.3
Noisier for Nossiter? Spell Checker is relentless when it comes to proper nouns, and its suggested replacements for one's own name can be humbling.

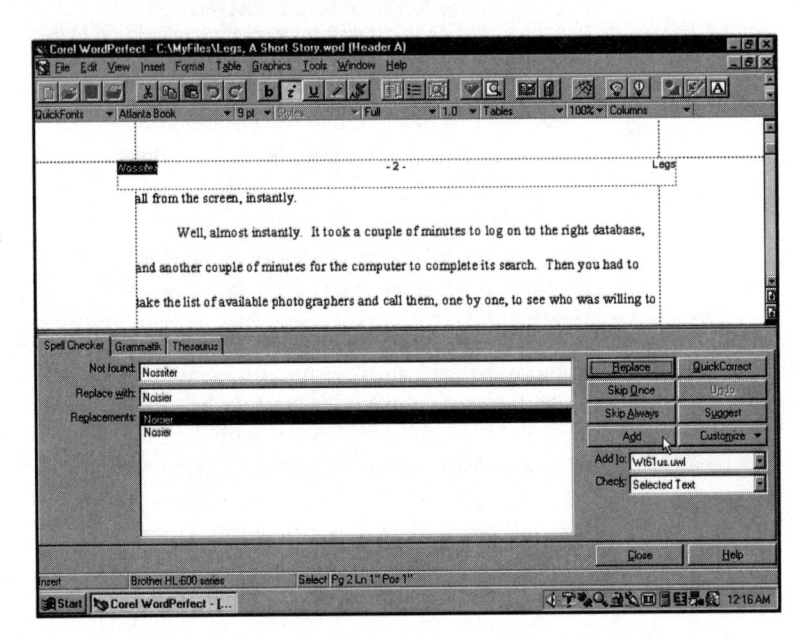

Some proper nouns, nicknames, and specialized terms that are spelled correctly will be marked by Spell Checker. You have several options when that happens. Click any of these buttons in the Spell Checker:

- Skip Once will ignore the word this time, but Spell Checker will stop if the word is found again.

- Skip Always is a better choice if it's a recurring word. Words that you skip Always will be ignored throughout the document. You can even close Spell Checker, then rerun it, and words you've skipped Always continue to be ignored. But when you close the document, always is over. Always, at least in this case, only lasts for as long as the document is open.

- In the case of a correctly spelled word that Spell Checker doesn't recognize, add it to the Spell Checker dictionary. Select WT61US.UWL on the Add to drop-down list and click Add. Whenever you run Spell Checker again, the added word will be ignored, just like the other correctly spelled words in your document.

- Some documents might have uncommon words peculiar to the subject of the document—a technical paper, for example, or an essay on Chaucer. As Spell Checker highlights each correctly spelled but unrecognized word, select Document Word List on the Add to drop-down menu and click Add. That adds the words to a supplementary dictionary that'll be used for that document only. Fiction writers fond of unusual character names find this feature especially useful.

Spell Checker finds all kinds of errors—even nonerrors

Here's a mistake I'm prone to make. Maybe you do it, too. I'll type "the the" when all I want is "the." Spell Checker catches double words like that and suggests replacing them with a single word. Spell Checker needs to be carefully monitored though, as shown in figure 8.4.

Spell Checker doesn't distinguish between "the the" and "had had." Just click the Skip Once button in situations like that.

Spell Checker catches other mistakes that aren't always mistakes, as in words with numbers in them, like the tax form 1040EZ.

Fig. 8.4
Some double words are really needed, but Spell Checker doesn't make the distinction.

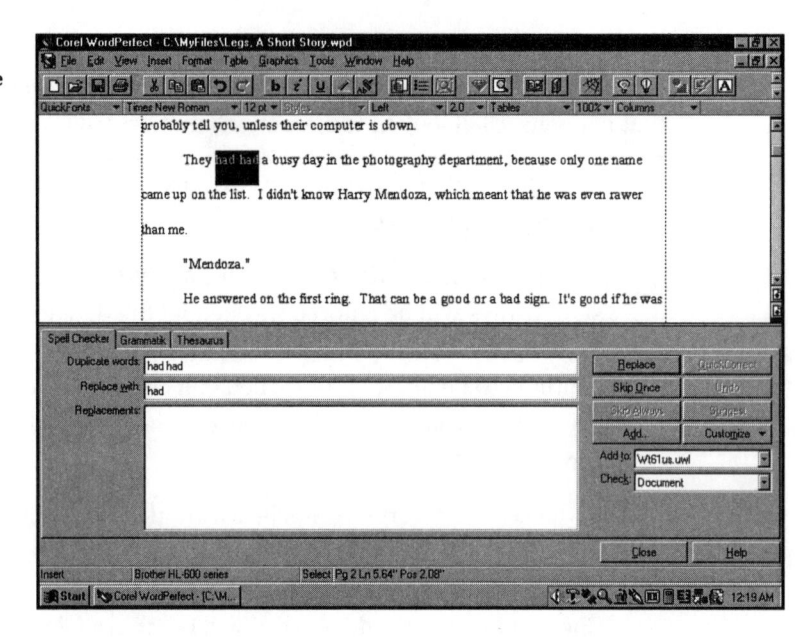

These features, helpful in the case of errors, are minor irritations when the document isn't in error. If they become major irritations, you can control the kinds of errors Spell Checker hunts down.

Click Customize in the Spell Checker for the menu shown in figure 8.5.

Fig. 8.5
The Customize menu gives you a measure of control over Spell Checker.

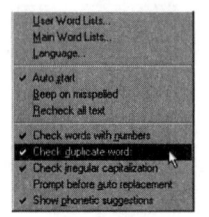

The kinds of errors that have a check mark beside them on the Customize menu will be flagged in your documents. Click the checked menu items to have Spell Checker ignore those sorts of "errors." Spell Checker is a great tool, but it needs to be watched.

Proofread, to catch what Spell Checker misses

Spell checkers and automobile air bags are knocked for the same reason: both can give you a false sense of security. Consider the sentence "This Pentium is fast, well-made, and expendable."

The word "expendable" is correctly spelled, so Spell Checker will ignore it. But it's the wrong word entirely in this context. *Expandable* is what's meant here, not *expendable*. A one-letter difference between words, but a big difference in meaning. It's a common, and easily made, error.

Spell Checker is no help for mistakes like that. Only a human proofreader will catch correctly spelled words that are just plain wrong in the context. But in spite of its limitations, Spell Checker has something else in common with air bags: we'd much rather have them than not.

QuickCorrect corrects as you type

At the back of every glittering parade is someone with a broom and dustpan cleaning up the debris. That's pretty much how QuickCorrect works: it corrects common typos and capitalization errors as soon as you hit the Spacebar to move to the next word.

Try it. Type **THe**, press the Spacebar, and watch the error get corrected to **The**, automatically. Same thing with **wierd**; type it and QuickCorrect transforms it to **weird** without your having to lift a finger.

Add your own mistakes to the QuickCorrect list

To see a list of all the words QuickCorrect fixes automatically, select Tools, QuickCorrect for the QuickCorrect dialog box shown in figure 8.6.

Fig. 8.6
The left-hand column might look familiar; those are all common typos and misspellings.

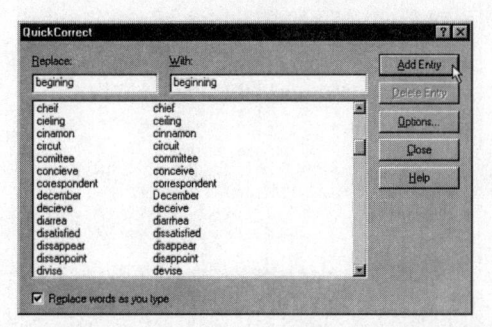

I often type "**begining**" when I want "**beginning**," so I'm adding it to the QuickCorrect list in figure 8.6. To add your own common typos to the list:

1. Click **T**ools, **Q**uickCorrect to pop up the QuickCorrect dialog box.

2. Type your typo in the **R**eplace edit box. In figure 8.6, I've typed **begining**.

3. Type the correction, **beginning**, in the **W**ith edit box.

4. Click **A**dd Entry and **C**lose when you're done. From now on, whenever I misspell "beginning," QuickCorrect will correct it for me.

Just make sure that R**e**place Words as You Type is checked in the QuickCorrect dialog box. Otherwise corrections won't be made automatically.

> **TIP** Click the **Q**uickCorrect button in the Spell Checker when you find common errors during a spell check. That adds the error and the correction to the QuickCorrect list.

What else does QuickCorrect correct?

Click the **O**ptions button in the QuickCorrect dialog box for the QuickCorrect Options dialog box shown in figure 8.7.

Fig. 8.7
QuickCorrect fixes other common mistakes besides typos and irregular capitalizations.

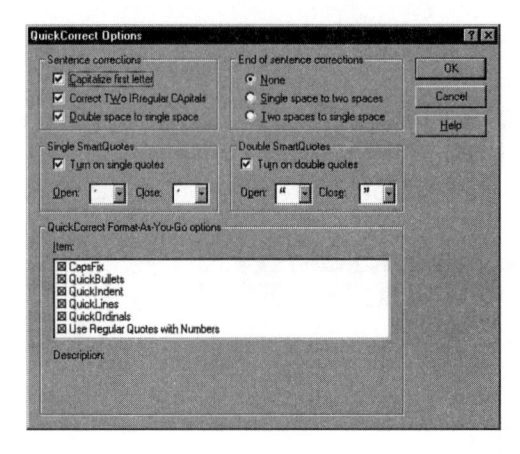

If you're Spacebar happy and tend to add two spaces after words instead of one, QuickCorrect can fix that for you as you type. Also, QuickCorrect eliminates single spaces at the end of sentences and omitted capitals at the beginning of sentences.

And if any of these automatic corrections are irritating rather than helpful, just deselect them.

TIP **Need the copyright or trademark symbols, © or ®?** Type (© for copyright or (® for registered trademark, and QuickCorrect will convert them to the appropriate symbols.

Q&A ***QuickCorrect is driving me nuts! Can I turn it off?***
Just deselect the Replace Words As You Type check box in the QuickCorrect dialog box. Errors will still be caught when you run Spell Checker, but they'll be left alone as you type.

I can't think of the right word!

You're sitting at your desk, typing away at a report. It's due at the end of the day, and time is running out. Then, you hit a roadblock—writer's block. What's the word for…? The word just won't come to mind. Or maybe you've used a word three times already and you need another way to say the same thing.

You could stare out the window and hope for inspiration. Or you can use WordPerfect's Thesaurus to find the word for you. Depending on how inspired you tend to be, that might save a lot of time.

> **Plain English, please!**
> A **thesaurus** is a dictionary of **synonyms** (different words with the same or similar meaning) and **antonyms** (words with opposite meanings). The original meaning of the Greek word "thesaurus" is treasury or storehouse, and a thesaurus is indeed a treasury of words.

Use the Thesaurus to say it another way

If you're having a hard time thinking of the right word, click the word for which you'd like a synonym; then click Tools, Thesaurus to pop up the Thesaurus, as shown in figure 8.8.

1. The Thesaurus automatically looks up the word at the insertion point and displays a list of synonyms and antonyms. If you want another word entirely, type a word close in meaning to the word you want in the Replace With edit box. We want synonyms for "nice" in the example in figure 8.8.

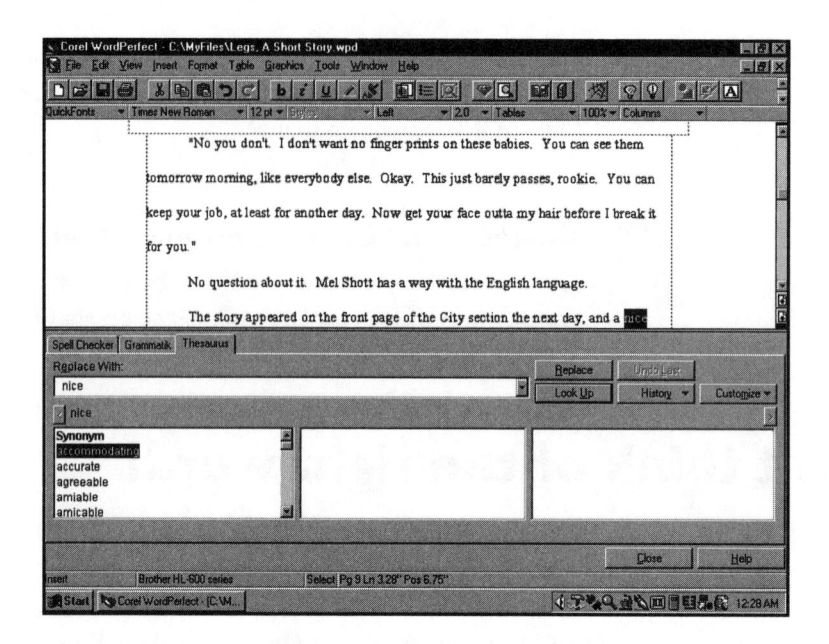

Part III *Getting the Words Right on Screen and Page*

Fig. 8.8
The Thesaurus is a storehouse of word choices.

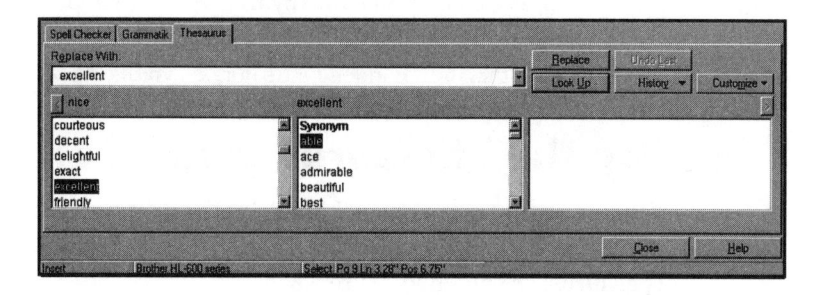

Fig. 8.9
Double-clicking "pleasant" produces another list of synonyms and antonyms in the second column.

2 Click Look Up. A list of synonyms appears in the first column. Scroll down to the bottom of the list for antonyms.

3 Each of the words in the column has a corresponding list of synonyms and antonyms associated with it. Browse the list, and double-click the word that's closest in meaning to what you're trying to say. That gives you another list of synonyms and antonyms in the second column, as shown in figure 8.9.

4 If nothing in the second list appeals to you, double-click any of the words to fill up the third column with yet another list of synonyms and antonyms.

Chances are, you'll find your word amongst all those choices.

Put the Thesaurus to work on your document

The Thesaurus is handy for improving a document. A letter to your office supply company, for example, dashed off in a hurry, might not be as clear as you'd like. Vague phrases such as "no good" might creep into your usually precise prose. An antonym for "good" might help, and the thesaurus can find one for you. Click the word; then click <u>T</u>ools, <u>T</u>hesaurus, as shown in figure 8.10.

Fig. 8.10
The right antonym can sharpen your prose.

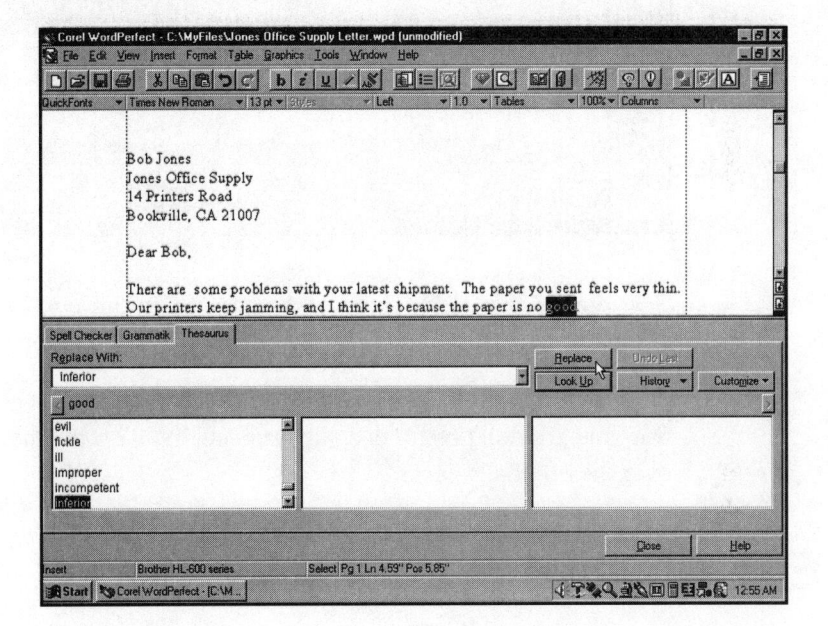

You'll find the antonyms way down on the Thesaurus' list of words. Just keep scrolling and you'll get there in the end. Replacing "no good" with "inferior" would be an improvement. Click <u>R</u>eplace to substitute "inferior" for "good," and then select "no" in the document and delete it. You can edit a document while the Thesaurus is running; just click in the document to move the insertion point to the desired spot. Click the Thesaurus again when you're done editing.

The word "wrong" is in both sentences in the second paragraph. Click the second occurrence; then click <u>L</u>ook Up in the Thesaurus, as shown in figure 8.11.

Fig. 8.11
The Thesaurus is helpful in the case of an overused word.

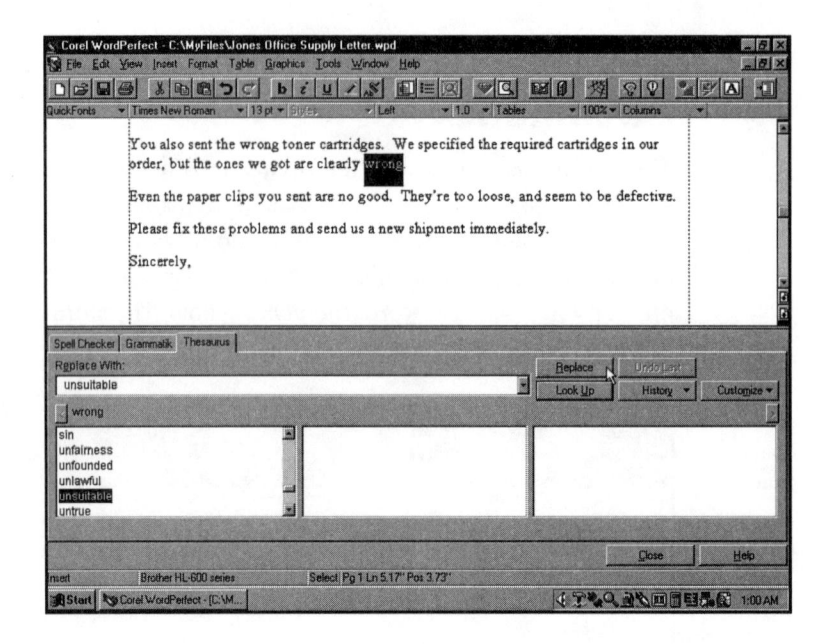

"Unsuitable" is a good substitute for "wrong" in this context. Select the word in the Thesaurus, and click Replace to pop it into the document in place of "wrong."

Our changes don't result in a masterpiece, but it's a distinct improvement over the original.

It's English, but is it Grammatikal?

Those same reports and term papers we labored over in school that came back with Sp. all over them might also have been peppered with teachers' annotations like "awk," or "run on."

Combing your documents for slips like those is the job of WordPerfect's Grammatik feature. Grammatik goes through your documents line by line, pointing out errors in grammar and usage along the way. Grammatik has one major advantage over your old teacher: you can adopt its corrections, or ignore them completely.

How do I use Grammatik?

Let's turn Grammatik loose on our corrected letter to Jones Office Supply, last seen in figure 8.11.

1 Open the document and choose Tools, Grammatik.

2 The Grammatik dialog box pops up and immediately seizes on what it reckons is the first error in the document, as shown in figure 8.12.

Fig. 8.12
Grammatik flags words it doesn't find in its dictionary.

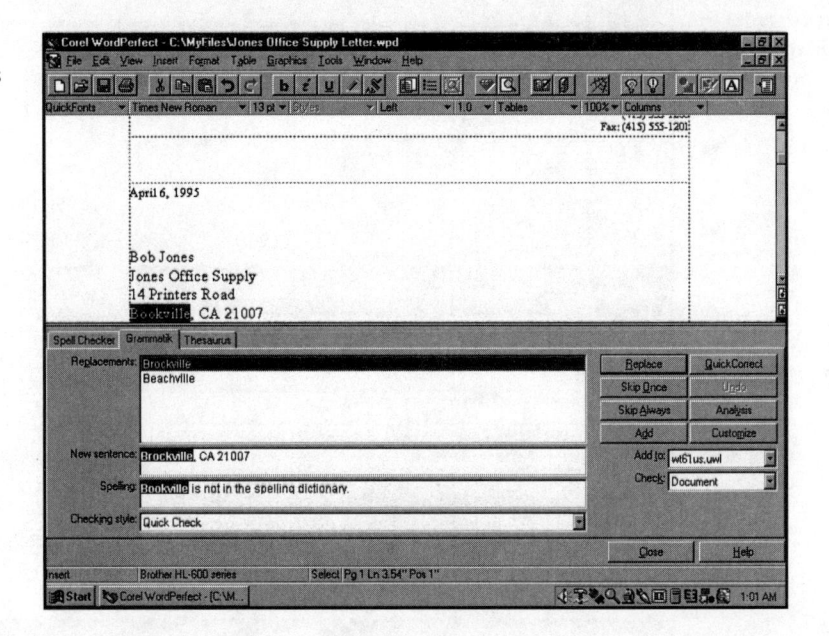

3 Grammatik doesn't recognize the place name "Bookville" (which doesn't exist, as far as I know, because I made it up). It *does* recognize Brockville and Beachville, wherever they may be, which is of no interest to us. This isn't an error, so we'll click Skip Always and carry on.

> **TIP** You can always add words to the Grammatik dictionary. Click A**d**d in the Grammatik dialog box, and the highlighted word is added to the default supplementary dictionary, WT61US.UWL, the same one used by Spell Checker.

4 Grammatik jumps on "clips," as in paper clips, as shown in figure 8.13.

5 Grammatik suspects that "clips" is missing the possessive apostrophe, as in "clip's." That's clearly an incorrect assessment in this case. However, if you think that Grammatik is really on to an error, you can get more information about the grammatical rule or term in question. Click the words in green in the grammatical rule box for definitions and

Part III *Getting the Words Right on Screen and Page*

explanations of Grammatik's rules. You'll get a Grammatik Help on Grammar window like the one in figure 8.14.

Fig. 8.13
Grammatik can be overzealous. It's prone to finding errors where none exist.

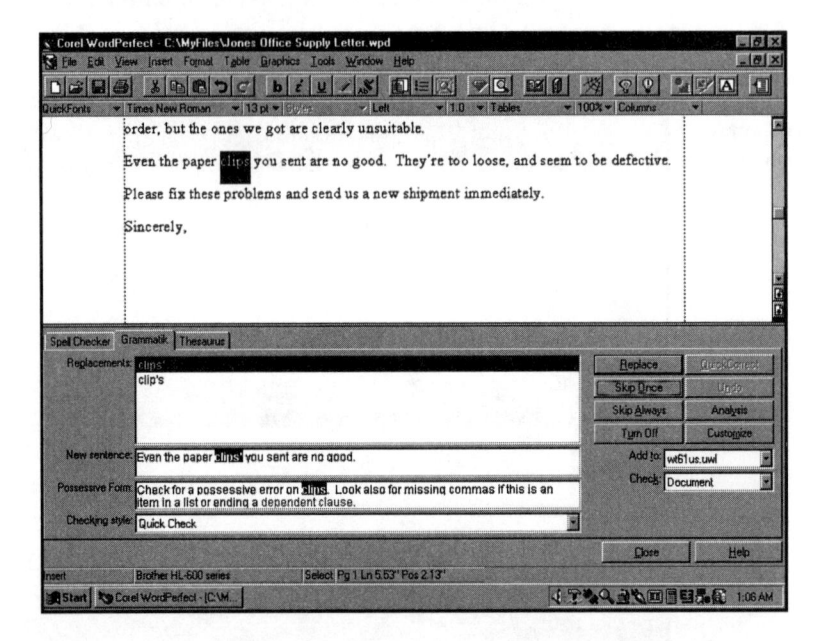

Fig. 8.14
Grammatik gives definitions and explanations of grammatical rules and terms on demand.

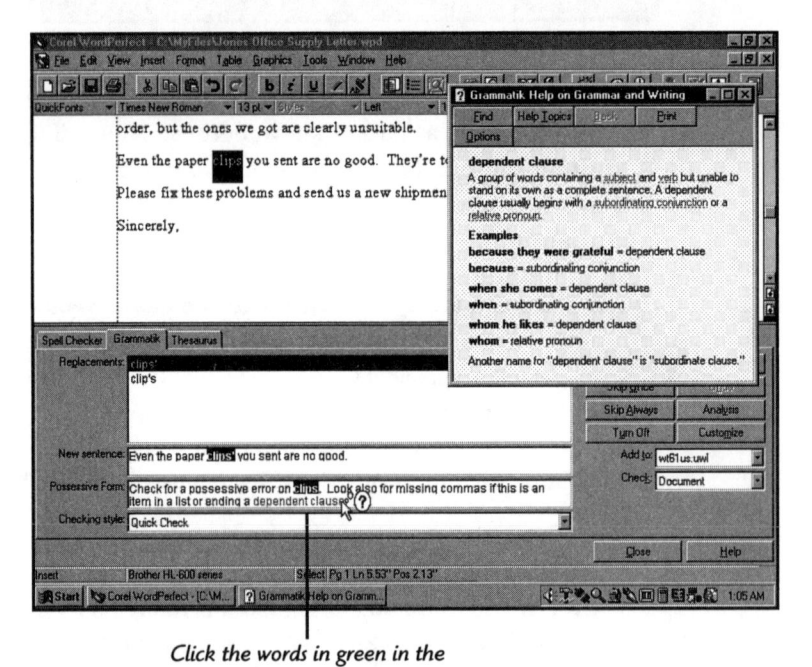

Click the words in green in the rule box for a Help window.

6 We'll close the Grammatik Help box and click Skip Once. That brings us to the next problem in our letter. Grammatik finds the object pronoun "you" following the noun "clips" to be awkward (see fig. 8.15). Here, Grammatik offers no Replacements; had it done so, we could have selected the replacement and clicked Replace to replace our word with Grammatik's. We could replace "the paper clips you sent" with "the paper clips that you have sent to us" on our own. But we won't bother. This letter's tone is informal, and the original formulation is fine.

7 Clicking Skip Once again gets us to the end of the grammar check. Although Grammatik didn't have much to offer in the way of improvements for our letter, we did learn something about a few grammatical terms.

My letter is informal. Can I tell Grammatik to lighten up?

Grammatik can be more useful if you adjust its Checking Style. For informal documents, try a less stringent option. To view Grammatik's checking options, click the Checking Style arrow for the drop-down list shown in figure 8.15.

Fig. 8.15
Grammatik varies checking criteria, depending on your choice in this list.

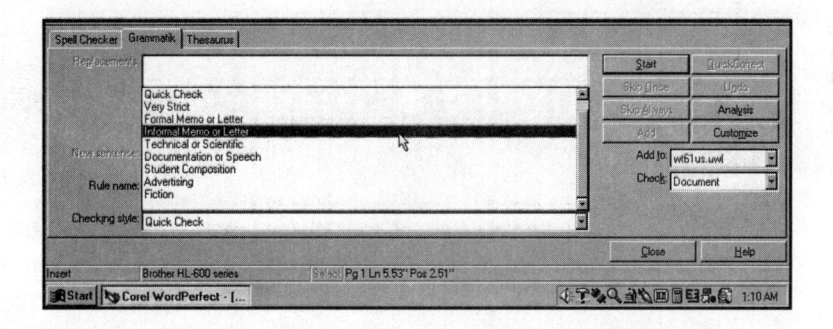

Grammatik offers a lot of interesting information

You may or may not find Grammatik to be a useful tool. Try it for final polish on important documents; if nothing else, you'll learn a fair amount of English grammar.

For those who like to put their writing under a powerful lens, Grammatik has some nifty options.

When Grammatik highlights a potential problem, click Analysis in the Grammatik dialog box, and select Parts of Speech. Your sentence is broken down into its component parts, as shown in figure 8.16.

Fig. 8.16
If grammatical analysis appeals to you, explore Grammatik's analysis feature. Click a word in the sentence for an explanation of the codes.

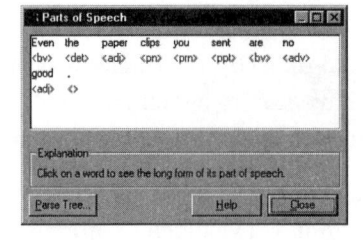

For a diagram of the indirect and direct objects in your sentence, click the Parse Tree button in the Parts of Speech dialog box. A display like the one in figure 8.17 pops up, showing the relation between the words in the sentence.

Fig. 8.17
If you're wondering about agreement questions, the Grammatik Parse Tree can supply answers.

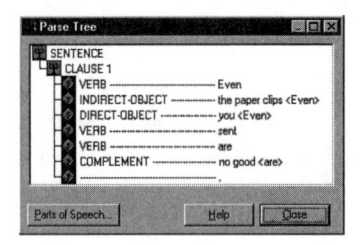

All I really want is a word count for this document

There are plenty of situations where you'll need an accurate word count of your document. If you submit a document for publication, a word count will probably be required. If you're getting paid by the word, there's no probably about it. Or you might just be curious about the number of hard-won words you've actually set down.

To get a word count, and quite a bit more besides, select File, Document, Properties while your document is open. That pops up the Properties dialog box. Click the Information tab, and you'll get all the data shown in figure 8.18.

If all you're looking for is a word count, this might be more than you need.

Fig. 8.18
The Information tab of the Properties dialog box tells you everything you want to know about your document.

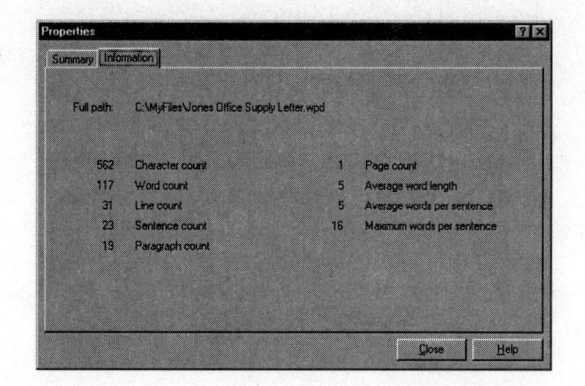

Properties	
Summary / **Information**	
Full path:	C:\MyFiles\Jones Office Supply Letter.wpd
562	Character count
117	Word count
31	Line count
23	Sentence count
19	Paragraph count
1	Page count
5	Average word length
5	Average words per sentence
16	Maximum words per sentence

[Close] [Help]

9

The Printer's Craft

● In this chapter:

- How do I print my document?
- I only want to print a few pages
- Can I print envelopes?
- Printing labels is easy!
- I want a one-page print job, but my document's two pages long
- How do I print several documents at once?

Created a great looking document? Nothing gets lost in the translation when you print from screen to page in WordPerfect................................

The best gadget for storing information is completely portable, easily searchable, and conveniently viewable. What is it? The printed page. It's still easier to read text in print than text on the screen. And carrying a document is much handier than lugging a computer, no matter how diminutive the machine.

Printed text isn't just convenient. Readers tend to treat print with respect. There are always exceptions—Charles Darwin used to rip big books in half to make them easier to handle. But, putting words in print gives them authority, and dignity, too. It's no accident that the printer is the most common computer accessory.

All of WordPerfect's formatting and editing features are designed to produce accurate and readable pages. When it's time to put those pages on paper, most of the work is already done. That makes the rest of the job—actually getting a printout—very easy.

Pick your printer

Before Windows came along, setting up a printer to work with your software was a job fraught with obscure commands, arcane terminology, and gray hairs. Nowadays, Windows handles the job for us. Before printing a document in WordPerfect, we just need to make sure that the current printer is the printer we want to use.

Glance at the WordPerfect status bar; if the displayed printer isn't the printer you want, double-click the status bar printer button for the Print to dialog box shown in figure 9.1.

Click the Name drop-down arrow for a list of your installed printers and select the one you want.

> **TIP** **If you have a fax/modem, a fax printer may be listed among the** available printers. Select the fax printer to send your fax; the document will print to a file on disk or directly to your fax software rather than to a printer. Just remember to select a regular printer for your other print jobs.

Fig. 9.1
The Printer tab of the Print to dialog box lets you switch printers.

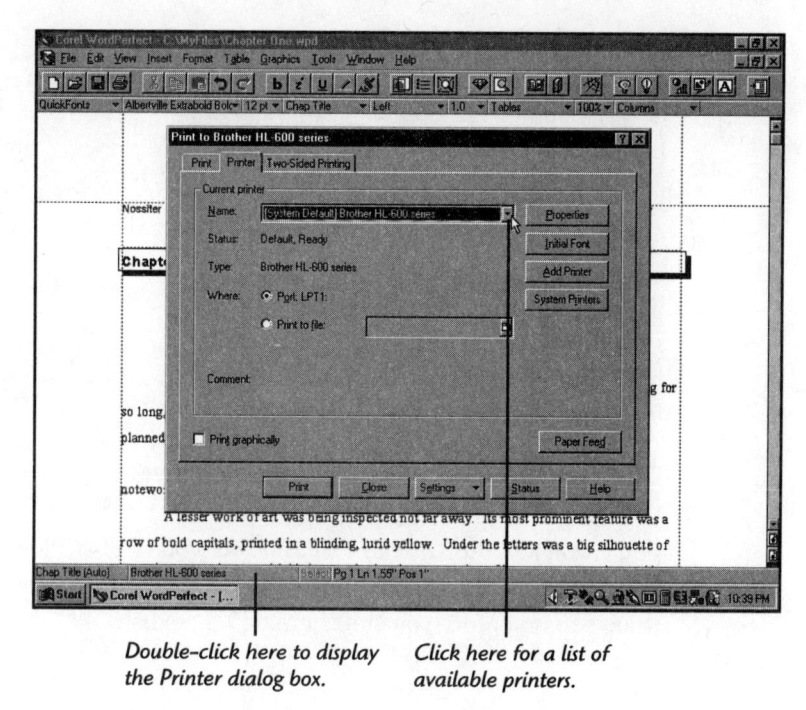

Double-click here to display the Printer dialog box.

Click here for a list of available printers.

How do I print this document?

You've finished writing your document. It's formatted and edited and spell checked. Print a copy, and you can go home. Or maybe you're still working on your document, and you want to print what you've done so far. Many people, including me, find that reading hard copy makes editing easier.

Either way, save your work with a click of the Save button on the Toolbar. Then, to print the active document:

1 Click the Print button on the Toolbar. That pops up the Print dialog box shown in figure 9.2.

2 There are plenty of options in the Print dialog box, and all the important ones are already selected for you. If you want to print one copy of all the pages of your document on the printer displayed in the dialog box, don't change anything. Just click Print.

3 That's all there is to it. WordPerfect displays a message that it's preparing the document for printing, the dialog box disappears, and the printout emerges from your printer.

Fig. 9.2
Click the Toolbar Print button to summon up the Print dialog box.

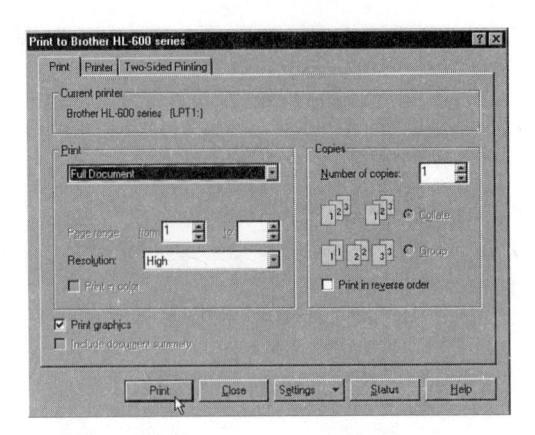

My printer's not printing! What do I do?

You've clicked the Toolbar Print button, you've also clicked the Print button in the Print dialog box, and your printer is still not printing. Time for the "things to do before you start cursing" checklist:

- Is the printer plugged in AND turned on?
- Is the cable between printer and computer securely connected at both ends?
- Is there paper in the printer's paper tray or sheet feeder?
- Is the correct printer selected in the WordPerfect Printer dialog box?

Although laughably obvious, any of the above can derail your print job—and I speak from bitter experience. If they all check out, you can at least isolate the problem. Turn your printer off, wait 10 seconds, and then turn it on again. My printer sometimes gets confused, and turning it off and on seems to sort it out.

Now, print a test page from your computer:

1 Double-click the Printer button on the status bar.

2 Click Properties in the Printer dialog box that pops up.

3 In the Properties dialog box, select the General tab and click Print Test Page.

If you can't print a test page from the computer, try printing a test page right from the printer to make sure it's working properly. You'll have to see your printer manual (you still have the manual, don't you?) for instructions on which printer buttons to press to do that.

If you can print test pages directly from your printer and also from Windows, you know that both the printer and the connection between computer and printer are working. If your WordPerfect document *still* won't print, try saving it with a different name. Click File, Save As, type a new name in the Name box, and click Save. Computer files can get corrupted, and renaming them might solve the problem.

Your renamed document still won't print? Go ahead and curse. Then, call WordPerfect tech support. For the phone number, press F1 to get the Help dialog box, click the Contents tab, and double-click Corel Support Services. Depending on where you live, double-click either Product Support in North America or Product Support WorldWide to see those critical phone numbers.

Q&A Why aren't the pages of my printout numbered?

The status bar displays page numbers as you move around in the document, but those numbers won't print. For printed page numbers, click Format, Page Numbering, Select. Choose a format and a Position in the Select Page Numbering Format dialog box, and click OK. See Chapter 7 for more information about page numbers.

Look before you leap: previewing your document layout

WordPerfect shows you what you're doing as you do it. When you change fonts, or apply boldface or italics to text, the editing window displays your changes. That's called **WYSIWIG** (pronounced "WIZZY-wig"), an acronym for What-You-See-Is-What-You-Get. It's a common feature of Windows programs.

Trouble is, what you see in the editing window is not exactly what you'll get on the printout. It's tough, for example, to gauge how margin settings will look on paper just by looking at the display on the screen. Since the editing window only displays about a third of the page at a time, you can't really tell how the whole page will look in print.

To see the whole page, click the Page/Zoom Full button on the Toolbar. That shrinks the page to fit the screen; detail is hard to make out, but you do get the big picture, as shown in figure 9.3.

Fig. 9.3
Use the Page/Zoom Full button for a preview of the printed page.

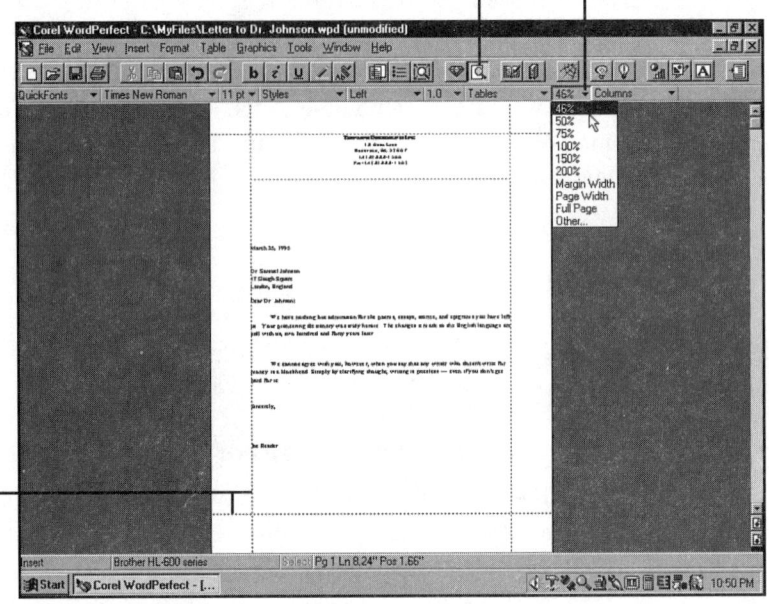

The Page/Zoom Full button

Click the Zoom button and select a different magnification from the list to see more detail.

Drag the Guidelines to adjust left, right, top, and bottom margins.

In the full page view shown in figure 9.3, you can see how your margin settings and text placement will look in print. To see more or less detail, use the Power Bar Zoom button.

All the editing and scrolling commands are available in full page view, so you can move from page to page, drag the Guidelines to change margins, and even edit text. This view is particularly handy if you're adjusting graphics or other large elements on the page.

Click the Page/Zoom Full button again to return to the normal editing view.

> **Q&A** *I'm looking at my document in full page view, and the text is all scrunched up toward the top of the page. And there's lots of white space at the bottom of the page! What do I do?*
>
> The quick fix: center the text on the page. Press Ctrl+Home to move the insertion point to the top of the document. Then Click Format, Page, Center. Choose Current Page and click OK to center the text.

I don't want to print the whole document

There'll be plenty of occasions when you'll want to print only a few pages of a long document, or only the page you're working on, or even just a section of one page.

To print only some of the pages in a document:

1 Click the Print button on the Toolbar; the Print dialog box pops up.

2 Type the range of pages you want to print in the Page range edit boxes. For example, type **3** in the from box and **6** in the to box to print pages 3 through 6, as shown in figure 9.4.

Fig. 9.4
This range prints pages 3 through 6.

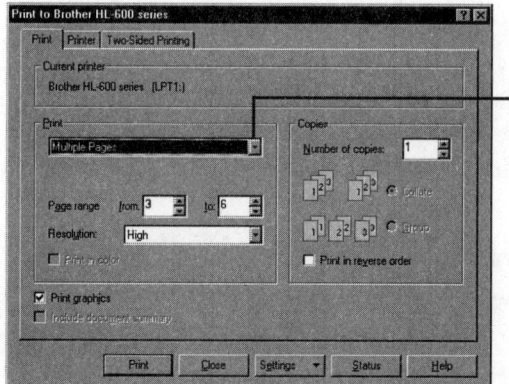

Click here to choose to print the current page, the full document, or multiple pages. When you enter a Page range, Multiple Pages is selected automatically.

3 Once you've entered the range of pages you want, click Print to send the job to the printer.

Refine print selections with Advanced Multiple Pages

WordPerfect makes it very easy to print exactly the pages you want in a long document. Advanced Multiple Pages lets you print individual pages, ranges of pages, or both. To specify the pages to print with Advanced Multiple pages:

1 Click the Print button on the Toolbar to pop up the Print dialog box.

2 Click the Print drop-down arrow in the Print dialog box, and select Advanced Multiple Pages.

3 Now click the Edit button that appears under the Print drop-down arrow.

4. The Advanced Multiple Pages dialog box appears. Want to print pages 3, 10, and 15? Type those page numbers, separated by a comma (no spaces), in the P̲age(s)/label(s) edit box, as shown in figure 9.5.

Fig. 9.5
Choose to print exactly what you want in the Advanced Multiple Pages dialog box.

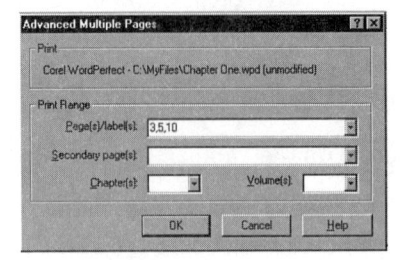

5. Once you've typed the pages you want to print in the P̲age(s)/label(s) edit box, click OK in the Advanced Multiple Pages dialog box. That takes you back to the Print dialog box; click Print to send your job to the printer.

Table 9.1 lists the ways you can specify pages to print in WordPerfect.

Table 9.1 Defining print ranges

Type this in the P̲age(s)/label(s) edit box of the Advanced Multiple Pages dialog box to print page(s)	
2	2 only
2,4,6	2 and 4 and 6
2–6	2 through 6
–6	from beginning of the document to page 6
6–	from page 6 to the end of the document

If you just want to print individual pages *and* a range, use a combination of hyphens and commas: 6,8,9–12 prints pages 6 and 8, and pages 9 through 12.

Q&A ***The Print button on the Toolbar is grayed out! What happened?***

If the insertion point is inside a header or footer, the Print button is grayed out. Click anywhere outside the headers or footers to restore the Print button.

All I want to print is one section of a page

You may want to see how a heavily formatted paragraph looks in print without printing the whole document.

Select the text you want to print, and click the Print button on the Toolbar. WordPerfect chooses the Selected Text option in the Print dialog box for you; just click Print and your selected text goes right to the printer. The selected text appears at its original location on the page on the printout, not at the top of the page as you might expect.

How do I print more than one copy?

With a computer and a printer, you can save yourself a trip to the photocopier. WordPerfect lets you print multiple copies of a single page, a range of pages, or a whole document. To print multiple copies:

1 Click the Print button on the Toolbar for the Print dialog box.

2 Click the arrows or type a number in the Number of copies box.

3 For collated copies (copies in the document's page order), select Collate. For multiple copies of individual pages (two or more copies of page 1, page 2, and so on), select Group.

4 Select Full Document, Current Page, or Multiple Pages on the Print drop-down list.

5 Click Print. If you want to print just a range of pages, type the page range in the from and to boxes. If you chose Current Page, you get only the page where you left the insertion point.

Other nifty print options

One of my printers is an inkjet model that's nice and quiet. It has one big disadvantage. Print jobs come out with the pages face up. That puts the first page at the bottom of the pile, with the last page on top—reverse page order. I used to reorder the pages by hand, but now I get WordPerfect to do it for me.

WordPerfect can print documents in reverse page order, so that on printers like my inkjet model, the first page winds up at the top of the output pile, the last page at the bottom.

To print in reverse page order, click the Print button on the Toolbar. In the Print to dialog box, click the Print in re_v_erse order check box, as shown in figure 9.6.

Fig. 9.6
Printing in reverse order is handy for printers that output in reverse order.

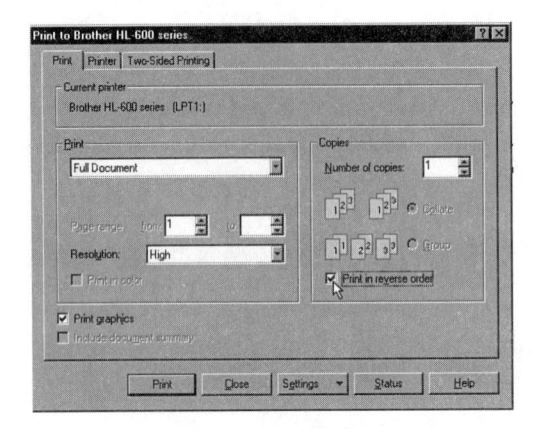

Click Print to send the job to the printer. The last page of your document will come out of the printer first, then the next to last page, and so on. If you print long documents on printers with reverse order output, this option will save you a lot of paper shuffling.

Here's a paper saver: print on both sides of the page

Some printers can print on both sides of a sheet of paper at the same time. That's called **duplexing**, a neat trick that my printer certainly can't do, and yours probably can't either.

WordPerfect lets you print on both sides of the page even if your printer doesn't do duplexing:

1 Click the Toolbar Print button; then click the Two-Sided Printing tab in the Print to dialog box.

2 Click the Front: odd pages (step 1) option under Manual.

3 Click Print to print your document's odd-numbered pages.

4 Put the stack of printed pages back in the printer. Make sure the correct side is facing up, which will depend on your printer, and repeat the steps to print the document's even-numbered pages. Just select Back: even pages (step 2) in step 2 of these instructions.

This will work, but depending on how your printer feeds paper and the order in which it prints pages, you might have to experiment with refeeding the pages for the even-numbered pages part of the print job. Try printing a few pages first. A little trial-and-error work will ensure success here.

Unless your printer *can* do duplexing, the Automatic by printer options in the Two-Sided Printing dialog box are grayed-out.

Curious about the Print as boo**k**let option in the Two-Sided Printing dialog box? That prints pages divided into columns, in the correct order for a booklet bound at the spine. (See Chapter 14 for more information on booklet printing.)

How do I print labels and envelopes?

Ever received a beautifully laser-printed letter, formatted to perfection, but mailed in an envelope addressed by hand? The sender obviously gave up on trying to master the intricacies of envelope printing. Same thing with labels; with some software, fitting the text onto a label is just more trouble than it's worth.

In WordPerfect envelopes and labels are as easy to print as ordinary pages.

Perfect envelopes, fast

To print an envelope:

1 Insert an envelope in your printer. With the letter still as the active document, click Fo**r**mat, En**v**elope. The Envelope dialog box shown in figure 9.7 appears.

Fig. 9.7
The Envelope dialog box grabs the mailing address right from the letter.

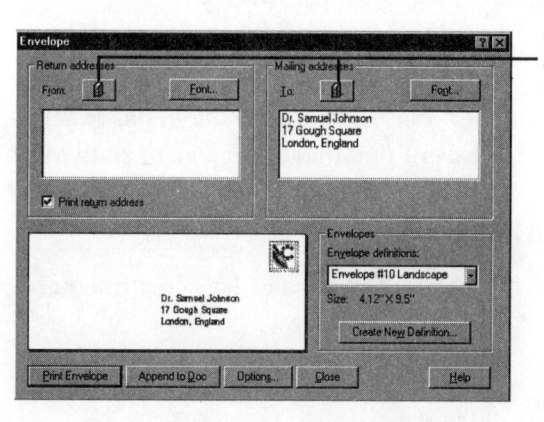

Click the Address Book buttons to insert addresses from your book.

2 If you've typed the mailing address on the letter, WordPerfect grabs it and automatically puts it in the Mailing addresses To edit box. You also can select an address before choosing Format, Envelope. Or click the Address Book button and make your selection there (see Chapter 12 for more information on the Address Book). Otherwise, just click the edit box and type it in yourself.

3 Click the From edit box and type in the return address, or click the Address Book button and select the return address from your book. Make sure the Print return address box is checked, or the return address won't print.

4 Select the correct envelope type and size from the Envelope definitions drop-down list. The default is a #10 envelope, the standard size.

5 Click Print Envelope to print.

> **Q&A** *I did all this and my envelope's still not printing! What gives?*
>
> Unless you have a printer with an envelope bin, WordPerfect assumes that you're feeding envelopes into the printer manually. Press the appropriate button on the printer to continue printing. It varies from printer to printer, but usually it's some variation of form-feed or Continue.

> **TIP** **To print USPS bar codes on your envelope, click Options... in the** Envelope dialog box, and select one of the USPS bar code position options. WordPerfect automatically translates your typed 5-, 9-, or 11-digit ZIP code into a bar code.

Printing labels is easy

You need to answer one crucial question before trying to print labels in WordPerfect: what kind of labels do you have? Once you know the make and model number of your labels, you're set. In this example, we're going to print an Avery 5162 Laser Printer label, a standard address label sheet available at any office supply store. Check your label package for the make and model number of your labels.

With that vital information in hand, let's create and print a label:

Chapter 9 *The Printer's Craft* **177**

1. If there's an open document in the current window, click the New Blank Document button on the Toolbar (if you don't, WordPerfect takes whatever you have in the editing window and tries to fit it onto labels). Then, click Format, Labels and the Labels dialog box shown in figure 9.8 appears.

Fig. 9.8
Scan the list of label types in the Labels dialog box for your make and model.

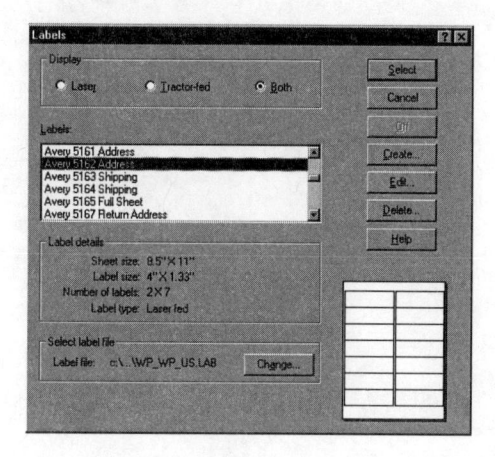

2. If you're printing laser sheet labels, click Laser under Display. That trims the very long list of labels to manageable proportions. Otherwise, leave the Both option selected to see all the label types.

3. Scroll down the list of Labels, and select your make and model number. In the example, we're using Avery 5162 Address labels.

4. Click Select and the editing window changes to display the first blank label on the sheet. If you're printing the first label on the sheet, type the information you want on the label. It looks like figure 9.9.

> **TIP** **If your address is in the Address Book, click the Address Book** button on the Toolbar, select the address you want, and click Insert. If you've typed the address you want in another open document, just select the address and copy and paste it into the labels editing window.

5. Press Ctrl+Enter to move the insertion point to the next label, and type the information for that label. As you move from label to label, the status bar page number indicator changes. Click the Page/Zoom Full button on the Toolbar to see the whole sheet of labels at once (see fig. 9.10). WordPerfect considers each individual label a **logical** page and numbers them accordingly. This sheet has 14 labels on it, so there

are logical pages 1–14 to choose from. The whole sheet is called a **physical page**.

Fig. 9.9
Type the address or any other information you want on the blank on-screen label.

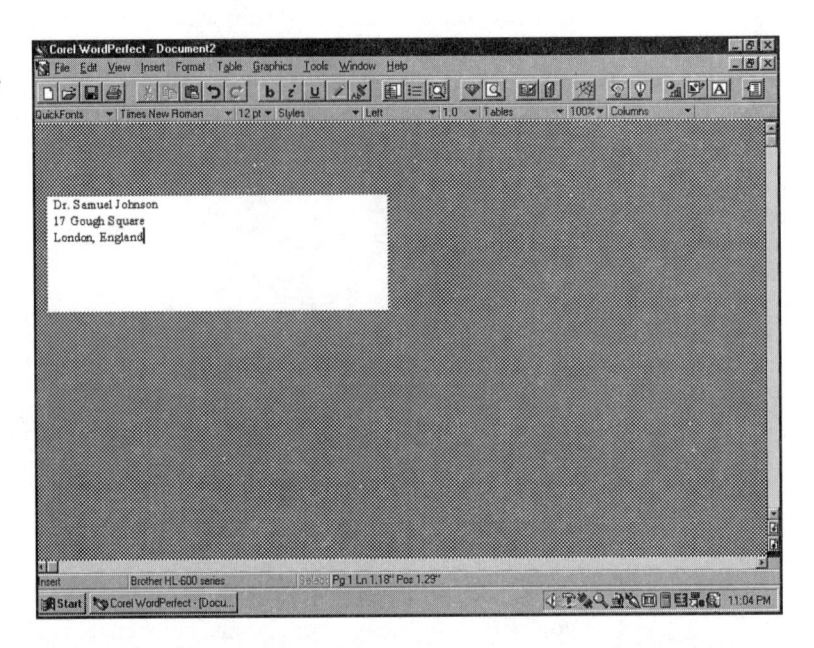

Fig. 9.10
As you add labels, the physical page begins to fill with completed labels.

The whole sheet is a physical page.

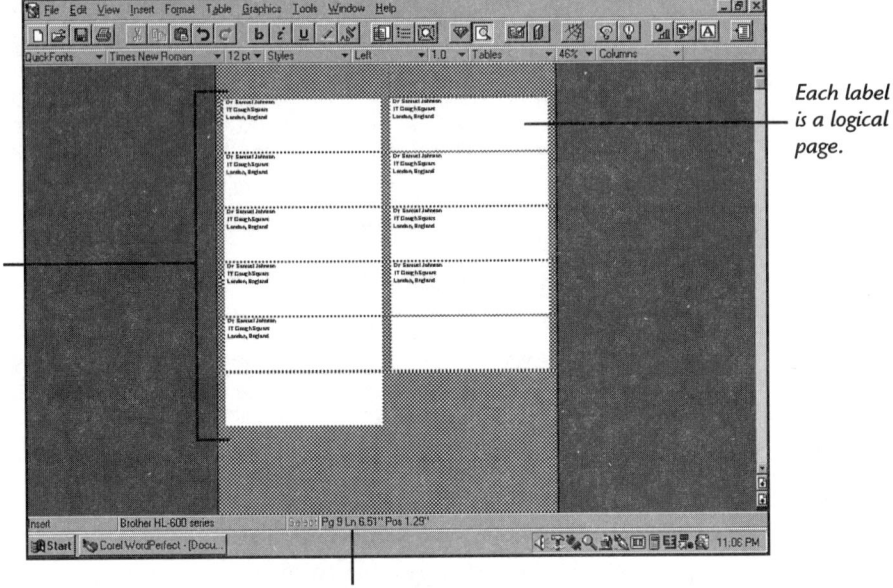

Each label is a logical page.

The status bar shows the logical page location of the insertion point.

6 Click the Zoom/Page Full button again to return to the previous view, so that you can see what you're doing. Continue typing (or copying and pasting) your label information until you're done.

7 Insert the sheet of labels in your printer, click the Print button on the Toolbar, and click Print to print your labels.

> **TIP** **Labels are expensive. If you're experimenting with this option, try** printing labels to regular sheets of paper first. When you're satisfied with the result, take the plunge and print your labels.

To print only certain labels on the sheet, click Multiple Pages in the Print dialog box; then enter the range of the labels' logical page numbers in the from and to Page range boxes.

If you want a whole sheet of the same label, type the information in the first label on the sheet; then copy and paste the information into all the other labels on the sheet. Press Ctrl+Enter to move the insertion point from label to label. (See Chapter 13 for information on automatically merging address information to labels.)

> **TIP** **If you don't want to waste unused labels on a sheet of labels, fill** the blank ones with your return address for use on packages and so on.

> **Q&A** *So why isn't my label printing?*
> Just as with envelopes, WordPerfect assumes you're feeding sheets of labels manually. Unless you actually place the label sheets in your paper tray like regular sheets of paper, you'll have to go over to your printer and press the appropriate button to continue printing from the manual feed.

> **TIP** **Format your labels the same way you format pages and para-** graphs. Click Format, Page, Center to center the text on the label, for example. You can change fonts, add borders, or add any other formatting touches you like.

Can I print several documents at once?

Want to print a document without bothering to open it? Or maybe you have several chapters, each in a different file, and you want to print them all at once. Either way, click the Open button on the Toolbar.

Right-click the file you want to print, and choose Print on the Quickmenu that appears. For more than one file, click the first file; then hold down the Ctrl key and click additional files (release the Ctrl key when you've selected all the files you want). Point at any of the selected files, right-click, and choose Print.

Figure 9.11 shows the Open dialog box with several selected files and the Quickmenu popped up.

Fig. 9.11
Print one file or many from the Open dialog box without the bother of opening them first.

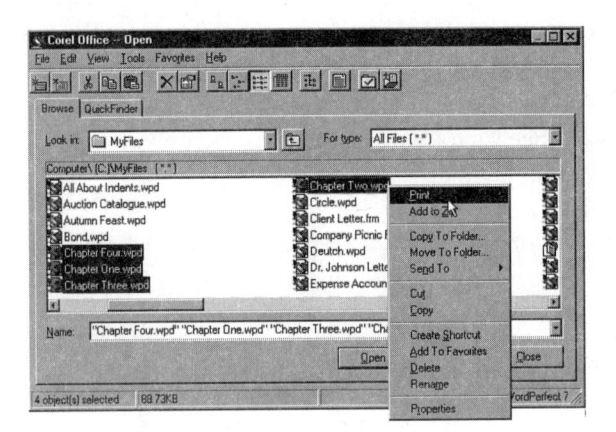

The last lines of my print job look lonely on their own page

Here's something that can complicate a simple print job: the last line or two of the document spills over onto an extra page. You could drive yourself nuts trying to adjust margins and font sizes to squeeze that last bit of text into the rest of the document. Or you can take the easy way out and let WordPerfect do the squeezing for you.

If the tail end of your print job looks orphaned on its own sheet of paper, click the Make It Fit button on the Toolbar. That pops up the Make It Fit dialog box shown in figure 9.12.

Fig. 9.12
Make It Fit shrinks or expands a document to fit on a specified number of pages

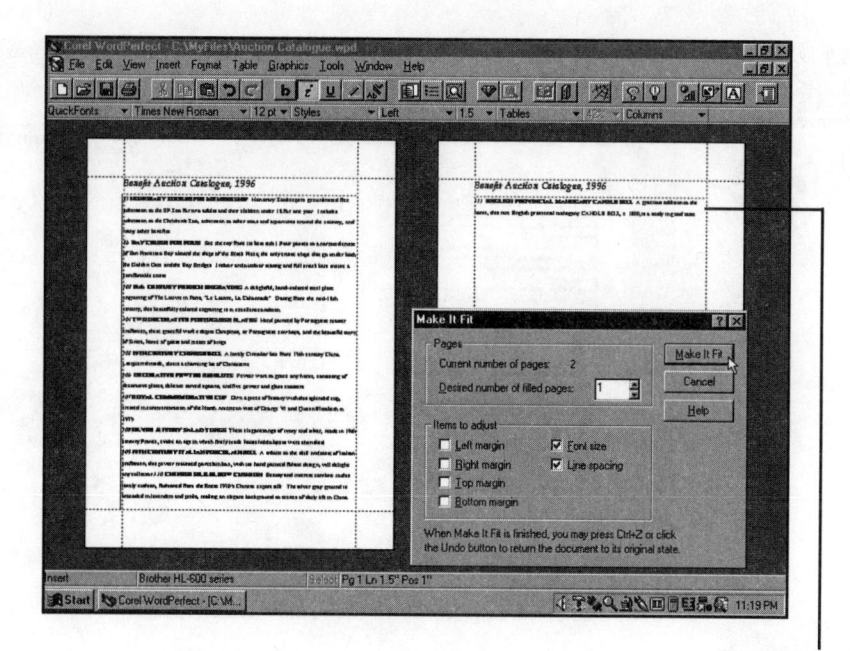

The last lines of this document wound up on an extra page.

If you have a two-page document that looks like the one in figure 9.12, enter 1 in the Desired number of filled pages edit box in the Make It Fit dialog box. By default, Make It Fit adjusts the line spacing and font size to shrink your two-page document down to one page. Choose different Items to adjust if you'd rather keep your line spacing and font size, and you want to use smaller margins instead.

Click Make It Fit when you've made your selections, and your orphaned last lines are reunited with the rest of the document's text, as seen in figure 9.13.

If you don't like what Make It Fit has done to your document, simply click the Undo button on the Toolbar. Try Make It Fit again with other Items to adjust selected to see if you get better results. Make It Fit is especially handy if you're faxing a document and you don't want to fax a last page with only a line or two on it.

Make It Fit also expands documents to a specified number of pages. If you've been asked for a two-page memo on the office paper clip shortage, but inspiration flagged after a single page, click the Make It Fit button and type a 2 in the Desired number of filled pages box. You'll wind up with a lot of white space, but you'll also have your two-page memo.

Fig. 9.13
Like magic, the two-page document is now a one pager, saving paper and a gray hair or two.

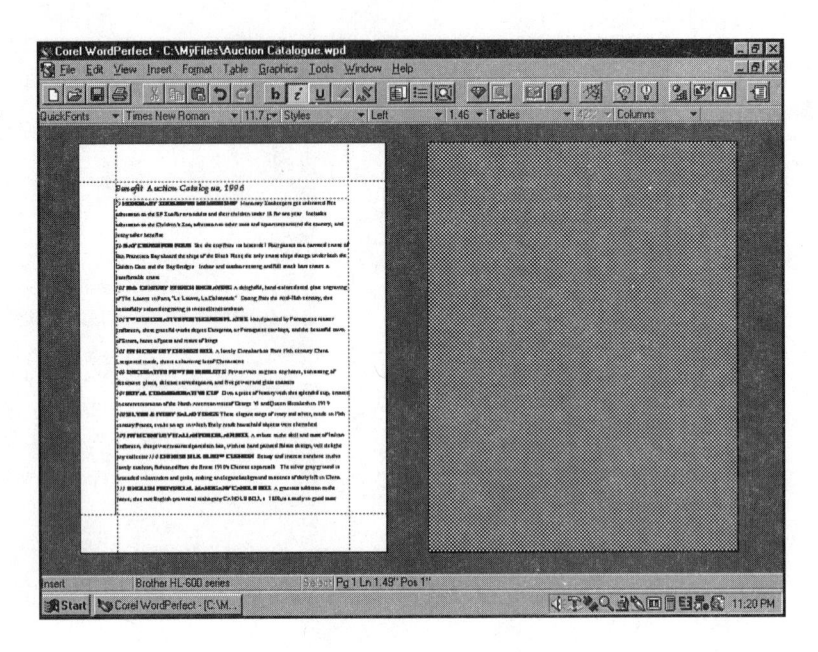

Part IV: Let WordPerfect Do Some of the Work for You

Chapter 10: **Templates: The Express Route to Fancy Documents**

Chapter 11: **Documents with Style(s)**

Chapter 12: **WordPerfect's Labor-Saving Devices**

Chapter 13: **Merges, for Letters by the Bushel**

10
Templates: The Express Route to Fancy Documents

● **In this chapter:**

- A template? Explain, please
- This memo packs a punch
- Need help with your newsletter? Call in the Expert
- Can I change the canned newsletter?
- How about my own template?

Like a mold for clay or a pattern in sewing, templates shape your text for professional-looking results. . . . . ▶

There's nothing quite like the image of a major-league pitcher poised on the mound. Against the backdrop of cropped green grass and neatly uniformed teammates, he's a stirring sight. Now imagine the same pitcher in blue jeans and a tee shirt, tossing a pickup game in a vacant lot.

The setting matters, for documents and for pitchers. Plain text might get the job done. Set in a perfectly formatted document, even mundane text can have lasting impact. WordPerfect's templates give you just that sort of setting. Templates take documents right from the sandlot to the Major Leagues.

What exactly is a template?

Just like a cookie cutter with raw dough, a **template** gives shape to your text. Templates save you the bother of choosing fonts, setting margins, or making other tricky formatting decisions. Each template is a collection of formatting commands saved in a special file. Opening the file gives you a ready-made, precision-formatted document. Just add text, and you're done. There are dozens of templates to choose from, for everything from greeting cards to purchase orders.

When do I use templates?

Templates provide everything you need for complex documents like newsletters, but they're easy enough to use for a simple memo.

In fact, dashing off a quick memo using one of the memo templates takes less time than trying to set it up yourself, and the results will be a lot more impressive. To write a memo using a template:

1. Click the New Document button on the Toolbar. That opens the Select New Document dialog box, which lists all the WordPerfect templates. Choose Main on the Group list of template categories as shown in figure 10.1.

2. Double-click <Memo Expert> on the Select template list. If you've already entered Address Book Personal Information, skip straight to step 3. If you haven't, WordPerfect prompts you to enter information about yourself: name, address, phone number, and so on. Doing so is highly recommended.

Fig. 10.1
WordPerfect organizes templates in categories by Group, and each Group has several templates from which you can choose.

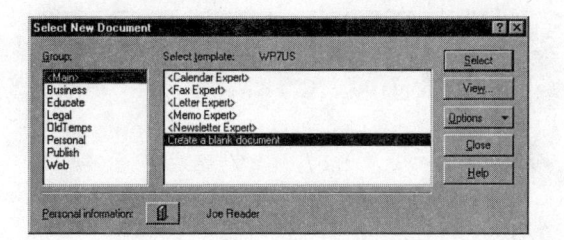

If the Personalize Your Templates message box appears, click OK, choose Person and OK in the New Entry dialog box, and then fill out the blanks in the Properties for New Entry dialog box that appears next. Type it now, and the information goes into the Address Book, where it's used and reused for all your memos, letters, and other documents (see Chapter 12 for details on the Address Book).

Once you finish with the Properties for New Entry dialog box, click OK, and then click Select in the Address Book to select your name as the memo's sender.

3 The Memo Expert dialog box pops up, with a full page view of the memo's layout behind it. Entering your Personal Information has already saved time—the From edit box is filled in with your name! Type the memo recipient's name in the To edit box; then fill in the Subject and CC edit boxes as needed. If you plan on leaving any of the edit boxes blank, make sure you deselect them by clicking the check boxes to remove the checkmarks (see fig. 10.2).

4 Click the Memo style drop-down arrow and take your pick from the list. The full page view behind the Memo Expert dialog box previews your choice, as seen in figure 10.3.

5 Now click OK in the Memo Expert dialog box. WordPerfect takes all the information you typed and puts each item in the appropriate spot in the document. Figure 10.4 shows the memo so far.

Q&A *I'm clicking OK in the Memo Expert dialog box, and all I get is an Entry Required message!*

You have a blank edit box that's also selected with a check mark. Click the check box to deselect the blank field; then click OK. WordPerfect doesn't let you proceed until you either enter information in the edit box or deselect it.

Fig. 10.2
Completing a template is like filling in the blanks on a form.

If you don't want one of these memo elements, deselect it.

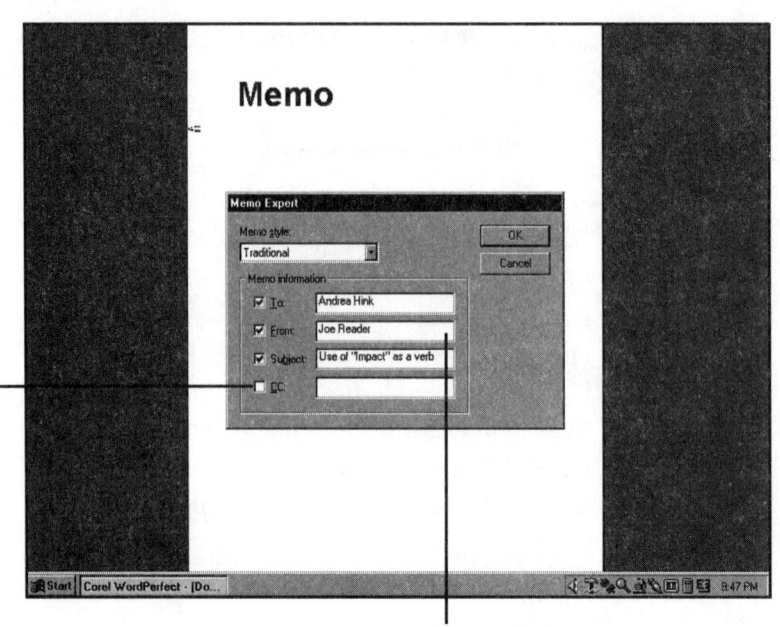

The From box is already filled in with your personal information, but you can change the name if you want to.

Fig. 10.3
Choose a memo style that suits you. All the formatting is already done, saving you the bother.

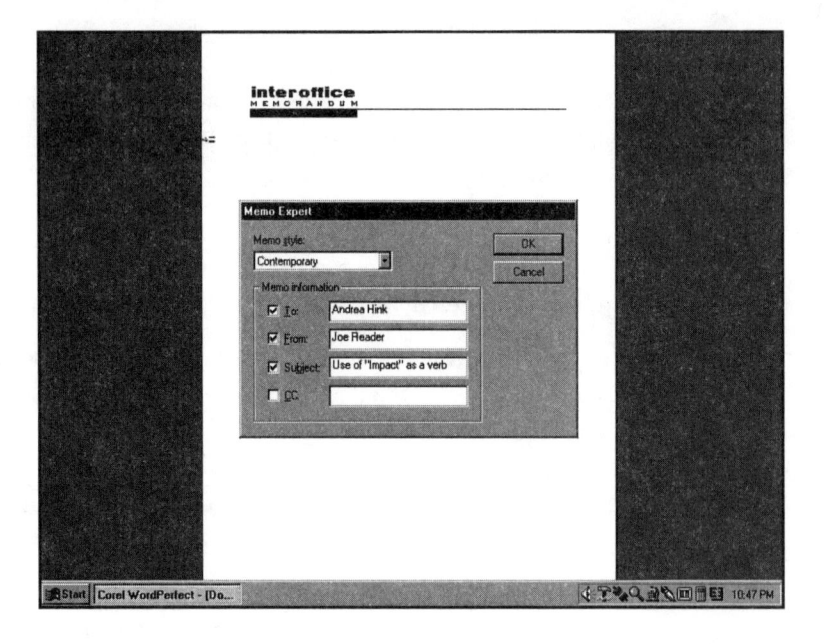

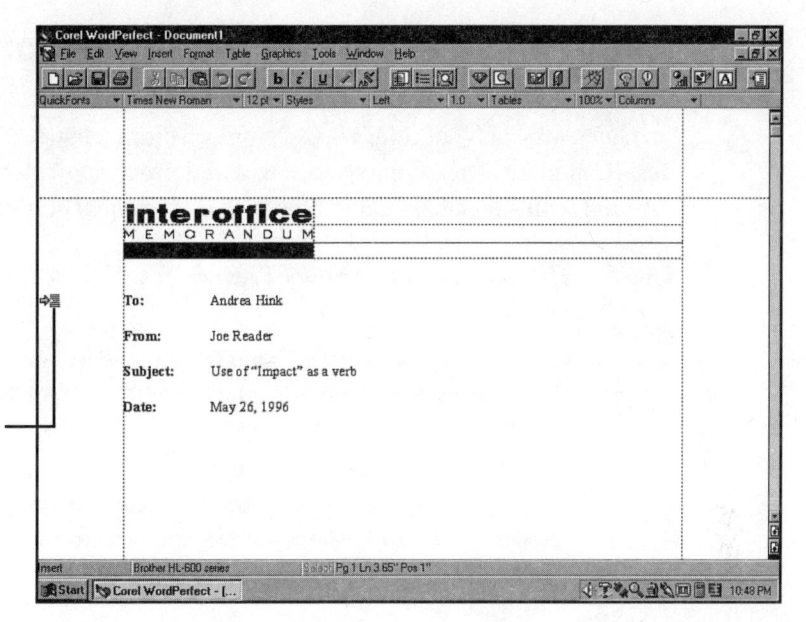

Fig. 10.4
The memo template includes the current date, one more item you needn't bother to add.

The Tab Set icon appears because the Memo Expert changed tab settings. It won't print when it's time to produce hard copy.

The memo has everything—date, subject, recipients, and sender—except the body text. Type that in, save the memo, and you're done.

Figure 10.5 shows the completed memo.

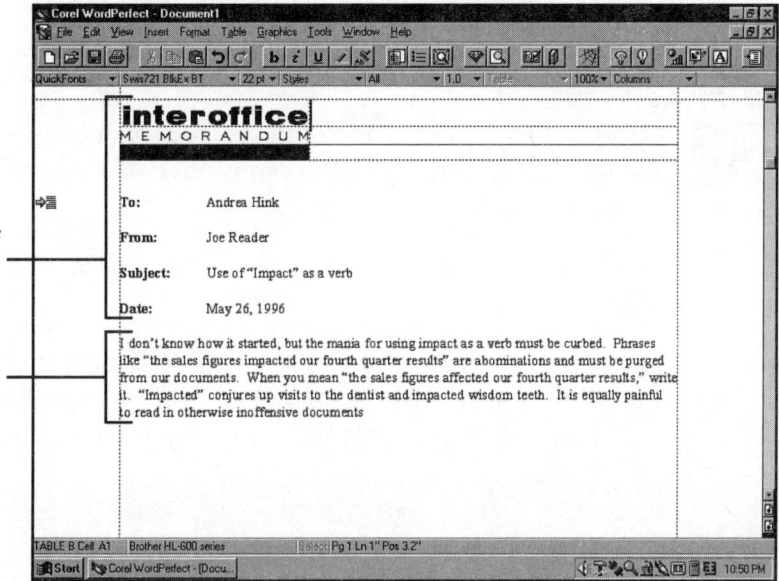

Fig. 10.5
Memos get added punch when they have the professional look of a WordPerfect template.

The title and template information is the masthead.

The body text is ordinary WordPerfect text.

Can I edit template information?

Maybe you misspelled one of the memo recipient's names. Or you might want to change the subject title. Whatever your editing changes, just put the insertion point where you want to edit and fire away. You can edit documents created with specialized templates with all the usual editing commands.

Q&A ***The status bar shows* TABLE B Cell A1. *What's that all about?***

You'll notice that the status bar displays references such as TABLE B Cell A1 when you move the pointer into the masthead of the memo, as shown in figure 10.5. That's because WordPerfect sometimes sets up the heavily formatted parts of templates, such as the masthead in this memo, in a table grid. For editing purposes, just ignore the cell references. They're covered in detail in Chapter 14, where you can find out more about WordPerfect tables.

Newsletter to write? Call in the expert

Newsletters are a great way to keep colleagues informed. Anyone who's had to write a newsletter knows that the actual text is the easy part; formatting the newsletter is the real chore. WordPerfect takes the sting out of setting up a newsletter. The Newsletter Expert handles all the formatting worries, leaving you more time to devote to the newsletter text.

Click the New Document button on the Toolbar and select the Main <u>G</u>roup. Double-click the <Newsletter Expert> and the editing window fills with a sample newsletter.

Then let the Newsletter Expert guide you through the creation of a newsletter:

1. Fill in the blanks in the Template Information dialog box that pops up. You'll need a newsletter title; add a subtitle, date, and the main headline. Press Tab or click Ne<u>x</u>t Field to move the insertion point from one edit box to another (see fig. 10.6).

Chapter 10 Templates: The Express Route to Fancy Documents

Fig. 10.6
Anything you enter here is changeable later, so you don't have to get it all right the first time.

2. Click OK when you're done. WordPerfect's gears whirl for a moment or two as it loads your preferences. That doesn't mean much on your first use of the Newsletter Expert, but the next time you use it, your prior settings will load automatically. That's handy, because any customizing you do now need only be done this one time. The Newsletter Expert dialog box appears next, as seen in figure 10.7.

Fig. 10.7
Change as much of the prefab newsletter as you want, or just accept the standard issue.

3 Click the Select element to modify drop-down arrow, and select any elements you want to change from the list. You can choose 1, 2, or 3 columns, change borders or fill in the title, change fonts, and even insert drop-caps at the beginning of the first paragraph. Or don't change anything and accept the defaults; they work fine too.

4 To change the appearance of the newsletter title, click the Select item to modify drop-down arrow and select Title options. Click the Small cap title check box and select Shaded Heavy Top on the Title border / fill drop-down list. The result is shown in figure 10.8.

Fig. 10.8
The title is the first thing readers see, and WordPerfect makes it easy to draw some attention to it.

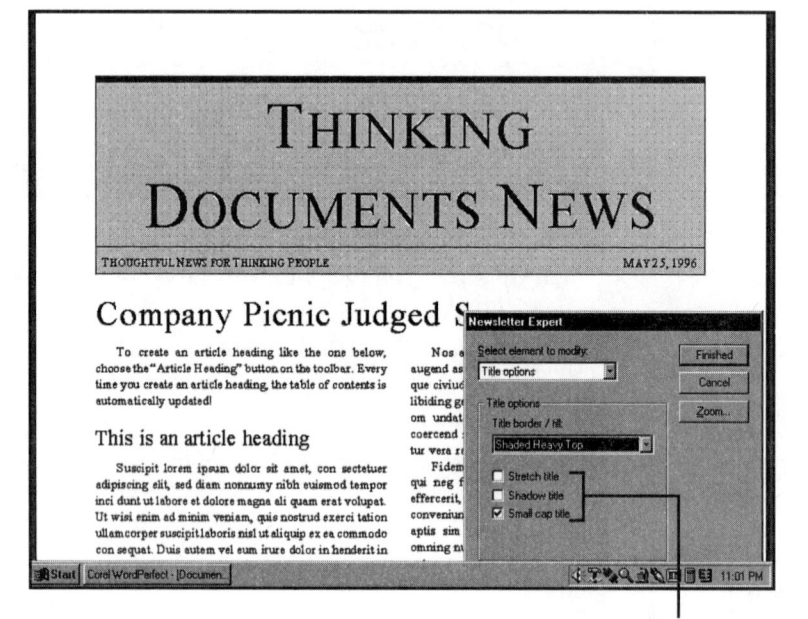

The dialog box options change as you select different items to modify.

5 Click Finished in the Newsletter Expert dialog box, and it's time to go to work. Select any of WordPerfect's remaining text; then start typing your own. WordPerfect's text is overwritten with your own material, as seen in figure 10.9.

6 When you finish writing the first article, press Enter. Click the Article Heading button that has appeared on the Toolbar (see fig. 10.10), and type your next article heading in the Article Heading dialog box. Click OK when you're done.

Fig. 10.9
The fastest way to get rid of the canned material: select it and then type your own.

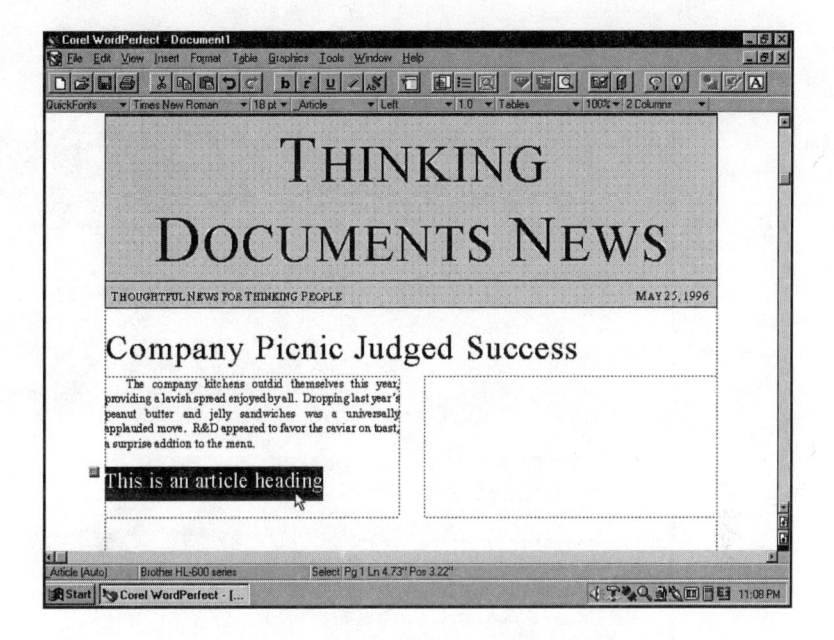

7. Heading finished? Notice how the Power Bar automatically displays the FirstPara style. Type the article's first paragraph, press Enter, and the style automatically switches to Body Text. Press Enter at the end of the article's body text, and click the Article Heading button on the Toolbar to enter your next article heading. You'll get the same cycle of FirstPara and Body Text styles when you press Enter after typing each. If the automatic sequence of styles gets out of whack, just click the Power Bar and select the correct style. Figure 10.10 shows the newsletter taking shape.

8. Once all the headings and articles are typed, click Tools, Generate, Table of Contents. The Table of Contents feature bar appears below the Power Bar. Click Generate on the feature bar and the Generate dialog box appears (see fig. 10.11).

9. Click OK in the Generate dialog box, and you'll get an instant table of contents at the end of the document. To see your table of contents, drag the vertical scroll button all the way down to the bottom of the scroll bar. To move the table of contents elsewhere in the newsletter, click it, and drag it to a new location with the four-headed arrow, as seen in figure 10.12.

Fig. 10.10
If the automatic style sequence goes awry, click the Power Bar Styles button and choose from the list to format the different newsletter elements.

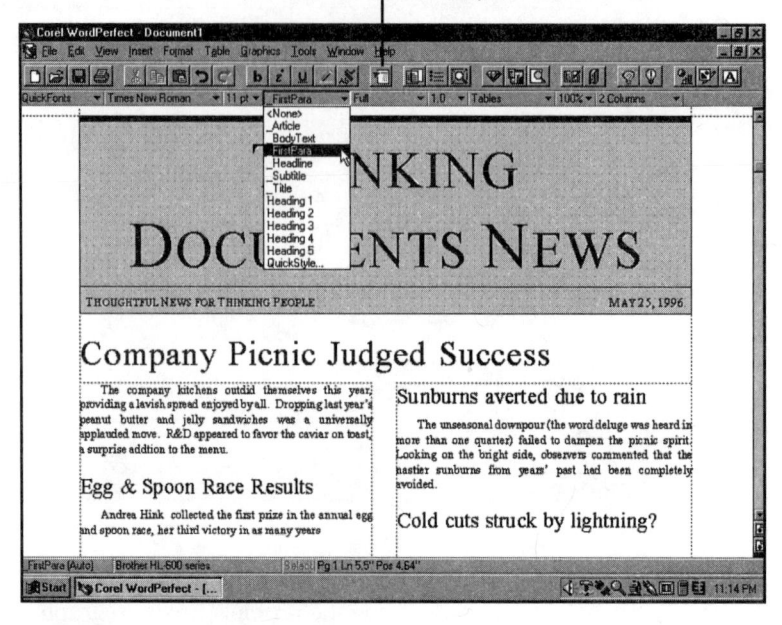

The Article Heading button appears on the Toolbar whenever you run the Newsletter Expert.

Fig. 10.11
Here's one dialog box whose options you can ignore for now; just click OK.

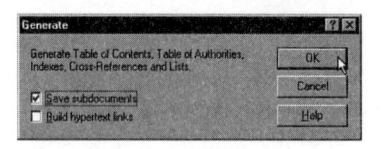

Click the Save button on the Toolbar to name and save your document, and your newsletter is done in record time.

As fast as you did the job this time, your next newsletter will be even faster. Any formatting changes you made in the Newsletter Expert dialog box will load the next time you cook up a newsletter. The job will be done so fast, in fact, that you'll have plenty of time to persuade somebody else to do the chore next time.

Fig. 10.12
You might want to put the table of contents on the first page of a multipage newsletter. If so, just drag it there.

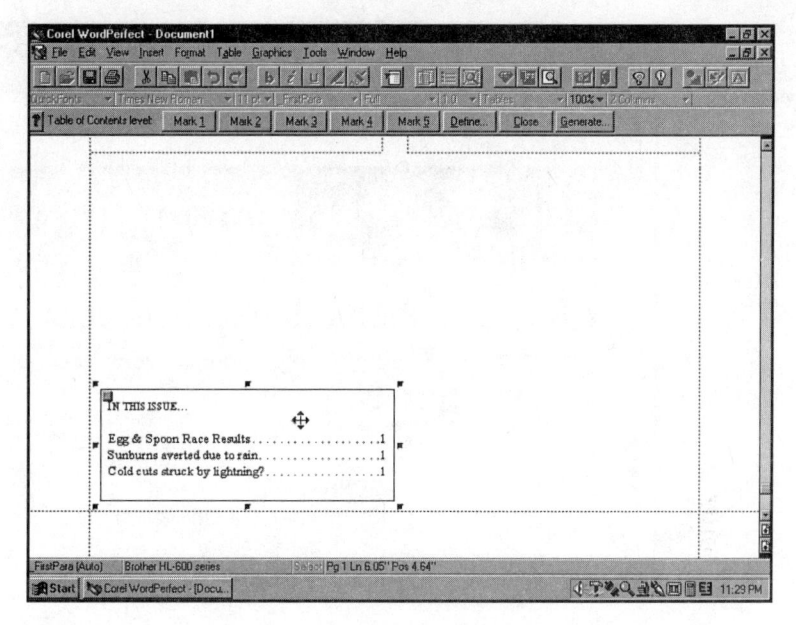

Can I create my own template?

Although the Newsletter Expert dialog box makes it easy enough to change the template's formatting, you may want to make formatting changes after you finish writing the newsletter. That lets you see how your own text looks with the new formatting. You might want to change fonts, for example, or shift the margins.

Formatting changes made outside the Newsletter Expert dialog box won't load the next time you run the Expert. But if you like your changes enough to reuse them, save your modifications as a new template.

Figure 10.13 shows the newsletter created in this chapter with some quick font changes.

Save your customized newsletter with a new file name, and close it. We'll call this effort Thinking News, Number 1. To save the customized newsletter as a new template:

1. Click the New Document button and select Options, New Template in the New Document dialog box. The template feature bar, shown in figure 10.14, displays.

Fig. 10.13
Customizing existing templates is easy with a few font changes.

Fig. 10.14
The template feature bar provides the tools for building your own template.

2. Click the Insert File button; then find and double-click the file name of your customized template document. Click Yes to insert the document and Yes again to overwrite existing styles.

3. The customized newsletter appears in the editing window. Click Exit Template and Yes to save the changes.

4. The Save Template dialog box pops up next (see fig. 10.15). Enter a Description of the template, the Template name, and click the Template group to which you want to add the new template.

5. Click OK and the template is saved. To reuse it, just select it from the list in the New Document dialog box.

There are plenty of other templates in WordPerfect 7, for all sorts of specialized documents (see Chapter 2 for details on the Letter Expert template). The next time you're stuck with the chore of producing such a document, click the New Document button on the Toolbar, and browse the list of templates

Chapter 10 *Templates: The Express Route to Fancy Documents* **197**

before you start. Chances are there's a template there that'll save you a lot of time. And if you don't see something suitable, make your own template, as we just did.

Fig. 10.15
Saving new templates preserves them for future use.

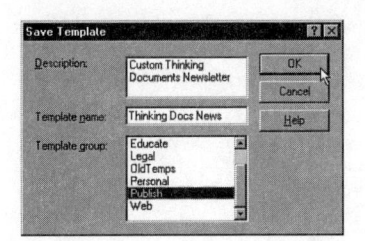

11

Documents with Style(s)

● **In this chapter:**

- I need some quick headings
- Can I copy formatiing from one paragraph to another?
- QuickFormat really is quick!
- Borders and fill make for stylish paragraphs
- How can styles save me time?
- I want my own style

Plain text is like white bread: functional, but not too exciting. WordPerfect's formatting tricks are jam for text>. . . . . . . ➤

Style isn't easy to achieve, or even to define. Lord Chesterfield, the 18th century wit, was an authority on the subject: "Style is the dress of thoughts," said Chesterfield. That's as neat a definition as we're ever likely to get, though not everyone is willing to concede Chesterfield the last word. Dr. Samuel Johnson skewered his contemporary in his own inimitable style: he'd thought Chesterfield "a lord among wits; but I find he is only a wit among lords."

True style is as hard to come by as it is to pin down, but not in WordPerfect. WordPerfect **styles** are collections of formatting commands that you can assemble and save. Use them to dress up your text, and you'll find that stylishness isn't so hard to achieve after all.

WordPerfect's canned headings, for instant style

The best style always feels unstudied and effortless. Great prose stylists work hard to hone their writing, but the reader isn't aware of their labors. We just admire the results. With WordPerfect's heading styles, you can achieve good results with absolutely no labor at all. Click a heading, click the Power Bar Styles button, choose one of the heading styles, and you're done.

There are five different heading styles to choose from, each one with a different emphasis. You might use Heading 1 for a document title, and Heading 2 for the most important topic headings. Subtopic headings are candidates for Heading 3, 4, and 5 styles, depending on their importance. Figure 11.1 illustrates how to use WordPerfect's built-in heading styles.

The selected heading style is applied to the current paragraph (the paragraph adjacent to or containing the insertion point). The paragraphs that follow or precede the current paragraph aren't affected. If none of the canned heading styles appeals to you, read on.

Fig. 11.1
For stylish documents in a hurry, use WordPerfect's built-in heading styles.

Use Heading 2 for important topics.

Click a heading in the document; then click the heading style to apply it.

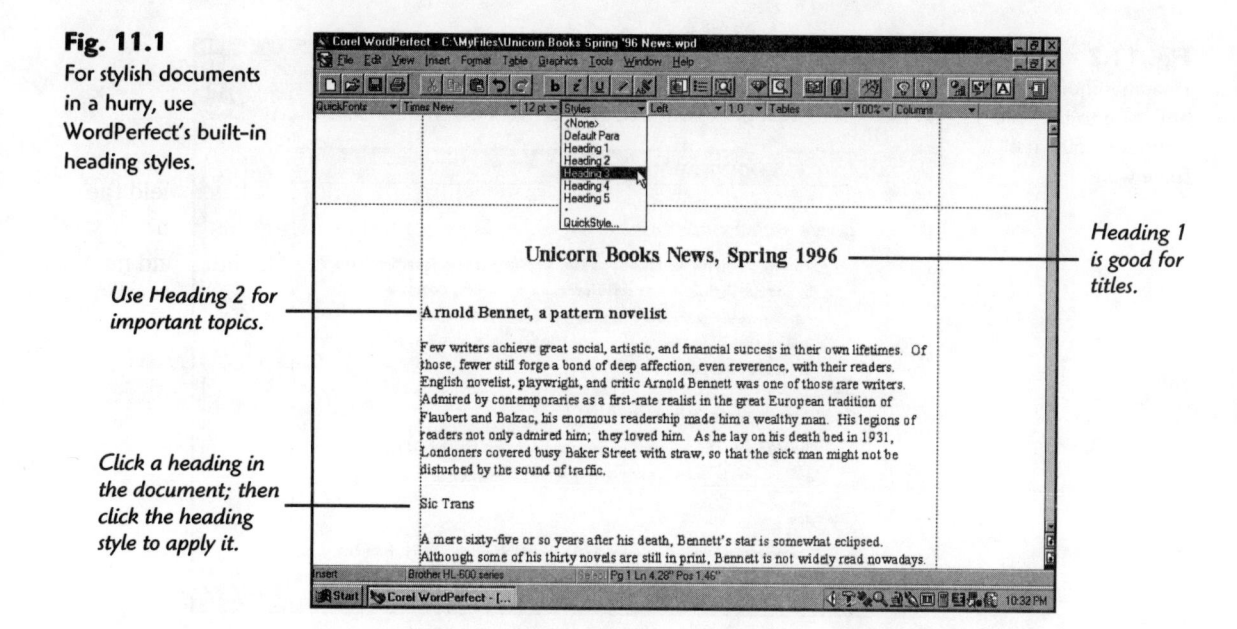

Heading 1 is good for titles.

QuickFormat provides quick style

WordPerfect's canned headings are fine, but you'll want your own heading styles as well. All the formatting features are so easy to use that perfecting a heading takes no time at all. Once you've whipped up a mix of formatting commands that looks right, wouldn't it be great if you could copy the formatting from that first heading and "paste" it on your other headings? You can!

QuickFormat grabs the formatting you've applied to text and paints it over unformatted text. It's just like mixing paints on a palette to get a particular shade, then dipping a brush in the paint and applying it to a plain surface.

QuickFormat starts with formatting

QuickFormat is especially handy for headings in a short report or newsletter.

The headings shown in figure 11.2 are on the plain side. We'll format the first heading and then use QuickFormat to copy the formatting to the other headings on the page.

To format text, then copy and apply the formatting elsewhere with QuickFormat:

Fig. 11.2
Headings should call attention to the text, but these could use some work.

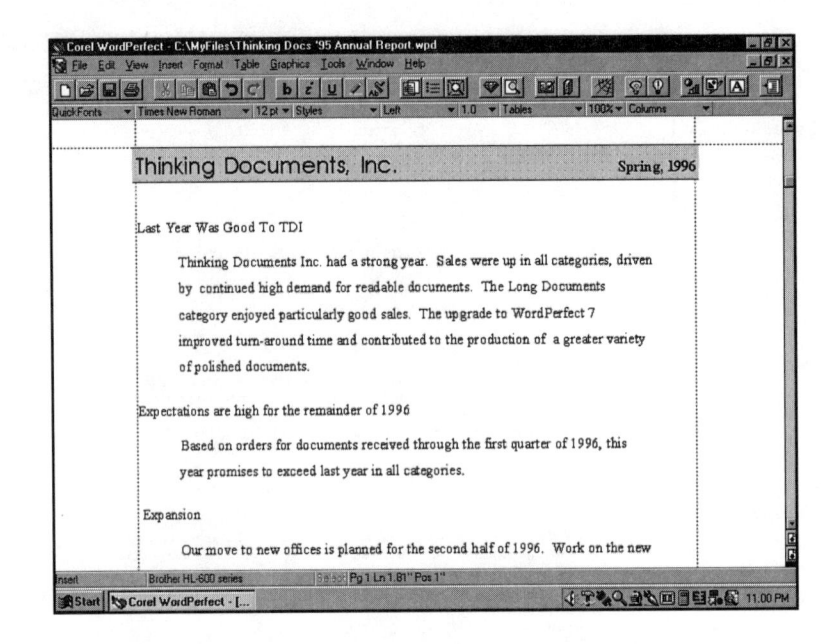

1. Triple-click the heading to select it. Click the Power Bar Font Face button, and select Arial to change fonts.

2. Click the Font Size button and choose 14 point. Click the Bold button on the Toolbar to apply boldface. Sans serif fonts (fonts without those little tails on the characters) like Arial work well in headings. A slightly larger size and boldface make them stand out.

3. To copy the formatting to the other headings, click the formatted heading. Then click the QuickFormat button on the Toolbar. That pops up the QuickFormat dialog box, shown in figure 11.3.

Fig. 11.3
With the insertion point in a heading, QuickFormat automatically selects Headings in the dialog box.

4. With Headings selected in the QuickFormat dialog box, click OK.

5. The pointer grows a little paint roller. Point at the heading you want to format and click. The text of the second heading instantly acquires the formatting of the first heading, as shown in figure 11.4.

Fig. 11.4
While the pointer sports that little paint roller, you can keep applying the copied formatting.

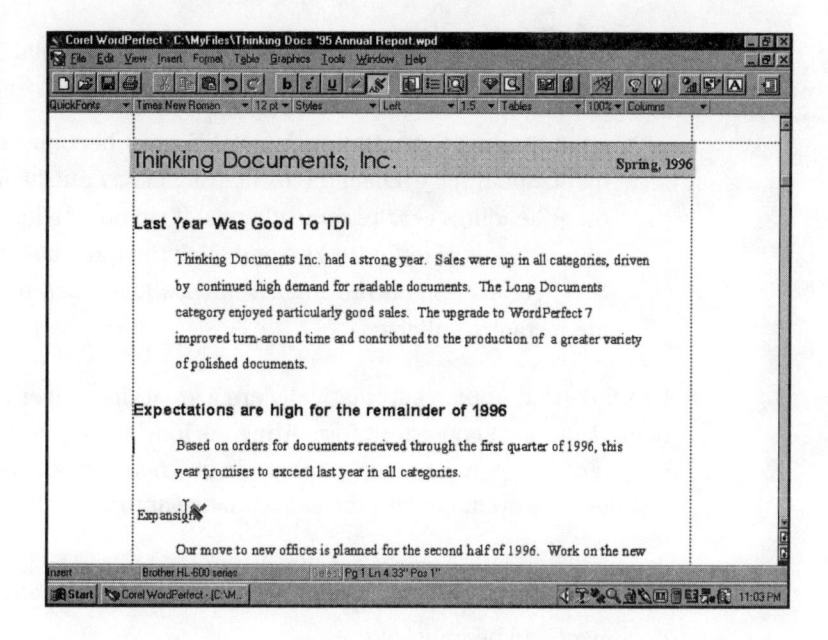

6 Click your other headings if you want them formatted the same way. When you finish, click the QuickFormat button on the Toolbar to turn off QuickFormat.

> **TIP** When you copy formatting with QuickFormat, WordPerfect names the formatting **QuickFormat1**. Use QuickFormat to copy a second batch of formatting, and you get **QuickFormat2**, and so on. Those numbered QuickFormats appear on the Power Bar Styles button list, along with the built-in headings we looked at earlier. To apply any of the numbered QuickFormats to the current paragraph, click the Power Bar Styles button and choose the QuickFormat you want from the drop-down list.

QuickFormat's magic trick: automatic updating

Once you've created a combination of font face and attributes you like, you can always select some text, click the QuickFonts button on the Power Bar, and apply that font to the selected text. So why bother with QuickFormat at all? For one thing, QuickFormat will copy other formatting attributes such as borders and fill (keep reading), not just fonts. QuickFormat can also save you time in two ways:

- You don't have to select text to apply a QuickFormat to it. Simply click the paragraph with the QuickFormat paint roller.

- Each heading formatted with QuickFormat becomes linked for automatic updating. Change the formatting in any one heading, and all the other headings get the same change. If we put the insertion point in any of the headings in figure 11.4 and click the Italic button on the Toolbar, that heading *and all the other headings formatted with QuickFormat* are instantly italicized.

Headings that update automatically are a great time-saver if you value documents with consistent formatting. As long as they're formatted with QuickFormat, you can make changes in one heading, and all your other headings are updated with the same change automatically.

Automatic updating works for WordPerfect's built-in heading styles as well. Italicize a Heading 2 heading, and all the other Heading 2 headings in the document will be italicized.

Can I copy formatting from character to character?

QuickFormat also works for individual characters, words, or sentences. Suppose we want to make all the initial capitals of `Thinking Documents Inc.` 28 points and bold. After formatting the first character, use QuickFormat to format the other characters:

1 Select the character and apply formatting to it. Use italics, boldface, a different font, whatever you like.

2 Click the QuickFormat button to display the QuickFormat dialog box. Select Characters and click OK; the pointer acquires a little paintbrush (see figure 11.5).

3 Drag through the text you want to format, as seen in figure 11.5.

4 When you release the mouse button, the formatting you've copied with QuickFormat is applied to the text.

Characters "painted" with the QuickFormat paintbrush aren't linked like headings formatted with the QuickFormat paint roller. Characters don't get a QuickFormat style, so they don't automatically update when you change one of the characters' attributes.

Fig. 11.5
When you QuickFormat text instead of paragraphs, the pointer acquires a paintbrush.

QuickFormat uses a paint roller to copy heading formats, and this paintbrush for character formats.

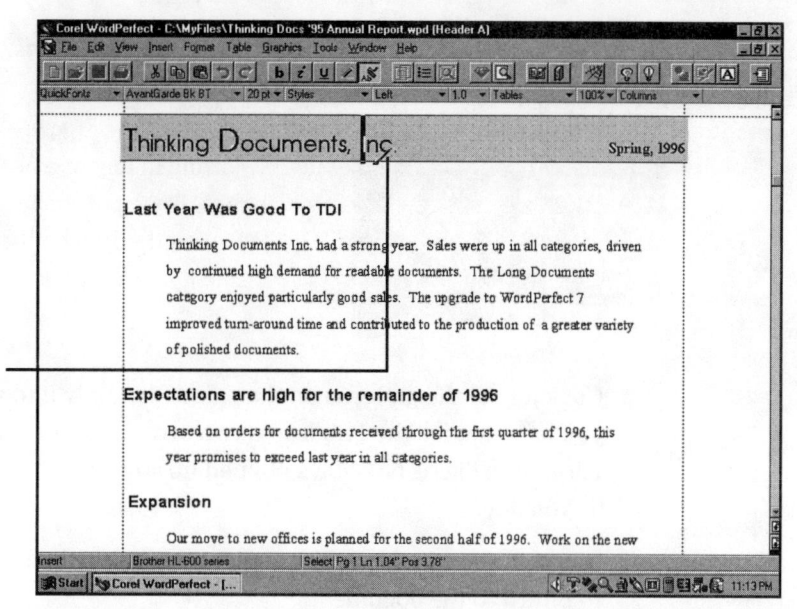

What is fill, and how do I use it?

That gray background seen in the heading in figure 11.5 is called **fill**. It's a pattern made up of lines or dots that "fills" in the background behind a paragraph. It's strictly decorative; use fill to make text or headings stand out from the rest of the document, but don't overdo it. Fill is something that a reader quickly gets his fill of.

> ### Plain English, please!
> **Fill** is a pattern that you can apply to paragraph backgrounds or to characters in the paragraph foreground. Fill can be different levels or shades of gray, or designs made up of dots and lines. **Borders,** cousins of fill, are lines in different thicknesses above, below, or around text. Borders also include shadow effects.

To apply fill to a paragraph:

1 Move the pointer to the left margin of the paragraph you want to "fill" and click the QuickSpot that appears.

2 In the Paragraph dialog box that appears, click the Fill drop-down arrow. You see a palette of fill patterns, as shown in figure 11.6.

Fig. 11.6
Fill patterns range from the subdued to the positively gaudy.

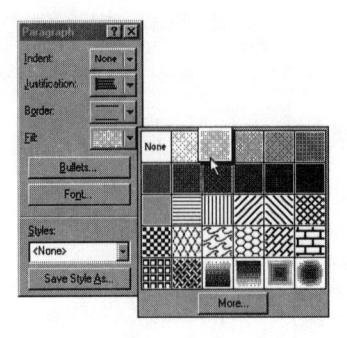

3. Click any of the patterns on the palette to apply it to your paragraph. If you hate it, click the Fill drop-down arrow and try another one. The Paragraph dialog box stays popped up so you can experiment as much as you like.

4. When you're satisfied, click anywhere outside the Paragraph dialog box to return to the document.

Applying borders works just like applying fill. Click the Border drop-down arrow in the Paragraph dialog box for any of the many border options.

Trial and error is the way to proceed with borders and fill. It's easy to mix and match from the Paragraph dialog box, and eventually you'll get the effect you want.

If you want to apply the same border and fill mix to several paragraphs, format the first one, and then use QuickFormat to apply the formatting to your other paragraphs. And to get rid of borders and fill, click the QuickSpot next to the formatted paragraph, and select None on the Border and Fill palettes.

Just what is a style?

Like a QuickFormat, you can use **styles** to apply formatting commands to text. There's one big difference: styles name the formatting you've assembled and save it for future use.

Instead of mixing paints on a palette to get a special shade, styles are like mixing the paints right in the can. Name your creation, label the can of paint, and—the next time you want that shade—just grab the can off the paint shelf.

Like those cans of paint, styles not only have names; there's even a shelf to store them on.

What can I do with styles?

Create styles for any headings or titles that need to be formatted the same way every time. Newsletter headlines are good candidates for a style; also report titles, section headings, and chapter titles.

You can apply several different styles in the same document for a consistent, professional look from one document to the next.

QuickStyles, for styles the quick way

There are two ways to get paint. You can go hiking to collect ores, grind them up for pigment, mix them with a liquid, and hope that you wind up with something usable. Or you can go to the hardware store and buy a can.

You have a similar choice with styles. You can make them from scratch, or you can use QuickStyles.

QuickStyles grab formatting from your document and turn it into a style. Created a heading whose formatting you'd like to preserve and use again? Use QuickStyles to turn it into a style.

To make a QuickStyle out of your formatting creation:

1 Click the paragraph whose formatting you're turning into a style; then click the Power Bar Styles button, and choose QuickStyle, as seen in figure 11.7.

2 That pops up the QuickStyle dialog box. Type a name for your style, and add a brief description, as shown in figure 11.8.

Create QuickStyles for entire paragraphs, single characters, or any selected text, exactly as we've created the chapter title style here.

Fig. 11.7
The Styles button shows the default styles; as you use other styles, they're added to the list.

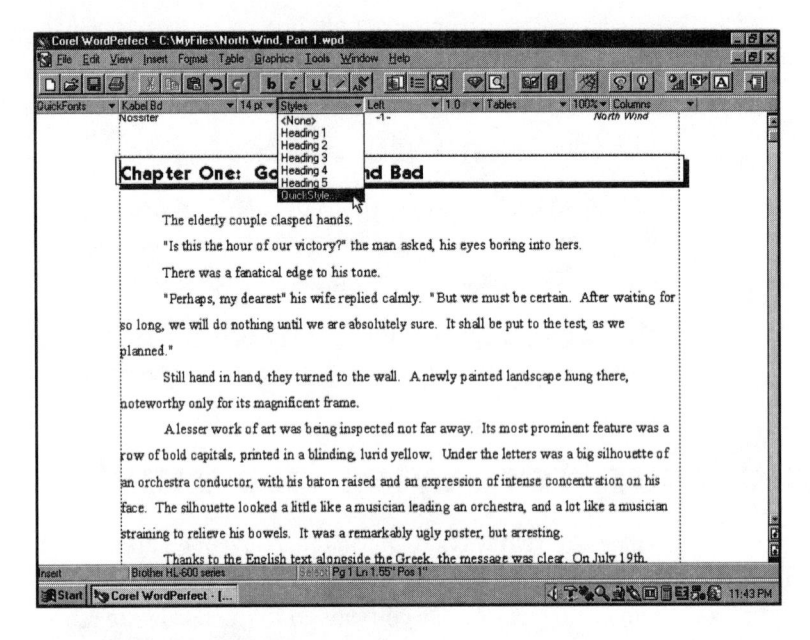

Fig. 11.8
Give your paragraph style a short name and a longer description.

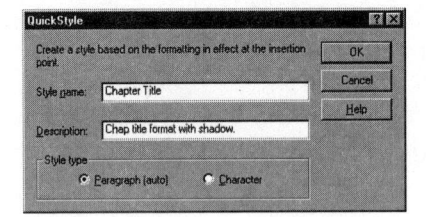

3 Click OK. The style name is added to the Power Bar Styles button list.

How do I apply my new style?

Creating a QuickStyle is quick; applying it is even quicker:

1 Click the paragraph you want to apply the style to; then click the Power Bar Styles button. In figure 11.9, we'll style that plain-looking chapter title.

2 Click the style you want, Chapter Title here, and the paragraph is instantly formatted in that style, as shown in figure 11.10.

Fig. 11.9
Once your style is created, apply it with two clicks.

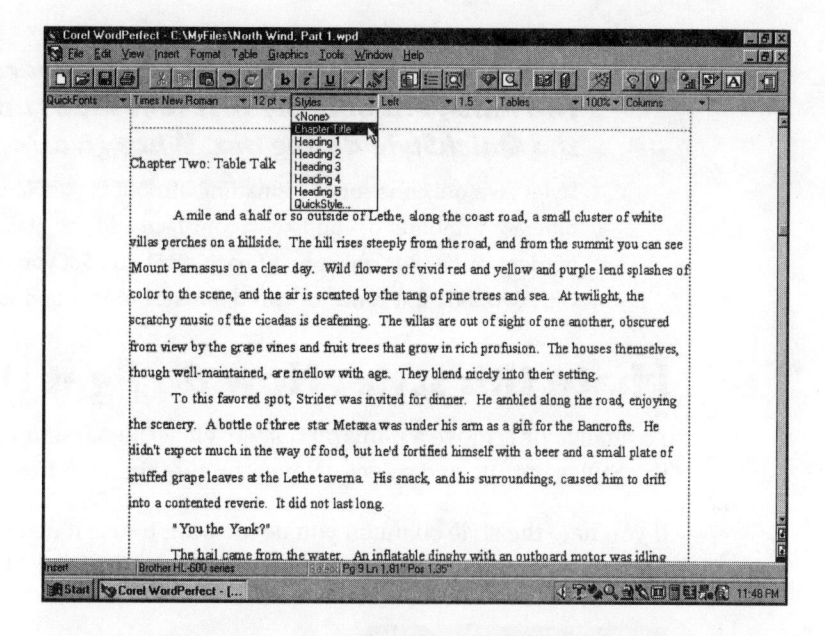

Fig. 11.10
Styles create consistent headings within documents, and from one document to another.

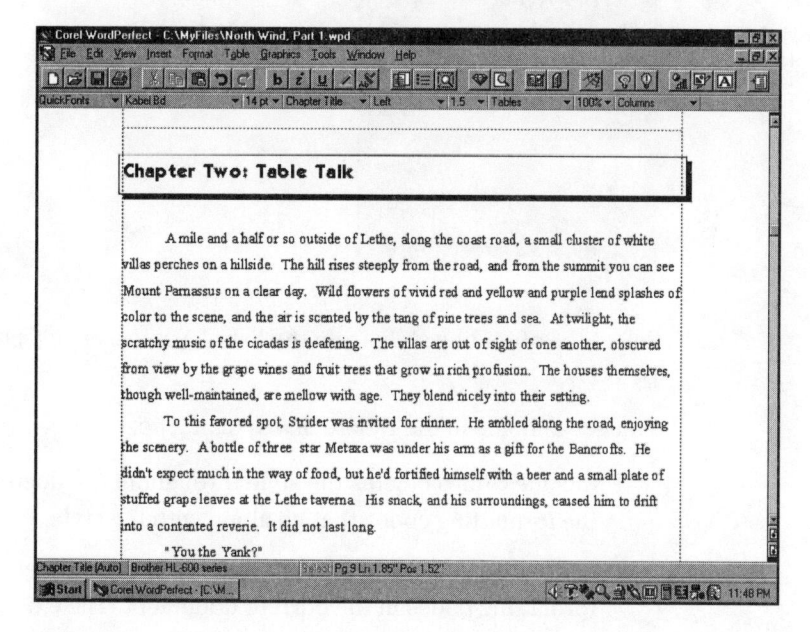

Q&A *I tried to create a QuickStyle from a paragraph with two fonts, but only the first font shows up when I quit the QuickStyle dialog box. What gives?*

Styles save only one set of formatting attributes. A style can have as many different attributes as you like—a font face and size, italics, boldface, borders, or fill. But only one of each attribute. So, you can't have a style with two different fonts, or two different borders, and so on.

I hate this style. How do I get rid of it?

To change or remove a paragraph style, click the paragraph, click the Power Bar Styles button, and select <None> or another style from the list.

If you hate the style so much you never want to use it again, select Fo_r_mat, Styles to see the Style List dialog box shown in figure 11.11.

Fig. 11.11
Manage styles in the Style List dialog box.

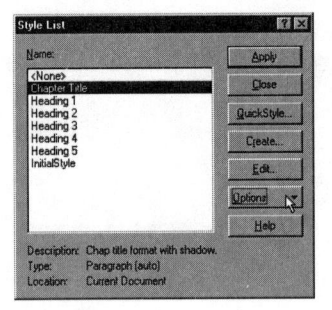

Select the offending style from the list of Names, click Options, and choose Delete.

You get a choice in the Delete Styles dialog box:

- Include Codes deletes the style throughout the document and removes the formatting codes that go along with the style.

- Leave Codes deletes the style from your style collection, but leaves the formatting codes in the current document. The existing formatting in the document won't change, but it'll no longer be a style.

Q&A *I accidentally applied a style to a paragraph. How do I get rid of the style?*

If you catch the mistake immediately, click the Undo button on the Toolbar. Otherwise, click the paragraph and select None from the Styles button on the Power Bar.

This style needs restyling

Even if you don't hate your style enough to delete it, you may find it mildly unsatisfactory. You might want to change a font, for example, or add or remove a border. If that's the case, just edit your style.

Click Format, Styles, Edit for the Styles Editor dialog box, shown in figure 11.12.

Fig. 11.12
Edit the formatting codes or add formatting commands from the Styles Editor menu bar.

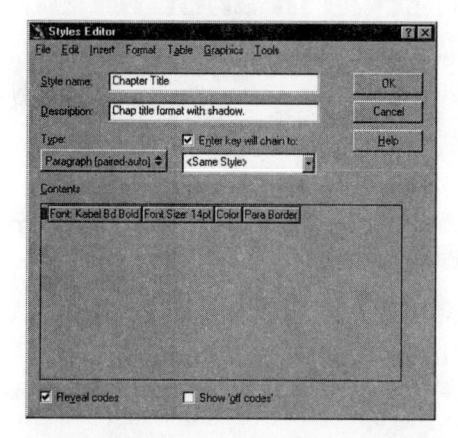

In the Styles Editor dialog box, make any changes you like to your style. Get rid of formatting codes by dragging them out of the Contents window. Add codes with the menu bar commands, which put all the WordPerfect formatting features at your disposal.

The Styles Editor dialog box also has a useful option for controlling the way styles are applied to your text as you type.

By default, if you select a style and begin to type, the style stays on until you turn it off or change it from the Power Bar. If you want to turn off a style when you press Enter at the end of the paragraph, click the Enter Key will Chain to: drop-down arrow and select <None>. Make sure the Enter key will Chain to: check box is checked before you click OK in the Styles Editor dialog box.

Concoct your style from scratch

If you know exactly what you want from a style, make it from scratch. Select Format, Styles, Create for the Styles Editor dialog box. Choose any formatting commands you like from the dialog box menu bar. The codes appear in the Contents window when you make your choices. Name and describe the style, and click OK to save it.

You might find it easier to create styles from formatted text with the QuickStyles command we've looked at already. You wind up with the same thing: a named style to apply to text. And with QuickStyles, you can get your style just right by experimenting on text first.

I want this style in another document

Styles you create in one document are saved with the document. They're also only available in that document. You might want to apply a style created in one document to text in other documents, too.

To grab a style from one document so you can use it in the current document, select Format, Styles, Options, Retrieve; you get the Retrieve Styles From dialog box shown in figure 11.13.

Either type the file name of the document with the style you want, or click the Select File button, and select the file from the list.

Choose the User Styles option button, and then click OK. Click Close in the Style List dialog box. The style appears on the Power Bar Select Style button in your current document.

Fig. 11.13
Share styles among documents by retrieving them into the current document.

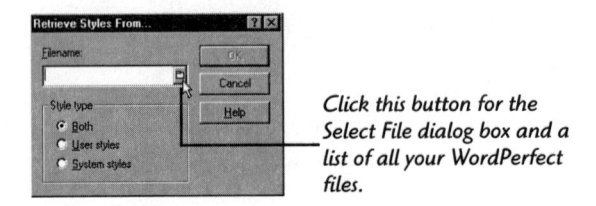

Click this button for the Select File dialog box and a list of all your WordPerfect files.

CAUTION **If WordPerfect prompts you to Overwrite Current Styles, answer** No, or you ay lose other styles in your current document.

12

WordPerfect's Labor-Saving Devices

● **In this chapter:**

- How can I trim these typing chores?

- WordPerfect abbreviations cut typing down to size!

- Put that little black book where it belongs—in WordPerfect

- What's a macro?

- Creating macros is easy...

- Playing macros is even easier!

Time spent on chores like typing is time stolen from thinking (or golf). WordPerfect has great gadgets to free you from routine jobs. . . . . ▸

Monday morning in the Age of Gadgets. The automatic alarm goes off. The automatic coffee maker goes on. Electric hair dryers compete with electric razors for air time. Toast springs eternal from electric toasters; less easily identified foodstuffs emerge from microwave ovens. Automatic garage doors open for our favorite mechanical marvel. Gadgets aren't necessities, but just picture Mondays without them.

WordPerfect's labor-saving devices aren't necessities either. But, if you value your hair dryer and coffee maker, take a minute to learn about macros, abbreviations, and the electronic address book. Put them to good use, and you'll have more time to figure out that VCR.

Save typing with abbreviations

We never stop to think about common abbreviations like Mr., Mrs., or Dr. Glance at Mr. on the page, and your mind automatically expands it to Mister. That's exactly what WordPerfect does with abbreviations.

Create a WordPerfect abbreviation, type it in a document, click it, and then press Shift+Ctrl+A to instantly expand it. Use abbreviations for words or phrases you type all the time. If you type your company name or address frequently, abbreviate it. Editors given to repeating phrases like "this is not clear," can abbreviate it to "tnc" and save themselves time. Government and corporate officials with acronym-laden documents find this feature particularly handy.

To create an abbreviation:

1. Select the text that you want to abbreviate and click Insert, Abbreviations, Create. Figure 12.1 shows selected text and the Create Abbreviation dialog box.

2. Type the abbreviation in the Abbreviation Name edit box shown in figure 12.1 and then click OK. Make the abbreviation as easy to remember as possible, using an obvious combination of letters. I've typed **tda** for Thinking Documents address.

Fig. 12.1
The more obvious you make the abbreviation name, the easier it'll be to remember.

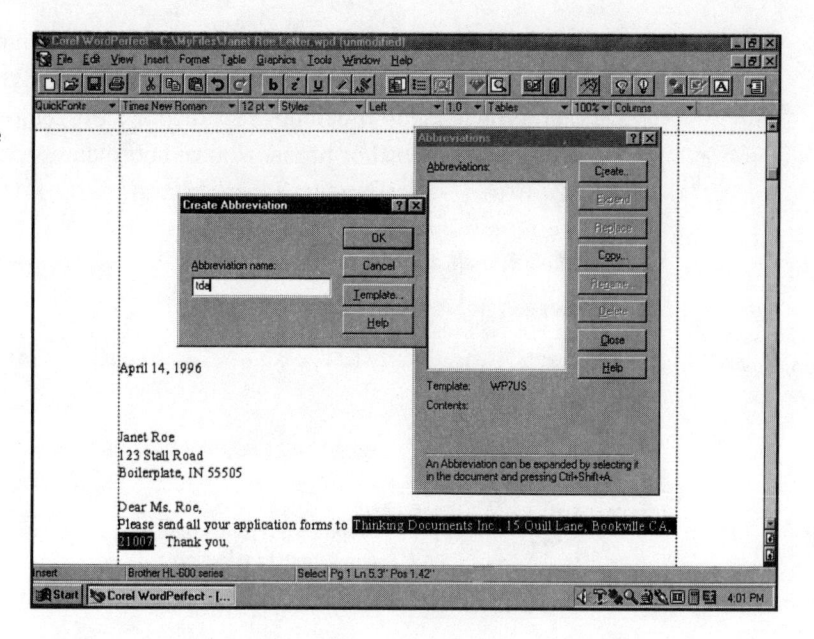

> **TIP**
>
> **Abbreviations are case-sensitive, which is a fancy way of saying** that if you name the abbreviation **TDA** with uppercase letters, you'll have to type **TDA** every time you use it. So **tda**, in lowercase, won't work. But because entries in Abbreviations are case-sensitive, you can use both **TDA** and **tda** as abbreviation names. That's handy if you want to abbreviate both the Thinking Documents address and "Theodore Delano Asquith."

> **Q&A**
>
> **I'm typing my lowercase abbreviation at the beginning of a sentence and it doesn't work! What's going on?**
>
> QuickCorrect is the culprit. QuickCorrect automatically capitalizes the first letter of a sentence, making lowercase abbreviations inoperable. You can out-persist QuickCorrect; it gives up after one, or sometimes two, corrections. Press Del or Backspace to get rid of the incorrectly capitalized letter, then retype the lowercase letter. Repeat the procedure if QuickCorrect corrects you again.

> **TIP**
>
> **If you find deleting and retyping a nuisance, you can also turn off** QuickCorrect's automatic capitalization: select Tools, QuickCorrect, Options for the QuickCorrect Options dialog box. Clear the Capitalize First Letter check box and click OK.

3 Click OK in the Create Abbreviation dialog box. Your new abbreviation is added to the list in the Abbreviations dialog box. Select the abbreviation on the list, and the dialog box displays the template where it's saved, and the word or phrase you've abbreviated, as shown in figure 12.2.

Fig. 12.2
The Abbreviations dialog box displays the abbreviation and what it stands for.

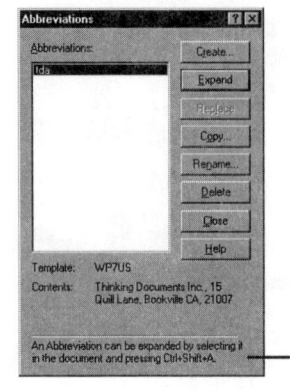

Despite what it says here, you don't have to select an abbreviation to expand it—clicking it is sufficient.

Click Close, and we're through. For a quick reminder of your abbreviations, just select Insert, Abbreviations to pop up the Abbreviations dialog box. Select an abbreviation and read the Contents to jog your memory.

Abbreviate your typing chores: use abbreviations

Once you've created an abbreviation, just type it wherever you want the word or phrase it represents. If you want to expand the abbreviation right away, position the insertion point in or adjacent to the abbreviation and press Shift+Ctrl+A. The abbreviation is instantly expanded. Otherwise, just keep typing, adding abbreviations as you go along.

Q&A Why can't I get this #$@! abbreviation to expand?

Chances are, you're not in or next to the abbreviation. Hitting the Spacebar after typing a word is the natural thing to do, but once the insertion point goes beyond the abbreviation, Shift+Ctrl+A won't work to expand it. Make sure the insertion point is in or adjacent to the abbreviation before pressing Shift+Ctrl+A.

How about expanding all my abbreviations at once?

Once you've created a collection of abbreviations, you can put your typing on the express train. Figure 12.3 shows a memo full of abbreviations (they're in boldface so you can see what's going on).

Fig. 12.3
Abbreviations save time; combined with a button to expand them, they'll save even more time.

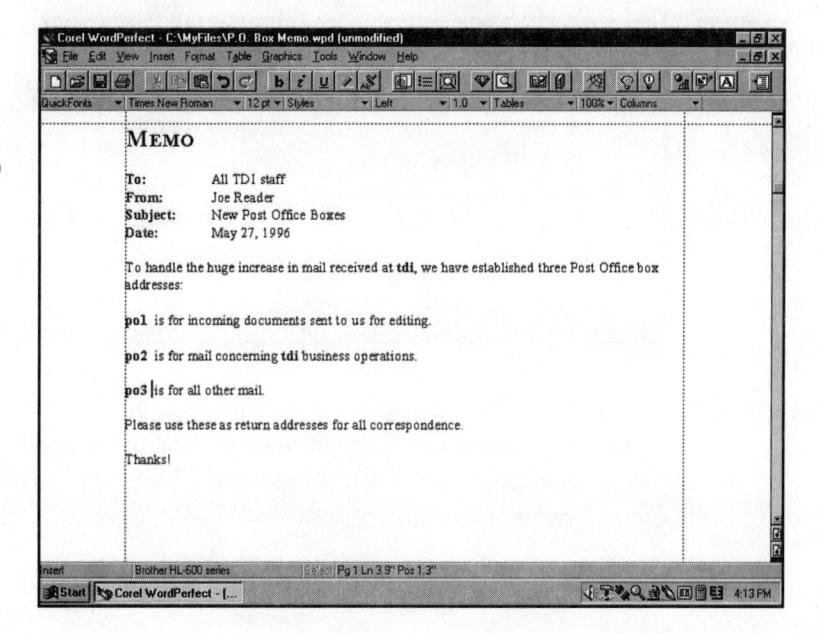

Typing the abbreviations is fast. Expanding each abbreviation as you work can slow you down, and going back and expanding each one is a nuisance. WordPerfect has a handy button that expands all your document's abbreviations at once, which takes care of both roadblocks. To get, and use, the Toolbar Expand All button:

1 Right-click the Toolbar for the Toolbar QuickMenu and select Utilities.

2 Click the Expand All button on the Toolbar. That expands all the abbreviations at once, as shown in figure 12.4.

3 To get the regular Toolbar back, right-click the Toolbar and select WordPerfect 7 on the QuickMenu.

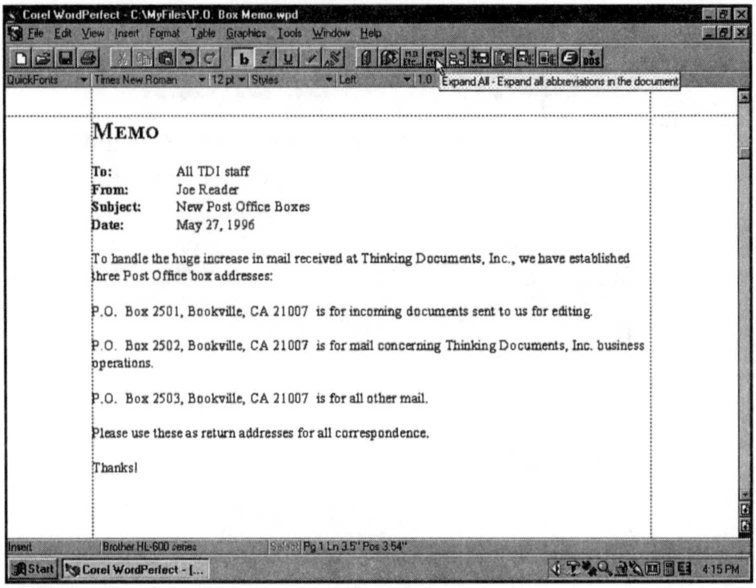

Fig. 12.4
Point at the other buttons on the Utilities Toolbar for their names and descriptions of what they do—some are pretty handy.

TIP **If you like this feature, you can add the abbreviations Expand All** button to the standard Toolbar. See Chapter 20 on how to rearrange and create toolbars.

I need to change these abbreviations

Click Insert, Abbreviations for the Abbreviations dialog box to do any of the following:

- Delete abbreviations: select the abbreviation from the list, and click Delete, Yes.
- Rename abbreviations: select the abbreviation from the list and click Rename. Type a new name in the Rename Abbreviation dialog box and click OK.
- Replace the text the abbreviation stands for: select the new text; then click Insert, Abbreviations and choose the abbreviation from the list. Click Replace, Yes to replace the old text with the new selection.

I want this abbreviation in another template

You might create an abbreviation in a letter template, but you need to use it in a report template. To copy an abbreviation from one template to another:

Chapter 12 *WordPerfect's Labor-Saving Devices* **219**

1 Click Insert, Abbreviations for the Abbreviations dialog box.

2 Click the Copy button for the Copy Abbreviation dialog box.

3 Select the abbreviation you want to copy from the Select Abbreviation to Copy list.

4 Click the Template to copy to drop-down arrow, and select a template, as shown in figure 12.5.

Fig. 12.5
Select a template from the drop-down list to copy your abbreviation to it.

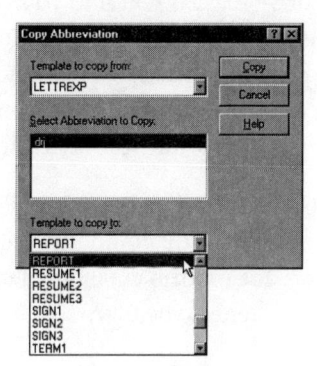

5 Click Copy and then Close in the Abbreviations dialog box.

TIP If you want to make the abbreviation for all of your new blank documents, copy the abbreviation to the WP7US template.

What's a macro?

As useful as they are, household and office gadgets are only tools to help us get the job done. They can't do the job for us. The fax machine is a terrific device, but if we want to send a fax, we still have to load the document, dial a number, and press a button to send it.

We'd rather have an assistant on call all the time to do chores like faxing for us. The kind of assistant who'll remember how to do any job just by watching us do it once. An assistant who then does the job flawlessly whenever we want it done.

We have a helper like that in WordPerfect: a **macro**. The Expand All button we used earlier is a macro supplied with WordPerfect. One click, and it executes many expand abbreviation commands, saving us the bother.

> **66 Plain English, please!**
>
> A **macro**, in computer lingo, is a single command that executes a large, or macro, number of other commands. **99**

How can I create my own macro?

Macros are great for any repetitive task. If you find yourself doing the same WordPerfect chore all the time, create a macro to do it for you. Turn on the macro recorder, do your chore, and then turn off the macro recorder. Creating a macro is no harder than doing the chore itself. Even if it involves dozens of steps, a macro will take care of the whole job with one command.

Here's one repetitive chore not covered by an existing WordPerfect feature: setting up a generic document header. You could use such a header to turn out quick, all-purpose stationery for reports and such. Let's record a macro called HEADER.WCM to create a generic header:

1. Click <u>T</u>ools, <u>M</u>acro, <u>R</u>ecord for the Record Macro dialog box shown in figure 12.6.

> **CAUTION** If you record a macro while you're working on a document, it's a good idea to save your work before you start recording the macro. You're unlikely to run into memory or program glitches while recording macros, but on those rare occasions when you might, you don't want to risk losing your work.

2. Type a name in the <u>N</u>ame box. We'll call this macro **header**, as shown in figure 12.6.

Why is it called a macro?

Macro, the opposite of micro, comes from the Greek. As a prefix, macro means large or long. Think of microscopic—too tiny to see unaided; and macroscopic, meaning visible to the naked eye. If your colleague's new promotion goes to his head, tell him he's macrocephalic, meaning big-headed. And if an author is putting you to sleep, he's becoming macrostylous, or long-styled.

Fig. 12.6
The Record Macro dialog box displays a list of the macros that come with WordPerfect and those that you create yourself.

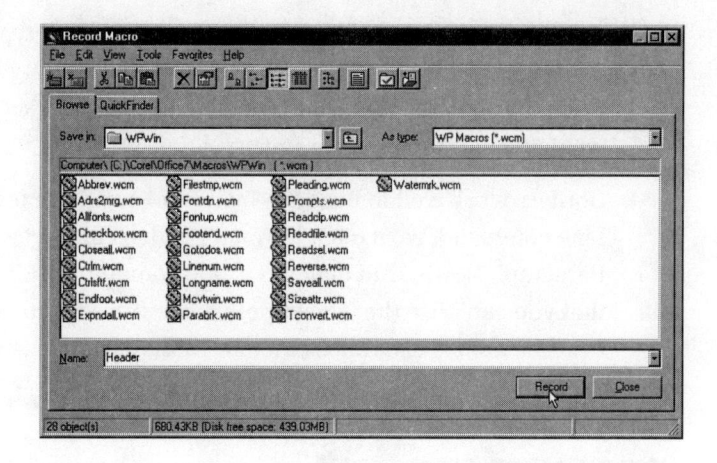

3. Click Record to turn on the macro recorder. The dialog box disappears and the macro feature bar pops up. Until we turn the macro recorder off again, every mouse click we make and every command we execute will be recorded.

Q&A *Why did my pointer turn into a circle with a line through it when I started recording my macro?*

Although you can use the mouse to click buttons and choose menu commands, you can't select text or move the insertion point with the mouse while recording a macro. The circle with a line across it (the international "NO" symbol) is a gentle reminder of that fact. Instead, use the arrow keys to move the insertion point and the Shift+arrow key combination to select text while recording macros.

4. With the macro recording, we'll start doing our chore. Click Format, Header/Footer, select Header A, and click Create.

5. We'll stick our company name in here, **Thinking Documents, Inc**. Use your company name, your own name, a font of your own choosing, or whatever other text you want in the header.

6. Press Shift+F7 to center the next text and click Number, Page Number on the header feature bar to insert page numbering if you want it. If you make a typing mistake while recording a macro, correct it and carry on, just as though you were editing an ordinary document. It's the end result of your typing and corrections that matters.

7. Press Alt+F7 to align the next text flush right, and type the document author's name if you want it there. All the formatting commands are available from the menu and Toolbar, so apply italics, boldface, and whatever else strikes your fancy.

8. Borders work well in headers. Instead of using the feature bar Insert Line command, we'll click Format, Border/Fill, Paragraph for the Paragraph Border/Fill dialog box and something more decorative. Note that you can't use the QuickSpots while you're recording a macro because mouse clicking inside the editing window isn't allowed.

9. Click the Border tab for the choice of borders shown in figure 12.7.

Fig. 12.7
The Paragraph Border/Fill dialog box offers more variety than the header feature bar Insert Line button.

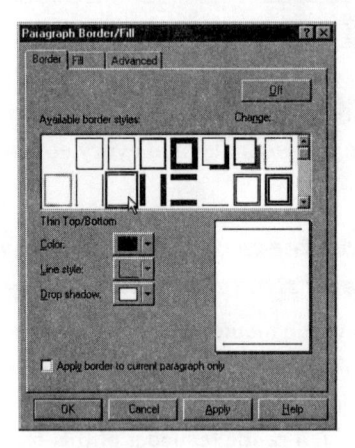

10. Click your choice from the Available border styles; I've selected the Thin Top/Bottom border, the third choice on the second row. Click OK once you've made your selection.

11. Click Close on the header feature bar, and click the Stop Macro button on the macro feature bar shown in figure 12.8.

The macro feature bar should vanish when you click the Stop Macro button. If it doesn't, click Options, Remove Macro Bar.

HEADER.WCM is born. It took a dozen or so steps to create this simple header. The next time we want it, a couple of clicks will take care of the whole thing.

Macros aren't confined to creating headers—any repetitive chore can be automated with a macro. Once you start creating macros, you'll wonder how you ever got along without them.

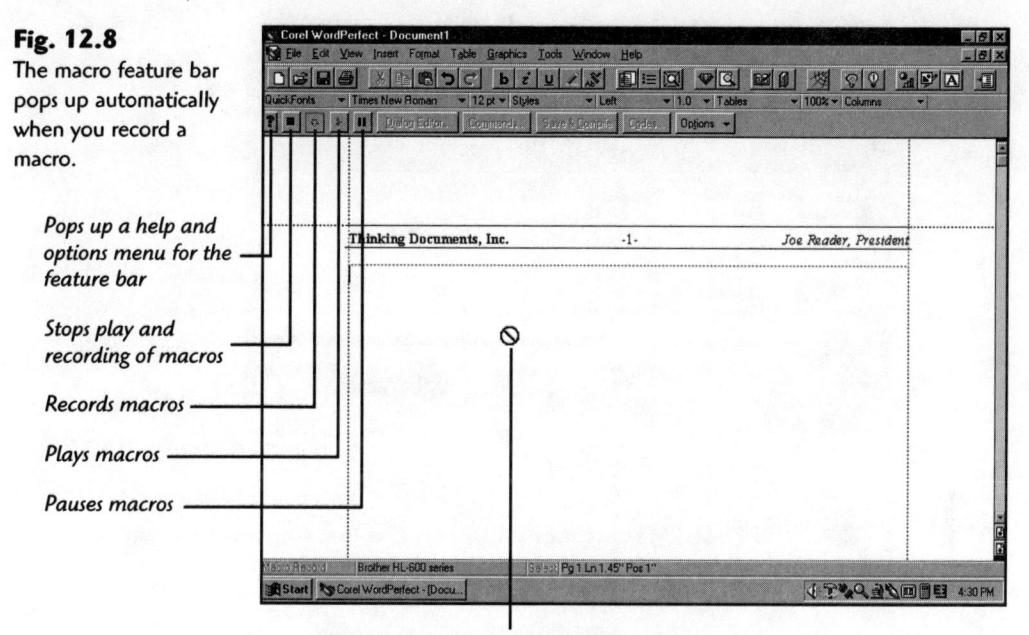

Fig. 12.8
The macro feature bar pops up automatically when you record a macro.

- Pops up a help and options menu for the feature bar
- Stops play and recording of macros
- Records macros
- Plays macros
- Pauses macros

The pointer takes this shape in the editing window while you're recording a macro.

How do I play it back?

Recording a macro is only as complicated as performing the task you record. Playing a macro back is always a snap, no matter how complex the underlying chore.

To play the HEADER macro you just created:

1 Click <u>T</u>ools, <u>M</u>acro, <u>P</u>lay for the Play Macro dialog box shown in figure 12.9.

2 Select a macro from the list; to play the macro we just created, scroll down to HEADER.WCM, and select it.

3 Click Play. All the typing we did and commands we issued while recording the macro are played back in the blink of an eye. The header pops into place on the page, and you're ready to write your document.

The macros on the list in the Play Macro dialog box are handy time-savers supplied by WordPerfect. Any of them can be run from Toolbar buttons, like the EXPNDALL.WCM macro we used to expand abbreviations. You can also play them from the Play Macro dialog box. Just select a macro and click Play.

Fig. 12.9
Macros are stored in files that can be renamed, deleted, and moved from the dialog box.

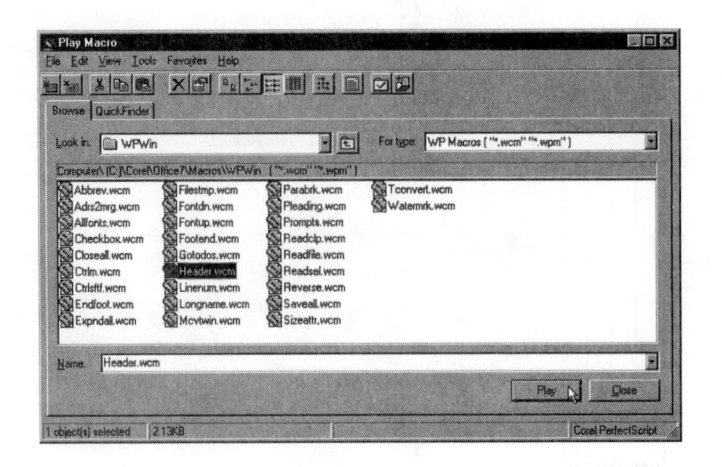

> **TIP** The **T**ools, **M**acros menu displays the last four macros you've used. Click one and then click OK to run it.

> **TIP** If you find a macro that's particularly useful, add it to your customized Toolbar. That way it'll never be more than a mouse click away. See Chapter 20 on how to do that.

This macro could use a few alterations

When you record your keystrokes and mouse clicks in a macro, some pretty amazing things go on behind the scenes. Macro recording sets in motion a kind of United Nations simultaneous translation team. As you perform them, your actions are translated, or **compiled**, into WordPerfect's macro language.

It's a language with its own vocabulary, punctuation, and syntax that's used to talk directly to WordPerfect. Normally, you communicate with the program through menus and buttons; the macro language bypasses the menus and issues commands directly to WordPerfect.

66 Plain English, please!

Macros consist of **commands** that WordPerfect understands. When you record a macro, WordPerfect arranges all the commands in the proper order, using correct **syntax**. We know syntax in English grammar as the rules that govern sentence construction. English isn't necessarily strict about syntax; writers break the rules all the time and call it poetic license. WordPerfect is more exacting. Macros require correct syntax in order to run. You can write macros, programming the commands yourself, as long as you use the proper syntax. WordPerfect's translation team sees to it that our actions are recorded with the proper syntax when we record macros. 99

Can I edit my macros?

Although macros are saved in the macro language, in other respects macro files are like ordinary WordPerfect files. All the program's editing features can be used in macro files. And, although macro language isn't English, it's close enough so that we don't have to learn it in order to edit it.

Why would you want to edit a macro in the first place? If you don't like the way it turns out, you can always delete the macro and start again. But, if you have a few minor alterations to make, editing the macro is often faster than re-recording the whole thing.

To edit a macro:

1 Click <u>T</u>ools, <u>M</u>acro, <u>E</u>dit for the Edit Macro dialog box.

CAUTION! **Editing macros can be a bit tricky. If you accidentally delete a** crucial punctuation mark, or even add a space in the wrong place, you can make your macro nonfunctional. Before you edit the macro, make a backup copy. Right-click the macro name in the Edit Macro dialog box, and choose Cop<u>y</u> To Folder on the QuickMenu. Choose a different folder in the Select Destination Folder For Copy dialog box that appears (one click of the Up One Level button takes you to the Macros folder, which is as good a place as any for your copy). Click C<u>o</u>py to finish the job.

2 Select the macro from the list in the Edit Macro dialog box, and click the Edit button. That puts the macro in the editing window and pops up the macro feature bar, as shown in figure 12.10.

Fig. 12.10
This is what the HEADER.WCM macro looks like in macro language.

Click in between the quotes to edit text in a macro.

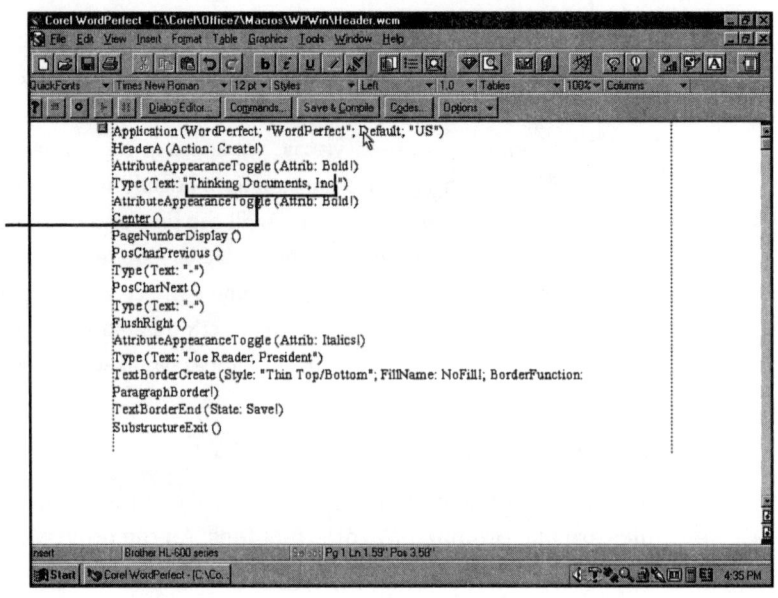

3. Most of your macro edits are likely to be changes in the text you typed while the macro was recording. Typed text appears in quotation marks inside parentheses preceded by Type and a space, as in `Type (Text: "Thinking Documents Inc.")` on line 7 in figure 12.10.

4. If you wanted a minor change, Inc. to Incorporated for example, just place the insertion point after the "c" in "Inc.," delete the period, and type **orporated**. Be careful not to move or delete any of the punctuation marks around the text.

5. When you finish editing your macro, click the Options button on the feature bar; then select Close Macro and click Yes to save the changes.

WordPerfect has an online macro guide

If you're inclined that way, WordPerfect has a complete online guide to macros. Press F1 for the Help Topics dialog box, click the Contents tab, and then double-click the Macros book icon to access it. There's help for problem macros, and what amounts to a manual for the macro language.

The macro language, PerfectScript, has a host of built-in commands that can make macros more useful. There are commands to do everything from typing today's date, to converting an angle in degrees to radians. To view the PerfectScript commands, choose Tools, Macro, Macro Bar, and click the Commands button on the macro feature bar that appears.

Your little black book is a click away

It's amazing how much vital information finds its way into an address book. Contacts, friends, family, and all the clues needed to get hold of them—it's all in there. Somewhere. If your address book is like mine, any alphabetical system you may have started with breaks down after a few months. Addresses and phone numbers change, entries are added and deleted, and in no time, that tidy little address book looks like a patchwork of crazy scrawls.

That's why you'll find the WordPerfect Address Book an invaluable adjunct to the program. It stores addresses and phone numbers in perfect alphabetical order no matter how much you edit the entries. It creates an automatic list of the names and numbers you access most often. And best of all, it'll stick any address you choose right into a WordPerfect envelope, label, or document of any kind. Putting a mass mailing together? WordPerfect's merge feature (see Chapter 13) can turn all your Address Book entries into mailing labels or envelopes automatically.

Add address entries to build your book

Add Address Book entries at will for whomever you plan to send documents, e-mail, or faxes. The Address Book can even dial phone numbers for you if you've got a modem. To add new entries to the Address Book:

1 Click the Address Book button on the Toolbar; then click the My Addresses tab in the Address Book dialog box.

2 Click <u>A</u>dd and the New Entry dialog box appears. Select Person or Organization and click OK.

3 If you selected Person in the New Entry dialog box, you'll see the Properties for New Entry dialog box shown in figure 12.11.

4 Type as much information as you care to store in the Properties for New Entry dialog box. Include phone numbers and e-mail addresses. If you fill in the <u>G</u>reeting box with something like Dear XYZ, that greeting can be used in the letter templates, saving you the bother of typing it every time.

5 Click OK to close the Properties for New Entry dialog box and return to the Address Book list display.

Fig. 12.11
Enter as many details as you wish about each new Address Book entry; type it once, and you'll never have to do it again.

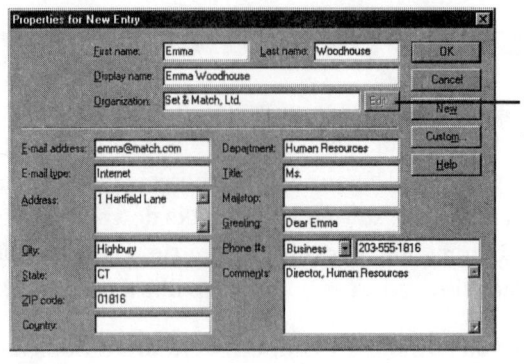

The Edit button is dimmed until you enter text in the Organization edit box, save the entry, and then return to the entry.

If your entry included an Organization name (see figure 12.11), the organization appears as a separate listing in the Address Book, identified by a little picture of an office building. To enter an address for the organization, click the listing in the Address Book and choose Edit, as shown in figure 12.12.

Fig. 12.12
Edit Address Book Organization listings to add a telephone number and address for the organization.

Organization entries are identified by a little picture of an office building.

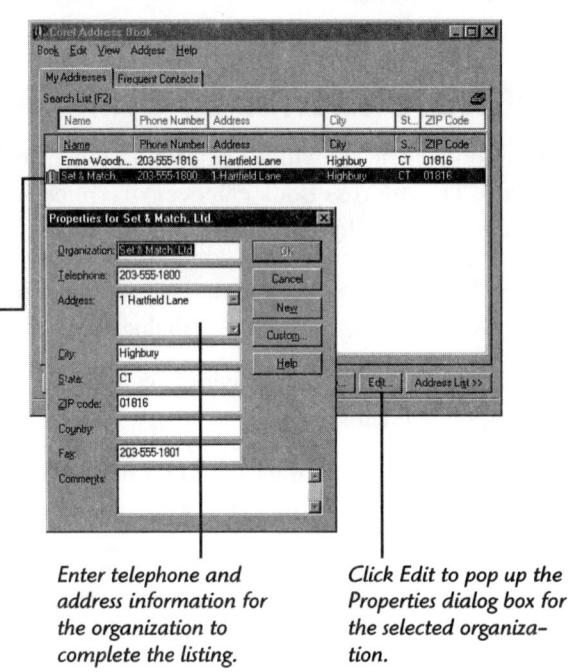

Enter telephone and address information for the organization to complete the listing.

Click Edit to pop up the Properties dialog box for the selected organization.

Click OK in the Properties dialog box shown in figure 12.12 to save the entry. To change any of the listings in the Address Book, select the listing and click Edit. Whenever you need your entry's address in a document or on an envelope or label, just click the Address Book button and double-click any of the entries. The address, neatly formatted, appears at the insertion point.

For all its virtues, that's one trick my little black book just can't do.

> **TIP** **Want to move an entry between address books? Just drag any** entry onto the tab of another book. To move an entry from the Personal Address Book to the My Addresses book, for example, click the Personal Address Book tab. Drag any entry on the list right onto the My Addresses tab. As you drag, the pointer is accompanied by a stick figure and a trash can. When the pointer is over an Address Book tab, the trash can vanishes. Release the mouse button, and the entry will drop into the address book whose tab you're pointing at. Don't release the mouse button until the trash can disappears; if you do, you'll delete your entry!

> **CAUTION** **Microsoft Exchange users might be tempted to click E̲dit, P̲refer-** ences in the Address Book and change their P̲referred profile from Corel Settings to Exchange Settings. **Don't do it!** As of this writing, a bug in the program will make your Address Book inoperative if you change profiles. The only fix if that happens is to remove the Corel WordPerfect Suite 7 from your computer and reinstall it.

13

Merges, for Letters by the Bushel

● **In this chapter:**

- What happens in a merge?

- Data files? Form files? Explain, please?

- You mean I already have a data file?

- Form files are very flexible

- I can do envelopes by the bushel too?

- How can I tell one dialog box from another?

Merges mass-produce documents on the assembly line principle, yet each finished document looks handmade . . . . ▶

Merging is a risky business, and recent history is full of mergers gone awry. Which isn't to say that mergers are always flops. When Maria Sklodowska (Marie Curie) married Pierre Curie, their merger resulted in the discovery of radioactivity and a shared Nobel prize in physics.

Word processor merges used to be seen as risky procedures, akin to hitching a big manufacturer to an investment bank. In WordPerfect, merges are more like the collaboration of the Curies: a sure thing.

What happens in a merge?

A WordPerfect merge produces documents on an assembly line. Henry Ford pioneered the idea when he built the Model T: you start with an empty shell of a car, systematically add parts from a supply bin, and end up with a finished automobile.

WordPerfect merges have the same three-part setup:

- The empty shell is called a **form file.** The form file is a document with blanks, such as a letter missing the recipient's name and address.
- The parts bin is called a **data file.** That's your WordPerfect Address Book, and it contains the items needed to fill in the blanks in the form file: names and addresses, for example. If you haven't had an opportunity to use the Address Book yet, now's your chance.
- **Merging** takes the data from the Address Book and sticks it in the appropriate blanks in the form file to produce finished documents.

When do I use a merge?

Like Henry Ford's assembly line, merges mass-produce finished products, quickly and with little effort. Whenever you have more than a couple of documents to produce, and the documents vary only slightly one from the other, use a merge.

With a merge, you can:

- Write one letter and send it to dozens of recipients, each letter personalized with the recipient's name and address.

- Produce labels by the gross, using one formatted label and a list of names and addresses.

- Create and update directories and other lists by merging data from the Address Book into a formatted document.

Those are some common uses of merges. Once you see how easy merges are, you'll think of plenty of other applications.

Merges start with a data file...

Here's a common chore: sending out letters announcing a change of address to your clients. A generic "Dear Sir or Madam" letter is fine, but maybe you'd like to personalize the letters to your best clients.

That's a fine opportunity for a merge. The body text is identical in each letter: the details of your new address. The only variations are the names and addresses of each client. The first step in a merge is assembling the data, all the names and addresses, and saving them in a file. Sounds like a lot of work? It isn't really. In fact, if you keep your WordPerfect Address Book updated, the job may already be done!

...And the data file is your Address Book

The Address Book is where you store the data for the merge. Exercise a little care in filling out your Address Book entries, and you'll build a powerful database with many handy uses, from sticking a single address in a quick envelope, to a mass mailing for an entire client list.

Click the Address Book button on the Toolbar, click Add in the Address Book. Then select Person in the New Entry dialog box and click OK. That pops up the Properties for New Entry dialog box (see fig. 13.1).

Although we aim to eschew jargon, here's some unavoidable database lingo that also happens to be merge-speak. You might not have thought of it exactly this way, but entries in the Address Book are actually made up of two building blocks: fields and records (see fig. 13.1).

- **Records** are like Rolodex cards. Each record contains all the information you want to use to fill in the blanks in a form file. Every entry stored in the Address Book is a record.

Fig. 13.1
The Address Book's Properties for New Entry dialog box provides the raw material for your merge.

Each item in the dialog box is a field.

The completed entries, consisting of all the fields, are records.

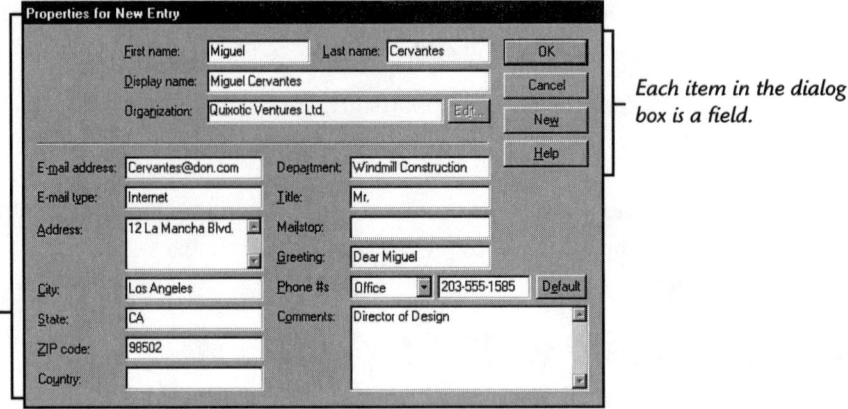

- **Fields** are separate items of data in a record. Last names, first names, company names, and street addresses are all distinct fields. The edit boxes in an Address Book record are fields.

Generally speaking, the more fields you include, the more flexible your records will be. The Address Book is a good place to store your records, because it breaks them down into many fields.

When you fill out the Properties for New Entry dialog box in the Address Book, enter your data with the idea of eventually putting each field in a letter, or on an envelope. In the Title field, for example, you'll want the appropriate title: Mr., Mrs., Ms., or Dr. The Comments field is more free-form, and you can use it for anything you like (see fig. 13.1 for one idea).

Once you get around to the merge itself, you can pick and choose which fields from the Address Book you want to use. You don't *have* to use them all, but fill in the fields as though you *might* use them all. Although the actual data entry isn't much fun, here's one consoling thought: you only have to enter a record once. Stick a client or contact or employee in your Address Book, and you can use and reuse the data as often as you like.

Form files are document shells

Entering your data in the Address Book is the biggest chore in a merge. Once that's done, creating a form file is a breeze. **Form files** contain the body text of your finished document with merge codes that'll be replaced by the Address Book fields in a merge.

Although the letter we're about to create will be written only once, after the merge, we'll have individualized copies to send to any of the people we select from the Address Book.

How do I make a form file?

Tackle the form file after you finish with your Address Book entries. Once you enter all your letter recipients in the Address Book, go ahead and close it (you can always open the Address Book again to add or edit your entries).

To create the form file:

1 Click the New Blank Document button on the Toolbar. In the blank document that appears, select Tools, Merge to pop up the Merge dialog box shown in figure 13.2.

Fig. 13.2
Here's the control panel for your merge. You already have a Data File—it's your Address Book.

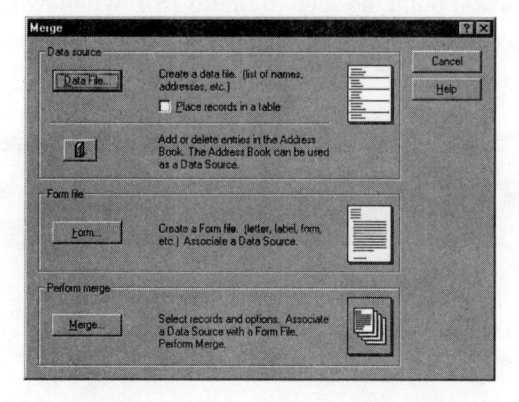

2 Click Form in the Merge dialog box to summon up the Create Form File dialog box.

3 In the Create Form File dialog box, choose the Associate an address book option and click the button below the option to choose which Address Book you want to use, as shown in figure 13.3.

4 Click OK in the Create Form File dialog box, and you're back in the editing window with the Merge feature bar displayed. Here's where we'll type our letter and insert all the codes that the merge will replace with Address Book data. As with any letter, the first thing we need is the return address. Since we already entered our personal information in the Address Book back in Chapter 2, here's our chance to dig it out and insert it in our form file (if you haven't entered your own name and

address in the Address Book, this might be a good time to take care of the chore). Click the Address Book button on the Toolbar, select the return address you want to use, and click Insert.

Fig. 13.3
Unless you created another address book, your data will be in the default My Addresses book.

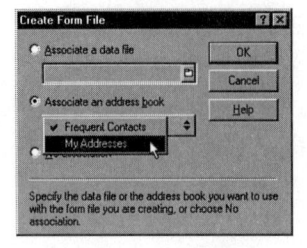

5. Now, we need the date. Press Enter twice to insert blank lines and click the Date button on the merge feature bar. That sticks the DATE code at the insertion point, as seen in figure 13.4. Whenever this generic letter is merged with the data file, the current date will appear where the DATE code is inserted.

Fig. 13.4
Merge codes like DATE appear in red on a color screen. The code will be replaced by the current date whenever the letter is used in a merge.

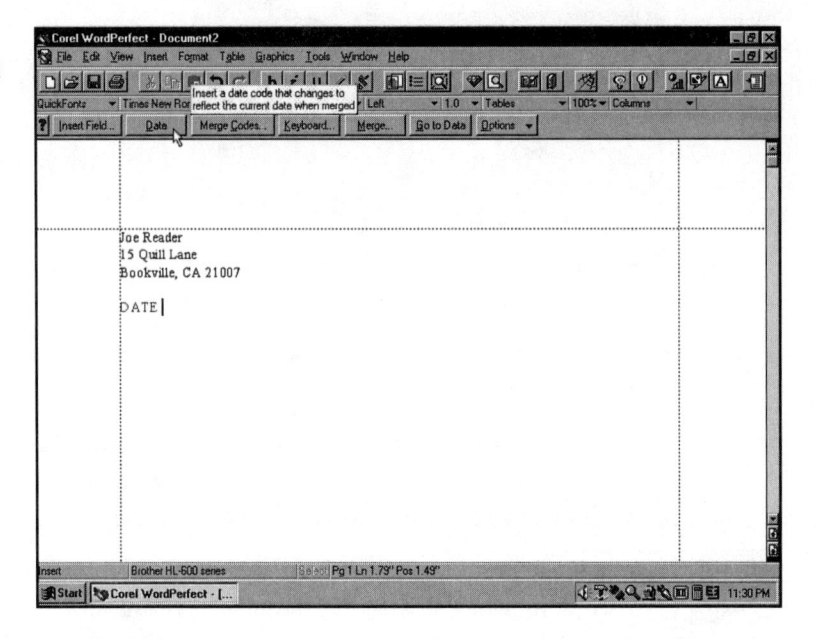

6. We want each recipient's address to appear at the top of the letter, followed by the salutation. Instead of typing each name and address, we'll insert the field names from the Address Book fields. The field names will act like blank lines in a form, waiting to be filled in with data

from the Address Book. Press Enter a couple of times to move the insertion point below the date.

7 Click the Insert Field button on the merge feature bar. The Insert Field Name or Number dialog box shown in figure 13.5 appears.

Fig. 13.5
The Insert Field Name or Number dialog box lists all the field names in the associated Address Book.

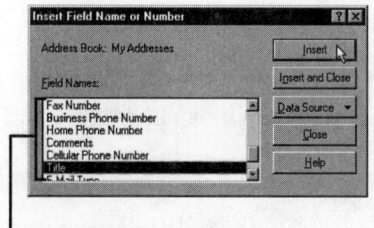

Each of these field names corresponds to a field in the Address Book.

8 Scroll down and select Title from the list of Field Names in the Insert Field Name or Number dialog box, and click Insert. The Title field is dumped into the form file at the insertion point, as shown in figure 13.6.

Fig. 13.6
The Insert Field Name or Number dialog box remains on the screen while you insert field names into the form file.

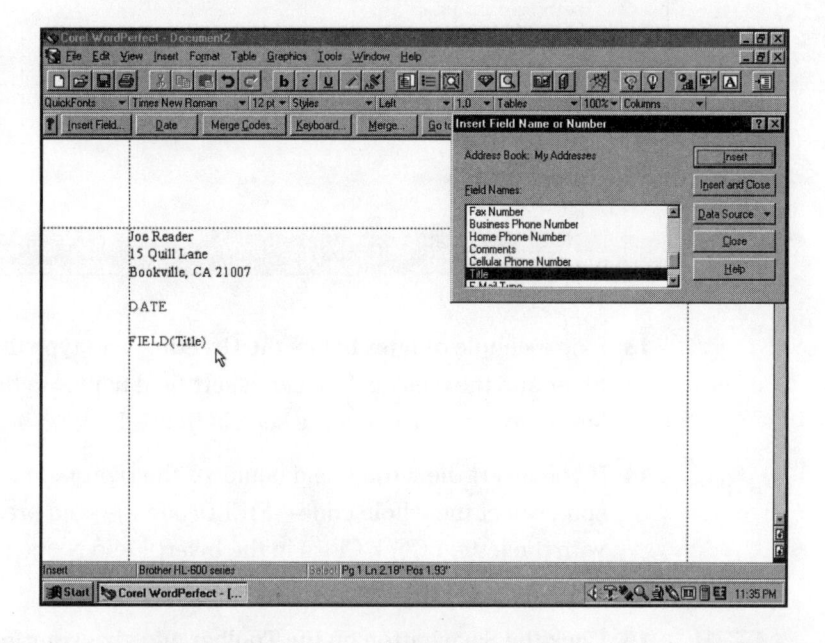

9 Insert a space with the Spacebar, select the Name field name from the Insert Field Name or Number dialog box, and click Insert. That puts the Name field one space over from the Title field, exactly where we want it.

Part IV Let WordPerfect Do Some of the Work for You

10. Press Enter to skip to the next line, and insert the Organization field name. Press Enter again; then insert the Address field name.

11. Press Enter to skip to the next line. We want the letter to read "city comma state," so insert the City field name, type a comma and a space; then insert the State field name. Put two spaces after the State field name, and insert the Zip field name.

12. Skip another couple of lines with the Enter key and insert the Greeting field name. So far, the form file looks like figure 13.7.

Fig. 13.7
As you set up a form file, visualizing the actual data in place of the merge codes helps you lay out the letter.

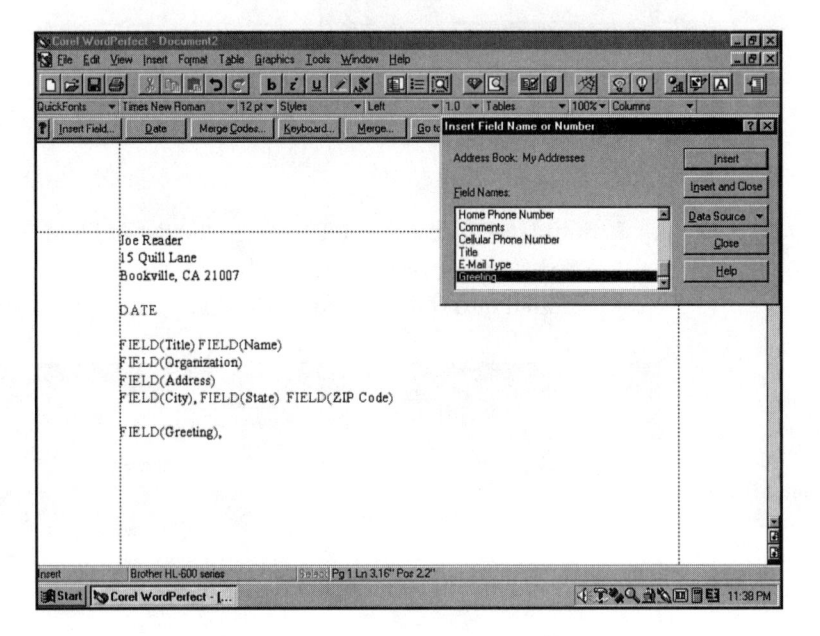

13. Skip a couple of lines below the Greeting, and type the body of the letter and the closing. You can insert field names in the body of the letter anywhere you like, as seen in figure 13.8.

14. If you insert the wrong field name, or the right field name in the wrong spot, select the whole code—FIELD(name)—and press Delete. Finished with the letter? Click Close in the Insert Field Name or Number dialog box.

15. Click the Save button on the Toolbar and give your form file a name. Any file name will do; WordPerfect keeps track of the fact that this is a form file for you.

Fig. 13.8
Put field names wherever they might be appropriate in the form file.

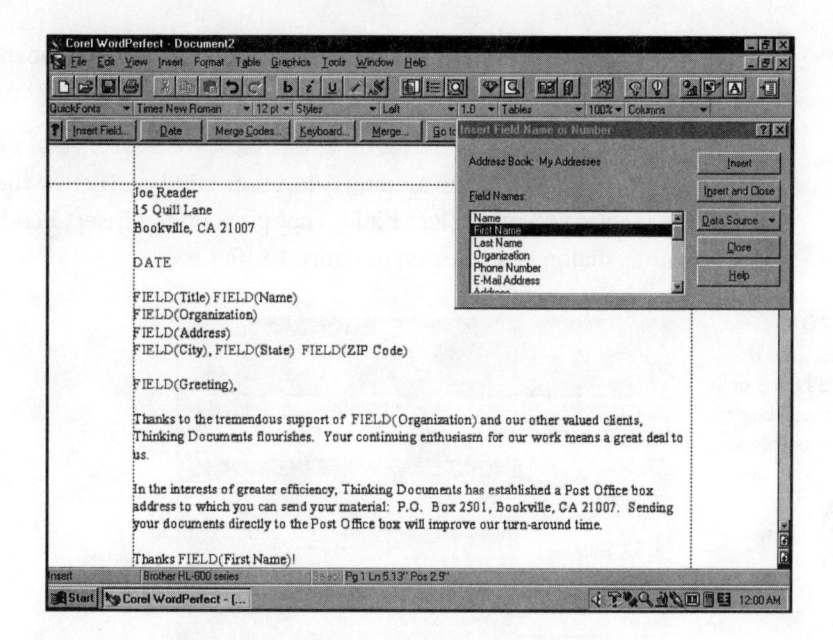

While we're at it, how about envelopes by the bushel, too?

Since we're making the extra effort to send "personalized" letters to our clients, we don't want to ruin the effect with impersonal mailing labels. It's easy to create form envelopes to go with our form letter. Set up the field names, and we'll get a slew of perfectly addressed envelopes.

To add envelopes to the form file:

1 Click the Merge button on the feature bar, and select Envelopes in the Perform Merge dialog box, as shown in figure 13.9.

Fig. 13.9
Unless you have a good reason not to, use the default Merge selections in the Perform Merge dialog box.

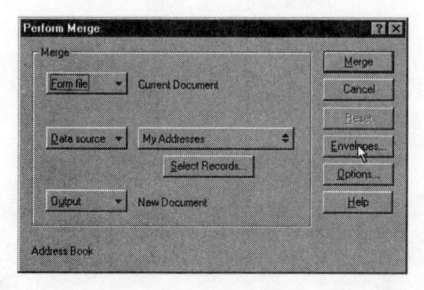

2 Select Envelopes and the Envelope dialog box appears. Click the From Address Book button, select the return address in the Address Book, and click OK.

3 Click inside the Mailing Addresses edit box (below the drop-down arrow), and select Field. That pops up the Insert Field Name or Number dialog box, as seen in figure 13.10.

Fig. 13.10
Insert fields from the Insert Field Name or Number dialog box to set up your envelope form.

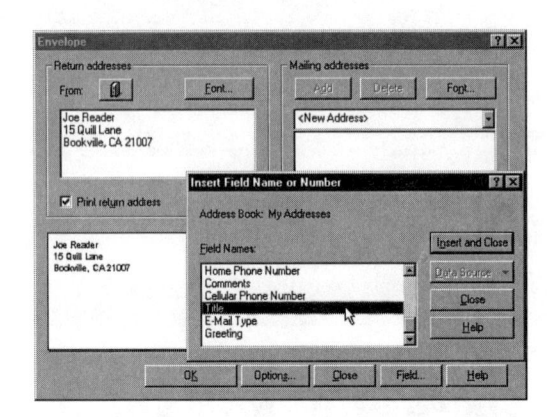

4 Select and then double-click field names to stick them in the right places in the Mailing Address edit box. Annoyingly, the dialog box closes after you insert a field name, so you'll have to keep clicking Field after each insertion. Remember to use spaces, commas, and Returns between the field names. The sample envelope window previews the final product as you work. When you're done, it'll look like figure 13.11.

Fig. 13.11
Putting field names where you want them is easy with a little practice.

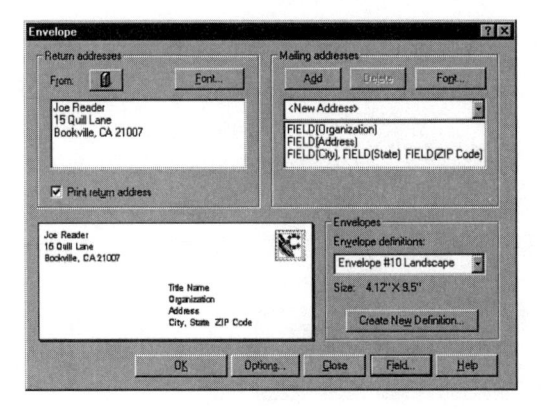

5 Click OK, and you're back at the Perform Merge dialog box, ready to merge the data file into the form file and the envelope.

Select your records; then bring it all together with a merge

As a few merger-mad companies discovered in the last decade, the best mergers are seamless. That's hard to achieve in business, but it's a snap in WordPerfect.

Once you set up your Address Book and form file, and add an envelope form if you want it, the real work is done. Only one chore remains: unless you're using every name in your Address Book, you'll want to select the names that you want to merge. To do that, click Select Records in the Perform Merge dialog box. That takes you back to the Address Book. Click the first record you want, and then Ctrl+click each additional record, as seen in figure 13.12.

Fig. 13.12
Unless you want a mailing for every entry in your Address Book, choose the entries you do want before merging.

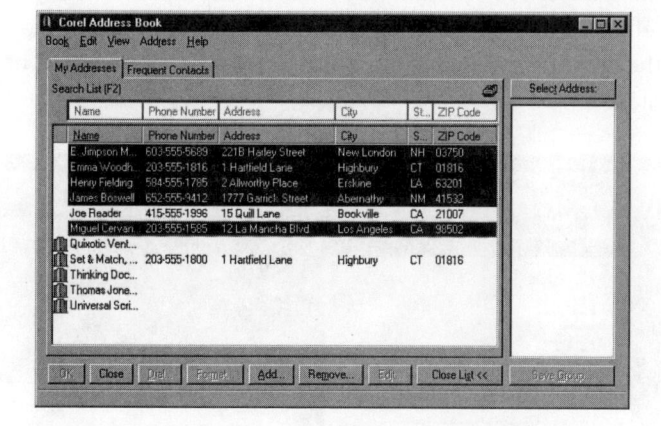

With all the records you want to merge selected, click Select Address. The names of the selected addressees appear together at the right of the Address Book, as seen in figure 13.13.

Click OK in the Address Book when you've selected the records to merge.

CAUTION The Address Book is finicky when it comes to selecting records for a merge. You have to click Select Address once you've made your selections, and you have to click OK, not Close, when you're done. Failure to do either or both will result in a merge that uses all your Address Book entries.

To finish the merge, click Merge in the Perform Merge dialog box.

Fig. 13.13
If you plan on merging the same names again, click the Save Group button and give the group a name.

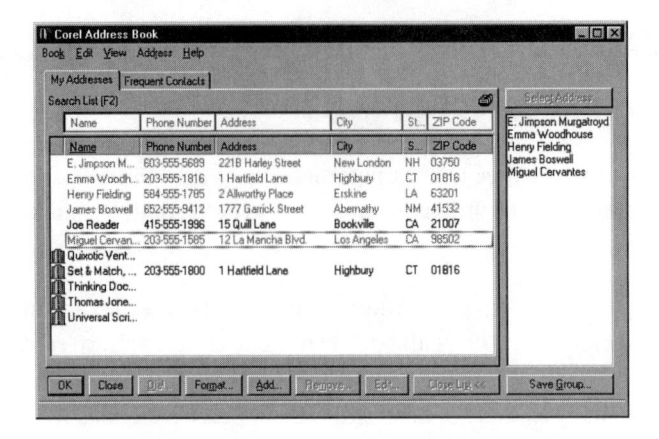

WordPerfect's gears whirl for a moment, and you wind up with a multipage document of letters and (if you went through the exercise) envelopes. Each letter is on a separate page; the envelope addresses are on separate pages at the end of the document. Figure 13.14 gives you an idea of what happens in a merge.

Fig. 13.14
This two-page view shows the last page of letters and the first page of envelopes.

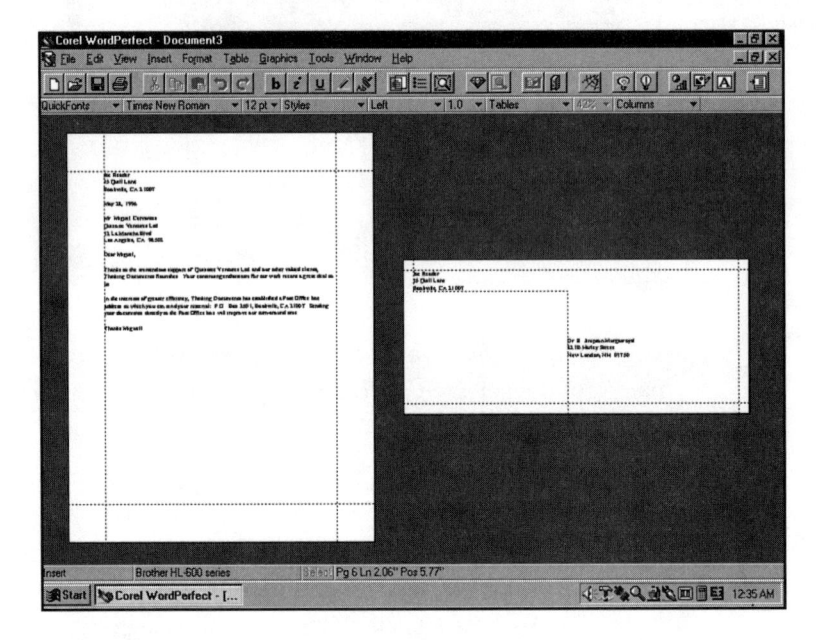

What do I do with this merge?

The idea behind this particular merge was to send out a mailing, so once the merge is completed, you'll want to print your letters and envelopes.

There's no need to save the merged document in this case. Since the data is stored in your Address Book, and the form file is already saved, you can remerge them any time. Need an updated merge to include new clients? Just add more records to the Address Book and perform another merge.

Q&A ***I don't have an envelope feeder! With letters and envelopes in the same document, how do I print them separately?***

Select File, Print. In the from edit box of the Print dialog box that appears, type the number of the first page of letters. Type the number of the last page of letters in the to edit box. Click Print, and you'll print all your letters. To print the envelopes one by one, move the insertion point to each envelope page, and click Current Page on the Print drop-down list in the Print dialog box. Click Print to print each envelope.

Here are a couple of other points concerning merges:

- Merging to labels is just as easy as merging to envelopes. See Chapter 9 for details on creating labels. Follow the same steps if you're merging to labels; just substitute merge codes for the names and addresses you'd otherwise type.

- If you use a database program such as Paradox, you might have data files with name and address information of the sort you'd use in a merge. Database files work fine in a merge, too; select them as your data source in the Perform Merge dialog box, instead of using the Address Book. WordPerfect form files will merge seamlessly with any compatible database file.

Merge bells and whistles

The sample merge we performed in this chapter was effective for what we wanted to accomplish. Most of the merges you're likely to want to do will be along similar lines.

There are also loads of sophisticated twists that you can introduce into a merge. Merge codes, inserted into your form or data files with the help of the feature bar, allow all sorts of merge tricks.

Click the Merge Codes button on the feature bar and the Insert Merge Codes dialog box appears, as shown in figure 13.15.

Fig. 13.15
WordPerfect's collection of merge codes is a sophisticated programming language.

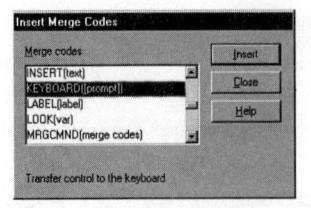

The Insert Merge Codes dialog box provides a brief explanation of each code when you select it from the list.

Part V: How to Be a Desktop Publisher

Chapter 14: **When Only Columns Will Do**

Chapter 15: **Dress Up That Text!**

Chapter 16: **Jazz Up a Document with Graphics**

Chapter 17: **In a Table, Anything Goes—with Ease**

14
When Only Columns Will Do

● **In this chapter:**

- Newspaper columns? Parallel columns? What's the difference?

- Newspaper columns are easy to work with

- How do I get quick columns?

- I need to adjust these columns

- I can't get these parallel columns to work!

Unvaried pages of text can be like boundless seas: impressive, but monotonous. Columns break the monotony by breaking up the page . . . . ▶

Journalists chasing a few columns of newspaper space are a tough breed. One early reporter set the standard for toughness, back in the days when columns supported buildings instead of newspaper publishers.

An ancient Greek soldier ran all the way to Athens to report a historic Greek victory over the Persians. The 25-mile run cost him his life, but that ultimate journalistic sacrifice hasn't been forgotten. That military messenger's exploit in reporting the battle of Marathon is celebrated every time a modern athlete runs a marathon.

WordPerfect columns won't confer that kind of immortality. On the other hand, setting up columns in WordPerfect is anything but a marathon job.

Why newspapers love newspaper columns

Imagine the morning paper without columns. You'd have long lines of text, marching from margin to margin across that wide page. It would be unreadable. As you read from left to right, your eyes take a quick breather at the right margin. Too much distance between margins, and your eyes start to feel like they're running a marathon.

Columns shorten the distance to the right margin, giving your eyes a break. They're used on any pages of dense text—think of dictionaries and encyclopedias. Columns also give pages a lively, vigorous look, which is why magazines and newsletters use them.

There are three basic kinds of columns:

- **Newspaper columns** wrap text from one column to the next. When you reach the bottom of one column, text flows to the top of the next column, just like wrapped text at the end of a WordPerfect line. Newspaper columns are easy to set up, and easy to edit. Figure 14.1 shows newspaper columns.

- **Balanced newspaper columns** are newspaper columns of even length. Figure 14.2. shows the same document as the one in figure 14.1 formatted with balanced newspaper columns. WordPerfect adjusts the text so that each column has an equal amount.

Fig. 14.1
Newspaper columns wrap text from one column to the next.

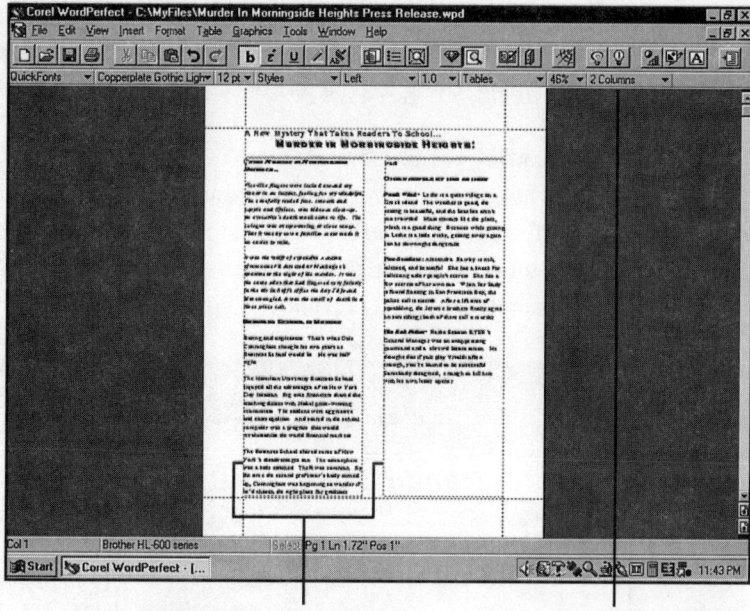

Column Guidelines indicate where your columns begin and end. Drag the Guidelines to adjust column widths and lengths.

The Power Bar Columns button displays the number of columns selected.

Fig. 14.2
If you plan to use balanced newspaper columns, type your text before applying the column formatting.

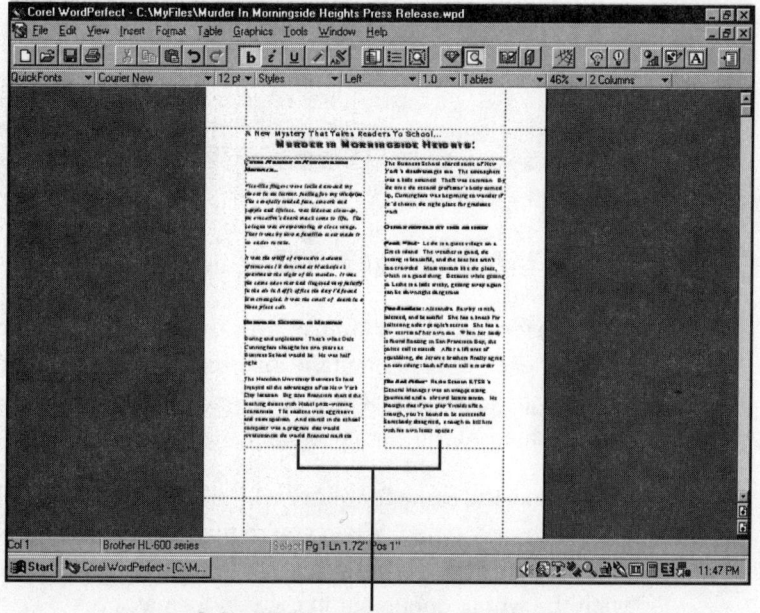

Balanced newspaper columns distribute text evenly across the columns.

> **TIP** You'll save yourself a lot of grief if you type your text with the default left and right margins first, and apply columns only when you finish typing. Trying to type text directly into columns can be—trying.

- **Parallel columns** place chunks of text in column rows across the page, just like a table. Parallel columns are often used to display related but different information side-by-side (dates and job descriptions in a résumé, or a script with actor's name, dialog, and stage directions, for example). Figure 14.3 shows parallel columns.

Fig. 14.3
Parallel columns are effective for specialized uses, but they can be tricky to deal with.

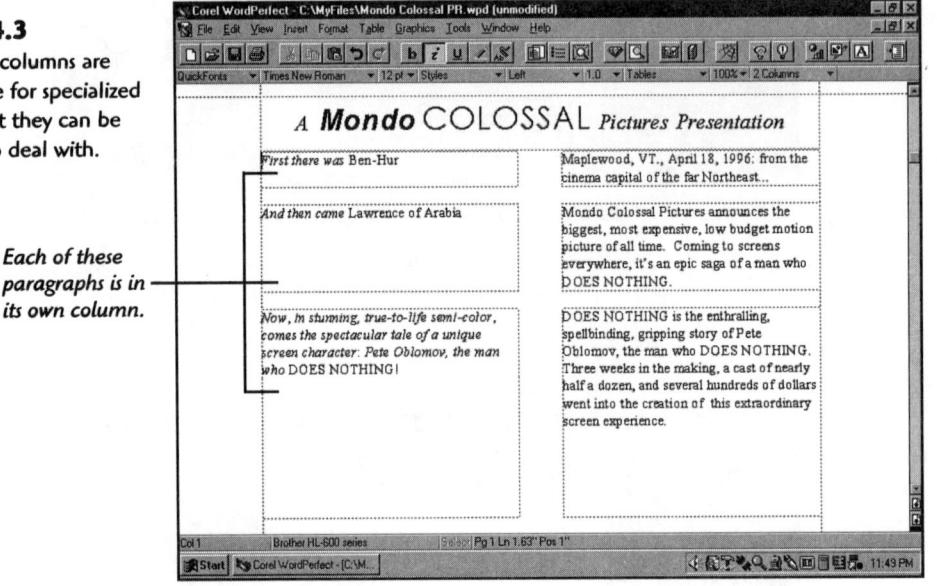

Each of these paragraphs is in its own column.

Fast columns with no fussing

WordPerfect gives you control over the number of columns on the page, the width of each column, and the amount of space between columns. You can tinker until you're absolutely satisfied. But, when all you want is two or three quick columns, you can get them without fuss.

This works the same for either a blank document or for a document that you've already typed. When you're ready to format the text in columns, move the insertion point to the spot where you want columns to begin. If you want the whole document in column format, press Ctrl+Home to go to the top of the document. Now, click the Columns button on the Power Bar. That gives you the menu of choices shown in figure 14.4.

Fig. 14.4
Choose the number of columns you want on the Power Bar list. The more columns you choose, the skinnier they'll be.

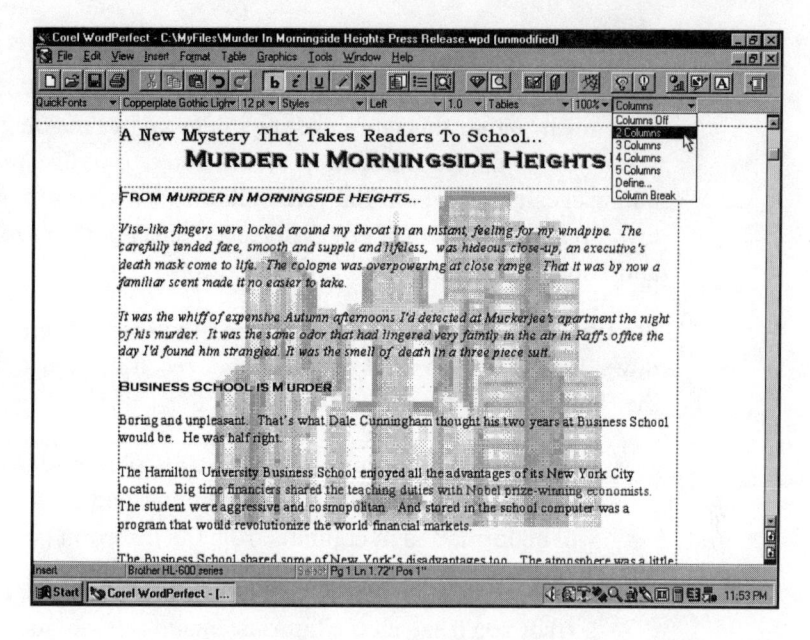

If you have text already, it's instantly formatted in columns. If you have a blank document, start typing. The red column Guidelines show you where your columns begin and end. If you don't see the column Guidelines, click View, Guidelines, and click the Columns check box in the Guidelines dialog box. Click OK to close the dialog box and return to your document.

To jump back and forth between columns for editing, move the mouse pointer wherever you want the insertion point, and click. To turn columns off again at the insertion point and return to ordinary lines of text, click the Power Bar Columns button and select Columns Off.

The Power Bar Columns button gives you regular newspaper columns. Despite the name, newspaper columns don't have to be used only for newspapers or newsletters. They're fine for reports or any text for which you want a column format.

Q&A

I turned on three columns to format this document, but I only see text in the first column. What happened?

You probably don't have enough text to fill the second and third columns yet. If you aren't going to add more text, consider using balanced newspaper columns. Press Ctrl+Home to go to the beginning of the document, click the Power Bar Columns button, and choose Define. In the Columns dialog box that appears, click Balanced newspaper and choose OK. That distributes what text you do have evenly between the three columns.

Where's the Power Bar Columns button?

Here you are reading about the Columns button on the Power Bar, thinking to yourself "either this guy's making things up or I'm going blind" because *you don't see a Columns button on the Power Bar.* The problem is neither failing eyesight nor authorial verisimilitude; it's your screen resolution. At lower resolutions, WordPerfect doesn't display portions of the Power Bar and Toolbar, including the Columns button.

See Chapter 1 for information on increasing your screen resolution in Windows. If your system can't handle higher resolutions, use the menu bar to get the Columns dialog box:

- Click Format, Columns, Define. In the Columns dialog box that pops up, select the Number and Type of columns, and click OK. The document will be formatted in columns from the insertion point on.

- Or, do as I did on my low resolution laptop: change the Power Bar font so that you'll see all the buttons, including Columns. Right-click the Power Bar and choose Options. In the Power Bar Options dialog box that appears, click Arial on the Font face list, and select 13 for a Font size. Click OK in the Power Bar Options dialog box, and you'll see the Columns button on your Power Bar.

How can I tell where column formatting begins and ends?

When you turn columns on, WordPerfect inserts a [Col Def] code into the text at the insertion point. Another [Col Def] code is inserted wherever you turn columns off. That makes it easy to put columns and regular text on the same page, as shown in figure 14.5. To see your column definition codes, open the Reveal Codes window (View, Reveal Codes or press Alt+F3).

You might want a heading or an introduction before your columns begin, and maybe a conclusion below your columns. Just use the Reveal Codes window to see where the [Col Def] codes are, and put the insertion point before or after the codes.

If you lose track of what column you're in, glance at the General Status button's column indicator on the status bar (see fig. 14.5).

Fig. 14.5
The Reveal Codes window shows you where columns begin and end on the page.

Columns begin at the opening [Col Def] code.

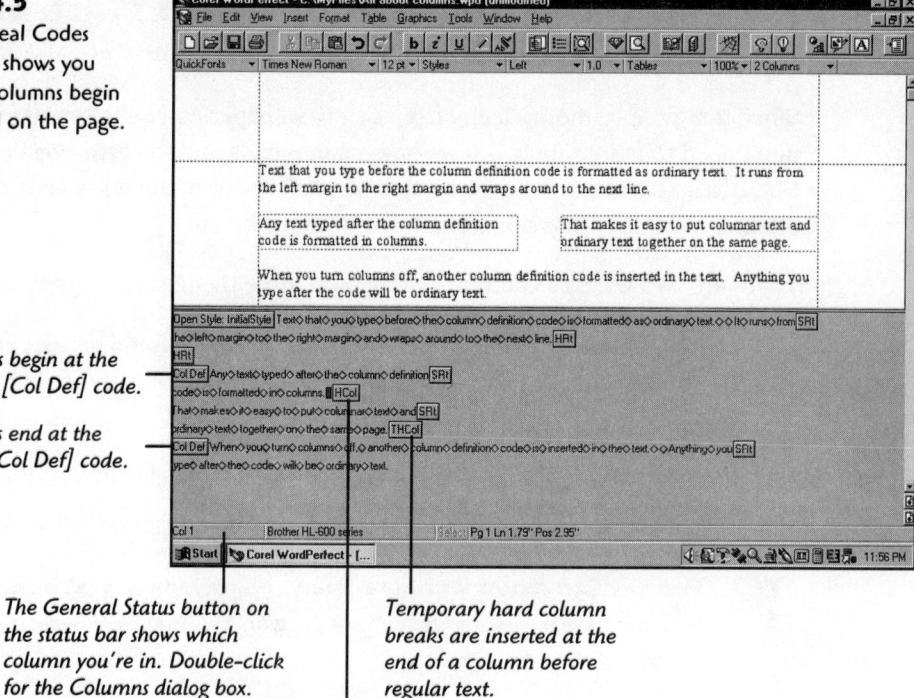

Columns end at the closing [Col Def] code.

The General Status button on the status bar shows which column you're in. Double-click for the Columns dialog box.

Temporary hard column breaks are inserted at the end of a column before regular text.

A hard column break, which WordPerfect inserts when you press Ctrl+Enter in a column.

> **TIP** When the General Status button on the status bar displays a column number, double-click it to pop up the Columns dialog box.

To get rid of columns, drag the first [Col Def] code out of the Reveal Codes window. That'll return your text to the normal, left margin to right margin lines.

Although columns start from wherever you put the insertion point when you turn them on, headers and footers in the document aren't affected by column formatting in the body text. If you want column formatting in headers and footers, you'll have to turn on columns *within* the header or footer.

How do I end one column and start another one?

Since text wraps automatically from one newspaper column to another, you don't need to worry about where one column ends and the next one begins. But, if you want to end a column at a particular spot in the text and start another column, you can insert a **hard column break**.

There are two ways to end one column and force the text to begin in another:

- Press Ctrl+Enter. That inserts a [HCol], or hard column break code (see fig. 14.5) to snap off one column at the insertion point and start another one.

- Or, for dedicated mousers, click Format, Columns, Column Break to insert a hard column break code.

> **TIP** **Pressing Ctrl+Enter within ordinary, noncolumnar text inserts a** hard page break, ending the current page and putting the insertion point at the top of the new page.

Default columns settings are usually fine...

The default columns you produce with the Power Bar Columns button are regular newspaper columns with 1/2-inch of space between them. The width of the columns themselves depends on how many columns you choose, your margins, and the paper size. WordPerfect automatically calculates column width for you: the more columns you select, the skinnier they get.

Figure 14.6 shows the default settings for two pages with the same text. Page one has two 3-inch columns, and page two has four 1 1/2-inch columns.

> **TIP** **If your columns are too skinny, decreasing the left and right page** margins will fatten them up a little. The margins are one-inch wide by default, but cut them down by half and columns within the margins gain an extra inch. To change margin settings, drag the Guidelines or press Ctrl+F8 for the Margins dialog box.

Fig. 14.6
The WordPerfect default column settings work, but if you're not satisfied, it's easy to make changes.

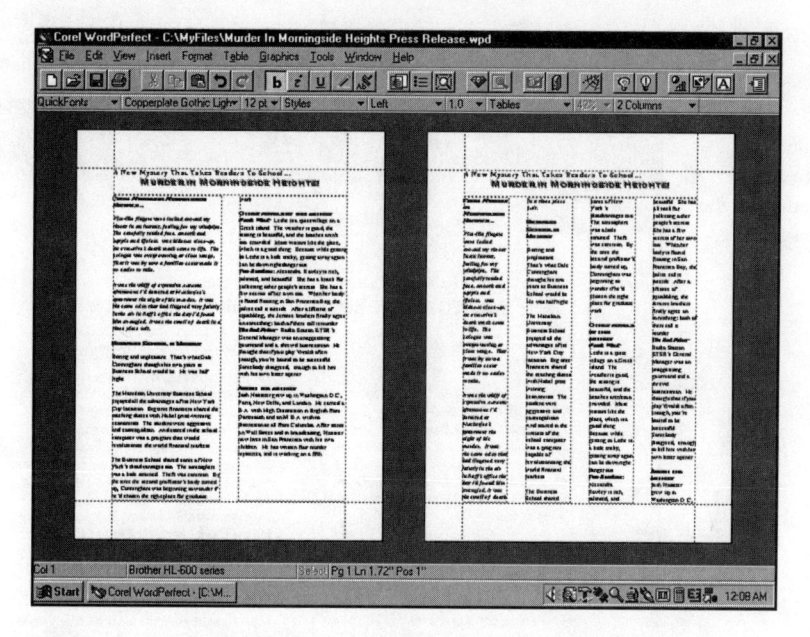

These columns need adjustment

The default settings work well for most uses. If you don't like the way the page looks with the defaults, change the settings. Add more or less space between columns, change the width of your columns, or create columns of unequal width.

> ❝ **Plain English, please!**
> The space between columns is called the **gutter** in page layout jargon. WordPerfect calls it **spacing between columns**. ❞

It's easy to make changes to any column setting. Drag a column Guideline, and the Guideline's QuickStatus indicator displays the changing width of the column, and of the space between that column and the adjacent column. Figure 14.7 shows you what happens when you drag a column Guideline.

Although it's fast and easy, there's one drawback to adjusting column widths with Guidelines. Dragging one column's Guideline changes the width for that column only; the other column (or columns) in the document do not change until you change them.

Fig. 14.7
Drag a column Guideline to adjust column widths and the spacing between columns.

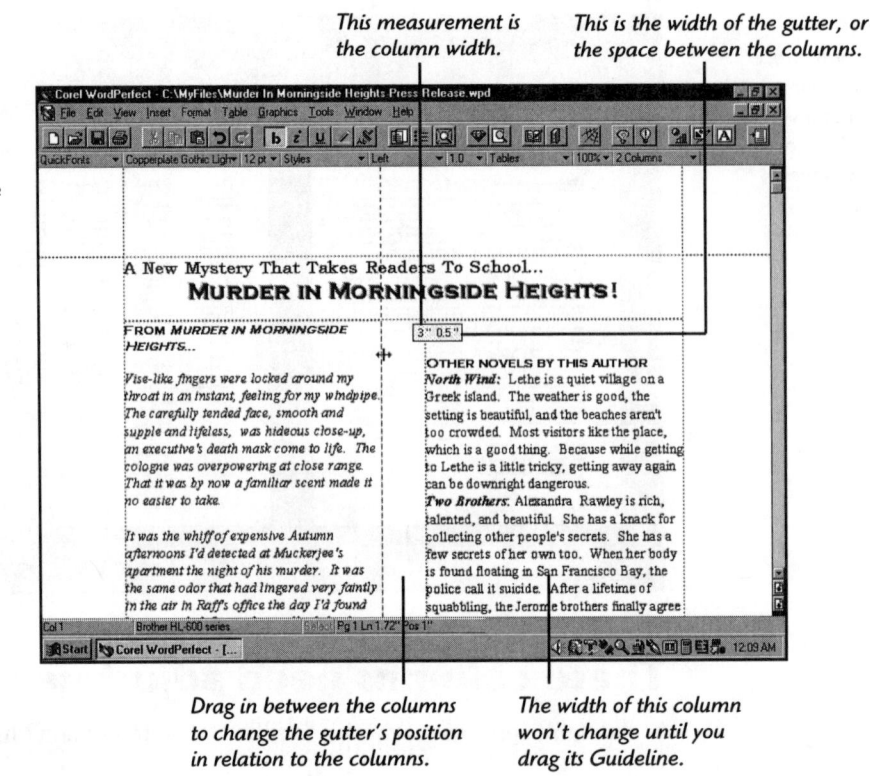

This measurement is the column width.

This is the width of the gutter, or the space between the columns.

Drag in between the columns to change the gutter's position in relation to the columns.

The width of this column won't change until you drag its Guideline.

Suppose you start out with two 3" columns with .05" of space between them, and then drag the left column's Guideline to make it wider. You'll get a wider left column, a narrower gutter, and a right column that's still 3" wide. To adjust the right column so that it's equal to the left column, you have to drag its Guideline as well.

With two columns on the page, it's not too difficult to adjust both so they remain of equal widths. With three or more columns, you might want to use the Columns dialog box (click For̲mat, C̲olumns, D̲efine to get it) to change your column widths. The Columns dialog box automatically adjusts all your columns, and the spaces between them, at once.

Q&A I'm dragging this Guideline, but I can't get my column width exactly where I want it!

Dragging the column Guidelines changes column widths in fixed increments. You can change from 3" to 3.06" to 3.13", but don't waste your time trying to drag a Guideline to a width of 3.1". You'll never get there.

How do I fine-tune my columns?

Of course, columns don't have to be evenly spaced. In fact, changing the pattern of the text on the page with columns of unequal width might help keep your readers from falling asleep. Still, the commonest sort of column layout, that seen in newspapers for example, usually calls for equal columns. If you have three or more columns to deal with, the easiest way to keep them of equal width is with the Columns dialog box.

The Columns dialog box is the column control panel

Let's use the Columns dialog box to format a three-column press release. We want to avoid anemic-looking skinny columns, so first we'll give ourselves a little extra room and widen the page margins. Drag the left margin Guideline left to .75", and drag the right margin Guideline to the right to .75". That gives us three-quarter-inch page margins, and an extra half-inch of space for the columns.

Now for the columns. If you're formatting an existing page of text, press Ctrl+Home to move the insertion point to the beginning of the document. Click the Power Bar Columns button and select Define (or choose Format, Columns, Define) for the Columns dialog box. To set up columns in the Columns dialog box:

1 Click the arrows next to the Columns edit box to pick the number of columns. You can have as many as 24 and as few as two. We'll click the up arrow once for three columns.

2 The values in the Column widths edit boxes change from 3.25" to 2", and Column 3 is added to the Column widths section of the dialog box. WordPerfect calculates the change in column widths for us, narrowing the columns to accommodate the third one.

3 We'll select Newspaper for column type. Newspaper columns are the easiest type to work with, and they work well for most uses.

4 Since our goal is robust-looking columns, we'll cut down on the space between them to give the columns themselves a little more heft. Click the Spacing between columns edit box and type in .3. That gives us three 2.13" columns, as seen in figure 14.8.

Fig. 14.8
If you don't like the look of skinny columns, cut down on the space between them.

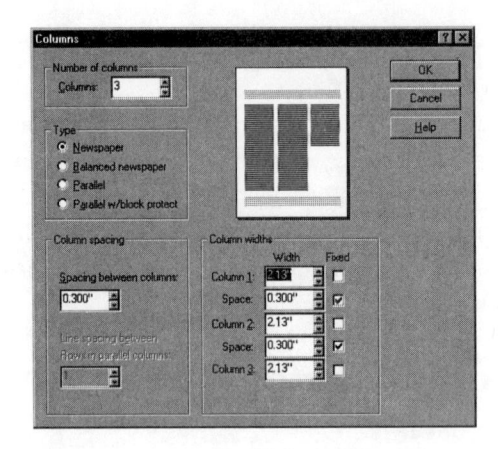

> **TIP** **If you're adjusting the column widths, clicking the arrows for** Column Widths changes widths in increments of .1". For a different value, just type it in the edit boxes. You can type fractions, such as 2 1/3, which WordPerfect automatically converts to 2.33.

5 Click OK in the Columns dialog box, and you're set. If you started with a page of text, presto chango, it's now in three columns. Otherwise, start typing. Your text will flow into the columns as you type it.

Figure 14.9 shows the results of our column formatting, with text and a header added.

If you're bent on further tinkering, just remember this: when you adjust column widths and gutter spacing between columns, the total width of the columns and the spaces between them is fixed by the page margin settings. WordPerfect adjusts each width and space when you make changes. But, no matter what adjustments you make, the total of the widths can't exceed the total space between margins.

How do I move around in these columns?

Typing and editing text in columns is the same as typing and editing in an ordinary page. Moving the insertion point from one column to another with the keyboard works a little differently though.

To move the insertion point from column to column, use the mouse just as you would ordinarily, and click wherever you want the insertion point.

Fig. 14.9
With a few adjustments, columns in WordPerfect will turn out exactly as you want them.

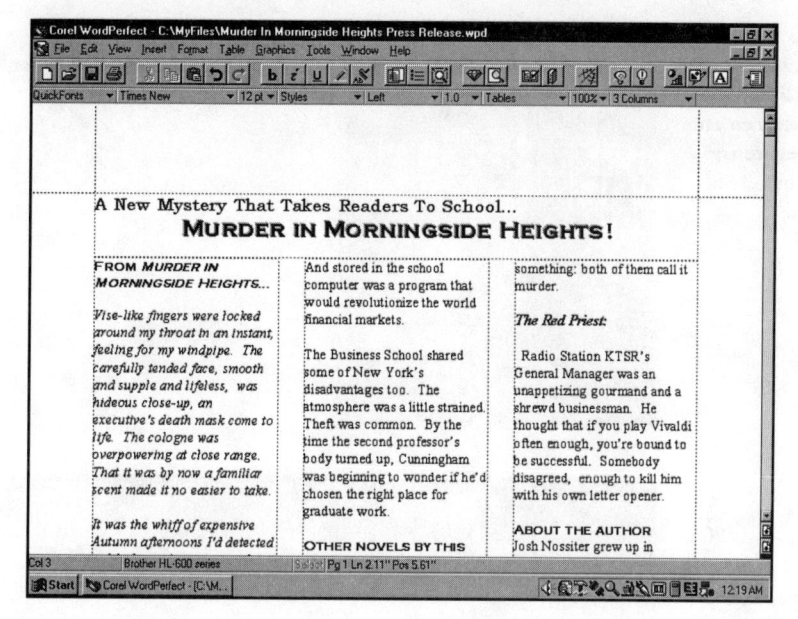

CAUTION You can't move to another column if it doesn't have any text yet!

These columns need borders

Putting borders between columns is a fast way to dress up a columnar page. WordPerfect has special border styles for columns. To add column borders:

1 With the insertion point anywhere within your columns, click Format, Border/Fill, Column, for the Column Border/Fill dialog box to appear.

2 Click the Border tab and scroll down the list of Available border styles. Figure 14.10 shows the Column Between border selected in the Column Border/Fill dialog box.

3 Click OK. Borders appear between each column, as shown in figure 14.11.

Fig. 14.10
The other column border style is Column All, which puts borders between columns and around the outside of the columns.

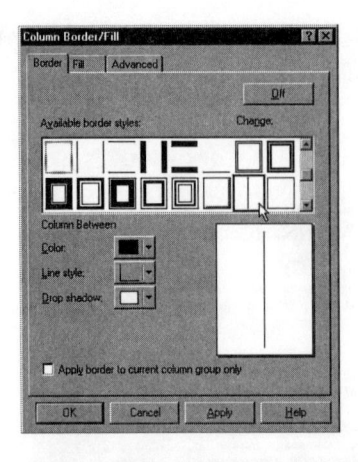

Fig. 14.11
Borders between columns add a decorative touch; the New York Times uses very skinny ones.

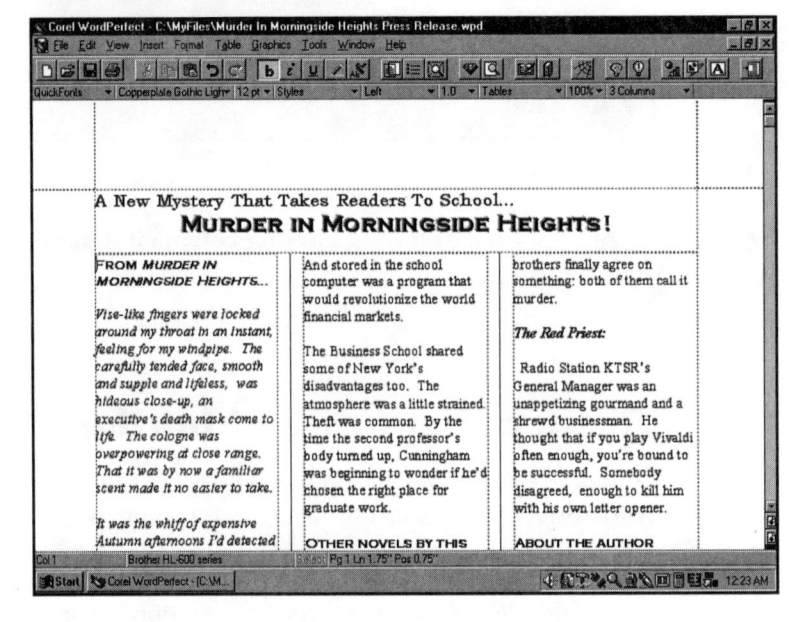

> **Q&A** **Why do I only get horizontal lines when I select Column Between borders from the Paragraph Border/Fill dialog box?**
>
> You're in the wrong dialog box. If you select Format, B<u>o</u>rder/Fill, Pa<u>r</u>agraph, you'll see the Column Between style, but the line is horizontal. For vertical column borders, you have to choose Format, B<u>o</u>rder/Fill, <u>C</u>olumn. That also goes for the Paragraph dialog box that pops up when you click a QuickSpot. Even though the B<u>o</u>rder palette in the Paragraph dialog box has a style that looks like it belongs in columns, it doesn't.

How do I get these parallel columns to work?

Parallel columns can be difficult to work with. It's also impossible to apply them to existing text. There is one sure-fire method to make parallel columns work:

1 Before you start typing text, click the Power Bar Columns button, and select Define.

2 Choose the number of columns you want, and select Parallel.

3 Click OK to return to the document, and type the first block of text in column 1 (first column from the left margin).

4 Press Ctrl+Enter to insert a hard column break after the text in column 1.

5 Type the first block of text in column 2. Press Ctrl+Enter to insert another hard column break after the text in column 2.

6 If you're using three columns, that puts the insertion point in column 3; if you have two columns, you go back to column 1. Either way, keep typing blocks of text and inserting hard column breaks after each block until you're done.

Figure 14.12 shows the hard column breaks after each block of text in two parallel columns.

Q&A *These parallel columns are tricky. Isn't there an easier way?*

Text formatted in parallel columns looks good, but tables give you the same effect with a lot less work. Entering text in a table is a snap, and you can turn off table lines so that the text looks just like parallel columns. You can even turn columnar text into a table. See Chapter 17 for more about tables.

Fig. 14.12
Parallel columns are doable, provided you insert hard column breaks after each block of text.

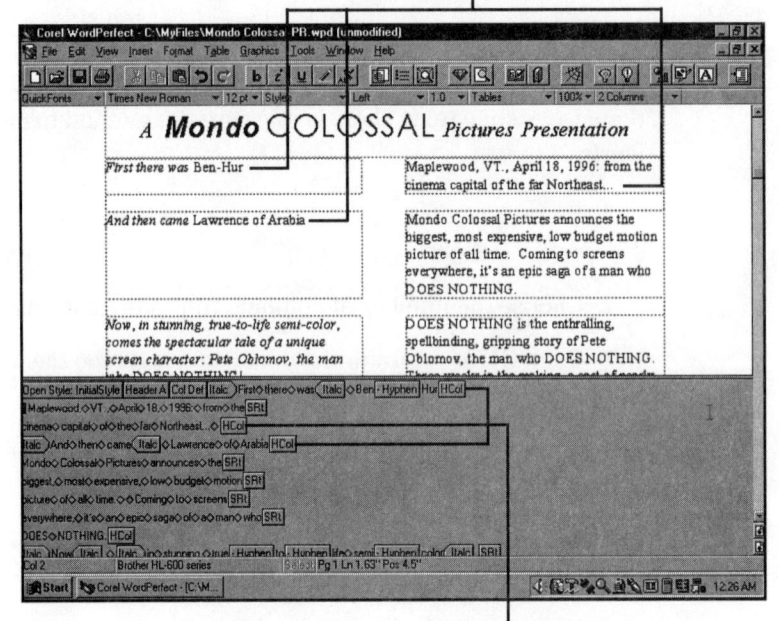

Insert hard column breaks after each block of text.

The hard column break codes show up in the reveal codes window.

15

Dress Up That Text!

● **In this chapter:**

- **With WordPerfect, you're the typographer**
- **TextArt gives text an artistic bent**
- **What's a watermark?**
- **How can I produce a typeset quality document?**
- **I need to use foreign characters**

With everything from typeset precision to a little show-biz, WordPerfect's bag of formatting tricks brings plain documents to life . . . . ▶

Why do we sit through bad movies, only to wonder "Why on earth didn't I walk out?" Something hooks us. It can be scenic settings or brilliant camera work. Or the hook might be more subtle, like the lighting or the atmosphere.

Pages of text have atmosphere and qualities of light, too. Those medieval illuminated manuscripts are so called because the gold leaf and art work "light up" the pages.

You don't get gold leaf in WordPerfect, but there are some nifty tools to brighten your pages. Formatting effects and decorative touches can help to hook a reader—even when the text itself isn't exactly a thriller.

Call in the typographer? No need. It's you!

The typographer's job is to take charge of the appearance of the page. How bright or dark the page looks, the impression it makes—brash or subtle, friendly or sophisticated—that's all in the typographer's hands.

Equipped with WordPerfect and your own good taste and judgment, you can be your own typographer.

I want to see what this font looks like before I use it

Like any good typographer, your first decision is the one that has the biggest impact on your pages: what font to use? Between WordPerfect and Windows, there are plenty of fonts to choose from. Chances are, you have other programs that installed still other fonts in your system. Faced with this cornucopia of type, where do you start?

Try the Font dialog box. It lists all the fonts you've installed in Windows, and there's a small preview window so you get an inkling of what the fonts look like. Click Format, Font or press F9 for the Font dialog box (see fig. 15.1).

Click an item on the Font face list, select a Font size, and then click any of the Appearance boxes to apply boldface, italics, and the other attributes. Your font creation appears in the lower left part of the dialog box.

Fig. 15.1
Preview fonts and their attributes before deciding on a font to use in your document.

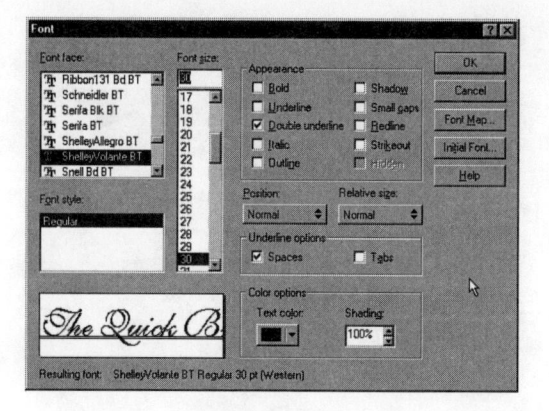

Want lighter text? Click the Shading down arrow and try a lower value in the Shading box. 100% is the most intense font color; anything less makes your text fainter by degrees. Once you click OK in the Font dialog box, new text takes on the combination of font face, size, and appearance that you've made. If you want to change the font of existing text, select the text first, then pop up the Font dialog box and make your selections.

How about a different color for this font?

Color printers are ubiquitous these days. And although a lot of documents sent over networks or by e-mail never get printed at all, your readers have color monitors. Splash some color over your text, and you'll draw your colleague's eye away from his solitaire game.

To color existing text, first select it. Then, to change the color of the current font:

1 Click Format, Font to bring up the Font dialog box.

2 Click the Text color button in the Font dialog box. A palette of colors appears; point at any of the colors in the palette, and the color jumps to the foreground in a little box, as seen in figure 15.2.

3 Once you've located the color you want, click it. Both the Text color button and the text in the preview window display the new color.

4 Click OK in the Font dialog box. Any new text that you type appears in the new color. If you selected text first, it's instantly transformed from black to whatever color you selected.

Fig. 15.2
Primary colors are in the top row of the palette, with shades below them.

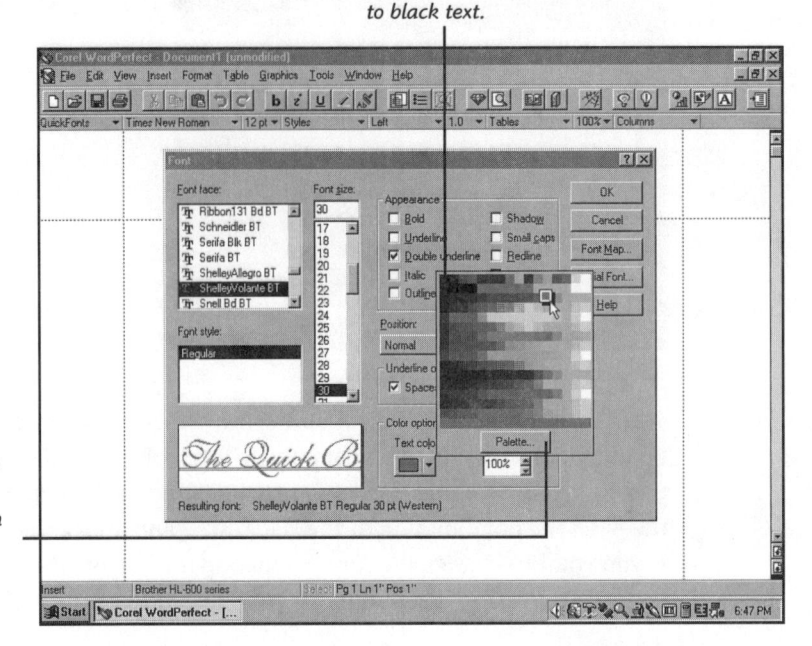

Click here to return to black text.

If none of the colors on display appeal to you, click the Palette button for a dialog box that lets you mix your own shade.

A little color spices up a document, but you don't want to overdo it. To return to black text, press F9 for the Font dialog box, click the Text color button, select black on the color palette (see fig. 15.2), and click OK.

Ever wonder why fonts have those odd names?

The invention of moveable type—letters carved in blocks of wood or engraved on bars of metal, arranged to form words, then inked and pressed against paper—revolutionized the world. Moveable type led to the printing press and the mass production of books and newspapers.

It all began with handwriting. The early font faces imitated written characters. Roman faces like Times New Roman, the WordPerfect default font face, are patterned on the writing style of the ancient Romans. Gothic or Black Letter faces like Braggadocio, with their upright, thick lines, recall the handwriting of medieval monks. Innovative designers like the 18th-century William Caslon gave font faces a more modern look. Caslon based his designs on shapes made by engravers' tools. Caslon Openface, a font you'll find in the Font dialog box, derives from Caslon's designs.

What are those symbols by the font names?

Click the Power Bar Font button. As you browse the list of font faces, you'll notice the symbols by the font names (see fig. 15.3).

Fig. 15.3
TrueType fonts were designed to work with Windows.

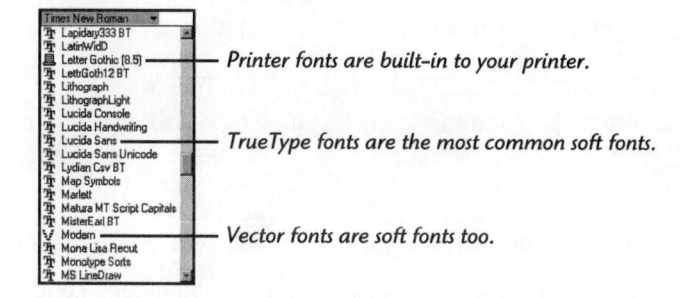

Printer fonts are built-in to your printer.

TrueType fonts are the most common soft fonts.

Vector fonts are soft fonts too.

TrueType and Vector fonts (see fig. 15.3) are **soft fonts.** All the information needed to display and print soft fonts is kept in files on your hard disk, and WordPerfect uses those files to generate the fonts automatically whenever they're selected.

TrueType is the Windows standard. TrueType fonts are **scaleable**, meaning that you can change their size. TrueType fonts are designed to look the same on the screen and the printed page, which makes them the best choice for most uses. WordPerfect and Windows both come with a slew of TrueType fonts, and any fonts installed in Windows are automatically installed in WordPerfect.

Vector fonts are like TrueType fonts; they can be sized, and they display and print with the same look. But where TrueType fonts are composed of zillions of little dots, Vector fonts are outlines, or "suggested shapes" for characters that WordPerfect fills in on the fly.

Printer fonts are built-in to your printer. The printer fonts you see listed in figure 15.3 are in my printer, but not necessarily yours. This only matters because, unlike TrueType fonts, WordPerfect may not display a selected printer font. It'll print, but you may see something different on the screen. If I select Brougham, for example, WordPerfect displays Courier. Printer fonts in a document look fine and print quickly, but if you send the document to others, they may have trouble getting the same results on their printers.

How do I add more fonts?

WordPerfect comes with over two hundred fonts, probably more than you'll ever need. They're found in the COREL\OFFICE7\APPMAN\WKSFILES\FONTS folder in the WordPerfect CD, and they install with the program. If you need still more fonts than you get with Windows and WordPerfect, you can add to your font collection. Buy them, on floppy disk or CD-ROM, or download them from an online information service.

When you add fonts, you install them in Windows. Once installed in Windows, they're automatically installed in WordPerfect.

To install new fonts:

1 Click the Start button and choose Settings, Control Panel.

2 Double-click the Fonts icon in the Control Panel dialog box.

3 In the Fonts dialog box that pops up, click File, Install New Font.

4 The Add Fonts dialog box appears. Insert the floppy or CD-ROM that holds your new font (if you have either one), and click the Drives drop-down arrow to select the appropriate disk drive. If the new font is on your hard disk, scroll down the Folders list and double-click the appropriate folder. Any fonts lurking in the folder or drives appear on the List of fonts, as seen in figure 15.4.

Fig. 15.4
Adding fonts to WordPerfect is a one-step job; just add them to Windows first.

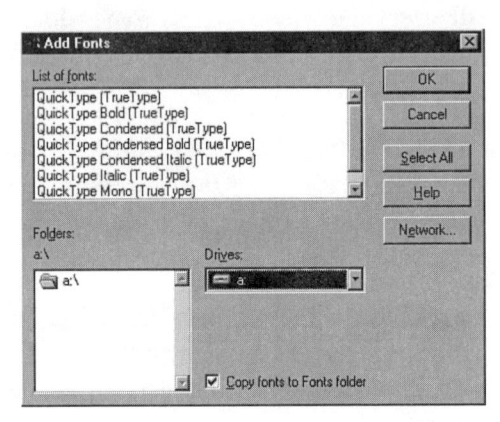

5 Select the fonts you want to add from the List of fonts and click OK to install them in Windows. Close the Fonts dialog box and the Control Panel. When you return to WordPerfect, you'll see the new font on the Power Bar fonts button list.

> **TIP** If you have no use for fonts like WP Cyrillic B, you can get rid of them. Deleting fonts you won't use saves memory and improves Windows' performance. Select the unwanted font in the Control Panel Fonts dialog box and press Delete. Click Yes in the Windows Fonts Folder message box that pops up to confirm the deletion. Once removed, you won't see the font on the WordPerfect list. If you change your mind and want the font back again, double-click the Recycle Bin icon on the Windows desktop, right-click the deleted font, and choose Restore from the shortcut menu.

> **TIP** You might want to see what you're deleting before you do it. To preview a font listed in the Control Panel Fonts dialog box, just double-click it.

TextArt, for text with an artistic bent

Giambattista Bodoni was an 18th century typographical genius, whose beautiful designs are still in use today. Pick up a copy of the *Washington Post*, and you'll see a Bodoni font in the newspaper's headlines; you'll also find Bodoni fonts in WordPerfect's Font dialog box. Bodoni compiled an *Inventory of Types* that covered all types of fonts. Far-seeing as he was, Bodoni couldn't have imagined TextArt.

TextArt turns fonts into silly putty. It lets you stretch, squeeze, and bend fonts into shapes like the one seen in figure 15.5.

Bending TextArt to your will

TextArt gives you an electronic crayon box to play with. Use TextArt to create banners, titles, and logos. Need to whip up a quick flyer for the company picnic? Here's what you do:

1 In a blank document, click Graphics, TextArt. In a moment or two, the editing window fills with the TextArt 7 dialog box and a big TextArt object.

2 The insertion point should be in the Type here edit box in the TextArt 7 dialog box. If not, click the edit box.

3 Type your text, but try to keep it short. The longer the text, the more distorted it gets, as you can see in figure 15.6.

Fig. 15.5
With TextArt, fonts assume mind-bending shapes.

Click a shape here, and the text bends to fit the shape.

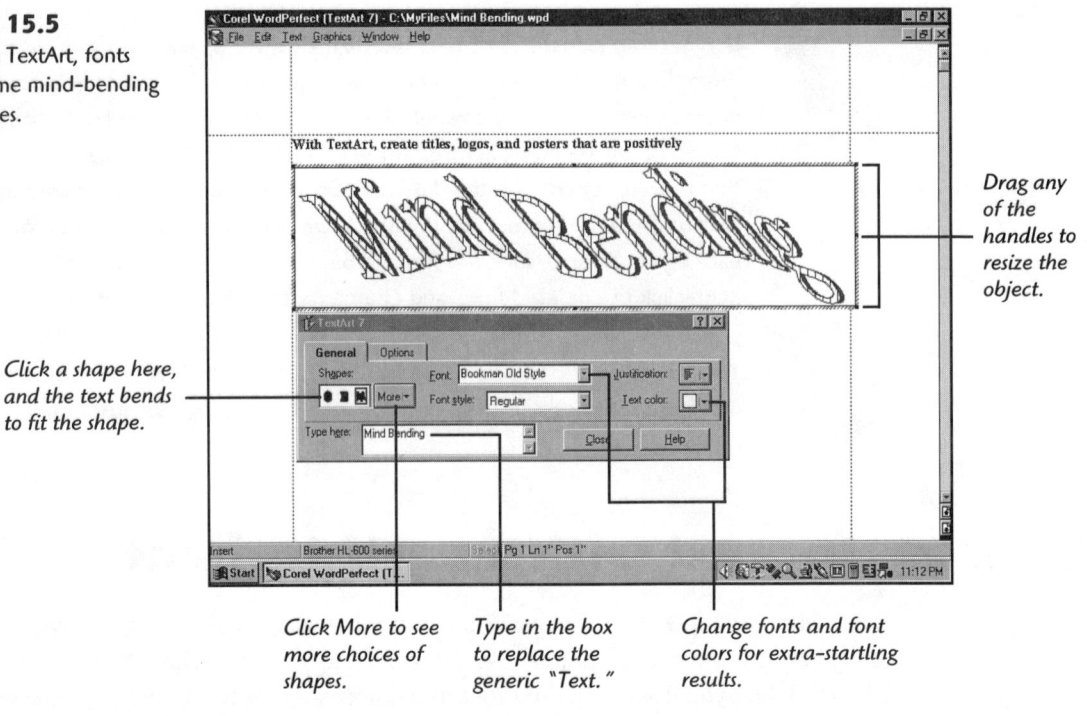

Drag any of the handles to resize the object.

Click More to see more choices of shapes.

Type in the box to replace the generic "Text."

Change fonts and font colors for extra-startling results.

> **TIP** **If the Type here edit box is too cramped for your typing style, type** your text in the WordPerfect document window first. Select the text; then click Graphics, TextArt. That puts you in the TextArt window, with your selected text transformed into TextArt.

4 Click More to see the full palette of shapes; click any of the shapes, and watch as the text you typed bends and stretches. Trial-and-error is the way to proceed here. And if no one is looking over your shoulder, it's fun to play around with.

5 Click the Options tab in the TextArt 7 dialog box to add patterns and shadow effects, and to change colors and character thickness. Experiment until you come up with something you like. Figure 15.6 shows what you can end up with.

> **TIP** **Those TextArt characters actually have two parts to them, an** outline of the character and "fill" inside the outline. When you first pop up TextArt, the outlines and the fill are the same color, so they look like solid characters. Click the Pattern button on the Options tab of the TextArt 7 dialog box and choose No Fill to see the outlines more clearly.

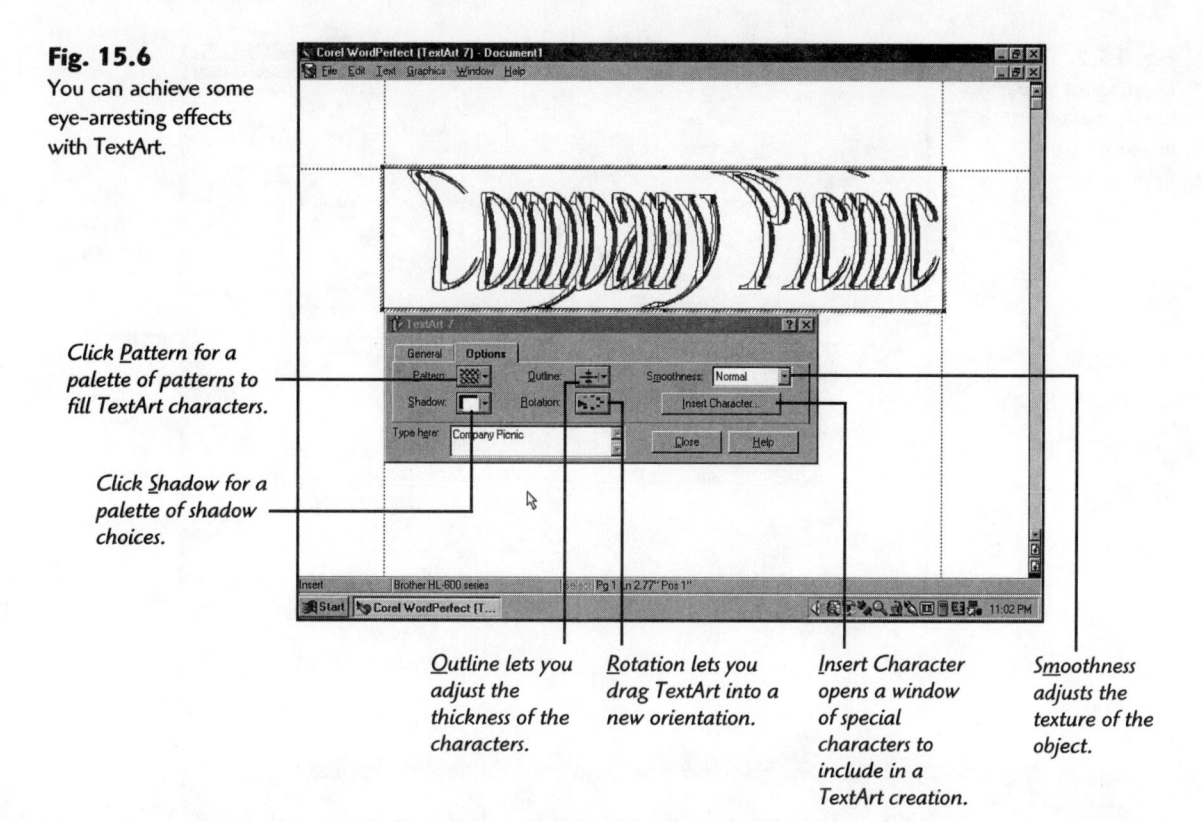

Fig. 15.6
You can achieve some eye-arresting effects with TextArt.

Click Pattern for a palette of patterns to fill TextArt characters.

Click Shadow for a palette of shadow choices.

Outline lets you adjust the thickness of the characters.

Rotation lets you drag TextArt into a new orientation.

Insert Character opens a window of special characters to include in a TextArt creation.

Smoothness adjusts the texture of the object.

6 Click the Rotation button, and drag any of the rotation handles shown in figure 15.7 to change the orientation of the characters. Click the Rotation button again to make the rotation handles disappear.

7 When you're satisfied with your creation, click anywhere outside the broken-line border to plop the image into a document. The editing window returns to normal, and the TextArt 7 dialog box disappears.

Editing TextArt

Once you've stuck TextArt into a document, you can save it for reuse, copy and paste it into other documents, or add text above, below, or around it. To save a TextArt creation as a WordPerfect image:

1 If you've inserted your TextArt into a document, click the TextArt object to select it. If you're still in the TextArt 7 editing window, you don't have to click the object; it's already selected.

Fig. 15.7
Rotating the characters is nifty, but distorts the image.

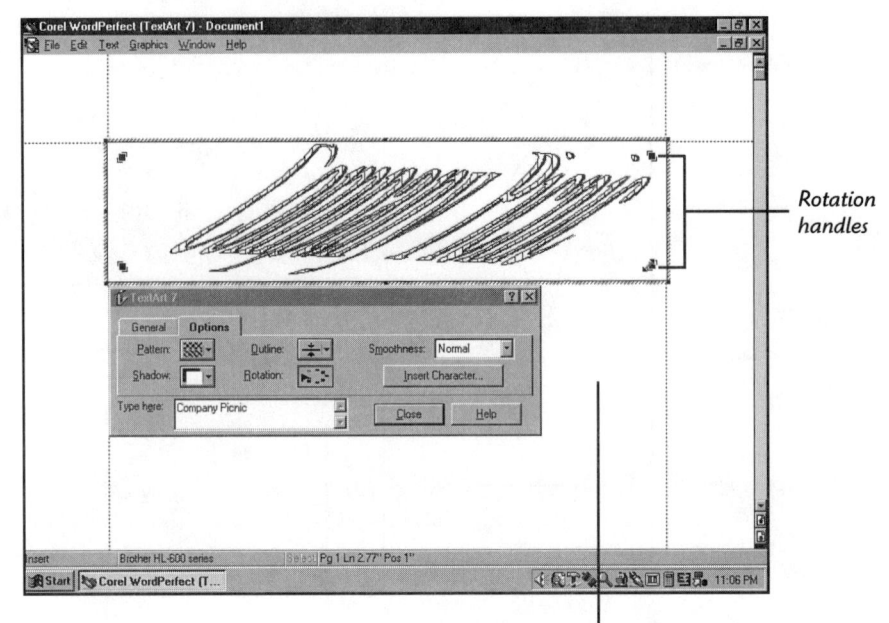

Rotation handles

Click outside the TextArt object to return to your document.

2 Choose File, Save As. The Save dialog box appears.

3 In the Save dialog box, choose Selected Image and click OK.

4 The Corel Office—Save As dialog box appears. Select a folder in which to save the TextArt object, type a name for the object, and click Save.

The default MyFiles folder is a fine home for TextArt object, but you might want to save your TextArt in the COREL\OFFICE7\GRAPHICS folder instead. If you do, your TextArt object will appear on the list of graphics files whenever you click the Toolbar Insert Image button.

To move TextArt on the page, put the pointer over the TextArt object and click. That pops up black square **sizing handles** around the object and the pointer turns into a four-headed arrow, as shown in figure 15.8.

Now, drag the object to a new spot on the page. Click outside the object to make the handles disappear and fix your TextArt in place.

To edit the object, just double-click it to get the TextArt dialog box back.

When you finish editing, click anywhere outside the object to return to the normal editing window.

Fig. 15.8
Drag the TextArt object anywhere you like, or size it to suit.

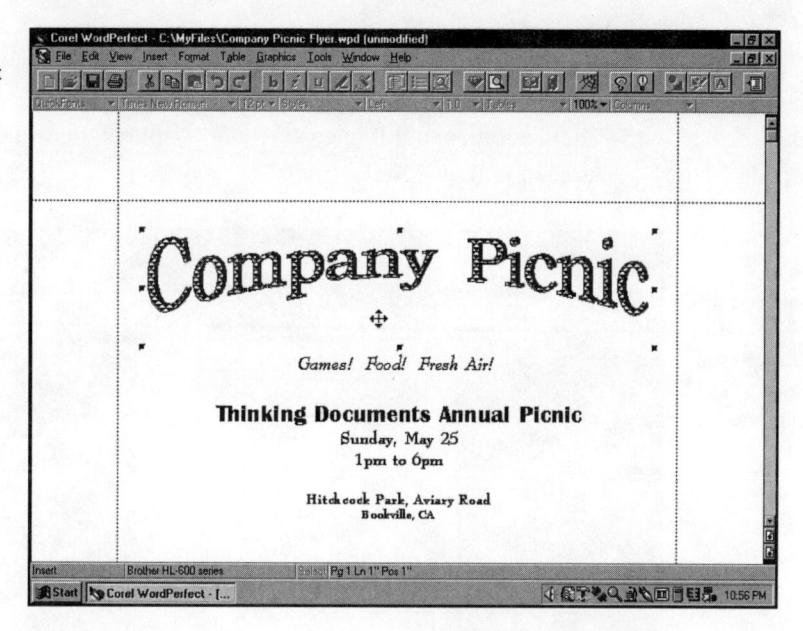

Create fancy stationery with watermarks

Take a sheet of good-quality stationery and hold it up to the light. That faint image you see is a **watermark**. It's usually the paper manufacturer's name, but sometimes, you'll find a design, or both. Paper makers have distinguished their work with watermarks for the past three hundred or so years.

WordPerfect watermarks are faint designs or characters in the background of the page that give a similar effect. You can use a WordPerfect image for a watermark, or use any document file to create your own.

WordPerfect images make great watermarks

As with headers and footers, watermarks repeat on every page of a document until you turn them off. Also like headers and footers, you can put up to two watermarks on a page. Start from a blank document, or stick a watermark directly into your current document.

To create a watermark in the current document:

   1 Click Format, Watermark.

2 In the Watermark dialog box that appears, select Watermark A, and click Create.

3 That switches to full-page view and displays the watermark feature bar, as seen in figure 15.9.

Fig. 15.9
If you start in a document with text in it, the document is still active even though you don't see it as you create a watermark.

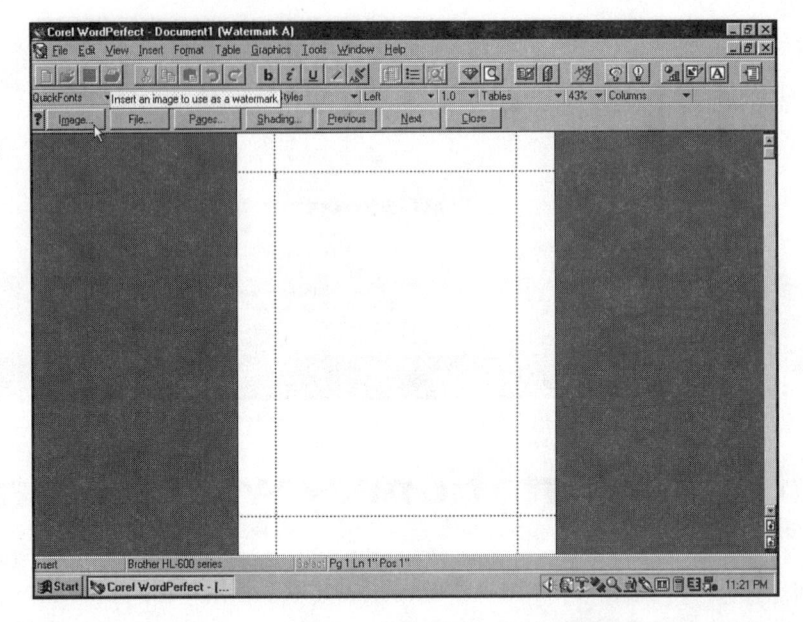

4 Click the Image button on the feature bar, and the Insert Image dialog box appears. The Graphics folder displayed in the Look in box is packed with images, and with folders filled with still more images. If you feel like browsing, double-click the QuickArt folder; then double-click the Standard.qad folder. The folders that appear next hold images (and other folders with images!) organized by category. Double-click your way through those and any further subfolders, and you'll see the thumbnail images shown in figure 15.10 (click the Large Icons button on the Insert Image dialog box toolbar to see them more clearly).

5 If you'd rather not work your way through the QuickArt folders and subfolders, just select one of the file names in the Graphics folder, and click the Preview button on the Insert Image dialog box toolbar to view the image. Figure 15.10 shows the Insert Image dialog box with a selected file being previewed.

Fig. 15.10
There's a great collection of image files stored in WordPerfect's Graphics folder.

Click the Preview button to view a selected image.

Double-click these subfolders for more art work.

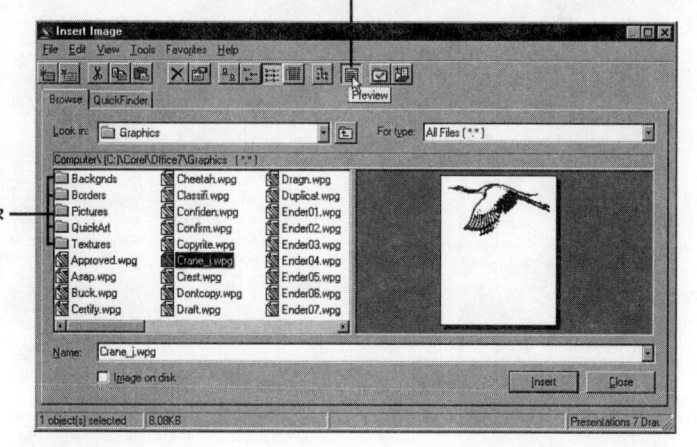

> **TIP** **Don't click the Preview button again after selecting a file to view.** Keep the button pushed in, and view the files one after another as you select them from the list.

6 Once you find an image you like, click <u>I</u>nsert in the Insert Image dialog box. Your selected image appears, faintly, centered in the watermark editing window.

7 Point at the image, and you'll see the four-headed arrow. Drag to move the image around on the page, or leave it centered. Point at any of the little handles. The pointer turns into a double arrow; drag to resize the image, as seen in figure 15.11.

8 For a fainter or darker image, click the <u>S</u>hading button on the feature bar, and enter a higher or lower value in the Watermark Shading dialog box.

9 Click <u>C</u>lose when you finish adjusting the image. That returns you to your document. If you had text in the document already, you'll see the watermark behind the text. Otherwise, type and edit your text as you would normally. Figure 15.12 shows a document with a watermark behind the text.

Fig. 15.11
Moving and resizing graphics in WordPerfect is easy with the mouse.

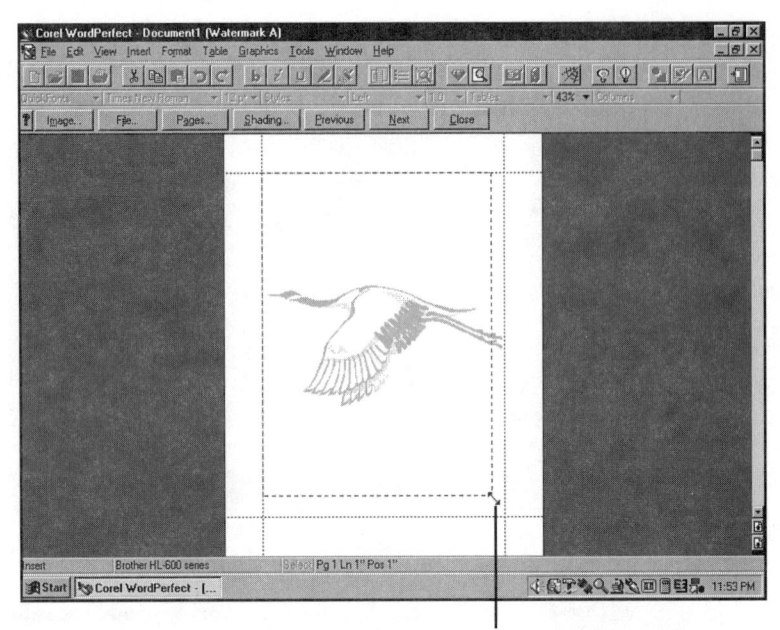

Drag one of the tiny handles around the image to resize it.

Fig. 15.12
The default shading value of 25% gives you a smooth image like this; reduce it too far and the image looks grainy.

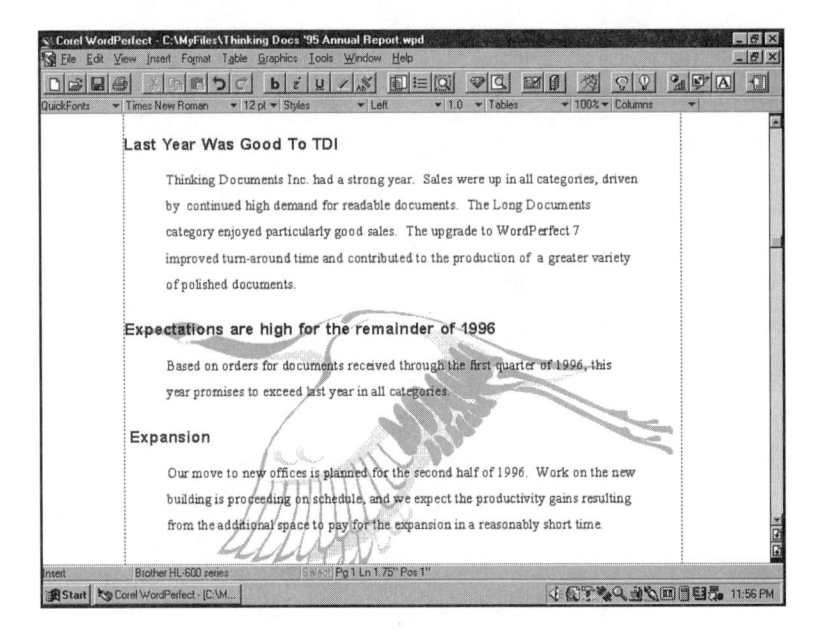

If you need to tinker with the watermark further, right-click the watermark (it doesn't matter if there's text in front of it) and select W<u>a</u>termark on the

Quickmenu. The Watermark dialog box appears; select Watermark A and click Edit.

To get rid of a watermark, open the reveal codes window (press Alt+F3), and drag the watermark code out the window. If you just want to discontinue it , choose Format, Watermark, choose the watermark you want to discontinue, and click Discontinue. That's handy if you don't want a watermark on every page of your document.

How do I create my own watermark?

Graphics (including those you create) that are saved as images are easy to use as watermarks. Just insert them into the watermark editing window as we just did. You can also turn any text or graphics file into a watermark. Here's one idea: create a logo with TextArt and save it as a document file. Then, use the file as a watermark.

Switch to the document in which you want the watermark. Select Format, Watermark, Create for the watermark editing window. Click the File button on the watermark feature bar, and double-click the file containing your TextArt logo. That pops it right into the watermark editing window.

Make any adjustments you want in the watermark editing window, click Close on the watermark feature bar, and you might wind up with something like figure 15.13.

Fig. 15.13
Combining features like watermarks and TextArt can save you a trip to the printer.

There's no outline, and a light gray was selected as the text color in TextArt.

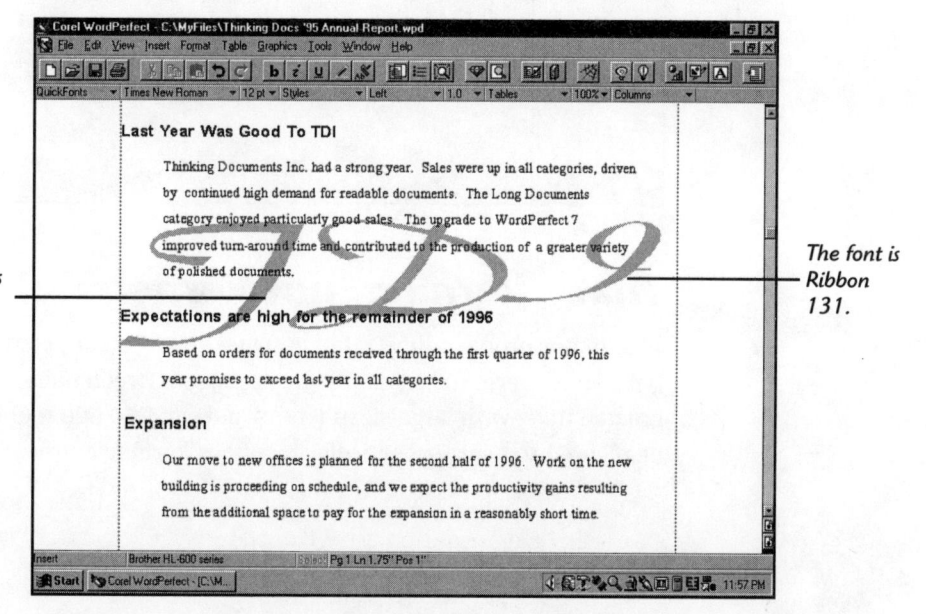

The font is Ribbon 131.

WordPerfect puts a typesetter on your desk

Documents created in WordPerfect and printed on a laser printer look almost like pages set and printed by a professional printer. The "almost" is partly because the spacing between letters in a typeset document is perfect. In WordPerfect, certain pairs of letters look as though they have minor variations in the amount of space between them.

It's subtle, but enough to give a perfectionist pause. Spacing variations are due to the shape of certain characters, and they're especially obvious in larger point sizes (see fig. 15.14).

Fig. 15.14
Lower case e's and n's are especially prone to the appearance of having extra space.

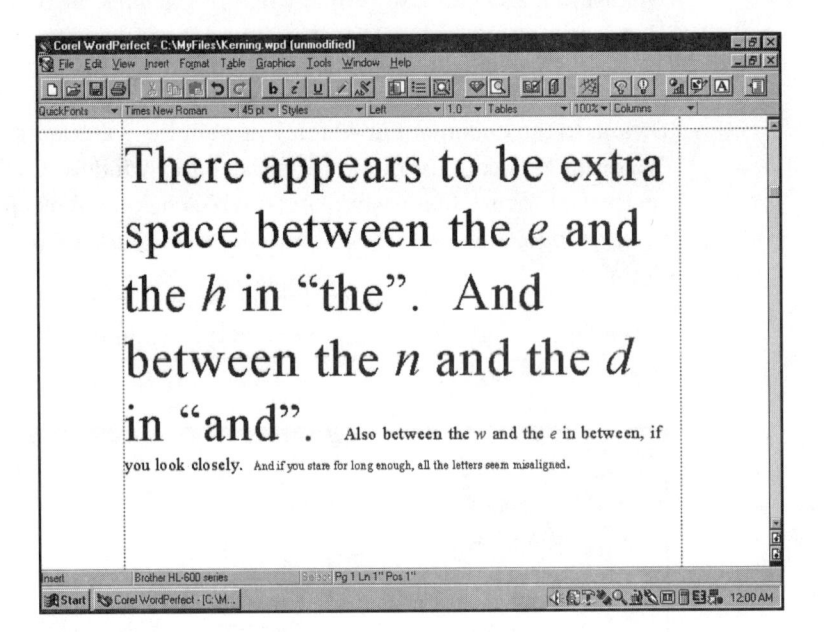

That's kerning, not kernel, Colonel

That minor problem illustrated in figure 15.15 can be fixed. **Kerning** is the typesetter's term for adjusting the spacing between pairs of letters. If you've created titles with large-sized letters and run into odd looking spacing, you'll be pleased to hear that WordPerfect does kerning automatically.

66 Plain English, please!

Kerning is so-called because the projecting parts of letters like "J" in metal type are called **kerns**. Computers often allow too much space between letters for kerns. That's especially obvious in cases like "A" and "V," which have complementary projections that could be placed closer together. 99

To turn on automatic kerning to fix spacing problems between letter pairs:

1 Select the text you want adjusted, or just put the insertion point at the beginning of the document.

2 Click Format, Typesetting, Word/Letter Spacing and the Word/Letter Spacing dialog box appears, as shown in figure 15.15.

Fig. 15.15
Kerning is usually needed only with very large point sizes, and you may very well never need it at all.

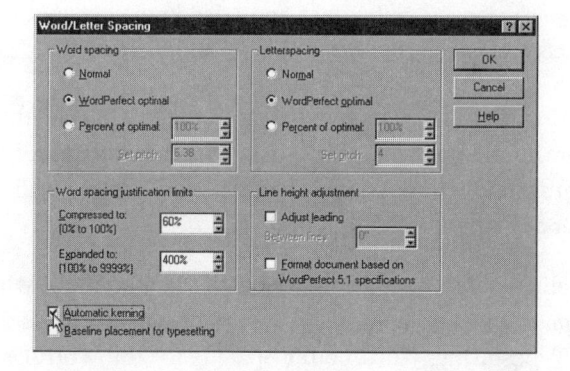

3 Select Automatic Kerning, and click OK.

Automatic kerning has one big drawback: it only works for certain pairs of letters. Worse, the letter pairs vary from font to font, so you can't know if automatic kerning will do the job for you until you try it.

If automatic kerning doesn't fix the problem, try manual kerning. Put the insertion point between the two characters you want to kern and select Format, Typesetting, Manual Kerning. That pops up the Manual Kerning dialog box. Click the Amount arrows to adjust spacing between the two letters, and observe the effect.

Q&A *How come the Manual Kerning choice on the Format, Typesetting menu is grayed-out?*

You've selected text. Manual kerning only works for two characters. Simply position the insertion point between the two characters and try again.

Line Spacing? Leading? What's that all about?

Adjusting the spacing between lines in WordPerfect is a snap—provided you want your lines to be single, one and a half, or double-spaced. Click the Power Bar Line Spacing button and take your pick. Choose Other on the Power Bar Line Spacing button to pop up the Line Spacing dialog box, and you can set your lines anywhere from .01 to 160 (really) lines apart.

TIP Type either fractions or decimals in the Line Spacing dialog box, whichever you prefer. 1.25 and 1 1/4 both work; just remember to put a space between the whole number and the fraction.

Line spacing takes the distance between the top of one line and the top of the line below it, and multiplies that distance (called **line height**) by whatever value you set. Adjusting line spacing will very likely be all that you need, but even finer adjustments are possible.

If you really need to, you can tinker with the amount of white space between the *bottom* of one line and the top of the line below it. To do that, select Format, Typesetting, Word/Letter Spacing for the Word/Letter Spacing dialog box (see figure 15.15).

Look under Line height adjustment and click Adjust leading. Then, click the Between Lines arrows to enter a new value.

66 *Plain English, please!*

Leading (pronounced "*LED-ding*," like pencil lead) is the typesetter's term for adjusting the space between lines. Typesetters working with metal type used thin strips of metal, often made of lead, to divide lines of type. The strips are called leads, and the more you added, the more space between lines you got. Hence, leading. **99**

How about letterspacing?

Full-justification is used in the body text of books to give the page a formal, balanced look. If you've tried full-justification, you'll have noticed something right away: in order to make a fully justified line flush with both the left and right margins, WordPerfect inserts a lot of space between words and letters.

Letterspacing and **Word Spacing** combat these unsightly spaces in justified text. Select Fo_r_mat, _T_ypesetting, _W_ord/Letter Spacing for the Word/Letter Spacing dialog box (see fig. 15.15). Select any of the following in the dialog box:

- Word Spacing and Letterspacing _N_ormal sets the amount of space between words and letters to the font manufacturer's specifications. _W_ordPerfect optimal, the default setting, uses the program's values for word and letter spacing for a particular font.

- P_e_rcent of optimal for word and letter spacing lets you fiddle with the values. Values less than 100% reduce the spaces between words and letters; values greater than 100% increase the spacing. Trial-and-error is the way to proceed here.

- **Pitch** is the number of characters-per-inch. When you select _S_et pitch and click the arrows to enter new values, you're directly controlling the number of characters-per-inch that are displayed and printed.

- Word spacing justification limits is like a vise for lines of text. If the words in a fully justified line are too close together, set a higher value than the default in the _C_ompressed to box. To reduce the spacing between the words, enter a lower value in the E_x_panded to box.

Pardon my French: inserting special characters

Suppose you have to write a letter in French (or Spanish or German). You haul out those old high school and college language texts, keep the dictionary handy, and laboriously churn out your letter. You're finally done, but there's one problem: how do you type all those accented characters?

WordPerfect solves the problem. Select _I_nsert, _C_haracter to pop up the WordPerfect Characters dialog box shown in figure 15.16.

Fig. 15.16
Click the Character Set button in this dialog box to choose from a variety of different character sets; Japanese or Cyrillic, for example.

Click any of the special characters, select Insert or Insert and Close, and the character is inserted at the insertion point.

The Number in the WordPerfect Characters dialog box identifies each character. There are fifteen sets of characters, for everything from ASCII to Japanese, numbered 0 through 14. Each character in each set is also numbered. So 1,71 is character set 1 (Multinational), character number 71, which happens to be ü.

How can I use the Characters dialog box more efficiently?

Lifting your fingers from the keyboard to click characters in the WordPerfect Characters dialog box is a nuisance. Here's a short cut: press Ctrl+W, type a character and punctuation mark combination, then press Enter.

For example, press Ctrl+W, type **a'**, press Enter, and á is inserted at the insertion point. Table 15.1 shows keyboard shortcuts for some common accented characters, with a couple of other special characters thrown in for good measure.

Table 15.1 Keyboard shortcuts for common accented characters

Press Ctrl+W; type...	Then, press Enter to get
a`	à
a'	á
e^	ê
u"	ü
c,	ç

Press Ctrl+W; type...	Then, press Enter to get
AE	Æ
n~	ñ
co	©
/2	–
/c	¢

Substitute any other letter for the letters in the first column of table 15.1 to get that letter accented with the accent marks in the second column.

16

Jazz Up a Document with Graphics

● **In this chapter:**

- How do I add a line to this document?

- My text could use a picture pick-me-up

- This graphic looks great, but it doesn't fit in my text!

- Can I move and resize a graphic?

- What's a text box?

Even the strongest text benefits from a choice graphic or two. And although writing forceful prose is hard work, inserting graphics in a WordPerfect document is always easy . . . . . ▶

A cliché is something we think all the time, but don't dare utter. Here's one: one picture is worth.... You get the picture. With images coming at us from every direction nowadays, we're tempted to treat that particular cliché as truth.

Not that it is. History might not have taken quite the turn it did if Jefferson had substituted a graphic for a ringing phrase like "Life, liberty, and the pursuit of happiness" in the Declaration of Independence.

Still, graphics generally enhance a document—especially if the document itself isn't exactly loaded with ringing phrases. You won't find any images likely to alter history in WordPerfect, but there is a huge collection of text-enhancing graphics.

Here's your line: graphics lines

You can do a lot with a line or two. Call attention to your text, break up a page, add a little visual interest; one well-placed line can be more effective than a more complex image.

WordPerfect makes inserting, moving, and editing lines a breeze. You also have a choice of vertical or horizontal lines in different weights and styles. And, if you don't like any of the choices offered, you can create your own line.

Here's the speediest way to insert a horizontal line in a WordPerfect document: type three hyphens ([-][-][-]) and press Enter. You get an instant single line that runs from the left margin to the right margin. Need a double-line instead? Type three equals signs ([=][=][=]) and press Enter. Don't put any spaces between the hyphens or equals signs, or QuickLines, as they're called, won't work. Like one of those trick ropes that stiffen when a magician waves his hand, QuickLines transform ordinary hyphens and equals signs into graphics lines as if by magic.

To get rid of a QuickLine, click it and press Delete.

Q&A *What if I really want three hyphens (or equals signs), not a graphics line?*

QuickLines, like most WordPerfect features, can be turned off. Click Tools, QuickCorrect, Options. Deselect the QuickLines check box in the QuickCorrect Options dialog box that appears, and click OK.

How do I get a line on more lines?

If a vertical line is what you need, click Graphics, Vertical Line for a line that runs from the top margin to the bottom margin of the page. Turned QuickLines off and want a horizontal line? Click Graphics, Horizontal Line for a line that goes from the left to the right margin. Figure 16.1 shows a full page view of a vertical line.

> 66 *Plain English, please!*
>
> What WordPerfect calls a **graphics line**—like the vertical and horizontal lines described here—is called a **rule** by typesetters. That's a straightforward bit of typesetting jargon: how do you add straight lines to a page? With a ruler. Incidentally, a QuickLine is the same thing as a horizontal graphics line, just a different way to produce it. 99

Fig. 16.1
The default lines run from margin to margin, top to bottom, or side to side.

Vertical lines inserted in the body of a page don't go in headers and footers.

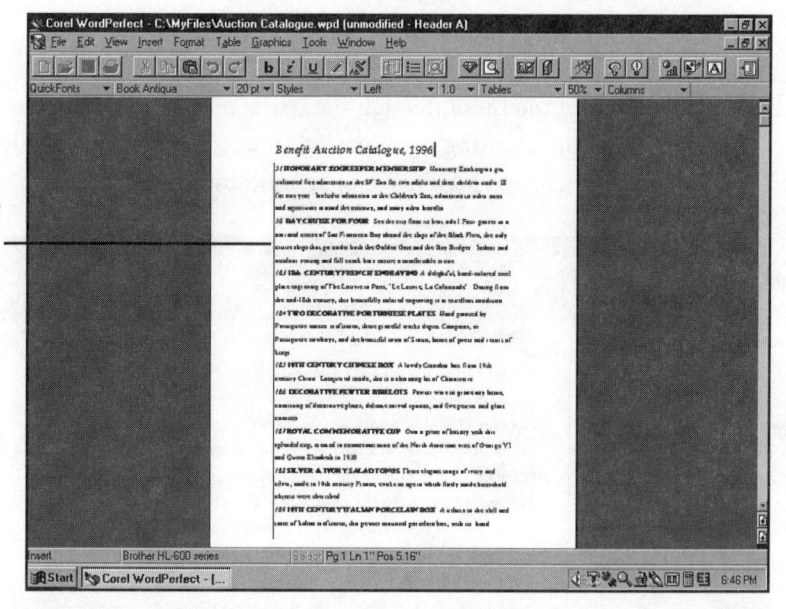

TIP **If you have a lot of graphics to insert in a page, you** might find the Graphics Toolbar handy. Right-click the Toolbar for the QuickMenu, and select Graphics. Clicking the Horizontal Line or Vertical Line buttons inserts either kind of line, just like the Graphics menu's Horizontal and Vertical Line commands.

Q&A ***I just inserted a horizontal line; now I've lost the flashing insertion point!***

The insertion point is still there, but it takes the shape of the line you inserted. It's hidden by the line, but if you look closely at the very beginning of the line, you'll see it faintly ticking away. When you start typing or when you press Enter, the insertion point comes out from hiding.

This line needs some work: move, resize, or delete it

Once inserted, either with the menu commands or the QuickLines trick, lines are easily moved, deleted, and formatted. You might divide your document with a vertical line, for example, and then want to move it to another spot on the page.

To move a line:

1. Put the tip of the pointer arrow on the line. The pointer changes direction, pointing right instead of left, when it's correctly positioned. Click once, and handles appear, as shown in figure 16.2.

Fig. 16.2
The pointer tip has to be right on the line if you want to select it.

Handles pop up when you select a line, and the pointer becomes a four-headed arrow.

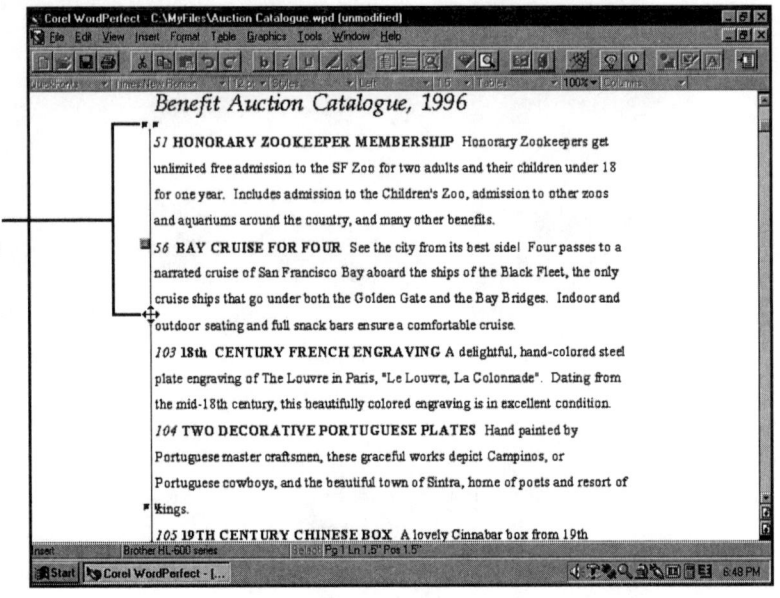

2. With the pointer anywhere along the line, just drag it to a new position. A broken outline of the line follows the pointer around; release the mouse button and the line snaps into place.

You can also use the mouse to change the width of a line. If you put the pointer directly over one of the handles, it turns into a double-headed arrow. Drag the double-headed arrow to thicken the line, as shown in figure 16.3.

Fig. 16.3
Like any WordPerfect graphic, you can drag the handles to move or resize.

Dragging a handle with the double-headed arrow makes the line thicker or thinner.

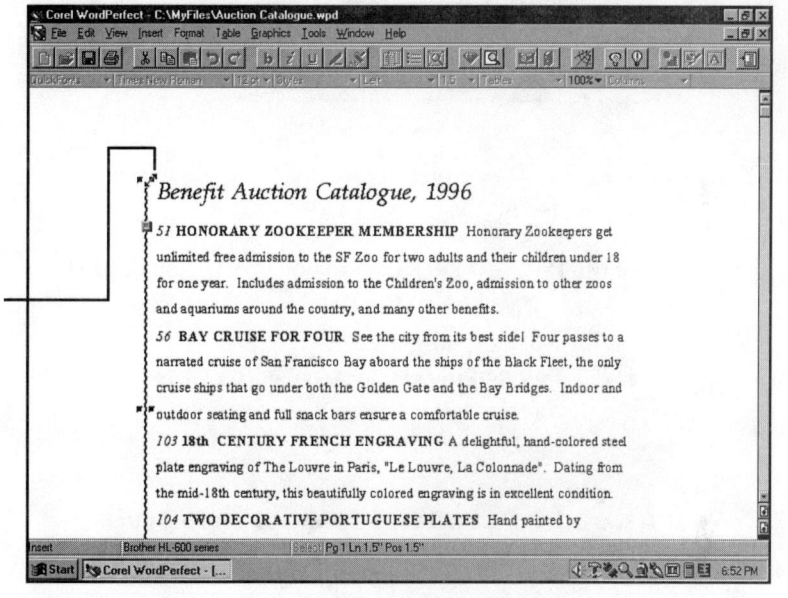

To get rid of the handles, click anywhere outside the line.

To delete the line, point at it, and click for the handles. Press the Delete key on your keyboard—the line is gone.

I want a fancier line

Lines make page dividers, and they can also be decorative, injecting a little visual stimulus into a document. WordPerfect gives you a whole palette of line styles.

For fancier effects, put the tip of the pointer on a graphics line. When the pointer changes direction and points right, double-click. That pops up the Edit Graphics Line dialog box. Under Line options, click the Line style drop-down arrow (not to be confused with the Line Styles button on the right of the dialog box!) for the palette of lines shown in figure 16.4.

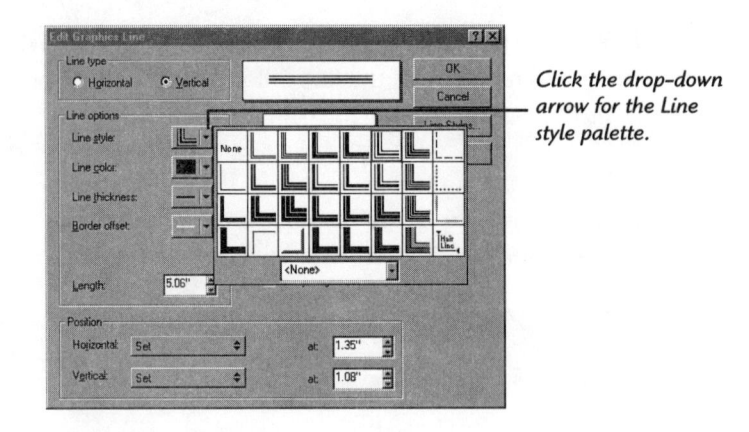

Fig. 16.4
These line styles look like wedges, but you get either vertical or horizontal lines.

Click the drop-down arrow for the Line style palette.

Click your choice on the palette, click OK, and your line is transformed into the selected style.

Use the Edit Graphics Line dialog box to adjust the length and position of your lines if you like. (I find the mouse easier for most line maneuvers.)

> **TIP** You can also right-click a line to pop up a QuickMenu of editing choices.

I need to create my own line style

If you don't like any of the line styles available in the Edit Graphics Line dialog box, create your own. Click the Line Styles button in the dialog box (not the Line style button; that gives you the palette of existing styles in figure 16.4).

In the Line Styles dialog box, click Create for the Create Line Style dialog box shown in figure 16.5.

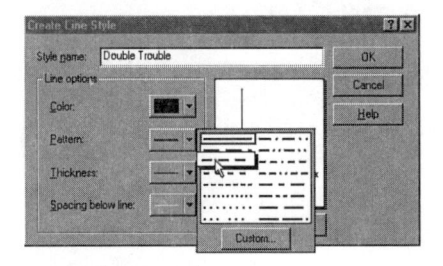

Fig. 16.5
Customizing a line is easy to do, and once you name your custom line, you can use it over and over again.

Select a Color, Pattern, or Thickness, type a name for your custom style in the Style Name edit box, and click OK when you're done.

Your custom style will appear on the Styles list in the Line Styles dialog box.

When text needs a pickup... add a picture

WordPerfect comes with a huge assortment of pictures, graphical messages such as Top Secret, and decorative borders and images that can add a little punch to your pages.

To stick a graphic into your document at the insertion point:

1 Look your document over and decide where the graphic ought to go. It's easy to move graphics around, but deciding on a position in advance will save you a little work. Move the insertion point to the spot where you want the graphic.

2 Click the Image button on the Toolbar. The Insert Image dialog box appears.

3 If you know which graphics file you want, just double-click it on the list. If you're browsing, click the Preview button in the Insert Image dialog box. As you select graphics file names, they appear in the viewer, as seen in figure 16.6.

Fig. 16.6
Click a file and it appears in the viewer. As you select files, leave the viewer on to see each one in turn.

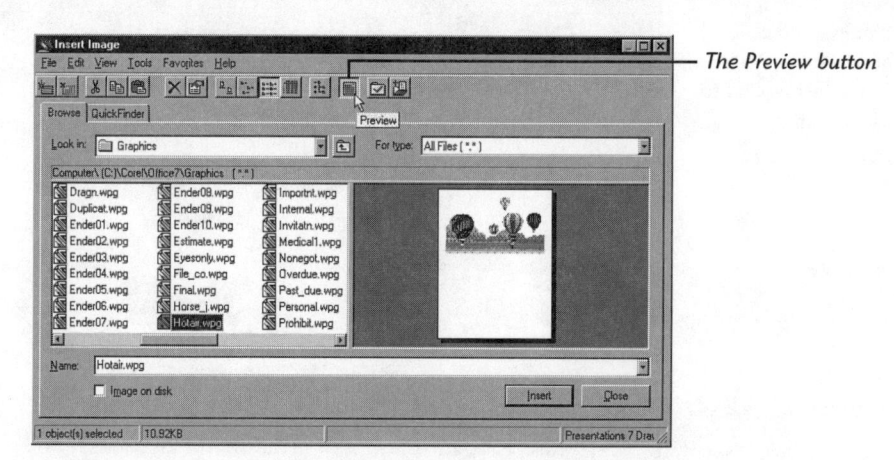

The Preview button

> **TIP**
> **There are more graphics in the Pictures, Borders, Backgnds, Textures, and QuickArt folders you'll see in the Insert Image dialog box. Double-click any of them to see more graphics files and folders.**

4. When you find a graphic you like, double-click it. The graphics image pops into place in your document at the insertion point.

5. If everything is perfect, click anywhere outside the graphic. If you need to make some adjustments (and you probably will), read on.

How do I fit this graphic on the page?

Popping a graphic into a document is easy. Once popped, you'll probably have to tinker with the graphic to fit it on the page. That's okay, because tinkering is easy, too.

This graphic pushed my text aside!

Like anything inserted in a WordPerfect document, whatever's already in place gets shoved aside to make room for the graphic. As you can see in figure 16.7, that isn't exactly what we want.

Fig. 16.7
Graphics (and any other inserted objects) unceremoniously shove existing text around to make room.

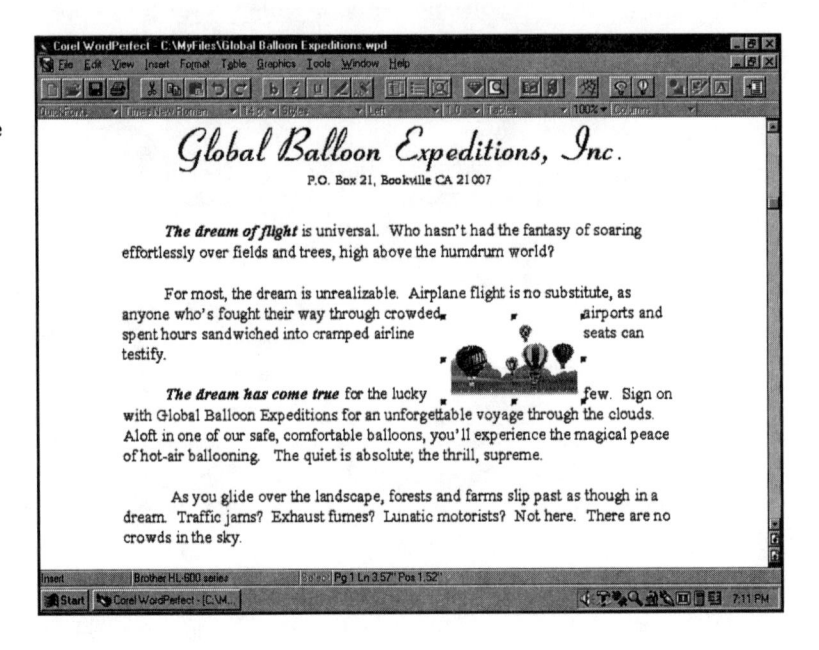

Chapter 16 Jazz Up a Document with Graphics

We want the text to snake around the graphic, instead of having our paragraph cut in half like the one in figure 16.7. That's called **wrapping**, and it's easily done.

To wrap text around a graphic:

1. Click the QuickSpot inside the graphic to pop up the Edit Box dialog box. In the Edit Box dialog box, click the Wrap text button for the menu shown in figure 16.8.

Fig. 16.8
The Edit Box dialog box gives you all the tools you need to fit graphics to the page.

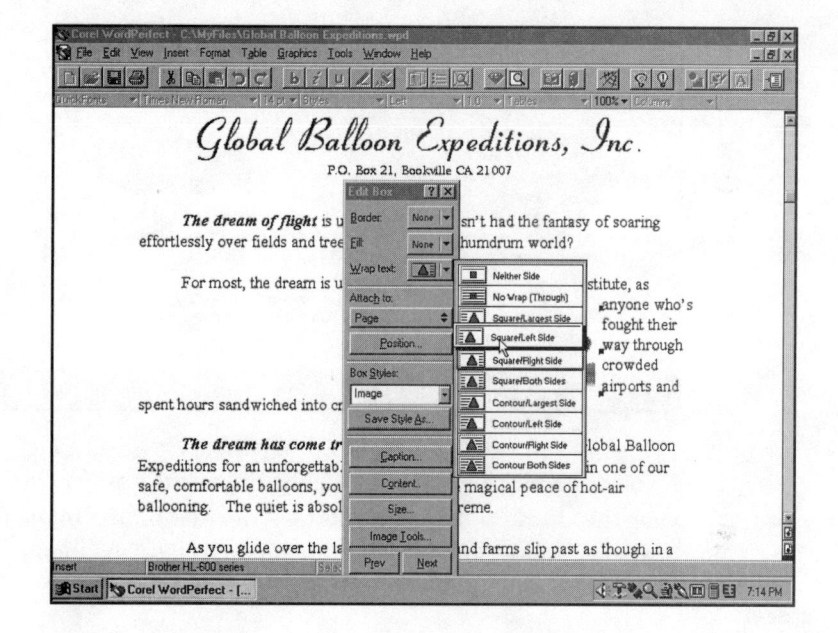

Q&A Why don't I see the QuickSpot inside my graphic?

If the graphic is selected (the handles will be visible), the QuickSpot can be hard to spot. Click outside the graphic to deselect it; then, move the pointer back over the graphic. You'll see the QuickSpot appear in the upper left-hand corner of the image.

2. The illustrations next to each choice on the Wrap Text menu are pretty self-explanatory. Trial-and-error is fine here, too; you can always come back and change wrapping options. We'll choose Square/Left Side to fit our text along the left side of the graphic. Wrapping text around the left side of a graphic is usually a safe choice. Since the eye reads from left to right, text wrapped around the right side can be difficult to read.

3 Once you make your selection on the Wrap Text menu, click anywhere on the page outside the Edit Box dialog box and the graphic to see a big improvement, as shown in figure 16.9.

Fig. 16.9
Wrapping text around a graphic integrates the text with the picture.

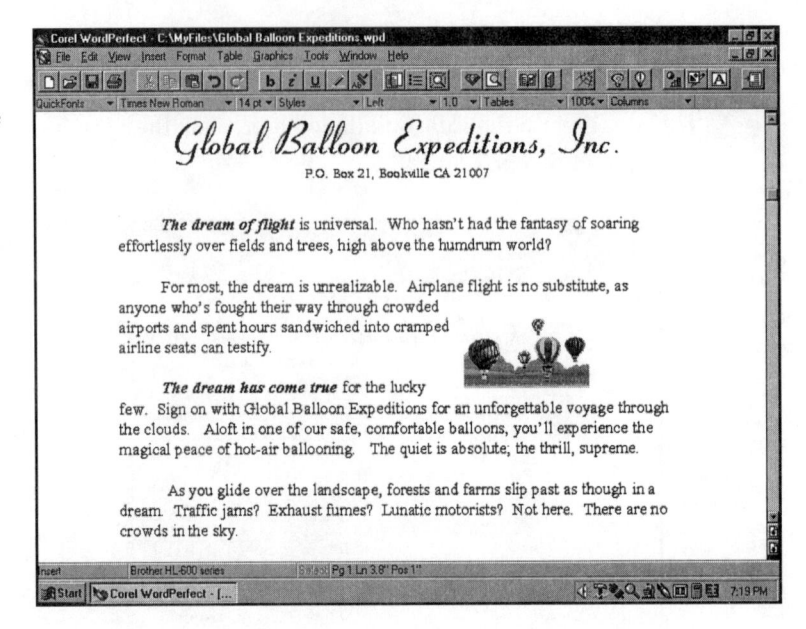

If you don't like the squared-off look, move the pointer over the graphic and click the QuickSpot. Now click the Wrap text button in the Edit Box dialog box and choose Contour/Left Side on the Wrap Text menu (refer to fig. 16.8). That gives you the effect shown in figure 16.10.

Text wrap has improved the way our graphic looks on the page, but we can still do better.

How do I resize this graphic?

Figures 16.9 and 16.10 show a graphic with text neatly wrapped around the left side of the image. We've also got a large blob of white space to the right of the graphic that doesn't look quite right.

We'll simply expand the graphic toward the right margin to fill in the space. Click the graphic to select it. The handles appear around the graphic; drag the handle in the lower-right corner over to the right margin to expand the image, as shown in figure 16.11.

Fig. 16.10
Contouring text around a graphic can really knit your text and image together.

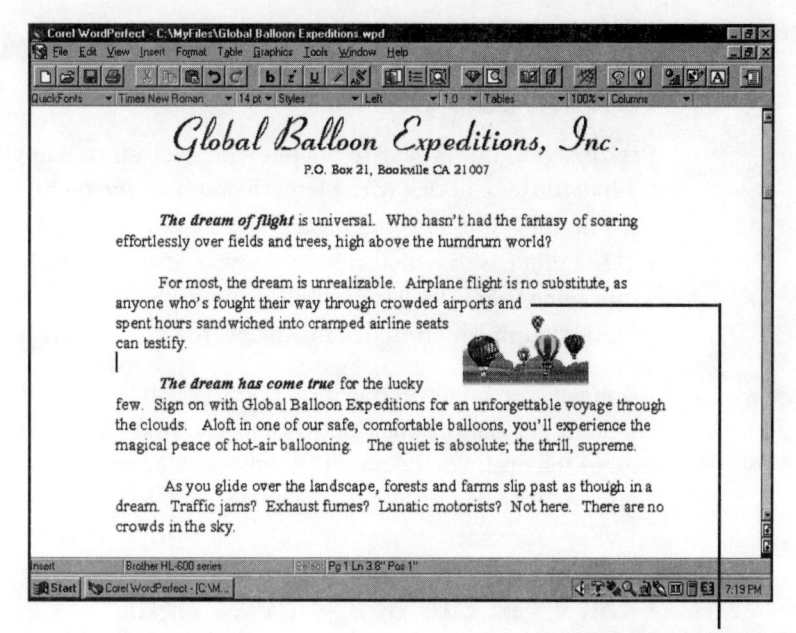

Contoured text follows the shape of the side of the image you select.

Fig. 16.11
When the pointer is over a handle, it becomes a double-headed arrow; drag to stretch the image in any direction.

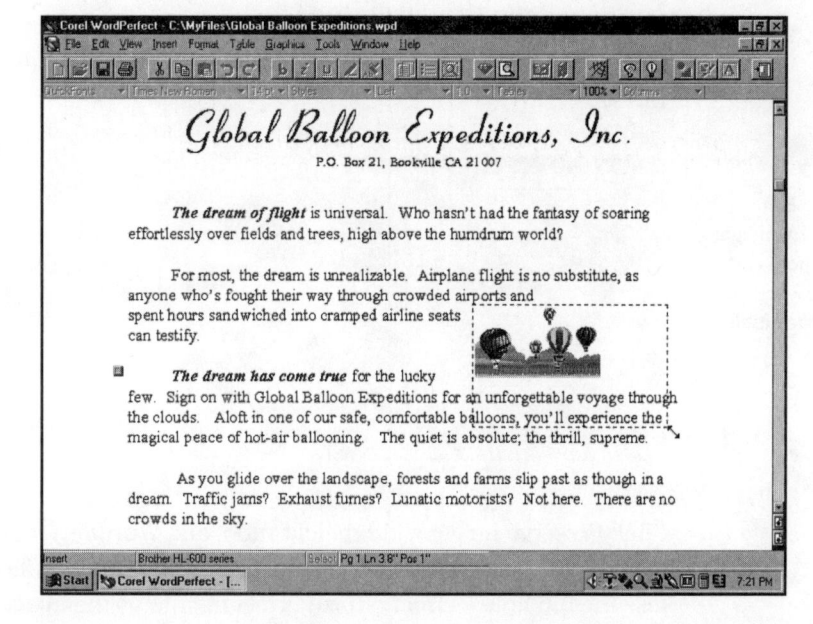

This graphic looks like a reflection in a fun house mirror

Resizing graphics is easy to do, but when you stretch anything, you distort it. It's like those balloons with pictures on them; the picture looks fine, until you blow up the balloon. Dragging a graphic's corner handle, as we did in figure 16.11, minimizes the distortion since you're expanding both height and width at the same time. Dragging a middle handle at the sides or the top of the graphic flattens or stretches the image, but you can fix it.

If you yank an image in one direction, you can tug it in the other direction to eliminate the distortion. That, with a little trial-and-error work, should take care of the problem. Of course, if you yank horizontally and then tug vertically, you'll be expanding the image in both directions, which may or may not be what you want.

I can't get this image quite right

If the yanking and tugging approach doesn't seem to work, there's another way to deal with resized image distortion.

Click the graphic's QuickSpot; then click the Content button in the Edit Box dialog box that pops up. That gets you the Box Content dialog box (see fig. 16.12).

Fig. 16.12
Clicking the Edit button takes you right to Presentations and a battery of gadgets to alter the image itself.

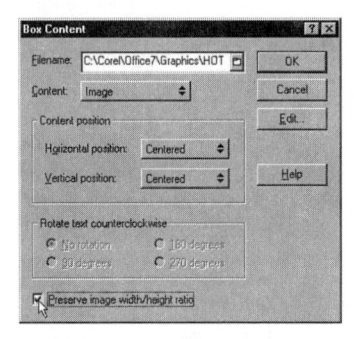

Click Preserve image width/height ratio, and WordPerfect automatically adjusts the image to prevent distortion as you resize it. Click OK, and you lose the fun house effect. WordPerfect maintains the image's original width-to-height ratio, no matter how high and wide you drag your graphic.

Retaining the original Height/Width ratio may still leave you with too much white space around the image. If so, deselect Preserve Image Width/Height Ratio in the Box Content dialog box, and go back to yanking and tugging.

You can also try resizing the box around the image. Click the graphic's QuickSpot and choose Size in the Edit Box dialog box. In the Box Size dialog box that appears, make sure Set is selected for both Height and Width; then try entering new values for Height and Width. Although the graphics box starts out fitted to the graphic, it doesn't stay that way when you start resizing. And, unfortunately, there's no automatic way to fit the contents of the box—your graphic—to the box itself once you've resized it. Trial and error is the only option here.

I just can't get this graphic right!

If you've yanked and tugged the image, fiddled with the Box Contents and Box Size dialog boxes, and still can't get the image quite right, consider starting over. If you've plucked an image from WordPerfect's collection, click to select it, and then press Delete to erase it from your document.

Now try Plan B: Drag to Create. Drag to Create lets you drag a graphics box to the size and shape you want. When the box is sized and placed, you pop the image of your choice right into it. At least, that's the idea. An image inserted this way may need to be fiddled with as well, but it's worth a shot. To insert an image into a document with Drag to Create:

1 Select Graphics, Drag to Create and click OK in the WordPerfect for Windows message box that pops up (if there's a check by Drag to Create, skip this step—it's already enabled).

2 Click the Image button on the Toolbar; then move the pointer into the editing window. The pointer turns into a little hand clutching a picture frame (but only when the pointer is actually *in* the editing window).

3 Position the pointer at the upper left corner of the area where you want the graphic, and drag toward the lower right corner. That picture frame the hand was clutching expands, as seen in figure 16.13.

4 Don't worry about placing the graphic with precision—it's easy to move it later on. You may get better results if you drag the lower-right corner of the box all the way over to the right margin. Release the mouse button at the lower right-hand corner of where you want your graphic, and the Insert Image dialog box appears.

Fig. 16.13
The broken-line box indicates the position and dimensions of the graphic.

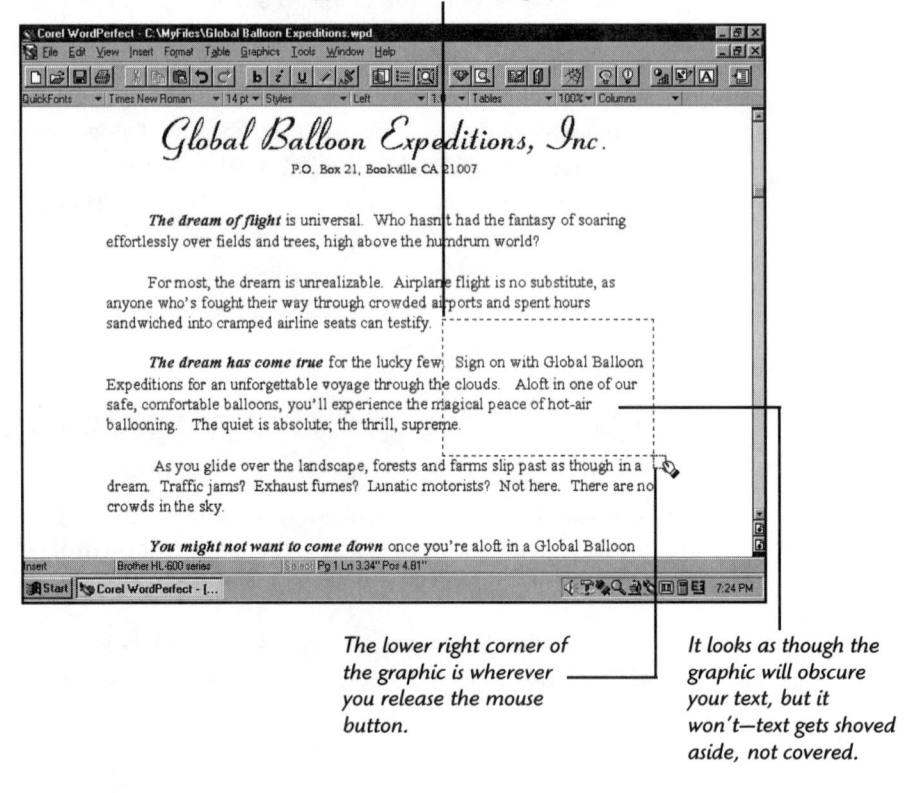

The point at which you start to drag is the upper left corner of the graphic.

The lower right corner of the graphic is wherever you release the mouse button.

It looks as though the graphic will obscure your text, but it won't—text gets shoved aside, not covered.

5. Double-click the image you want to use. The graphic image pops into place in your document, inside the box you've already created.

6. Now, click the graphics QuickSpot to see the Edit Box dialog box, and choose a text wrapping option. Click anywhere outside the dialog box and the graphic, and with any luck, you'll have your graphic where you want it.

How do I move a graphic around?

Moving graphics is straightforward. Click the graphic to select it, and slide the pointer over the image until you get the four-headed arrow. Now, just drag to move the graphic anywhere you like. If you've selected a text wrapping option, text wraps automatically in the new location.

What about a caption?

If your graphic needs further explanation, add a caption. Click the graphic's QuickSpot, and choose Caption in the Edit Box dialog box. The Box Caption dialog box appears (see fig. 16.14).

Fig. 16.14
Choose the Caption position in the Box Caption dialog box; the preview window reflects your choices.

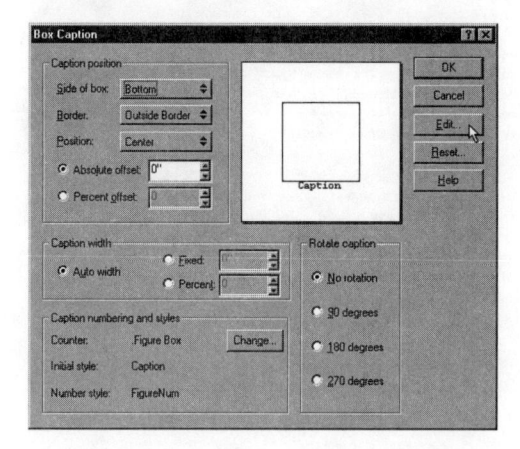

Put the caption below, above, or to one side of the image with your choice on the Side of Box button. With a caption above or below the graphics box, you can also center, left- or right-justify the caption text by clicking the Position button.

When you've settled on the caption's position, click Edit. That puts the insertion point at the selected caption position. Press Backspace to get rid of the generic **Figure 1** and type your own text. Click anywhere outside the graphic when you finish typing to remove the Edit Box dialog box. You'll wind up with something like figure 16.15.

To edit your caption further, right-click the graphic, and choose Edit Caption on the QuickMenu.

> **TIP** If you lose the graphic's QuickSpot during any of these maneuvers, moving the pointer over the graphic should get it back. Or right-click the graphic and take your pick of items on the QuickMenu.

Fig. 16.15
A caption describes images that aren't self-explanatory or conveys information that doesn't fit in the body text.

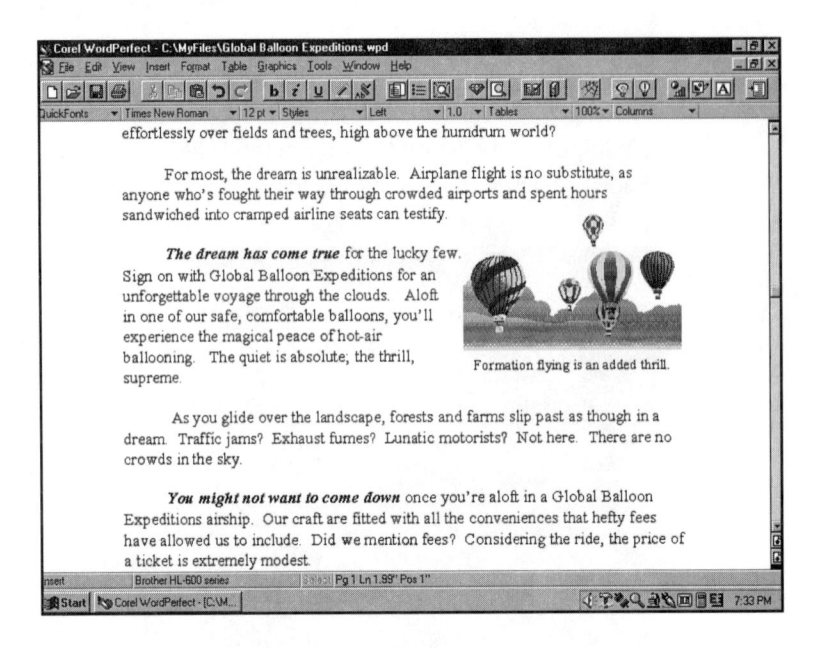

Just what is a graphics box?

WordPerfect puts graphics inside a box. When you move or resize an image, you're actually moving and resizing the box that contains the image. It's as though you were stretching or compressing a canvas by changing the size of the picture frame around it.

There are different styles of boxes for images, text, tables, and a particularly nifty style for buttons.

Click the graphic's QuickSpot; then click the Box Styles drop-down arrow and take your choice of box styles.

I need to make this text stand out

A **text box** is just what you'd expect: a graphics box containing text instead of an image. Text boxes make important information jump out at the reader.

To create a text box:

1. Move the insertion point to where you want the text box, and click the Text Box button on the Toolbar (or select Graphics, Text Box). You'll get two heavy black lines with the insertion point between them.

2 Type your text.

3 Change the font if you want to. Click outside the text box, move the pointer over the text box, and the QuickSpot appears. Click the QuickSpot to change the borders, or to add fill if you want it. Click outside the Edit Box dialog box and the text box, and you'll see something like figure 16.16.

Fig. 16.16
Text boxes call attention to an important message.

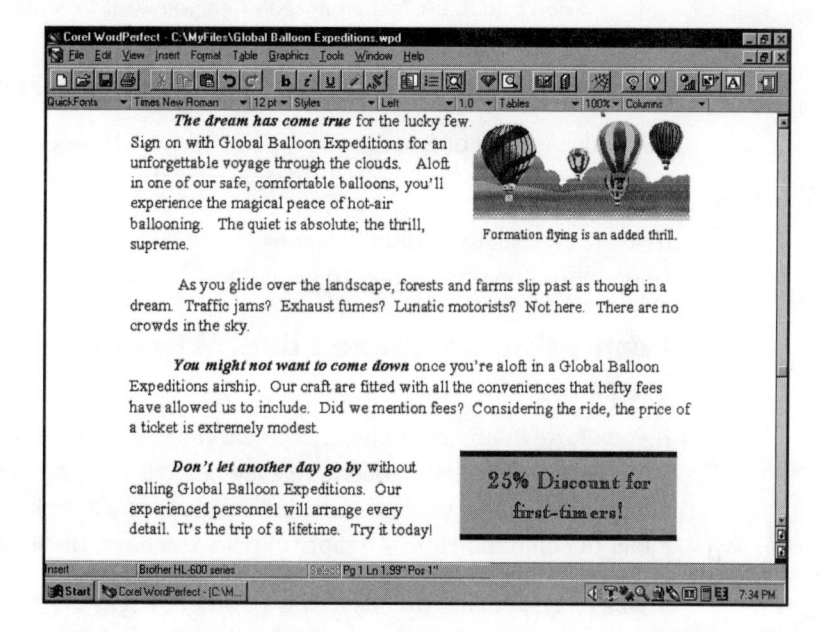

> **TIP** **The default Text Box Style gives you the two heavy black lines** shown in figure 16.17. To get rid of them, click the text box QuickSpot; then click the Border button in the Edit Box dialog box and choose None.

Editing text in a text box is a snap. Just double-click the box—that puts the insertion point inside it for easy editing. Click anywhere outside the box when you're done.

To move a text box around on the page, just click to select it and then drag with the four-headed arrow. You can wrap text around the box, too; click the text box QuickSpot, and take your pick of text wrapping options in the Edit Box dialog box.

CAUTION **Double-clicking an image has a dramatically different effect.** You'll think your system has ground to a halt, but actually it's WordPerfect's gears whirring as it loads Presentations. That's the Corel WordPerfect Suite's built-in drawing program, which we look at in Chapter 19. You can use the Presentations tools to edit your image, but you might find they're more than you want. To exit Presentations and return to your document, click anywhere outside the graphics box. And to avoid Presentations, right-click (don't double-click) an image when you want to make changes.

How do I get rid of graphics boxes?

Deleting any kind of graphics box, image, text, whatever, is the easiest part of inserting graphics. Just click the graphics box and press Delete.

If you decide that you didn't want to delete your graphic after all, click the Undo button on the Toolbar to get it back.

I can't find an image I like. Where can I find more graphics?

If you chose the recommended "Typical" installation of the Corel WordPerfect Suite, you got a pretty fair selection of graphics images to choose from. Once you've examined them all, you'll probably want more. It's a fact of computing life: the more clip art you have, the more you'll want.

That's okay, because there's a slew of other images the "Typical" installation doesn't include lurking on your Corel WordPerfect Suite CD. If you have a keen desire for a bigger selection of images, and over 30 megabytes of free hard disk space in which to store them, you can vastly increase your WordPerfect graphics collection.

First, check to make sure that the extra graphics aren't installed: click the Image button on the Toolbar; then double-click the QuickArt folder in the Insert Image dialog box. If you see the Premium.qad folder listed, skip the following steps. The additional QuickArt images are installed already. Double-click the Premium.qad folder, and select any of the subfolders therein to view scads of extra graphics.

If there is no Premium.qad folder listed in the QuickArt folder, go ahead and add the extra art work to your "Typical" WordPerfect installation:

1. Exit WordPerfect, the DAD, and any other Corel WordPerfect Suite 7 applications that might be running. Insert your Corel WordPerfect Suite CD, and the Corel WordPerfect Suite 7 CD-Rom dialog box will appear in a moment or two.

2. Click the WordPerfect Suite Setup button.

3. Keep clicking Next or Yes until you get to the Installation Type dialog box. Once there, select Custom.

4. Click Next until you see the Custom Installation dialog box. Select Optional Shared Components in the Custom Installation dialog box, and then click Components.

5. In the Optional Shared Components dialog box that appears, select Graphics and click Components.

6. That gets you the Graphics dialog box. Select QuickArt and click Components.

7. We've finally arrived at our destination: the QuickArt dialog box. Click the Additional QuickArt check box. Now, keep clicking OK or Next until you get to the Ready to Install dialog box. Click Install, and the additional QuickArt will be installed to your hard drive.

To view all the QuickArt you've just installed, run WordPerfect, and click the Image button on the Toolbar. Double-click the Premium.qad folder in the Insert Image dialog box; then browse the various subfolders. Inside them are dozens of images to satisfy your craving for more graphics. For now, at any rate.

Figure 16.17 shows the QuickArt in one of the many (many!) Premium.qad subfolders.

Fig. 16.17
QuickArt displays thumbnails of the underlying artwork. Click the Preview button for a closer look.

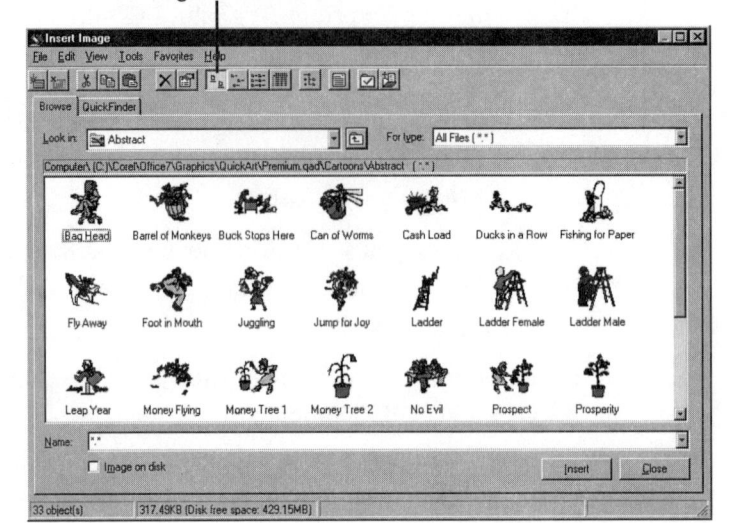

QuickArt thumbnails are easier to see if you click the Large Icons button.

17

In a Table, Anything Goes—with Ease

● **In this chapter:**

- **Just what is a table?**
- **How do I make a table?**
- **This table needs editing**
- **WordPerfect is a spreadsheet too?**
- **I don't want my table to look like a table**
- **My table needs a facelift**

WordPerfect tables bring order to graphics, text, and numbers. They'll even figure your mortage payment for you! . . . . . ▸

When elected officials "table" legislation, they're delaying (if not killing) it. Shelved would be a better word, but it wouldn't do to say so to constituents expecting action.

Those constituents would be better served with a WordPerfect table. In WordPerfect, tables are tools for action with myriad uses. Lists, directories, and even graphics all belong in tables. Tables organize and analyze information of any kind, in large amounts or small. You might say that tables put data on the table.

What exactly is a table?

How many busy days have you started by grabbing a scrap of paper and jotting down something like this?

To-dos:	Calls:
Pick up dry cleaning	Joe, re: contract
Return library books	Plumber!!
Finish Jones project	...

That's a table. We use them all the time to organize information. Tables are handy because they make entering data easy. Tables also make data easy to read at a glance.

Create a quick table

WordPerfect tables make managing data especially easy. Using columns or tabs to organize written information works after a fashion, but as you add and delete items, keeping a neat columnar structure can be a real chore.

Here's one use for a table: you have several clients to meet, and you need to note your expenses for the accounts department. With a table, it's easy to enter, organize, and even calculate your data. To build a table:

1 How many rows and columns do you need? A rough idea of a table's structure is helpful at the outset, but you can always add rows and columns later. We want headings for Client, expense Item, and Amount, so that gives us three columns. And we have three client meetings planned, with each client on a separate row. Add a row for the column headings, and we have four rows in all.

2. Click the Tables button on the Power Bar, hold the mouse button down, and drag across three columns and four rows. 3-4 appears at the top of the button's display, as seen in figure 17.1.

Fig. 17.1
Keep pressing the mouse button as you select columns and rows with the Power Bar Tables button.

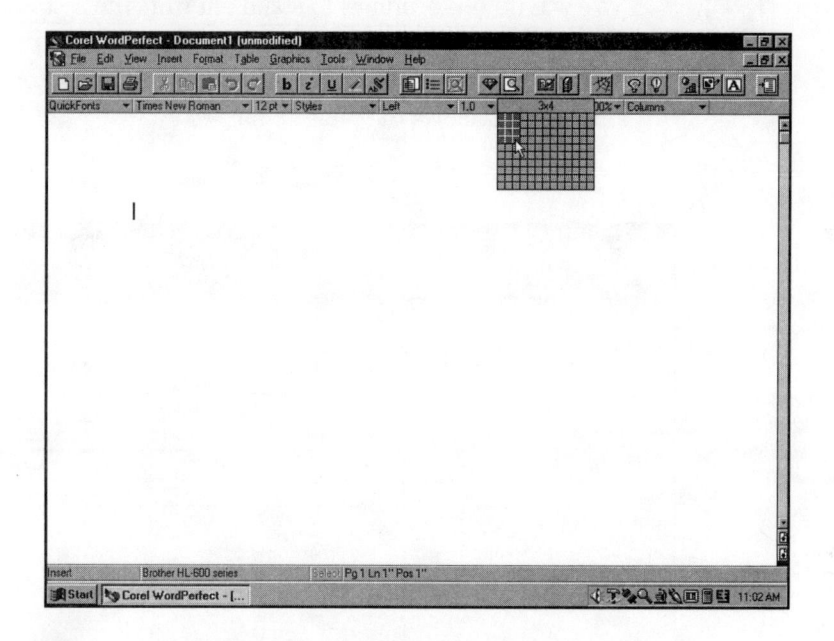

Q&A *I keep clicking the Power Bar Tables button, and that little display disappears on me!*

You have to click and hold the Power Bar Tables button. Don't release the mouse button until you've selected the number of columns and rows you're after.

TIP **If you wind up with the wrong number of rows or columns, just** click the Undo button on the Toolbar and try again.

3. When you release the mouse button, a grid of three columns and four rows snaps into place on the document, with the insertion point in the first box of the grid. The boxes in the grid are called **cells**. Type the heading for the first column in the first cell.

TIP **The tables Toolbar appears when you create a table. Put the** insertion point outside the table, and the standard Toolbar reappears. Click anywhere inside the table to get the tables Toolbar back.

4   When you finish with the first heading, press Tab to move the insertion point into the second cell on the top row. Type in the second heading, and do the same thing for the third.

5   We want those headings to stand out from the rest of the information on the table, so we'll put them in boldface. Drag across all of the cells in the top row to select them; then click the Bold button on the Toolbar. Figure 17.2 shows the table so far.

Each column has a heading to identify its contents.

Fig. 17.2
Drag across whole rows and columns, or click single cells to select them.

When the pointer points left, click to select the cell; double-click to select the row.

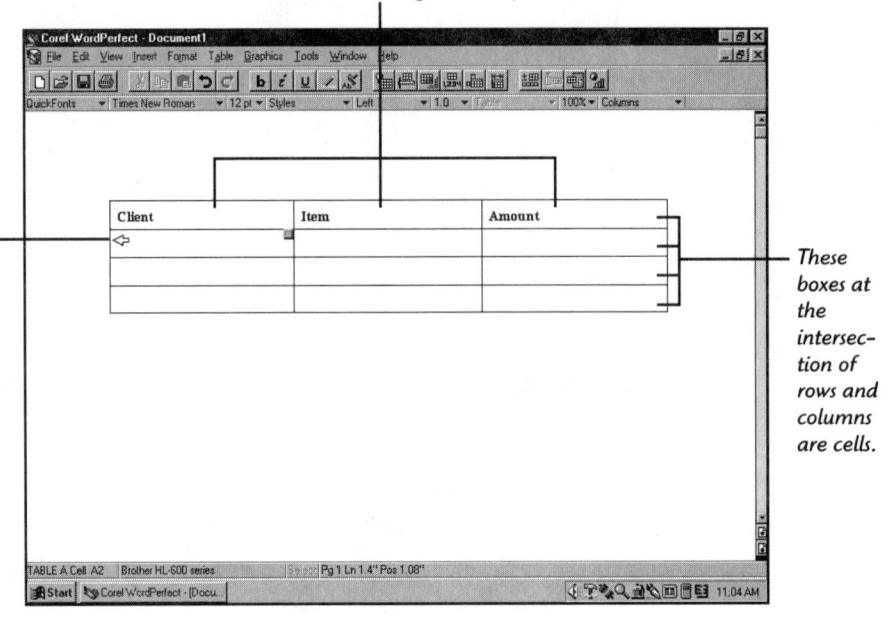

These boxes at the intersection of rows and columns are cells.

TIP **As you drag across cells in a table, the pointer points left. The** same thing happens if you point very carefully at vertical lines in a table. And if you point with equal care at the horizontal lines, the pointer points up. When the pointer changes direction like that, click to select the cell the pointer is in. When the arrow points up, double-click to select a column; when the arrow points left, double-click to select a row.

6 Now type the rest of the information in the table. In this example, it's client names, expense items, and amounts. Feel free to enter the data shown in figure 17.4 for the exercise, or type your own data. Use Tab, Back Tab, or the arrow keys to move the insertion point from cell to cell.

TIP **If you reach the end of your table and need another row, just** press the Tab key in the last cell. A new row pops into place right below the last row.

7 When you enter numbers in a table, just type the plain digits. It's easier to format the numbers (with dollar signs or commas, for example) after you've typed them. When your data is entered, select all the cells you want to format, and then click the Numeric Format button on the Toolbar. That pops up the Properties for Table Numeric Format dialog box shown in figure 17.3.

Fig. 17.3
The Preview window displays the various number formatting options, but the number shown ($1,234) has nothing to do with your data.

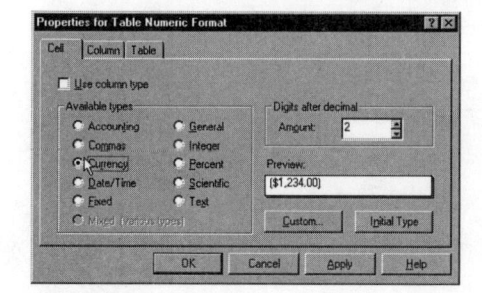

8 On the Cell tab of the Properties for Table Numeric Format dialog box, select Currency and click OK. The selected cells are formatted with dollar signs and two decimal places.

TIP **If you want to format all the numbers in your table the same way** (as currency, percents, whatever), click the Table tab in the Properties for Table Numeric Format dialog box and make your selection. That'll format the numbers in the whole table, saving you the bother of selecting cells.

9 Need a title? If the table is at the very top of the document, you're probably wondering how to get the insertion point out of, and above, the table. Here's how to do it: press Ctrl+Home twice, press Enter twice, then press the Up arrow key twice. That moves the table down two lines, and positions the insertion point one blank line above it.

> **Q&A** ***I pressed Ctr+Home twice in this table, and now I've lost the insertion point!***
>
> The insertion point's not lost. It's just hiding. Look closely at the left border of the first cell in the table, and you'll see the insertion point ticking away next to the border line. Press Enter; then press the Up arrow key, and the insertion point will come out of hiding.

10 To add a centered title once you have the insertion point over the table, press Shift+F7 and start typing. The finished table looks like figure 17.4.

Fig. 17.4
Tables display data in an organized way.

When a table's at the top of a document, press Ctrl+Home twice to move the insertion point just outside the top left table border line.

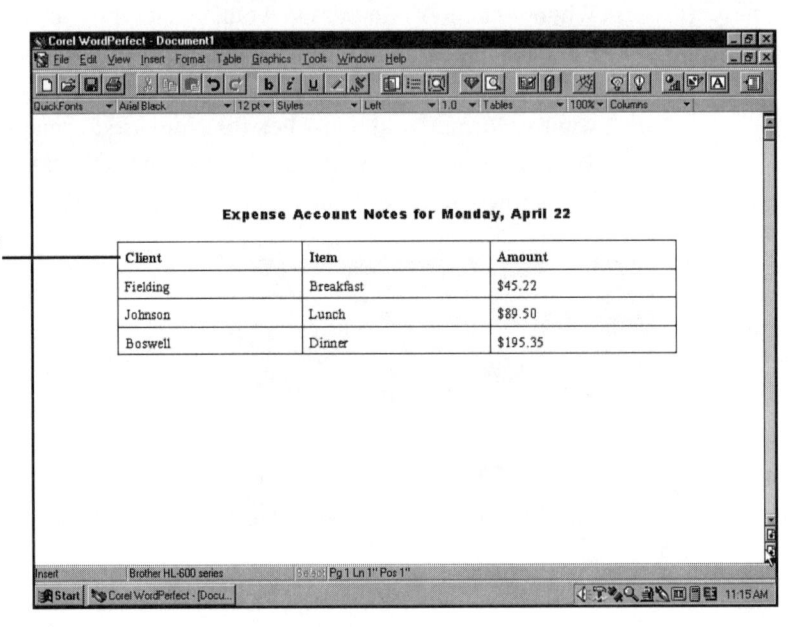

How do I edit this table?

Tables give you a lot of control over your data. By breaking up data into cells on a grid, tables let you operate on a single item, several items, or all your data at once.

Think of a street map. It's a mass of data that's saved from being a mess of data by its grid structure. Any decent map has letters and numbers around the perimeter that help you locate particular streets. Looking for Jones Street? The map's index tells you Jones is in C3, so you locate 3 on the map's perimeter and run your eye over to the area where 3 intersects with C.

Tables have the same setup:

- Columns are identified by letters.
- Rows are identified by numbers.
- Each cell, the intersection of a column and a row, is identified by the corresponding column letter and row number. Cell C3 in a table is the cell in column C, row 3. A cell's identifying column letter and row number is called the **cell reference** or **cell address**.

Those numbers and letters that identify rows and columns are called row and column **indicators**. To display them, click the Row/Column Indicators button on the Tables Toolbar. If you move the insertion point outside the table, both the indicators and the Tables Toolbar vanish. Click inside the table to make them reappear.

How do I add rows and columns to this table?

Suppose we need to fit another client meeting in the already heavy day we're tracking in the table shown in fig. 17.4. We'll just add another row to the table:

1 We met this client over drinks, so we need to squeeze a new row in between Lunch and Dinner (see fig. 17.4). Right-click anywhere in row 4 and choose Insert on the QuickMenu. That pops up the Insert Columns/Rows dialog box shown in figure 17.5.

Anatomy of a WordPerfect table

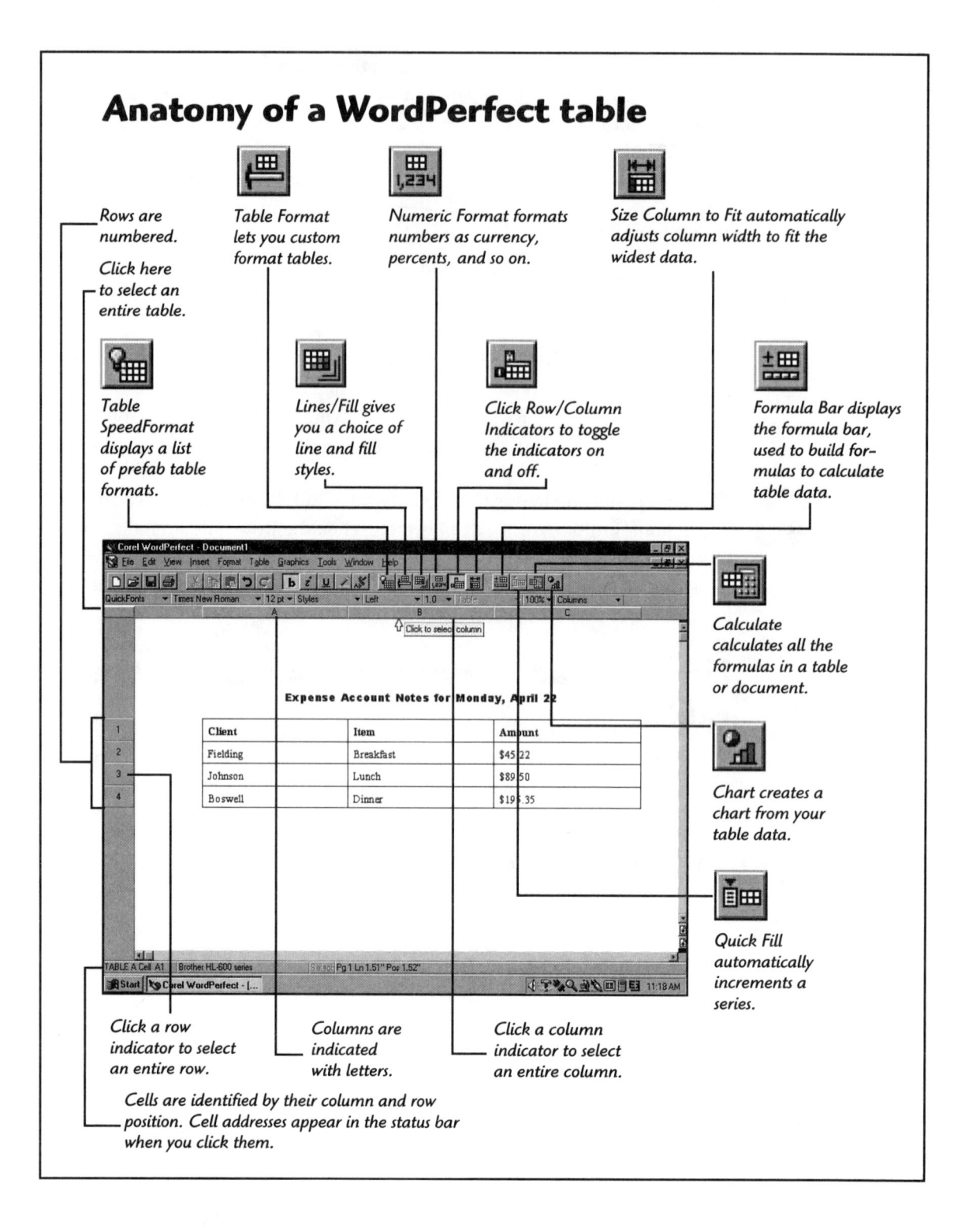

Rows are numbered. Click here to select an entire table.

Table Format lets you custom format tables.

Numeric Format formats numbers as currency, percents, and so on.

Size Column to Fit automatically adjusts column width to fit the widest data.

Table SpeedFormat displays a list of prefab table formats.

Lines/Fill gives you a choice of line and fill styles.

Click Row/Column Indicators to toggle the indicators on and off.

Formula Bar displays the formula bar, used to build formulas to calculate table data.

Calculate calculates all the formulas in a table or document.

Chart creates a chart from your table data.

Quick Fill automatically increments a series.

Click a row indicator to select an entire row.

Columns are indicated with letters.

Click a column indicator to select an entire column.

Cells are identified by their column and row position. Cell addresses appear in the status bar when you click them.

Expense Account Notes for Monday, April 22

Client	Item	Amount
Fielding	Breakfast	$45.22
Johnson	Lunch	$89.50
Boswell	Dinner	$195.35

Fig. 17.5
Use the Insert Columns/Rows dialog box to add rows and columns, and to control their placement in the table.

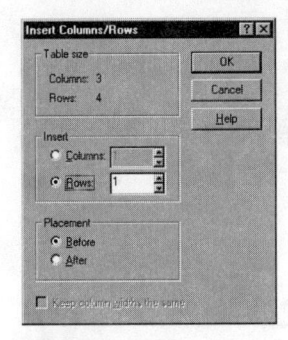

> **TIP** The default placement choice is **B**efore; when you squeeze in new rows and columns, click the row or column *after* the inserted one. That saves you the bother of selecting **A**fter in the dialog box.

> **TIP** A quick way to insert a row at the insertion point: press Alt+Ins. Likewise, press Alt+Del to delete a row at the insertion point.

2 In the Insert Columns/Rows dialog box, Table Size displays the current size of the table. We're inserting 1 **R**ow, with Placement **B**efore row 4, the selected row. Click OK, and the new row pops into place, as shown in figure 17.6.

Fig. 17.6
Inserting columns works the same way as inserting rows.

Click a column or row indicator to select entire rows and columns.

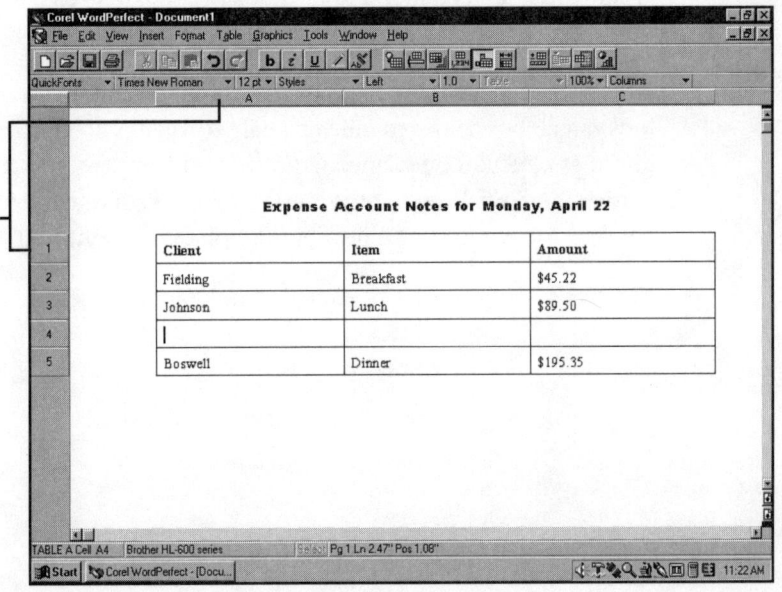

3 Now, just type the data into the newly inserted row.

Deleting rows and columns is equally easy. Click a row or column indicator to select the row or column, and press Delete. The Delete dialog box shown in figure 17.7 appears.

Fig. 17.7
The Delete dialog box offers the choice of getting rid of just the data, or the entire row or column.

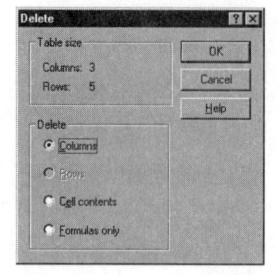

Select Rows or Columns to delete the whole row or column. Click OK, and the cells and all they hold vanish. If you want to leave blank cells in place but delete their contents, select Cell Contents, and click OK.

This cell doesn't look big enough for my data...

When you hold a balloon under the water tap, it swells as you fill it. Empty the water out, and the balloon shrinks.

Cells work the same way, except they won't burst if you overfill them. They look small, but cells expand vertically to accommodate whatever you type into them. As you type, lines wrap with soft returns, just like they do in the editing window. Pressing the Enter key works like it does in the editing window too—you start a new paragraph in the same cell.

Figure 17.8 shows cells stretched to hold additional lines of text.

Fig. 17.8
I pressed Enter after the client name, and typed the firm name on a new line.

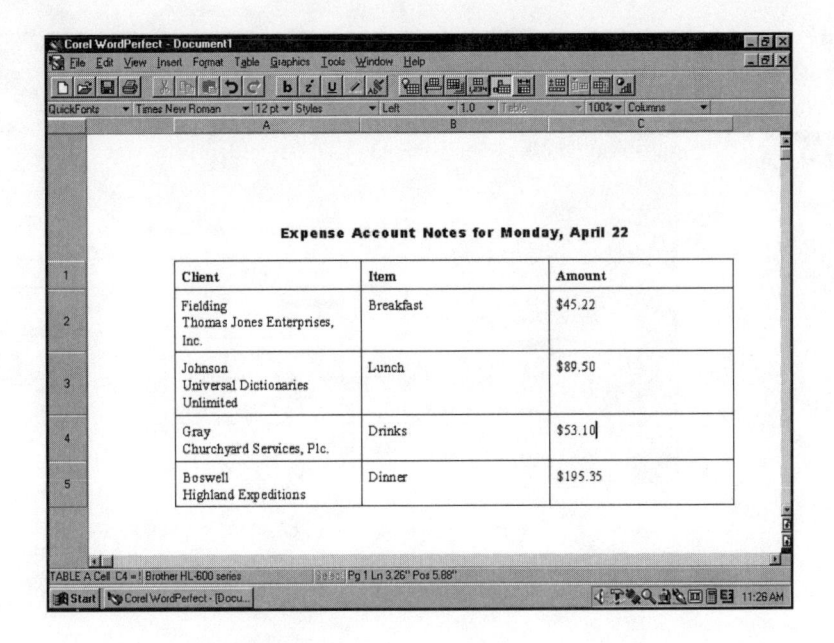

I want wider cells

Text typed in cells wraps at the right cell border line. That's handy for fast data entry, but your table might wind up looking too long and skinny if you have a lot of cells with several lines in them.

You can fix that problem by widening the column. Click anywhere in the column you want to widen; then click the Size Column to Fit button on the Toolbar.

The selected column instantly stretches to the width of the length of the longest line in the column, as shown in figure 17.9. If you select more than one column, all selected columns adjust at once.

Fig. 17.9
Adjusting column widths is easily done, and can make for a more readable table.

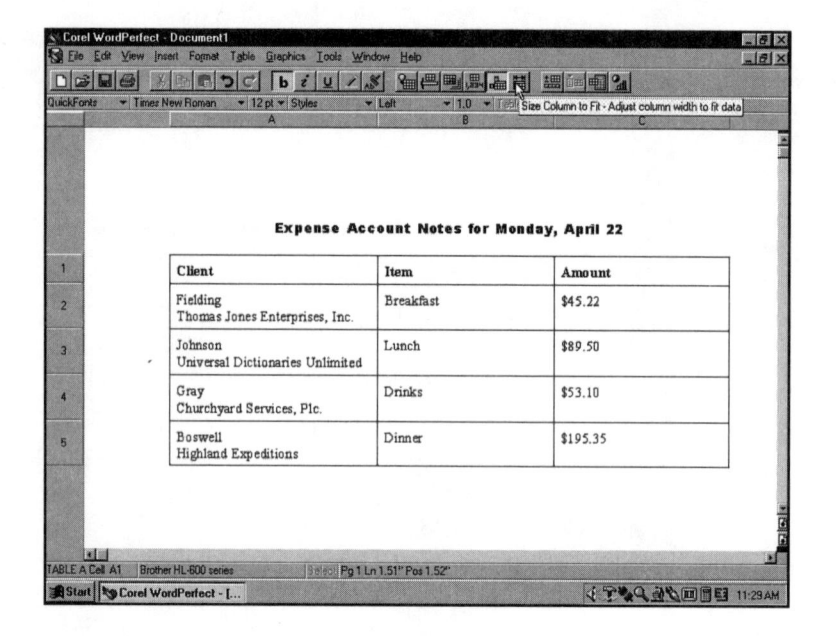

Adjusting column widths is a drag

If you have one cell with a very long line in it, you might not want the Size Column to Fit button to stretch all the cells in the column to the length of that one line. You want *most* of the entries to fit on one line, but it's okay if a few of them wrap.

In that case, just point at the right border line of the column you want to widen. The pointer turns into a black double-arrow; now drag to widen the column, as shown in figure 17.10.

When you're satisfied with the new column width, release the mouse button. The column border line snaps into the new position.

Fig. 17.10
The broken line follows the pointer around as you drag the double arrow.

The QuickStatus box indicates the changing widths of the adjacent columns as you drag.

Tables are spreadsheets, too

With a calculator, a scrap of paper, and a pencil, we can get through a lot of arithmetic in little time. A spreadsheet takes care of arithmetical chores even faster. **Spreadsheets** combine the easy editing features of a word processor with the calculating might of the most powerful scientific and financial calculators. WordPerfect has a built-in spreadsheet, and it's a dandy.

We've used tables so far in this chapter to organize text. Let's use WordPerfect's spreadsheet features to turn our table into an electronic calculator.

The formula bar turns tables into calculating machines

To make a spreadsheet out of your table, click the Formula Bar button on the Toolbar. That puts the formula bar at the top of the editing window, as shown in figure 17.11.

Fig. 17.11
The formula bar turns WordPerfect into a powerful calculator.

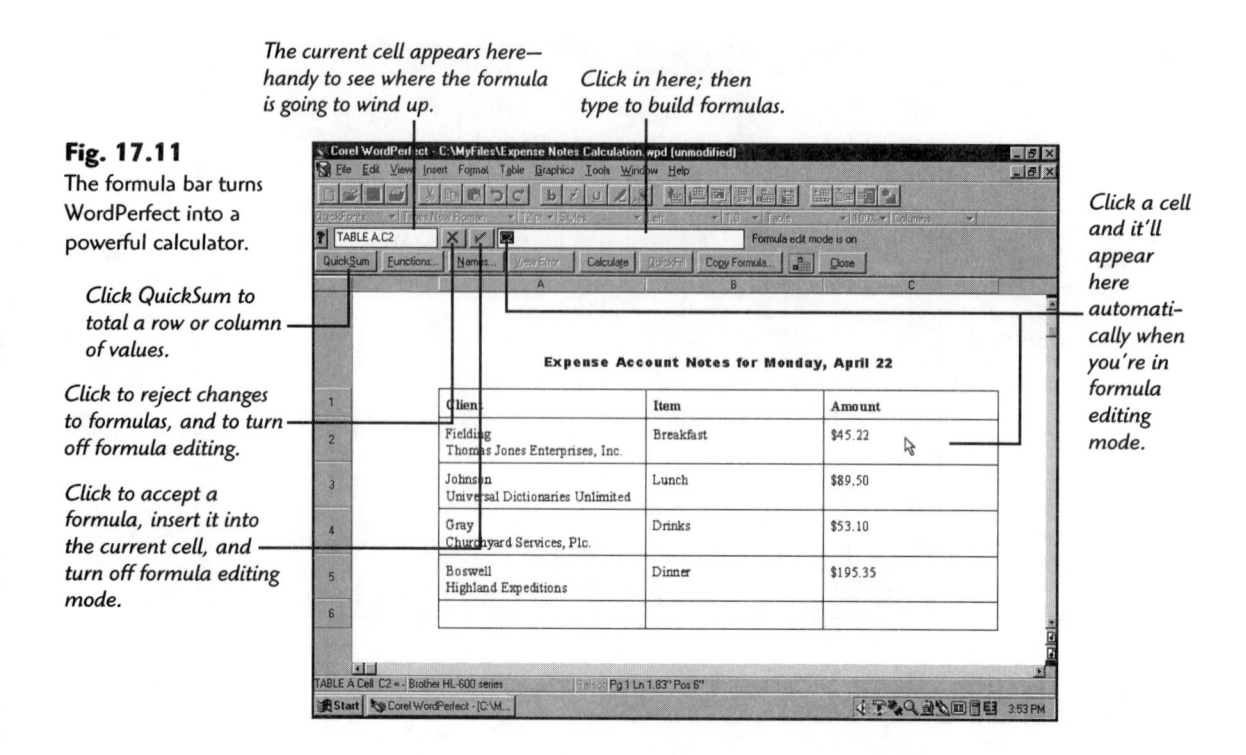

Click QuickSum to total a row or column of values.

Click to reject changes to formulas, and to turn off formula editing.

Click to accept a formula, insert it into the current cell, and turn off formula editing mode.

The current cell appears here—handy to see where the formula is going to wind up.

Click in here; then type to build formulas.

Click a cell and it'll appear here automatically when you're in formula editing mode.

You use **formulas** and **functions** to calculate data in WordPerfect:

- A **formula** is like a recipe; a series of steps that operate on ingredients to produce a final result. Formulas use **values** as ingredients. 8 and 12 are examples of values; 8+12=20 is a formula.

- **Operators** are the instructions in the formula recipe. They determine what happens to the values in a formula. + is an operator; so are – and *.

- **Functions** are ready-made formulas, a bit like buying your soup in a can instead of making it yourself. The ingredients in a function are called **arguments**. For example, AVE(A1:A3) tells WordPerfect to give us the average of all the values in cells A1 through A3.

How do I add up a column of numbers?

Of all the gadgets in WordPerfect, the SUM function is one of the handiest. One click of the Sum button on the formula bar adds all the values in a row or column. We'll use SUM to add up the values in column C of our table (see fig. 17.11).

Chapter 17 *In a Table, Anything Goes—with Ease* **319**

1. We need to add another row to the table in figure 17.11 for our total. Since we're putting the row at the very end of the table, just click the last cell in row 5 and press Tab. That tacks a new row at the bottom of the table.

2. In cell B6 in the new row, type **Total:**.

3. We want the total to appear in cell C6; click C6, then click QuickSum on the formula bar. The values in column C are totaled with a SUM function, and the result appears in C6, as shown in figure 17.12.

Fig. 17.12
When you click the QuickSum button, all the values in a column or row are totaled. Text is ignored.

Clicking the QuickSum button puts a SUM function in the active cell; the function's arguments are in parentheses.

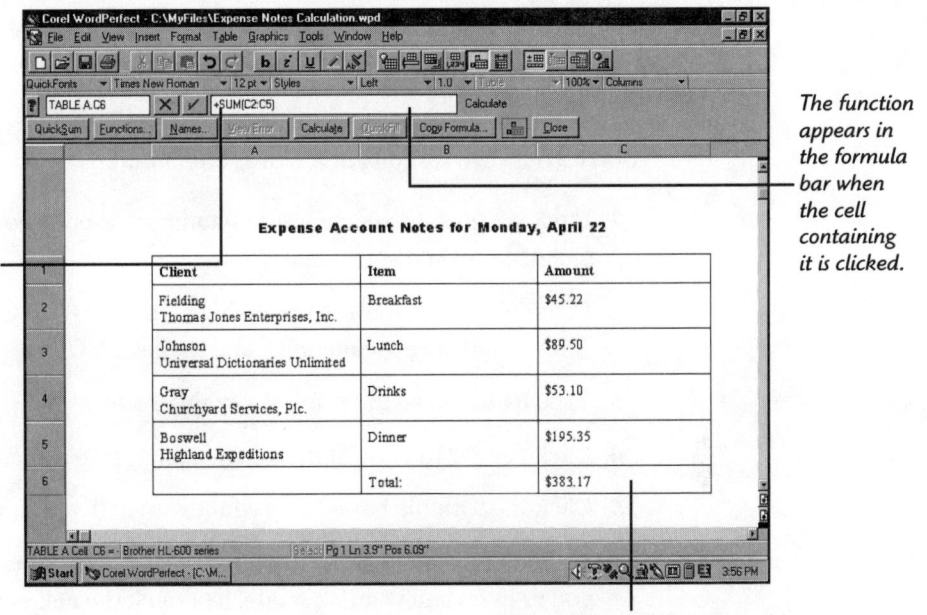

The function appears in the formula bar when the cell containing it is clicked.

Only the result of a formula or function appears in the cell.

You'll have noticed that the function uses cell references (C2:C5 in figure 17.12) instead of the actual values as its arguments. That's true of all WordPerfect functions and formulas. That way, you can change the values in the cells referenced by the function, without having to change the function itself.

> **66 Plain English, please!**
>
> The reference C2:C5 refers to all the cells from C2 through C5. That's called a **range**. Ranges are groups of two or more cells. **Range references** consist of the first and last cell addresses in the range, separated by a colon. **99**

How do I write my own formula?

We used one of WordPerfect's canned formulas—the SUM function—to total our amounts in figure 17.12. Writing your own formula is equally easy.

Suppose that we get reimbursed for only 80% of our total expenses. We'll add another column to show our reimbursement for each item, and write a formula to calculate 80% of each amount.

To write our own formula in a WordPerfect table:

1 First, we need to add another column: right-click column C for the QuickMenu, and select Insert.

2 In the Insert Columns/Rows dialog box, select 1 Columns and click After to add a new column D, and then click OK.

3 Type **Reimburse** in D1 for a column heading.

4 Click cell D2 to make it the active cell.

5 Click the formula bar editing window to activate formula editing mode.

6 You don't have to type cell references into WordPerfect formulas. While you're in formula editing mode, just click the cell you want to reference, and the cell address is automatically dumped into the formula. Here, we'll click cell C2 to put the cell reference C2 in the formula bar editing window. Our formula will now use whatever value happens to be in C2.

7 Type ***.8** in the formula bar editing window. That multiplies the value in C2 by .8, or 80%.

8 Click the Check Mark button on the formula bar. That completes the formula and puts it in cell D2. Only the result appears in D2; the formula appears in the formula bar when D2 is the active cell. If your efforts go awry while you're creating a formula, just click the Undo button on the Toolbar to erase your last action. When everything is right, it looks like figure 17.13.

Fig. 17.13
Formula building is mostly a process of clicking cells and typing operators.

Click inside the formula editing window to edit your formulas.

The + sign at the beginning of the formula is added automatically when you click the check mark button.

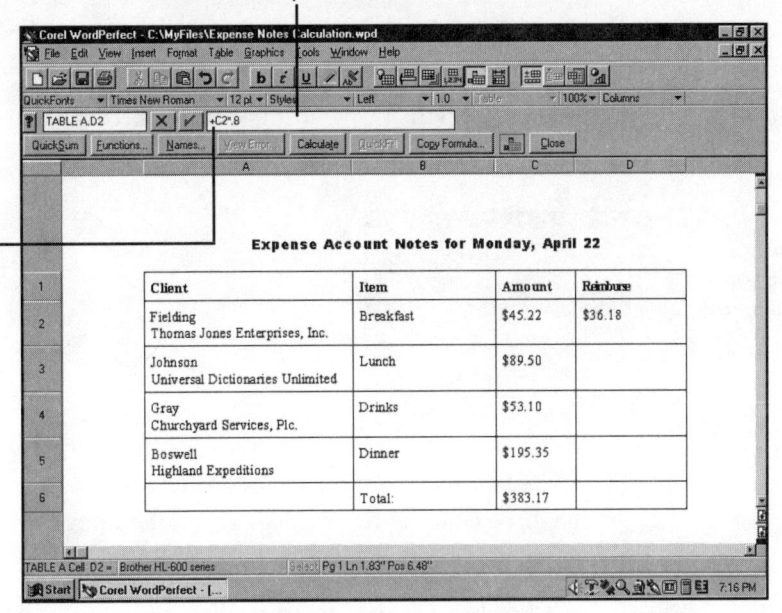

Can I copy this formula?

Write a formula in a table once, and you can use it again and again by copying it to other cells. It's not only a big time-saver; copying formulas also helps to avoid spreadsheet errors.

Some references are relative

We can copy the formula to the other cells in column D, and the cell reference automatically changes to reflect the new rows. C2 in our formula is a **relative** reference; it changes relative to where you place the formula. For example, if you copy the formula in D2 to D3, the formula automatically changes to multiply 0.8 times cell C3.

Think of the formula as a marksman and the cell reference as his target. A relative reference is just like a moving target, tracked by the marksman wherever it goes. The result is that we can copy the formula and get the correct result wherever the formula is copied.

To copy the formula in D2 to the other cells in column D:

1. Click cell D2 to make it the active cell, and click the Copy Formula button on the formula bar.

2. That pops up the Copy Formula dialog box shown in figure 17.14 as it appears after you make the following changes.

Fig. 17.14
The Copy Formula dialog box lets you copy formulas to rows or columns.

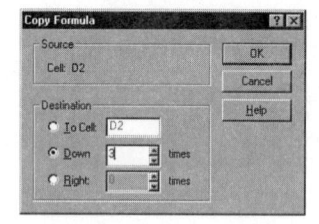

3. Select Down and enter 3 in the Times edit box to copy the formula to the three cells below D2. Click OK in the Copy Formula dialog box.

4. The formula is copied to the other three cells, with the results displayed in the cells, as seen in figure 17.15.

Fig. 17.15
Copying formulas saves you a lot of typing.

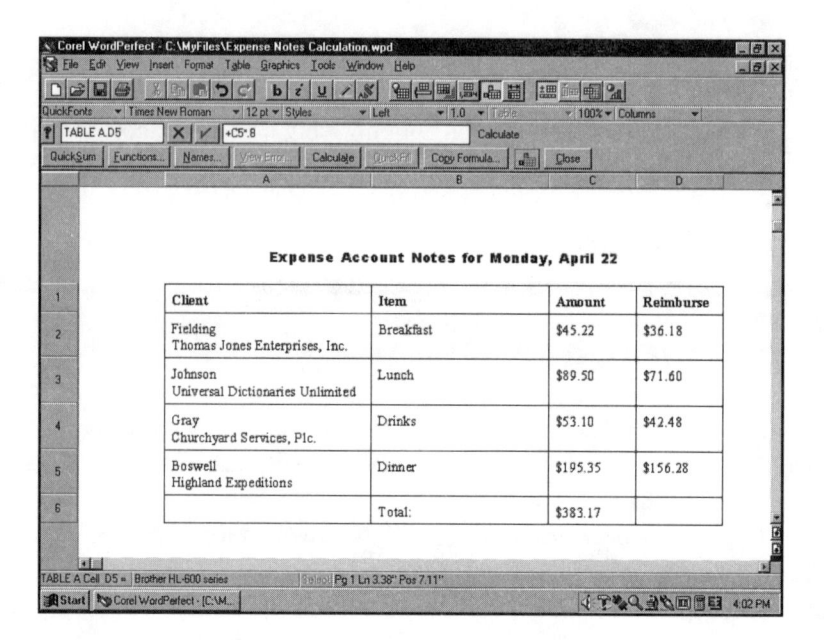

To total the amounts in column D, click cell D6, and then click the QuickSum button on the formula bar.

SUM is just the beginning

WordPerfect is a serious spreadsheet. SUM is just one of many functions that you can use to calculate data in tables. To browse the selection of functions in WordPerfect, click the Functions button on the formula bar and the Table Functions dialog box shown in figure 17.16 appears.

Fig. 17.16
The PMT function is a handy mortgage calculator.

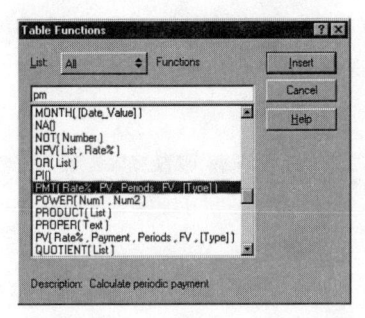

There are functions to analyze investments and to calculate the number of days between two dates, just to mention two of many.

Can I put this table in another document?

You'll probably want to import tables into other documents. Our expenses table, for example, might well have to be justified with a supporting memo. To stick a table in another document, just select the table, cut or copy it, and paste it wherever you like.

For something fancier, try importing a table in a graphics box. With a table in a graphics box, you can wrap text around it, add a caption, and manipulate it like any other graphics object.

A default table extends from the left to the right margin, so it starts life too wide for a graphics box. With a few alterations to cut your table down to size, it'll fit perfectly.

To import a table into another document as a graphics box:

   1 First, make the table smaller to fit it into a graphics box. Point at any border line in the table. When the pointer turns left or up, triple-click to select the whole table (or click Edit, Select, Table). With the table selected, click the Font Size button on the Power Bar and select 8 on the drop-down menu.

2. With the table still selected, click the Size Column to Fit button on the Toolbar. Choose a smaller font for your title as well. If the title is centered, the alignment will be off; click at the beginning of the title; then press Backspace to delete the Center code to fix that. To make your table even more compact, delete any blank lines between the title and the table. Now, you have a smaller, but still readable, table (see fig. 17.17).

Fig. 17.17
Smaller fonts and fitted columns make for a more compact table.

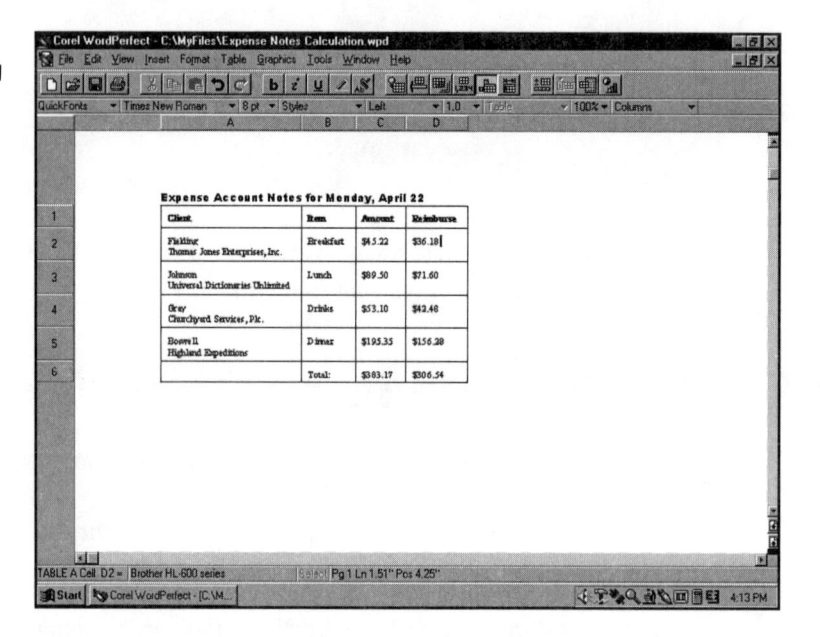

3. Save your table (and give it a file name if you haven't already).

4. Open the document in which you want the table, and click Graphics, Custom box.

5. In the Custom Box dialog box, select Table from the Style Name list, and click OK. A graphics box for your table appears in the document at the insertion point.

6. Right-click the graphics box and choose Content on the QuickMenu. The Box Content dialog box appears.

7. Enter the table's file name in the Filename edit box, and click OK.

Chapter 17 *In a Table, Anything Goes—with Ease* **325**

   8. The table pops into the graphics box. Click the QuickSpot and make your choices in the Edit Box dialog box to wrap the text, add a caption, or change the box style.

   9. Close the Edit Box dialog box when you're done. Figure 17.18 shows a 75% zoomed view of what you might end up with.

Fig. 17.18
Wrapping supporting text around a table knits the table and the document together.

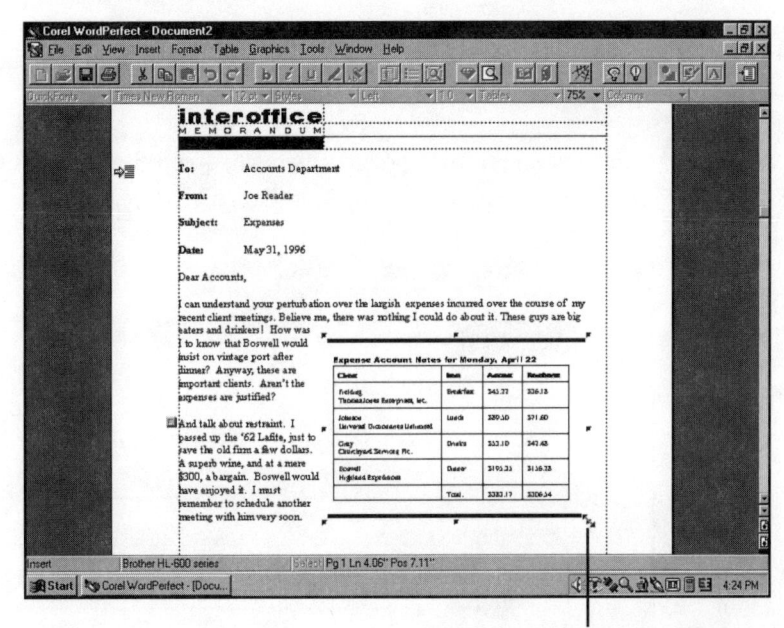

If part of your table is cut off, drag a box corner handle to expand the box.

If your imported table needs further adjustments, see Chapter 16, which covers editing graphics in detail.

This table could use a facelift

You can use tables to create custom forms, invoices, and any other document that lends itself to tabular form. To create tables like that, all the WordPerfect formatting and editing tools and features are at your disposal.

When your table is only in need of a quick change of clothes, click the Table SpeedFormat button on the Toolbar. That pops up the Table SpeedFormat dialog box shown in figure 17.19.

Fig. 17.19
There's a wardrobe of formats for tables here, including some startling effects!

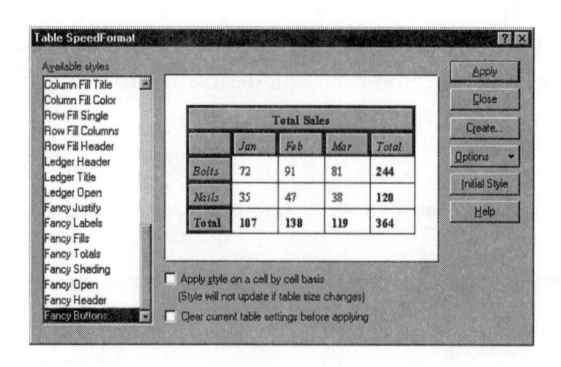

Click a style on the Available Styles list, and then click Apply. Your table is instantly transformed, as seen in figure 17.20.

Fig. 17.20
The Header Fill Column style is a good choice for a speedy table makeover.

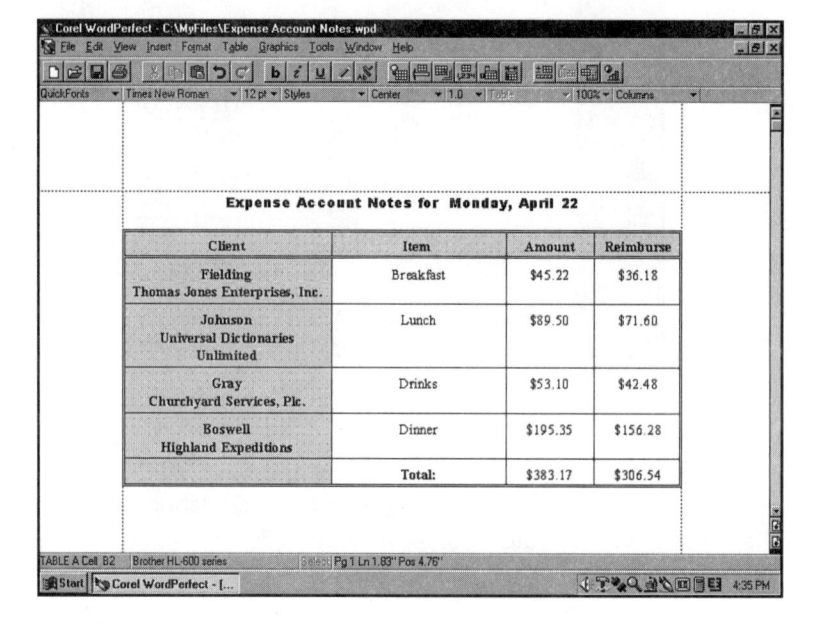

If you don't like the way your table makeover turns out, click the Undo button on the Toolbar, click the Table SpeedFormat button, and pick another style from the list.

> **TIP** Spreadsheets like Quattro Pro right-align cells with numeric data. If your data has the same number of decimal places (as they would in a currency format), the decimal points all line up. To right-align numeric data

in a WordPerfect table in the same way, drag through the cells containing the data to select them; then click the Power Bar Justification button and choose Right.

What else can I do with tables?

When you put your books away, you probably put them on a bookshelf. There they'll sit, securely side by side, until you need them again. That beats stacking them in a corner any old way, or tossing them in a pile on your desk.

Tables are like bookshelves for information that needs to be arranged and presented side by side. And if you turn off the borders and gridlines, tables are indistinguishable from the parallel columns we looked at in Chapter 14, with one big advantage over their twin: tables are far easier to use. Adding and deleting text in a table is a snap; the same can't be said for parallel columns.

Table cells can hold graphics and just about anything else that you'd put in a document. Figure 17.21 shows some uses for tables that look anything but tabular.

Put a graphic and some fancy text side by side in a table, and you have an instant logo.

Fig. 17.21
If you turn off the gridlines and table borders, you have all the advantages of a table that doesn't look like a table.

Side-by-side information you might want to put in parallel columns will be much easier to work with in a table.

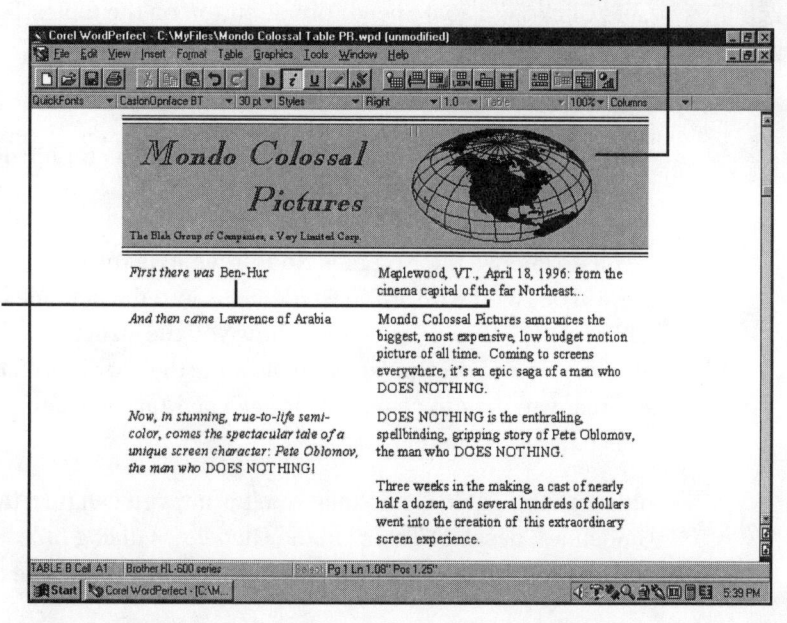

Can I turn these parallel columns into a table?

You might find tables so much more useful than parallel columns that you'll want to convert them. You can also convert those tabbed columns we all tend to use when we're in a hurry. If the text in figure 17.21 reminded you of text last seen in parallel columns back in Chapter 14, that's because it *was* text in parallel columns. It was a nuisance to deal with, so I converted it to a table.

To convert your own columns to tables:

1 Select the columns you want to turn into a table.

2 Click Table, Create to pop up the Convert Table dialog box.

3 Select either Parallel column or Tabular column in the Convert Table dialog box if you have to. WordPerfect will determine which type you have, so you can probably skip this step.

4 Click OK to convert your columns to a table.

Tables don't have to look like tables

To turn off table borders so your table doesn't look like a table:

1 Click the Table SpeedFormat button on the tables Toolbar. The Table SpeedFormat dialog box appears.

2 Select No Lines No Border from the list of Available Styles.

3 Click Apply, and your table will look like a graphic design, a columnar document, or anything but a table.

If you do choose the No Lines No Border style for your table, the table cells are still outlined with Table Guidelines, dotted black lines around the cell and table borders. Table Guidelines show you the structure of your table. Like the blue dotted Margin Guidelines that frame the WordPerfect editing window, and that you drag to change your page margins, you can drag Table Guidelines to adjust column widths.

Although the Table Guidelines won't print, you can turn them off. Click View, Guidelines, deselect Tables in the Guidelines dialog box, and click OK to turn off the Guidelines. If you *still* see dotted lines around the table cells and borders, those are **table gridlines**. Gridlines look and act just like Table Guidelines, and they can be dragged to alter column widths. Click View, Table Gridlines to toggle them on and off.

My data is out of sorts

Lists are a natural for tables. And once you build a list, you'll want to sort it alphabetically. With a table, nothing could be easier. To sort a list:

1 Enter your data in the table. If you're cataloguing your library for example, you'd have a column for the author's name, another column for the book title, a third column for the shelf location, and so on.

2 An alphabetical sort by author would be logical in such a table. Select the cells containing author names.

3 Click Tools, Sort and the Sort dialog box appears, as shown in figure 17.22.

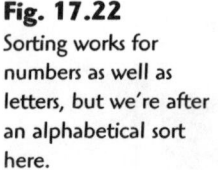

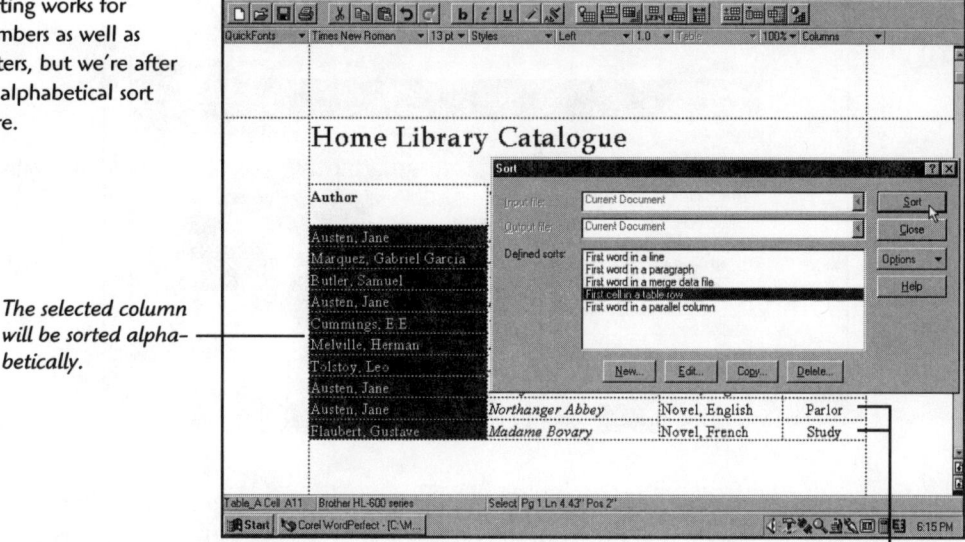

Fig. 17.22
Sorting works for numbers as well as letters, but we're after an alphabetical sort here.

The selected column will be sorted alphabetically.

Data in each row will be shifted together with each sorted name in the first column.

4 Select First cell in a table row on the list of Defined sorts (see fig. 17.22).

5 Click **S**ort, and your table is instantly arranged alphabetically by author.

Now that your table is sorted, click the Table SpeedFormat button and take your pick of the canned formats. Or add your own decorator touches. Filling in the top row, for example, makes your column headings stand out.

To add fill to a table row:

1 Click any cell in the top row, and point at a vertical gridline until the arrow turns left.

2 Double-click to select the row; then click a QuickSpot in the row.

3 That pops up the Table Tools dialog box. Click the **F**ill button, and then click your choice of fills (see fig. 17.23).

Fig. 17.23
Use the Table Tools dialog box or the Toolbar buttons to redecorate your tables, whichever you find handier.

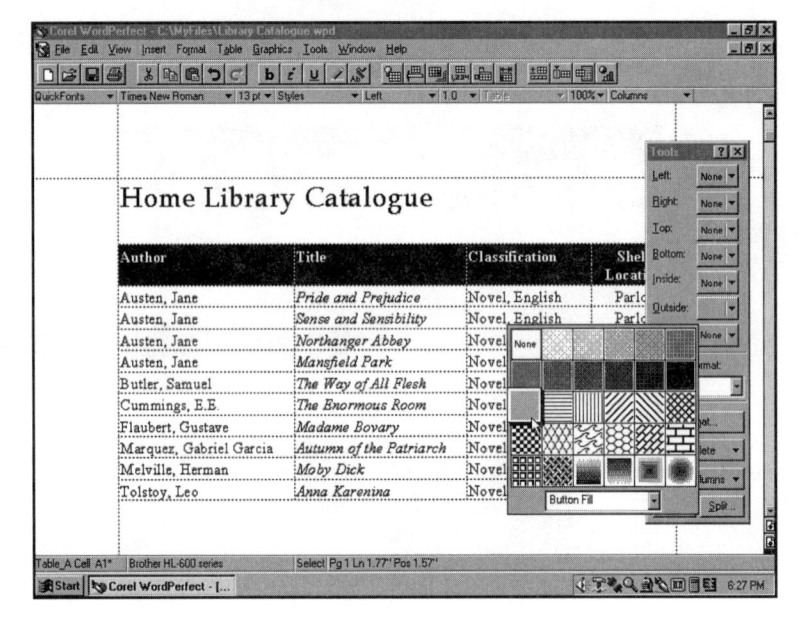

The table Tools dialog box has all the table formatting gadgets you'll need. You get the same tools from the table Toolbar, so use either one. Multiple ways to do the same thing? WordPerfect always tries to cater to every taste.

Part VI: Getting the Most Out of WordPerfect

Chapter 18: **Documents, Big and Small, Few and Many**

Chapter 19: **Presentations 7 for Instant Artists**

18 Documents, Big and Small, Few and Many

● **In this chapter:**

- An outline can help you organize a document

- Master documents, master big files!

- I need a table of contents

- Can I see more than one document at once?

- I'm drowning in files! What can I do about it?

WordPerfect helps take the sting out of writing jobs big and small. And when you've done many such jobs, WordPerfect makes all your hard-won files easy to get . . . . ▶

Novelists and publishers like to provide value for money. That's why our beach reading is so bulky. But when a publisher is his own novelist, the large economy size in books comes into its own. Samuel Richardson was an 18th-century publisher whose novel *Clarissa* ran to seven big volumes. Although not a page-turner by modern standards, its sheer bulk commands respect.

We're unlikely to match Richardson's output (or his profits), but when our documents grow in size and number, WordPerfect is up to the job. There's a powerful file manager to cope with large numbers of documents, and a battery of features to help deal with big documents.

Outlining organizes documents

When an office building goes up, a skeleton of girders gets fleshed out, step-by-step, with wiring, plumbing, outer walls, and so on. An outline is like a skeleton of girders in a document; you lay out the document's topics and headings, then flesh them out with text.

Any document that can be broken down into topics and subtopics is a good candidate for an outline. Finished outlining? WordPerfect converts your outline to the actual headings and subheadings in the document.

Outlines help you present the information in a document logically, and WordPerfect makes using outlines very convenient. WordPerfect assigns a number or letter to each topic and subtopic in an outline, in a sequence that reflects the relative importance of the topics and subtopics. The most important topics become the highest level in the outline sequence, the next most important topics are the next outline level, and so on down to the lowest outline level and the least important topics.

How do I create an outline?

Say we're a film studio preparing a report for our bankers on the subject of our most recent releases. This report needs to be carefully written, so we want to outline it first. Each movie release, and the report's introduction and conclusion, will be our main topics. Any subtopics will go beneath the main topics in the outline sequence.

Chapter 18 *Documents, Big and Small, Few and Many* **335**

To create an outline:

1. Click <u>T</u>ools, <u>O</u>utline. You will see the outline feature bar, the numbered line for your first outline item, and a stylized numeral one in the left margin. That stylized "1" stands for outline level one, the outline level for the most important topics.

2. Type **Introduction** on the numbered first line and press Enter. That skips to the next line, automatically numbered with a 2. So far, our outline looks like figure 18.1.

Fig. 18.1
Once you turn on outlining, simply type your first heading and press Enter.

Click the left arrow to promote the current line to the next higher outline level.

Click the right arrow to demote the current line to the next lower level.

Level icons indicate the outline level; 1 is the highest level, for major topic headings.

Q&A Why can't I see my level icons?

Drag the horizontal scroll button to the left to display the left margin. If you still don't see the level icons, click <u>O</u>ptions on the feature bar and select Show Level <u>I</u>cons.

66 *Plain English, please!*

Outline **levels** refer to the relative importance of items in the outline. Level 1 is for the most important items, such as chapter titles; level 2 is for major topics in the chapter; and so on, all the way down to level 8. In WordPerfect's outline style, levels are marked by I, A, 1, a, (1), and so on—the same system we all learned in school. Each level aligns at a tab stop. 99

3. The introduction is a major heading, making it a level 1 item. We want a subtopic or two under that major heading, so we'll demote the second line to a level 2 item. Click line 2, and click the right arrow on the feature bar (refer to fig. 18.1).

TIP Don't like mousing around with the outline feature bar arrows?
Press Tab to demote the current outline item one level. Shift+Tab promotes the current item one level. Press Tab or Shift+Tab repeatedly to promote or demote the current item several levels. Shift+Tab a level 1 item, and it cycles straight to the lowest outline level, level 8. Tabbing a level 8 item promotes it to level 1.

4. That indents the line, the 2. turns into an a., and the level icon changes to a stylized 2 to indicate that it's a level 2 line. Type the subtopic heading and press Enter. The result looks like figure 18.2.

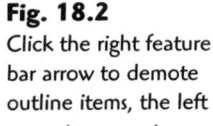

Fig. 18.2
Click the right feature bar arrow to demote outline items, the left arrow to promote them.

The original level icon acquires a – sign, indicating that there are displayed subordinate items.

The level icon indicates a level 2 item.

Pressing Enter begins a new level 2 line for a second subtopic.

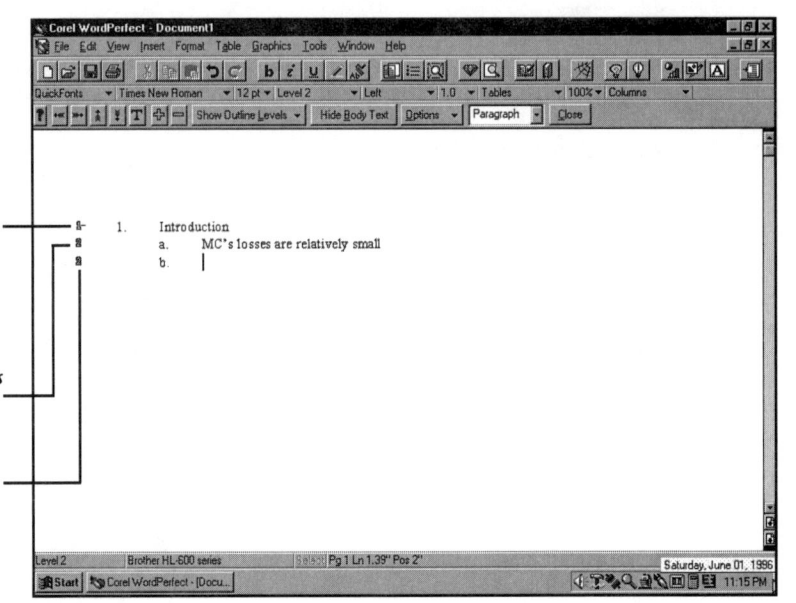

Chapter 18 *Documents, Big and Small, Few and Many* **337**

5 Type the second subtopic heading and press Enter at the end of the line for an additional subtopic.

6 For level 3 subtopics under a level 2 subtopic, click the right arrow on the feature bar; type the headings, pressing Enter after each one.

7 When you're ready for a new level 1 item, click the left arrow on the feature bar on a new line, repeatedly if necessary, until you get a number 2. and a level 1 icon in the left margin.

8 Continue to press Enter at the end of each line. Click the left and right arrows on the feature bar to promote and demote items, and type your headings. Add a title, and as the outline takes shape, it looks like figure 18.3.

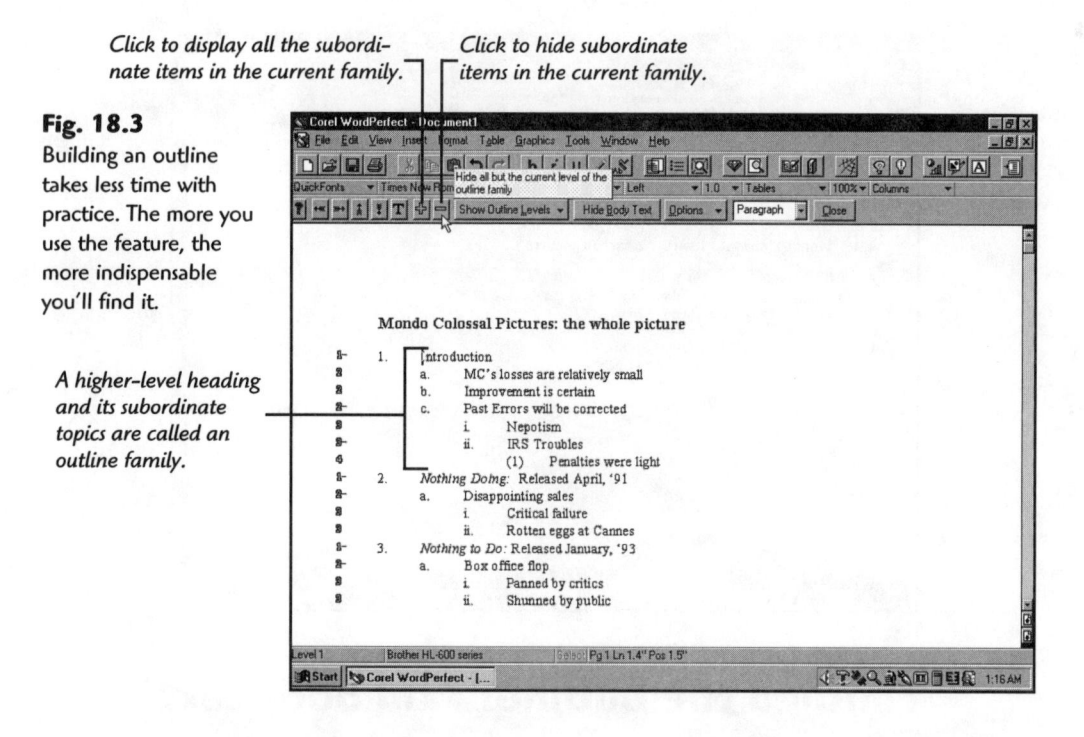

Click to display all the subordinate items in the current family.

Click to hide subordinate items in the current family.

Fig. 18.3
Building an outline takes less time with practice. The more you use the feature, the more indispensable you'll find it.

A higher-level heading and its subordinate topics are called an outline family.

As you build up your outline, a sea of subtopics can become confusing to look at. Put the insertion point next to a higher-level item, and click the + and – buttons on the feature bar to hide or display subordinate items within outline families (see fig. 18.3).

> **Plain English, please!**
>
> An **outline family** is an outline item and its subordinate items; for example, a level 1 item and all the level 2, 3, and so on, items below it. Or a level 2 item and its subordinate items—the parent item in an outline family can be an item of any level.

TIP Double-click a level icon to toggle on and off the display of subordinate items in the outline family.

Figure 18.4 shows the same outline with only the level 1 outline items in the first two topics displayed.

Fig. 18.4
Outlines are less confusing to look at when you hide subordinate items, especially as you work on new items.

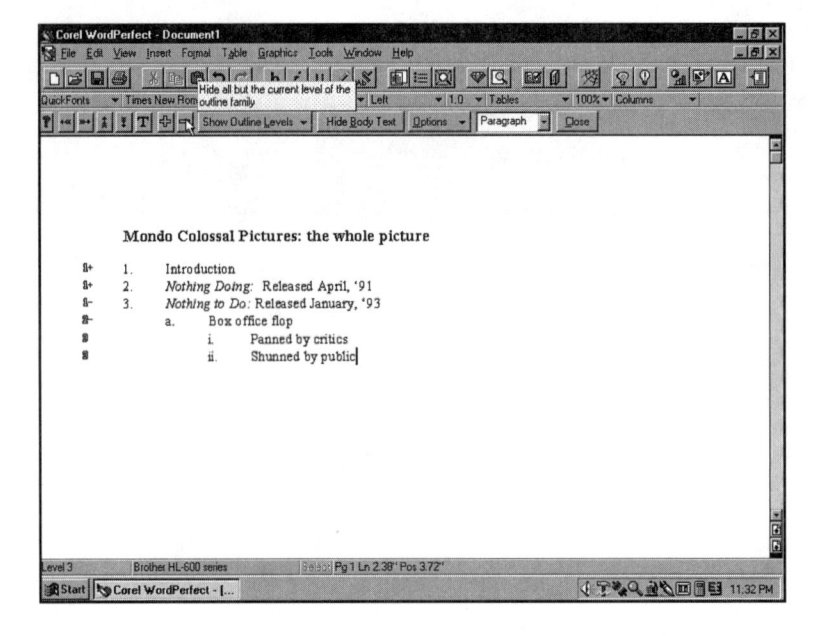

Finished the outline? Add body text

The idea behind an outline is to help you organize a document. Once you finish the outline, you have a few options for adding body text. If you don't plan to use the outline items as section headings in your document, do either of the following:

- Turn off outlining: click Options on the feature bar and select End Outline. Then, type your body text at the end of the outline if you want it in the same document.

- Or save your outline and open a new document for body text. You can print the outline and refer to the printout as you write.

If you do want your outline items as document section heads, add body text within the outline. That puts the outline right under your nose, for easy reference. What's more, you can convert all your outline items to headings in the document. That saves you from retyping them, and it gives you a ready-made structure for your document.

Save your outline first. To add body text to an outline:

1 Press Enter at the end of the line with the outline item under which you want to add text.

2 Click the T button on the feature bar. That converts the line to body text.

> **TIP** Keyboard fans can press Ctrl+H to convert the current outline item to body text; press Ctrl+H to convert body text to an outline item.

3 Type your text. Repeat steps 1 and 2 for any other outline items under which you want to add text. Figure 18.5 shows an outline with body text.

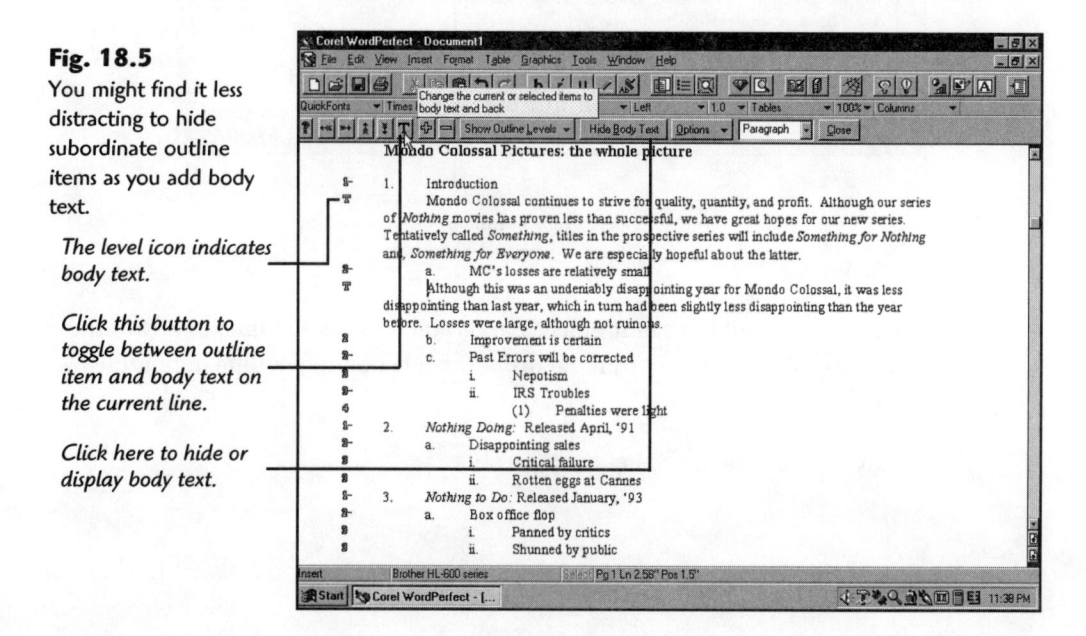

Fig. 18.5
You might find it less distracting to hide subordinate outline items as you add body text.

The level icon indicates body text.

Click this button to toggle between outline item and body text on the current line.

Click here to hide or display body text.

To toggle the display of body text, click the Show [or Hide] **B**ody Text button.

How do I get rid of these outline numbers and letters?

Our body text is lined up where we want it, under the appropriate outline items. To complete the document, convert all the outline items to headings.

Click the drop-down arrow on the outline definitions list on the feature bar (see figure 18.6), and select Headings. Figure 18.6 shows you what happens.

Fig. 18.6
Two clicks turns an outline into a report.

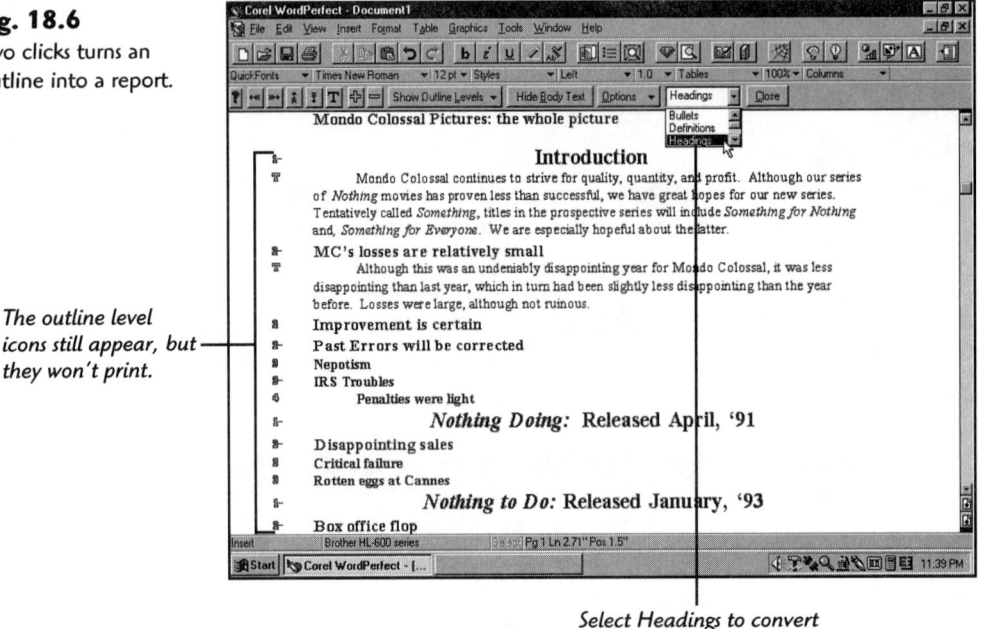

The outline level icons still appear, but they won't print.

Select Headings to convert your outline items into document headings.

To display the outline again, select Paragraph, Bullets, Outline, or any of the other outline definitions from the drop-down list on the outline definitions button.

Figure 18.7 shows the Bullets outline style.

Fig. 18.7
Choose whatever outline style you like; you can switch back and forth between the definitions any time.

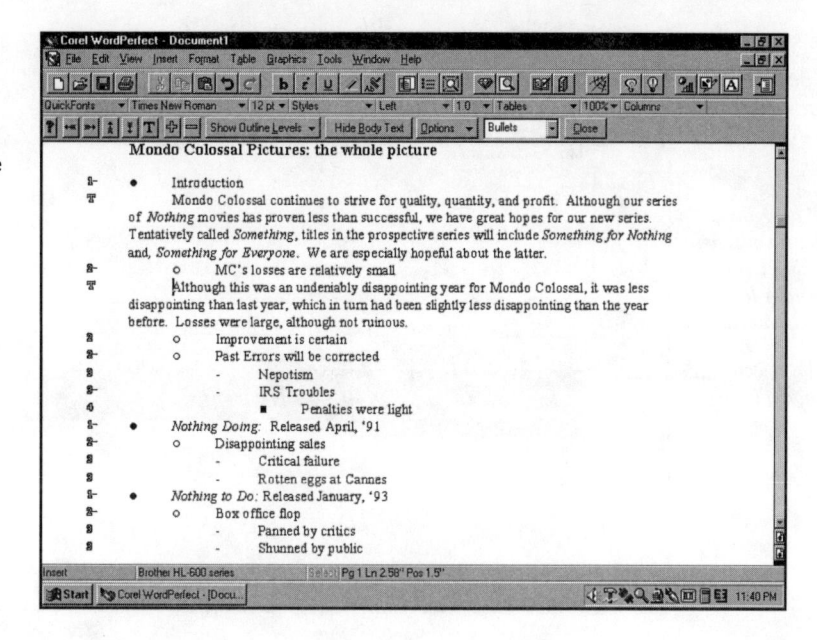

I need to move this outline item

Outlines change. You'll want to move items up or down, and back again, as your thinking about the final document changes.

To move a single outline item, put the insertion point anywhere within the item, and click the up or down arrow on the feature bar.

To move an outline family up or down:

1 Point at the outline level icon. The pointer turns into a two-headed white arrow.

2 Click once to select the entire family.

3 Drag the two-headed arrow up or down. A solid line moves with the pointer, indicating where the selected text is going to wind up. Figure 18.8 shows an outline family on the move.

> **TIP** **You can also convert an existing document to outline form.** If you're working on a report with a confusing number of topics, click Tools, Outline to turn on Outline mode. Then, use the feature bar to convert body text to outline items and to promote or demote items you've converted. In outline form, you'll see your document a lot more clearly.

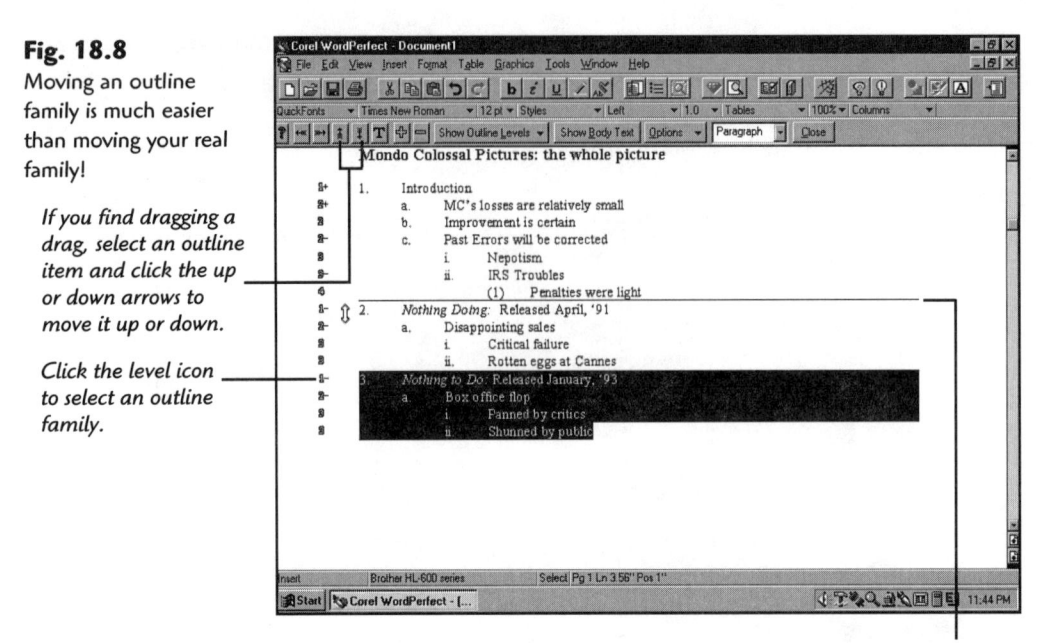

Fig. 18.8
Moving an outline family is much easier than moving your real family!

If you find dragging a drag, select an outline item and click the up or down arrows to move it up or down.

Click the level icon to select an outline family.

As you drag, the solid line indicates where the family's moving.

This big document is cumbersome

If you work with large documents in WordPerfect, you'll notice that the program can slow down quite a bit when those documents are open. Editing chores such as Find and Replace sometimes seem to happen in slow motion when you're working with large files.

It would be more convenient to break up that big file into smaller files, provided you could put them back together again when you want to. That's exactly what a **master document** does.

Master documents hold the pieces, called **subdocuments**, of a large document in the form of icons. You can work in the individual subdocuments, those pieces of the large document. When you want all the pieces assembled again, you expand the master document. That's handy if you want to print the whole thing, or Find and Replace throughout the document. When you finish, you collapse the master document again.

How do I create a master document?

Setting up a master document is easy. Suppose we have four chapters of a novel on our hands, in four different files. The files are named Chapter One,

Chapter 18 *Documents, Big and Small, Few and Many* **343**

Chapter Two, and so on. The novel's title is *North Wind*. We'll create a master document called North wind that will hold our individual chapters as subdocuments.

To create a master document:

1 Click the New Blank Document button on the Toolbar to open a new document.

TIP **You can turn an existing document into a master document; just** open it and go through the steps we're about to take.

2 Click File, Document, Subdocument to pop up the Include subdocument dialog box.

3 Select the first file you want as a subdocument from the Filename list in the Include subdocument dialog box. In the example, it's the Chapter One file, as shown in figure 18.9.

Fig. 18.9
Regrettably, you can't select more than one file at once.

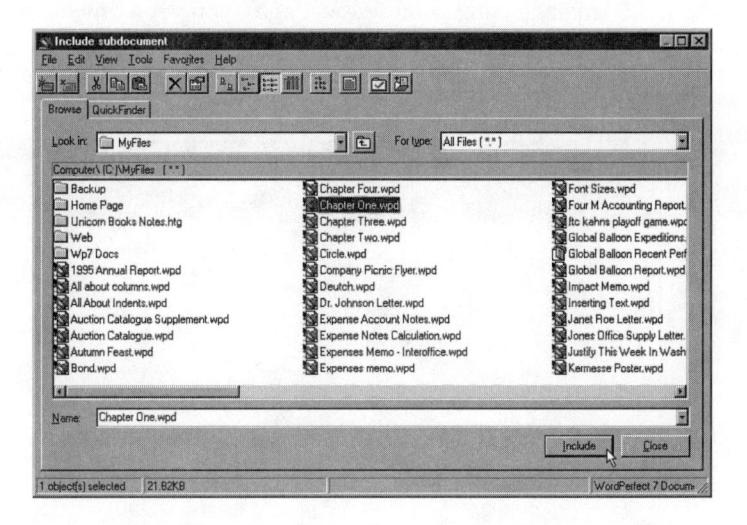

4 Once you make your selection, click Include. The dialog box disappears, and what happens next depends on what view mode you're in. In draft view (click View, Draft), you see a shaded comment bar across the editing window, as shown in figure 18.10.

Fig. 18.10
The subdocument's file name appears in draft view.

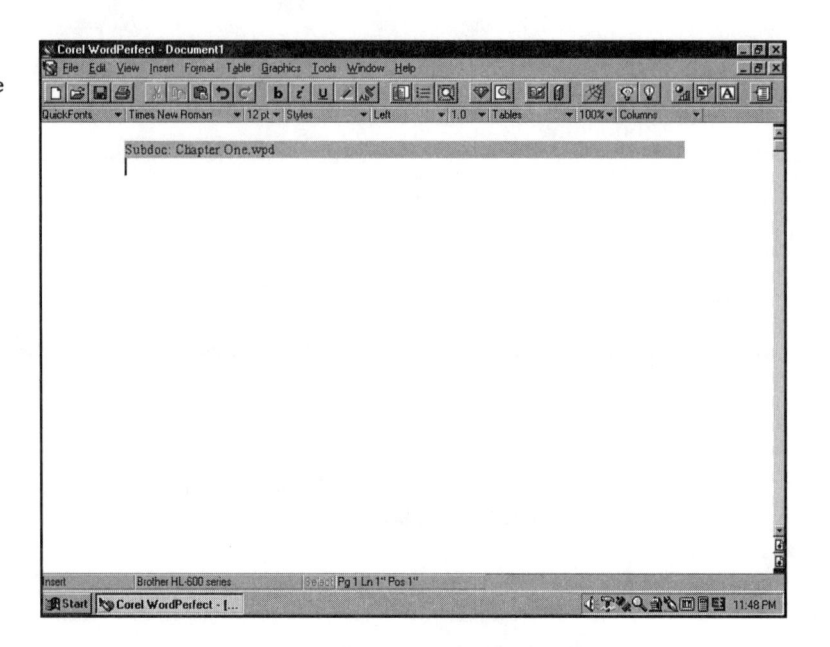

5 In page view (click View, Page), you get a tiny document icon in the left margin. Click the icon, and a balloon appears with the subdocument's file name in it, as shown in figure 18.11.

Fig. 18.11
Subdocuments look like this in page view when you click the subdocument icon.

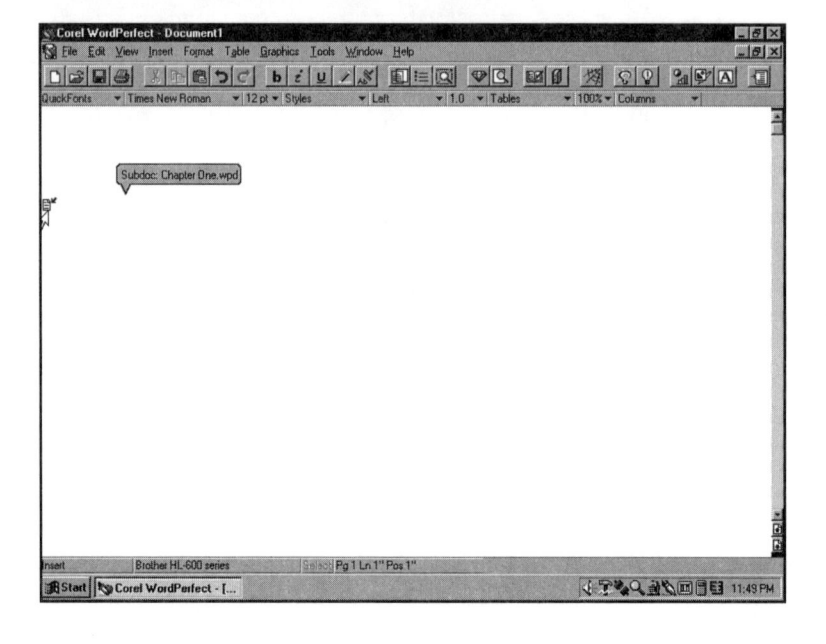

Chapter 18 *Documents, Big and Small, Few and Many*

Q&A *I don't see that subdocument icon!*

On lower resolution monitors, you might not see the subdocument icon. It's tiny, and it's also parked on the extreme left of the editing window. Drag the horizontal scroll button all the way to the left and you'll see it. If your screen resolution is set at 800 × 600, you can't miss the subdocument icon.

6. Press Enter to skip to the next line. Click File, Document, Subdocument for the Include Subdocument dialog box to appear, and select the next file from the list. Click Include (or double-click the file name), and repeat for all the files you want as subdocuments.

TIP **You can also right-click the subdocument icon and select** Subdocument from the QuickMenu for the Include subdocument dialog box.

7. Add a header or any text (an introduction, for example) that you want in the master document. Click the Save button on the Toolbar to save the master document. It might look like figure 18.12.

Fig. 18.12
The master document is a good place for a title page or a table of contents.

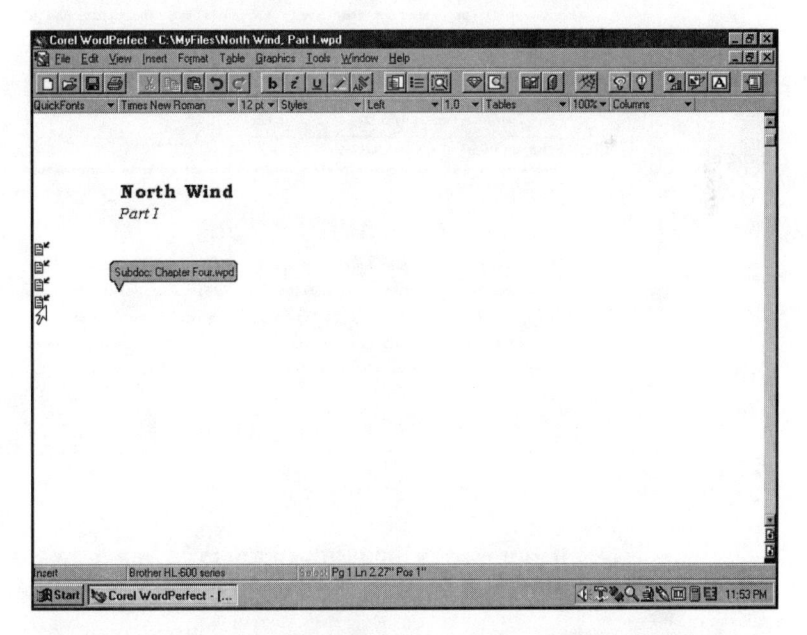

I want my document in one piece!

Our one-page master document, shown in figure 18.12, is like a collapsed telescope—it's small, but there's more to it than meets the eye.

To snap it open and combine the four subdocuments into one file, click File, Document, Expand Master and the Expand Master Document dialog box appears (see fig. 18.13).

Fig. 18.13
Click the Mark button to select all or none of your subdocuments in one step.

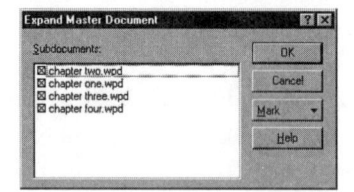

Select any or all of your subdocuments, and click OK. WordPerfect tells you it's expanding subdocuments, and after a moment or two, your selected subdocuments appear on the screen, as shown in figure 18.14.

Fig. 18.14
Subdocuments are strung one after the other when expanded.

Shows end of one subdocument

Shows the beginning of the next subdocument

Click a subdocument icon to display the balloon.

> **TIP** If you want your subdocuments to begin on a new page, press Ctrl+Enter to insert a hard page break at the end of each subdocument.

What can I do with this expanded document?

Expanded master documents are especially useful for Find and Replace operations. If you have a word change to make, and the word occurs in all your chapters, you don't have to open each chapter file to make the change; just perform the Find and Replace in the expanded master document.

Here are a couple of other things to keep in mind when you expand subdocuments:

- If your subdocuments include page number codes, pages will be numbered consecutively from the first page of the first subdocument to the last page of the last subdocument. Printing an expanded master document prints all your subdocuments with the correct pagination. Don't put new page number codes in your subdocuments; those change the pagination from the code to the end of the document.

- In expanded master documents, formatting changes from the point at which any new format codes are encountered. If subdocument 1 has 1" margins, for example, subdocuments 2, 3, and 4 will get 1" margins as well. But if one of those subdocuments has a different margin setting, the margins will change from that point on.

Put the expanded document away again

Once you print or edit an expanded master document, there's no need to save it—that just takes up disk space. Instead, condense the master document into subdocuments again. You have the option of saving any changes in each subdocument when you do that.

To condense an expanded master document, either double-click one of the subdocument icons or select File, Document, Condense Master for the Condense/Save Subdocuments dialog box shown in figure 18.15 to appear.

Each subdocument is listed twice; choose to save and/or condense any or all of the subdocuments. Click OK when you've made your selections, and the subdocuments shrink back to icons.

Fig. 18.15
If you make editing changes in the expanded master document, save them in the subdocuments.

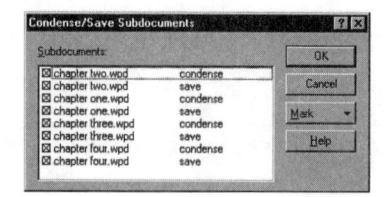

> **TIP** If you do try to save an expanded master document, WordPerfect gives you the option of condensing it first. Click <u>Y</u>es to condense the subdocuments when the message box appears.

Viewing a condensed master document

If your subdocuments have hard page breaks to begin or end them, the subdocument icons will appear on separate pages in a condensed master document in page view.

You might find it handier to view condensed master documents in Draft mode instead. This lets you view all the subdocument comment bars in one window, as shown in figure 18.16.

Fig. 18.16
Viewing a condensed master document in Draft mode is handy if your subdocuments are divided with hard page breaks.

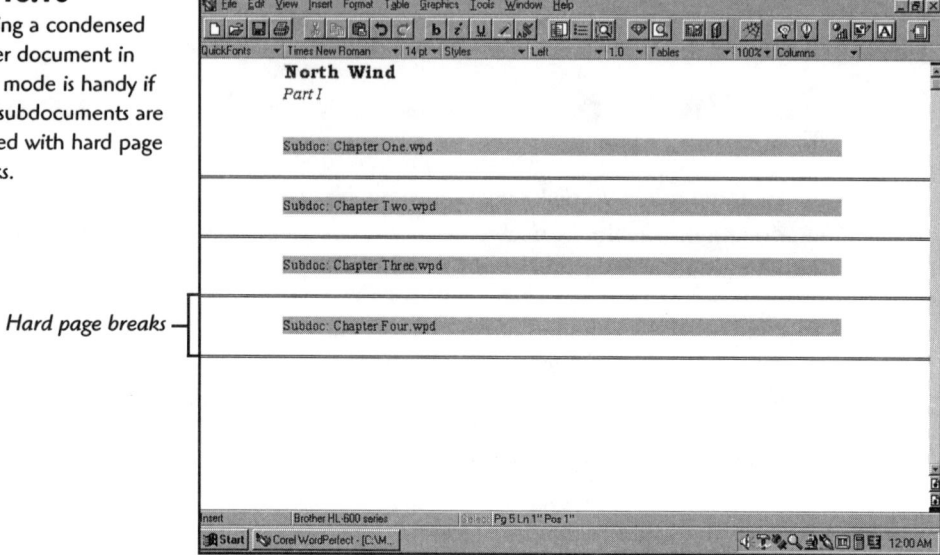

Hard page breaks

I need a table of contents

A table of contents is like a road map to your document. It's a good organizational tool for the document's author and a convenience for the reader. That's especially true in a large document with many sections.

To create a table of contents:

1 With your document open, click Tools, Generate, Table of Contents. That pops up the Table of Contents feature bar shown in figure 18.17.

Fig. 18.17
Tables of contents have heading levels like outlines.

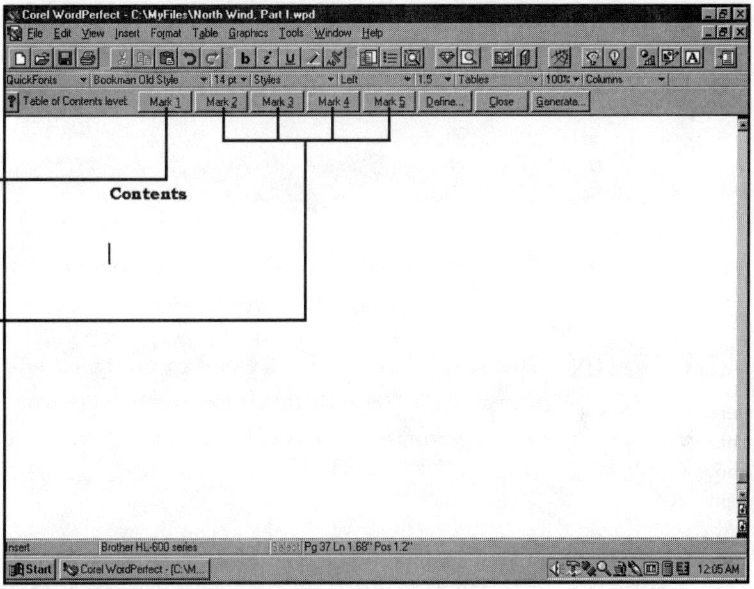

Click for chapter headings.

Click for subtopics on different levels.

2 Like outlines, tables of contents have different levels of headings, labeled 1 through 5. Level 1 is for the most important headings, such as chapter titles or section heads; levels 2 through 5 can be used for subtopics within chapters or sections. You don't have to use all the different levels; just as many as you need. Select the text you want to appear in the table of contents for your first level 1 heading and click the Mark 1 button on the feature bar.

3 Move the insertion point to the next heading you want to appear in the table of contents. Figure 18.18 shows a level 2 heading in Chapter One. Select the text and click the Mark 2 button on the feature bar.

Fig. 18.18
Mark text for level 2 headings you want in the table of contents and click the Mark 2 button.

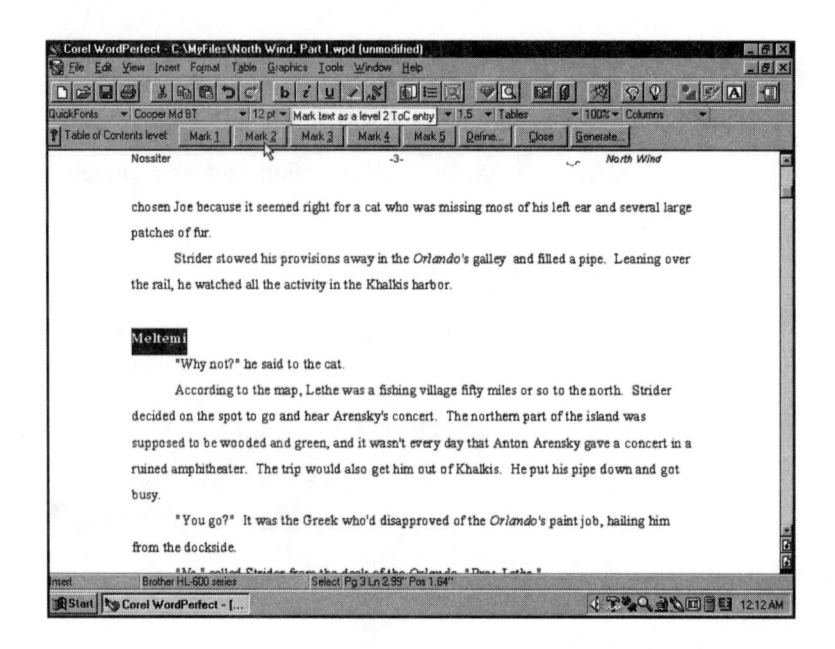

4. Go through the entire document. Mark the text for table of contents headings, and click the appropriate Mark button on the feature bar.

CAUTION The text you mark for a table of contents will have the same formatting in the TOC that it has in the document. If you mark chapter headings formatted in 30pt Poster Bodoni, they'll turn up in the TOC in the same font. The quick fix: change the TOC font after you generate the TOC.

TIP Find and Replace is a handy tool for marking table of contents text. Use it to search for text such as "Chapter" or even for formatting. If you format your heading text in a different font, for example, click Edit, Find and Replace and the Find and Replace Text dialog box appears. Select Type, Specific Codes, and double-click Font in the Specific Codes dialog box. Select the font you're looking for on the Find font drop-down list. Click Find Next, and you'll go straight to text formatted in that font.

5. When you finish marking text, move the insertion point to the page where you want the table of contents. If you want your TOC at the

beginning of the document, press Ctrl+Home; then press Ctrl+Enter to insert a blank page on page one. Or press Ctrl+End, and then press Ctrl+Enter to put a blank page at the end of the document. Either way, click the blank page to make it the active page.

6 Click the <u>D</u>efine button on the feature bar. That pops up the Define Table of Contents dialog box shown in figure 18.19.

Fig. 18.19
You can tinker with styles and page numbering options, but all you really need here is to set the number of levels.

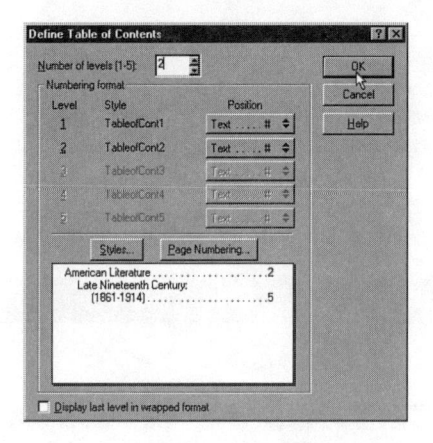

7 Click the arrows to set the <u>N</u>umber of levels you want in your table of contents. Here, we're using two levels.

8 Click OK. WordPerfect displays a message saying <<Table of Contents will generate here>> wherever you left the insertion point. Now, click <u>G</u>enerate on the Table of Contents feature bar and the Generate dialog box appears. Click OK in the Generate dialog box. WordPerfect's gears whirl for a moment, and your table of contents appears, as shown in figure 18.20.

If your TOC picked up text formatting—font faces and styles, for example—from the document that you don't want in the TOC, just change the TOC formatting. The TOC in figure 18.20 uses the same font (KabelBd in different sizes) that was used for the document text I marked. To change it, select the TOC and choose a different font on the Power Bar Font Face drop-down list.

Fig. 18.20
This is the default table of contents. It's serviceable, but if you want a different look, tinker with the settings in the Define Table of Contents dialog box.

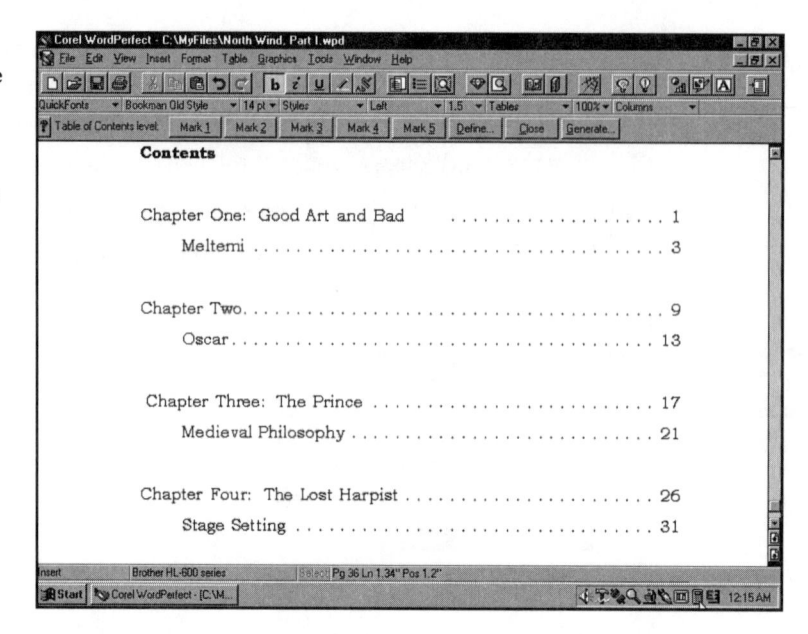

I want to see lots of files at the same time

When you're working in several different files, it's helpful to display them together. That's especially true if you're working on subdocuments and master documents. Comparing subdocuments side by side before you expand them helps you spot things like inconsistent formatting from document to document.

To view multiple files:

1 Click the Open File button on the Toolbar and select the files you want from the list. Click the first file; then Ctrl+click the other files to select them all. WordPerfect lets you open up to nine files at the same time.

2 Click OK in the Open File dialog box, and the files open one after the other in separate full-screen windows.

3 Click Window, Tile Side by Side for the screen arrangement shown in figure 18.21.

Drag the window borders to resize them. To scroll in a document window, click anywhere in the window to activate it; then use the scroll bar.

Fig. 18.21
With four files open, you don't see too much of each file.

Click to minimize or maximize document windows.

Click anywhere in the document window to activate it.

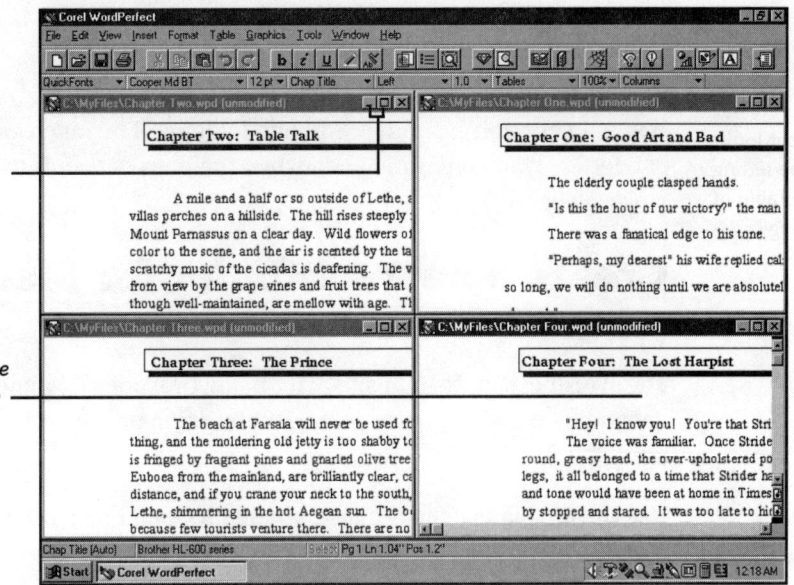

And if you want to get windows out of sight fast, click the Minimize button. That reduces a document window to an icon at the bottom of the screen. Click the Full Screen button in the icon to restore the document.

> **TIP** Double-click a document window title bar to maximize it.

How do I manage all these files?

Computers are wonderful because they remember everything you tell them. The curse of the computer is that it *does* remember everything. It doesn't take long before you accumulate more files than you know what to do with.

Here's a strategy you might try to manage large file collections:

- Create a new subfolder to hold all your documents of a particular type—letters, for example.

- Use QuickFinder (see Chapter 2) to locate all your letter files and to move them into the new subfolder.

With all your correspondence in one folder, it'll be much easier to find any one letter. That comes in handy when the boss demands to see a letter you wrote a year ago.

Create a new subfolder for files of one type

The WordPerfect file management dialog box pops up under different names depending on what you're doing. But by any name, it's a powerful file manager.

Use the file management dialog box in its Open File guise to create a new subfolder:

1 Click the Open File button on the Toolbar to pop up the CorelOffice—Open dialog box, one of the file management dialog box's many aliases.

2 By default, the Open dialog box displays the MyFiles folder. That's fine, because you can create as many subfolders as you want right in the MyFiles folder, and you'll always know where they are.

> **TIP** If you want the Open dialog box to open with a folder other than MyFiles, Click Edit, Preferences for the Preferences dialog box. Double-click the Files icon, and enter a new folder name and path as the Default document folder. Click OK to save the change.

3 Click File, New, Folder, and a new subfolder appears in the MyFiles folder. You'll notice it's called New Folder, a name that begs to be changed (see figure 18.22).

4 Now, type your new folder name. Call it whatever you like. This one is called Letters, 1996.

5 Press Enter to save the name change, and your new folder is born.

For now, the Letters, 1996 folder is empty. We'll use QuickFinder to fill it up.

Fig. 18.22
You can do all your file chores, including renaming folders, from the file management dialog boxes.

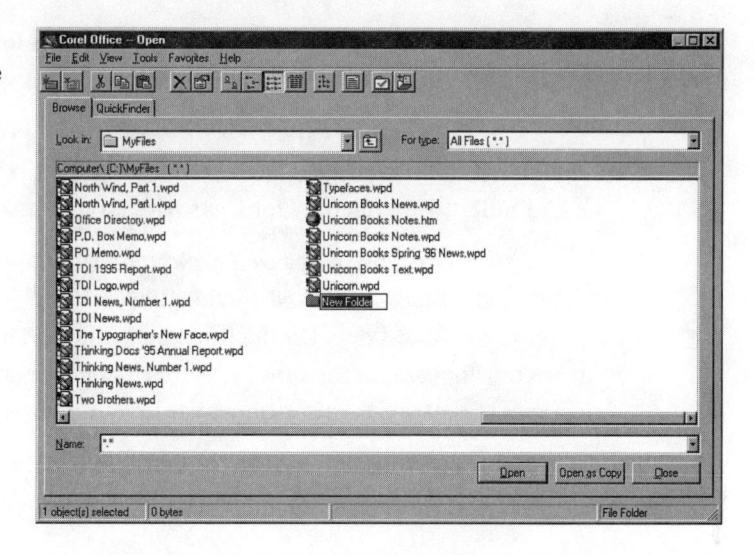

Let QuickFinder gather your files together

Most of us create a document, name and save it in a hurry, and then promptly forget all about it—which is fine, until you want the document again. If your file names are like mine, remembering what you called the file might not be so easy. QuickFinder can help you out.

Let's use QuickFinder to find all the letters we've stored in WordPerfect. Those letters might not have obvious names, but QuickFinder will search through the text in the files to find text that might only be found in a letter. To put QuickFinder to work:

1 Click the Open File button on the Toolbar to pop up the CorelOffice— Open dialog box.

2 Click the Quickfinder tab. If this is your first use of QuickFinder, you'll get the QuickFinder Fast Search Setup Expert. Click Pre-Search to have QuickFinder index your hard disk. It only takes a few moments now, and it'll speed up all your subsequent QuickFinder searches.

3 Once the QuickFinder Fast Search Setup Expert finishes its work, we're back in the QuickFinder tab of the Open dialog box. We're interested in finding all our letters, and the one thing they'll probably have in common is the salutation. In other words, "Dear...." Type **Dear** in the Content edit box.

4. Trouble is, the word "dear" is likely to crop up in a lot of documents that aren't letters. We want "Dear" with an uppercase D. Click Ad‐vanced.

5. Click Match case in the Advanced Find dialog box. That'll force QuickFinder to search only for Dear with an uppercase D.

6. We can further refine our search for letters. Double-click the word "Dear" in the Words edit box to select it. Now, click the Components option button and select On the first page. Since a letter's salutation invariably appears on the first page, this maneuver should eliminate documents that aren't letters in which Dear, uppercase D, might appear.

7. Click Insert and the search code for first pages is dumped into the Words box, enclosing the word we're looking for (see figure 18.23).

Fig. 18.23
Search Tools allow you to refine QuickFinder searches so that you'll find only what you're looking for.

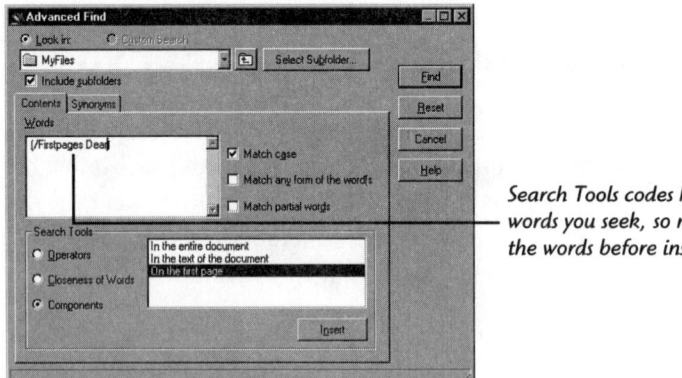

Search Tools codes have to enclose the words you seek, so make sure you select the words before inserting codes.

> 66 **Plain English, please!**
>
> Wondering about the **Operators** choice among the Search Tools? Opera‐tors act on text the way mathematical operators like + and – act on numbers. The search operator AND, for example, is just like a + sign for text. Search for Jerry&Jones, and you'll find every file in which the words "Jerry Jones" occur. 99

8. Click Find, and you bounce back to the QuickFinder tab of the CorelOffice—Open dialog box. The list of files in which QuickFinder found "Dear" on the first page appears, as seen in figure 18.24.

Fig. 18.24
QuickFinder really is quick. Use it to search your entire drive for missing files if you need to.

Click the file; then click the Preview button to view its contents.

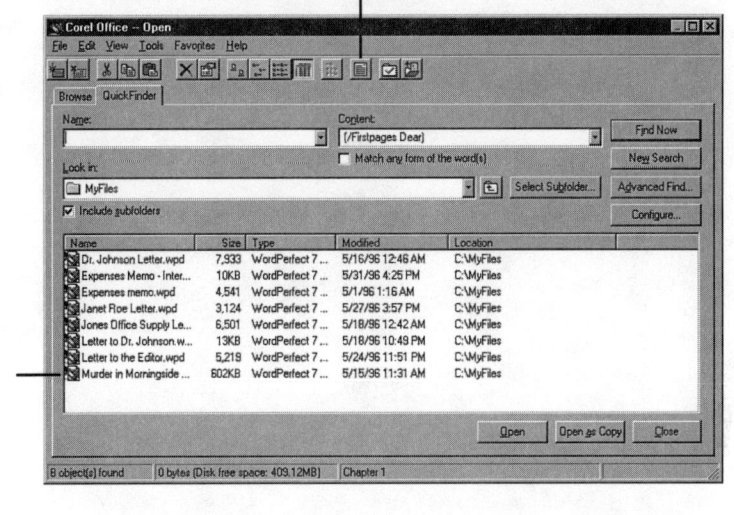

I happen to know that this file isn't a letter.

9. QuickFinder seems to have found all our letters, and more besides. If you're not sure that a particular file really belongs on the list, select it and click the Preview button to examine it.

10. To move the letters to the Letters, 1996 folder we created earlier, click the first file in the list, and then Shift+click the last file to select them all.

11. Click the Cut button on the Open dialog box Toolbar to put your selected files in the limbo of the Windows Clipboard.

12. Now, click the Browse tab of the Open dialog box, double-click the Letters, 1996 folder to open it, and click the Paste button on the Open dialog box Toolbar. All the files you cut from the MyFiles folder are now pasted into the MyFiles/Letters, 1996 subfolder, and your file reshuffle is completed.

13. As a final time-saver, with the Letters, 1996 folder still open, click the Add to Favorites button on the Open dialog box Toolbar. That puts the Letters, 1996 folder in a special folder that holds shortcuts to your most-often-used folders.

The next time we need to look at an old letter, we can cut down on search time by flipping right to the Letters, 1996 folder in any of the file management dialog boxes. Just click the Go to Favorites button and double-click the Letters, 1996 folder. And when we write new letters, we can save them right to the new folder.

It's a bit of a chore to set up, but after you've accumulated a few hundred letters, you'll be glad you did it!

19

Presentations 7 for Instant Artists

● **In this chapter:**

- What is Presentations, and what do I do with it?

- How can I tailor clip art to my text?

- This drawing needs some work

- Can I create a quick chart for this document?

- What else should I know about charts?

Lines of text and rows of numbers have their place—and so do deserts and ice fields. Plain documents perk up with the change of scenery provided by WordPerfect's built-in drawing program, Presentations 7 . . . . ➤

Leonardo da Vinci filled thousands of pages with notes on everything from helicopters to human anatomy. The text is obscure—it's in mirror writing. The drawings, which cover every page, are sharper than photos. When Leonardo wanted clarity, he drew a picture.

WordPerfect gives you two ways to make your point with pictures. Charts describe numbers in colorful images, and there's an easy-to-use charting feature built into the program.

WordPerfect's drawing feature, Presentations, is an electronic drawing board. Use it to draw anything—diagrams, sketches, even a copy of Leonardo's Mona Lisa.

What can I do with a drawing program?

"Words fail me." "I was speechless." Artists know what to do in situations like that: they draw a picture. Nonartists can use WordPerfect's Presentations. Presentations puts a gallery of images at your disposal, together with the tools to customize them any way you like. Change colors and textures, add your own free-hand creations, and spice up any document with a picture or two. Altered to suit, the right image can emphasize a point, inject a little humor, or simply provide some eye relief.

Can't find the image you want? Make your own!

There are plenty of clip art images included with WordPerfect, and inserting them in documents is easy to do (see Chapter 16 for details.) But if you've browsed the clip art collection and can't find exactly what you need, just create your own. You don't have to start from scratch. You can customize any of the existing images to fit your text.

One of the WordPerfect images is a prancing pony. But what if you need a unicorn? It's easy to make the transformation. To customize a clip art image in Presentations:

1 Click the Draw button on the Toolbar (or select Graphics, Draw) to run Presentations 7, the WordPerfect drawing program. In a moment or two, the Presentations drawing window and Toolbars appear on the screen. Now click the Chart or Graphic Tools button on the left-hand toolbar, as shown in figure 19.1.

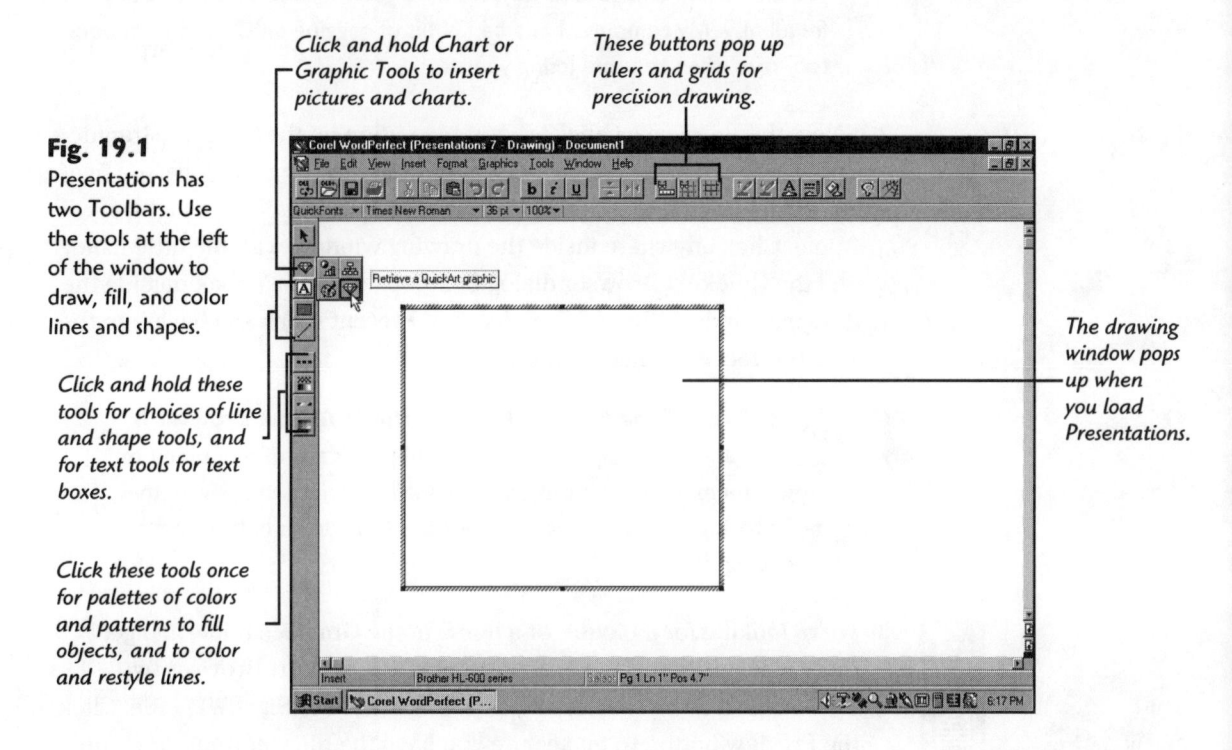

Fig. 19.1
Presentations has two Toolbars. Use the tools at the left of the window to draw, fill, and color lines and shapes.

Click and hold Chart or Graphic Tools to insert pictures and charts.

These buttons pop up rulers and grids for precision drawing.

Click and hold these tools for choices of line and shape tools, and for text tools for text boxes.

Click these tools once for palettes of colors and patterns to fill objects, and to color and restyle lines.

The drawing window pops up when you load Presentations.

Three Cheers for OLE

OLE (pronounced just like the bullfighter's cheer, and the acronym for **Object Linking and Embedding**) is an amazing feature of Windows programs. It allows you to create an object in one program, Presentations for example, and embed it in another program, such as WordPerfect. An object can be anything: a drawing, a clip art image, a chart, or even a document.

Embedding an object is like pulling a grape from the bunch and dropping it into a bowl of jello—with one big difference: an embedded OLE object is linked to the original. Create a chart in Quattro Pro, embed it in WordPerfect, and any editing you do in the Quattro Pro chart also changes the chart you embedded in WordPerfect. That would be like peeling another grape in the bunch and having the embedded grape lose its skin too. Mind-boggling, but it really does work. Depending on how much memory you have and the speed of your computer, OLE might work a little slowly. To perform these OLE tricks, your computer has to run several programs simultaneously.

CAUTION

OLE taxes your computer's processing power and memory. When you create and embed OLE objects, it's a good idea to save your work frequently. My computer has a bad habit of gagging on OLE; if yours does too, save often to avoid losing your work.

2. Select the Retrieve a QuickArt graphic option on the Chart or Graphic Tools button, and move the pointer into the drawing window (see figure 19.1). The pointer arrow turns into a little hand clutching a picture frame. Click anywhere inside the drawing window with the little hand, and the QuickArt Browser dialog box pops up. (Don't click outside the drawing window; that takes you out of Presentations and back into the WordPerfect document window!)

TIP

Each of the folders shown in the QuickArt Browser is stuffed with clip art images; double-click any of the folders to browse them. When the clip art thumbnails pop into the viewer, they might be too tiny to see clearly. Click the Large Icons button to make them bigger.

3. We're looking for a picture of a horse in the Graphics folder. To get there, click the Up One Level button in the QuickArt Browser two times. Scroll down the file list, and select the HORSE_J.WPG file. Click the Preview button to make sure you have the file you want, or if you're just browsing (see figure 19.2).

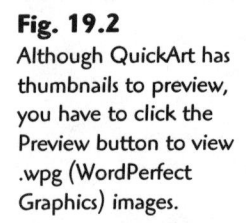

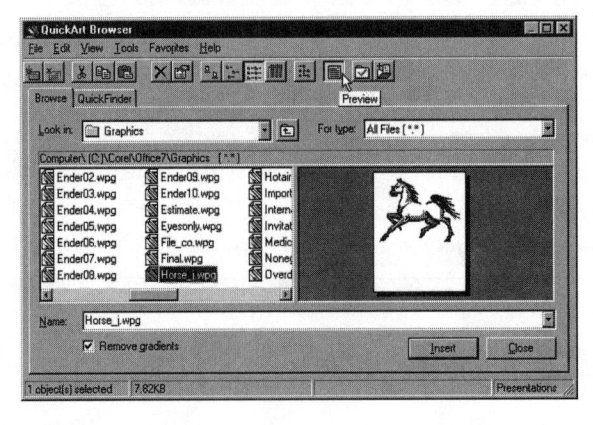

Fig. 19.2
Although QuickArt has thumbnails to preview, you have to click the Preview button to view .wpg (WordPerfect Graphics) images.

Chapter 19 *Presentations 7 for Instant Artists* **363**

    4 Click Insert to pop your selected graphic into the Presentations drawing window. That gets us the better part of our Unicorn; all we need now is the horn. Click and hold the Closed Object Tools button on the Presentations toolbar and select the Ellipse tool, as shown in figure 19.3.

Fig. 19.3
Select from this palette of shapes to add filled objects to your drawings.

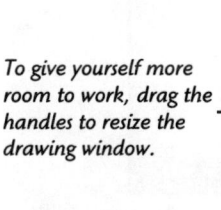

To give yourself more room to work, drag the handles to resize the drawing window.

Create your drawing anywhere within the drawing window; then drag it into place when it's finished.

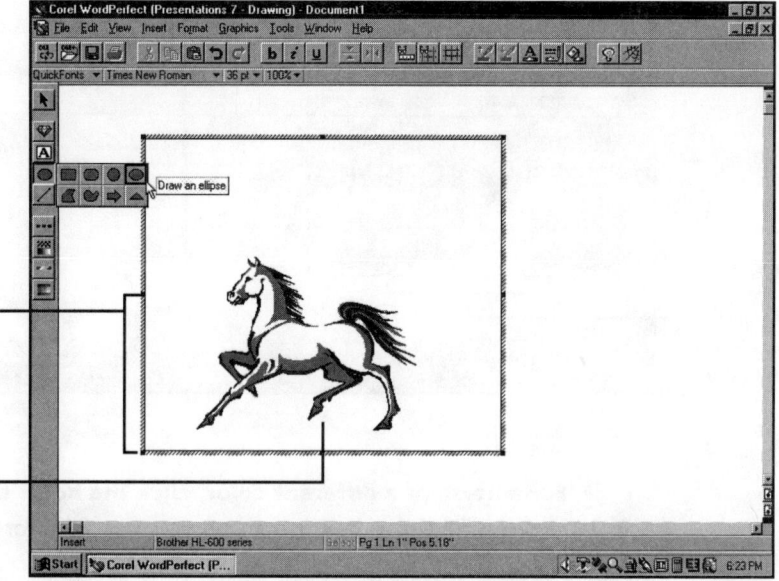

    5 With the Ellipse tool selected, the pointer turns into a crosshair when it's in the drawing window. Position the crosshair wherever you want the beginning of the ellipse; then drag to wherever you want the ellipse to end and release the mouse button. Use any blank spot in the drawing window for your ellipse; you can drag it into place when it's finished. For ideas on where to draw the ellipse and what shape to make it, see figure 19.4.

    6 The ellipse fills in automatically, and we'll change the fill color. With the ellipse still selected, click the Fill Colors button at the bottom of the drawing Toolbar. You'll see a double palette of colors, one for the ellipse's background color, the other for the ellipse's pattern or fill color, as shown in figure 19.4.

Part VI Getting the Most Out of WordPerfect

Fig. 19.4
The default fill color is blue, but you can easily change it.

These sizing handles appear around an object after you drag to create it.

To change the fill color of the selected object, click your choices from the palettes.

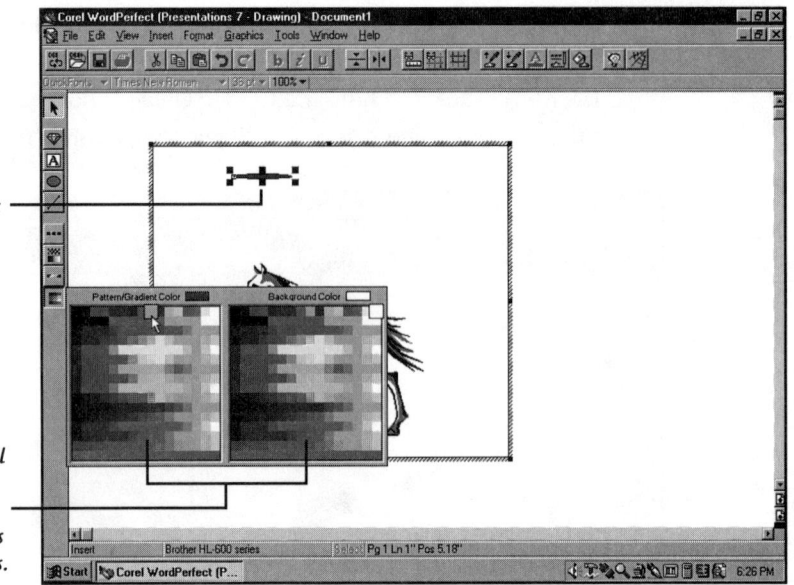

> **TIP** **For a horse of a different color, click the horse to select it; then** click the Fill Colors button and choose a new fill color from the palette.

7 For a solid fill, leave the Background color white and take your choice from the Pattern/Gradient Color palette. We're adding a pattern, so I've selected a bone shade for the background color and a light gray for the pattern color.

8 To add a pattern, click the Fill Attributes button on the Toolbar, and take your choice on the palette of patterns.

> **TIP** **If you don't see your pattern in the selected object, the pattern** color is being washed out by the background color. Click the Fill Colors button and adjust either, or both. A dark pattern color against a light background color will make the pattern stand out.

9 Our horn is looking a little more like a horn, but it's not at the right angle. Right-click the object and select Rotate on the Quickmenu. Rotation handles appear around the object; drag a handle to rotate the object to the angle you want, as seen in figure 19.5.

Fig. 19.5
Rotating objects is a handy way to blend together different elements in a drawing.

To flip a selected object horizontally or vertically, click these buttons.

10. With our horn at the correct angle, right-click the horn and choose Select on the QuickMenu. Now drag the horn into position on the unicorn's head. Drag any of the object's sizing handles to make it longer, shorter, fatter, or skinnier.

TIP **With several objects bunched together in the drawing window, it's** not always easy to figure out which object you've selected when you click it. If that's the case, click View, Selected Object Viewer on the Presentations menu bar. That pops up the Selected Object Viewer window. Now click any object, or portion of an object, in the drawing window; your selection appears in the Selected Object Viewer (see figure 19.6).

11. When everything looks about right, here's the final touch to make our custom image easier to resize or move: right-click a blank spot in the drawing window and choose Select All. That selects both the horse image and our horn; point anywhere within the selected images, right-click, and select Group from the Quickmenu. With the objects in the drawing grouped in this way, they'll stay together when moved, and change together if resized.

Fig. 19.6
The Selected Object Viewer makes editing images much easier.

The selected object or chunk of an object appears in the viewer.

Click an area of your image to select it.

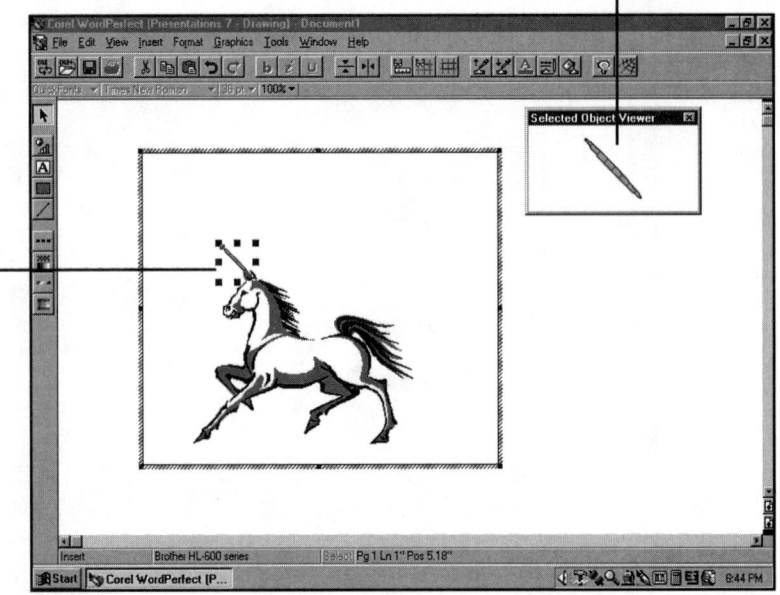

> **TIP** To edit either of the objects separately again, right-click the image, and select Separate on the QuickMenu. Then click the element you want to edit.

12 You'll probably want to shrink the image before putting it in a document. First, drag one of the drawing's corner handles toward the center of the image (see figure 19.7). With the drawing itself cut down to size, drag one of drawing *window's* corner handles toward the center of the drawing to shrink the graphics box.

13 Now, click anywhere outside the drawing window to shut down Presentations and pop the drawing into your document.

The drawing winds up in the document at the insertion point. Simply drag it to move it around on the page. If you want text to wrap around the image, click the QuickSpot and choose one of the wrapping options. At the end of the day, you'll have something that looks like figure 19.8.

Fig. 19.7
You won't want your creation to take up too much of the document page, so cut it down to size before inserting it.

Click anywhere outside the drawing window to close Presentations and insert the drawing into the document.

To avoid too much white space around the image in the document, drag the drawing window corners to shrink it.

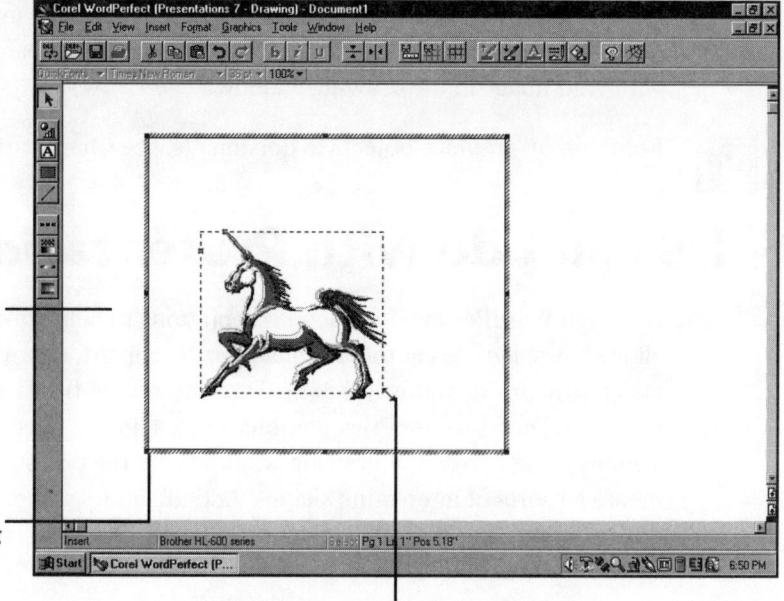

First, shrink the drawing by dragging a corner toward the center of the image.

Fig. 19.8
Once you find your way around the Presentation tools, you can alter any image in the clip art collection to fit your text.

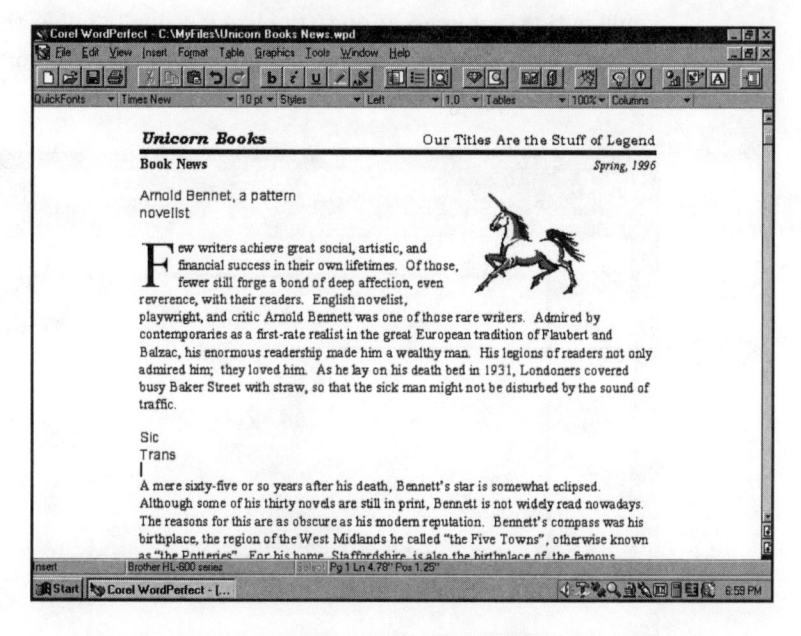

Part VI *Getting the Most Out of WordPerfect*

If you need to do further work on your drawing after it's inserted into a document, just double-click the image. That sends you back to Presentations with your image in the drawing window.

For more on graphics objects in documents, see Chapter 16.

What else can I do with Presentations?

Although WordPerfect designed Presentations to help you produce elaborate slide shows, it's a great tool for customizing clip art, as we've just seen. It's also terrific for doodling. Click the Draw button on the Toolbar (or select Graphics, Draw) to run Presentations, click a line or filled shape tool on the Toolbar, drag across the drawing window with the crosshair, and you can create all sorts of interesting shapes. Add fill colors and patterns, and your doodle might start to look like art. If that's the case, you can help it along with some artistic editing.

How can I reshape this object?

If you look closely at an active object in the Presentations drawing window, you'll notice that in addition to the black sizing handles, there's a smaller, unfilled handle at the corner of a rectangle or near the curve of an oval. That's an editing handle, shown in figure 19.9

Fig. 19.9
Use the editing handles to reshape an object.

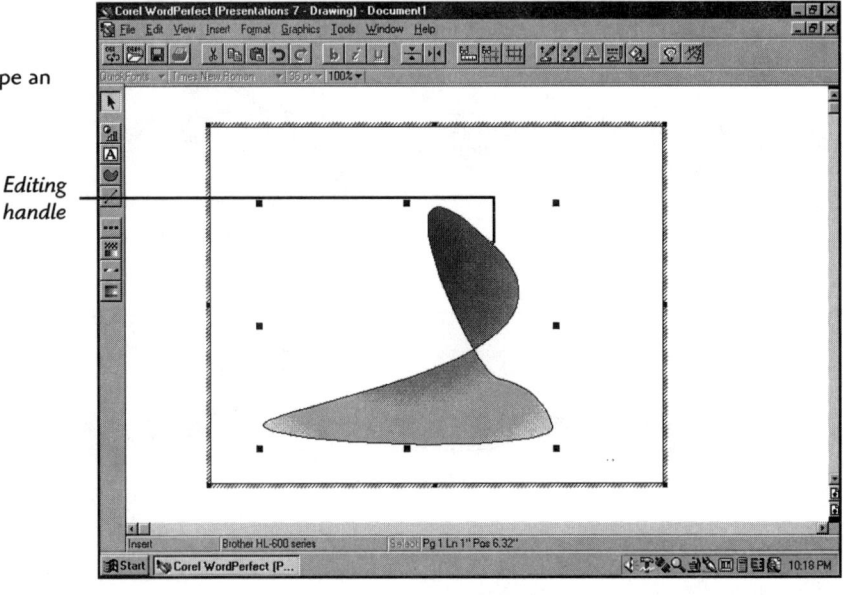

Editing handle

Double-click anywhere in the object, and more editing handles pop up along the perimeter of curved objects, or at the corners of pointed objects. Point at any editing handle and the pointer turns into a crosshair. Now drag to reshape the object, as shown in figure 19.10.

Fig. 19.10
Drag the editing handles to create eye-catching shapes.

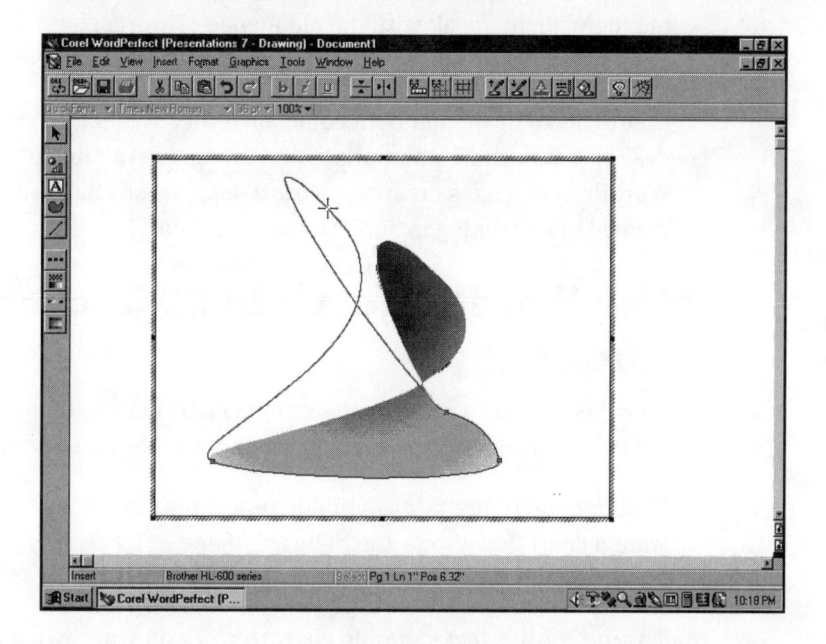

You can also use editing handles to twist curved lines into knots.

Q&A *I keep pointing at the editing handle, but I don't get a crosshair to drag it with!*

Double-click the object to make the editing handles appear first; then drag with the crosshair. Or right-click the object for the QuickMenu and select Edit Points to pop up the editing handles. If you don't see the Edit Points choice on the QuickMenu, choose Edit Group, right-click the object again, and then choose Edit Points.

TIP **For perfectly straight horizontal and vertical lines, press the Shift** key as you drag with the crosshair.

Can I make charts in WordPerfect?

Numbers tell stories just as words do. Annual reports, marketing studies, and similar documents rely on numbers to make their point. To a trained eye, numbers might speak with the eloquence of words; but for the rest of us, there isn't a lot of poetry and drama in tables of numerical data.

Charts make those numbers come alive. Just as a photo enlivens a dry description, a chart summarizes and dramatizes a table of numbers. Since WordPerfect makes creating charts a snap, use a chart whenever a document in need of enlivening includes numerical data.

Use WordPerfect's built-in chart for fast results

WordPerfect has a ready-made sample chart built right into the program. Just enter your own numbers and labels, and you have an instant chart.

Suppose you're preparing a billing report for a small accounting practice. You want a chart that shows the billings generated by each of the four partners for each quarter of 1994.

To put WordPerfect's sample chart to work on your own data:

1 Click the Chart button on the Toolbar (or select Graphics, Chart) and the Presentations Chart window appears, as shown in figure 19.11.

2 The sample chart reflects the data and the labels in the sample Datasheet. All you do is enter your own data in the rows and columns of the Datasheet, as shown in figure 19.12.

> **TIP** To format numbers with dollar signs, or any other way, select the cells and click the Format button on the Toolbar. Make your selections in the Format dialog box that pops up; then click OK. For details on formatting data in tables, see Chapter 17.

3 The chart now shows the four partners' names and their billings for the four quarters, but it still needs some work. Double-click the Title of Chart label to pop up the Title Properties dialog box shown in figure 19.13.

Chapter 19 *Presentations 7 for Instant Artists* **371**

The labels and numbers in the Datasheet produce this chart; change the Datasheet and the chart changes too.

Fig. 19.11
WordPerfect's sample chart is a handy place to start creating your own chart.

The Y-axis shows the values in the rows of the Datasheet.

The chart legend is the key to the chart.

The data in each row is a data series, and each cell is a data point.

The X-axis shows the categories in the Datasheet columns.

Fig. 19.12
Enter your own labels and values in the Datasheet to create your own chart.

Your typed labels replace the sample labels in the chart as soon as you press an arrow key or Enter in the Data Sheet.

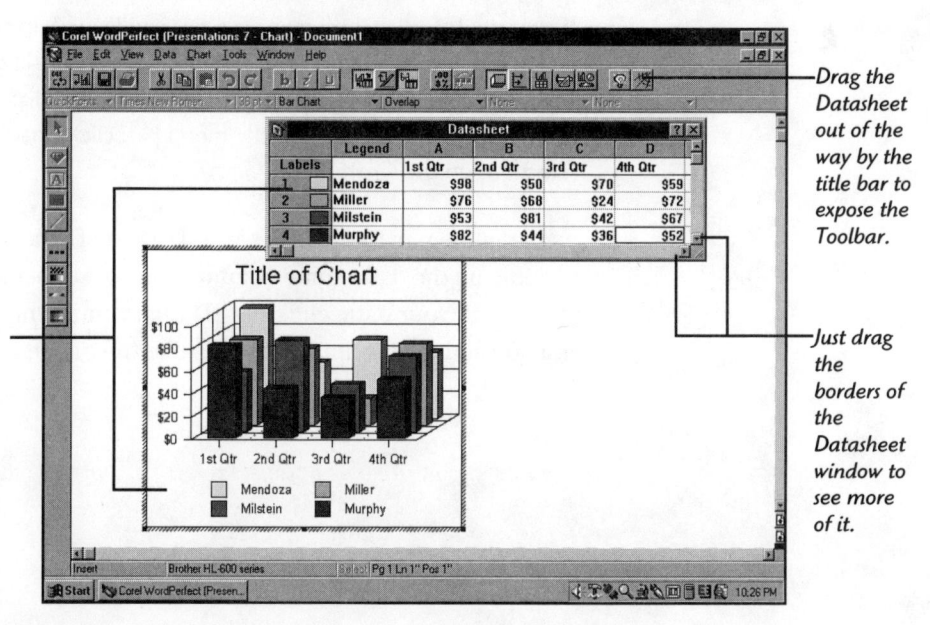

Drag the Datasheet out of the way by the title bar to expose the Toolbar.

Just drag the borders of the Datasheet window to see more of it.

Part VI Getting the Most Out of WordPerfect

Fig. 19.13
Chart titles and all the labels in a chart should tell the readers everything they need to know about the chart.

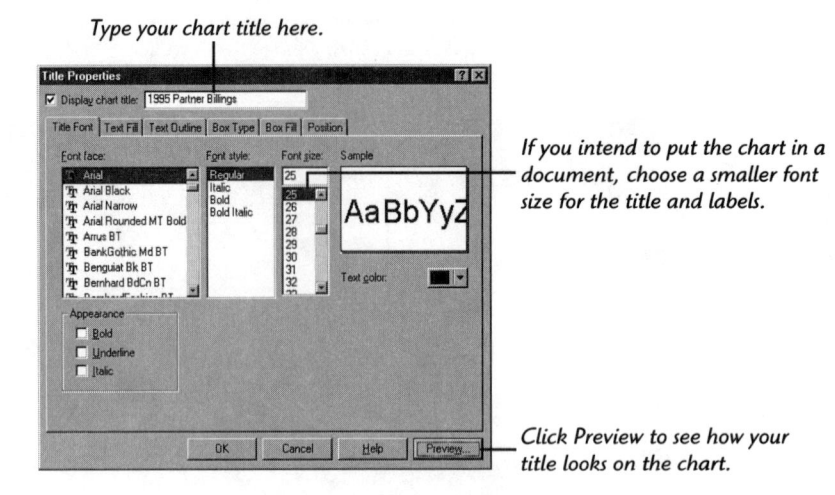

Type your chart title here.

If you intend to put the chart in a document, choose a smaller font size for the title and labels.

Click Preview to see how your title looks on the chart.

4. Everything in the chart is an object that you can select, format, and move. To add a title for the Y-axis, double-click the Y-axis to pop up the Primary Y Axis Properties dialog box. Click the Title Font tab, type in the Display title edit box, and click OK. Double-click the X-axis and follow the same steps if you want an X-axis title. Figure 19.14 shows the result of adding chart and Y-axis titles.

> **Q&A** *I can't seem to double-click the right object in this chart!*
>
> If your double-click is off by a little bit, you'll wind up with the wrong dialog box. Annoying, for sure. Try this instead: right-click the object you want (the X-axis, Y-axis, whatever) and choose the dialog box you want from the QuickMenu. Or use the menu bar: click Chart and make your selections on the Chart menu.

5. The chart shown in figure 19.14 is a 3D chart. Those look fine, but depending on the data, some columns may obscure others. If that happens with your data, click the 3D Chart button on the Toolbar to transform the chart into a 2D type like the one in figure 19.15.

Chapter 19 *Presentations 7 for Instant Artists* **373**

The Auto Redraw button is activated by default. It automatically redraws the chart when you change the Datasheet.

Click the View Datasheet button to hide or display the Datasheet.

Fig. 19.14
With informative titles and labels, the reader knows at a glance what the chart is meant to convey.

Double-click here for the Primary Y Axis Properties dialog box.

You'll want to select smaller font sizes for the legend and axis titles if you put the chart in a document.

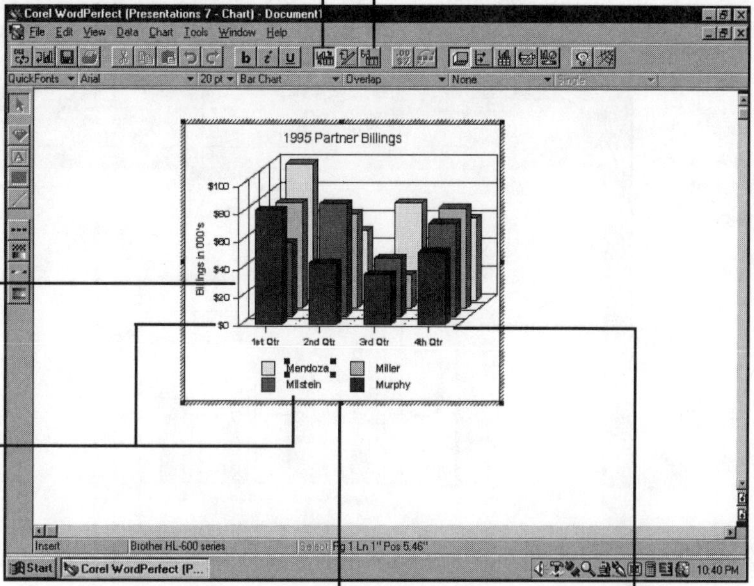

Click objects in the chart to select them; handles pop up to show you your selection.

Double-click here and the X-Axis Properties dialog box appears.

Click here to toggle between 3D and 2D charts.

Fig. 19.15
The difference between 2D and 3D charts is largely aesthetic; click the 3D Chart button to toggle between them.

2D charts might be less dramatic than their 3D cousins, but they can be easier to read.

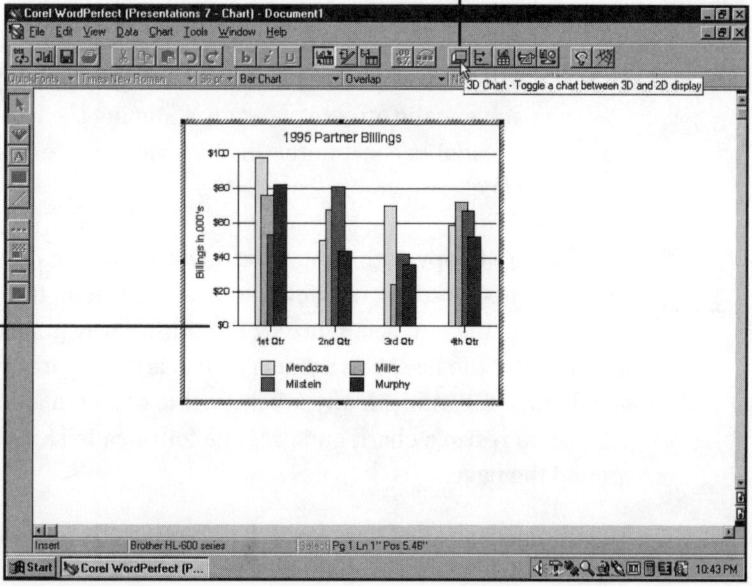

Fig. 19.16
WordPerfect has plenty of eye-catching ways to format charts, but sometimes simpler is clearer.

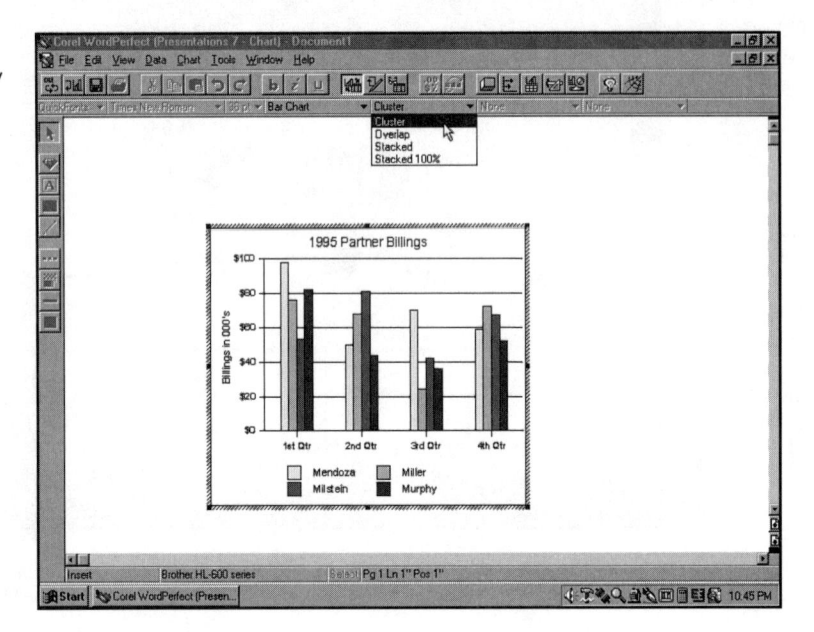

6. The bars in the chart shown in figure 19.15 overlap one another. That too, is a neat visual effect, but in this case, it makes the chart harder to read. Click the Overlap button on the Power Bar and select Cluster. That makes the chart clearer, as you can see in figure 19.16.

7. Our chart is just about finished. Wider bars might better convey the different partners' performances, though. Click the Layout button on the Toolbar and the Layout dialog box shown in figure 19.17 appears.

8. Click the arrows or drag the scroll button in the Width edit box until you achieve the effect you want. Widening the bars to 70 gives us a more readable chart here. Click Preview to see your alterations; then click OK when you're satisfied.

When you're happy with your chart, click anywhere outside the graphics box cross-hatched borders, or click the Close button on the Toolbar (the second button from the left; see figure 19.17). Either way pops the chart into a document at the insertion point. You can add text or save the chart as a stand-alone file. As with any other graphic object in a document, drag the handles to resize a chart, and drag the four-headed arrow to move the chart around the page.

To edit the chart, just double-click it to return to the chart editing window. Figure 19.18 shows the chart we've created in a document with added text.

Chapter 19 *Presentations 7 for Instant Artists* **375**

Or click the Close button to shut down Presentations and return to WordPerfect.

Fig. 19.17
You can edit every detail of your charts until the chart says exactly what you want it to say.

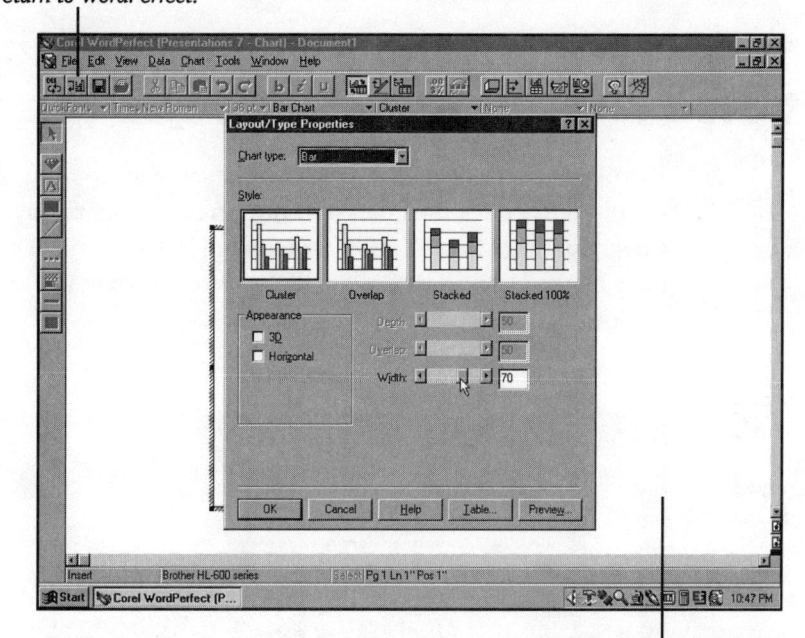

Click outside the chart window to return to your WordPerfect document with the chart inserted.

Fig. 19.18
Once the chart was placed in a document (just click outside the graphics box), I added some text and a header.

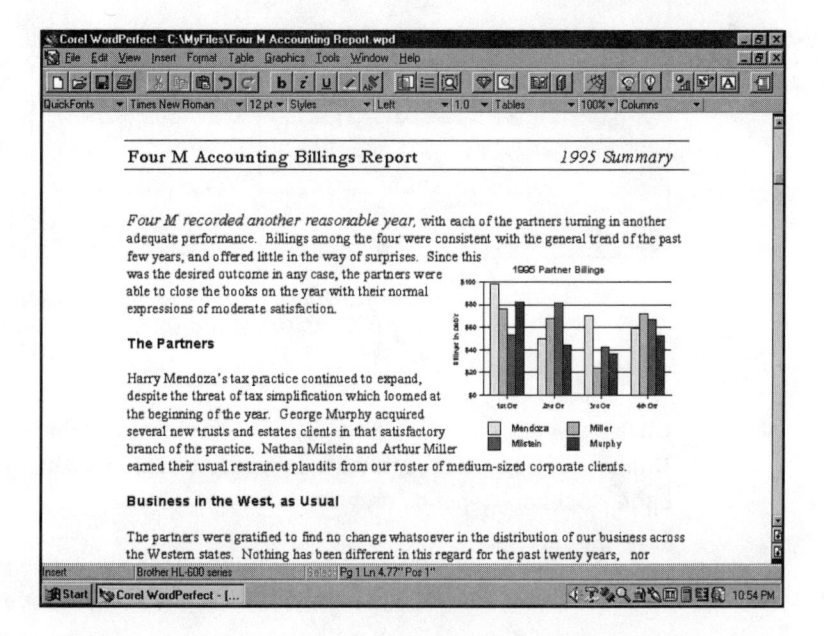

TIP To wrap text around a chart, click the chart's QuickSpot and choose one of the text wrapping options. That's what I did in figure 19.18.

What else should I know about charts?

WordPerfect has dozens of chart formats to choose from. To alter an existing chart, double-click the chart to return to the Presentations Chart window. Click the Data Chart Types button on the Power Bar and select Gallery. That pops up the Data Chart Gallery dialog box shown in figure 19.19.

Click the Data Chart Types button on the Power Bar to change chart types.

Fig. 19.19
WordPerfect has a chart for every type of data, and each chart type has several subtypes to choose from.

Click the 3D check box to view the 3D chart types.

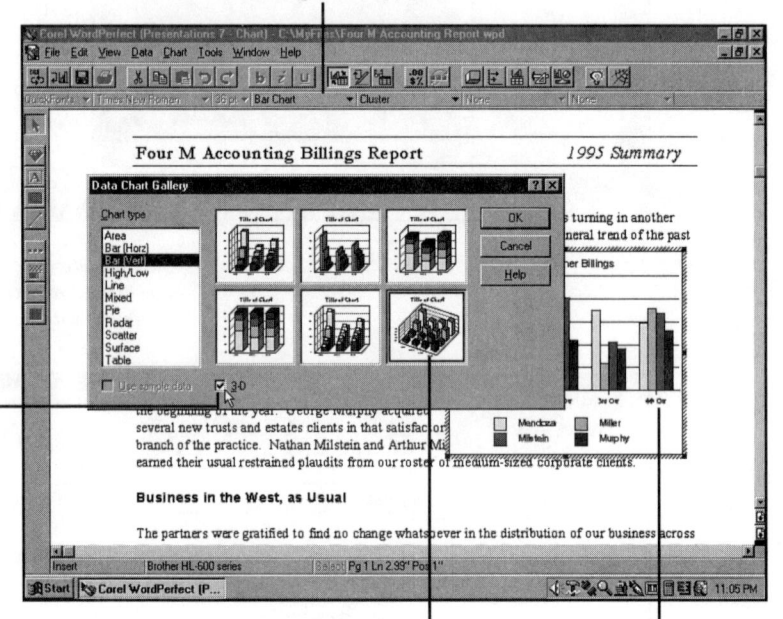

This angled 3D bar chart is a good choice if your 3D bars obscure each other.

Double-click an existing chart to summon up the Presentations Chart window.

Click a selection on the Chart Type list to view the gallery of subtypes. Double-click any one of them to instantly transform your chart. The best choice of chart depends on your data:

- Bar charts such as the ones in figure 19.18 show comparisons among different items in one period of time, or changes in different items over several periods (annual sales and expenses for one year or several, for example). If you find the chart in figure 19.18 too plain, a different type of 3D bar chart might work for your data, and add a little drama, as seen in figure 19.20.

Fig. 19.20
Make your selections in the Data Chart Gallery for instant chart makeovers.

Click outside the chart window to return to your document when you finish editing a chart.

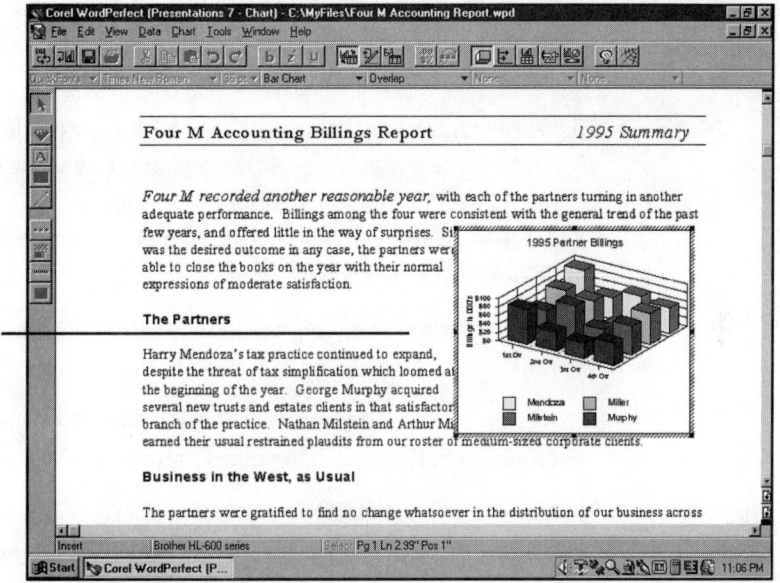

- Use pie charts to show the relationship between the parts and the whole. Pie charts only show one data series (different budget items as parts of the total budget, for example). Figure 19.21 shows WordPerfect's selection of pie chart choices.

Fig. 19.21
Use pie charts to illustrate the parts and the whole.

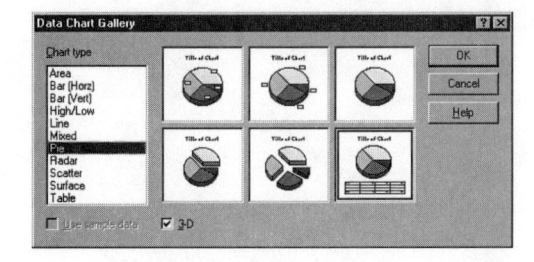

- Line charts show changes over time for one item or several (your stock's performance over the past six months against the Dow, for example). Figure 19.22 shows the selection of line charts.

Fig. 19.22
Line charts dramatize changing values over time.

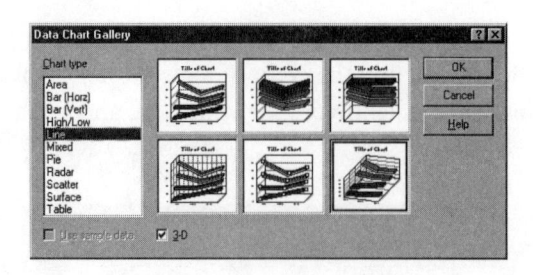

- High/Low charts are like line charts, with the addition of high/low bars along the data series. They show high and low values in a single time period as well as changing values over many periods. One common use of high/low charts is to show a stock's performance in one day and over the course of many days.

- Area charts show changing values over time, like line charts, and proportional relationships, like pie charts.

- Scatter charts are often used in statistics to show the strength of the relationship between single values and a mean value.

- Radar charts illustrate differences between each data series, and between many data series simultaneously. They're sometimes used in complex project management applications.

Part VII: Expert WordPerfect Features for Non-Experts

Chapter 20: **Customizing WordPerfect**

Chapter 21: **Import, Export, Convert: Sharing Files Between Programs**

Chapter 22: **Share Documents with the Office and the Rest of the World**

20
Customizing WordPerfect

● **In this chapter:**

- I want to see more document, fewer gadgets
- How can I work more efficiently?
- I'm tired of the same old buttons
- How do I add my own Toolbar button?
- What is the Equation Editor?

Fried eggs or scrambled? Brown shoes or black? Bus to work or drive? Rearrange WordPerfect the way you order your day: entirely to suit your tastes . . . . ➤

When you buy a shirt in a hurry, you tend to grab whatever's handy. Then, you get home and find that it doesn't quite fit. I hate it when that happens.

Buy your shirts from a Jermyn Street tailor in London, and they'll be custom-made exactly the way you want them. Just be prepared to take out a second mortgage to pay the bill.

As you use WordPerfect, you may find that aspects of the program don't suit your style. Like a shirt that doesn't fit perfectly, some WordPerfect features get the job done, but just don't feel quite right. That's no problem: there are plenty of ways to customize WordPerfect for a perfect fit, and none of them will cost you a cent.

I want to see more words and fewer gadgets

Some people keep their papers and office supplies in untidy desktop heaps. Others can't work unless their desks are pristine. WordPerfect adapts to both styles. There are two quick ways to change what you see in the document window:

- Click View, Toolbars/Ruler for the Toolbars dialog box. Deselect any of the Available Toolbars to hide features such as the status bar, Toolbar, or Power Bar. To get any of them back, select the item from the Toolbars dialog box again.

- For a completely austere look, click View, Hide Bars. The Hide Bars Information dialog box appears, as shown in figure 20.1.

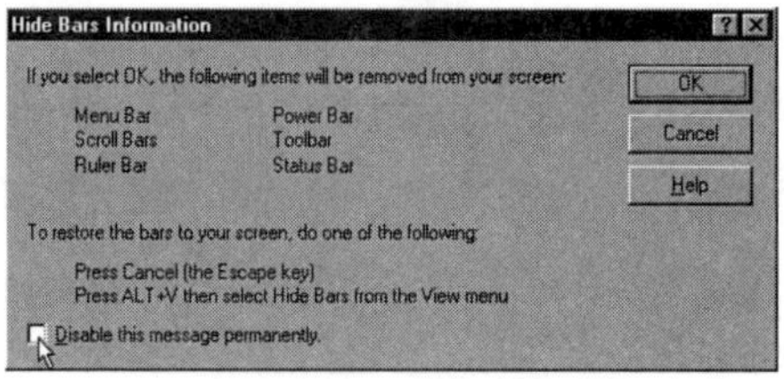

Fig. 20.1
You can even hide the dialog box by clicking the Disable this message permanently check box.

Click OK in the Hide Bars Information dialog box, and you'll see the document window shown in figure 20.2.

Fig. 20.2
For a look of stark simplicity, hide all the WordPerfect bars.

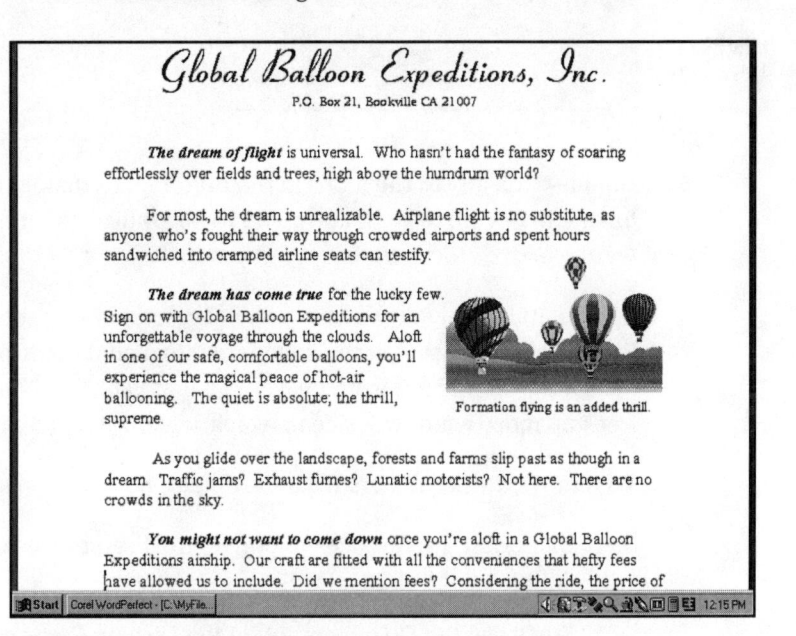

To get everything back again, press the Esc key.

> **TIP** **Documents with graphics can slow WordPerfect down. To bring** the program back up to speed, click View, and make sure Graphics isn't checked. (If it is checked, just click it.) That hides the document's graphics. You're left with the outline of the graphics boxes so you can still see their placement on the page.

Can I save my document window's custom look?

The View menu offers quick adjustments to the look of the document window, but you have to make your adjustments every time you run WordPerfect.

To see your custom look whenever you run the program, click Edit, Preferences and the Preferences dialog box appears (see fig. 20.3).

Fig. 20.3
Customize WordPerfect's operations from the Preferences dialog box.

Double-click any of the icons in the Preferences dialog box. That pops up further dialog boxes that allow you to customize all kinds of WordPerfect features.

For example, you may use the vertical scroll bar less the more you use WordPerfect, relying on the keyboard movement controls instead. You can banish the scroll bars from the screen; that gets rid of an unused feature and frees up more window space in which to view documents.

To remove the scroll bars from the default document display:

1 Click Edit, Preferences to pop up the Preferences dialog box, and double-click the Display icon.

2 You'll see the Document tab of the Display Preferences dialog box, with the choices shown in figure 20.4.

Fig. 20.4
If aspects of the WordPerfect screen are more hindrance than help, deselect them here.

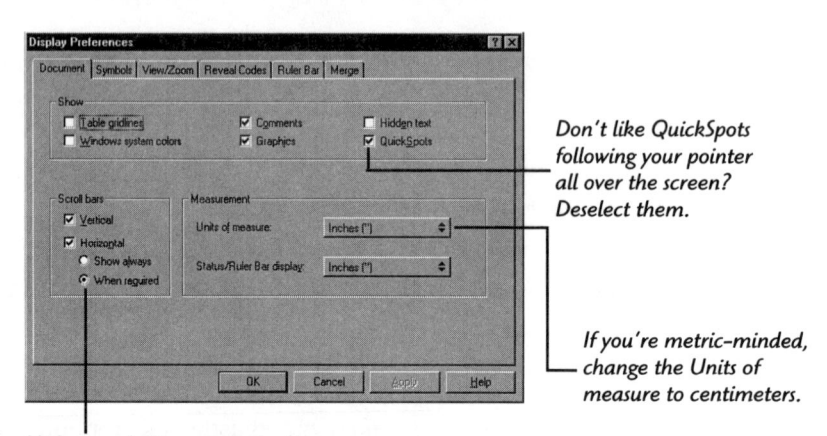

Don't like QuickSpots following your pointer all over the screen? Deselect them.

If you're metric-minded, change the Units of measure to centimeters.

Higher resolution screens don't see the horizontal scroll bar unless it's needed. Lower resolution screen users can select the same option.

3 If you never want to see the scroll bars, deselect Vertical and Horizontal Scroll bars. If you're not a fan of QuickSpots, you can deselect those too.

4 Once you make your choices, click OK in the Display Preferences dialog box; then, click Close in the Preferences dialog box.

Selections made in the Preferences dialog box are in effect whenever you run WordPerfect. All choices are changeable; just reverse the previous steps to restore the scroll bars (or any other feature you banish) to the display.

Speed up your work: keep your most used features in reach

Between the Toolbar and the Power Bar, there are many WordPerfect features a mouse click or two away. You might find that you hardly ever use some of those features, while other features that you do want aren't on the default bars.

WordPerfect lets you create your own Toolbar, with only the features you want on it. When you name and save the Toolbar, it'll appear on the Toolbar menu along with the other Toolbar choices. It's like buying a toolbox from the hardware store, removing the tools you don't use and adding ones that you do use.

How to create a custom Toolbar

The idea behind a custom Toolbar is to put the tools *you* want in reach. I'm going to create a Toolbar I'll call Useful, with the features I use most often on it. You can make your own choices for your own useful Toolbar.

To create the Useful Toolbar:

1 Right-click the Toolbar and select Preferences from the QuickMenu. That pops up the Toolbar Preferences dialog box shown in figure 20.5.

Part VII *Expert WordPerfect Features for Non-Experts*

Fig. 20.5
Click a choice on the Available toolbars list, and the specialized Toolbar buttons pop up on the Toolbar.

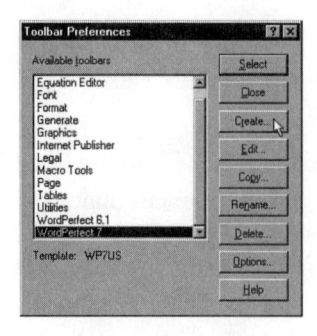

2. Click Create in the Toolbar Preferences dialog box and the Create Toolbar dialog box appears (see fig. 20.6). Type a name in the New Toolbar name edit box.

Fig. 20.6
If you want the Toolbar assigned to a particular template, click the Template button and make your choice; otherwise, it goes in the standard template.

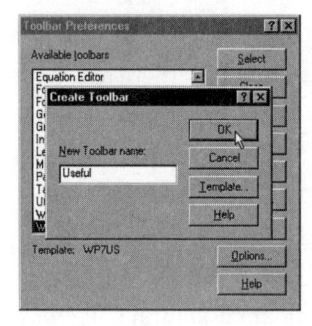

3. Click OK in the Create Toolbar dialog box. That pops up the Features tab of the Toolbar Editor dialog box. Click the Feature categories drop-down arrow.

4. Select Edit from the Feature categories drop-down list, and a list of editing features appears in the Features list, as shown in figure 20.7. Select a feature, click Add Button, and the button for the feature appears in the blank Toolbar at the top of the editing window, as shown in figure 20.7.

Fig. 20.7
When you select a feature, a picture of the corresponding button and its description appear in the dialog box.

The button appears here.

Read the description of the selected button here.

Select a feature from the list and click Add Button.

Drag a separator onto the Toolbar if you want one.

   5. Continue to select feature categories and features and add them to the Toolbar. If you change your mind about a button you've added, just drag it off the Toolbar. The pointer becomes a little trash basket, as shown in figure 20.8. When you release the mouse button, the dragged Toolbar button gets thrown out.

Fig. 20.8
Throw a button in the trash if you want to; you can always add it back if you change your mind.

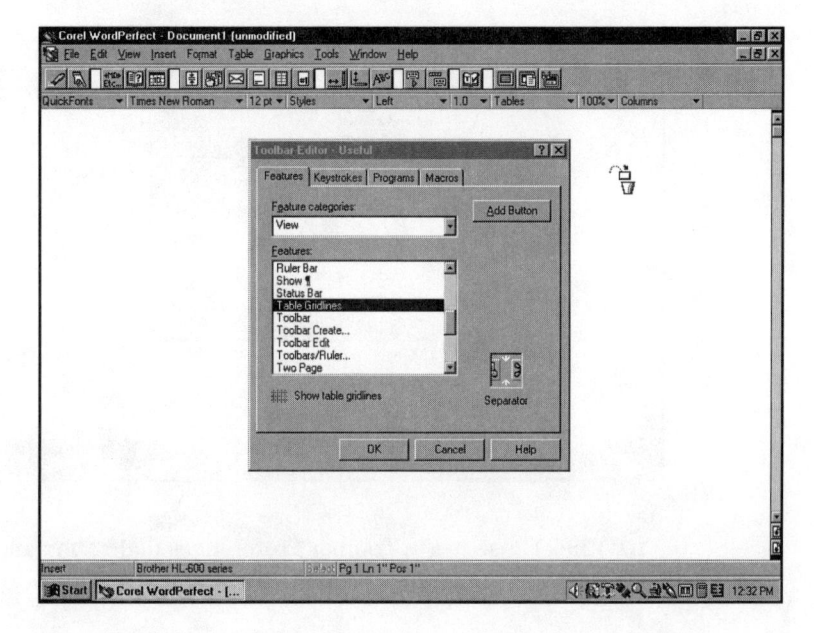

CAUTION When you drag a button off the Toolbar, keep dragging until the trash can appears. If you release the mouse button too soon, the Toolbar button you're trying to get rid of might wind up on the Power Bar!

6. To add a space between buttons, click the Separator button and drag a separator onto the Toolbar.

7. To change the location of a button, just drag it where you want it to go.

TIP If dragging buttons becomes a drag, double-click an item on the Features menu. That pops the corresponding button right onto the Toolbar.

8. Explore the list of features. If you work with many documents at once, for example, consider File features such as Close All, which closes all open documents at the same time (it prompts you to save modified documents first).

9. When you've added all the buttons you want, click OK. Your new Toolbar is added to the list of Available Toolbars in the Toolbar Preferences dialog box, as shown in figure 20.9.

Fig. 20.9
The Useful Toolbar is listed and on-screen. I inserted separators in between groups of buttons from different feature categories.

10. Click Close in the Toolbar Preferences dialog box and you return to the default Toolbar and the editing window.

Whenever you want the Useful Toolbar, just right-click the current Toolbar and select Useful on the QuickMenu. All the buttons are fully functional; they even have their own QuickTips in case you forget what the button does.

If you want to add or remove buttons, click Edit, Preferences, and double-click the Toolbar icon. Select Useful from the Available Toolbars list in the Toolbar Preferences dialog box; then click Edit.

If you add more buttons than there's room for on a Toolbar, a second row of buttons is created automatically. Scroll arrows appear on the right of the Toolbar so you can flip from row to row.

How about changing an existing toolbar?

You don't have to build a new Toolbar from scratch. Make a copy of an existing Toolbar, then modify it:

1 Right-click the Toolbar and select Preferences on the QuickMenu.

2 In the Toolbar Preferences dialog box that pops up, click Copy.

3 In the Copy Toolbar(s) dialog box, take your pick from the Select Toolbars to copy list and click Copy.

4 You'll see the Overwrite / New Name dialog box. Type a new name for the copied Toolbar in the To Object edit box and click OK.

5 Back in the Toolbar Preferences dialog box, select your newly named copy and click Edit. Now, rearrange the Toolbar in the Toolbar Editor dialog box, adding and subtracting buttons as we previously did.

6 Click OK when you're done, close the Toolbar Preferences dialog box, and the new Toolbar is ready for use.

Tired of the same old buttons? Change 'em!

You glance up from your labors to those familiar office fixtures, looking for inspiration. None is forthcoming. Maybe those familiar fixtures are just too familiar. So, you discreetly slip the boss's portrait off the wall and into an unused drawer. Instantly, the office is a more inspiring place.

A little office redecorating freshens the outlook, and you can do the same kind of thing in WordPerfect. Change the look of WordPerfect's interior, and you might find the results positively inspiring.

To change the Toolbar's appearance:

1 Right-click the Toolbar for the QuickMenu, and select Preferences to pop up the Toolbar Preferences dialog box.

2 Click Options and the Toolbar Options dialog box appears. To change the Toolbar to text buttons, like the ones on the Power Bar, select Text. For a completely different look, change the font as well (see figure 20.10.).

Fig. 20.10
Altering the appearance of the WordPerfect editing window is like moving furniture around in the house—not strictly necessary, but it makes for a change.

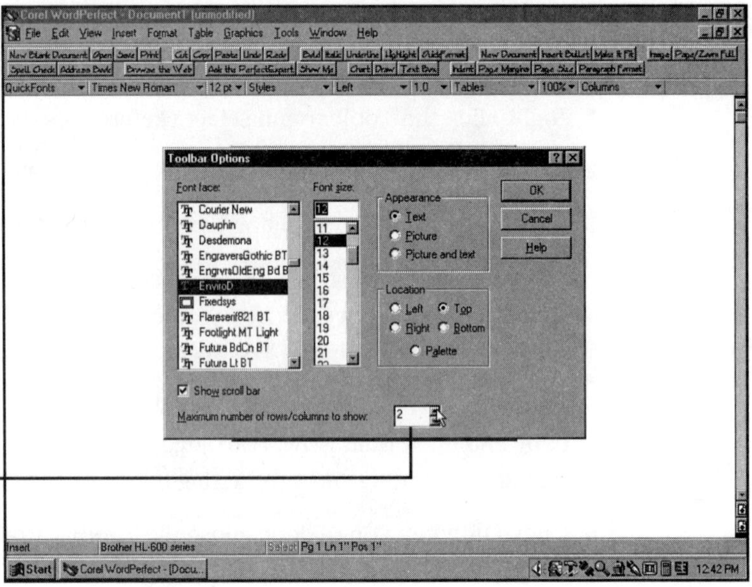

Change the number of Toolbar rows displayed to see more buttons.

3 Click the arrows for Maximum Number of Rows/Columns to Show to display more buttons at the same time.

4 If you like icons and text, select Picture and text for the effect shown in figure 20.11. Since the changes are immediate, if you don't like the result, you can try something different before choosing OK.

Fig. 20.11
Depending on how much of the editing window you're willing to give up, your remodeling choices are limitless.

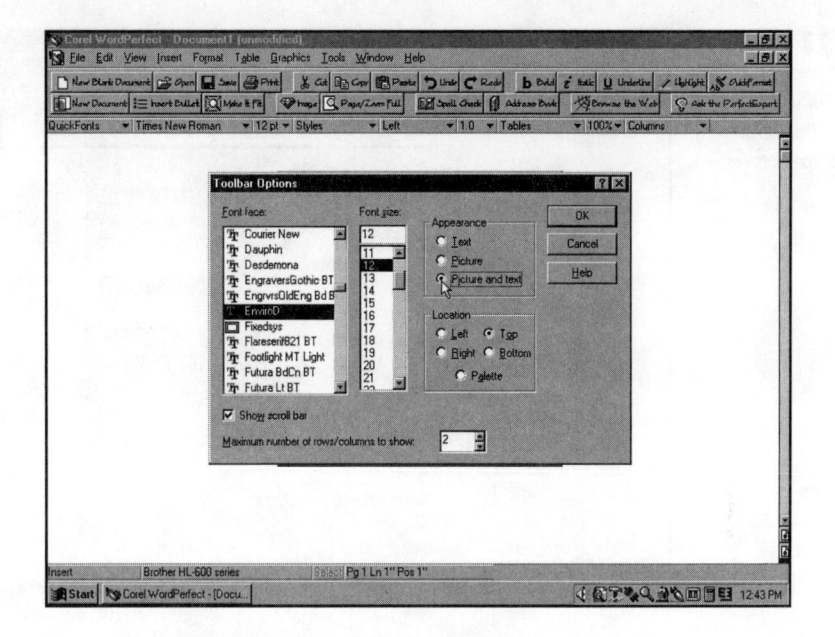

5. Choose a new Location to park the Toolbar on the bottom or on either side of the editing window if you want to. Palette arranges the Toolbar buttons on a floating palette that you can drag around the screen.

6. Click OK in the Toolbar Options dialog box and Close in the Toolbar Preferences dialog box when you're done.

The changes you make to the Toolbar's appearance are saved from one WordPerfect session to the next.

If you change your mind about your changes, select Picture and Top in the Toolbar Options dialog box to return to the default Toolbar look and location.

Power Bar remodeling is possible, too

For compulsive remodelers, change the Power Bar as well. Right-click the Power Bar for the QuickMenu, and select Edit to add or remove buttons in the Toolbar Editor dialog box. Add buttons from the list of Features, or drag them off the Power Bar to get rid of them again.

While you're at it, change the way the Power Bar looks. Right-click the Power Bar and select Options from the QuickMenu for the Power Bar Options dialog box. Select Picture for the Power Bar look shown in figure 20.12.

Fig. 20.12
For those who insist on icons and more icons, the Power Bar can be converted to pictures.

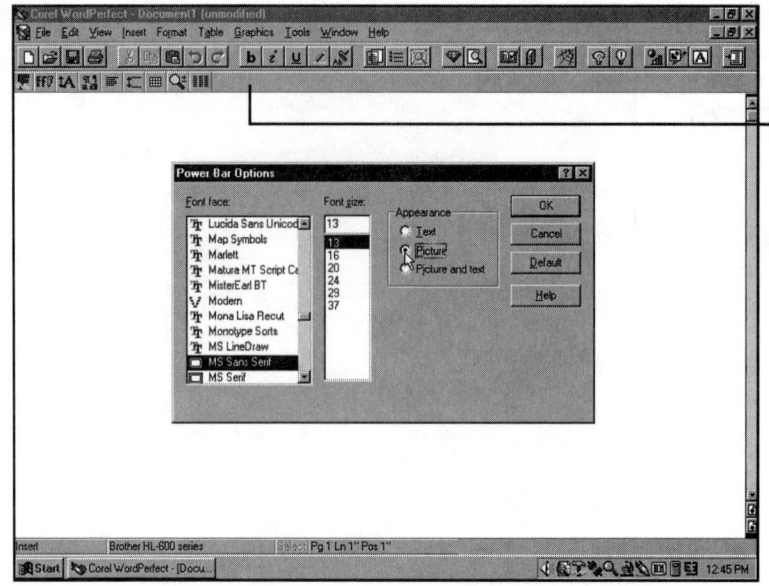

The picture Power Bar gives you more room to add features of your own choosing.

The one big advantage of converting the Power Bar to pictures: you give yourself lots more room for added features. To add more buttons to the "picture" Power Bar shown in figure 20.12, right-click the Power Bar, and select Edit on the QuickMenu. Select Feature categories and Features in the Toolbar Editor - Power Bar dialog box, and drag your choices onto the Power Bar. Click OK when you're satisfied with your beefed-up Power Bar.

Click Default in the Power Bar Options dialog box to return to the default text buttons.

Change the status of the Status Bar

The Status Bar down on the bottom of the WordPerfect window keeps you informed about your current page number and other useful things. Like the Power Bar and Toolbar, the Status Bar can be altered to suit, and you can make it even more useful with a couple of quick additions.

Want some handy Status Bar buttons to insert the date and time in a document? Right-click the Status Bar and choose Preferences on the QuickMenu. In the Status Bar Preferences dialog box that pops up, click the Date and Time check boxes, as shown in figure 20.13.

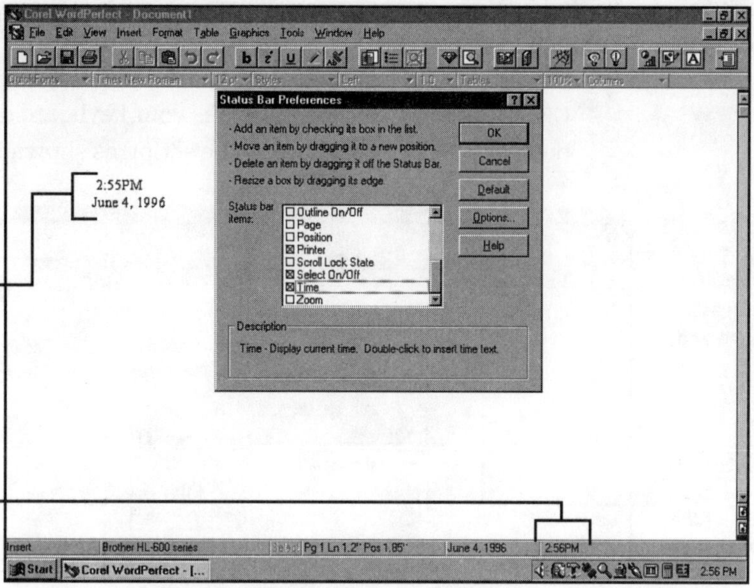

Fig. 20.13
Scroll down the Status bar items list and check the gadgets you'd like to see on your own Status Bar.

Double-click the date or time display to insert either at the insertion point.

Buttons appear on the Status Bar when you select items in the Status Bar Preferences dialog box.

Add any other items that you'd like to see on the Status Bar; then click OK in the Status Bar Preferences dialog box. Whenever you need to insert the date or time in a document, just double-click the date or time display on the Status Bar.

Short of buttons? Create your own

Redecorating WordPerfect's interior, while fun, may or may not be useful. It really depends on how strongly you feel about what you see on the screen every day.

Here's one custom feature that might really come in handy: adding a Toolbar button that types text for you. Suppose you have to type your name and title in dozens of memos and letters every day. You can add a Toolbar button that automatically types that text for you.

Here's how to do it:

   1 Right-click the Toolbar for the QuickMenu, and select Edit to pop up the Toolbar Editor dialog box.

   2 In the Toolbar Editor dialog box, click the Keystrokes tab.

3. Type the text you want played back when you click the new button in the Type The Keystrokes This Button Plays edit box.

4. Click Add Keystrokes. That saves your keyboard script and adds a button to the Toolbar to play the script, as shown in figure 20.14.

Fig. 20.14
The Keystrokes feature is handy for repetitive typing jobs, such as typing your name and title.

Click the new button, and the text you typed will be inserted at the insertion point.

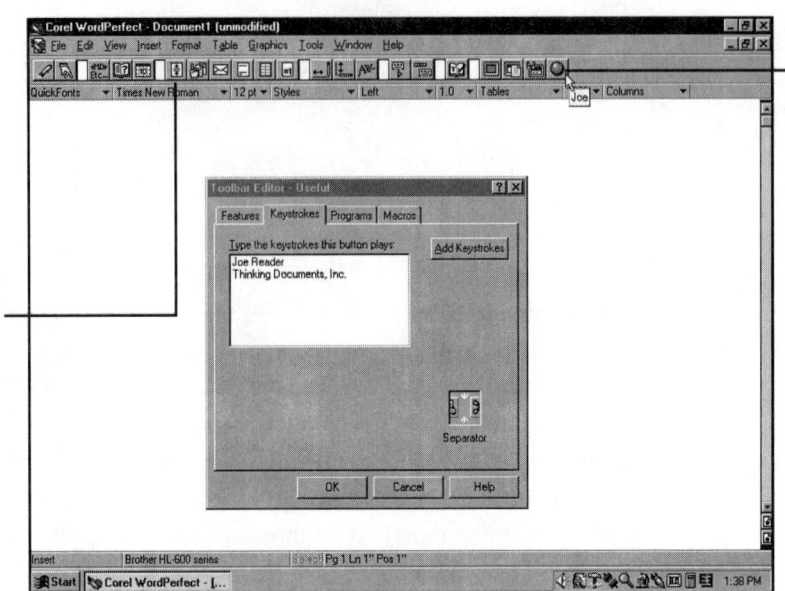

Add a new button to any Toolbar you like. I added the new button to the Useful Toolbar we created earlier.

5. Click OK in the Toolbar Editor dialog box, and your new Toolbar button is ready to use. It even has its own QuickTip.

Q&A *How come I don't see my new Toolbar button?*
If you added the button to the WordPerfect 7 Toolbar, there's no room on the first row of Toolbar buttons for the addition, so it's been placed in a second row. Click the scroll arrows at the right of the Toolbar to display the rows of buttons.

Can I change the way this button looks?

One thing you'll notice right away if you create several custom buttons to play keyboard scripts: all the new buttons look the same. You can fix that by drawing your own button.

Chapter 20 *Customizing WordPerfect* **395**

To change the look of any Toolbar button:

1. Right-click the Toolbar for the QuickMenu, and select Edit to pop up the Toolbar Editor dialog box.

2. Display the button whose appearance you want to change. If it's not already visible, click the scroll buttons at the right of the Toolbar.

3. Double-click the button you want to edit. That pops up the Customize Button dialog box (see fig. 20.15).

Fig. 20.15
Use the Customize Button dialog box to edit QuickTips and to change a button's appearance.

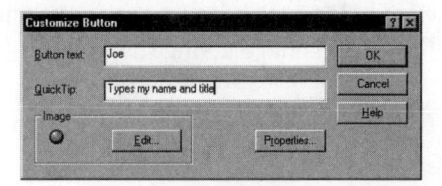

4. If you want, type new text for the QuickTip and the Button Text, that little label that appears when you point at a button. You might want this to say something like "Types my name and title."

5. To change the way the button looks, click Edit to pop up the Image Editor dialog box shown in figure 20.16.

Fig. 20.16
The Image Editor displays an enlarged (and distorted) picture of the Toolbar icon.

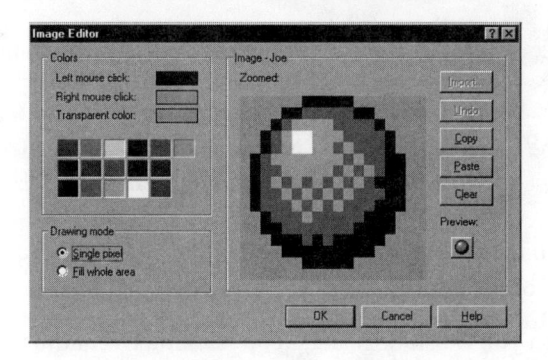

6. In the Image Editor dialog box, you have two choices: you can edit the existing image, or click Clear and start from scratch. In either case, make sure the Single pixel option is selected as the Drawing mode.

> **❝ Plain English, please!**
>
> The image you see on your screen is composed of zillions of tiny little dots of color. Seen together, the eye is fooled into thinking that they're solid images. Those tiny dots are called **pixels**. ❞

7. Click a color from the palette with the left mouse button. If you're adept at mousing, drag in the Zoomed Image area to draw your new image. Otherwise, click to add squares of color one at a time, and build your image that way. Just keep in mind that each of those squares is a single tiny pixel. They only look big because they're zoomed. Figure 20.17 shows a Toolbar button image taking shape.

Fig. 20.17
I cleared the original image first; notice the normal-sized button in the Preview section of the dialog box.

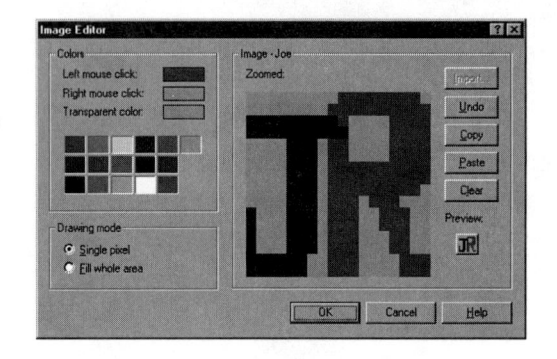

8. Click or drag with the right mouse button to erase mistakes.

> **TIP** To erase, make sure the selected color in the Right Mouse box is the background color. It is by default; if you've changed the background, just click the background color on the palette with the right mouse button.

9. For background color, click Fill whole area, click a color, then click in the Zoomed Image area.

10. When you finish drawing, keep clicking OK in the various dialog boxes to return to the editing window. Figure 20.18 shows the finished button on the Toolbar, complete with custom QuickTip.

Chapter 20 *Customizing WordPerfect* **397**

Fig. 20.18
My custom buttons give me a renewed appreciation for the artistry of WordPerfect's icon creators.

Custom math quizzes? Use the Equation Editor

WordPerfect is a program so rich in features that some will be used rarely, if ever. The Equation Editor may be one such feature. Unless, of course, you're a math teacher preparing an exam, or a financial analyst who needs the formula for net present value in a report, or you simply have a yen for typeset-quality equations. If so, WordPerfect's Equation Editor can create them.

To use the Equation Editor, click Graphics, Equation. If the Drag to Create option is selected, drag the little graphics hand to create a graphics box and release the mouse button. Either technique pops up the Equation Editor, as seen in figure 20.19.

Fig. 20.19
The Equation Editor has all the tools you need to create typeset-quality equations in your documents.

Click the Commands button to access palettes of mathematical symbols, characters, and functions.

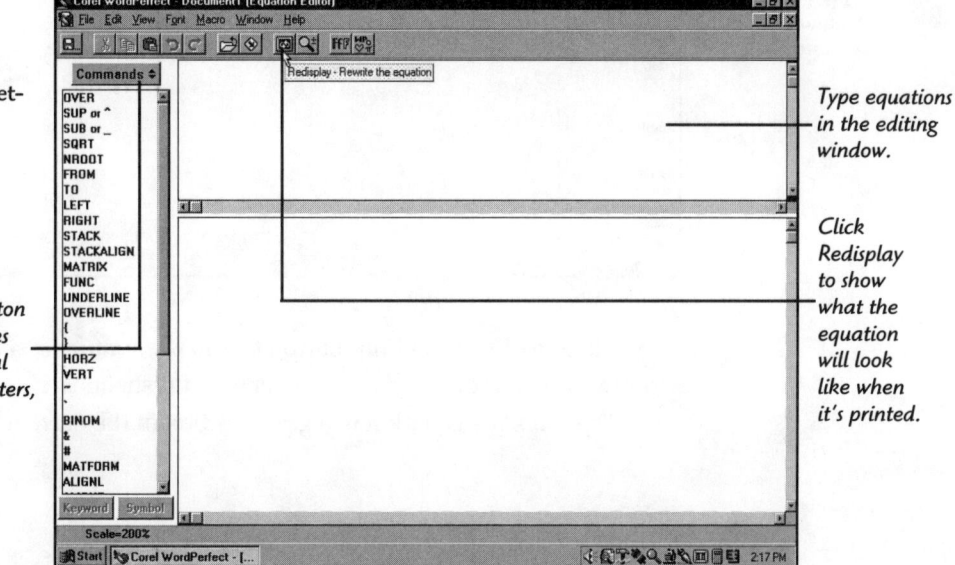

Type equations in the editing window.

Click Redisplay to show what the equation will look like when it's printed.

Create a simple equation with the Equation Editor

To use the Equation Editor to write equations:

1 Click Graphics, Equation to pop up the Equation Editor (drag the graphics box to size and release the mouse button if Drag to Create is turned on).

2 To create the equation for the area of a circle, Πr^2, type **Area = pi r^2** in the editing window. Make sure you leave a space between **pi** and **r^2**.

3 Click the Redisplay button on the Toolbar (refer to fig. 20.19) to display the equation in the display window, as shown in figure 20.20.

Fig. 20.20
Equations are typed into the editing window and then displayed in the display window when you click Redisplay.

Click the Close button to pop the equation into a document.

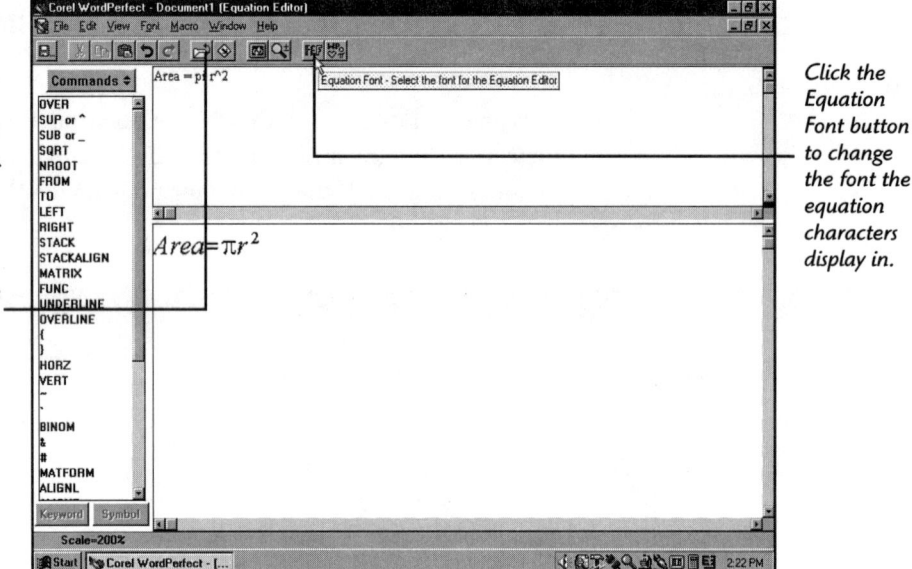

Click the Equation Font button to change the font the equation characters display in.

4 Click the Equation Font button to edit the font face, size, and attributes of the equation characters. When you finish, click Close on the Toolbar. That puts the equation in a graphics box in the current document.

With your equation in the current document, you can click the equation's QuickSpot and make your selections in the Edit Box dialog to add a border, fill, or make other formatting changes. To move the equation around on the page, click it and drag.

Although few of us will write our own math text books, WordPerfect gives us all the tools we need should the need arise (see fig. 20.21).

Fig. 20.21
Even if publication isn't your aim, custom math lessons might help the kids with their homework.

This drawing was created with Presentations, the WordPerfect Suite's built-in drawing program; click the Draw button on the Toolbar to run Presentations.

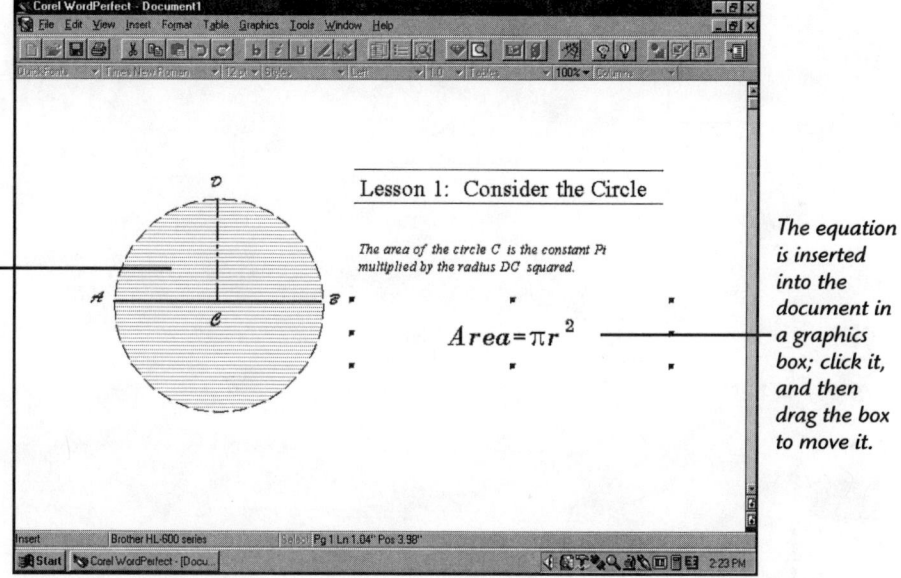

The equation is inserted into the document in a graphics box; click it, and then drag the box to move it.

Lesson 1: Consider the Circle

The area of the circle C is the constant Pi multiplied by the radius DC squared.

$$Area = \pi r^2$$

21

Import, Export, Convert: Sharing Files Between Programs

● **In this chapter:**

- I need to convert this file to a WordPerfect document

- How do I copy things from one program to another?

- Just what is a link?

- How do I use menus in Windows?

- I want my Presentations graphic in a WordPerfect document

Slipping files between briefcase and file cabinet is uncomplicated. Shunting files in and out of WordPerfect from other programs is even easier. There are no file labels to come unstuck, and there's no dust to blow off ancient file folders . . . . ➤

Anthony Trollope wrote dozens of fine novels, including those Masterpiece Theater regulars, the Palliser stories. 140 years ago, he also gave England its first mailboxes. Before Trollope, sending a letter meant a hike to the post office.

The mailbox made exchanging documents a lot easier. Windows and WordPerfect do for file exchanges between applications what the mailbox does for sending letters: they make the job simple, fast, and reasonably foolproof.

How can I turn this file into a WordPerfect 7 document?

Give a speech at the United Nations, and your non-English speaking audience will understand you. Your words are converted into Chinese, Spanish, Arabic, and the other UN languages by simultaneous translators.

That's pretty much how WordPerfect file conversions work. If you open a file written in a different application, the program translates it to WordPerfect 7 automatically. You don't have to do a thing.

Take your old WordPerfect for DOS files, supposing you have any (and millions do). Many of us still have scores of documents created in WordPerfect's earlier, pre-Windows incarnations, and chances are they look something like figure 21.1.

To convert a file from an older version of WordPerfect:

1 Click the Open file button on the Toolbar to pop up the Open File dialog box.

2 Double-click the folder where your old file is located; then double-click the file itself. WordPerfect's simultaneous translator goes to work, and the Conversion dialog box appears. This is one dialog box that doesn't require any further input from you; just sit back and watch.

3 The file appears in the editing window in WordPerfect 7 more or less the same way it looked in WordPerfect 5.0, as shown in figure 21.2.

Fig. 21.1
Print preview, WordPerfect 5.0 for DOS style. This is about as close to WYSIWYG as you got in those days.

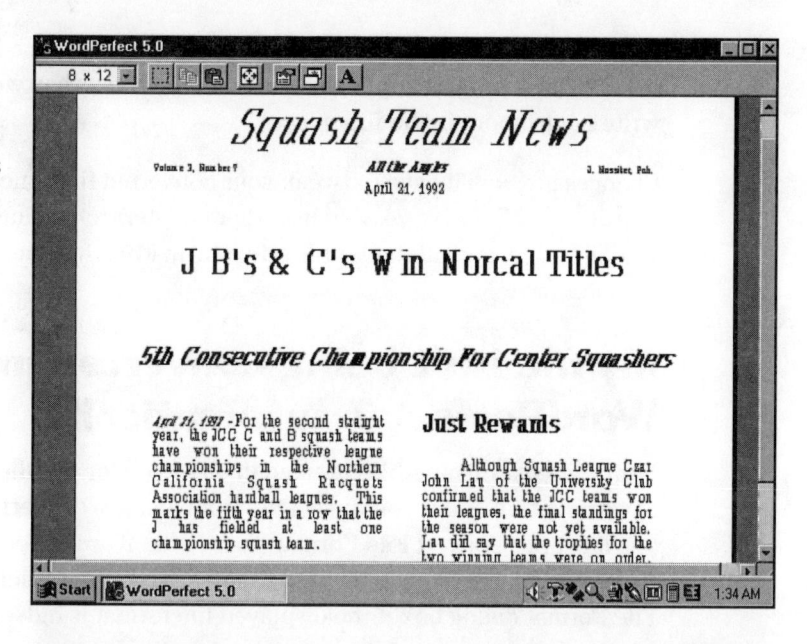

Fig. 21.2
WordPerfect's file conversion isn't perfect, but it's close.

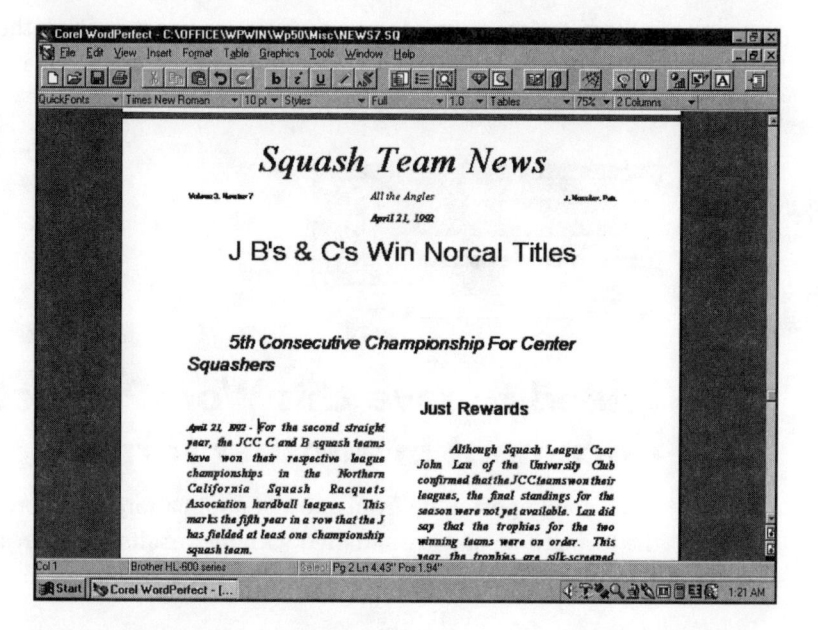

Although WordPerfect does a pretty good job of converting files from older versions of itself, the conversion isn't always perfect. The older the version of the program it was created in, and the more heavily formatted the document, the less faithful to the original the WordPerfect 7 version will be.

In the case of the file in figure 21.2, WordPerfect 7 got the basic layout right, but the fonts weren't duplicated perfectly (not that they were anything to write home about in the first place).

Chances are, you'll have to tweak your converted files once you open them in WordPerfect 7. As we've seen in earlier chapters, changing fonts and formats is easily done, and all the WordPerfect formatting features are available for the job.

My file isn't being converted into WordPerfect 7 automatically

WordPerfect converts files created in older versions of the program without any prompting, but if you open a file from a non-WordPerfect application, you'll get the Convert File Format dialog box. WordPerfect guesses your file's format, and most likely the guess will be correct. Just click OK in the Convert File Format dialog box if the displayed file format is indeed the correct one.

If WordPerfect guesses wrong, you can correct it. Click the Convert file format from drop-down arrow in the Convert File Format dialog box and select the correct format, as shown in figure 21.3.

Fig. 21.3
It's unlikely that you'll have to second-guess WordPerfect's file format choice, but you can if you have to.

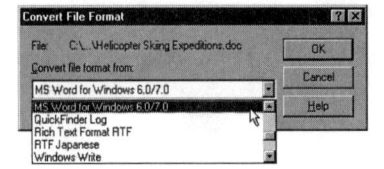

I need to save this WordPerfect document in another format

Once you import a file from another application into WordPerfect 7, tweak the formatting, and are satisfied with the results, you can save the file as a WordPerfect document.

If you have to save the file in another format, you can do that, too. Why would you want to?

You might, for example, want to edit your AUTOEXEC.BAT file in WordPerfect. If you save the AUTOEXEC.BAT file as a WordPerfect document, Windows will ignore it. You have to save system files such as

Chapter 21 *Import, Export, Convert: Sharing Files Between Programs* **405**

AUTOEXEC.BAT as ASCII files for your editing changes to be recognized by Windows.

To save a file in a format other than WordPerfect 7, click File, Save As and the Save As dialog box appears. Click the As type drop-down arrow, and select the format you want (see fig. 21.4).

Fig. 21.4
Windows system files such as AUTOEXEC.BAT and CONFIG.SYS have to be saved as ASCII files.

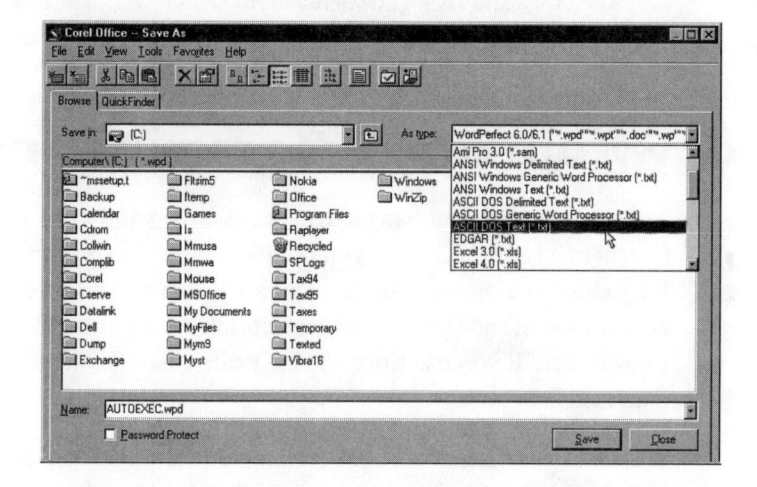

WordPerfect saves you from Save errors

Clicking the Save button on the Toolbar is a good habit to get into as you work on WordPerfect documents. Clicking Save regularly saves you from losing your work in the event of application or system hang-ups.

But what happens if you click the Save button when you're working on a non-WordPerfect 7 document, such as a system file?

WordPerfect saves you from yourself. The Save Format dialog box pops up, as shown in figure 21.5.

Fig. 21.5
Don't worry if you automatically reach for the Save button; WordPerfect lets you pick your Save format.

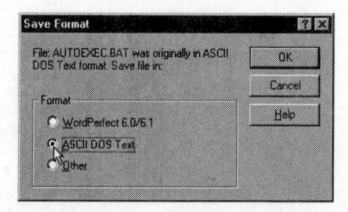

Simply select the ASCII DOS Text choice in the Save Format dialog box, and click OK.

Q&A *Help! I accidentally saved my DOS system file as a WordPerfect 7 document!*

That's easy to do, especially if you're a click-before-you-look type like me. Just resave the file as ASCII text. Click File, Save As for the Save As dialog box. Select ASCII DOS Text from the As type drop-down list (refer to fig. 21.4), and click Yes when you're asked if you want to replace the WordPerfect 7 file you created by mistake.

Can I copy from one program to another?

Although WordPefect has its own spreadsheet and database features (see Chapters 13 and 17), when you outgrow them you'll want applications with a little more horsepower for those chores. And you've already got them. One component of the Corel WordPerfect Suite is a powerful spreadsheet called Quattro Pro. If you use Corel Office Professional, you also have Paradox, a database program.

Whatever your Windows application, you can copy, cut, and paste text and objects between programs to your heart's content. If the applications support

There's no need to be ANSI about ASCII

ASCII and ANSI are a couple of computer terms that get tossed around casually, as though normal (as in noncomputer) people know instinctively what they mean. ASCII (pronounced "ASK-ee") is an acronym for American Standard Code for Information Interchange. When you type characters on your keyboard, your computer translates them into combinations of 0s and 1s—binary digits. Exactly which combination of binary digits represents a particular keyboard character varies from one computer program to another.

ASCII standardizes keyboard character-binary digit equivalents. It's a standard set of binary digit combinations that represent a standard set of keyboard characters. Since all PC programs use ASCII, WordPerfect can read an ASCII file written in Microsoft Word with no problems.

ANSI (pronounced "AN-see") stands for American National Standards Institute, an organization originally founded to establish standard ways of representing things such as screw threads in engineers' drawings. In computer lingo, ANSI is a standard character set, like ASCII, but with the addition of graphical and formatting characters. Windows and Windows applications use the ANSI standard, so if you write a file in the Windows Notepad, you can open it in WordPerfect.

Chapter 21 *Import, Export, Convert: Sharing Files Between Programs* **407**

OLE (all the Corel WordPerfect Suite applications do), you can even edit pasted material without leaving WordPerfect. (See Chapter 19 for more information about editing OLE objects.)

How do I put my Quattro Pro object in a WordPerfect document?

Here's the easiest way to insert a Quattro Pro object in a WordPerfect document. It works for maps, charts, spreadsheets, and any other chunk of Quattro Pro you care to send over to WordPerfect:

1 With both Quattro Pro and WordPerfect running, switch to your Quattro Pro object.

> **TIP** **Tired of mousing around? Here's the keyboard way to switch from** application to application in Windows: hold down the Alt key and press Tab repeatedly. As you press Tab, you cycle through icons for each active application, which appear in a box on the screen. When you get to the application you want, release the Tab and Alt keys.

2 Click the object to select it. The handles will pop up, as shown in figure 21.6.

Fig. 21.6
Graphics objects in Quattro Pro behave just like graphics objects in WordPerfect; click to select them, and right-click for the QuickMenus.

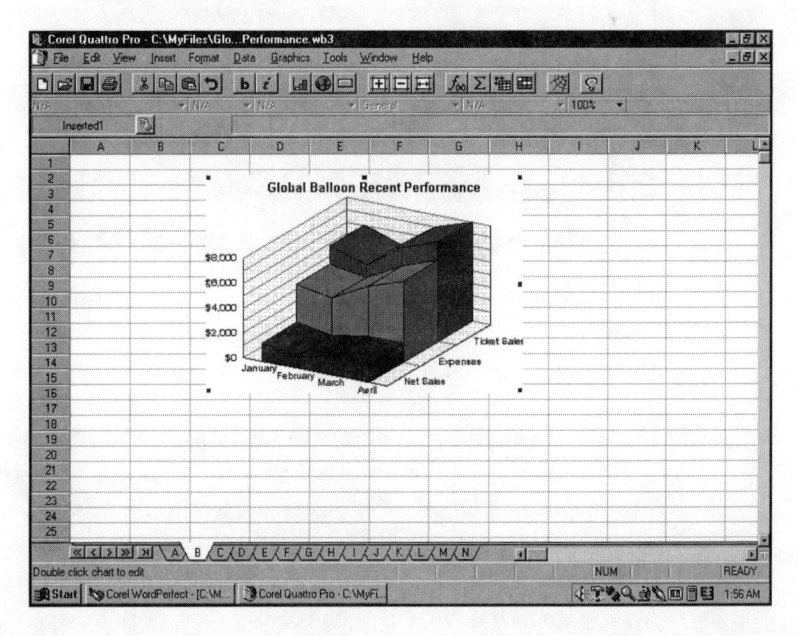

Part VII Expert WordPerfect Features for Non-Experts

3. With the object selected, click the Copy button on the Toolbar. That copies it to the Windows Clipboard.

4. Switch to your WordPerfect document, and put the insertion point where you want the object to appear.

5. Click the Paste button on the Toolbar and your Quattro Pro object pops into the WordPerfect document, as shown in figure 21.7.

Fig. 21.7
You needn't be precise about where you place imported graphics in a WordPerfect document; you can easily move and resize them.

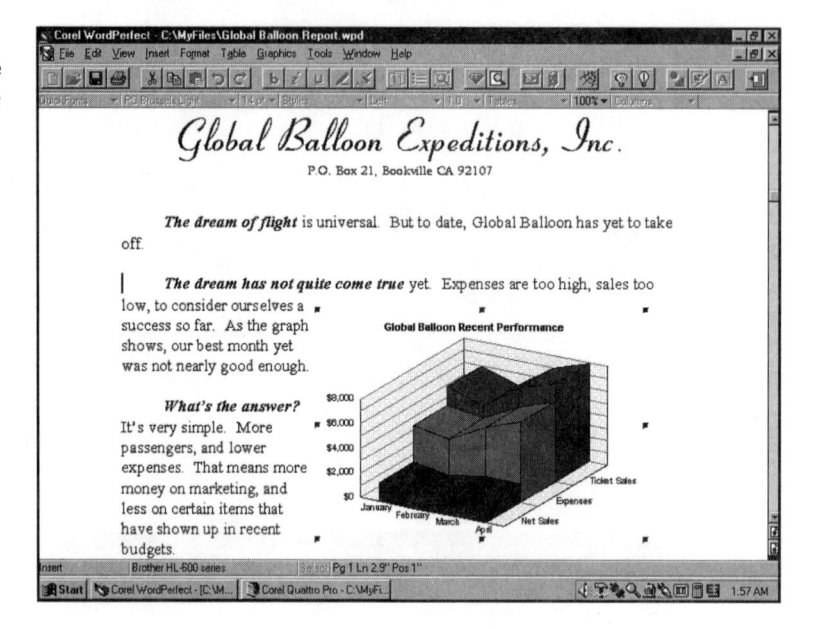

Edit embedded objects with the application that created them

Embedding an object, as we just did with that Quattro Pro chart, creates a copy that you can edit using the same application that created it. It's as though the object takes a chunk of its original application with it.

CAUTION If you copy an object in Quattro Pro, shut down Quattro Pro, and then paste it in WordPerfect, you'll be pasting an empty graphics box. Copied Quattro Pro objects are sent to the Windows Clipboard; close Quattro Pro, and the program clears the Clipboard automatically. If you want your Quattro Pro object embedded in WordPerfect, leave both programs running when you copy and paste between them.

Chapter 21 *Import, Export, Convert: Sharing Files Between Programs* **409**

Here's how to edit a Quattro Pro object embedded in WordPerfect:

CAUTION **Make sure you save whatever you're working on before you try this.**

1 In WordPerfect, double-click the embedded Quattro Pro object.

2 A broken border appears around the graph, and the Quattro Pro graphics Toolbar pops up right over your WordPerfect document, as shown in figure 21.8.

Fig. 21.8
Opening an embedded Quattro Pro object opens Quattro Pro as well—without leaving WordPerfect.

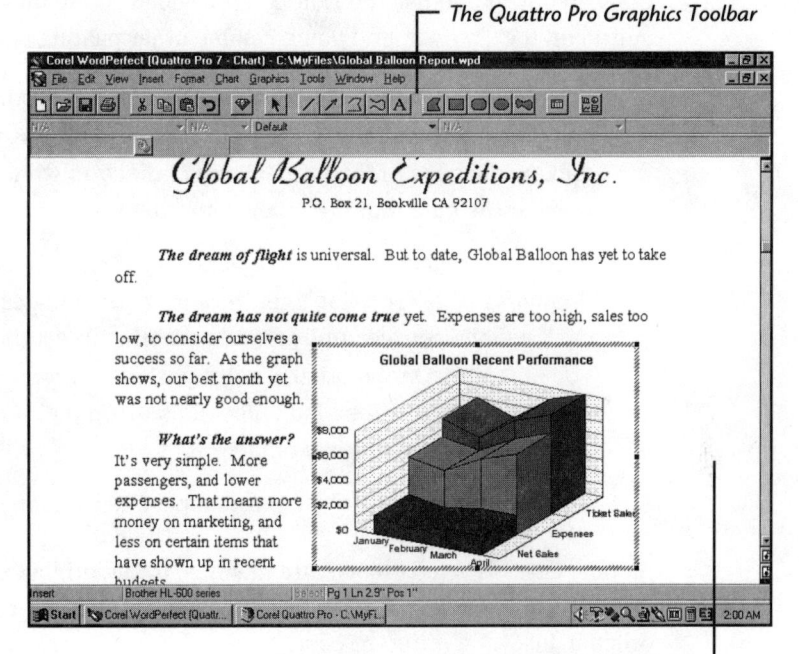

The Quattro Pro Graphics Toolbar

Click outside the graphics box to shut down Quattro Pro and return to WordPerfect.

3 Use the Quattro Pro tools to edit the graph. When you're done, click anywhere outside the graphics box to close Quattro Pro and return to WordPerfect.

66 Plain English, please!

In case you run across the terms in online help (or elsewhere), in OLE jargon, the application that created an object is called the **source**. The

> application in which you embed the object is the **container**. In the example, Quattro Pro is the source, and WordPerfect is the container. 99

What's a link?

Providing both applications are running, copying and pasting from one OLE application to another creates an **embedded object**, as we saw in figure 21.8.

Copy an object and use the Edit, Paste Special command instead of the Paste button on the Toolbar, and you get some other pasting options:

- If you **link** OLE objects, any changes you make in the original object show up automatically in the linked copy. Use links when you plan on making changes to the original object that you want to appear in the copy. If the data that underlies your graph is going to change, use a link.

- Pasting an object as a **picture** inserts it as an ordinary Windows graphics image. You don't get the automatic updates of a link, and you can't use the source application to edit the object the way you can if you embed it. On the other hand, a pasted picture needs less memory than a linked or embedded object. Paste as a picture if you just want a static copy of the original object.

- Linked or embedded objects can appear as icons in your document.

In most cases, copied objects are identical to the originals, no matter what paste method you use. But, if the copy doesn't faithfully reproduce the original, just try a different paste choice.

Link one application to another for fast updates

Linking an object to a copy is like setting off a controlled chain reaction in a lab experiment. Change the underlying data for a linked object, and you'll change both the original object and the copy as well.

To set up a link between a Quattro Pro object and a WordPerfect copy:

Chapter 21 Import, Export, Convert: Sharing Files Between Programs 411

1 Save your Quattro Pro file. Click the Quattro Pro object to select it; then click the Copy button on the Toolbar.

2 Click the WordPerfect icon on the Windows Taskbar or press Alt+Tab to flip to WordPerfect. Move the insertion point to the spot in the document where you want the object to appear.

3 Click Edit, Paste Special and the Paste Special dialog box appears, as shown in figure 21.9.

Fig. 21.9
Select an option from the list, and read the moderately helpful descriptions of what will happen next in the Result box.

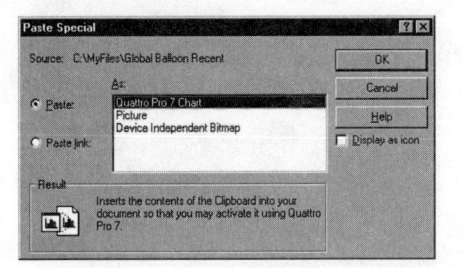

66 *Plain English, please!*

Select Paste As Picture and you'll get an eyeful of jargon concerning the Windows' **Metafile** format or the **Device Independent Bitmap**. It just means you're copying the object as a regular graphics image without links to any other program. 99

4 Click Paste link; then click OK. The linked object is pasted into the document at the insertion point.

Once you've pasted your linked object, you can move it around or resize it, just as you would with an ordinary graphics image.

Double-click the object to edit it, and the source application (Quattro Pro) opens. The original object appears, as shown in figure 21.10.

As you edit the object, or change the underlying data in the Quattro Pro table, the changes show up immediately in the linked copy in WordPerfect.

When you're done editing, click File, Exit in Quattro Pro to return to WordPerfect.

Fig. 21.10
When you open a linked object, you actually make your edits in the original object.

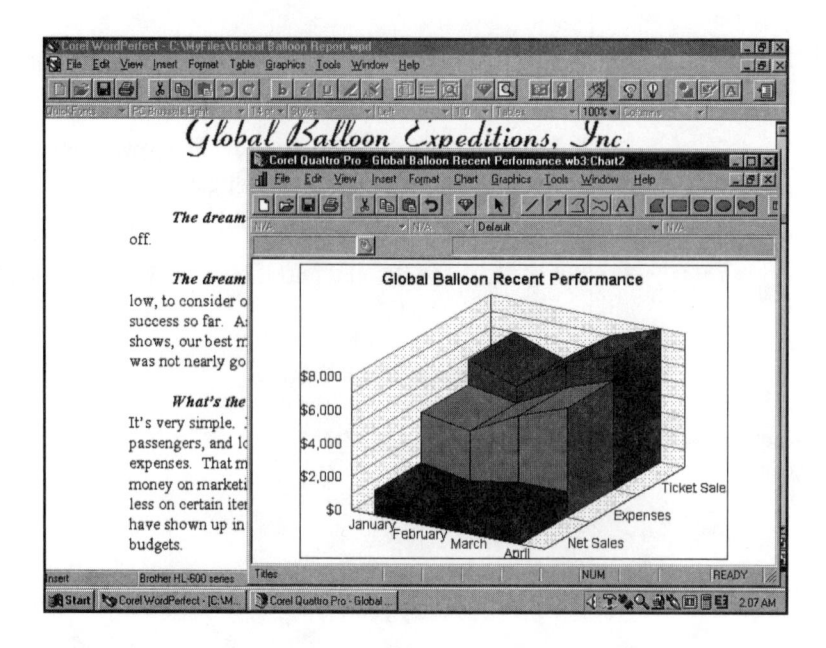

Keep up your links, or break them

Once you have linked objects in two OLE applications, the copied object is updated automatically when you make changes in the original. The underlying data can be changed only in the source (original) program; you can't make changes in WordPerfect, for example, and see those changes in Quattro Pro.

Suppose you try a few what-if scenarios with your Quattro Pro data, and you don't want those changes to show up in the WordPerfect copy of the your graph. If you don't want automatic updates, click Edit, Links for the Links dialog box shown in figure 21.11.

Fig. 21.11
Use the Links dialog box to control updates between linked objects.

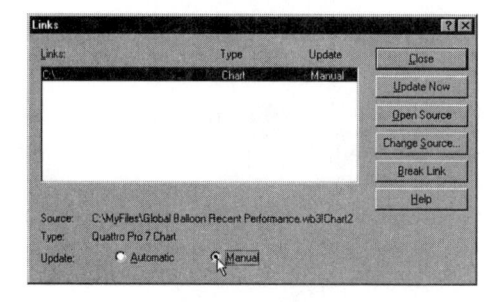

Click Manual in the Links dialog box, and changes you make in the original object won't be reflected in the copy until you return to the Links dialog box and click Update Now.

Can I stick my Presentations graphic in a WordPerfect document?

Corel WordPerfect Suite users have a nifty program called Presentations that's used to create drawings, graphics of all kinds, and slide shows.

If you've done any drawing in WordPerfect, you may have used Presentations without knowing it. Presentations is the WordPerfect drawing feature. It's also a stand-alone program, and if you've created graphics in Presentations and you want them in a WordPerfect document, nothing could be easier.

Inserting a Presentations graphic in WordPerfect is just like inserting a Quattro Pro graph. Presentations is another OLE application, so you can embed, link, or copy the graphic as a picture.

Unless you really need to link your Presentations graphic to the WordPerfect copy, pasting it with a click of the WordPerfect Toolbar Paste button is the simplest choice.

To paste a Presentations creation as a graphic in WordPerfect:

1 Click the Presentations graphic to select it, as shown in figure 21.12.

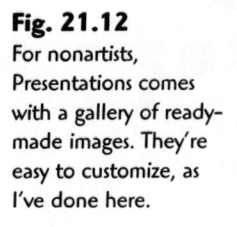

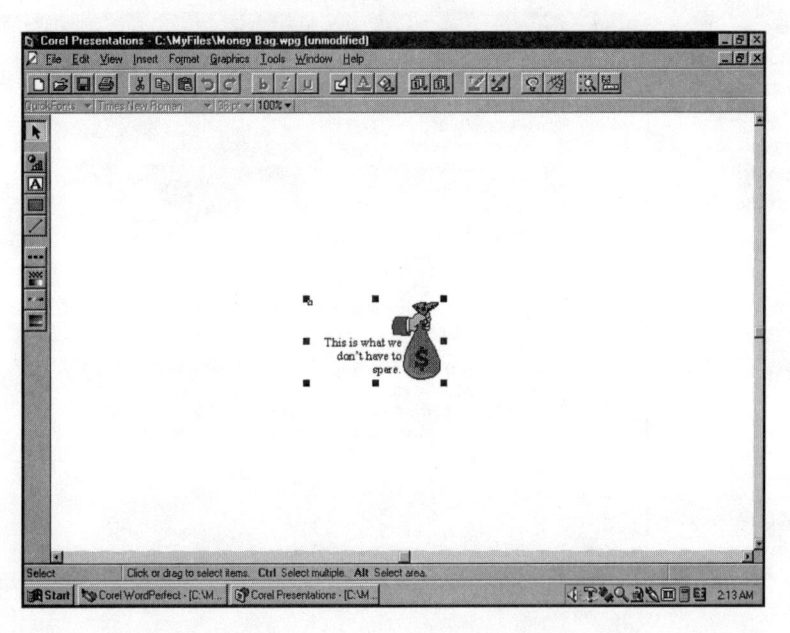

Fig. 21.12
For nonartists, Presentations comes with a gallery of ready-made images. They're easy to customize, as I've done here.

2 Click the Copy button on the Toolbar.

3 Press Alt+Tab or click the WordPerfect icon on the Windows Taskbar to flip to WordPerfect. Move the insertion point to the spot where you want the graphic.

4 Click <u>E</u>dit, Paste <u>S</u>pecial and the Paste Special dialog box appears (see fig. 21.13).

Fig. 21.13
Selecting the WPG20 format gives you the most faithful copy; choosing Presentations 7 Drawing embeds the graphic in WordPerfect.

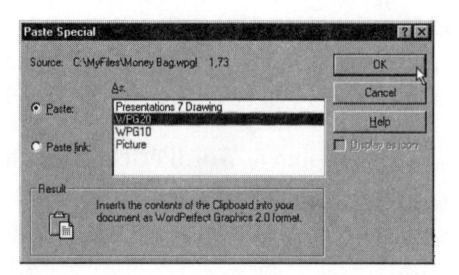

5 Select Paste <u>A</u>s WPG20 graphic and click OK.

6 The Presentations graphic pops into your WordPerfect document at the insertion point, as shown in figure 21.14.

Fig. 21.14
Like any other inserted graphics image, you can move and resize the pasted Presentations creation by dragging with the mouse.

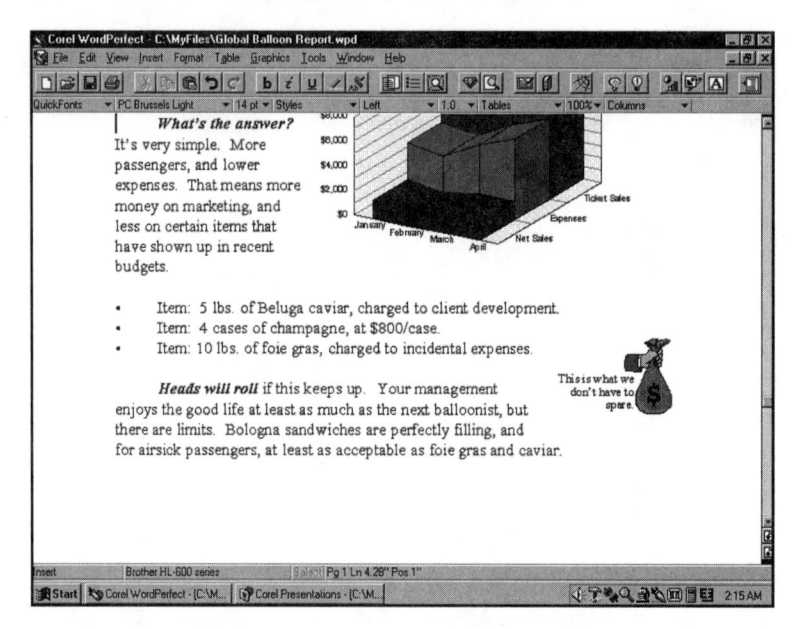

To edit a pasted Presentations graphic, just double-click it. That'll pop up all the Presentations tools and editing features.

22
Share Documents with the Office and the Rest of the World

● **In this chapter:**

- E-mail is saving me a fortune in stamps
- How do I publish my work on the World Wide Web?
- This document's not mere text; it's Hypertext
- How can I send my readers to the best Web sites?
- There's no place like a home page

The neighborhood used to be the people and places close by. Nowadays, the whole world is the neighborhood, and it's no farther than your own desktop. . . . . >

We moderns are good at inventing and discovering, and maybe not so good at putting our inventions and discoveries to practical use. We went to the moon almost 30 years ago, and we still haven't figured out what to do with it. We split the atom, with decidedly mixed results. We invented television, a marvel that "permits millions of people to listen to the same joke at the same time, and yet remain lonesome" as T.S. Eliot put it.

Now we have computers in every corner of the world, hooked together over the Internet. We've only a dim understanding of what that means for the future, but the Internet may be our greatest breakthrough yet.

Unlike some other advances, the Internet is already useful. Write a joke for TV, and if millions laugh, you won't hear them. Write your joke in WordPerfect, post it on the World Wide Web with WordPerfect's Internet Publisher, and you may well find your e-mail inbox overflowing with LOL's. That's e-mail for "laughed out loud."

Save shoe leather, postage stamps with e-mail

No matter what your missive, WordPerfect's technology slices, dices, and presents your work impeccably and speedily, like a food processor with a pile of vegetables. But to send that perfect letter, you have to turn the clock back 100 years or so. Stuffing envelopes, licking stamps, and making the trek to the nearest mailbox are tasks that haven't changed much since the horse-and-buggy era.

Except that now you can skip those old-fashioned chores. E-mail brings correspondence into the 20th century. A click or three sends that handsome document you've just crafted out into cyberspace and straight onto your recipient's computer screen.

Here are a few things to keep in mind when you send e-mail from WordPerfect:

- If your mail recipient is a WordPerfect user, send your e-mail as a WordPerfect document. Readers will see exactly the document you sent, even if it's loaded with formatting—borders, multiple fonts, graphics, tables, and the like.

- If the e-mail recipient doesn't use WordPerfect, Windows word processors such as Microsoft Word will do a reasonable job of converting your files in a way that approximates the original. It won't be a perfect match, especially if the document is heavily formatted. If you have a WordPerfect document laden with formatting and an e-mail recipient who doesn't use WordPerfect, the Corel WordPerfect Suite includes a program called Envoy that solves the translation problem. Send the document as an Envoy file, and the recipient will see an exact copy.

- Just sending a quick e-mail note? Select your text, and send it.

How do I send an e-mail note from WordPerfect?

When you want to send a message in plain text to somebody down the hall, or on the other side of the world, WordPerfect and Windows do the job together. All you need is a modem, an online service provider, and Windows e-mail program, Exchange (if you use another e-mail program, that'll work too).

To send an e-mail message right from WordPerfect:

1 Type your message; then select the text. If the document is text only, press Ctrl+A to select the whole thing.

2 Click File, Send. The Choose Profile dialog box pops up. Chances are you already will have set up Microsoft Exchange, the Windows e-mail program. If so, accept the default MS Exchange Settings and click OK. If you haven't set up Exchange yet, this is a good time to do it. Click New and follow the prompts through the Inbox Setup Wizard. Figure 22.1 shows the Choose Profile dialog box.

> **TIP** **GroupWise users don't have to bother with the Choose Profile** dialog box. Click File, Send, and GroupWise launches automatically, with your WordPerfect document ready for delivery.

Part VII *Expert WordPerfect Features for Non-Experts*

Fig. 22.1
You've probably already set up Microsoft Exchange, the e-mail program bundled with Windows. If not, click New and read the tip below.

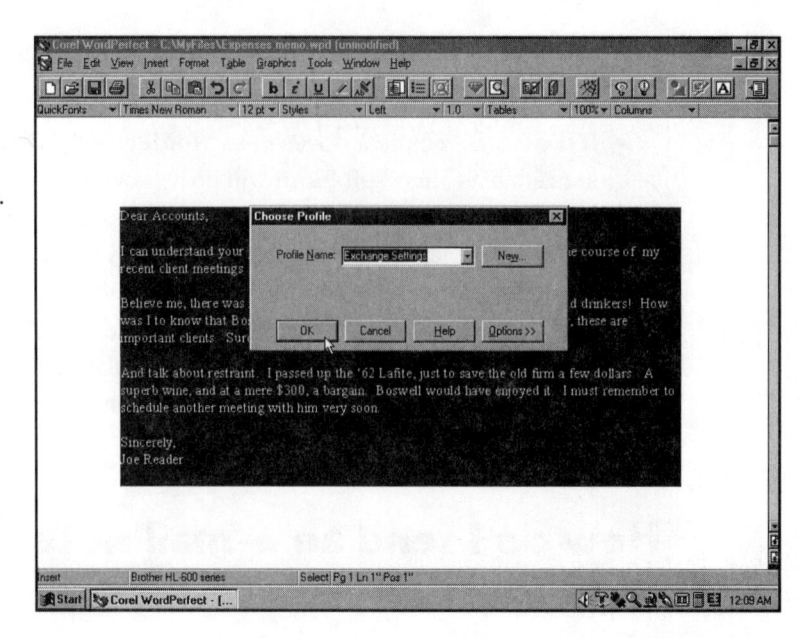

> **TIP** Those who haven't yet set up MS Exchange can save themselves a lot of bother in the Inbox Setup Wizard with this bit of advice: deselect Microsoft Mail on the Use the following information services list. If you don't, you'll wind up learning more about the ins and outs of MS Exchange than you'll want to know.

3 Once you click OK in the Choose Profile dialog box, your selected text is dumped into the New Message - Microsoft Exchange dialog box that appears, as seen in figure 22.2.

Fig. 22.2
Here's your message, ready to hit the ether as soon as you choose an addressee.

Click Send once you've chosen someone to send the message to.

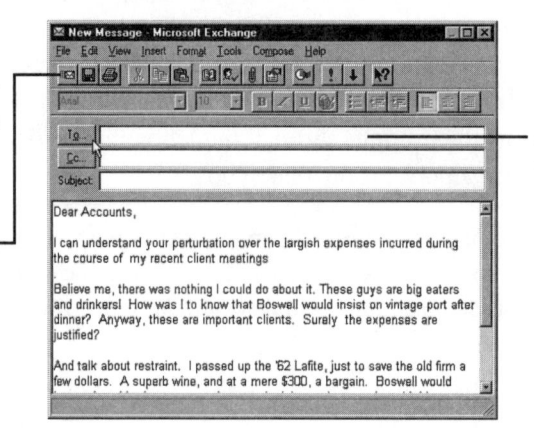

Don't try to type the name in here yourself. Click To to select a recipient for your e-mail.

Chapter 22 *Share Documents with the Office and the Rest of the World* **419**

4 Click T*o* in the New Message dialog box to summon up your Address Book. This is not your WordPerfect Address Book; it's the MS Exchange Address Book. If you've been dutifully recording names and addresses in the WordPerfect Book, this may come as a nasty surprise, but the two address books don't talk to each other (at least in this dialog box. See Chapter 12 for information on how to copy addresses from the WordPerfect Address Book to the Exchange book). Either double-click a recipient's name in the Address Book, or click *N*ew to add one. Your recipient's name should appear in the T*o* box in the Address Book, as seen in figure 22.3.

Fig. 22.3
If you've been using the Exchange Address Book all along, you'll feel right at home here.

Select a name; then click Cc to add one or more carbon copy recipients.

If the recipient's name isn't already in your book, you'll have to add it. Click New to do that.

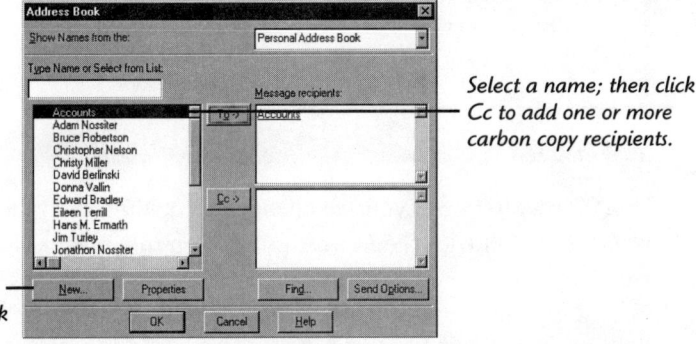

CAUTION

Exchange is a handy, though quirky, program. One of its quirks: you can't just type a recipient's name in the To or Cc boxes. Well, you *can*, but your e-mail won't go anywhere. Exchange has to know the correct address of any mail recipient, and the only way to set up that vital information is by adding the recipient to the Address Book.

5 Click OK in the Address Book to close it and return to the New Message dialog box. Your recipient's name appears, underlined, in the T*o* edit box. Type a Subject if you want one.

6 Now, click the Send button on the New Message Toolbar. That closes MS Exchange and returns you to your document in WordPerfect.

7 Here's another Exchange quirk: the Send button doesn't exactly send your message. Instead, it deposits the message in the MS Exchange Outbox. When you're ready to really send your e-mail, click the Start button on the Windows taskbar and choose Programs, Microsoft Exchange to run Exchange. Now, click Tools, Deliver Now Using, All Services. Log on to your information service or Internet provider, and your mail is finally on its way. Exchange automatically logs off when it's sent and retrieved all your mail. Figure 22.4 shows Exchange about to fire off some mail.

Fig. 22.4
It takes a few steps to get here, but after you've done it once, sending e-mail from WordPerfect really is a snap.

If you want a last look at your message before it goes, click the Outbox folder; then double-click the message. Make sure you click the Send button again once you've had your look.

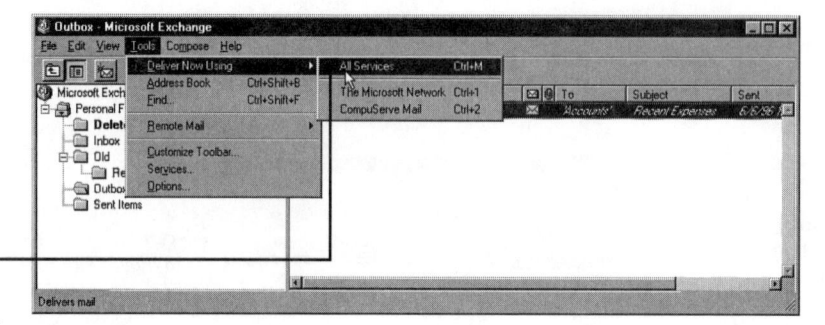

Don't forget to check your Exchange Inbox after you've sent your mail. Mine is usually filled with the newest pothole on the information highway: junk e-mail.

I'm e-mailing this document to another WordPerfect user

When you're sending mail to fellow WordPerfect users (WordPerfecters? WordPerfectos?), and you want to send an entire document, don't select any text first. Save your document first. Leave the document open and click File, Send. Then follow the steps we took previously. Your document appears in the Exchange New Message dialog box as an icon. If you want to include a note with the document, just click the New Message editing window and start typing, as seen in figure 22.5.

> **CAUTION** Your WordPerfect document has to be open before you click File, Send. If you try to send e-mail from WordPerfect from a new blank document, you'll send a blank document.

Fig. 22.5
E-mail recipients will get both the note and the document icon, just as they appear here.

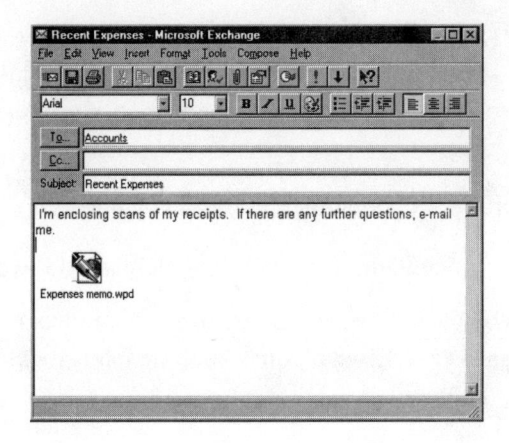

Click the icon; then drag it to move it around the editing window. Your e-mail recipient will get the document icon and any text you include with it in her own Inbox. To open a document icon, simply double-click it.

> **TIP** Even though there's no Undo button on the Exchange Toolbar, Undo still works. Press Ctrl+Z to undo your last action.

Envoy, for e-mail recipients who don't use WordPerfect

Strange as it may seem to the converted, some people use word processors other than WordPerfect. Despite this handicap, you can send them your WordPerfect documents in a form that'll preserve every last formatting detail, no matter what word processor they have.

WordPerfect accomplishes this magic trick with a program in the Corel WordPerfect Suite called Envoy. Envoy packages your WordPerfect document in a special viewer. The viewer and the document arrive at their destination in an Envoy icon; the e-mail recipient double-clicks to run the viewer and open the document at the same time. The beauty of it is that the recipient needn't have the Envoy program on his computer. Envoy files of this kind can be sent to anyone, because the program sends a chunk of itself along with the document.

The chunk of Envoy that accompanies the document is called a **runtime** version; it's a small clone of the program that's created just to display your document. Use Envoy whenever you send a non-WordPerfect user a heavily formatted document.

To send a WordPerfect document as an Envoy file:

1 Save your document; then click File, Publish to Envoy.

2 The Envoy Viewer opens with the document displayed, as seen in figure 22.6. This is exactly what your e-mail recipients will see when they get the file.

Fig. 22.6
Envoy produces a faithful replica of your original WordPerfect document that anyone can read.

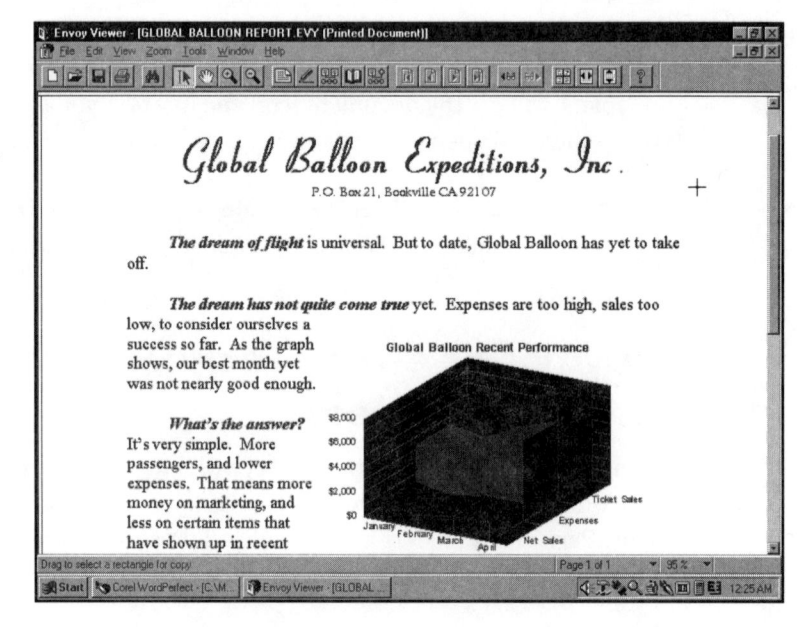

3 Click the Save button on the Envoy Toolbar. In the Save As dialog box that appears, click the Save as type drop-down arrow and select Envoy Runtime Files (*.exe) as I've done in figure 22.7.

Fig. 22.7
All we're doing in Envoy is saving the file in the special Envoy runtime format.

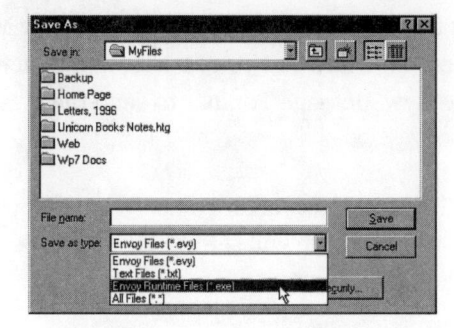

4. Type a name in the File name edit box, and click Save.

5. Click the Close button at the right of the Envoy title bar to shut the program down. You'll get a message from Envoy prompting you to save the file before closing the program; click No in the Envoy Viewer message box.

6. Your Envoy file is ready to send. Click the Start button on the Windows Taskbar and choose Programs, Microsoft Exchange.

7. When the Inbox dialog box appears, click the New Message button on the Toolbar.

8. Click To to select a recipient and type a Subject if you want one.

9. Click the Insert File button on the New Message dialog box Toolbar. That pops up the Insert File dialog box; click your way to the MyFiles folder, where you'll find the icon for your Envoy file (see fig. 22.8).

Fig. 22.8
Envoy files have a distinctive icon that makes them hard to miss in a sea of WordPerfect documents.

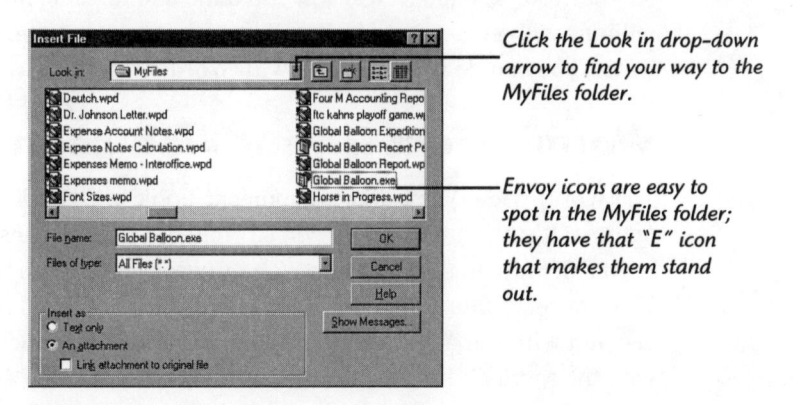

Click the Look in drop-down arrow to find your way to the MyFiles folder.

Envoy icons are easy to spot in the MyFiles folder; they have that "E" icon that makes them stand out.

10 Double-click the Envoy file to stick it into the New Message dialog box editing window. Add any text you care to, and then click the Send button on the New Message Toolbar to send the message to the Exchange Outbox.

If you're ready to fire off the file, click Tools, Deliver Now Using, All Services. The recipient of your Envoy file will see exactly what we saw in figure 22.6: a replica of the original document.

I want the whole world to read this document!

All writers want readers, though getting them hasn't always been easy. Even a genius like Theodore "Dr. Seuss" Geisel had to try more than two dozen publishers before he found one willing to put his first book before the public. The result was readers in the millions for Geisel, and riches on the same scale for his publisher. History is mum on the fate of the two dozen or so who turned him down.

WordPerfect users can find millions of readers without beating down the doors of myopic publishers. We don't even have to leave our desk chairs. Any WordPerfect document can be published on the World Wide Web with WordPerfect's Internet Publisher. On the Web, it can be read by the teaming legions of Net surfers from around the world. There's absolutely no guarantee that your document will win you fame and fortune, nor indeed that millions will, in fact, read it. But, if you want to submit your work to the world, you can do so very easily with WordPerfect.

WordPerfect is your Web connection

The World Wide Web is like an immense book, with millions of pages and authors. It's a dynamic book, whose contents change constantly, and you need software, in the form of a Web browser, in order to "read" it. The Corel WordPerfect Suite comes with all the software you need to set up an Internet account with the AT&T WorldNet Service, and to surf the World Wide Web with the service's built-in browser.

If you don't already have an Internet account and browser, now's the time to get both. You'll need to have your modem properly installed and connected. You'll also need your Corel WordPerfect Suite CD.

With those essentials in hand, close any applications you might be running (including WordPerfect) and insert the Corel WordPerfect Suite CD in your CD-ROM drive. In a moment or two, the Corel WordPerfect Suite 7 CD-ROM dialog box appears. Click the Internet Service Setup button, and follow the prompts to set up the AT&T WorldNet Service.

The setup program installs software that lets you browse the Web. It also establishes your account with the AT&T WorldNet Service. Patience is required: there are many screens to plow through. Make sure you understand the pricing structure of an AT&T WorldNet Service account; while access to the Internet isn't necessarily expensive, it's not free. AT&T long distance customers do get a bargain, however. For them, five hours of Internet browsing per month is completely free of charge (unless your call to the service is a toll call). That's a very good deal for newcomers to the Web who are just getting their feet wet.

I'm lost in Cyberspace

Like any other subculture, the Internet has spawned its own language and customs, many of which will seem strange to newcomers. Take the language. Please. Adjectives such as "hot" and "cool," nouns like "zine" and "cyberspace," and the many variants of the verb "to surf" are seen at every turn. The jargon of the Internet is a strange brew of California beach town and science fiction, which isn't altogether surprising. Although the World Wide Web was invented in Europe (at CERN, the European particle physics lab), many of its devotees hail from our own left coast. Science fiction being the reading of choice among computer adepts, the mingling of sci fi and Beach Boys was inevitable.

Cyberspace is a word invented by William Gibson, author of a science fiction yarn called *Neuromancer* (Gibson himself reportedly doesn't use computers at all). It usually refers to the whole realm of computers linked together on the global Internet network. To **surf** the Web means to browse, more or less aimlessly, among the millions of documents posted on the World Wide Web. A **zine** is an electronic magazine, along with its variants **e-zine** and **web-zine**.

If you're drawing a blank at any of the terms in common use on the Web, visit one of the many glossaries or **FAQ**s (acronym for frequently asked questions). An outfit called the Internet Literacy Consultants maintains a good glossary of Internet terms. The **URL** (Uniform Resource Locator, or address) is http://www.matisse.net/files/glossary.html. Microsoft has a jazzier, graphical introduction to the World Wide Web that's also worth visiting. You'll find it at http://www.msn.com/tutorial/default.html. Type either URL in the Location edit box of your Web browser and press Enter to go straight to the right page. You can also enjoy and profit from the World Wide Web without knowing anything about its arcana; it's pretty user-friendly, which is why it was invented in the first place.

How do I publish my document on the Web?

WordPerfect uses its own special codes and conventions to format documents, and the World Wide Web has an entirely different set of codes and conventions. The WordPerfect Internet Publisher converts WordPerfect documents to the World Wide Web format, **HTML**, which stands for Hypertext Markup Language. The Internet Publisher also converts HTML documents into WordPerfect format, and lets you create an HTML document from scratch.

> ❖❖ *Plain English, please!*
>
> **Hypertext** is what makes the World Wide Web tick. It's a formatting language that allows the insertion of special codes to link documents together. Hypertext links are like cross-references in an encyclopedia, but without the page flipping. Click the links in a hypertext document (they're usually underlined words), and you travel automatically to other documents. Those document addresses are embedded in the link. The WordPerfect Internet Publisher lets you insert the hypertext links of your choice in any Web documents you create. ❞❞

If this stew of jargon and acronyms is beginning to make your eyes glaze over, it's not surprising. What is surprising is the ease with which you can put a Web page together in WordPerfect:

- Open the document you want to publish on the Web. It can be pretty much anything that's neither libelous nor otherwise likely to get you in trouble. The Web is a large-spirited place, but there are laws and limits.

- Convert your document to HTML with the Internet Publisher. It's automatically saved and displayed in HTML format. Use the Internet Power Bar to add hypertext links.

- Post your document on the Web through your Internet service provider.

Not all WordPerfect formatting features can be converted to HTML. Columns, drop caps, fill, headers and footers, page numbering, tabs and indents, vertical lines, and watermarks won't make the transition. Nor will borders and font changes. You'll want to bear that in mind as you create your document.

Chapter 22 *Share Documents with the Office and the Rest of the World* **427**

Substitutes for some of these features are easily added with the Internet Publisher tools. Figure 22.9 shows a document before it's converted to HTML.

Fig. 22.9
If you're creating documents for publication on the Web, skip WordPerfect features that won't be converted. Some of the formatting seen here will disappear in the HTML version.

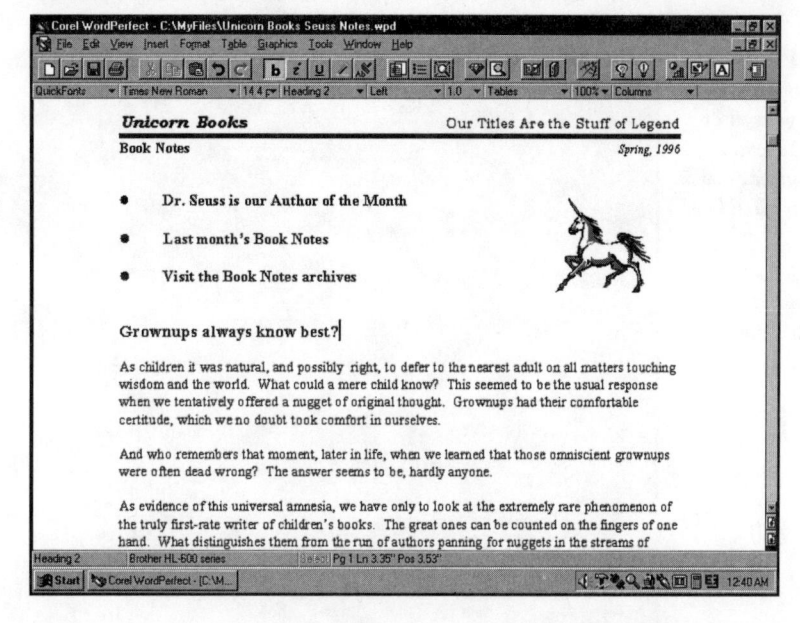

To create a Web document from an existing WordPerfect document:

1. Save your document, and leave it open. Click File, Internet Publisher, and the Internet Publisher dialog box appears (see fig. 22.10).

Fig. 22.10
Here's your Internet control center; you can even surf the Web from WordPerfect.

2. Click Format as Web Document in the Internet Publisher dialog box; then click OK in the Internet Publisher message box that pops up next. The document undergoes its transformation to HTML, and the Internet Publisher Toolbar appears, as seen in figure 22.11.

Fig. 22.11
HTML format isn't compatible with all of WordPerfect's features, so your document may not look too much like the original.

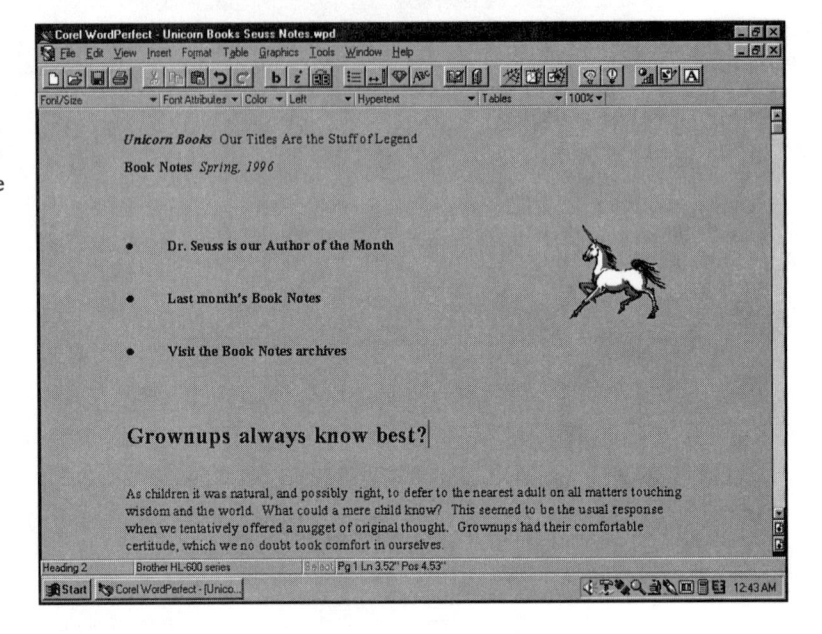

3. Although the document in figure 22.11 lost something in translation, the Internet Publisher Toolbar and Power Bar give you a lot of formatting scope.

- Click the Font/Size button on the Power Bar to add headings.
- Insert bullets, horizontal lines, and TextArt with the Toolbar tools (see Chapter 15 for details on TextArt). WordPerfect lets you dress up your text even in HTML format.

TIP To turn an existing title into TextArt: select the title, and then click the TextArt button. The selected title appears automatically in the TextArt edit box.

4. Click Format, Text/Background Colors to pop up the Text/Background colors dialog box. Choose a new color scheme for the page background and text. To add wallpaper, click the Browse button next to the

Chapter 22 *Share Documents with the Office and the Rest of the World* **429**

Background wallpaper text box. Investigate the folders filled with wallpaper schemes in the Background wallpaper dialog box that appears. Figure 22.12 shows the Text/Background Colors dialog box.

Fig. 22.12
You can go to town with a wild color scheme for your Web page, though something tasteful will separate your page from the herd.

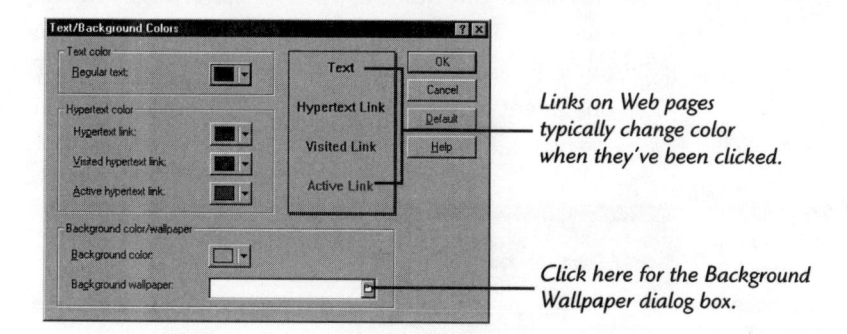

Links on Web pages typically change color when they've been clicked.

Click here for the Background Wallpaper dialog box.

5. To see how your document will actually look when it's in a reader's Web browser, click the View in Web Browser button on the Toolbar. That summons up the Web browser with your document in it. When you're ready to return to the Internet Publisher, click the Close button in the browser's title bar. Figure 22.13 shows the document viewed in the Web browser.

Fig. 22.13
Print preview, World Wide Web style. Web surfers with different browsers may not see exactly what we have here.

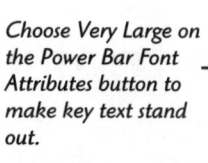

The subtitles were centered.

Choose Very Large on the Power Bar Font Attributes button to make key text stand out.

The background color was changed to white in the Text/Background colors dialog box.

The title was converted to TextArt.

6 Once you're satisfied with the document, save it in HTML format. Click the Publish to HTML button on the Toolbar to summon up the Publish to HTML dialog box. Enter a new path and file name in the Publish to edit box if you want to; otherwise, keep the existing name and path, and click OK. The Web document will have the same name as the original, but a different extension, as in FILE NAME.HTM. The original .wpd document won't change. Figure 22.14 shows the Publish to HTML dialog box.

Fig. 22.14
If you're going to keep Web documents in a special folder, choose it here. Otherwise, just click OK.

7 WordPerfect's gears whirl for a moment while it makes the conversion. Once the process is finished, exit the document without saving it. Click the document Close button, and choose No when you're prompted to save your changes. You don't want to change your original .wpd file, and you've already saved your work in a new .htm file.

Now you have a Web page ready to post on the World Wide Web. You may not get *millions* of readers, but you'll certainly get some.

If you want to edit your Web document further, click the Open button on the Toolbar and double-click the file, or choose it from the File menu if it appears there. The Convert File Format dialog box appears, prompting you to Convert file format from HTML. Just click OK to open your file. That'll bring back the Internet Publisher Toolbar, with your file in the editing window. When you finish editing, click the Publish to HTML button on the Toolbar to save the changes.

Hypertext links send readers on side trips

You've seen them in this book: "see Chapter 10..." and the like. Cross-references like that steer readers to related information. They're useful, and they can also be maddening, especially if a cross-reference steers you to a magazine you threw out a week ago.

Hypertext links are like automatic cross-references, except that the reader doesn't have to leaf through a book to get to "Chapter 10" or search through the recycling bin for an old magazine. Instead, the reader clicks the link and goes straight to the cross-reference. If you've spent any time browsing the World Wide Web, you've used hypertext links many times. Every time, in fact, you clicked an underlined word or a graphic in a Web document and wound up in another Web page.

Add hypertext links to an existing or new Web document, or to an ordinary WordPerfect file. There are two kinds of hypertext links:

- **Bookmark** links connect words within a document to send readers to another spot in the text. If you discuss Dwight D. Eisenhower's presidency of Columbia University on page 5 of your text, and you have a short history of Columbia on page 110, create a bookmark link. The reader clicks the underlined Columbia University on page 5, and the document scrolls to page 110 in the blink of an eye. That's a handy feature in a long document.

- **Document** links send readers across cyberspace to other documents on the Web. If your document mentions Columbia University, link the mention to the Columbia University Home page on the Web. One click takes your reader directly there, because the address, or URL, of the Columbia Home page is embedded in the link.

Bookmark links turn ordinary text into Hypertext

Reading a book is easy. You just turn the pages. Reading documents on the World Wide Web isn't as convenient, because you can only read one screen at a time. With an open book, you can glance back and forth across the pages, and up and down a single page. With a Web document, you have to scroll, scroll, scroll.

Bookmark links are the way to beat the Web document scrolling blues. Set up Bookmark links within a document, and readers can click the underlined words to jump around in the text. Since a reader can see only about a third of a Web page at a time, many Web sites use the top third of the page as a table of contents. It's often in the form of a bulleted list. Each heading on the list has a link to text further down in the page. A reader clicks the topic she's interested in, and the link takes her directly to the text. Web pages set up this way ensure that Web surfers won't miss critical information as they breeze past the page.

Figure 22.15 shows a bulleted item at the top of a document that we're going to turn into a hypertext link to the text at the bottom of the document.

Fig. 22.15
Since Web surfers can't see the whole document at once, use hypertext links to send them to key portions of the text.

This bulleted item is going to be the underlined text readers will click.

Here's the material we want Web surfers to read when they click the underlined link.

To create hypertext links:

1 Open a Web document created with the WordPerfect Internet Publisher, and select the word or words in the text you want your readers to go to when they click the link.

2 Click the Hypertext button on the Internet Publisher Power Bar and choose Bookmark, as seen in figure 22.16.

Fig. 22.16
Select the words you want readers to go to before you click the Power Bar Hypertext button.

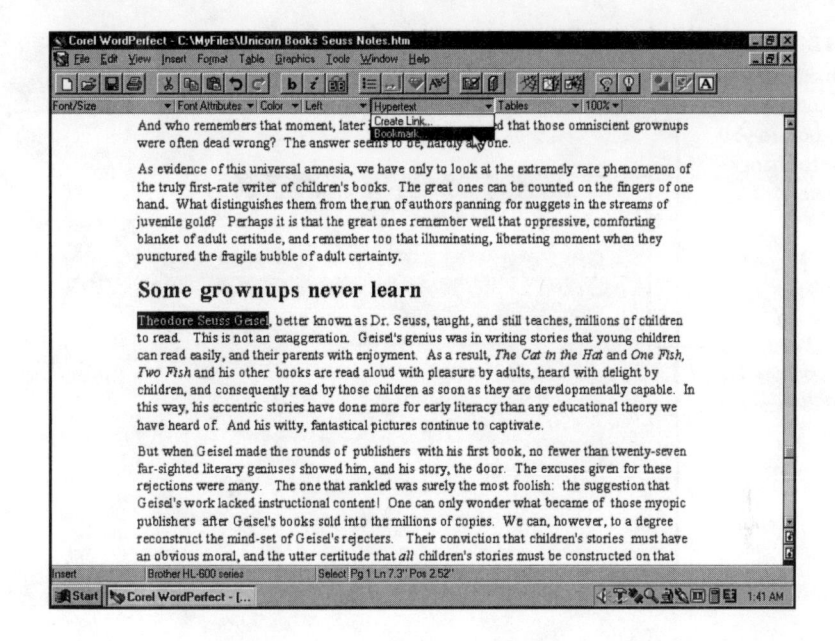

3 Click Create in the Bookmark dialog box that pops up. Your selected text appears in the Create Bookmark dialog box shown in figure 22.17.

Fig. 22.17
Don't type a new Bookmark name; your selected text is already in the edit box.

4 Click OK in the Create Bookmark dialog box, and the Bookmark and Create Bookmark dialog boxes disappear.

5 Now, we set up the hypertext link. Like pressing an elevator button for your floor, clicking the link will take readers to the Bookmark we created. The link appears as underlined text in the document. Select the text for the underlined link, click the Hypertext button on the Power Bar, and choose Create Link. That pops up the Create Hypertext Link dialog box shown in figure 22.18.

Fig. 22.18
The Bookmark name appears automatically in the edit box, so you don't have to change anything here.

This text will be underlined, and readers will click it to go to the bookmark we've created.

6. Click OK in the Create Hypertext Link dialog box. The link is automatically underlined, and it's now connected to the Bookmark we created. Figure 22.19 shows the underlined, linked text.

Fig. 22.19
When the pointer is over a hypertext link, it turns into a pointing hand.

Whenever a reader clicks the underlined text shown in figure 22.19, the document will scroll to the text we first selected as our bookmark. To create other cross-references in the same document, just follow the same steps for other selected text. If you're in the habit of creating long and complex documents, your readers will thank you for the convenience.

To get rid of a link, select the underlined text, click the Power Bar Hypertext button, and choose Remove Link.

Q&A *I can't seem to get rid of this link!*

Here's a WordPerfect quirk: if your Bookmark link is at the end of a line, you can't remove the link by selecting the text first. You have to use the keyboard arrow keys to position the insertion point inside the underlined text. Then, click the Power Bar Hypertext button and choose Remove Link.

Create Bookmark links like this one in ordinary WordPerfect documents, too. Open your document and click Tools, Hypertext/Web Links. You'll get the Hypertext feature bar instead of the Power Bar button we just used, but the idea is the same. Select text; then click the Bookmark button on the feature bar to create Bookmarks and the Create button on the feature bar to create links.

I happen to know this great Web site...

With the millions of Web pages on the Internet, it's impossible for anyone to visit more than a relative few. That's why so may Web pages consist of nothing more than links to other Web pages. Everyone has favorite spots on the World Wide Web, and the need to share them with others seems universal.

There are plenty of practical reasons to put links to other Web documents in your own Web page. Scientists and scholars can direct readers to other sites of interest; businesses like to point potential customers to Web sites that might help them make a sale; writers might have links to sites with online editions of their work; the possibilities are endless.

WordPerfect makes linking sites on the World Wide Web to text in a Web page extremely easy:

1 Open a Web document produced with the WordPerfect Internet Publisher, and select the text you want to link to a Web page. The selected text will appear either with an underline or a button, your choice, once the link is set up.

2 Click the Hypertext button on the Power Bar and choose Create Link.

66 Plain English, please!

What's in a **URL**? Universal Resource Locators on the Web have some things in common. All share the http://www. prefix, and though the other elements of the URL vary, they give you clues as to what a Web site might be about. The bit that follows the www. in the prefix is called the domain name. In the URL http://www.mcp.com, mcp.com is the **domain name**. The domain name is the giveaway: the .com in mcp.com stands for commercial organization (that happens to be Macmillan Computer Publishing's Web site). If the domain name has an .edu suffix, it's an academic institution such as a college. Nonprofits like National Public Radio have an .org suffix, and government sites have domain names that end in .gov. 99

3 In the Create Hypertext Link dialog box that appears, select Document. If you know the URL of the Web page you're linking, type it in the Document edit box, as shown in figure 22.20.

Fig. 22.20
URLs, as addresses, lean toward the practical rather than the poetic.

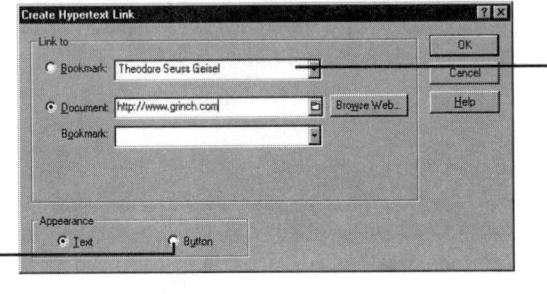

Any Bookmarks you might have on the page appear here. Just ignore them.

Want a link that looks like a button? Click here.

4 If you don't know the URL of the Web site you're linking, click the Browse Web button. That summons up the Web browser; log on and go to the Web site you want to link. Now, switch back to WordPerfect, and you'll see the current Web site's URL entered in the Document editing box. With the URL correctly typed or automatically entered from the current Web site, click OK in the Create Hypertext Link dialog box. (If you logged on to the Web to get the URL, don't forget to sign off again!)

5 Your Web site link is now forged. The link is either underlined or appears as a button in your Web document, and one click will send you, or your readers, straight to the linked site.

To edit a link, right-click the underlined text or button, and choose Edit Hypertext/Web Link on the QuickMenu.

To remove a link, select the link text, click the Hypertext button on the Power Bar, and choose Remove Link. If your link is a button, put the insertion point adjacent and to the left of the button (it'll look like the button's border is flashing) and choose Remove Link from the Power Bar Hypertext button. If the insertion point is to the right of the button, this won't work.

Q&A *So how do I get my page on the Web?*

Now that you've created your Web page, you'll want to post it on the World Wide Web. Many, but not all, service providers allow subscribers to maintain their own pages. The procedure varies from provider to provider, and you'll have to contact your particular provider for details.

Building a home page? Call in the Web Page Expert

One common (and justified) criticism of the Web: there's too much junk on it. There's wheat aplenty out there, but far more chaff. Wading through the latter to get to the former can be a bit of a chore. Of course, the same thing might be said of many other institutions.

Build your own home page, and you'll be doing your bit to improve the tone of the Web. Like a book cover, a home page catches the eye of passing Web surfers. A home page is also the introduction to whatever other material you're putting on the Web.

Try the WordPerfect Web Page Expert for home page construction. The Expert gives you a Web page template, and expert guidance in filling it in with your own material.

To summon up the Web Page Expert, click File, Internet Publisher. In the Internet Publisher dialog box that appears, click New Web Document. That brings up the Select New Web Document dialog box; double-click Web Page Expert on the Select template list.

You'll get a preformatted Web page and the Web Page Expert dialog box shown in figure 22.21.

Fig. 22.21
Like all the WordPerfect templates, the Web Page Expert gives you off-the-rack formatting.

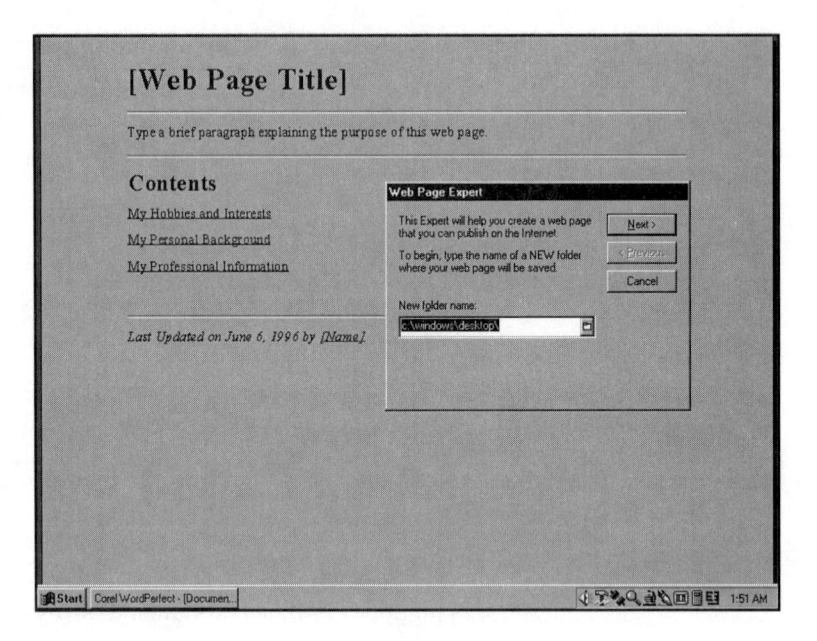

Type the name of a new folder in the Web Page Expert dialog box, and click Next. Then, let the Expert guide you through the creation of a Web page. Add links to other documents on your Web site or elsewhere on the Web. When you finish formatting and editing, click the Publish to HTML button on the Toolbar to save your work.

If enough *Using Corel WordPerfect 7 for Windows 95* readers publish on the Web, those Web critics may well have to turn their attention elsewhere.

Action Index

Edit documents

When you need to:	Turn to page
Check your grammar	158
Check your spelling	148
Cut and Paste	77
Find and Replace	82
Get a word count	162
Insert the date	33
Select text	73
Type text in a document	32
Undo and Redo	77
Zoom a document view	27

Format characters

When you need to:	Turn to page
Add a drop-cap	98
Add fonts	268
Change fonts	92
Insert accented characters	281
Preview font changes	264
Change the font color	265

Format documents

When you need to:	Turn to page
Add headers and footers	130
Add paragraph borders	120
Add paragraph fill	205
Adjust column widths	257
Adjust margins with Guidelines	104
Center text	113
Change margin settings	104
Clear/change tab stops	107
Copy formatting with QuickFormat	201
Create a newsletter	190
Create custom page numbers	126
Indent paragraphs	110
Justify text	114
Turn on columns	250
Use bulleted or numbered lists	116
Put a decorative border around the page	140
Present side-by-side information in a table	306

Cut down on typing chores

When you need to:	Turn to page
Create abbreviations	214
Edit a macro	225

Action Index 441

When you need to:	Turn to page
Play a macro	223
Record a macro	220
Insert addresses from the Address Book	227
Print a bushel of letters (or envelopes)	242
Sort a list automatically	25

Insert graphics

When you need to:	Turn to page
Add a decorative line	286
Create a poster title	269
Create a quick chart	370
Decorate the page with a watermark	273
Insert an image	291
Move and resize a graphic	294
Wrap text around a graphic	293
Customize a clip art image	360
Add to WordPerfect's clip art collection	302

Print

When you need to:	Turn to page
Print envelopes	175
Print labels	175

continues

When you need to:	Turn to page
Print multiple files	180
Print multiple pages	171

Manage documents

When you need to:	Turn to page
Create a table of contents	349
Find files with QuickFinder	355
Organize files in a new subfolder	353
Outline a document	335
Preview documents	169
Save files	41

Change the way you work with WordPerfect

When you need to:	Turn to page
Prevent the DAD from appearing on the Taskbar	14
Add your own Toolbar buttons	389
Customize the WordPerfect screen	382
Draw your own Toolbar button	394

Share Documents with the Office and the World

When you need to:	Turn to page
Put a Quattro Pro chart in a WordPerfect document	407
Send a WordPerfect document by e-mail	417
Send WordPerfect documents to non-WordPerfect users	421
Create a Web page	437
Set up the Internet software	424

Index

Symbols

+ key, star bullets (keyboard commands), 117
\> key, triangular bullets (keyboard commands), 117
1 Document command (Window menu), 39–41
2 Document command (Window menu), 40
3D Chart button, 372

A

abbreviations
    creating, 214
    deleting, 218
    documents, expanding all, 217–218
    expanding, 216
        troubleshooting, 216
    renaming, 218
    templates, copying to, 218–219
    troubleshooting, 215
Abbreviations command (Insert menu), 214
accented characters
    displaying, 281–282
    keyboard shortcuts, 282–283
activating automatic kerning, 279

Add Button, 386
Add Fonts dialog box, 268
Add to Favorites button, 357
adding
    buttons to toolbars, 389
    columns in tables, 313–314
    columns of numbers to spreadsheets, 318–320
    rows in tables, 313–314
    typos to QuickCorrect list, 153–154
    words to Spell Checker dictionary, 151
    see also inserting
Address Book
    creating merges, 233–234
    editing, 228–229
    entries
        building, 227–229
        detailing, 227–229
        moving, 229
    inserting
        entries into documents, 37–41
        entries onto envelopes, 176
Address Book button, 227
Address Book dialog box, 227

adjusting
    columns
        settings, 255–256
        with Guidelines, 256
    Grammatik criteria when checking documents, 161
    letterspacing, 281
    spacing
        between lines, 280
        on pages, 136–137
        tab stops, 107–109
    see also customizing; editing; modifying
Advanced Find dialog box, 356
Advanced Multiple Pages dialog box, 172
aligning
    text, 112–113
        documents, 32–33
        text flush right, 112
Alt+F3, Reveal Codes (keyboard commands), 80-81, 107
Alt+F4, exit (keyboard commands), 16
Alt+F5, page mode (keyboard commands), 27–28
Alt+Ins, inserting row (keyboard commands), 313
Alt+Page Down, top of next page (keyboard commands), 70

Alt+PageU, top of previous page (keyboard commands), 70
analyzing sentence structure with Grammatik, 162
antonyms, viewing in Thesaurus, 156–158
applying
    boldface to text, 89
    borders to paragraphs, 206
    color to fonts, 265–266
    color to text, 265–266
    fill to paragraphs, 205–206
    formatting styles to tables, 326–327
    italics to text, 89–90
    outline effects to fonts, 94–95
    QuickFormat to headings, 201–203
    QuickStyle to paragraphs, 208–210
    shading arrows to text, 95–96
    shadow effects to fonts, 94–95
    special effects to Drop-caps, 99–101
    special effects to lines, 289–291
    styles in newsletters, 193
    subscript to text, 95
    superscript to text, 95
    TextArt to fonts, 269
    underlines to text, 90–91
area charts, 378
Article Heading button, 192–193
Article Heading dialog box, 192–193
Ask the PerfectExpert dialog box, 52–53

AT&T WorldNet Service
    help features for WordPerfect, 63
    installing, 425
    World Wide Web, connecting, 424–425
automatic kerning
    activating, 279
    disadvantages, 279
automatic numbering
    lists, 119
    turning off, 120

B

Back button, 59–60
backgrounds, applying fill, 205
Backgrounds folder, 292
balanced newspaper columns, 248
bar charts, 376
Begin Find at Top of Document command (Options menu), 85
block protection, utilizing, 139
Bold button, 89
boldface, applying to text, 89
Bookmark dialog box, 433
bookmark links in Web documents
    creating, 432–435
    removing, 435
Border button, 120–121
Border/Fill button, 99–100
Border/Fill command (Format menu), 140
borders
    applying to paragraphs, 206
    deleting, 120–121, 206

    deleting from tables, 328–329
    inserting
        columns, 259–260
        pages, 140
        paragraphs, 120–121
    paragraphs, applying, 206
    selecting, 140–141
    styles, selecting, 120–121
    turning off, 140–141
Borders folder, 292
Box Caption dialog box, 299
Box Content dialog box, 296
breaking links to objects, 412
building
    entries for Address Book, 227–229
    home page with Web Page Expert, 437–438
bullets, creating in paragraphs, 117–118
Bullets button, 117
buttons
    3D Chart, 372
    Add, 386
    Add to Favorites, 357
    adding to Status Bar, 392–393
    Address Book, 227
    appearance, customizing, 395–397
    Article Heading, 192–193
    Back, 59–60
    Bold, 89
    Border, 120–121
    Border/Fill, 99–100
    Bullets, 117
    Cancel, 26
    Center Page, 137
    Character Set, 282
    Chart, 370

Chart or Graphic
  Tools, 362
Close, 14–15
Columns, 250
Commands, 226
Content, 296
Copy, 40–41, 77,
  219–229, 411
Copy Formula, 322
Create, 131
Cut, 77, 357
Data Chart Types, 376
Define, 351
displaying help with
  QuickTip, 21
Draw, 360
Equation Font, 398
Expand All, 217–218
Fill Attributes, 364
Fill Colors, 364
Find Next, 83–84
Font Size, 93–94, 202
Font/Size button, 428
Format, 370
Formula Bar, 317
Full Screen, 353
Functions, 323
General Status, 253
Help, 26, 61
Hide Body Text, 340
Horizontal Line, 287
Hypertext, 432
Image, 274, 291
Image Editor, creating,
  395–397
Indent, 111
Insert Field, 237
Insert File, 196–197
Insert Line, 132
Internet Service
  Setup, 425
Italics, 90
Justification, 114–115
Keep Together, 139
keyboard scripts,
  playing, 393–394
keystrokes, creating,
  393–394

Large Icons, 362
Layout, 374
Line Spacing,
  136–137, 280
Line Styles, 290
Make It Fit, 180
Merge Codes, 243
Minimize, 353
New Blank Document,
  36–38, 177, 235, 343
New Document,
  36–38, 186
Next Page, 28–29
Numeric Format, 309
Open, 180
Open File, 352
Open file, 402
Options, 154–155
Overlap, 374
Page Border, 140
Page Numbering,
  126, 128
Page/Zoom Full,
  27–28, 35, 169–170
Parse Tree, 162
Paste, 40–41, 77, 408
Pattern, 270
PerfectExpert, 52
Position, 95
Power Bar Columns,
  251
Power Bar Font, 267
Power Bar Font Face,
  92–93, 202
Power Bar Justifica-
  tion, 114–115
Power Bar Styles,
  117, 194, 200, 203
Preview, 44–45
  274, 291
Previous Page, 28–29
Print, 47, 168
Printer, 168
Publish to HTML, 430
QuickFonts, 96–97, 203
QuickFormat, 203
QuickSum, 319
Redo button, 78

Replace, 149–150
Replace All, 83–84
Resume, 150
Rotation, 271
Row/Column Indica-
  tors, 311
Save, 41–42,
  167–168, 345, 405
Save Group, 242
Separator, 388
Shading, 275
Show Body Text, 340
Show Me, 53–54
Side of Box, 299
Size Column to Fit, 315
Skip Always, 151
Skip Once, 151
Spell Check, 148–149
Stop Macro, 222
Sum, 318
Suppress, 136
T, 339
Table SpeedFormat,
  325
Tables, 307
Text Box, 300
Text color, 95, 265
Underline, 90–91
Undo, 71
User Styles option, 212
Vertical Line, 287
Web Browser, 429
Wrap text, 293

C

Cancel button, 26
Caption command
  (QuickMenu), 299
captions
  editing, 299–300
  inserting into
    graphics, 299
cells
  addresses in
    tables, 311
  expanding widths in
    tables, 314–316
  tables, 307–310

Center command
(Format menu),
137, 170
Center Page button,
137
Center Page(s) dialog
box, 137
centering
pages, 137
text in documents,
113–114
Change Display Type
dialog box, 20
changing, *see* editing;
modifying
Character Set button,
282
characters
QuickFormat, 204
QuickStyles, 207–208
Characters command
(Insert menu), 281
Chart button, 370
Chart command
(Graphics menu), 370
Chart or Graphic Tools
button, 362
charts
area, 378
bar, 376
creating, 370–376
formatting numbers,
370–372
high/low, 378
inserting labels, 370
line, 377
moving within documents, 374–376
pie, 377
radar, 378
scatter, 378
Choose Profile dialog
box, 417
choosing, *see* selecting
clearing tab stops,
107–109

clip art
customizing, 360–368
selecting for Presentations, 362–366
Close button, 14–15
Close command (File
menu), 23–24
codes
[Col Def] code, 252
[HCol], 254
documents, 79–82
find option, 84
merges appear as color
red, 236–237
modifying in text,
81–82
replace option, 84
revealing in documents, 79–82
viewing in text, 80–81
Codes command (Match
menu), 84–85
Codes dialog box,
84–85
Collate command (Print
menu), 173
Color command (Graphics menu), 291
colors, applying
fonts, 265–266
text, 265–266
Column Border/Fill
dialog box, 259
Column Break command (Format
menu), 254
columns
adding
in spreadsheets,
318–320
to tables, 313–314
borders
inserting, 259–260
troubleshooting,
260
breaks, inserting, 254

Columns dialog box,
controlling, 257–258
converting into tables,
328
default widths,
modifying, 254–255
entering text, 251
expanding widths in
tables, 315–317
formatting codes,
viewing, 252–253
Guidelines, adjusting,
256
numbers, selecting,
251
parallel, creating,
261–262
settings, adjusting,
255–256
tables, 307–310
converting, 328
text, entering, 258–259
types
balanced newspaper, 248–250
newspaper,
248–250
parallel, 248–250
widths, troubleshooting, 256
Columns button, 250
viewing, troubleshooting, 252
Columns command
(Format menu), 252
Columns command
(View menu), 251
Columns dialog box,
251
controlling column
settings, 257–258
commands
Edit menu
Find, 82–84
Find and Replace,
350

commands

Links, 412
Paste Special, 410
Preferences, 354–355
Replace, 82–84
Restore, 72
Select, 323
Table, 323
Undelete, 72
Undo/Redo History, 78
File menu
  Close, 23–24
  Condense Master, 347
  Document, 343
  Exit, 16, 43
  Expand Master, 346
  Folder, 354
  Install New Font, 268
  Internet Publisher, 427
  New, 354
  Print, 47, 180, 243–244
  Properties, 162–163
  Publish to Envoy, 422
  Save As, 169, 272, 405
  Send, 417
  Subdocument, 343–345
Format menu
  Border/Fill, 140
  Center, 137, 170
  Column Break, 254
  Columns, 252
  Create, 211–212, 277
  Define, 252
  Discontinue, 136, 277
  Drop-Cap, 99
  Edit, 211
  Envelope, 175–176
  Flush Right, 112
  Flush Right with Dot Leaders, 113
  Font, 94–95, 264
  Fonts, 25–26
  Header/Footer, 221
  Headers/Footers, 131–132
  Keep Text Together, 138
  Labels, 177
  Manual Kerning, 279–280
  Margins, 106–107
  Page, 124
  Page Numbering, 126
  Paragraph, 112
  Retrieve, 212
  Styles, 210
  Suppress, 136
  Text/Background Colors, 428
  Typesetting, 279
  Watermark, 273–277
  Word/Letter Spacing, 279
Graphics menu
  Chart, 370
  Color, 291
  Components, 303
  Custom Box, 324
  Drag to Create, 297
  Draw, 368
  Equations, 397
  Horizontal Line, 287
  Patterns, 291
  Text Box, 300
  TextArt, 269
  Thickness, 291
  Vertical Line, 287
Insert menu
  Abbreviations, 214
  Characters, 281
  Date, 33–34
  Date Code, 33–34
  Date Text, 33–34
Match menu
  Codes, 84–85
Open menu
  Find Now, 46
  Pre-Search, 46
Options menu
  Begin Find at Top of Document, 85
  Define a Bookmark, 59–60
  Display a Bookmark, 59–60
  Exit Template, 196
  New Template, 195–196
  Show Level Icons, 335
PerfectScript, 226
Print menu
  Collate, 173
  Group, 173
QuickMenu
  Caption, 299
  Create, 386
  Insert, 311
  Picture, 391
  Preferences, 385
Start menu
  Change Display Type, 20
  Control panel, 20
  Delete, 14
  Open, 16
  Settings, 20
Table menu
  Create, 328
  Sort, 329
Tools menu
  Deliver Now, 420
  Edit, 225
  Form, 235
  Generate, 193, 349
  Grammatik, 159
  Hypertext/Web Links, 435
  Macro, 220
  Merge, 235

Outline, 335–338
Play, 223–224
QuickCorrect,
   118, 153, 215, 286
Record, 220
Remove Links, 435
Select Records, 241
Spell-As-You-Go, 22
Table of Contents,
   193, 349
Thesaurus, 155
Type menu
   Word Forms, 85–86
View menu
   Columns, 251
   Draft, 26-27,
      29, 343
   Guidelines,
      104, 251
   Hide Bars, 382
   Page, 26–27, 344
   Reveal Codes,
      79–80, 252–253
   Selected Object
      Viewer, 365
   Table Gridlines, 329
   Toolbars/Rulers,
      382
   Toolbar/Ruler,
      107–108
   Two-Page, 27
   Zoom, 28–29
Window menu
   1 Document, 39–41
   2 Document, 40
   Tile Side by Side,
      352
Commands button, 226
**completing projects
   with QuickTasks,
   54–55**
**Components command
   (Graphics menu), 303**
Compuserve
   connecting, 63
   help features for
      WordPerfect, 63

**Condense Master
   command (File menu),
   347**
**Condense/Save
   Subdocuments dialog
   box, 347**
**conditional end of page
   option, 139**
connecting
   Compuserve, 63
   World Wide Web
      through AT&T
      WorldNet Service,
      424–425
Content button, 296
**contouring text around
   graphics, 294**
**Control panel command
   (Start menu), 20**
**Control Panel dialog
   box, 268**
**controlling columns
   with Columns dialog
   box, 257–258**
**Conversion dialog box,
   402**
**Convert File Format
   dialog box, 404, 430**
**Convert Table dialog
   box, 328**
converting
   columns into tables,
      328
   documents
      HTML format,
         426–430
      outlines, 341–342
      WordPerfect format,
         402–406
   files automatically to
      WordPerfect
      format, 404
   older WordPerfect
      files, 402–404
   outline section heads
      to document head-
      ings, 339–341

**Copy Abbreviation
   dialog box, 219**
**Copy button, 40,
   77, 219–229, 411**
Copy dialog box, 225
**Copy Formula button,
   322**
**Copy Formula dialog
   box, 322**
**Copy Toolbar(s) dialog
   box, 389**
copying
   abbreviations to other
      templates, 218–219
   files to diskettes, 45
   formulas in tables,
      321–322
   Quattro Pro objects to
      WordPerfect docu-
      ments, 407–408
   QuickFormat, 203
   spreadsheet formulas,
      321–322
   text, 77
      to other documents,
         39–41
   toolbars, 389
**Corel Desktop Applica-
   tion Director icon, 14**
**Corel Office Save As
   dialog box, 41–42**
**Corel Support Services
   technical hotline, 169**
**Corel WordPerfect Web
   site, 62**
**correcting documents
   with Grammatik,
   159–161**
**Create Abbreviation
   dialog box, 214**
**Create Bookmark
   dialog box, 433**
Create button, 131
**Create command
   (Format menu),
   211–212, 277**
**Create command
   (QuickMenu), 386**

Create command (Table menu), 328
Create Form File dialog box, 235
Create Hypertext Link dialog box, 433
Create Line Style dialog box, 290
Create Toolbar dialog box, 386
creating
abbreviations in documents, 214
bookmark links in Web documents, 432–435
bullets in paragraphs, 117–118
buttons
in Image Editor, 395–397
that type keystrokes, 393–394
charts, 370–376
custom toolbars, 385–389
custom watermarks, 277
documents from templates, 186–189
documents with Letter Expert template, 35–38
dot leaders, 112–113
Drop-caps, 98–99
envelope merges, 239–240
equations with Equation Editor, 398
footers in documents, 134–135
form files, 235–240
headers in documents, 131–132
headers in macros, 221–223
home pages for WWW, 437–438
hypertext links in Web documents, 431–435
macros, 220–223
master documents, 343–345
memos from templates, 186–189
merges with Address Book, 233–234
newsletters from templates, 190–195
numbered lists, 119–120
outlines, 335–338
parallel columns, 261–262
QuickStyle, 207–208
subfolders for like files, 354–355
tables, 306–310
templates, 195–196
text boxes, 300–302
watermarks in current documents, 273–277
Ctrl+B, boldface (keyboard commands), 89
Crtl+Backspace, deleting word adjacent to (keyboard commands), 71–72
Ctrl+C, copy (keyboard commands), 40–41
Crtl+Delete, deleting to end of line (keyboard commands), 71–72
Ctrl+down arrow, beginning of next paragraph (keyboard commands), 70
Crtl+End, end of document (keyboard commands), 70
Ctrl+Enter, hard column breaks (keyboard commands), 254
Crtl+F4, Close (keyboard commands), 23
Ctrl+F5, Draft mode (keyboard commands), 27–28
Ctrl+F6, document switcher (keyboard commands), 39
Ctrl+F8, margins (keyboard commands), 106–107
Ctrl+H, convert outline items (keyboard commands), 339
Crtl+Home, beginning of document (keyboard commands), 70
Ctrl+I, italics (keyboard commands), 90
Ctrl+left arrow, one word to left (keyboard commands), 70
Ctrl+right arrow, one word to right (keyboard commands), 70
Ctrl+U, underlining (keyboard commands), 90–91
Ctrl+up arrow, beginning of previous paragraph (keyboard commands), 70
Ctrl+V, paste (keyboard commands), 40–41
Ctrl+X, cut (keyboard commands), 40–41
Current Page option, 47
Custom Box command (Graphics menu), 324
Custom Installation dialog box, 303
Custom Page Numbering dialog box, 128
Customize Button dialog box, 395

customizing
  buttons appearance, 395–397
  clip art images in Presentations, 360–368
  lines, 290–291
  newsletter elements within templates, 192–195
  page number fonts, 129
  page numbers, 128–131
  toolbar appearance, 390–391
  watermark images, 275–277
  see also adjusting; editing; modifying
Cut button, 77, 357
cutting text, 77

D

DAD (Desktop Application Director)
  displaying programs, 13–16
  launching WordPerfect, 13–16
  other Windows 95 programs, launching, 13
  reducing size, 15
  restarting, 15
  Windows 95 taskbar, deleting, 13–16
DAD Properties dialog box, 15
data
  entering in tables, 309
  sorting in tables, 329–330
Data Chart Gallery dialog box, 376
Data Chart Types button, 376

data files
  components
    fields, 233–234
    records, 233–234
  flexibility of records, 234
  merge component, 232
Date Code command (Insert menu), 33–34
Date command (Insert menu), 33–34
Date Text command (Insert menu), 33–34
dates, inserting into documents, 33–34
default margins in WordPerfect, 104
Define a Bookmark command (Options menu), 59–60
Define button, 351
Define command (Format menu), 252
Define Table of Contents dialog box, 351
defining
  file searches for QuickFinder, 355–357
  print ranges, 172
Delete command (Start menu), 14
Delete dialog box, 314
Delete Styles dialog box, 210
deleted text, restoring, 78
deleting
  abbreviations, 218
  borders, 120–121, 206
  from tables, 328–329
  buttons from toolbars, 388
  DAD from Windows 95 taskbar, 13–14
  fill, 206
  fonts, 269

  graphics boxes, 302
  lines within documents, 289
  outline letters, 340–341
  outline numbers, 340–341
  paragraph styles, 210
  QuickLines, 286
  text, 71–72
    boxes, 302
    replace option, 86
  watermarks, 277
Deliver Now command (Tools menu), 420
depositing e-mail messages in Microsoft Exchange Outbox, 419–420
Desktop Application Director, see DAD
detailing Address Book entries, 227–229
dialog boxes
  Add Fonts, 268
  Address Book, 227
  Advanced Find, 356
  Advanced Multiple Pages, 172
  Article Heading, 192–193
  Ask the PerfectExpert, 52–53
  Bookmark, 433
  Box Caption, 299
  Box Content, 296
  Center Page(s), 137
  Change Display Type, 20
  Choose Profile, 417
  Codes, 84–85
  Column Border/Fill, 259
  Columns, 251
  Condense/Save Subdocuments, 347
  Control Panel, 268
  Conversion, 402
  Convert File Format, 404, 430

Convert Table, 328
Copy, 225
Copy Abbreviation, 219
Copy Formula, 322
Copy Toolbar(s), 389
Corel Office Save As, 41–42
Create Abbreviation, 214
Create Bookmark, 433
Create Form File, 235
Create Hypertext Link, 433
Create Line Style, 290
Create Toolbar, 386
Custom Installation, 303
Custom Page Numbering, 128
Customize Button, 395
DAD Properties, 15
Data Chart Gallery, 376
Define Table of Contents, 351
defined, 25–26
Delete, 314
Delete Styles, 210
Display Preferences, 384
Display Properties, 19–20
Document Initial Font, 96
Drop Cap Border/Fill, 99–101
Edit Box, 293
Edit Graphics Line, 289
Edit Macro, 225
Envelope, 175, 240
Expand Master Document, 346
Find, 58–59
Find and Replace Text, 83, 85–86, 350
Find Setup Wizard, 58–59

Font, 26, 84, 94, 264
Format, 370
Generate, 193
Go To, 75–76
Grammatik, 159–161
Headers/Footers, 131
Help Online, 63
Help Topics, 57, 226
Hide Bars Information, 382
Image Editor, 395
Include Subdocument, 345
Insert Columns/Rows, 311
Insert Field Name or Number, 237
Insert File, 44–45
Insert Image, 274, 291
Insert Merge Codes, 243
Installation Type, 303
Internet Publisher, 427
Keep Text Together, 138
Labels, 177
Layout, 374
Letter Expert, 37–38
Line Spacing, 136
Links, 412
Make It Fit, 180
Manual Kerning, 279–280
Margins, 106–107, 254
Memo Expert, 187
Merge, 235
Microsoft Exchange, 418
New Document, 195–196
New Entry, 36, 187–190
New Message, 419
Newsletter Expert, 191–195
obtaining help, 61
Open, 44–45
Open File, 352, 402

Open file, 180
Optional Shared Components, 303
Overwrite/New Name, 389
Page Border/Fill, 140
Page Numbering Font, 129
Page Numbering Options, 129
Pages, 134
Paragraph, 111, 205
Paragraph Border, 222
Paragraph Border/Fill, 222, 260
Parts of Speech, 162
Paste Special, 411
PerfectExpert, 52
PerfectExpert's Upgrade Help, 60
Perform Merge, 239
Play Macro, 223
Power Bar Options, 252, 391
Preferences, 354, 383
Primary Y Axis Properties, 372
Print, 47, 167–168
Print to, 166–167
Properties, 162–163
Properties for New Entry, 36, 187, 227
Publish to HTML, 430
QuickArt Browser, 362
QuickCorrect, 118, 153–154
QuickCorrect Options, 215, 286
QuickFormat, 202
QuickStyle, 207
QuickTasks, 54–55
Ready to Install, 303
Record Macro, 220
Rename Abbreviation, 218
Retrieve Styles From, 212
Save, 272

Save As, 42, 272, 405
Save Format, 405
Save Template, 196
Select Device, 20
Select New Document, 36–38, 89, 186
Select New Web Document, 438
Select Page Numbering Format, 126
Sort, 329
Specific Codes, 350
Status Bar Preferences, 392
Style List, 210
Styles Editor, 211
Suppress, 136
Table Functions, 323
Table Numeric Format, 309
Table SpeedFormat, 325
Table Tools, 330
Template Information, 190–191
Text/Background colors, 428
TextArt, 272
TextArt 7, 269
Title Properties, 370
Toolbar Editor, 386
Toolbar Options, 54, 391
Toolbar Preferences, 54, 385
Toolbars, 107, 382
Two-Sided Printing, 175
Undelete, 72
Undo/Redo History, 78
Values, 130
Watermark, 274
Watermark Shading, 275
Web Page Expert, 438
Word/Letter Spacing, 279
WordPerfect Characters, 281

dimmed menu items, 23–24
Discontinue command (Format menu), 136, 277
diskettes, copying files, 45
Display a Bookmark command (Options menu), 59–60
Display icon, 384
Display Preferences dialog box, 384
Display Properties dialog box, 19–20
displaying
  accented characters, 281–282
  buttons, 17-20
  outline levels, 337–338
  programs through DAD, 13–16
  toolbars for WordPerfect, 17-20
  see also viewing
Document command (File menu), 343
Document Initial Font dialog box, 96
document windows
  modifying, 382
  scroll bars, removing, 384–385
documents
  abbreviations, creating, 214
  Address Book, inserting, 37–41
  adjusting line spacing, 280
  aligning text, 32–33
  applying fonts, troubleshooting, 95–96
  codes, 79–82
  columns, selecting, 251
  converting to HTML formats, 426

copying text, 39–41
dates, inserting, 33–34
defining print ranges, 172
dot leaders, inserting, 112–113
Envoy, viewing, 421–424
exiting, 43
expanding all abbreviations, 217–218
fonts, modifying, 93–94
fonts overview, 91–92
footers, creating, 134–135
full page view, troubleshooting, 170
Grammatik
  correcting, 159–161
  utilizing, 158–162
graphic lines, inserting, 286–291
graphics
  inserting, 291–292
  moving, 298
  placing into box, 297–298
  resizing, 296–297
Guidelines, utilizing, 105–109
headers
  creating, 131–132
  editing, 135
  inserting second, 133–134
HTML format, converting, 427–428
indenting methods, 109–112
insertion points, placing, 68–70
layout, previewing, 169–170
Letter Expert template, creating, 35–38
lines
  applying special effects, 289–291

deleting, 289
moving, 288–289
margin measurements, 107
modifying HTML formatting, 428
multiple copies, printing, 173
naming, 42–43
other formats, saving to, 404–405
outlines, converting, 339–342
page numbering, troubleshooting, 169
pages
   expanding, 181–182
   shrinking, 180–181
pasting text, 39–41
print range, setting, 171
printing, 47, 167
   Current Page option, 47
   Multiple Pages options, 47
   reverse order, 173–174
publishing guidelines for WWW, 426
Quattro Pro objects
   copying, 407–408
   editing, 409–410
QuickFonts features, 96–97
retrieving, 44
retrieving styles, 212
reveal codes, 79–82
saving, 41–42
saving to HTML format, 430
scrolling, 28–29
searching with QuickFinder, 45–46
sending
   through Envoy to non-WordPerfect users, 422–424

   via e-mail to other WordPerfect users, 420–421
setting margins, 104–109
storing in MyFiles, 42–43
table of contents
   generating, 349–352
   selecting text, 349–350
tables, importing, 323–325
templates
   creating, 186–189
   selecting, 36–38
   utilizing, 35–38
text
   centering, 113–114
   copying, 39–41
   entering, 32–33
   pasting, 39–41
TextArt, inserting, 271–273
Thesaurus, 155-158
two-sided printing, 174–175
unopened, printing to, 180
utilizing Drop-caps, 98–99
viewing
   in Web Browser, 429
   options, 26–29
   side by side, 352–353
watermarks, creating, 273–277
Web site, linking, 436
word count, obtaining, 162–163
WordPerfect, converting, 402–406
wrapping text, 32
WWW publishing, 427–430
zooming, 27–28

dot leaders
   creating, 112–113
   inserting in documents, 112–113
double spacing text, 136–137
double-indented paragraphs, 110
Draft command (View menu), 27, 29, 343
Drag to Create command (Graphics menu), 297
dragging
   graphics, 296
   Guidelines to set margins, 105–109
   toolbar to different desktop positions, 20
Draw button, 360
Draw command (Graphics menu), 368
Drop Cap Border/Fill dialog box, 99–101
Drop-Cap command (Format menu), 99
Drop-caps
   creating, 98–99
   defined, 98–99
   special effects, applying, 99–101
duplexing, 174–175

E

e-mail
   messages, sending, 417–420
   obtaining addresses from Microsoft Exchange, 419–420
   send guidelines, 416–417
   sending
      documents to other WordPerfect users, 420–421
      through Envoy, 422–424

through Microsoft
Exchange,
417–420
**Edit Box dialog box,
293**
**Edit command (Format
menu), 211**
**Edit command (Tools
menu), 225**
**Edit Graphics Line
dialog box, 289**
**Edit Macro dialog box,
225**
Edit menu commands
Find, 82–84
Find and Replace, 350
Links, 412
Paste Special, 410
Preferences, 354–355
Replace, 82–84
Restore, 72
Select, 323
Table, 323
Undelete, 72
Undo/Redo History, 78
editing
Address Book,
228–229
advice on macros,
225–226
captions, 299–300
headers, 135
information within
templates, 190
macros, 225–226
Quattro Pro objects to
WordPerfect docu-
ments, 409–410
text
in text boxes,
301–302
with Undo/Redo
options, 78–79
see also adjusting;
customizing; modify-
ing
electronic mail, *see*
e-mail

embedded objects
linking, 410
modifying, 410
**End, end of line (key-
board commands), 70**
entering
body text in news-
letters, 193
text in columns,
251, 258–259
text in documents,
32–33
entries
detailing in Address
Book, 227-229
moving between
Address Books, 229
**Envelope command
(Format menu),
175–176**
**Envelope dialog box,
175–176, 240**
envelopes
Address Book,
inserting, 176
merges, creating,
239–240
printing, troubleshoot-
ing, 175–176
size, selecting, 176
USPS (United States
Postal Service) bar
codes, printing, 176
Envoy
documents, sending to
non-WordPerfect
users, 422–424
e-mail, 422–424
saving files, 423–424
viewing sent docu-
ments, 421–424
Envoy icon, 421
Equation Editor
equations, creating,
398
**Equation Font button,
398**

equations
appearance, modifying,
399
creating with Equation
Editor, 398
**Equations command
(Graphics menu), 397**
**Exit command (File
menu), 16, 43**
**Exit Template com-
mand (Options menu),
196**
exiting
documents, 43
outlines, 338–339
**Expand All button,
217–218**
**Expand Master com-
mand (File menu),
346**
**Expand Master Docu-
ment dialog box, 346**
expanding
abbreviations, 216
cell widths in tables,
314–316
column widths in
tables, 315–316
documents to fit
desired number of
pages, 181–182
graphics selection,
302–303
master documents, 347
subdocuments, 347

F

**F1, comprehensive help
option (keyboard
commands), 55**
**F7, indent (keyboard
commands), 112**
**fields in data files,
233-234**
File menu commands
Close, 23–24
Condense Master, 347

Document, 343
Exit, 16, 43
Expand Master, 346
Folder, 354
Install New Font, 268
Internet Publisher, 427
New, 354
Print, 47, 180, 243
Properties, 162–163
Publish to Envoy, 422
Save As, 169, 272, 405
Send, 417
Subdocument, 343–345
files
  automatic conversion to WordPerfect format, 404
  diskettes copying, 45
  Envoy, saving, 423–424
  folders, pasting, 357
  management strategies, 353–354
  multiple viewing, 352–353
  naming conventions, 42–43
  older WordPerfect, converting from, 402–404
  other formats, saving from, 404–405
  QuickFinder, searching, 45-46, 355–357
  saving as WordPerfect document, troubleshooting, 406
  subfolders, creating, 354–355
Files icon, 354
fill, 205–206
  deleting, 206
  paragraphs, applying, 205–206
Fill Attributes button, 364
Fill Colors button, 364
Find and Replace command (Edit menu), 350

Find and Replace Text dialog box, 86, 350
Find command (Edit menu), 82–84
Find dialog box, 58–59
Find Next button, 83–84
Find Now command (Open menu), 46
find option
  codes, 84
  text, 82–84
Find Setup Wizard dialog box, 58–59
Flush Right command (Format menu), 112
flush right text alignment, 112
Flush Right with Dot Leaders command (format menu), 113
Folder command (File menu), 354
folders
  fonts location, 268–269
  pasting files, 357
Font command (Format menu), 94–95, 264
Font dialog box, 26, 84, 94–95, 264
Font Size button, 93–94, 202
Font/Size button, 428
fonts
  colors, applying, 265–266
  default, modifying, 96
  defined, 91–92
  deleting, 269
  folder location, 268–269
  installing, 268–269
  modifying attributes, 93–94
  outline effects, applying, 94–95
  page numbers, customizing, 129

  previewing, 264–265
  Sans Serif, 97–98
  Serif, 97–98
  shadow effects, applying, 94–95
  TextArt, applying, 269
  Times New Roman, 92–93
  troubleshooting, 95–96
  types
    Printer, 267
    soft fonts, 267
    TrueType, 267
    Vector, 267
Fonts command (Format menu), 25–26
Fonts icon, 268
footers
  creating in documents, 134–135
  suppressing, 136
Form command (Tools menu), 235
form files
  creating, 235–240
  merge component, 232
  using other database programs in WordPerfect, 243
Format button, 370
Format dialog box, 370
Format menu commands
  Border/Fill, 140
  Center, 137, 170
  Column Break, 254
  Columns, 252
  Create, 211–212, 277
  Define, 252
  Discontinue, 136, 277
  Drop-Cap, 99
  Edit, 211
  Envelope, 175–176
  Flush Right, 112
  Flush Right with Dot Leaders, 113
  Font, 94–95, 264
  Fonts, 25–26

Header/Footer, 221
Headers/Footers, 131–132
Keep Text Together, 138
Labels, 177
Manual Kerning, 279–280
Margins, 106–107
Page, 124
Page Numbering, 126
Paragraph, 112
Retrieve, 212
Styles, 210
Suppress, 136
Text/Background Colors, 428
Typesetting, 279
Watermark, 273–277
Word/Letter Spacing, 279

formatting
  characters with QuickFormat, 204
  numbers
    for charts, 370–372
    in tables, 309–310
  text with QuickFormat, 201–203

Formula Bar button, 317

formulas
  copying, 321–322
  Equations Editor, 398
  spreadsheets, 318
  writing, 320–321

Full option, text justification, 115–116

Full Screen button, 353

functions
  PMT, 323
  sample list, 323
  spreadsheets, 318
  SUM, 318

Functions button, 323

G

General Status button, 253

Generate command (Tools menu), 193, 349

Generate dialog box, 193

generating table of contents, 349–352

Go To dialog box, 75–76

Grammatik
  correcting grammatical errors in documents, 159–161
  criteria, adjusting, 161
  grammatical analysis, viewing, 162
  help window, viewing, 159–161
  sentence structure analysis, 162
  utilizing in documents, 158–162

Grammatik command (Tools menu), 159

Grammatik dialog box, 159–161

graphics
  Backgrounds folder, 292
  Borders folder, 292
  captions, inserting, 299
  creating watermarks, 277
  dragging, 296
  height/width ratio, 297
  inserting in documents, 291–292
  lines, inserting, 286–291
  moving within documents, 298
  pasting into WordPerfect, 413–414
  Pictures folder, 292
  placing into box on documents, 297–298
  QuickArt folder, 292
  resizing in documents, 296–297
  selection, expanding, 302–303
  text
    contouring, 294
    wrapping, 293–294
  Textures folder, 292

graphics boxes
  deleting, 302
  importing tables, 323–325

Graphics menu commands
  Chart, 370
  Color, 291
  Components, 303
  Custom Box, 324
  Drag to Create, 297
  Draw, 368
  Equations, 397
  Horizontal Line, 287
  Patterns, 291
  Text Box, 300
  TextArt, 269
  Thickness, 291
  Vertical Line, 287

graphics objects
  copying into WordPerfect documents, 407–408
  editing in WordPerfect documents, 409–410

Group command (Print menu), 173

Guidelines
  adjusting column width, 256

dragging to set margins, 105–109
setting margins, 104–109
Guidelines command (View menu), 104, 251
gutters, 255

H

Hanging-indented paragraphs, 110
hard column break, 254
hard returns in text, 33
Header/Footer command (Format menu), 221
headers
creating
in documents, 131–132
in macros, 221–223
editing, troubleshooting, 135
even pages, selecting, 132
inserting second type into documents, 133–134
odd pages, selecting, 132
placing text, 131–132
suppressing, 136
Headers/Footers command (Format menu), 131–132
Headers/Footers dialog box, 131
headings
QuickFormat, applying with, 201–203
styles selection, 200
height/width ratio for graphics, 297
Help button, 26, 61

help features
AT&T WorldNet Service, 63
Compuserve, 63
dialog boxes, 61
F1, 55
Find, 58–59
PerfectExpert, 52–55
QuickTasks, 53
technical hotline for Corel Support Services, 169
WordPerfect on the Web, 62
Help icon, 59–60
Help Online dialog box, 63
Help Topics dialog box, 53, 57–59, 226
Hide Bars command (View menu), 382
Hide Bars Information dialog box, 382
Hide Body Text button, 340
high/low charts, 378
Home, beginning of line (keyboard commands), 70
home pages, building with Web Page Expert, 437–438
Horizontal Line button, 287
Horizontal Line command (Graphics menu), 287
horizontal lines, troubleshooting, 287–288
HTML (Hypertext Markup Language)
documents
converting, 426–430
modifying, 428
saving, 430
viewing in Web Browser, 429

Hypertext button, 432
hypertext links
bookmark, 431
document, 431
overview, 430–431
Web documents
creating, 431–435
removing, 435
Hypertext/Web Links command (Tools menu), 435
hyphens, transforming into graphic lines with QuickLines, 286

I

icons
Corel Desktop Application Director, 14
Display, 384
Envoy, 421
Files, 354
Fonts, 268
Help, 59–60
modifying toolbars, 390–391
outline level, 335
Recycle Bin, 269
red stop sign, 53
subdocument, 345
tab bar, 109
Toolbar, 389
WordPerfect, 15–16
Image button, 274, 291
Image Editor
buttons, 395–397
icons, 395–397
Image Editor dialog box, 395
images
QuickArt folder, 274
selecting for Presentation, 362–366
importing tables to other documents, 323–325

Include Subdocument
dialog box, 343, 345
Indent button, 111
indented paragraphs,
110
indenting options for
documents, 109–112
indicators, viewing
tables,
311–317
Insert Columns/Rows
dialog box, 311
Insert command
(QuickMenu), 311
Insert Field button,
237
Insert Field Name or
Number dialog box,
237
Insert File button,
196–197
Insert File dialog box,
44–45
Insert Image dialog
box, 274, 291
Insert Line button, 132
Insert menu commands
Abbreviations, 214
Characters, 281
Date, 33–34
Date Code, 33–34
Date Text, 33–34
Insert Merge Codes
dialog box, 243
inserting
Address Book
entries into docu-
ments, 37–41
entries on enve-
lopes, 176
body text to outlines,
338–341
borders
around columns,
259–260
around paragraphs,
120–121

on pages, 140
captions into graphics,
299
column breaks, 254
data in tables, 309
dates into documents,
33–34
dot leaders in docu-
ments, 112–113
graphic lines in
documents, 286–291
graphics into docu-
ments, 291–292
page numbers, 126–130
second header in
documents, 133–134
TextArt images into
documents, 271–273
titles for tables,
309–310
watermark images, 275
see also adding
**insertion points,
placing in documents,
68–70**
**Install New Font
command (File
menu), 268**
**Installation Type dialog
box, 303**
installing
AT&T WorldNet
Service, 425
fonts, 268–269
WordPerfect, graphics
selection, 302–303
**Internet Publisher,
converting documents
to HTML format,
426–430**
**Internet Publisher
command (File menu),
427**
**Internet Publisher
dialog box, 427**
**Internet Service Setup
button, 425**

italics, applying to text,
89–90
Italics button, 90

J - K

Justification button,
114–115
Justify All option, text
justification, 115–116
**Keep Text Together
command (Format
menu), 138**
**Keep Text Together
dialog box, 138**
**Keep Together button,
139**
kerning
automatic, 279–280
defined, 278–279
manual, 279–280
key words, utilizing in
QuickFinder, 46
keyboard commands
(+ key) star bullets,
117
(> key) triangular
bullets, 117
Alt+F3 (Reveal Codes),
107
Alt+F4 (exit), 16
Alt+F5 (page mode),
27–28
Alt+Ins (inserting row),
313
Alt+PageDown (top of
next page), 70
Alt+PageUp (top of
previous page), 70
Ctrl+B (boldface), 89
Crtl+Backspace
(deleting word
adjacent to), 71–72
Ctrl+C (copy), 40–41
Crtl+Delete (deleting
to end of line), 71–72

Crtl+End (end of document), 70
Ctrl+Enter (hard column breaks), 254
Crtl+Home (beginning of document), 70
Ctrl+down arrow (beginning of next paragraph), 70
Ctrl+F4 (close), 23
Ctrl+F5 (Draft mode), 27–28
Crtl+F6 (document switcher), 39
Ctrl+F8 (margins), 106–107
Ctrl+H (convert outline items), 339
Ctrl+I (italics), 90
Ctrl+left arrow (one word to left), 70
Ctrl+right arrow (one word to right), 70
Ctrl+U (underlining), 90–91
Ctrl+up arrow (beginning of previous paragraph), 70
Ctrl+V (paste), 40–41
Ctrl+X (cut), 40–41
End (end of line), 70
F7 (indent), 112
Home (beginning of line), 70
PageDown (top of editing window), 70–71
PageUp (top of editing window), 70
selecting text, 73
Shift+Ctrl+A (expand) abbreviation, 214
Shift+F1 (online help), 50–51
keyboard scripts, operating with buttons, 393–394
keyboard shortcuts for accented characters, 282–283

L

labels
 feeding to printer, troubleshooting, 179
 format, modifying, 179
 inserting into charts, 370
 merge printing, 243
 multiple copies, printing, 179
 print range, setting, 179
 printing, 176–179
 selecting types for print job, 177–179
Labels command (Format menu), 177
Labels dialog box, 177
Large Icons button, 362
launching
 other Windows 95 programs from DAD, 13
 WordPerfect
  from DAD, 13–16
  from desktop icon, 15–16
  from Windows 95 start menu, 13
Layout button, 374
Layout dialog box, 374
leading, 280
Letter Expert dialog box, 37–38
Letter Expert template, 35–38
letterspacing, 281
line charts, 377
Line Spacing button, 136–137, 280
Line Spacing dialog box, 136
Line Styles button, 290
lines
 custom, naming, 291
 customizing, 290–291
 deleting within documents, 289
 inserting in documents, 286–291
 moving within documents, 288–289
 spacing, adjusting, 280
 special effects, applying, 289–291
linking
 embedded objects, 410
 objects, 410
 Quattro Pro objects to WordPerfect, 412
 Word Perfect documents to Web sites, 436
links
 breaking, 412
 defined, 410
Links command (Edit menu), 412
Links dialog box, 412
lists, creating, 119–120
logical pages, 177–178

M

Macro command (Tools menu), 220
macros
 advice on editing, 225–226
 creating, 220–223
 defined, 220
 editing, 225–226
 headers, creating, 221–223
 playing, 223–224
 recording, troubleshooting, 221
 syntax importance, 224–225

Make It Fit button, 180
Make It Fit dialog box, 180
Manual Kerning command (Format menu), 279–280
Manual Kerning dialog box, 279–280
margins
　dragging Guidelines, 105–109
　Guidelines feature, 104–109
　measurements, 107
　ragged left, 114
　ragged right, 114
　setting in paragraphs, 104–109
Margins command (Format menu), 106–107
Margins dialog box, 106–107, 254
master documents
　condensed, viewing, 348
　creating, 343–345
　defined, 342
　expanding, 347
　saving, 345
Match menu commands
　Codes, 84–85
mathematical equations
　appearance, modifying, 399
　creating with Equation Editor, 398
Memo Expert
　template, 186–189
　troubleshooting, 187
Memo Expert dialog box, 187
memos, creating, 186–189
menus, dimmed, 23–24
Merge Codes button, 243
Merge command (Tools menu), 235
Merge dialog box, 235
merges
　Address Book, creating, 233–234
　codes, red color, 236–237
　common uses, 232–233
　envelopes, creating, 239–240
　labels, printing, 243
　overview, 232
　printing, troubleshooting, 243
　printing output, 242–243
　records, selecting, 241–242
messages
　depositing in Microsoft Exchange Outbox, 419–420
　e-mail, sending, 417–420
　receiving in Microsoft Exchange Inbox, 420
Microsoft Exchange
　Address Book, e-mail addresses, obtaining, 419–420
　Inbox, receiving e-mail messages, 420
　Outbox, depositing e-mail messages, 419–420
Microsoft Exchange dialog box, 418
Minimize All Windows command, 17–19
Minimize button, 353
modifying
　codes in text, 81–82
　columns default widths, 254–255
　default font setup, 96
　document windows, 382
　embedded objects, 410
　equations appearance, 399
　existing toolbars, 389
　fonts, 93–94
　HTML documents, 428
　label format, 179
　mathematical equations appearance, 399
　Power Bar, 391–392
　screen resolution for monitors, 17–20
　size of text, 95
　table appearance, 330
　table of contents format, 351–352
　text, 77
　　styles, 211
　toolbar icons, 390–391
　see also customizing; editing
monitors
　pixels and screen resolutions, 17
　screen resolution, modifying, 17–20
mouse
　Double-clicking in text, 74
　pointer shape, viewing, 20
　Quadruple-clicking in text, 74
　right button functions, 24–25
　selecting text, 74
　　by dragging, 74–75
　Triple-clicking in text, 74
　two-headed arrow, 20
　white arrow, 20
moving
　Address Book entries, 229
　charts in documents, 374–376
　graphics within documents, 298

lines in documents, 288–289
numbers on pages, 127–128
outline levels, 341–342
TextArt in documents, 272–273
multiple files
viewing, 352–353
Multiple Pages options, 47
multiple printing
documents, 173
labels, 179
MyFiles, document storage, 42–43

N

naming
custom
created lines, 291
templates, 196–197
documents, 42–43
files, 42–43
subfolders, 354–355
New Blank Document button, 177, 235, 343
New command (File menu), 354
New Document button, 36–38, 186
New Document dialog box, 195–196
New Entry dialog box, 36, 187–190
New Message dialog box, 419
New Template command (Options menu), 195–196
Newsletter Expert dialog box, 191–195
Newsletter Expert templates, 190–195
newsletters
body text, entering, 193

styles, applying, 193
templates
creating, 190–195
customizing, 192–195
newspaper columns, 248
Next Page button, 28–29
numbered lists, creating, 119–120
numbering
formats, 126-127
pages, 124–130
styles, 119
numbers, formatting tables, 309–310
Numeric Format button, 309

O

Object Linking and Embedding, see OLE
objects
coloring in Presentations, 363
copying to WordPerfect documents, 407–408
editing in WordPerfect documents, 409–410
embedded, linking, 410
grouping in Presentations, 365–366
linked, pasting, 411–412
linking, 410
breaking, 412
reshaping in Presentations, 368–369
rotating in Presentations, 364–365
obtaining
e-mail addresses from Microsoft Exchange Address Book, 419–420

help with PerfectExpert, 52–55
word count in documents, 162–163
OLE (Object Linking and Embedding)
troubleshooting memory, 362
Open button, 180
Open command (Start menu), 16
Open dialog box, 44–45
Open File button, 352, 402
Open File dialog box, 352, 402
Open dialog box, 180
Open menu commands
Find Now, 46
Pre-Search, 46
operators in spreadsheets, 318
Optional Shared Components dialog box, 303
Options button, 154–155
Options menu commands
Begin Find at Top of Document, 85
Define a Bookmark, 59–60
Display a Bookmark, 59–60
Exit Template, 196
New Template, 195–196
Show Level Icons, 335
ordinary paragraphs, 110
orphans, 138
Outline command (Tools menu), 335–338
outline effects, applying to fonts, 94–95

outline level icons, 335
outlines
   body text, inserting, 338–341
   converting from documents, 341–342
   creating, 335–338
   exiting, 338–339
   letters, deleting, 340–341
   levels
      demoting, 336–338
      displaying, 337–338
      moving, 341–342
      promoting, 336–338
   numbers, deleting, 340–341
   section heads, converting, 339–341
   theory, 334
Overlap button, 374
Overwrite/New Name dialog box, 389

P

Page Border button, 140
Page Border/Fill dialog box, 140
Page command (Format menu), 124
Page command (View menu), 26–27, 344
Page Numbering button, 126, 128
Page Numbering command (Format menu), 126
Page Numbering Font dialog box, 129
Page Numbering Options dialog box, 129
Page Toolbar, page setup options, 124
Page/Zoom Full button, 27–28, 35, 169–170

PageDown, top of editing window (keyboard commands), 70–71
pages
   borders, inserting, 140
   centering, 137
   expanding document to fit, 181–182
   footer limits, 131
   header limits, 131
   number codes, troubleshooting, 129
   numbering, 124–130
   numbers
      customizing, 128–131
      inserting, 126–130
      positioning, 127–128
      starting point on documents, 130
      suppressing, 136
   shrinking document to fit, 180–181
   spacing, adjusting, 136–137
   test, printing, 168–169
Pages dialog box, 134
PageUp, top of editing window (keyboard commands), 70
Paradox, 243
Paragraph Border dialog box, 222
Paragraph Border/Fill dialog box, 222, 260
Paragraph command (Format menu), 112
Paragraph dialog box, 111, 205
paragraphs
   applying
      fill, 205–206
      styles, troubleshooting, 210
   borders, inserting, 120–121

   bullets, creating, 117–118
   double-indented, 110
   formatting with QuickSpots, 110–112
   hanging-indented, 110
   indented, 110
   margin setting, 104–109
   ordinary, 110
   QuickStyles, 207–208
   styles, deleting, 210
parallel columns, 250
   creating, 261–262
Parse Tree button, 162
Parts of Speech dialog box, 162
Paste button, 40, 77, 408
Paste Special command (Edit menu), 410
Paste Special dialog box, 411
pasting
   files into other folders, 357
   linked objects, 411–412
   Presentations graphics into WordPerfect, 413–414
   text, 77
      to other documents, 39–41
Pattern button, 270
Patterns command (Graphics menu), 291
PerfectExpert, obtaining help, 52–55
PerfectExpert button, 52
PerfectExpert dialog box, 52
PerfectExpert Upgrade Help dialog box, 60
PerfectScript
   commands, viewing, 226
   macro language, 226

Perform Merge dialog box, 239
physical pages, 177–178
Picture command (QuickMenu), 391
pictures, adding to Power Bar, 392
Pictures folder, 292
pie charts, 377
pitch, 281
pixels, 17
placing
  graphics into documents, 297–298
  insertion points in documents, 68–70
  text in headers, 131–132
Play command (Tools menu), 223–224
Play Macro dialog box, 223
playing
  keyboard scripts with buttons, 393–394
  macros, 223–224
PMT function, 323
point size, 94
Position button, 95
Power Bar
  adding
    buttons, 392
    pictures, 392
  appearance, modifying, 391–392
  difference between toolbar, 21
Power Bar Columns button, 251
Power Bar Font button, 267
Power Bar Font Face button, 92–93, 202
Power Bar Justification button, 114–115
Power Bar Options dialog box, 252, 391

Power Bar Styles button, 117, 194, 200, 203
Pre-Search command (Open menu), 46
Preferences command (Edit menu), 354–355
Preferences command (QuickMenu), 385
Preferences dialog box, 354, 383
Presentations
  clip art images, customizing, 360–368
  coloring objects, 363
  graphics, pasting, 413–414
  grouping objects, 365–366
  images, selecting, 362–366
  reshaping objects, 368–369
  rotating objects, 364–365
preventing
  orphans, 139
  widows, 139
Preview button, 44–45, 274, 291
previewing
  document layout, 169–170
  fonts, 264–265
Previous Page button, 28–29
Primary Y Axis Properties dialog box, 372
Print button, 47, 168
  troubleshooting, 172
Print command (File menu), 47, 180, 243–244
Print dialog box, 47, 167–168
Print menu commands
  Collate, 173
  Group, 173

print ranges
  labels, 179
  settings, 171
Print to dialog box, 166–167
Printer button, 168
Printer fonts, 267
printers
  installed, viewing, 166–167
  selecting for print jobs, 166–167
printing
  Current Page option, 47
  documents, 47, 167
    in reverse order, 173–174
    troubleshooting, 168
  envelopes, 175–176
  labels, 176–179
  merge output, 242–243
  merges to labels, 243
  multiple copies
    documents, 173
    labels, 179
  Multiple Pages options, 47
  page ranges, troubleshooting, 47
  test pages, 168–169
  two-sided documents, 174–175
  unopened documents, 180
  USPS bar codes on envelopes, 176
Properties command (File menu), 162–163
Properties dialog box, 162–163
Properties for New Entry dialog box, 36, 187–190, 227
Publish to Envoy command (File menu), 422

Publish to HTML
button, 430
Publish to HTML dialog
box, 430
publishing documents
on WWW, 427–430

Q

Quattro Pro objects
copying to
WordPerfect documents, 407–408
editing in WordPerfect
documents, 409–410
linking to WordPerfect,
410–412
QuickArt Browser
dialog box, 362
QuickArt folder
graphics location, 292
images, 274
QuickBullets, 117–118
QuickCorrect
correcting typos, 153
eliminating extra
spacing between
words, 154–155
fixing capitalization,
154–155
typos, adding, 153–154
QuickCorrect command
(Tools menu),
118, 153, 215, 286
QuickCorrect dialog
box, 118, 153–154
QuickCorrect feature,
153-155
QuickCorrect Options
dialog box, 215, 286
QuickFinder
file searching capabilities, 45–46
key words, utilizing, 46
searching
files, 355–357
documents, 45–46

QuickFinder Fast
Search Setup Expert,
355
QuickFonts, 96-97
QuickFonts button,
96–97, 203
QuickFormat
applying to headings,
201–203
automatic updating
feature, 203–204
copying, 203
formatting
characters, 204
text, 201–203
paint roller, 204
QuickFormat button,
203
QuickFormat dialog
box, 202
QuickLines
deleting, 286
hyphens, transforming,
286
QuickMenu, 74
QuickMenu commands
Caption, 299
Create, 386
Insert, 311
Picture, 391
Preferences, 385
QuickSelect, 74
QuickSpot, 23
viewing in graphics,
troubleshooting, 293
QuickSpots, 110-112
QuickStyle
applying to paragraphs,
208–210
characters, 207–208
creating, 207–208
paragraphs, 207–210
text, 207–208
troubleshooting, 210
QuickStyle dialog box,
207
QuickSum button, 319

QuickTasks, 54-55
QuickTasks dialog box,
54–55
QuickTip buttons, 21
quitting, *see* exiting

R

radar charts, 378
ragged left
margins, 114
ragged right
margins, 114
Ready to Install dialog
box, 303
Record command
(Tools menu), 220
Record Macro dialog
box, 220
records
data files
components,
233–234
flexibility, 234
selecting for merges,
241–242
Recycle Bin icon, 269
red cross-hatchings
(Spell-As-You-Go
feature), 22
red stop sign icon, 53
Redo button, 78
Remove Links command
(Tools menu), 435
removing
bookmark links, 435
hypertext links, 435
scroll bars from
document windows,
384–385
Rename Abbreviation
dialog box, 218
Replace All button,
83–84
Replace button,
149–150
Replace command (Edit
menu), 82–84

replace option
   codes, 84
   deleting text, 86
   text, 82–84
replacing
   word forms in text, 85–86
   words with Thesaurus, 157–158
resizing graphics
   alternatives to dragging, 296–297
   in documents, 296–297
Restore command (Edit menu), 72
restoring deleted text, 78
Resume button, 150
Retrieve command (Format menu), 212
Retrieve Styles From dialog box, 212
retrieving
   documents, 44
   styles from documents, 212
Reveal Codes command (View menu), 79–80, 252–253
revealing codes in documents, 79–82
reversing document print order, 173–174
Rotation button, 271
Row/Column Indicators button, 311
rows
   adding to tables, 313–314
   in tables, 307–310

S

Sans Serif fonts, 97–98
Save As command (File menu), 169, 272, 405
Save As dialog box, 42–43, 405
Save button, 41, 168, 345, 405
Save dialog box, 272
Save Format dialog box, 405
Save Group button, 242
Save Template dialog box, 196
saving
   documents, 41–42
      in other formats, 404–405
      to HTML format, 430
   files
      in other formats, 404–405
      to Envoy, 423–424
   master documents, 345
   subdocuments, 347–348
   templates, 195–196
   TextArt images, 271–273
scatter charts, 378
screen resolution
   adjusting monitors, 17–20
   displaying
      toolbars for WordPerfect, 17–20
      WordPerfect buttons, 17–20
   pixels, 17
   troubleshooting, 20
scroll bars, 28–29
   removing from documents, 384–385
searching
   documents with QuickFinder, 45–46
   files with QuickFinder, 45–46, 355–357
   URLs, 436
   words in Thesaurus, 156

Select command (Edit menu), 323
Select Device dialog box, 20
Select New Document dialog box, 36, 89, 186
Select New Web Document dialog box, 438
Select Page Numbering Format dialog box, 126
Select Records command (Tools menu), 241
Selected Object Viewer command (View menu), 365
selecting
   border styles, 120–121, 140–141
   columns for documents, 251
   envelope size, 176
   even pages for headers, 132
   headings styles, 200
   images for Presentations, 362–366
   labels for print jobs, 177–179
   numbering styles for lists, 119
   numbers of columns, 251
   odd pages for headers, 132
   printers for print jobs, 166–167
   records for merges, 241–242
   templates, 36–38, 186–187
   text
      by dragging mouse, 74–75

for table of contents
from document,
349–350
with keyboard
commands, 73
with mouse, 74
with QuickMenu, 74
with QuickSelect,
74
**Send command (File
menu), 417**
sending
documents via e-mail
to other WordPerfect
users, 420–421
e-mail
guidelines, 416–417
messages, 417–420
through Envoy,
422–424
through Microsoft
Exchange,
417–420
**sentence structure,
analyzing with
Grammatik, 162**
Separator button, 388
Serif fonts, 97–98
setting
margins in paragraphs,
104–109
page numbers on
documents, 130
print range
documents, 171
labels, 179
table of contents levels,
351–352
**Settings command
(Start menu), 20**
shading arrows, 95-96
Shading button, 275
shadow effects, 94-95
**Shadow Pointer, 23,
68-70**
**Shift+Ctrl+A, expand
abbreviation (keyboard commands),
214**

**Shift+F1, online help
(keyboard commands), 50–51**
**Show Body Text
button, 340**
**Show Level Icons
command (Options
menu), 335**
**Show Me button,
53–54**
**shrinking documents to
fit desired number of
pages, 180–181**
**Side of Box button,
299**
**single spacing text,
136–137**
**Size Column to Fit
button, 315**
**Skip Always button,
151**
Skip Once button, 151
soft fonts, 267
soft returns in text, 33
**Sort command (Table
menu), 329**
Sort dialog box, 329
**sorting data in tables,
329–330**
spacing
kerning, 278–279
lines, adjusting, 280
special effects
applying to Drop-caps,
99–101
applying to lines,
289–291
**Specific Codes dialog
box, 350**
**Spell Check button,
148–149**
Spell Checker
double words, 151–152
limitations, 152–153
misspelled words,
148–150
options, 151

replacement words,
suggesting, 150
utilizing, 148–150
words, adding to
dictionary, 151
**Spell-As-You-Go
command (Tools
menu), 22**
**Spell-As-You-Go
feature**
adding words to list,
146–147
checking text spelling,
146–147
red cross-hatchings, 22
spell-checking, 22
turning on/off, 22, 147
spreadsheets
columns, adding,
318–320
creating from table
functions, 317–318
formulas, 318
copying, 321–322
writing, 320–321
functions, 318
operators, 318
Start menu commands
Change Display Type,
20
Control panel, 20
Delete, 14
Open, 16
Settings, 20
starting, *see* **launching**
**Status Bar, adding
buttons, 392–393**
**Status Bar Preferences
dialog box, 392**
Stop Macro button, 222
storing
documents in MyFiles,
42–43
TextArt images,
272–273
**Style List dialog
box, 210**

styles
   applying
      in newsletters, 193
      reformatting to
         tables, 326–327
   defined, 206–207
   documents retrieval,
      212
   heading selections, 200
   modifying, 211
**Styles command
   (Format menu), 210**
**Styles Editor dialog
   box, 211**
**Subdocument command
   (File menu), 343–345**
subdocument icon, 345
subdocuments
   defined, 342
   expanding, 347
   saving, 347–348
   viewing icon, trouble-
      shooting, 345
subfolders
   creating, 354–355
   naming, 354–355
**subscript, applying to
   text, 95**
Sum button, 318
SUM function, 318
**superscript, applying to
   text, 95**
Suppress button, 136
**Suppress command
   (Format menu), 136**
**Suppress dialog box,
   136**
suppressing
   footers, 136
   headers, 136
   page numbers, 136
**synonyms, viewing in
   Thesaurus, 156–158**

T

T button, 339
tab bar icon, 109

tab stops
   adjusting, 107–109
   clearing, 107–109
**Table command (Edit
   menu), 323**
**Table Functions dialog
   box, 323**
**Table Gridlines com-
   mand (View menu),
   329**
Table menu commands
   Create, 328
   Sort, 329
**Table Numeric Format
   dialog box, 309**
table of contents
   format, modifying,
      351–352
   generating, 349–352
   levels, setting, 351–352
   selecting text, 349–350
**Table of Contents
   command (Tools
   menu), 193, 349**
**Table SpeedFormat
   button, 325**
**Table SpeedFormat
   dialog box, 325**
**Table Tools dialog box,
   330**
tables
   appearance, modifying,
      330
   as spreadsheets,
      317–318
   borders, deleting,
      328–329
   cell address, 311
   cell widths, expanding,
      314–316
   columns, 307–310
      adding, 313–314
      expanding widths,
         315–317
   creating, 306–310
   data
      entering, 309
      sorting, 329–330

   formatting styles,
      applying, 326–327
   formulas
      copying, 321–322
      writing, 320–321
      importing to other
         documents, 323–325
   indicators, 311–317
   rows, 307–310
      adding, 313–314
   titles, inserting,
      309–310
Tables button, 307
**taskbar, deleting DAD
   from, 13–14**
**technical hotline for
   Corel Support Ser-
   vices, 169**
**Template Information
   dialog box, 190–191**
templates
   copying abbreviations,
      218–219
   creating, 195–196
      documents,
         186–189
      memos, 186–189
      newsletters,
         190–195
   custom, naming,
      196–197
   customizing newsletter
      elements, 192–195
   defined, 186
   information, editing,
      190
   Letter Expert template,
      35–38
   Memo Expert, 186-189
   Newsletter Expert,
      190–195
   saving, 195–196
   selecting, 186–187
      for documents,
         36–38
**test pages printing,
   168–169**

text
   aligning, 112–113
      documents, 32–33
      flush right, 112
   block protection, 139
   boldface, applying, 89
   boxes, creating, 300–302
   centering, 113–114
   codes
      modifying, 81–82
      viewing, 80–81
   color, applying, 265–266
   columns, entering, 251
   conditional end of page option, 139
   contouring around graphics, 294
   copying, 77
   cutting, 77
   deleted, restoring, 78
   deleting, 71–72
   double spacing, 136–137
   editing, 78-79
      in text boxes, 301–302
   entering
      in columns, 258–259
      in newsletters, 193
      into documents, 32–33
   find feature, 82–84
   fonts overview, 91–92
   hard returns, 33
   headers, placing in, 131–132
   Insert modes, 69–70
   inserting in outlines, 338–341
   italics, applying, 89–90
   justification, 114–116
   justified
      Full option, 115–116
      Justify All option, 115–116
   keystrokes button, 393–394
   letterspacing, 281
   modifying, 77
      fonts, 93–94
   orphans, preventing, 139
   pasting, 77
   QuickFormat, 201-203
   QuickStyles, 207–208
   ragged left
      margins, 114
   ragged right
      margins, 114
   replace feature, 82–84
   selecting
      dragging mouse, 74–75
      keyboards, 73
      mouse, 74
      QuickMenu, 74
      QuickSelect, 74
   shading arrows, applying, 95–96
   single spacing, 136–137
   size, modifying, 95
   soft returns, 33
   Spell-As-You-Go feature 146–147
   subscript, applying, 95
   superscript, applying, 95
   triple spacing, 137
   Typeover mode, 70–71
   undeleting, 71–72
   underlines, applying, 90–91
   utilizing TextArt, 269
   widows, preventing, 139
   word forms, replacing, 85–86
   word spacing, 281
   wrapping documents, 32–33

Text Box button, 300

Text Box command (Graphics menu), 300

text boxes
   creating, 300–302
   deleting, 302
   editing, 301–302

Text color button, 95, 265

text strings, 85

Text/Background Colors command (Format menu), 428

Text/Background colors dialog box, 428

TextArt
   creating watermarks, 277
   effect on fonts, 269
   images
      saving, 271–273
      storing, 272–273
   inserting images into documents, 271–273
   moving in documents, 272–273
   utilizing, 269–271

TextArt 7 dialog box, 269

TextArt command (Graphics menu), 269

TextArt dialog box, 272

Textures folder, 292

Thesaurus
   antonyms, viewing, 156–158
   synonyms, viewing, 156–158
   words
      replacing, 157–158
      searching, 156

Thesaurus command (Tools menu), 155

Thickness command (Graphics menu), 291

Tile Side by Side command (Windows menu), 352

Times New Roman, 92–93
Title Properties dialog box, 370
titles, inserting in tables, 309–310
Toolbar Editor dialog box, 386
Toolbar icon, 389
Toolbar Options dialog box, 54, 391
Toolbar Preferences dialog box, 54, 385
toolbars
   adding buttons, 389
   appearance, customizing, 390–391
   copying, 389
   custom, creating, 385–389
   difference between Power Bar, 21
   deleting buttons, 388
   inserting space between buttons, 388
   multiple rows of buttons, 389
   viewing buttons, troubleshooting, 394
Toolbars dialog box, 107–108, 382
Toolbars/Rulers command (View menu), 382
Tools menu commands
   Deliver Now, 420
   Edit, 225
   Form, 235
   Generate, 193, 349
   Grammatik, 159
   Hypertext/Web Links, 435
   Macro, 220
   Merge, 235
   Outline, 335–338
   Play, 223–224
   QuickCorrect, 118, 154, 215, 286

   Record, 220
   Remove Links, 435
   Select Records, 241
   Spell-As-You-Go, 22
   Table of Contents, 193, 349
   Thesaurus, 155
Toolsbar/Ruler command (View menu), 107–108
transforming hyphens with QuickLines, 286
triple spacing in text, 137
troubleshooting
   abbreviation expansion, 216
   abbreviations, 215
   adjusting column width, 256
   applying paragraph styles, 210
   borders around columns, 260
   Columns button, viewing, 252
   documents
      fonts, 95–96
      full page view, 170
      page numbering, 169
   editing headers, 135
   horizontal lines, inserting, 287–288
   label feed to printer, 179
   macro recording, 221
   Memo Expert, 187
   memory problems with OLE (Object Linking and Embedding), 362
   page number codes, 129
   page numbers, viewing, 128
   posting Web page, 437
   print button grayed out, 172

   printing
      documents, 168
      envelopes, 176
      merges, 243
      page ranges, 47
   QuickBullets, 118
   QuickStyle, 210
   saving files as WordPerfect documents, 406
   screen resolution, 20
   toolbar buttons, viewing, 394
   viewing
      QuickSpot in graphics, 293
      subdocument icon, 345
TrueType fonts, 267
turning off
   automatic numbering, 120
   borders, 140–141
   QuickBullets, 118
   Spell-As-You-Go feature, 147
Two-Page command (View menu), 27
two-sided printing, 174–175
Two-Sided Printing dialog box, 175
Type menu commands, Word Forms, 85–86
typefaces, *see* fonts
Typeover mode, 70-71
Typesetting command (Format menu), 279
Typography, 98
typos, adding to QuickCorrect list, 153–154

U

Undelete command (Edit menu), 72
Undelete dialog box, 72

undeleting text, 71–72
Underline button, 90–91
underlines, applying to text, 90–91
Undo button, 71
Undo/Redo History command (Edit menu), 78
Undo/Redo History dialog box, 78
Undo/Redo option, 78-79
URL (Universal Resource Locators)
    defined, 436
    searching, 436
User Styles option button, 212
USPS (United States Postal Service) bar codes, 176
utilizing
    block protection in text, 139
    conditional end of page option for text, 139
    Grammatik in documents, 158–162
    Guidelines in documents, 105–109
    key words for QuickFinder, 46
    Memo Expert template, 186–189
    QuickCorrect feature, 153–155
    Spell Checker, 148–150
    templates for documents, 35–38
    TextArt, 269–271
    Thesaurus feature in documents, 155–158

V

Values dialog box, 130
Vector fonts, 267
Vertical Line button, 287
Vertical Line command (Graphics menu), 287
View menu commands
    Columns, 251
    Draft, 26–27, 29, 343
    Guidelines, 104, 251
    Hide Bars, 382
    Page, 26–27, 344
    Reveal Codes, 79–80, 252-253
    Selected Object Viewer, 365
    Table Gridlines, 329
    Toolbars/Rulers, 382
    Toolbar/Ruler, 107–108
    Two-Page, 27
    Zoom, 28–29
viewing
    antonyms in Thesaurus, 156–158
    codes in text, 80–81
    column formatting codes, 252–253
    condensed master documents, 348
    document display options, 26–29
    documents sent with Envoy, 421–424
    documents side by side, 352–353
    grammatical analysis with Grammatik, 162
    Grammatik's help window, 159–161
    HTML documents in Web Browser, 429
    installed printers in WordPerfect, 166–167
    mouse pointer shape, 20
    multiple files, 352–353
    PerfectScript commands, 226
    synonyms in Thesaurus, 156–158
    see also displaying

W

Watermark command (Format menu), 273–277
Watermark dialog box, 274
Watermark Shading dialog box, 275
watermarks
    creating in current documents, 273–277
    custom, creating, 277
    deleting, 277
    images
        customizing, 275–277
        inserting, 275
Web Browser button, 429
Web documents
    creating
        bookmark links, 432–435
        hypertext links, 431–435
    removing
        bookmark links, 435
        hypertext links, 435
Web Page Expert, 437-438
Web Page Expert dialog box, 438
Web pages, troubleshooting, 437
Web sites
    Corel WordPerfect, 62
    linking documents, 436

widows, 138
Window menu commands
　　1 Document, 39–41
　　2 Document, 40
　　Tile Side by Side, 352
Windows 95
　　deleting DAD from taskbar, 13–16
　　installing fonts, 268–269
　　launching other Windows 95 programs from DAD, 13
word count, 162-163
Word Forms command (Type menu), 85–86
word spacing, adjusting, 281
Word/Letter Spacing commands (Format menu), 279
Word/Letter Spacing dialog box, 279
WordPerfect
　　buttons, displaying, 17–20
　　converting older files, 402–404
　　default margins, 104
　　form files, 243
　　graphics selection installation, 302–303
　　launching from desktop icon, 15–16
　　launching from Windows 95 start menu, 13
　　screen resolution and toolbars, 17–20
WordPerfect Characters dialog box, 281
WordPerfect icon, 15–16
words
　　adding to Spell Checker dictionary, 151

　　double (Spell Checker), 151–152
　　misspelled (Spell Checker), 148–150
　　replacing
　　　　with Spell Checker, 150
　　　　with Thesaurus, 157–158
　　searching in Thesaurus, 156
.wpd document extensions, 41–42
Wrap text button, 293
wrapping
　　graphics around text, 293–294
　　text, 32-33
writing
　　formulas in tables, 320–321
　　spreadsheet formulas, 320–321
WWW
　　connecting through AT&T WorldNet Service, 424–425
　　creating documents, 427–430
　　home pages, creating, 437–438
　　hypertext links, 426
　　publishing guidelines, 426
　　Web page linking, 417–419

X-Y-Z

Zoom command (View menu), 28–29
zoom percentage, 27–28
zooming in documents, 27–28

GET CONNECTED
to the ultimate source of computer information!

The MCP Forum on CompuServe

Go online with the world's leading computer book publisher! Macmillan Computer Publishing offers everything you need for computer success!

Find the books that are right for you!
A complete online catalog, plus sample chapters and tables of contents give you an in-depth look at all our books. The best way to shop or browse!

➤ Get fast answers and technical support for MCP books and software

➤ Join discussion groups on major computer subjects

➤ Interact with our expert authors via e-mail and conferences

➤ Download software from our immense library:
  ▷ Source code from books
  ▷ Demos of hot software
  ▷ The best shareware and freeware
  ▷ Graphics files

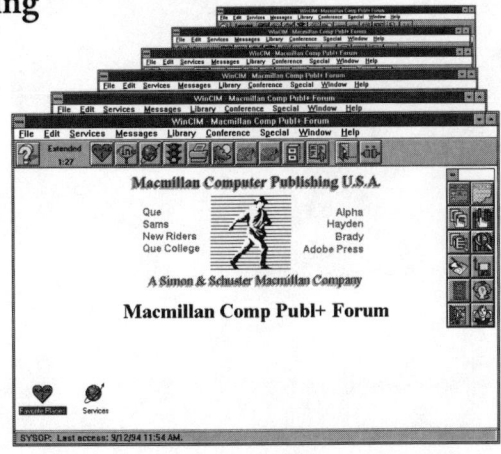

Join now and get a free CompuServe Starter Kit!

To receive your free CompuServe Introductory Membership, call **1-800-848-8199** and ask for representative #597.

The Starter Kit includes:
➤ Personal ID number and password
➤ $15 credit on the system
➤ Subscription to *CompuServe Magazine*

Once on the CompuServe System, type:

GO MACMILLAN

for the most computer information anywhere!

MACMILLAN COMPUTER PUBLISHING

CompuServe

Check out Que® Books on the World Wide Web
http://www.mcp.com/que

As the biggest software release in computer history, Windows 95 continues to redefine the computer industry. Click here for the latest info on our Windows 95 books

Make computing quick and easy with these products designed exclusively for new and casual users

Examine the latest releases in word processing, spreadsheets, operating systems, and suites

The Internet, The World Wide Web, CompuServe®, America Online®, Prodigy® —it's a world of ever-changing information. Don't get left behind!

Find out about new additions to our site, new bestsellers and hot topics

In-depth information on high-end topics: find the best reference books for databases, programming, networking, and client/server technologies

A recent addition to Que, Ziff-Davis Press publishes the highly-successful *How It Works* and *How to Use* series of books, as well as *PC Learning Labs Teaches* and *PC Magazine* series of book/disk packages

Stay on the cutting edge of Macintosh® technologies and visual communications

Find out which titles are making headlines

With 6 separate publishing groups, Que develops products for many specific market segments and areas of computer technology. Explore our Web Site and you'll find information on best-selling titles, newly published titles, upcoming products, authors, and much more.

- Stay informed on the latest industry trends and products available
- Visit our online bookstore for the latest information and editions
- Download software from Que's library of the best shareware and freeware

Copyright © 1996, Macmillan Computer Publishing-USA, A Viacom Company

Complete and Return this Card for a *FREE* Computer Book Catalog

Thank you for purchasing this book! You have purchased a superior computer book written expressly for your needs. To continue to provide the kind of up-to-date, pertinent coverage you've come to expect from us, we need to hear from you. Please take a minute to complete and return this self-addressed, postage-paid form. In return, we'll send you a free catalog of all our computer books on topics ranging from word processing to programming and the internet.

☐ Mrs. ☐ Ms. ☐ Dr. ☐

Name (first) _____ (M.I.) __ (last) _____
Address _____
City _____ State __ Zip _____
Phone _____ Fax _____
Company Name _____
Email address _____

Please check at least (3) influencing factors for purchasing this book.

- Front or back cover information on book ☐
- Special approach to the content ☐
- Completeness of content ☐
- Author's reputation ☐
- Publisher's reputation ☐
- Book cover design or layout ☐
- Index or table of contents of book ☐
- Price of book ☐
- Special effects, graphics, illustrations ☐
- Other (Please specify): _____ ☐

How did you first learn about this book?

- Saw in Macmillan Computer Publishing catalog ☐
- Recommended by store personnel ☐
- Saw the book on bookshelf at store ☐
- Recommended by a friend ☐
- Received advertisement in the mail ☐
- Saw an advertisement in: _____ ☐
- Read book review in: _____ ☐
- Other (Please specify): _____ ☐

How many computer books have you purchased in the last six months?

- This book only ☐
- 3 to 5 books ☐
- 2 books ☐
- More than 5 ☐

4. Where did you purchase this book?

- Bookstore ☐
- Computer Store ☐
- Consumer Electronics Store ☐
- Department Store ☐
- Office Club ☐
- Warehouse Club ☐
- Mail Order ☐
- Direct from Publisher ☐
- Internet site ☐
- Other (Please specify): _____ ☐

5. How long have you been using a computer?

☐ Less than 6 months ☐ 6 months to a year
☐ 1 to 3 years ☐ More than 3 years

6. What is your level of experience with personal computers and with the subject of this book?

	With PCs	With subject of book
New	☐	☐
Casual	☐	☐
Accomplished	☐	☐
Expert	☐	☐

Source Code ISBN: 1-7897-0141-3

7. Which of the following best describes your job title?
- Administrative Assistant ☐
- Coordinator ☐
- Manager/Supervisor ☐
- Director ☐
- Vice President ☐
- President/CEO/COO ☐
- Lawyer/Doctor/Medical Professional ☐
- Teacher/Educator/Trainer ☐
- Engineer/Technician ☐
- Consultant ☐
- Not employed/Student/Retired ☐
- Other (Please specify): _____ ☐

8. Which of the following best describes the area of the company your job title falls under?
- Accounting ☐
- Engineering ☐
- Manufacturing ☐
- Operations ☐
- Marketing ☐
- Sales ☐
- Other (Please specify): _____ ☐

9. What is your age?
- Under 20
- 21-29
- 30-39
- 40-49
- 50-59
- 60-over

10. Are you:
- Male
- Female

11. Which computer publications do you read regularly? (Please list)

_____
_____
_____
_____
_____
_____
_____

Comments: _____

Fold here and scotch-tape to

BUSINESS REPLY MAIL
FIRST-CLASS MAIL PERMIT NO. 9918 INDIANAPOLIS IN

POSTAGE WILL BE PAID BY THE ADDRESSEE

ATTN MARKETING
MACMILLAN COMPUTER PUBLISHING
MACMILLAN PUBLISHING USA
201 W 103RD ST
INDIANAPOLIS IN 46290-9042

NO POSTAGE
NECESSARY
IF MAILED
IN THE
UNITED STATES

QUE® has the right choice for every computer user

From the new computer user to the advanced programmer, we've got the right computer book for you. Our user-friendly *Using* series offers just the information you need to perform specific tasks quickly and move onto other things. And, for computer users ready to advance to new levels, QUE *Special Edition Using* books, the perfect all-in-one resource—and recognized authority on detailed reference information.

The *Using* series for casual users

Who should use this book?

Everyday users who:
- Work with computers in the office or at home
- Are familiar with computers but not in love with technology
- Just want to "get the job done"
- Don't want to read a lot of material

The user-friendly reference
- The fastest access to the one best way to get things done
- Bite-sized information for quick and easy reference
- Nontechnical approach in plain English
- Real-world analogies to explain new concepts
- Troubleshooting tips to help solve problems
- Visual elements and screen pictures that reinforce topics
- Expert authors who are experienced in training and instruction

Special Edition Using for accomplished users

Who should use this book?

Proficient computer users who:
- Have a more technical understanding of computers
- Are interested in technological trends
- Want in-depth reference information
- Prefer more detailed explanations and examples

The most complete reference
- Thorough explanations of various ways to perform tasks
- In-depth coverage of all topics
- Technical information cross-referenced for easy access
- Professional tips, tricks, and shortcuts for experienced users
- Advanced troubleshooting information with alternative approaches
- Visual elements and screen pictures that reinforce topics
- Technically qualified authors who are experts in their fields
- "Techniques form the Pros" sections with advice from well-known computer professionals

Copyright © 1996, Macmillan Computer Publishing-USA, A Viacom Company